D0152321

SECOND EDITION

Staffing Organizations

SECOND EDITION

Staffing Organizations

BENJAMIN SCHNEIDER
UNIVERSITY OF MARYLAND

NEAL SCHMITT
MICHIGAN STATE UNIVERSITY

WAVELAND
PRESS, INC.
Prospect Heights, Illinois

For information about this book, write or call:

Waveland Press, Inc.
P.O. Box 400
Prospect Heights, Illinois 60070
(708) 634-0081

Cover photo © Armando F. Mola.

Acknowledgments appear on pages 476-478, which constitute a legal
extension of the copyright page.

Copyright © 1986, 1976 by HarperCollins Publishers, Inc.
1992 reissued by Waveland Press, Inc. under arrangement with
HarperCollins Publishers, Inc.

ISBN 0-88133-672-6

*All rights reserved. No part of this book may be reproduced,
stored in a retrieval system, or transmitted in any form or by
any means without permission in writing from the publisher.*

Printed in the United States of America

7   6   5   4   3   2

FOR BRENDA
FOR KARA

PREFACE

Since the first edition of this book appeared, interest in formal processes for staffing organizations has exploded. This is especially true with respect to theoretical and psychometric issues surrounding different forms of validity analysis and the importance of job analysis as the fundamental base for staffing practices. Much of this explosion in interest was pushed by federal legislation mandating certain staffing procedures. These procedures, put forth in documents and court cases, were primarily socially motivated; they attempted to insure that the staffing policies of organizations would not stand in the way of equal opportunity regarding access to jobs.

Major advances have also come from the scientific community as it explores basic behavioral, psychological, and statistical issues relevant for the study of human behavior at work. Because staffing is both a practical and theoretical problem, the interplay of the real world of work and theoretical constructs has produced a set of robust insights and findings. Examples are as diverse as validity generalization, new forms of established interest inventories, new kinds of employment interviews, and the use of simulations as selection procedures.

A result of the increased interest in formal processes for staffing organizations was a thorough investigation of the role of these procedures in denying various subgroups equal access to employment. As we show in the text, a tremendous amount of research indicates that formal selection procedures were *not* the culprit; society at large was. The evidence indicates that artificial discrimination may exist but it is not generally attributable to the professionally developed tests, interviews, or job simulations used by organizations to assess applicants for jobs. Organizations *can* develop and use these formal mechanisms for evaluating job candidates and, at the same time, take action to create equal access to jobs. Doing this will both create an effective work force and correct past artificial denial of job opportunity.

The bottom line is that if organizations adopt appropriate job analysis, assessment, and validation techniques, effective strategies for finding employees with good potential can be developed. People who will be more productive, produce higher quality work, give better service, be absent less, and be less likely to become a turnover, can be selected. We have made significant advances in estimating the utility of our personnel selection procedures; i.e., we can make estimates of the relative benefits compared to developmental and implementation costs.

We hope that student readers of this book will come away with the feeling that people who will be more effective can be selected and that they will also learn some ways of making this happen. At a minimum they will be aware of some of the opportunities to make good personnel staffing decisions and some of the pitfalls of trying the seductive "quick fix." We have presented many operational examples in the text so that the novice to the topic will be able to see how some of these procedures look and work. The examples, combined with a comprehensive yet straightforward writing style make the material available to senior undergraduate students as well as graduate students in business administration, psychology, labor and industrial relations, and related programs.

Our hope is that practitioners in personnel, human resources management, labor relations, and so forth will also use the book. While the procedures and options we describe may look idealized, our examples should make them real enough to use. The extensive coverage we give to a wide variety of issues in staffing, from recruitment to cost benefit analysis and from job analysis to interviewing, should help create new ideas for effective staffing strategies. Perhaps of most interest will be Chapters 8–10, which are devoted to the various kinds of assessment techniques that now exist for gathering data on job applicants. However, each chapter contains material that is as up-to-date as we could find so the book will be a valuable desk reference as well as a useful source of various staffing procedures.

Readers familiar with the first edition will be surprised at how the book has grown; Roger Holloway, our editor, certainly was! As we noted at the beginning of the Preface, however, there has been an explosion of knowledge and techniques in the past ten years. In addition, the issues are so salient to corporate personnel and legal officers that the need to be relatively comprehensive had to be satisfied. Finally, if you double the number of authors, . . .

Speaking of authors, it isn't always easy to work with another person on a project like this. Both of us continue to marvel at how much we still like each other. The fact is that we had no fights, or major disagreements; we each seemed able to accept what the other had to say since invariably he was right. We've now done two projects together and we are looking forward to the third.

Of course, we didn't do this book by ourselves. Brenda and Kara, Lee, Rhody, and Krista all allowed us the chance to write. In fact, Lee helped tremendously in the preparation of the Instructor's Manual that accompanies the text. Beth Rubin did the major part of that Manual and she deserves plaudits for her insightful discussion suggestions and questions.

On a more technical level, a number of our colleagues agreed to help us by carefully reviewing both the first edition and this revised version. Useful critiques and enthusiasm for the first book were obtained from Charles H. Fay, Rutgers, the State University; Michael D. Hawkins, University of Washington; Stephan Schuster, California State University, Northridge; and Thomas G. Swenson, Naval Postgraduate School, Monterey. Irwin L. Goldstein, University of Maryland, College Park; Elaine D. Pulakos, Personnel Decisions Research Institute, Minneapolis; and Hannah R. Hirsh, United States Office of Personnel Management all read this new edition and gave us line-by-line commentary to help us tighten it up and make it as readable as possible. As with the first edition, Lyman Porter's comments proved invaluable, especially in helping us order things so that they made the most sense.

Finally, the real workers. At Maryland, Deborah Evans astounded us with her speed and the quality of her work, especially when she was hit with ''I need it tomorrow.'' At Michigan State, Arline Jennex, Mary Scott, and Marcy Schafer provided nearly instant turnaround on several versions of this text and added many helpful editorial comments as well.

As you can see, this is not a two-person product. We thank all of the people we named for their help.

Benjamin Schneider
Neal Schmitt

CONTENTS

6

VALIDATION STRATEGIES 217

7

THE UTILITY OF PERSONNEL
SELECTION PRACTICES 260

11

STAFFING ORGANIZATIONS: REVIEW AND IMPLICATIONS   407

APPENDIX

UNIFORM GUIDELINES ON EMPLOYEE SELECTION PROCEDURES   439

AUTHOR INDEX   466

SUBJECT INDEX   472

ACKNOWLEDGMENTS   476

SECOND EDITION

Staffing Organizations

INTRODUCTION

AIMS OF THE CHAPTER

In this first chapter of *Staffing Organizations* we want to set a foundation against which you can view contemporary issues in staffing an organization. To provide this background information we first define staffing, then provide a way of understanding where staffing fits into the prediction and understanding of employee behavior in organizations. After the framework, a brief history of important concepts and procedures underlying staffing is presented.

STAFFING ORGANIZATIONS DEFINED

Staffing may be defined as the processes involved in finding, assessing, placing, and evaluating individuals at work. These processes operate through the acts of recruiting, selecting, appraising, and promoting individuals. *Organizations* adds breadth and scope to these processes and indicates how important the characteristics of the job and organization are in the entire staffing process. The organization not only influences the staffing process itself, but also the kinds of people who will be recruited, selected, and promoted. This is so because people are the staff of organizations; the best staffing programs take great care to specify the kinds of people who will be effective and satisfied with the job and the organization into which they are hired. In brief, then, the aims of staffing an organization are to improve organizational function and effectiveness by attracting, selecting, and retaining people who will facilitate the accomplishment of both organizational and individual goals.

Figure 1–1 presents a working framework as a convenient way to think about the many factors that influence an individual's behavior at work. As you can see, there are at least four major categories of issues that can influence behavior:

1. **Individual attributes.** This refers to kinds of characteristics people bring with them to work and/or learn after entering the organization through both formal and informal training and interaction with coworkers and the system at large. Most staffing systems attempt to identify the individual characteristics that will increase the probability that people hired will be able to do the work they are hired for and will enjoy the work long enough to repay the organization's investment in the hiring process. A lot of evidence presented later indicates that people who bring job-relevant skills and abilities with them are likely to perform better and that when people come

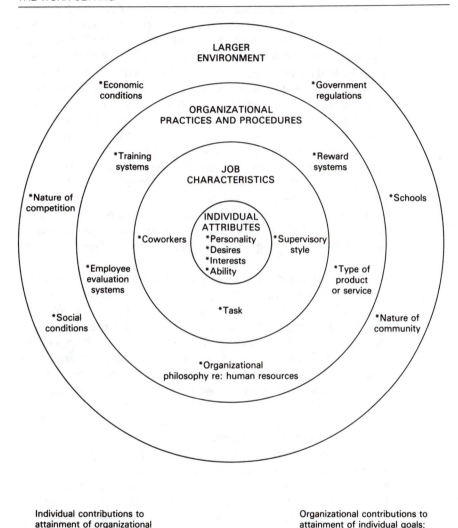

Individual contributions to attainment of organizational goals; satisfactoriness.

Organizational contributions to attainment of individual goals; satisfaction.

with certain expectations about what the job and organization will be like, and those expectations are fulfilled, then the people will be more satisfied, committed, and will stay longer. We call it *satisfactoriness* when people meet the performance standards set for them at work. When people's own expectations are met, then we refer to *satisfaction* (Lofquist and Dawis, 1969).

2. **Job characteristics.** When we think about a person's job, we tend to be quite restrictive in our thinking and picture the task(s) at which they work. By doing this we ignore a number of other immediate job-relevant issues, namely the others with whom people work and the persons people work for. Anyone who has worked knows that these interpersonal facets make the task more or less completeable and interesting. So, not only the way the task is designed affects satisfactoriness and satisfaction but the other people connected with carrying out the task also play an important part.

We won't pay too much attention to the role of the supervisor and coworkers in determining performance and satisfaction in this text. It's not that these issues are unimportant; it's just that we have focused on the task for which people will be hired. In most cases we will ignore the interpersonal issues and call the sum total of the task a job (as in job analysis). The reader will have to remain cognizant of the strong social effects on peoples' work performance.

3. **Organizational practices and procedures.** We will also ignore the characteristics of organizations as an influence on employee behavior and attitudes. Again, not because the issues listed (like training programs, reward systems, and the philosophy of management toward people) are unimportant but because our focus will be on the individual attribute-task characteristic match. Entire books exist on the effects of organizational practices and procedures on behavior at work, and many of them also detail the role of coworkers and supervisors. These books go by various titles but the two main areas they fall under are *organizational psychology* and *organizational behavior.*

The two primary concerns with organizational practices and procedures in this book will be in understanding the importance of organizational goals on the kinds of people hired by an organization and the way organizational conditions can actually constrain individual effectiveness. We will argue that the best staffing systems are those that are designed around a careful specification of organizational goals. The logic goes this way: an organization that is able to be specific about its goals probably has defined a set of jobs such that if those jobs are performed well, the goals will be accomplished. The chore for the staffing specialist becomes one of finding people able to meet the goals of specific jobs. As we will show, many, if not most organizations, have done a poor job of specifying their goals, and this makes finding people who are able and willing to do the job well difficult. That is, if the standards against which people will be evaluated once they are on the job are vague and/or changing, it is going to be difficult to predict who will be able to do the job well.

With respect to constraints on effectiveness, we will argue that even when an organization has a staffing program that effectively identifies potentially competent workers, simply hiring those workers may not make organizational performance as good as it could be. The reason for this is that organizations can either constrain or facilitate behavior by the way they are structured and managed. Given that organizations can literally "hold down" the level of performance of competent workers, it will become clear that an organization that assumes it can solve all of its productivity problems just by hiring a few more good people will be in for some rude shocks.

4. **Larger environment.** The issues listed here, like the nature of competition and federal regulations, have played an increasingly important role in the way organizations staff themselves. Thus, an organization requiring highly skilled people in an environment filled with competitors for those same people will behave differently from one that does not face these circumstances. For example, companies in the Silicon Valley have difficulty attracting and retaining qualified computer hardware development people. And, perhaps the most obvious external force on current staffing procedures has been U.S. Government legislation concerning equal employment opportunity. Both here, in Chapter 1, and throughout the book this influence on staffing will be presented in considerable detail.

One feature of Figure 1-1 that is not obvious is the *reciprocal* nature of these four critical elements. By reciprocal here we mean that the four features interact with each other and influence each other. So, for example, the kinds of people who get attracted to, selected by, and remain in a particular job will influence the kinds of pay and incentive systems of the organization and even the nature of the larger environment in which the organization functions. That is, different kinds of people seem to start up different kinds of organizations and those organizations end up competing in different kinds of environments—people who start halfway houses are not the same as those who start banks (Schneider, 1983a, 1983b). We think it is clear that organizations are differentially effective to the extent that the four elements in Figure 1-1 fit or match each other. In other words, the kinds of people in an organization should fit their jobs, the technology should fit the industry, and so forth (Thompson, 1967). It will become clear in the remainder of the book that "fit" and "match" are central constructs in staffing organizations.

The above discussion should help pinpoint the emphasis of this book: we are concerned with fitting the attributes of people to jobs in legal ways that permit the organization to be effective in accomplishing its goals. To make this happen, we must have considerable information about the jobs to be staffed (Chapter 2), the standards against which the effectiveness of the staffing process will be evaluated (Chapter 3), how to find sufficient staff both externally and internally (Chapter 4), the various ways of evaluating or choosing good staffing procedures (Chapters 5 and 6), the costs and benefits of good staffing programs (Chapter 7), and the variety of procedures available to help make staffing decisions (Chapters 8, 9 and 10).

Prior to exploring all these issues we want to give you a flavor of the historical roots of the procedures and conclusions we will present. This is not a very long history, encompassing only about 100 years in terms of methods like those used today. As we will discover, however, some of the concepts on which those methods rest are quite a bit older.

HISTORICAL FOUNDATIONS OF STAFFING

Individual Differences

The fact that people differ from each other in important ways has been known and recognized at least as long as the existence of the written word. It is clear, further, that early peoples not only recognized these differences, but made use of them—not everyone performed the same functions in the hunt, not everyone was a chief, and the medicine man was often selected after some competition.

Aristotle suggested the use of measures of physical prowess for the selection of soldiers. Plato, speaking of soldier-selection for the Republic, not only described the physical characteristics required, but also the kind of "personality" necessary—obviously implying that not everyone possessed the proper type of personality. The discussion follows:

> Then it will be our duty to select, if we can, natures which are fitted for the task of guarding the city?
> It will.
> And the selection will be no easy matter, I said; but we must be brave and do our best.
> We must.
> Whereas, I said, they [those selected] ought to be dangerous to their enemies, and gentle to their friends; if not they will destroy themselves without waiting for their enemies to destroy them.
> True he said.

What is to be done then? I said; how shall we find a gentle nature which has also a great spirit, for the one is the contradiction of the others? (Plato, 1952, pp. 319–20).

Reading further in Plato we find a discussion of differences in personal attributes among women:

One woman has a gift of healing, another not; one is a musician, and another has no music in her nature?
Very true.
And one woman has a turn for gymnastic and military exercises, and another is unwarlike and hates gymnastics? (Plato, 1952, p. 359)

Those same differences are the subject of this book. How do we identify people with knowledge, skill, ability, and personality to perform well at a set of tasks we call a job?

Given the very early and continuing interest in identifying how people differ from each other, it is surprising that the refinement of psychological methods of measuring the range and kind of individual differences did not take place until the later 1800s. We specify *psychological* here because actually the first recorded *scientific* study of individual differences was accomplished by early astronomers, who depended upon human observation of the heavens for their calculations. They found that observers did not agree with each other on such things as the speed with which heavenly bodies moved across the sky. Astronomers thus had to "calibrate" different observers; to do this they had to "measure," in some degree, how people differed from one another (see Boring, 1950).

Darwin

The belief that individuals differ from each other in important ways that determine or are related to differences in work behavior underlies the science of staffing. This philosophy can be traced historically to the work of Charles Darwin (Jenkins and Paterson, 1961), whose theory of natural selection showed that those organisms best suited to an environment are the most likely to survive and prosper (a notion termed *functional utility*). Darwin's work provides a rationale for the scientific study of staffing, and subsequent research in statistics and testing provided the procedures for relating the capabilities of individuals to their performances in organizations (schools, business and industry, the military, etc.)

Many early contributors to the psychology of testing and education probed the uses of psychology in relation to the concept of functional utility and Darwin's theory of evolution.

The effect of this Darwin theory upon the development of psychology was tremendous . . . As we shall see presently, Francis Galton seized at once upon the notion of mental inheritance and brought out evidence in favor of it. Out of that activity grew the whole business of studying individual differences in mental capacities and of psychological assessment by means of mental tests, the business which the Americans took over and promoted (Boring, 1950, pp. 471–72).

The Correlation Coefficient

For the science of staffing, a most important breakthrough in procedures was due to the Englishman, Sir Francis Galton. Galton sought a way to determine his belief that the mental capabilities of parents were co-related with the mental capabilities of their children. He collected considerable evidence to document his hypothesis but was having trouble summarizing his conclusions in a single index showing the relationship between parents' and childrens' intelligence. A colleague, Karl Pearson, solved Galton's problem in 1896 by developing what is now called the Pearson Correlation Coefficient—*correlation* for short.

The statistical concepts underlying correlation will be presented in Chapter 5. Here it is important to stress the utility of the correlation—in one number we can summarize how well two kinds of data collected on a group of people are related. For example, if one knew that fifty people differed in their mechanical ability, one might wonder whether these differences in ability were related to differences in their performance as auto mechanics. Their mechanical ability test scores could be correlated with an assessment of successfulness as an auto mechanic.

The Correlation Coefficient is the statistical procedure used to indicate the degree of relationship. With this statistical tool, psychologists are not only in a position to study individual differences but are able to relate differences of various kinds to each other. The point cannot be overemphasized that this correlational procedure, this ability to establish statistical relationships, is at the very foundation of the science of staffing organizations.

Mental Tests

Alfred Binet and Theophile Simon, two French experimental psychologists, approached the problem of identifying children of subnormal intelligence—children who would not benefit from the typical school system. Galton, in contrast, was not very interested in practical matters; his concern was with documenting the extent and nature of individual differences and their interrelationships.

Thus, while Binet and Simon were not the first authors of psychological tests, they were the first to demonstrate the practical usefulness of testing procedures—they were the first to *validate* their mental test. By validate we mean that they showed that assessments made of people's ability to respond correctly to mental problems at one point in time were predictive of how well they actually behaved (in school) at a later point in time. They wrote in 1905 about *validity:*

> The use of tests is today very common, and there are even contemporary authors who have made a specialty of organizing new tests according to theoretical views, but who have made no efforts to patiently try them out in schools. Theirs is an amusing occupation, comparable to a person's making a colonizing expedition into Algeria, advancing always upon the map, without taking off his dressing gown. We place but slight confidence in the tests invented by these authors and we have borrowed nothing from them. All the tests which we propose have been repeatedly tried, and have been retained from among many which after trial have been discarded. We can certify that those which are here presented have proved themselves valuable (Binet and Simon, 1948, pp. 415–16).

The process of "trying" tests and continuing to use only those that prove valuable is known as *validating* a test. It is the process of validation that distinguishes the science of staffing from armchair guesswork in the prediction of behavior. This process of validation and the development of mental tests are two of the most important technological contributions of psychology to staffing.

The Binet-Simon Scales, as noted above, were not the first mental tests, although they became (as the Stanford-Binet Intelligence Test) the most frequently used, individually administered measure of childhood general scholastic aptitude. In England, Galton had developed a series of tests of physiological capabilities (hearing, hand strength, and so forth), and in 1890 in the United States, Cattell proposed that a series of ten tests could be used ". . . in discovering the constancy of mental processes, their interdependence, and their variation under different circumstances" (1948, p. 347). Cattell suggested that these tests would also be ". . . perhaps, useful in regard to training, mode of life or indication of disease."

The ten tests Cattell proposed were:

1. Dynamometer pressure
2. Rate of movement
3. Sensation areas
4. Pressure causing pain
5. Least noticeable difference in weight

6. Reaction time for sound
7. Time for naming colours
8. Bisection of a 50 cm. line
9. Judgment of 10 seconds time
10. Number of letters remembered on once hearing (1948, p. 347)

In spite of the fact that Cattell coined the term "mental tests," it is clear from this list that in 1890 testing was not as we know it today.

Compare Cattell's mental tests with the Binet-Simon indicators of intelligence. A seven-year-old should:

1. Indicate omissions in a drawing
2. Give the number of fingers
3. Copy a written sentence
4. Copy a triangle and a diamond
5. Repeat 5 figures
6. Describe a picture
7. Count 13 single sous (coins)
8. Name 4 pieces of money (Binet and Simon, 1948, p. 420)

The Binet-Simon scales had a different purpose from Cattell's tests. Cattell was primarily interested in understanding the *range* of individual differences, and he suggested that his measures would "perhaps be useful" in accomplishing this purpose. Binet and Simon on the other hand, made the *usefulness* of their measures a criterion for the success of their work. They were interested in the constancy of mental processes and the range of individual differences *primarily as these processes and differences were useful to society.* They felt that the ability to identify subnormal intelligence (and, conversely, identify normals who had been heretofore deemed subnormal) offered proof that psychology was "in a fair way to become a science of great social utility."

This very functional orientation to the assessment of people's attributes proved quite effective. During World War I, large-scale assessments of soldiers were attempted—the armies of England, France, and especially the United States were staffed through the use of mental tests. The fairly successful use of tests of individual differences in ability during World War I was carried over into civilian pursuits after the war. Perhaps the primary reason for this was the development of tests that could be administered to groups of people rather than to one person at a time. Hull's book *Aptitude Testing* (1928) provided a useful summary of the range and kind of individual differences, and of the utility of tests in staffing all kinds of organizations (to staff schools with pupils as well as to staff manufacturing and service organizations with semi-skilled, skilled, and clerical employees). Viteles' (1932) book summarized the early knowledge related to the effectiveness of tests in government, business, and industry in the U.S. while by 1935 Welch and Miles had published a practical guide in England that summarized validated procedures for selecting weavers, salesmen, dressmakers, machine workers, cigarette packers, tram drivers, and engineers, among others.

Not only psychologists were writing about the success of studying individual differences as a means of identifying the more from the less capable. By 1923, *Personnel Management* by Scott and Clothier was in its first of five editions. These authors were already oriented toward matching the skill requirements of tasks to the ability of workers. In their book they stated their view of the essential principles of individual differences as follows:

> First, one individual differs from another in those personal aptitudes, those special abilities with which he is equipped and which he is able to contribute to the work of his company in exchange for his salary. Second, individuals differ in interest and motive and respond best to varying stimuli. Third, the same individual changes from day to day and from year to year in ability (both degree and kind) and in interest. Fourth, different kinds of work require different kinds of personal ability in the persons who are to perform them. Fifth, granting equal ability, different kinds of work are done best by persons who, temperamentally, are particularly interested in them. Sixth, the work in each position in a company changes as time goes on; duties are added and taken away. Sometimes the change is negligible, sometimes it is great. In the measure in which it takes place, a similar change is apt to take place in the abilities and interests the work requires of the worker. Seventh, environment—working conditions, supervision, relations with the employer and with fellow employees, opportunity and so forth—exercises a tremendous influence on personal efficiency and consequently on group production (p. 12).

Points six and seven—the impact of kinds of work and the working environment on people—did not receive much early attention from those interested in staffing organizations; the individual, as noted earlier, was viewed as the sole factor in performance. However, beginning with the 1930s, changes in the general society and in the prevailing kinds of psychological research, resulted in a new emphasis in understanding the behavior of people at work. This emphasis was on the role of the work situation as a determinant of performance and satisfaction.

CHANGES IN SOCIETY SINCE 1930

Over the past fifty years a number of changes in society generated increasing concern for the impact of situations on behavior. Not the least of these was the Great Depression.

The Depression

American society was founded on the idea that the individual was the center of society; if anything good was to happen, it would be a function of personal effort and ability. The philosophy of pre-depression America, then, was that an individual who worked hard could overcome all kinds of obstacles and ultimately succeed. The Great Depression revealed flaws in this way of thinking. People who were able and who were willing to work hard could not find work; they sold apples on streetcorners or, if less fortunate, stood in soup lines to prevent starvation.

One remedy for the problems of the Depression, or at least a way to combat its overwhelming effects, was the creation of programs like the Civilian Conservation Corps (CCC), which was capable of creating jobs for large segments of the population. The establishment of such programs, and the subsequent homogenization of people with wide individual differences in the same place, doing the same kind of work, were to have an influence on the way people thought about the impact of situations on behavior.

The Depression was over when the U.S. became involved in World War II. However, the impact of the Depression on the way people thought left a lasting imprint: like it or not, the positive or negative impact of a situation can be of great consequence to the individual.

World War II

The war may have removed the burden of the Depression from people, but it also created another negative situation over which individuals had little control. The war again demonstrated people's lack of total control over their own destinies, no matter how hard they tried. One could hypothesize that the establishment of the United Nations was an attempt to create a *positive* situation out of the lessons of the war, a situation whose impact on people would be to foster and facilitate people's potential to respond to positive rather than negative stimuli. The important point, however, was that situations, rather than individuals alone, began to be regarded as having controlling influences on people's behavior.

While the war had negative consequences for people in general, it was also the final proving ground for the social utility of the methods and concepts of personnel selection. Literally millions of men had to be selectively assigned to fill all kinds of jobs, and *new* jobs as well—pilots were required, and submarine personnel, and thousands of officers had to be commissioned. Psychologists were assigned to interview, test, appraise, and place personnel. These psychologists were successful and, especially in the Army Air

Corps, they developed large-scale programs that were effective in identifying men who would be more likely to succeed as pilots. In addition, in all the branches of the military, success in identifying those who would perform effectively as officers and leaders was achieved. By the end of the war, a fairly clear set of procedures was available for placing people in those jobs for which they had the highest probability of success (Thorndike, 1949).

Personnel psychology, with its emphasis on individual differences in ability, reached its zenith during World War II. Both sides in this war found the application of systematic procedures for staffing the war machines effective, but not as effective as they had hoped. As mentioned earlier, with changes occurring in society and in psychology's orientation to the study of behavior, it became increasingly necessary to reevaluate the importance of the individual versus the importance of environment as the primary causative factor regarding behavior.

The Depression, World War II, and the postwar era saw a change in the way people began to think about the role of the situation in satisfying people's needs. The change was from the viewpoint that "people are supreme and control their own destiny" to "people can be supreme if they create situations that facilitate their becoming supreme." Perhaps this involves not so much a change in the way people think as an expansion of their thinking to include the impact of situations on people's behavior and feelings. Failure and success were no longer attributed exclusively to the individual but to the situation in which the individual functioned as well.

Equal Employment Legislation

Certainly there are many conditions in the United States of a social and societal nature that influenced the way we think about each other, and our role in society. We can name numerous events that evoke frequently painful memories—the war in Viet Nam, starvation in Bangladesh and Ethiopia—as well as the joys associated with accomplishment like those experienced by the landing of a man on the moon or the national sense of pride associated with hosting of the Summer Olympics in 1984. From a staffing point of view, however, the most important event was the passage of the 1964 Civil Rights Act during the Johnson administration.

The Act had several parts (called Titles). For example, one Title dealt with voting rights. For staffing purposes, the most important title was Title VII because it dealt with employment. Thus, it dealt with all forms of employment issues—pay, promotion, working conditions—including selection. Title VII made it illegal to use age, race, sex, national origin, or religion as a basis for making a hiring decision. One outcome of this legislation was a close examination of procedures that were being used for making these kinds of decisions.

Because written tests constituted a prevalent source of information used in making hiring decisions, some employees who felt they had been denied employment because of poor performance on a test brought suit against that company arguing that the test had wrongfully discriminated against them. By wrongfully discriminated they meant that the test was used to discriminate against them because they were black, or female, or older. This was a very serious charge because paper and pencil tests and all measures of people used to collect information as a basis for making employee decisions are designed to discriminate more capable from less capable persons. So, what some claimants were arguing was that these tests were discriminating against them because of their sex or race and not because they were more or less capable.

While we will review case law concerning what has transpired since the middle to late 1960's in Chapter 8, here it is important to summarize a few key points concerning the influence of legislation on personnel selection:

1. From the standpoint of the staffing process, the most important outcome of numerous court cases and tremendous effort on the part of personnel researchers has been a focus on job relevance in the design of measures used as a basis for making selection decisions. In brief, tests used for making hiring decisions are today far more likely to accurately reflect the demands of jobs than was perhaps true prior to federal Equal Employment Opportunity (EEO) pressures.

2. Thorough review of what tests do in providing information to decision-makers has revealed that tests are not wrongfully discriminating. This is not to say that tests do not make discriminations among people, for that is precisely what they are designed to do. But they do not make wrongful, i.e., unwarrantedly biased, discriminations. In the language of the prestigious National Academy of Sciences (NAS) report on ability testing:

> The Committee has seen no evidence of alternatives to testing that are equally informative, equally adequate technically, and also economically and politically viable, . . . and little evidence that well-constructed and competently administered tests are more valid predictors for a population subgroup than for another: individuals with higher scores tend to perform better on the job regardless of group identity (National Academy of Sciences, 1982, p. 144).

What the National Academy of Sciences was saying, then, is that the presumed bias of tests against different subgroups based on sex, race, and so on had not been demonstrated to exist. And, further, that the tests were really quite useful.

3. Another interesting outcome of the legal battles was a definition of a test. Typically we think of a test as an examination of some kind responded to with paper and pencil, usually on some form of answer sheet. We think a test is like the multiple choice exam we took in some college course. In fact, industrial psychologists and the *Uniform Guidelines on Employee Selection Procedures* (1978) have defined the word "test" in much broader terms and the courts have adopted this definition. In brief, a test is defined as any form of collecting information on individuals when that information is used as a basis for making an employment decision. So, interviews are tests, as are application blanks, training programs which some people may fail, performance appraisals used as a basis for making promotions (which, obviously are selection decisions), and any other kind of information used for making employment decisions.

We've tried in the rest of the book to continually remind the reader about this definition of a test because many of the most important technical principles underlying the evaluation of selection procedures require us to include all sources of information used in making decisions in our definition of a test.

4. The finding by the National Academy of Sciences referred to above made it clear that an attack on tests was not going to be viable as a way to redress past discriminations in the employment world. There is no doubt that there have been such discriminations.

One way in which the courts have mandated the equal representation of various subgroups in an organization's work force is by means of application of the *four-fifths rule.* An organization is "violating" the four-fifths rule if the rate at which it employs minority individuals is less than four-fifths the rate at which it employs members of the majority group. When this is true, the organization must show that its hiring procedures are based on people's ability to perform important job tasks, not on the basis of their ethnic or gender status.

As noted at the beginning of this section, we will cover a number of the court cases that resulted in these conclusions later in the text. Here it is important to note that the cases brought to the courts may have been a mistake in that they attacked paper and pencil tests when the tests themselves were probably not at fault. On the other hand, too much poor quality personnel selection work had been going on with companies buying off-the-shelf procedures with little demonstrable validity or utility, blindly applying them as a basis for hiring their people. Though many may disagree, federal intervention may have improved the quality of the selection procedures employed and, thus, improved organizational functioning. In this vein, most companies failed to recognize that the pain they suffered when suits were brought against them probably resulted in their eventually implementing a far more effective selection program than they had had previously. On the other hand, legal costs have been tremendous. As we will show in Chapter 7, an efficient selection system can have very rapid dollar benefits for an organization in terms of productivity. The moral here is that the pressure to be accurate in selection decisions should have long term positive consequences for organizations.

UNDERSTANDING WORK BEHAVIOR

Scientists, being people, respond to the *Zeitgeist,* or climate of the times. Occasionally scientists anticipate the climate of the times and are prepared to facilitate change in a societally useful way. With such issues about what causes what, a chicken versus egg kind of question arises, but it is clear that during and just after World War II psychologists began making in-depth studies of the impact of situations on people's behavior. Studies of leadership, management style, organizational reward systems, power, the effects of formal and informal groups, and so forth were accomplished both in social psychology laboratories and in field settings.

While Darwin suggested early on that survival was dependent upon the fitness of the organism, of equal importance to him was his concept of the environment as a sculptor, molding the behavior (and psychology) of the organism. The molding process was thought to encourage behavior that was appropriate to the ever-changing environment. Only those organisms so deviant from the environment in form and function, or so rigid in form and function that they could not adapt, failed to survive. Although Darwin had stressed understanding the role of the environment as a determinant of the behavior of organisms, early psychologists concentrated on the assessment of which organisms could adapt rather than on understanding the environments to which they had to adapt.

After World War II, however, there was a veritable explosion of interest and research that addressed the impact of the work environment on work motivation in particular and work behavior in general. In fact, between about 1955 and 1965, a number of books appeared about the role of the work environment in human motivation and in the general quality of life that have had a lasting effect on the study of behavior at work. Perhaps the father of this surge in both scholarly and practical theorizing was Kurt Lewin.

Lewin

Before and during World War II, the work of Kurt Lewin showed the importance of the social environment on people's behavior. In one set of experiments he showed how young boys' behavior depended upon whether their teacher was democratically or autocratically oriented. In another study, during the war, he was able to obtain the cooperation of housewives in serving kinds of meat they had previously found distasteful (beef lung, for example) by having groups of women discuss the problem and come to a consensus about the benefits of these meats (cf. Marrow, 1970).

Lewin's notion that behavior is a function of *both* person and environment had a tremendous impact on the study of humans at work. This impact extends into theories of motivation and management, which stress the concept of person and situation alike.

Vroom

V. H. Vroom's (1964) theory of motivation illustrates Lewin's concepts. Vroom's statements regarding motivation take the following form: people work to obtain rewards that in turn enable them to obtain other things they value (time off, a car, etc.); people put forth effort only to the extent that they perceive a relationship between effort and rewards that are valued. This view of human motivation is one that conceptualizes a system of values attached to particular rewards, establishes an environmental relationship between effort and reward, and determines the extent to which workers can be expected to perform at the level necessary to obtain rewards. Note that individuals may differ in the rewards they desire so that two people in the same environment may not be equally "motivated."

The implications of this theory for understanding human behavior at work are great. For example, Vroom suggests that employee effort is a function of individual desires and organizational feedback; i.e., the relationship the organization creates between worker effort and worker rewards. This truly involves an interaction between individual and organizational characteristics. A second implication of this theory is that people are thinking, rational, decision-makers; they are organisms that make choices about *what* work to do and *where* to work. The decisions are based on some assessment of the extent to which the work will be instrumental in obtaining desired rewards.

Vroom's (1964) work tied together much of the early work in psychology concerning studies of learning and motivation as well as studies of behavior in the work setting. His theory seemed to offer a relatively parsimonius way to summarize findings in occupational choice, job satisfaction, and motivation.

While the optimism surrounding Vroom's formulation has not been fully realized (Campbell and Pritchard, 1976), his formula^{..}on was important because it directed the efforts of work psychologists to worker motivation and the role of the work situation in facilitating motivation. Other theorists came along to push this mode of thinking, and today there are literally thousands of studies that can be attributed to Vroom's influence.

Maslow/McGregor

Vroom's (1964) theory was focused on individuals and individual rationality—i.e., thinking, decision-making people. An alternative view on worker motivation was promoted by McGregor (1960), following the theories of Maslow (1954). McGregor's portraits of worker motivation are more inclusive and less individual since they emphasize workers, in general (Schneider, 1985). These theories, and others (e.g., Argyris, 1957; Herzberg, Mausner, and Snyderman, 1959), emphasized *feelings* as the major goal of human behavior. For example, feelings of security, or self-esteem or self-actualization were pictured as goals toward which workers moved. In recent years, these portrayals of human motivation have been very influential in the design of new organizations and the renewal of old ones as organizations attempt to improve the general quality of life at work (Beer, 1980).

Depending upon an organization's views of what motivates people, different strategies for motivating workers may be adopted. If an organization takes the view that people want to experience self-actualization, then jobs are designed in ways that permit people to display their abilities. Supervision is rather loose and designed to be supportive rather than directive. On the other hand, if the organization takes the view that employees desire warm, interpersonal relationships, then the organization concentrates on creating work groups, selecting coworkers by peers, establishing open channels of interpersonal communication, reducing interpersonal conflict, and so forth. The important point here is that, depending upon one's philosophy or theory regarding the motivational bases of behavior, one adopts certain guidelines and procedures vis-a-vis employees that are consistent with those prior conceptions.

Therefore, organizations—through their policies and procedures, the way they design jobs, the procedures they implement for appraising and developing employees and for staffing their organizations—should be inherently active in shaping the work environment. According to the Darwinian concept of adaptation, the environment changes as a function of universal and unalterable forces. This is not so with organizations, even though it occasionally appears as if they have lost control over their own internal environments. Later we will discuss how organizations *do* have control, and how the proper exercise of this control affects the outcome of the total staffing effort.

Schmidt and Hunter

The impact of thinking about motivation and the role of the environment on behavior has made the study of work behavior more comprehensive and the understanding of the multiple influences on behavior clearer. However, staffing researchers will continue to emphasize the point that it is, ultimately, the people in the organization who make things happen. If this is true, and we believe it is, some recent developments in personnel selection research itself are very important. This breakthrough, primarily driven by the research of Schmidt and Hunter (e.g., Schmidt and Hunter, 1981), has revealed that carefully developed tests of cognitive abilities are valid for a wide range of jobs in a wide range of job situations.

This finding is so important because prior to the Schmidt and Hunter results, staffing specialists thought that each time they wanted to select people for a new job, they would have to design a new test. Further, they imagined that even if they had a valid test for a job in one situation, if they moved to a new situation (with, ostensibly, the same job) they would need a new test. It is easy to see that having certain kinds of tests be valid for whole classes of jobs and for those classes of jobs regardless of the situation in which the job existed would be a major breakthrough.

In a series of clever studies, Schmidt and Hunter presented the idea that validity does indeed generalize across many types of jobs and situations. While the details of their work are saved for discussion in Chapter 8, here we can summarize their major conclusions.

General cognitive ability tests (paper and pencil aptitude tests similar to the ACTs or SATs taken prior to entry into college) demonstrate consistent validity across the entire domain of white collar and pink collar jobs (Hunter and Hunter, 1984). In fact, the more the job requires intellective abilities as identified through job analysis, the more useful these tests are for predicting job performance. Jobs requiring more mechanical abilities are less well predicted by paper and pencil tests of cognitive ability but performance on more mechanical jobs is better predicted by psychomotor tests. For this reason, in Chapter 8 we discuss a variety of types of ability tests useful in selecting employees.

In order to allow the conclusions cited above, Schmidt and Hunter figured out why it looked like the same tests might not work for seemingly similar jobs or even seemingly identical jobs that existed in different companies. They showed that researchers frequently reached a conclusion that a test was not valid because the number of people on whom the test was tried was too small. To be more precise they showed that conclusions about the validity of tests were frequently inaccurate because of the small numbers of people involved when the tests were tried. They also showed, quite convincingly, that the widely different results regarding test validity for similar jobs in different situations were also due to the small sample sizes in these studies.

We note here, and will repeat this again later, that Schmidt and Hunter were able to accomplish their breakthrough because of the existence of very large numbers of carefully reported validity studies. Their results do not mean that validity studies are no longer necessary, nor do their results mean that any test, regardless of who or how it is put together, will be valid. One of the purposes of this book is to teach the methods and procedures for doing and reporting careful validity studies so accomplishments like those of Schmidt and Hunter will be possible in the future as well.

The validity generalization findings and Equal Employment Opportunity (EEO) legislation have overlapping histories in that one of the outcomes of the validity generalization findings was the National Academy of Sciences (NAS) report on testing supporting the use of paper and pencil tests of cognitive ability in making hiring decisions, regardless of the subgroup (by race or sex, for example) on whom the test was being used. Thus, one of the things Schmidt and Hunter were able to show was that tests did not make artificial or unwarranted discriminations against persons as a function of their race or sex or age or national origin. Again, we will detail these issues later, but the Schmidt and Hunter findings are so important that they belong in this history chapter; they have only begun to have their full impact on the processes and procedures by which organizations are staffed.

SUMMARY

Considerable background information has been presented in this chapter and some of it may seem somewhat contradictory. For example, first we introduced the idea that many individual, job, organizational, and environmental factors influence people's behavior in the work setting. At the end of that discussion, however, was the idea that all of those factors were in reciprocal relationship, with people interacting with each other to determine many of those factors at the same time those factors were, in turn, influencing them. Following this discussion, we presented a brief history of ideas relevant to staffing organizations. This discussion emphasized both the role of individual differences in understanding individual behavior and the role of situational factors beyond individual control in influencing the behavior of people.

A subtle but important distinction had been introduced—the distinction between predicting and understanding the behavior of *individuals* and predicting and understanding the behavior of people in the *aggregate*. This is an important distinction, and one that will be introduced and reintroduced from time to time. In general, though, it refers to the idea that staffing researchers are always concerned with making a choice from a pool of applicants and the challenge is to make the best choice—to choose the best individual. At the same time, however, staffing researchers need to maintain an organizational perspective and be sensitive to the cumulative effects of decisions on the functioning of the organization, in the aggregate. To do this, staffing specialists need to remember that pay, leadership, job design, and management philosophy will all influence organizational performance at least as much as selection decisions will. So, the people responsible for staffing organizations cannot feel that the total burden of responsibility for the success and failure of the organization is on them. On the other hand, they must be sensitive to the cumulative effects of what they do because, in the aggregate, the result of a comprehensive staffing program will help determine the very organizational factors that are reflected in organizational effectiveness.

It is clear that most of this book will emphasize the making of choices among applicants for a job, i.e., it will focus on the individual and not on the cumulative effects or overall organizational performance. We do not yet, unfortunately, know very much about the cumulative effects of staffing on organizational performance (Schneider, 1983a, 1983b), nor about how staffing practices might be differentially important depending upon the needs of the organization (Olian and Rynes, in press), but work like that developed by Schmidt and Hunter suggest that the effects can be very positive indeed. We proceed under that assumption.

REFERENCES

Argyris, C. (1957). *Personality and organization*. New York: Harper.

Beer, M. (1980). *Organization change and development: A systems view*. Santa Monica, CA: Goodyear.

Binet, A., and Simon, T. (1948). The development of the Binet-Simon scale. In W. Dennis (Ed.). *Readings in the history of psychology.* New York: Appleton-Century-Crofts.

Boring, E. G. (1950). *History of experimental psychology,* 2nd ed. New York: Appleton-Century-Crofts.

Campbell, J. P., and Pritchard, R. D. (1976). Motivation theory in industrial and organizational psychology. In M. D. Dunnette (Ed.). *Handbook of industrial and organizational psychology.* Chicago: Rand McNally.

Cattell, J. M. (1948). Mental tests and measurements. In W. Dennis (Ed.) *Readings in the history of psychology.* New York: Appleton-Century-Crofts.

Herzberg, F., Mausner, B., and Snyderman, B. (1959). *The motivation to work,* 2nd ed. New York: Wiley.

Hull, C. L. (1928). *Aptitude testing.* Tarrytown, NY: World.

Hunter, J. E., and Hunter, R. F. (1984). Validity and utility of alternative predictors of job performance. *Psychological Bulletin, 96,* 72–95.

Jenkins, J. J., and Paterson, D. G. (Eds.). (1961). *Studies in individual differences: The search for intelligence.* New York: Appleton-Century-Crofts.

Lofquist, L. H., and Dawis, R. V. (1969). Adjustment to work. New York: Appleton-Century-Crofts.

Marrow, A. J. (1970). *The practical theorist.* New York: Basic Books.

Maslow, A. H. (1954). *Motivation and personality.* New York: Harper.

McGregor, D. M. (1960). *The human side of enterprise.* New York: McGraw-Hill.

National Academy of Sciences (1982). *Ability testing: Uses, consequences, and controversies,* Vol. 1. Washington, DC: National Academy Press.

Olian, J. D., and Rynes, S. L. (in press). Organizational staffing: Integrating practice with strategy. *Industrial Relations.*

Plato (1952). *The dialogues of Plato* (Trans. by B. Jowett). Chicago: Encyclopedia Britannica.

Schmidt, F. L., and Hunter, J. E. (1981). The future of criterion-related validity. *Personnel Psychology, 33,* 41–60.

Schneider, B. (1983a). An interactionist perspective on organizational effectiveness. In D. Whetten and K. S. Cameron (Eds.). *Organizational effectiveness: A comparison of multiple models.* New York: Academic Press.

Schneider, B. (1983b). Interactional psychology and organizational behavior. In L. L. Cummings and B. M. Staw (Eds.). *Research in organizational behavior,* Vol. 5, Greenwich, CT: JAI.

Scott, W. D., and Clothier, R. C. (1923). *Personnel management.* New York: McGraw-Hill.

Thompson, J. D. (1967). *Organizations in action.* New York: McGraw-Hill.

Thorndike, R. L. (1949). *Personnel selection.* New York: Wiley.

Uniform guidelines on employee selection procedures. (1978). *Federal Register, 43,* 38290–38315.

Viteles, M. S. (1932). *Industrial psychology.* New York: Norton.

Vroom, V. H. (1964). *Work and motivation.* New York: Wiley.

Welch, H. J., and Miles, G. H. (1935). *Industrial psychology in practice.* London: Sir Isaac Pitman & Sons.

JOB ANALYSIS IN THE ORGANIZATIONAL CONTEXT

AIMS OF THE CHAPTER

The orientation of this book toward staffing organizations emphasizes first the organization and then the staff. That is, the burden of responsibility for what staff does *in* the organization is placed *on* the organization.

This chapter furnishes a basic concept for defining what jobs and organizations are, of what they are comprised, and how they can be described in human terms; i.e., in terms that allow them to be staffed with humans. We will attempt to describe the organizations in which people work and the jobs at which they work.

From a staffing viewpoint the purpose of job and organizational analysis is really very simple—to discover the kinds of people the organization needs in order to be effective. The information collected to achieve the staffing purpose, however, can serve many functions—as a basis for designing training programs and wage and salary (compensation) programs, for job redesign, organizational renewal and change, etc. In other words, job and organizational analyses, because they describe the work setting in human terms, can be useful as a basis for any human-related program in organizations.

Our view of the interrelationship among organizations, tasks, and worker qualifications is aptly expressed in Figure 2–1, adapted from Sidney Fine (Fine, 1980). When the organization and the work fit the worker qualifications and the motivation of the workers, the result will be optimal in terms of individual and organizational productivity and worker growth and satisfaction.

For staffing purposes, job and organizational analyses serve three major functions:

1. Job analysis is a means for identifying the human behaviors necessary for adequate job performance. Based on the identification of such behaviors, theories about the kinds of people the job requires (usually in terms of KSAs— *knowledge, skills, or abilities*) can be formulated and procedures (tests, exercises, interviews) for identifying such people can be developed. The procedures can then be submitted to a test of their effectiveness. The process of testing the procedures is, in fact, a test of hypotheses derived from the job and organizational analyses. This process of testing hypotheses or theories is at the very heart of a systematic staffing program and recalls Binet and Simon's comments about ''testing the test;'' about ensuring that the hypothesis or theory is valid. One can see that the job and organizational analyses on which such programs are based are important determinants of the ultimate effectiveness of a staffing program.

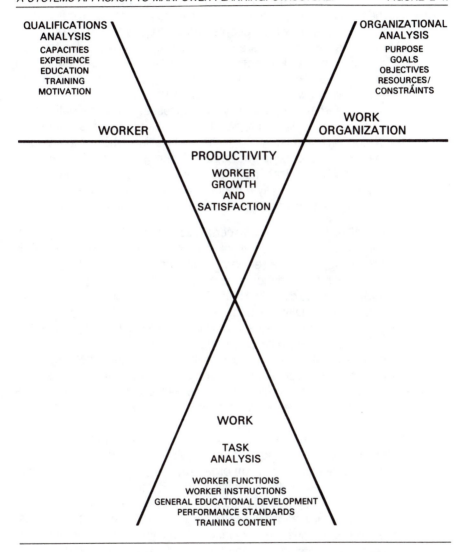

Another outcome of identifying necessary human behaviors is the development of standards against which the behavior of workers, and, therefore, the effectiveness of the staffing program, can be evaluated. If we know what behaviors are required for adequate performance, we can evaluate performance against those standards. (Procedures for identifying the worker behaviors necessary for adequate job performance are discussed in Types of Job Analysis Techniques later in this chapter.)

2. Job analysis identifies the rewards the job itself offers to the humans who do the job. Just as there are individual differences in the degree to which people can perform adequately on a job, there are individual differences in the degree to which the rewards that jobs offer will be satisfying to people. (Some procedures for identifying the kinds of rewards jobs offer are discussed under the section on Reward Attributes of Jobs.)

3. Organizational analysis is necessary because of the clear findings regarding the impact of organizational features, aside from the job, on human behavior in the work setting. Such organizational features as leadership and supervision, organizational reward systems, and organizational style have direct effects on employee behavior and thus play a major role in understanding and predicting aggregate levels of performance and productivity.

What this means is that certain conditions of jobs and organizations seem to be capable of generally suppressing or generally enhancing the work-relevant behaviors of people. By *generally* suppressing or enhancing we mean that it is in the organization as a whole that the condition has its effect and that different individuals tend to be equally affected.

For example, it is clear now that when organizations establish clearly specified, difficult but attainable goals for employees and provide employees feedback on their performance that aggregate performance levels are high (Locke & Lathan, 1984). These specific goals are interpreted similarly by all workers; the goals have a general, pervasive, effect on all employees for whom the goals are set.

It is still true, of course, that workers who have more of the qualifications a job requires will outperform people who fail to meet the qualifications. But, in organizations where the goal-setting procedures exist, it is possible for the performance of people with *less than average* qualifications to be as good as people who have *average* qualifications in another organization that fails to set goals. So, organizational performance is a function of both the qualifications of workers and the conditions under which they work; it is the combination that is important (Schneider, 1978). In Chapter 5 we will show statistically, the importance of this issue for understanding employee performance and organizational productivity.

Prior to detailing the various procedures for performing job analyses so we can specify the kinds of qualifications workers need, and the reasons for considering the organizational context, we first examine potential effects that the larger environment in which organizations operate can have on organizational and individual performance.

THE LARGER ENVIRONMENT

The larger environment in which organizations operate plays an important role in the way organizations design jobs and supervise people, and indeed, in the way people in organizations go about making decisions (cf. Beer, 1980; Katz and Kahn, 1978).

Burns and Stalker (1961), for example, conceptualize the "style" of organizations to be a function of the larger environment in which the organization operates. They suggest that this larger environment determines how an organization goes about accomplishing its goals. They note that, when the larger environment is stable, a *mechanistic* type of organization may be most effective. In a changing and unstable environment, an *organic* type of organization may be best. Burns and Stalker hypothesize that some differences in job and organizational designs may result from differences in the turbulence of the external world. Table 2–1 summarizes some of these differences in mechanistic and organic organizations.

The stability of the external environment seems to be a function of the volatility or perceived predictability of some or all of the following systems outside the organization with which organization members must deal:

1. The nature of the customer
2. The nature of the supplier
3. The nature of the competition
4. The nature of the sociopolitical environment
5. The nature of technology

We can hypothesize that an organization's design for management strategies and jobs through which it hopes to be effective is related to the nature of its external world. This is a relationship (rather than a one-way street) in the sense that while the larger environment affects organization management philosophy and job design, the organization's creativeness in identifying and effectively meeting the requirements of the external world will in turn have an effect on that external world. Thus customer demands, when met, result in less customer volatility (Schneider, Parkington, and Buxton, 1980). Less customer volatility, in turn, may result in a more mechanistic form of organization and job design, which again may spur a subsequent stimulation of customer volatility, and so on.

We address the larger environment issue to emphasize that jobs and organizations do not just independently exist; they are caused by understandable phenomena. We can conclude that organizations operating in different kinds of larger environments will develop different kinds of jobs. It follows that these jobs will require

TABLE 2-1. *MECHANISTIC AND ORGANIC ORGANIZATIONAL FORMS.*

MECHANISTIC	ORGANIC
1. Tasks are broken into very specialized abstract units	1. Tasks are broken down into subunits, but relation to total task of organization is much more clear
2. Tasks remain rigidly defined	2. Adjustment and continued redefinition of tasks through interaction of organizational members
3. Specific definition of responsibility that is attached to individual's functional role only	3. Broader acceptance of responsibility and commitment to organization that goes beyond individual's functional role
4. Strict hierarchy of control and authority	4. Less hierarchy of control and authority sanctions derive more from presumed community of interest
5. Formal leader assumed to be omniscient in all matters	5. Formal leader not assumed to be omniscient in all matters
6. Communication is mainly vertical between superiors and subordinates	6. Communication is lateral between people of different ranks and resembles consultation rather than command
7. Content of communication consists of instructions and decisions issued by superiors	7. Content of communication is information and advice
8. Loyalty and obedience to organization and superiors is highly valued	8. Commitment to tasks and progress and expansion of the firm is highly valued
9. Importance and prestige attached to identification with organization itself	9. Importance and prestige attached to affiliations and expertise in larger environment

From G. Zaltman, R. Duncan, and J. Holbek, *Innovations and organization* (New York: Wiley, 1973), p. 171. Reprinted by permission.

(and attract) different kinds of people. It is not surprising, then, as noted earlier, that organizations differ from each other as a result of the kinds of people who work there; hospitals attract, recruit, and select people who are different from those found in advertising companies. This idea of the affinities of people for being attracted to, selected by, and staying with particular organizations will be referred to throughout the book. Our concern now will be to understand what jobs are and how they can be described.

TYPES OF JOB ANALYSIS TECHNIQUES

In conjunction with the idea that jobs and organizations are ultimately dependent on each other (i.e., jobs exist in organizations), we will adopt Dunnette's definition of a job: "... a relatively homogeneous cluster of work tasks carried out to achieve some essential and enduring purpose in an organization (1966, p. 91)."

For our purposes, the value of this definition of a job is that it points out the essentially organizational nature of tasks and jobs; jobs do not just exist, they exist in organizations. Because they are created in organizations, jobs are, in fact, explicit statements by organizations of what they believe to be the most appropriate means for accomplishing their goals. While these explicit statements, jobs, may have been fostered without careful consideration of how the job contributes to some essential and enduring organizational purpose, jobs nevertheless help organizations tell employees about their goals, about how the goals are to be accomplished, and about how the organization views its human resources. Unfortunately, many organizations slide into their goals, and therefore, the jobs they create and their desires of employees are frequently poorly defined.

Such poor definition may have serious consequences for organizations, since we know that the nature or character of jobs is related, to some degree, to all of the following (Hackman & Oldham, 1980):

1. The amount of job satisfaction a worker experiences at work
2. The styles of leadership which will be most effective in supervising employees
3. The effectiveness of the organization
4. The motivation of employees

In short, the way jobs are designed can have important implications for many behavioral phenomena at work including ultimate organizational effectiveness. Of course, if the way jobs are designed is so important, then having effective procedures for describing jobs is similarly important. From a staffing point of view, job analysis is of central importance.

In defining jobs we believe it is important to distinguish between what is *required* of the employee and what *rewards* the job offers. The *job requirement* approach utilizes traditional methods to identify what the worker does on the job and the attributes he or she must bring to the job. In defining *worker rewards,* we consider what the job offers the worker in the way of fulfilling the kinds of psychological experiences people may desire from their work. Traditionally, most of the emphasis has been on detailing what characteristics a worker must have to perform effectively. Throughout this book, we argue that organizations must consider the satisfaction and commitment of employees. Rewards, both monetary and psychological, are important determinants of satisfaction and commitment; hence we believe they must be an integral part of job analysis and job description. In what follows, we first outline traditional procedures to define worker requirements, and then turn to a discussion of worker rewards.

A number of procedures have been devised for describing the demands jobs make on people—for describing what the job requires in terms of individual attributes. Once carried out, these procedures allow for the (relatively) unambiguous specification of acceptable performance and, as a result, help an organization identify the kinds of individuals it should recruit, select, develop, promote, and retain.

It has been noted that:

> The foundation for any selection and classification (staffing) program is a rich background of information about the job or jobs with which the program has to deal and a discriminating analysis and organization of that information (Thorndike, 1949, p. 3).

There are a number of procedures for gathering and organizing such information. We will discuss five of these approaches and will then propose a combination of approaches which we think more adequately satisfies several of the reasons for which job analyses are performed.

Functional Job Analysis

In 1977, the fourth edition of *The Dictionary of Occupational Titles* (DOT) was issued by the United States Employment Service. The publication of the DOT was important for two reasons. First, the DOT includes information on approximately 20,000 jobs that is potentially useful in determining job requirements or in confirming the information one might have gathered about a similar job. Second, the DOT describes a classification which amounts to a theory of work and a well defined methodology for gathering information concerning a job.

One major contribution of the work of Fine and his colleagues was the standardized manner in which they wrote task statements. This standardized form has been widely adopted by job analysts; its purpose was to clearly articulate the nature of different jobs to supervisors, trainers, recruiters, and other users of job information.

Task statements should include five types of information:

1. The subject of the task statement is assumed to be the worker or job incumbent.
2. The action performed requires an explicit, concrete verb. Verbs which point to a process such as "develops", "prepares", or "assesses" are undesirable.
3. The immediate objective of the work should be defined.
4. A task statement should identify the tools, equipment, or work aids a worker uses.
5. The task statement should include the type of instructions given to the worker.

An example of a complete edited task statement taken from Fine and Wiley (1974) is given below:

> Asks client questions, listens to responses, and writes answers on standard intake form, exercising leeway as to sequence of questions, in order to record basic identifying information.

In this task statement, "asks client questions, listens to responses, and writes answers" are the *actions* required. The immediate objective of the action is the recording of "basic identifying information", and the *tools, equipment, and work aids* were the "standard intake form" and a pen. The *instructions* included using the form but exercising discretion with respect to the sequence of questions asked.

When a task statement includes these pieces of information, staffing personnel have the basis upon which they can infer the worker qualifications needed to perform the task. The information required to write task statements is gathered by reviewing existing materials concerning the job and by interviewing job incumbents and their supervisors. Trained job analysts, however, write the task statements and provide the ratings discussed below. An example of a completed task analysis form for the job of an industrial/organizational psychologist is presented in Figure 2–2. Note the completed task analysis form includes information on the training and performance standards relevant to the task and a series of ratings of this task along the top. We turn next to a discussion of these ratings.

Functional job analysis is also a conceptual system used to define the level and orientation of worker activity. Fine assumes that the tasks people do can be organized along three dimensions that reveal the extent of their involvement with *data, people,* or *things.* The actions on each of the three dimensions are classified by the three worker function scales depicted in Figure 2–3 (see Fine & Wiley, 1974, p. 10). As can be seen in the figure, the actions or functions in each of these scales are actually examples of behavior ranging from the simple to more complex. There are two ways of

FIGURE 2-2. *FUNCTIONAL JOB ANALYSIS TASK STATEMENT AND RATINGS*

TASK CODE:

WORKER FUNCTION LEVEL AND ORIENTATION						WORKER	GENERAL EDUCATIONAL DEVELOPMENT		
DATA	%	PEOPLE	%	THINGS	%	INSTRUCTIONS	REASONING	MATH	LANGUAGE
3B	85	1A	5	1A	10	3	4	4	5

GOAL:

OBJECTIVE:

TASK: Writes report of validation study, outlining the procedures followed, the results obtained, and the conclusions drawn using standard reporting procedures and some discretion in the way the material is presented in order to comply with organization's reporting requirements.

(To Perform This Task)

PERFORMANCE STANDARDS	TRAINING CONTENT
DESCRIPTIVE:	FUNCTIONAL:
1. Writes clearly and legibly.	1. How to write report of validation study.
2. Writes on a level appropriate to the audience.	2. How to express oneself in non-technical terms.
3. Report is complete and accurate.	3. How to interpret results of a validation study.
4. Format of report follows the standard reporting procedures.	
	SPECIFIC:
NUMERICAL:	1. Knowledge of validation procedures used and results obtained.
1. Report includes all of the following: procedures, validity, reliability, norms, differential validity, test bias.	2. Knowledge of standard reporting procedure.
2. Report is completed within X amount of time from completion of validation study.	
3. X% feel level of report is understandable.	
(To These Standards)	*(Worker Needs This Training)*

DATA	PEOPLE	THINGS
0 Synthesizing	0 Mentoring	0 Setting Up
1 Coordinating	1 Negotiating	1 Precision Working
2 Analyzing	2 Instructing	2 Operating-Controlling
3 Compiling	3 Supervising	3 Driving-Operating
4 Computing	4 Diverting	4 Manipulating
5 Copying	5 Persuading	5 Tending
6 Comparing	6 Speaking-Signaling	6 Feeding-Offbearing
	7 Serving	7 Handling
	8 Taking Instructions-Helping	

Adapted from Figure 1 of Fine and Wiley, (1974) p.10.

comparing and measuring the behavioral requirements of any task in a job. Jobs can be described in terms of their *level* of involvement with Data, People, and Things—ranging from the relatively complex at the top of the scales in Figure 2–3 to the relatively simple at the bottom of the same scales. The *orientation* of a worker with respect to Data, People, or Things can be described by the percent of time spent on each of the three dimensions. When a given task has been assigned Functional Level and Orientation scores for Data, People, and Things, the worker's total involvement with the specific facets of that task—mentally (Data), physically (Things), and interpersonally (People)—is obtained. Similarly, a job comprised of *many* tasks can be given Functional Level and Orientation ratings. For example, a college professor's job might be described as follows:

Area	Functional Level	Orientation
Data	Synthesizing (0)	30%
People	Mentoring (0)	60%
Things	Handling (7)	10%

The worker function scales provide a means to compare all tasks and jobs. These worker function scales are used as the basis for the fourth (Data), fifth (People), and sixth (Things) digits of the DOT code that is assigned to each of the jobs described in the latest revision of the DOT.

The first digit in the DOT code represents the major category of work as follows:

1. Professional, technical, managerial occupations
2. Clerical and sales occupations
3. Service occupations
4. Farming, fishing, forestry and related occupations
5. Processing occupations

6. Machine trades occupations
7. Bench work occupations
8. Structural work occupations
9. Miscellaneous

The second and third digits represent greater degrees of specificity. For example, a DOT code of 15 represents a Professional, Technical, or Managerial occupation (1) in Entertainment and Recreation (5) while a code of 152 represents an occupation in Music.

A supplement to the DOT (Selected Characteristics of Occupations Defined in the DOT, 1981) offers additional information concerning the worker traits associated with job incumbents in these classifications. Since it deals with worker traits, this information is relevant to staffing personnel interested in Selection and Training. The traits required for job holders were rated by the job analyst who collected the original information and include the following categories:

1. Mathematical and Language Development (Training Time)
2. Specific Vocational Preparation (Training Time)
3. Aptitudes (nine aptitudes as measured by the General Aptitude Test Battery are rated on a 5-point scale)
4. Physical Demands (six categories)
5. Environmental Conditions (seven categories)

Training time embraces both the general educational development (Mathematical and Language Development) and any specific vocational preparation needed for a worker to acquire knowledge, skills, and abilities (KSAs) necessary for a job. Mathematical and Language Development includes formal or informal education or work experience that contribute to a worker's acquisition of language or math skills. Specific vocational preparation includes time required to learn techniques or acquire information necessary for successful job performance in a specific job-worker situation. Experience in lower level jobs, apprenticeships, in-plant and on-the-job training, and vocational programs are all examples. While the information concerning training time may be more useful in a counseling context than a selection context, knowledge of the amount of training and type of training typically required for effective performance on a job can lead to the hypothesis that certain knowledge, skills, and abilities have been acquired and are needed by job incumbents.

General aptitude requirements are indicated in terms of nine different aptitudes. For each of these nine aptitudes a digit from 1–5 expresses the average level of a given aptitude for persons employed in that job in comparison to the level of aptitude in the general working population where 1 = the top 10 percent of the population; 2 = top third exclusive of the top 10 percent; 3 = middle third of the general population; 4 = bottom third exclusive of the bottom 10 percent; and 5 = bottom 10 percent. For example, a 1 on Numerical ability means the average performance of workers on the job in question ranks in the top 10 percent of the general population. The aptitudes used by the DOT in its description of job requirements are as follows: (Note that these nine aptitudes are the basis of the General Aptitude Test Battery discussed in Chapter 8.)

- INTELLIGENCE: General learning ability. The ability to "catch on" or understand instructions and underlying principles. Ability to reason and make judgments. Closely related to doing well in school.
- VERBAL: Ability to understand meanings of words and ideas associated with them and to use them effectively. To comprehend language, to understand relationships between words, and to understand meanings of whole sentences and paragraphs. To present information or ideas clearly.
- NUMERICAL: Ability to perform arithmetic operations quickly and accurately.
- SPATIAL: Ability to comprehend forms in space and understand relationships of plane and solid objects. May be used in such tasks as blueprint reading and in solving geometry problems. Frequently described as the ability to "visualize" objects of two or three dimensions, or to think visually of geometric forms.
- FORM PERCEPTION: Ability to perceive pertinent detail in objects or in pictorial or graphic material; to make visual comparisons and discriminations and see slight differences in shapes and shadings of figures and widths and lengths of lines.
- CLERICAL PERCEPTION: Ability to perceive pertinent detail in verbal or tabular material. To observe differences in copy, to proofread words and numbers, and to avoid perceptual errors in arithmetic computation.
- MOTOR COORDINATION: Ability to coordinate eyes and hands or fingers rapidly and accurately in making precise movements with speed. Ability to make a movement response accurately and quickly.
- FINGER DEXTERITY: Ability to move the fingers and manipulate small objects with the fingers rapidly or accurately.
- MANUAL DEXTERITY: Ability to move the hands easily and skillfully. To work with the hands in placing and turning motions.

Physical demands are broken into six categories: 1) strength requirements; 2) climbing and/or balancing; 3) stooping, kneeling, crouching, and/or crawling; 4) reaching, handling, fingering, and/or feeling; 5) talking and/or hearing; and 6) seeing.

Environmental conditions are the physical surroundings a worker is likely to experience. They are described in terms of seven dimensions: 1) inside, outside, or both; 2) temperature changes and extremes of cold; 3) temperature changes plus extremes of heat; 4) moisture and humidity; 5) noise and vibration; 6) hazards; and 7) fumes, odors, toxic conditions, dust, and poor ventilation.

As should now be clear, the DOT represents a rich source of information concerning the work a job incumbent does and the worker characteristics which discriminate between good and bad performers on the job—for over 20,000 jobs! This information can be used to suggest what measures of individual differences to include in a selection battery. This DOT should be extremely helpful in suggesting what a researcher should expect to find in a job analysis and what he or she may have missed with respect to a given job. This information could also be given to job applicants as screening material. For example, some job applicants may be unaware of the harsh physical demands and working conditions characteristic of some jobs.

The Job-Element Approach

The U.S. Civil Service under the direction of E. S. Primoff has used the job element approach (Primoff, 1975) to identify the worker characteristics associated with good job performance. Job elements in his approach are defined as abilities, skills, knowledge, and personal characteristics that are necessary to perform a job. The job elements are identified in a brainstorming session in which the job analyst defines what he or she means by a job element, gives examples, and then asks a group of expert job incumbents to identify such elements. The brainstorming session seeks to identify individual differences in job performance. The directions one gives to this group are very important; a typical set of directions provided by Primoff (1975, p. 9) follows:

> We would like to list the abilities, knowledges, skills and personal characteristics that are necessary for the job of _____. What ability must an employee have? What makes an employee superior? In what areas have you had trouble when employees are weak?

The identified elements are then typed onto a form containing four scales similar to that in Figure 2–4. Expert job incumbents and/or supervisors are asked to rate each element on each scale.

From these ratings, the *Item Index* of an element is computed by multiplying the values in the "To pick out superior worker" and "Practicality" ratings and adding the "Trouble likely" rating.

Item Index = (To pick Superior × Practicality) + Trouble Likely

For example, in Figure 2–4 we have three job elements that might

FIGURE 2-4. *JOB-ELEMENT BLANK FOR HAND CALCULATION—FACE PAGE*

Rater's Name and Grade _____

Job Rated: Title and Grade _____
Title & Installation _____

Element	Barely acceptable workers 2 All have 1 Some have 0 Almost none have	To pick out *superior* worker 2 Very important 1 Valuable 0 Does not differentiate	Trouble likely if not considered 2 Much trouble 1 Some trouble 0 Safe to ignore	Practicality. Demanding this element, we can fill 2 All openings 1 Some openings 0 Almost no openings	$S \times P$	Trouble	Item Index: $S \times P + T$	Total Value: Item Index + S $- B - P$
Ability to add 2-digit numbers	2	0	2	2	0	2	2	−2
Can cook hamburgers	0	1	1	0	0	1	1	2
Can scrub floors	1	1	1	2	2	1	3	1

be necessary elements for a person working in a local Mac-Donalds:

1. Ability to add 2-digit numbers
2. Can cook hamburgers
3. Can scrub floors

The Item Index for "Ability to add 2-digit numbers" would be (0 × 2) + 2 or 2. For the element, "Can cook hamburgers," the Item Index would be (1 × 0) + 1 or 1.

The *Total Value* of an element is calculated by adding the totals of the Item Index and "To pick out superior worker" and subtracting the values for "Barely acceptable workers" and for "Practicality." So, for the element "Ability to add 2-digit numbers":

Total value = (Item Index + To pick superior) − (Barely acceptable + Practicality)

Total value = (2 + 0) − (2 + 2)

Total value = 2 − 4

Total value = −2

A third value, the *Training Value,* of an element can be calculated by:

1. Reversing the score for the element in the "Practicality" column
2. Multiplying "To pick superior" times this reversed "Practicality" rating
3. Adding the "To pick superior" and "Trouble likely" ratings to the product and subtracting the "Barely Acceptable" rating

Following this formula through, we see that the Training Values for the first two elements in Figure 2–4 are (0 × 0) + 0 + 2 − 2 = 0 and (1 × 2) + 1 + 1 − 1 = 4 respectively. This means that it is far more likely that we would have to train people to cook hamburgers (Training Value = 4) than to add 2-digit numbers (Training Value = 0).

We can see from these calculations that what Primoff (1975) attempted to do was to be systematic *and* realistic in describing worker characteristics required for jobs. The job element approach is systematic in that each job is described in terms of its own elements but according to the same issues ("Barely acceptable workers," "To pick out superior workers," etc.).

The procedure is realistic in two ways. First, the job element approach helps decide whether the element is a characteristic workers must have when they come to the job or whether it is something more likely to require training. The second way in which It is realistic concerns the use of the "Practicality" column, in particular, and the other columns as well. This means that while a particular applicant characteristic may be very desirable ("much trouble likely if not considered") it may be impractical to expect it. In the job element approach, then, we apportion the responsibility for having acceptable workers to selection or training, depending upon the practicality associated with the desirability of hiring workers who can perform various elements.

Use of the job element approach to establish test batteries for selection has several advantages, not the least of which is the relative ease with which data is gathered from many people. Second, the job element approach deals directly with establishing worker characteristics, thus circumventing the problem of inferring the ability requirements of a position based on task or duty statements. An interesting application of the job element approach is the use and documentation of past achievements as the basis on which to select employees (see Schmidt, Caplan, Bemis, Decuir, Dunn, & Antone, 1979). In Chapter 10, we present an example of this approach.

Position Analysis Questionnaire

Beginning in the 1950's, Dr. Ernest J. McCormick and his colleagues at Purdue University began a program of research which led to the development of a job analysis instrument called the *Position Analysis Questionnaire* (PAQ). Instead of requiring a job analyst to produce a narrative description of tasks for the PAQ, the job analyst or expert job incumbent makes ratings of a job on 194 descriptors. These descriptors are elements of work activity and the analyst judges the degree to which the element is present.

The development of the PAQ was based on the assumption that there was a commonality across jobs which was a result of workers doing similar things and not as a result of the technology used or the product produced. McCormick has called these common activities that workers do *worker-oriented variables* (actual behaviors) as opposed to the latter set of variables, which he called *job-oriented variables.*

The first three sections of the PAQ have worker behavior descriptors that are based on an information processing model. That is, the behaviors specified have to do with either *securing information, processing information,* or *outputting behavior.* Three additional sections were added to the PAQ because they define important requirements even though they are not part of the information processing model. The fourth part consists of *interpersonal*

FIGURE 2-5.   SAMPLE ITEMS FROM THE POSITION ANALYSIS
QUESTIONNAIRE

---

2.   MEDIATION PROCESSES

2.1   DECISION-MAKING AND REASONING

Decision-making (indicate by code the level of decision-making (typically) involved in the job, considering: the number and complexity of the factors that are taken into account; the variety of alternatives available; the consequences and importance of the decisions; the background experience, education, and training required; the precedents available for guidance; and other relevant considerations. The examples given for the following codes are only suggestions.)

Code	Level of Decision
1	Low ("decisions" in selecting parts in routine assembly, items in a warehouse, pasting labels on cartons, tending automatic machines, etc.)
2	Below average ("decisions" in operating a wood planer, dispatching a taxi, lubricating an automobile, etc.)
3	Average ("decisions" in setting-up machine tools for operation, diagnosing mechanical disorders of aircraft, ordering office supplies several months in advance, etc.)
4	Above average ("decisions" in determining production quotas, making personnel decisions such as promoting and hiring, etc.)
5	High ("decisions" in approving corporation annual budget, recommending surgery, selecting the location for a new plant, etc.).

---

activities such as communication requirements, interpersonal relationships, personal contacts, and supervision and coordination. The fifth section deals with *physical working conditions* as well as the *psychological and social aspects* of the job. The final section includes *miscellaneous items* regarding work schedules, uniform requirements, job demands, and level of responsibility.

As indicated here, a group of experienced job incumbents responds to each of the descriptors in the PAQ on an appropriate Likert-format scale: Extent of Use, Importance, Time Spent, or various special scales. A sample item measuring the degree of mediation processes with a special rating scale is given in Figure 2–5. Studies of interrater reliability have indicated that different raters give essentially identical ratings to the tasks in a job (see McCormick, Jeanneret, & Mecham, 1972).

The quantitative nature of the responses to the PAQ permits the application of a statistical procedure called *factor analysis* to be used in isolating the major underlying dimensions of job behavior across a large number of jobs. Factor analyses allow us to answer the question: what kinds of behavior characterize work behavior? The Functional Job Analysis and DOT answer to this question is Data, People, and Things, but these are very general behavioral categories. Factor analyses of the ratings of 536 different jobs in relation to the 194 elements in the PAQ indicated that jobs tend to differ from each other on five important dimensions:

1. Having decision-making/communication/social responsibilities. (This dimension reflects activities involving considerable
amounts of communication and interaction with people, as well as
responsibilities associated with decision-making and planning
functions, such as might be the case with a general foreman.)
2. Performing skilled activities. (This dimension is characterized by activities in which technical devices or tools tend to be
used, and in which there is an emphasis on precision, recognizing
differences, and manual control, such as in the case of tool-and-die
makers.)
3. Being physically active/related environmental conditions.
(This dimension is characterized by activities involving considerable movement of the entire body or major parts of it, along with such
environments as those of factories, shops, etc.)
4. Operating vehicles/equipment. (This dimension is characterized by some aspect of the operation or use of vehicles or
equipment, typically involving sensory and perceptual processes
and physical functions.)
5. Processing information. (This dimension is characterized
by a wide range of information-processing activities such as in the
case of budget officers or editors, in some instances accompanied
by the use of machines such as office machines [McCormick &
Ilgen, 1980]).

The data base maintained to interpret the PAQ is perhaps as
useful as the instrument itself. Responses to the PAQ can be sent
to PAQ Services in Logan, Utah for scoring. The resultant PAQ
analysis provides an estimate of the various worker attributes predictive of success in a given job and a comparison of this job with
other job classifications for which data are available. Percentile
scores of the job on each of the 32 PAQ dimensions (based on
more detailed factor analyses reported in McCormick, Jeanneret,
& Mecham, 1972) describe the levels of both the mental and physical characteristics that are required in the job and the level of each
which is required by the job. In addition, predicted scores on the
subtests of the *General Aptitude Test Battery* (GATB) and estimated
validities of the subtests for the job in question are provided. The
McCormick et al. (1972) paper describes the development of this
data base.

It should be noted that in providing validities for the job, this
technique produces information similar to that provided by subject
matter experts in the Civil Service methodology described here.
McCormick et al. (1972) based their assertions on the relationship
between the validities of the test and attribute ratings while the job
element methodology bases it directly on the judgments of subject
matter experts.

The ability to describe a large number of jobs with a constant set of descriptors yields another very important outcome: jobs can be compared to each other and similar jobs can be clustered into job families. This comparison capability allows one job analyst to compare a specific job to other similar jobs, providing considerable breadth of analytic information. In later chapters we will discuss additional uses of job clusters in the development of predictors to help make staffing decisions; for now it is sufficient to note that jobs can be clustered together on the basis of many kinds of information in addition to the similarity of actual worker activities involved. Jobs may be grouped on the basis of ability, temperament and/or interest requirements, or on the basis of common activities, or on the basis of the kinds of rewards people obtain from them.

We will discuss the relative advantages and disadvantages of various job analysis techniques later in this chapter, but the PAQ has one peculiar limitation: its reading level. Application of the Flesch formula by the authors indicated college reading skills are necessary to use the PAQ, which may present a problem for both job incumbents and job analysts in some situations.

Task Inventories

A job or task inventory is a structured job analysis questionnaire consisting of a list of tasks which are relevant to some occupational area. As such, they represent a job-oriented approach to job analysis as defined by McCormick (1976). Incumbents or supervisors are required to respond to inventories such as that depicted in Figure 2–6. Developing task inventories has been most popular with the Personnel Division of the Air Force Human Resources Laboratory (Morsh & Archer, 1967). In its final form, the job inventory consists of a set of tasks and several response scales. The respondent checks each task that he or she does and the task is then rated for "Time Spent" and "Significance to Position." The list of tasks included in an inventory should include all of the tasks that might be performed by a job incumbent. The tasks are usually grouped into similar broad categories called duties.

While it might seem most appropriate to have respondents answer the "Time Spent" dimension in terms of hours per week or percentage of time per task, research has generally indicated that a "relative time spent" scale is more desirable than direct estimates (Christal, 1974). When people are asked to give direct estimates, some raters report spending 300% of their time, or 120 hours per week. This could well be because workers' tasks overlap, but it could also be because they have reason to emphasize

PORTION OF A JOB INVENTORY DEVELOPED UNDER AIR FORCE
CONTRACT (41(609)–3162) FOR THE JET ENGINE MECHANIC.
DEVELOPED BY LIFSON, WILSON, FERGUSON, AND WINICK.

FIGURE 2–6.

DUTY: REPAIRING AND MAINTAINING JET ENGINES	CHECK √ IF DONE	TIME SPENT 1. Very much below average 2. Below average 3. Slightly below average 4. About average 5. Slightly above average 6. Above average 7. Very much above average	SIGNIFICANCE TO POSITION 1. An insignificant part 2. A very minor part 3. A minor part 4. A moderate part 5. A substantial part 6. A very substantial part 7. A most significant part
1. Adjust afterburner nozzles			
2. Adjust maintenance trailers			
3. Analyze inspection findings to determine extent of repair needed			
4. Apply safety wire to engine components			
5. Arrange for space for engine parts prior to disassembly			

the difficulty of their job when job analysis information is collected
and over-estimate time spent on tasks.

Because the list of tasks involved in the performance of a job
is likely to differ across jobs, task inventories must be developed
separately for each occupational area. Furthermore, developing a
single task inventory is a time-consuming process. The steps used
to develop a task inventory are presented below based on McCormick (1976) and Morsh and Archer (1967):

1. Explore source material. The job analyst should read
materials that describe the occupation of interest: training materials, instructional manuals for equipment, organizational charts and
directives, technical reports, and texts. Job incumbents are also
asked to supply lists of task statements.

2. Develop a preliminary inventory with major duty areas
each of which includes several tasks. Task statements from the
various sources are organized into a consistent form and written so
as to describe actual job activities in clear and unambiguous language and so that the rating scales with which they are used make
sense.

3. Review the inventory. Several experts in the occupational

area who are instructed to supply missing tasks and edit those already in the preliminary inventory review the inventory.

4. The analyst reviews the suggestions and constructs a final inventory which incorporates these suggestions. The final form usually includes an open-ended question asking incumbents to write in task statements which may have been omitted.

Research has shown that task inventories have acceptable interrater and test-retest reliability. For example, ratings from the same expert at two different time periods (spaced 1 to 2 weeks apart so real job changes do not take place) result in rank-ordering tasks in very similar fashion (see McCormick, 1976, for data from three unpublished studies). Similarly, the rank-ordering of tasks by "time spent" and "percent performing" ratings were highly similar.

The second aspect of the validity of task-oriented inventories involves the question of whether or not appropriate KSAs can be derived from the job inventory data. Deriving ability requirements from task statements requires an additional judgment on the part of a job analyst or personnel selection specialist that the performance of a given task *requires* certain skills or abilities. There is little available evidence on the comparability of various job analysis techniques, and hence, little information on this aspect of validity.

In summary, task oriented job inventories are reliable instruments when used to collect information on what tasks are required. The Air Force has used them successfully for years to monitor the changes that occur in jobs as a result of technological advances and/or personnel changes. Further, a computerized method called CODAP has been developed to summarize job analysis ratings. But, task inventories are expensive and time-consuming to develop, and they must be developed separately for every occupation one is interested in. Use of task inventories to establish knowledge, skill, and ability requirements also demands that someone decide what abilities will indicate individual differences in job performance. On the other hand, Prien (1977) takes the position that some form of task-oriented job analysis will be necessary when one is interested in constructing content-valid tests. The use of a combination of worker-oriented and job-oriented methods has, in fact, been proposed by those interested in establishing the content validity of selection procedures (Levine, 1983).

Critical Incidents Methodology

Flanagan (1954) proposed using a method which focuses on the things a worker does which distinguish that person as an effective or ineffective employee. Flanagan's method has been appropriately labeled the critical incident technique. An incident is defined as any observable human activity that is "sufficiently complete in itself to permit inferences and predictions to be made about the person performing the act" (Flanagan, 1954, p. 327). In order to be critical, an incident should occur in a situation in which the purpose or intent of the act seems clear to the observer and where its consequences are sufficiently definite to leave little doubt about the effects.

The critical incidents technique requires the following steps:

1. Agreement must be obtained regarding the goals and objectives of the job in question. Thus, the eventual users must be involved at the outset in helping specify the dimensions of performance for which critical incidents will be generated.

2. Plans need to be made about the incidents to be gathered. These plans specify relevant issues such as the place, the persons, the conditions, and the activities. For example, one plan might be to "collect incidents on the behavior of a grocery store clerk at a checkout line during peak hours of customer flow."

In addition *who* will be doing the observing needs to be decided. This decision should begin by considering people who are very familiar with the job (Subject Matter Experts or SMEs). At a minimum, the people who are charged with developing examples of effective and ineffective behaviors should receive some exposure to the job and its objectives. Flanagan (1954) suggests that in every case, plans should be made to specify the qualifications of the observers, the characteristics of the group to be observed, and the behavior (its relevance to some general organizational objective) to be observed.

3. Data must be collected. This can take the form of an interview or questionnaire, but it is easier if observers and/or reporters record information fairly close in time to the occurrence of behavior and if they know in advance the kinds of information that will be required.

In collecting data, it might be useful to ask observers to answer a series of questions (an example of answers for an incident involving emergency telephone operators is given below) about each incident observed as follows:

a. *What were the circumstances leading to the incident?* (Answer: Caller had called the emergency number repeatedly using abusive language, but reporting no problem.)

b. *What did the operator do that made you think she or he was a good, average, or poor performer?* (Answer: Operator "told off" the caller and angrily hung up.)

c. *What were the consequences of the operator's behavior in the critical incident?* (Answer: Considerable adverse publicity for the emergency center because caller reported the incident, and all conversations were tape recorded.)

d. *How effective do you feel this example of performance was* (circle one)?

1 ② 3   4   5   6   7
Extremely   About   Extremely
ineffective Average effective

4. Analyze the data. The data-collection process results in a mass of incidents descriptive of effective and ineffective behaviors in particular (critical) situations. For selection purposes, the data need to be sorted into dimensions of behavior that seem to characterize particular facets of job performance. For example, in the case of a grocery store check-out clerk, some dimensions of performance might be "courtesy," "accuracy," and "packaging," with each dimension being specified by examples of critical effective and ineffective behavior. These dimensions, then, become the focus of selection after specification of the KSAs required.

In summary, if the job analyst is successful in completing the steps above he or she should have a list of incidents which are behavioral and observable, a list of the situational factors involved, and judgments concerning the criticalness and importance of the incidents.

For the past 20 years, critical incidents methodology has been adapted to develop performance measures rather than as a job analysis technique (e.g., Smith and Kendall, 1963; Latham and Wexley, 1981). This adaptation represents the most widely used form of critical incidents methodology and is described in Chapter 3 on performance criteria.

The strength of the critical incidents approach lies in the emphasis placed on the observation of behavior that is critically important to successful job performance; that is, behaviors that discriminate effective from ineffective performers. On the other hand, several deficiencies have been noted in the use of the critical incidents approach in establishing the KSA requirements of a job. Most basic is the fact that nothing in the methodology leads to an explicit statement of ability requirements; one must still make a judgment concerning what knowledge, skills or abilities indicate individual differences in the capacity of a job applicant to perform an effective critical incident and to avoid ineffective critical incidents. In addition, job tasks which everyone masters and which they spend most of their time doing may never show up in a list of *critical* incidents. This criticism is not really relevant to personnel selection, since such tasks by definition can have nothing to do with individual differences in ability to perform the job. Finally, emphasis on incidents may lead to a fragmented view of the job in which one is unable to ascertain how various elements or tasks fit together.

COMPARISONS AND COMBINATION OF JOB ANALYSIS APPROACHES

Comparisons of Job Analysis Methods

Systematic methods of gathering job analysis data have received increasing attention by psychologists interested in selection and test validation. Professional guidelines on test use prepared by The American Psychological Association and the Society for Industrial and Organizational Psychology as well as the 1978 Uniform Guidelines on Employee Selection Procedures published jointly by the Departments of Labor and Justice, the Equal Employment Opportunity Commission Council, the Civil Service Commission and the Civil Rights Commission, all emphasize the importance of job analysis. In addition, court cases involving alleged discrimatory hiring have used the adequacy of job analysis as one criterion by which to judge validity studies (though the detail necessary in the job analysis may be far less than the courts typically seem to demand).

Thompson and Thompson (1982), for example, reviewed 26 court cases concerned with the requirements for an adequate job analysis. Their conclusions may be summarized as follows:

1. A job analysis must be performed on the job in question.
2. Results of the job analysis need to be in written form.
3. Multiple sources of information need to be utilized in the job analysis process:
   • Interviews with incumbents, supervisors and administrators
   • Training manuals and other written materials
   • Actual observation
   • Surveys and inventories of relevant tasks, duties and activities
4. Specification of KSAs must be included and the design of predictors must be based on these KSAs.

Since job analysis is a critical first step in establishing a variety of staffing problems and the tremendous effort and expense associated with job analyses, it is not surprising that several efforts have been made to compare job analysis methodologies.

Levine, Bennett, and Ash (1980) have compared critical incidents, job elements, PAQ, and task inventory approaches to job analysis in terms of their similarity in producing similar test plans. Each of these four job analysis methods was used to analyze four classes of jobs; then 64 personnel selection specialists used the job analysis reports to construct test plans. The four job analysis techniques were compared on four criteria:

1. *Informational reports* such as how good a picture of the job each report gives, how easy the report is to work with, and how much confidence one has concerning the exam plan developed were collected from each study participant.

2. *Costs incurred* in developing the job analysis report and in reviewing the report and constructing exams from it were evaluated for each method.

3. *The quality of the exam* plans was rated by "occupational experts" and the researchers.

4. Finally, measures of *how many exam techniques were proposed, how many constructs they measured,* and *the weights each construct received were obtained.* *

Perhaps the most striking result, and also the most important relative to this chapter, is that there were relatively few significant differences among job analysis methods. More specifically, small effects were observed for exam plan content, exam plan quality, or costs incurred in developing exam plans. The critical incidents technique resulted in somewhat higher ratings when differences did occur; the PAQ and critical incidents technique were less favored by the study participants; and study participants reported a great deal of difficulty with the PAQ language level. While the study does have limitations duly noted by the authors, they conclude that the relative lack of impact of job analysis methods on the criteria indicates that any method may do equally well.

It may be, as Levine et al. (1980) suggest, that a person who is familiar with test development can study a brief job description, spend some time talking with job incumbents and supervisors, and then produce an exam plan as good as someone who has gone through an extensive and expensive job analysis. However, it must be noted that their conclusions are based totally on the similarity of exam plans, not how *good* the exam plans and tests turned out to be as predictors of job performance. What is really needed, then, is evidence that the selection instruments developed are similar and that the validities for tests developed after different job analyses are the same. Consequently, the data that are really needed to compare job analysis methodologies were not collected.

Recently, Levine and his colleagues (Levine, Ash, Hall, & Sistrunk, 1983; Levine, 1983) have reported another study in which

---

*In this project, any difference that may have existed regarding familiarity with the job(s) being studied and/or the job analysis method(s) being used were taken into account when comparing job analysis methods.

they evaluated seven different methods of job analysis (the five discussed in this chapter plus threshold traits analysis (Lopez, Kesselman, & Lopez, 1981; and ability requirements scales (Fleishman, 1975). Their study involved ratings of the seven methodologies by 93 persons whose average experience in job analysis work was over six years. They included persons affiliated with universities, federal, state, and local government agencies, and private business and consulting firms. These job analysis "experts" provided ratings concerning the usefulness of each technique for eleven different purposes.

Of the five analysis techniques we discussed earlier, Levine's experts' opinions were as follows:

1. Functional job analysis serves best the widest variety of purposes, and is considered mediocre (rating of 3) only for purposes of worker mobility, efficiency and safety, work force planning, and legal requirements.
2. The task inventory method also is rated relatively highly for a variety of purposes.
3. The PAQ is perceived to be most useful for job classification and evaluation purposes and of least use for efficiency/safety purposes.
4. The job element approach is rated best in establishing personnel requirements and specifications and rated lowest for efficiency/safety purposes.
5. The critical incident technique was viewed as particularly useful for performance appraisal purposes but not widely useful for other personnel functions.
6. The major conclusion of Levine's survey is that the purpose for which the job analysis is done should dictate the method used.

Levine (1983) also collected data regarding the perceived practicality of each technique. Table 2–2 defines the considerations Levine asked the job analysis experts to rate. This is a good list to retain because these are issues to be considered whenever a choice of job analysis methods needs to be made. The responses of the experts can be briefly summarized as follows:

1. The PAQ is perceived as the most practical.
2. Functional job analysis and task inventories are perceived as relatively practical across a wide variety of concerns.
3. The job elements method is considered versatile and ready to use, but mediocre on most other criteria.
4. The critical incident method is seen as least practical.

While these survey data should be supplemented with evidence as to which method actually leads to more valid selection procedures, more efficiently designed workplaces, or better safety

TABLE 2–2. *PRACTICAL CONCERNS IN THE SELECTION OF A JOB ANALYSIS METHOD.*

(1) *Occupational Versatility.* This indicates the extent to which the method is suitable for analyzing a variety of jobs rather than only one or two.

(2) *Standardization.* This indicates the extent to which a method may yield data in the form of norms (similar to a standard IQ score) so that jobs analyzed in different settings can be compared (as people can be compared on IQ scores). An impractical method would be one in which the outcome of jobs analyzed in different situations can't be compared. A practical method would allow for easy comparisons between jobs that had been analyzed in different settings.

(3) *Respondent and User Acceptability.* This indicates the degree to which a job analysis method, including all of its data gathering and reporting aspects, is found to be acceptable to people who supply job analysis information and to people who use it. An impractical method would be difficult to sell. For example, a method may be unacceptable because it requires too much time away from the worker's job. On the other hand, a practical method would be enthusiastically embraced by respondents and users alike.

(4) *Amount of Job Analyst Training Required.* This indicates the degree to which training is required for someone to be able to put the method into use without supervision. An impractical method would be one in which the job analyst would need an extended period of training in order to use the method. A practical method would be one in which analysts might read the descriptive material supplied by the developer of the method and begin using it immediately.

(5) *Readiness for Use.* This refers to whether or not a method has been tested and refined enough to be considered ready to use in its current form. An impractical method is one in which the total procedure has to be retested and redesigned completely for each use. A practical method can be put to use pretty much as it stands.

(6) *Sample Size.* This indicates the number of respondents or sources of information that the method requires in order to get dependable data. An impractical method is one for which a large number of respondents or sources of information are required. A practical method on the other hand would require very few sources of information.

records, etc., they do indicate the relative strengths and weaknesses of the various available procedures. They also suggest that a combination of procedures may be best. Regardless of the method used, it will always be useful to plan for all the ways that a job analysis might be used by the organization. This means that a job analysis must be related to larger organizational goals, practices, and procedures. In a number of job analysis situations we confronted, we found it convenient to use a combination of methods to obtain the widest possible applicability of the results. Levine (1983) expressed a similar viewpoint and outlined the following procedure, which he labeled C-JAM for *Combination Job Analysis Method.* As we describe this "hybrid" approach, it will be easy to see how various aspects were borrowed from the five techniques described previously.

(7) *Usability of Scales and Instruments.* As opposed to readiness for use, which refers to the entire job analysis procedure, this concern is suggested as an indicator of the extent to which scales and data gathering instruments required by a method may be used as they stand. Obviously, when scales may be used as they stand, they are more practical than those which have to be designed and constructed anew to fit particular jobs.

(8) *Reliability.* This concern indicates to what degree the method will yield similar results if it were applied to the same job a second time. An impractical method would be one in which a reapplication might bear little resemblance in its results to the original set of results for a particular job. A practical method is one in which virtually identical outcomes would occur each time a method were reapplied to a particular job.

(9) *Cost.* Cost refers to the cost of materials, the cost of the required training and the total staff time invested in the job analysis effort multiplied by staff salaries, as well as the salary of the clerical support staff needed to prepare forms and reports. An impractical method would be prohibitively costly to use. A practical method would be relatively cheap.

(10) *Quality of Outcome.* This concern indicates whether a particular method will produce high quality information that can serve many organizational purposes. In other words, it indicates how versatile a method is with respect to purposes as opposed to jobs. An impractical method is not at all versatile. High quality outcomes may be expected for at most only one of the 11 organizational purposes that job analysis might serve. On the other hand, a practical method is highly versatile. High quality outcomes may be expected for virtually all 11 organizational purposes.

(11) *Time to Completion.* This indicates in terms of calendar time how long it takes on the average to complete a job analysis study using a particular method assuming analysts are already trained. An impractical method would take a great deal of time, a matter of many months. A very practical method would take relatively little time, a matter of a few hours or days.

From Levine, F. L. (1983).

Combination Job Analysis Method or C-JAM

One begins using C-JAM with a review of existing job descriptions and training manuals as well as interviews and observations of the job incumbents. The job analyst then meets with a group of five to eight subject matter experts to generate a list of task statements. First, any special environmental conditions (shift work, toxic chemicals, heat, noise) are noted. Then, the job analyst provides a definition of a task and examples of the tasks generated from her or his preliminary review of the job and the group is asked to generate additional tasks. These task statements can be done in written form, but for job incumbents who are not used to writing, it can be done orally with the job analyst or an assistant recording the tasks. The analyst then edits, deletes duplicate tasks, and groups the tasks into major dimensions as she or he views them. This process

TABLE 2-3.   TASK RATING SCALES.

1. Time spent—a measure of time spent per week doing a task relative to all other tasks within a given job.
   1 = Rarely do
   2 = Very much below average
   3 = Below Average
   4 = Average (approximately 1/2 tasks take more time, 1/2 take less)
   5 = Somewhat more than average
   6 = Considerably more than average
   7 = A great deal more than average

2. Task Difficulty—difficulty in doing a task correctly relative to all other tasks within a single job.
   1 = One of the easiest of all tasks
   2 = Considerably easier than most tasks
   3 = Easier than most tasks performed
   4 = Approximately 1/2 tasks are more difficult, 1/2 less
   5 = Harder than most tasks performed
   6 = Considerably harder than most tasks performed
   7 = One of the most difficult of all tasks

3. Criticality/Consequences of Error—the degree to which an incorrect performance would result in negative consequences.
   1 = Consequences of error are not at all important
   2 = Consequences of error are of little importance
   3 = Consequences are of some importance
   4 = Consequences are moderately important
   5 = Consequences are important
   6 = Consequences are very important
   7 = Consequences are extremely important

From Levine, (1983).

can be repeated with two or three groups of subject matter experts or until new groups fail to add novel tasks. A final group meets to edit the combined lists of tasks (tasks are best written to conform with the functional job analysis statements described earlier), and review the grouping of tasks into behavioral dimensions.

The next step involves subject matter experts rating each of the tasks on three aspects of the task: Time Spent, Task Difficulty, Criticality. Since this is a written task (literally, a task inventory) a larger group of job incumbents can be included, though accurate ratings can be obtained with a relatively small number of task raters (five to ten). The three scales recommended by Levine (1983) for rating each task are reproduced in Table 2-3.

Raters should be instructed to make their ratings based on the job in general rather than their own particular position. For each task an *overall task importance* value is computed by multiplying *difficulty* times *criticality* ratings and adding *time spent* ratings. While this method of combination seems to make logical sense (that is, a task must have some degree of criticality *or* difficulty), little research is available on appropriate methods of determining

EXAMPLE OF TASKS AND ASSOCIATED KSAOs FOR THE STAFF SELECTION, EVALUATION, AND DEVELOPMENT DIMENSION.	TABLE 2–4.

A. Two Tasks in Staff Selection, Evaluation, and Development Dimension of Job Performance
   1. Observes teachers' classroom performance to evaluate their performance and provide feedback to teachers.
   2. Confers with other principals and/or district personnel to coordinate educational programs across schools.
B. Four KSAOs Written for the Staff Selection, Evaluation, and Development Dimension of Job Performance
   1. Knowledge of curricula in various subject matter areas in own school as well as the district.
   2. Knowledge of appropriate instructional behavior in various subject matter areas.
   3. Sensitivity in dealing with observational intrusions in classrooms.
   4. Knowledge of school and district organizational chart and programs/facilities/personnel.

task importance. The job analyst can then produce a list of tasks organized by major functional categories in order of importance.

The next phase focuses on generating the human attributes required for performing each of the tasks or major functional dimensions. Human attributes are generally defined as *knowledge, skills, abilities, and other characteristics* (KSAOs). Though the distinction is occasionally ambiguous:

1. Knowledge is usually defined as the degree to which a job incumbent is required to know certain technical material.
2. A skill indicates adequate performance on tasks requiring the use of tools, equipment, and machinery.
3. Abilities are physical and mental capacities to perform tasks not requiring the use of tools, equipment, or machinery.
4. Other characteristics include personality, interest, or motivational attributes that indicate a job incumbent *will* do certain tasks, rather than whether they *can* do those tasks.

An example of KSAOs generated for the Staff Selection, Evaluation, and Development dimension of school administrator performance is given in Table 2–4. KSAOs are usually generated in small group meetings of four to eight subject matter experts. When the group is satisfied that a relatively complete list of KSAOs has been generated, the job analyst edits, removes duplicates, and has the list typed. This list is then rated by the subject matter experts, again on a series of scales such as those in Table 2–5.

If one uses these scales to determine personnel selection procedures, a clear majority of the subject matter experts should indicate that an item is necessary for newly hired workers and that it would be practical to expect that newly hired workers possess a

TABLE 2-5. *EXAMPLE OF A FORM FOR RATING KSAOs OF A PERSONNEL SPECIALIST.*

KSAO's	NECESSARY FOR NEW WORKERS YES or NO (Circle One)	PRACTICAL TO EXPECT YES or NO (Circle One)	EXTENT OF TROUBLE LIKELY 1 = Very Little or None 2 = To Some Extent 3 = To a Great Extent 4 = To a Very Great Extent 5 = To an Extremely Great Extent (Enter Your Rating)	DISTINGUISH SUPERIOR WORKER From Average 1 = Very Little or None 2 = To Some Extent 3 = To a Great Extent 4 = To a Very Great Extent 5 = To an Extremely Great Extent (Enter Your Rating)
Knowledge of item construction	YES or NO	YES or NO	3	3
Ability to communicate with angry/confused examinees	YES or NO	YES or NO	4	4
Knowledge of item analysis statistics, difficulty indices, and item-total correlations	YES or NO	YES or NO	2	3

Adapted from Levine, (1983).

given KASO. There must also be some consensus that lack of a particular KASO would produce trouble for the individual, his or her coworkers, or the organization. That is, the mean of the Trouble Likely Scale should be at least 1.5. Given the KASO is necessary, practical, and, if ignored, could produce trouble, then the most useful KASOs from a selection perspective are those which receive high "Superior" ratings. These are the KASOs on which the subject matter experts see the greatest individual differences; hence, informed selection *can* produce the greatest change in employee effectiveness. Items and tests would be selected and/or constructed to measure those KSAOs that pass the criteria mentioned here for the first three items and are highest on the scale, indicating that the KASO distinguishes Superior Workers from Average Workers.

For example, if we have the pattern of ratings for the three KSAO items for the job of personnel specialist shown in Table 2–5, we would develop three items or groups of items for any test (or other kind of predictor) because all three are *necessary* for newly hired workers. All three items are possessed by many applicants, so it is *practical* to select on these items, all would *produce some trouble* if ignored, and there are *differences among current employees' performance* on these items. We would expect that the ability to communicate with confused/angry examinees would be the most valid predictor of effectiveness because of the perception that the range of individual differences is greatest for this item.

In constructing items for an exam, we should go back to the task analysis part of the job analysis to determine the content of the exam. Frequently, a KSAO will be relevant for several tasks; in this case, test items are written using the tasks which are judged most important. Consideration of the tasks is critical when we use a content validation strategy (see Chapter 6). We must use items that are representative of important job tasks.

If we want to use the job analysis results for training, we need to know if new workers needed to have a KASO; if not and this item also distinguishes Superior from Average workers, then training on the KASO would be appropriate. If it is practical to require a KASO in the labor market, it may be cost effective to select for the characteristic; however, selecting on these attributes may eliminate otherwise excellent applicants who lack particular educational or job experience. Again, tasks associated with KSAOs that are considered important for training would be used as the basis for determining training content. Other uses of a job analysis conducted in this manner are discussed in Levine (1983).

Construction of Job Families

The ability to group jobs in a meaningful way is important for a number of practical reasons: development of appropriate promotional ladders and career paths; administration of performance appraisal systems (when do differences among jobs necessitate different systems and methods of appraisal?); and the ability to develop selection and training procedures that generalize across organizations and similar jobs. Statistically, researchers developed solutions to this problem that examined differences among jobs (for example, see Arvey & Mossholder, 1977) and similarities among jobs (for example, Mobley & Ramsey, 1973). The relative statistical advantages of one approach versus the other are not nearly as important as (1) the type of information about jobs which is collected; that is, whether it is worker- or task-oriented; and (2) what practical, behavioral differences exist among the job groupings.

After reviewing alternative grouping strategies, Pearlman (1980) concluded that grouping either on the basis of the *nature of jobs* or on the basis of *human attributes* that most directly account for individual differences in job performance are equally appropriate. While statistical analysis can provide useful guidelines to make job grouping decisions, the ultimate criterion ought to be whether or not the groupings have real behavioral meaning or practical consequences. Validity generalization research reviewed in Chapter 8 indicates that for selection purposes at least very broad job families such as clerical, managerial, or unskilled labor are sufficient in that measures of similar human attributes predict performance within these groups.

Summary

We have presented a great deal of information about a variety of procedures that have been developed to isolate the human behaviors required to effectively perform jobs and for estimating the KSAOs that, in turn, are required for those behaviors. Job analysis, then, is a strategy for first identifying behaviors and then identifying the KSAOs that are likely to yield those behaviors.

Research on job analysis hints at the conclusion that various job analysis techniques may yield similar kinds of outcomes, at least as far as *plans* for predictors are concerned. There is even some suggestion that extensive *and* expensive job analysis techniques are unwarranted (Schmidt, Hunter, & Pearlman, 1981) but, as noted, the courts seem to be quite clear regarding the need for a job analysis as we have discussed them.

We presented Levine's (1983) C-JAM in detail because it captures much of what is happening in contemporary job analysis applications (cf. Gael, 1983; Goldstein, 1986). C-JAM is a good summary by itself.

One issue that has not been addressed so far concerns the specification of KSAOs for jobs *that do not yet exist* or for jobs that exist in a particular form today but will change tomorrow, perhaps then requiring a person with somewhat different KSAOs. One of your authors has been involved in a project of the latter type. The job of telephone order taker was going to change to telephone order taker *and salesperson.* The job analysis was conducted with *subject matter experts* (SMEs or people who were familiar with the present job and involved in planning the future job and its objectives). This same group of people provided estimates of the KSAOs required to carry out both the old and the new set of tasks. Based on those KSAOs, a set of predictors was developed to predict performance on the new job prior to its actual existence. Methodologies designed to predict requirements (selection, training, etc.) of new jobs are only beginning to appear (Ford and Wroten, 1984). Given rapidly changing technology, these methodologies are certainly going to be necessary.

In the next section of this chapter, we turn to a consideration of whether people will find their jobs rewarding. That is, will they be motivated to take a particular job and remain in that job and organization?

REWARD ATTRIBUTES OF JOBS

While we now have a good feel for the kinds of job analysis procedures useful in specifying the KSAs people need to handle a particular job, some elements are still missing. The job analysis procedures already described implicitly focus on job productivity (sales produced, turnaround time, programs written). That is, in all the descriptions of procedures, the standards of performance for which KSAs are identified concern productivity. What kind of data do we need on a job if some other standards such as employee satisfaction, employee commitment, and employee absenteeism and/or turnover are also important standards of performance? This question requires a focus on the *reward attributes* of tasks rather than the *job requirements.*

If a job analysis was going to focus on the attributes of jobs that workers would find enjoyable/satisfying such that they wanted to come to work, on what facets of a job would it focus? According to an extensive review of the literature, the most important issue is mentally challenging work (Locke, 1976). Over the years, the issue of mentally challenging work has been specified in more concrete terms.

Turner and Lawrence. A job analysis procedure yielding data on the reward characteristics of jobs was developed by Turner and Lawrence (1965). Their procedure yields information on job features such as variety, autonomy, challenge, feedback, and responsibility. Turner and Lawrence presented data on the extent to which 47 different jobs potentially offered intrinsic rewards (that come from performing the work itself) that people might desire. Some representative jobs are presented as Table 2–6 in the order in which they were rated on a scale of intrinsic rewards.

Turner and Lawrence's research was based on a humanistic view of people, which suggests that a task high on intrinsic rewards leads directly to worker satisfaction. They were surprised to find, however, essentially a zero relationship between the level of intrinsic reward existing in jobs and the job satisfaction of the people working. Instead they were able to show that, whether jobs higher in intrinsic rewards resulted in higher job satisfaction depended on a person's background. This way of thinking about job satisfaction suggests that people who desire high levels of intrinsic rewards can

TABLE 2-6. *JOBS RANKED BY INTRINSIC REWARD CHARACTERISTICS.*

JOB TITLE	INTRINSIC REWARD SCORE
Paper Machine Operator	63
Tool and Die Maker	59.4
Automatic Screw Machine Operator (including setup)	53
Railroad Sectionman (Track Maintenance)	50
Railroad Locomotive Airbrake Repairman	46
Aluminum Extrusion Inspector	44
Railroad Blacksmith	42
Aluminum Remelt Furnace Tender	40.9
Telephone Wireman and Pole Climber	37.9
Hand Pastry and Roll Maker	35.4
Bakery Order Filler and Shipper	32
Washing Machine Pump Assembler	30
Railroad Track Rebuilding Crewman	29
Cake Oven Operator	26
General Warehouseman and Fork Lift Truck Operator	25.9
Bread Wrapping Machine Operator	23.6
Foundry Molder	23.3
Warehouse Order Picker	23
Heavy Hydraulic Press Operator	17
Automatic Washing Machine Assembly Line Operator	14.8

From A.N. Turner and P.R. Lawrence, *Industrial Jobs and the Worker: An Investigation of Response to Task Attributes* (Boston: Division of Research, Harvard Business School, 1965), p. 33. Reprinted by permission.

be satisfied merely with the performance of their required tasks. Turner and Lawrence concluded that:

> . . . management needs to be aware of the unintended consequences that may result from any selection policy favoring workers whose values and behavior are noticeably different from the prevailing norms of a particular [job] setting (1965, p. 121).

By this they mean that differences in people's desires (what they call values) should be matched to job differences in reward characteristics, just as the ability requirements of jobs must be matched to differences in individual ability.

Hackman and Lawler.   A number of researchers have developed more refined strategies for assessing the reward characteristics of jobs. Hackman and Lawler (1971) did some early research, and subsequent refinements in their early work have resulted in the *Job Diagnostic Survey* (JDS) (Hackman & Oldham, 1975). The JDS is the basic assessment technique for diagnosing jobs so that people with the appropriate kinds of desires can be placed with the highest probability of job satisfaction. It should be noted, parenthetically, that Hackman and Oldham did not intend that their measure be used in staffing organizations. They noted that ''. . . the instrument [JDS] is designed to be of use both in the diagnosis of jobs prior to their redesign, and in *research and evaluation* activities aimed at assessing the effects of redesigned jobs on the people who do them (p. 159)." They later caution against the use of the JDS in selection and placement because the descriptions of jobs may not be accurate. However, this caution assumes that the person doing the JDS is the same person to be selected or placed on the job. When the JDS is completed by others, the caution is probably not necessary, especially since Hackman and Oldham showed that external observers, incumbents, and supervisors are able to agree quite closely in describing different jobs.

In any case, after a careful review of the literature, Hackman and Lawler isolated four "core" dimensions of jobs, and Hackman and Oldman postulated a fifth (Task Significance). These five core dimensions are defined as follows:

1. *Skill Variety.* The degree to which a job requires a variety of different activities in carrying out the work which involve the use of a number of different skills and talents of the employee.

2. *Task Identity.* The degree to which the job requires completion of a "whole" and identifiable piece of work—that is, doing a job from beginning to end with a visible outcome.

3. *Task Significance.* The degree to which the job has a substantial impact on the lives or work of other people—whether in the immediate organization or in the external environment.

4. *Autonomy.* The degree to which the job provides substantial freedom, independence, and discretion to the employee in scheduling the work and in determining the procedures to be used in carrying it out.

5. *Feedback from the Job Itself.* The degree to which carrying out the work activities required by the job results in the employee obtaining direct and clear information about the effectiveness of his or her performance (Hackman & Oldham, 1975, pp. 161–162).

The measurement of these job reward characteristics has received considerable attention and been the subject of some controversy. Much of the research is summarized, quite critically, by Roberts and Glick (1981). They argued that asking people to describe their jobs in terms such as variety or autonomy yielded information that could not really be trusted to accurately represent the job. Subsequent research, however, has supported the Hackman and Lawler (1971) conclusion that reports on these reward attributes represent real job characteristics (Griffin, Welsh, & Moorhead, 1981).

The reader should compare these five job reward characteristics or dimensions with the five dimensions isolated by McCormick. We can see that the Hackman and Lawler/Hackman and Oldham conceptualization represents a clearly different psychological orientation. Further, one can see that combining the two kinds of analyses would yield a very rich view of jobs—both in terms of the kinds of KSAs required (especially ability) and the kinds of rewards offered. Further, this combination of analytic procedures enhances the probability that people who can perform the job effectively as well as be satisfied with it can be found. If this combination could be achieved, then organizations would be more likely to recruit competent individuals who will experience job satisfaction and remain in the organization.

Note that this conclusion does not mean that people who are more competent will necessarily also be the same people who are more satisfied. However, it does say that it should be possible to identify people who are *likely* to be both competent and satisfied. In the past, staffing programs have focused almost exclusively on individual competence—we are encouraging an additional focus on individual job satisfaction as another important outcome and the specification of the reward attributes of tasks so people with appropriate reward desires can be located. Or, as we will outline in Chapter 4, this information can be used to provide an accurate portrayal of what a job has to offer an interested applicant.

IMPACT OF THE ORGANIZATIONAL CONTEXT

A second major issue left unexplored in traditional job analysis procedures concerns the following question: given two organizations that are in the same industry (so they have the same kinds of jobs) hiring people with equivalent KSAs, why does one organization consistently outperform the other? In other words, are the KSAs of employees the only determinant of organizational effectiveness? Answering this question requires an approach to job analysis that includes specifying the organizational conditions in which the job will be performed.

In Chapter 3 we show how organizational conditions come into play when evaluating the performance of individual workers; the concern is for how one *person* in a job may work under different conditions than another person in the same job, and thereby perform differently (better or poorer). Here we are concerned with a different level of the problem: how some organizations create generally superior or inferior conditions for workers as a group, keep-

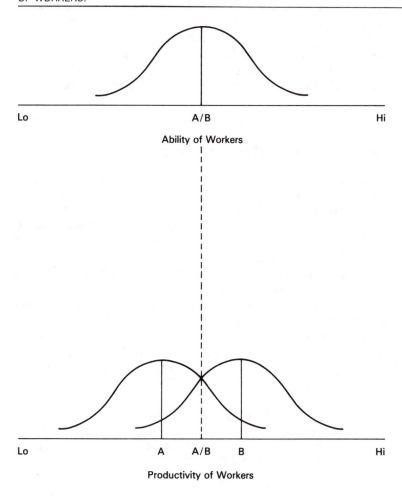

ing the general level of effectiveness higher or lower than would be expected given the qualifications (KSAs) of those who are hired.

This is an important issue because staffing procedures are designed, ultimately, to produce organizations that can compete and survive. It is, then, one thing to hire tomorrow more competent people than are being hired today, but it may be another thing to be competitive and survive. We know how to hire more competent people—that is what this book is about—but we also know that hiring people with more competence to do particular jobs does not assure organizational effectiveness.

Perhaps Figure 2–7 will make the issue clear. The top of Figure 2–7 shows the distribution of the ability of workers in organizations A and B. The bottom of the figure shows, however, that the distributions of productivity are not equal, that productivity in organization B is superior to productivity in organization A. Our contention is that certain organizational attributes, such as supervisory practices, have an impact on people that is essentially independent of the impact of their competence level as reflected in their KSAs (Schneider, 1978).

Dimensions of the Organizational Context

In discussing job analysis we specified a number of dimensions requiring analysis. The job analysis technique of the Department of Labor specified Data, People, and Things, and McCormick's Position Analysis Questionnaire postulated five major dimensions for analysis, as did the worker rewards Job Diagnostic Survey of Hackman and his associates.

Research on organizations also suggests that there are certain dimensions of importance: the goals of the organization, the organization's reward system, and the existing climate of personal relationships. Generally speaking then, organizational analysis attempts to provide a broad picture of the goals and human resources management practices of an organization. Typically, it relates to some or all of the elements set forth in Schein's definition of an organization:

> An organization is the planned coordination of the activities of a number of people for the achievement of some common explicit purpose or goal, through division of labor and function, and through a hierarchy of authority and responsibility (Schein, 1980, p. 15).

Organizational goals. From a staffing point of view an organization's goals may be the most important feature of the organization. In one way or another goals may help determine the kinds of jobs an organization designs. These jobs, in turn, are determinants of the standards against which employee performance will be evaluated and employee satisfaction generated. By implication, of course, if the behaviors required for effective performance differ as a function of organizational goals, then organizational goals also determine what kind of people will be required by and satisfied in the organization. In Chapter 3, the issue of goals will be discussed more completely.

Organizational style. The way an organization sets up its "hierarchy of authority and responsibility" determines its organizational style. Thus, while two organizations may have the same goals, the way they go about achieving those goals may differ. Of course, once an organization has a goal, there may be some consequent limitations placed on the way it may accomplish the goal. For example, a public service agency will not function in the same way as an automobile manufacturer—at least not insofar as the main service versus product business is concerned.

Earlier in this chapter we discussed mechanistic and organic styles of organizations and their emphasis on the external environment as the style determinant (Burns & Stalker, 1961). There are also other models for organizational styles, however, that emphasize the kinds of assumptions organizational management makes about the nature of workers. For example, McGregor (1960) noted that, basically, managers can make two different kinds of assumptions about employees, each of which dictates a particular style of behavior toward them.

One style, he said, was the result of Theory X. This theory assumes that workers are basically lazy, work only for money, and lack the desire and ability to assume responsibility, etc. When management follows the guidelines of Theory X, workers are closely supervised, rewarded primarily in terms of money, treated as if they were ignorant and unfeeling, and thought to be incapable of and lacking the desire for making decisions. Theory Y makes the opposite kind of assumption about people. Its usage results in management's creation of a climate that demonstrates to workers (1) its values for human resources; (2) its desire to help people do their job better rather than to punish them for doing it poorly; and (3) its belief that workers want to and can assume responsibility—a belief that is demonstrated by shared decision-making responsibility with lower-level employees.

Schein (1980) has called McGregor's Theory X the *Rational-Economic Man* assumption, and Theory Y the *Self-Actualizing Man* assumption. Schein also mentions the *Social Man* theory some managers have about workers. This theory of what motivates people has probably received more research attention than the others because the idea of Social Man generates such topics as Leadership/Supervision, T-Groups/Sensitivity Training, and Participation in Decision-Making. Generally speaking, the research evidence suggests that:

1. Leaders who personally treat their subordinates in a more considerate as well as task-oriented fashion will have lower absen-

teeism in their work groups, lower levels of grievances, and higher levels of satisfaction.

2. Interpersonal skills may be learned and attitudes toward treating others with more interpersonal competence can be changed. Whether the changed attitudes result in using new skills may depend upon the stimulation of opportunities to use the new skills in the work place.

3. Employee participation in decisions results in employees feeling that they have increased power and control over their own lives, and also in their feeling more committed to the decisions that have been made.

The Social Man organizational style seeks to involve employees in more interpersonal relationships with management. Then those relationships are used both to satisfy workers' desires for social contact and power and to achieve organizational goals.

Organizational reward system.   In previously discussing the worker-rewards characteristics of jobs, our interest was primarily in the content of jobs and in their potential fulfillment of people's desires for variety, autonomy, and so forth. However, the discussion of organizational style suggests that some people have other desires, desires that can only be fulfilled by promoting particular kinds of authority systems and procedures for supervising employees. And still a third way the larger organization has an impact on people concerns the patterns of rewards and punishments the organization designs; how the organization dispenses the rewards it has available. Two theories dominate present thinking along these lines—the equity of rewards (cf. Adams, 1963, 1965) and whether or not rewards are tied to performance (cf. Porter and Lawler, 1968; Vroom, 1964). A comprehensive treatment of how organizations can use reward systems more effectively is presented by Lawler (1981). In Chapter 4, we discuss the implications of these reward systems for employee recruitment.

Effects of the Organizational Context on Productivity

The tendency of staffing researchers and practitioners has not been to examine the leadership and motivation practices of organizations as much as to focus on jobs—and even then rarely to study worker reward aspects. However, jobs do not exist in a vacuum. Because job/person interaction is the ultimate focus of staffing decisions, it is important to understand external conditions that may affect interaction. Thus, the basic staffing model is to assess job and person characteristics and predict the outcome of their interaction. However, if organizational conditions (aside from the immediate attributes of the job) cause workers to behave in particular ways, then the staffing process may work more or less effectively than would be predicted on the basis of worker attributes alone. We will attempt to illustrate this point by describing some research on productivity in organizations.

Research on productivity in organizations shows that when certain characteristics of the organization are changed, people with the same basic levels of competence improve their productivity significantly. Such changes as the following consistently yield increased productivity (Katzell & Guzzo, 1983):

1. *Work redesign* used to enhance motivation ranges from the enrichment of individual jobs to the enrichment of the jobs of work units or teams.

2. *Supervisory methods* that allow for variation in the degree of influence or participation in decisions that a supervisor gives to subordinates usually has a positive impact. Research findings support the popular view that democratic supervision is better liked *and* pays off in productivity as well.

3. *Organizational restructuring,* concerned with patterns of responsibility, authority, activity, and communication, seems to have an effect beyond those face-to-face effects that occur as a result of supervisory style changes in a work group. In some situations, at least, organizational structuring seems to be a precondition for productivity improvement.

4. Some *decision-making techniques* affect the quality of decisions and the manner and frequency with which decisions are implemented.

A similar point of view has been expressed by Peters and O'Connor (1980); namely, that organizations can do much to facilitate or constrain the performance of employees. They suggest that systematic differences in work situations (organizations or units within an organization) exist and determine whether or not employees can be maximally effective. Their list of situational resource variables in included as Table 2–7.

If these kinds of changes yield improved productivity from people of equivalent levels of ability or competence, or if they serve as important constaints on productivity, then we can infer that organizations that are more like the changed organizations are going to be more effective. If this is true, then merely finding competent

TABLE 2-7. *SITUATIONAL RESOURCE VARIABLES RELEVANT TO PERFORMANCE.*

1. *Job-Related Information.* The information (from supervisors, peers, subordinates, customers, company rules, policies, and procedures, etc.) needed to do the job assigned.
2. *Tools and Equipment.* The specific tools, equipment, and machinery needed to do the job assigned.
3. *Materials and Supplies.* The materials and supplies needed to do the job assigned.
4. *Budgetary Support.* The financial resources and budgetary support needed to do the job assigned—the monetary resources needed to accomplish aspects of the job, including such things as long distance calls, travel, job-related entertainment, hiring new and maintaining/retaining existing personnel, hiring emergency help, etc. This category does not refer to an incumbent's own salary, but rather to the monetary support necessary to accomplish tasks that are a part of the job.
5. *Required Services and Help from Others.* The services and help from others needed to do the job assigned.
6. *Task Preparation.* The personal preparation, through previous education, formal company training, and relevant job experience, needed to do the job assigned.
7. *Time Availability.* The availability of the time needed to do the job assigned, taking into consideration both the time limits imposed and the interruptions, unnecessary meetings, non-job-related distractions, etc.
8. *Work Environment.* The physical aspects of the immediate work environment needed to do the job assigned—characteristics that facilitate rather than interfere with doing the job assigned. A helpful work environment is one that is not too noisy, too cold, or too hot; that provides an appropriate work area; that is well-lighted; that is safe; and so forth.

Reprinted with permission from Peters and O'Connor, (1980).

people may not result in the kinds of effectiveness that were hoped for.

We believe the following:

1. More competent people on a job will outperform less competent people on that job.
2. Performance of the same jobs in two different organizations with people of the same levels of competence may produce or result in different levels of effectiveness.
3. It is very important for organizations to ask themselves if their lack of effectiveness is attributable to the competence of workers or to the way the organization is managed.

Because of the potentially great impact organizations may have on the outcomes of staffing decisions, it is important for an organization to determine its own stance on various "style" factors. Unfortunately, we are not able to be as specific about these factors as we were with respect to job analysis. Leadership practices, reward systems, general interpersonal relationships, and organizational goals are all important targets of analysis. All these factors

SCHEMATIC FOR UNDERSTANDING THE ROLE OF JOB AND
ORGANIZATIONAL ANALYSIS IN THE STAFFING PROCESS.

FIGURE 2–8.

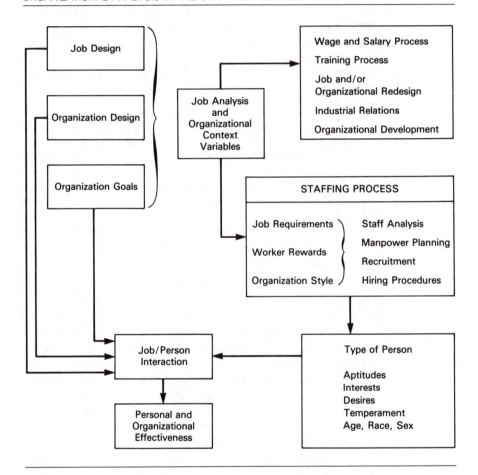

affect potential success or failure in explaining and/or predicting
how well people actually will do their jobs and how satisfied they
will be with what they do. These issues will be addressed again,
especially in Chapters 8, 9, and 10.

INTERACTION OF THE ORGANIZATIONAL
CONTEXT AND JOB ANALYSIS

Figure 2–8 schematically shows the role of job analysis and considerations regarding the organizational context. These analyses are,
of course, the necessary foundation for translating the material and

psychological context in which people work into terms useful for staffing that environment with humans. The result of the translation is a set of procedures for attracting and selecting people. The effective selection process discovers people who will help the organization achieve its goals while at the same time achieving their own goals in interaction with the context.

Figure 2–8 also shows that job analysis information and considerations regarding the organizational context must be translated into at least four different processes:

1. The Industrial Relations Process, including labor/management negotiations, wage and salary administration, and so forth;
2. The Training Process, including skills training, management training, etc.
3. The Organization Development Process, including organizational renewal, job enrichment and enlargement, structural redesign, etc.; and
4. The Staffing Process, including manpower planning, recruitment, selection, development, and evaluation or appraisal.

All factors affecting person/job interaction are fair game for staffing personnel because the effectiveness of staffing procedures is a function of the outcomes of this interaction. Thus, poorly designed jobs that result in poor performance, high turnover (as a result of dissatisfaction), or alienation cannot be compensated for by better staffing procedures. Organizational diagnoses may show that revised or new training procedures are required, or that job enlargement is necessary, or that staffing procedures indeed are where the emphasis should be. Organizations may effectively move toward achieving their goals by many routes, only one of which is through the implementation of various staffing policies and procedures. The contribution of the staffing procedures to the prediction of performance must be compared to what may be expected from other sources (i.e., job redesign, changes in management philosophy, or training, etc.) and various human resource efforts must be consistent with each other.

It has been proposed (Guion, 1965) that about half the behavior we observe in organizations is due to individual (person) characteristics, and the other half to situational variables (job and organizational characteristics). We hope the reader of this book will become a believer in regarding both people and situational factors as explanations for behavior. This point of view sets up the situation so that organizations and the people in them will profit maximally. Job and organizational analyses can help an organization understand the nature of its situation and thus the nature of the staffing problem.

SUMMARY

In this chapter we tried to show that jobs do not exist in a vacuum; the kinds of jobs in an organization are a function of its goals and the larger environment. We reviewed five job analysis procedures: (1) functional job analysis; (2) job elements; (3) Position Analysis Questionnaire; (4) task inventory approach; and (5) the critical incident technique. A job analysis which combined an interest in identification of tasks and worker requirements was presented as a means of accommodating the widest range of purposes for which job analyses are conducted. The importance of identifying (1) job requirements, (2) worker rewards, and (3) the larger context of the job was stressed. We maintain that the philosophy of understanding jobs and job context is necessary for developing the staffing process and for evaluating the potential contribution to the accomplishment of organizational goals. The importance of organizational goals and measurement of the degree to which goals are accomplished are the focuses of Chapter 3.

REFERENCES

Adams, J. S. (1963). Toward an understanding of inequity. *Journal of Abnormal and Social Psychology, 67,* 442–456.

Adams, J. S. (1965). Injustice in social exchange. In L. Berkowitz (Ed.). *Advances in experimental social psychology* (Vol. 2). New York: Academic Press.

Arvey, R. D., and Mossholder, K. M. (1977). A proposed methodology for determining similarities and differences among jobs. *Personnel Psychology, 30,* 363–374.

Beer, M. (1980). *Organization change and development: A systems view.* Santa Monica, CA: Goodyear.

Burns, T., and Stalker, G. M. (1961). *The management of innovation.* London: Tavistock.

Christal, R. E. (1974). *The United States Air Force occupational research project* (US AFHRL Technical Report No. 73–75).

Dictionary of Occupational Titles. (1977). U. S. Department of Labor, Washington, DC.

Dunnette, M. D. (1966). *Personnel selection and placement.* Belmont, CA: Wadsworth.

Fine, S. A. (1980). Personal communication.

Fine, S. A., and Wiley, W. W. (1974). An introduction to functional job analysis. In F. A. Fleishman & A. R. Bass (Eds.). *Studies in personnel and industrial psychology* (3rd ed.). Homewood, IL: Irwin.

Flanagan, J. C. (1954). The critical incident technique. *Psychological Bulletin, 51,* 327–355.

Fleishman, E. A. (1975). Toward a taxonomy of human performance. *American Psychologist, 30,* 1127–1149.

Ford, J. K., and Wroten, S. P. (1984). Introducing new methods for conducting training evaluation to program redesign. *Personnel Psychology, 37,* 651–666.

Gael, S. (1983). *Job analysis: A guide to assessing work activities.* San Francisco: Jossey-Bass.

Goldstein, I. L. (1986). *Training: in organizations: Needs assessment, 2nd ed.* Monterey, CA: Brooks/Cole.

Griffin, R. W., Welsh, A., and Moorhead, G. (1981). Perceived task characteristics and employee performance: A literature review. *Academy of Management Review, 6,* 655–664.

Guion, R. M. (1965). *Personnel testing.* New York: McGraw-Hill.

Hackman, J. R., and Lawler, E. E., III. (1971). Employee reactions to job characteristics. *Journal of Applied Psychology, 55,* 259–286.

Hackman, J. R., and Oldham, G. R. (1975). Development of the job diagnostic survey. *Journal of Applied Psychology, 60,* 159–170.

Hackman, J. R., and Oldham, G. R. (1980). *Word redesign.* Reading, MA: Addison-Wesley.

Katz, D., and Kahn, R. L. (1978). *The social psychology of organizations* (2nd. Ed.). New York: Wiley.

Katzell, R. A., and Guzzo, R. A. (1983). Psychological approaches to productivity improvement. *American Psychologist, 38,* 468–473.

Latham, G. P., and Wexley, K. N. (1981). *Increasing productivity through performance appraisal.* Reading, MA: Addison-Wesley.

Lawler, E. E., III. (1981). *Pay and organization development.* Reading, MA: Addison-Wesley.

Levine, E. L. (1983). *Everything you always wanted to know about job analysis.* Tampa, FL: Mariner Publishing Co.

Levine, E. L., Bennett, L. J., and Ash, R. A. (1980). Exploratory comparative study of four job analysis methods. *Journal of Applied Psychology, 65,* 524–535.

Levine, E. L., Ash, R. A., Hall, H., and Sistrunk, F. (1983). Evaluation of job analysis methods by experienced job analysts. *Academy of Management Journal, 26,* 339–347.

Locke, E. A. (1976). The nature and causes of job satisfaction. In M. D. Dunnette (Ed.). *Handbook of industrial and organizational psychology.* Chicago: Rand McNally.

Locke, E. A., and Latham, G. P. (1984). *Goal setting: A motivational technique that works!* Englewood Cliffs, NJ: Prentice-Hall.

Lopez, F. F., Kesselman, G. A., and Lopez, F. E. (1981). An empirical test of a trait-oriented job analysis technique. *Personnel Psychology, 34,* 479–502.

McCormick, E. J. (1976). Job and task analysis. In M. D. Dunnette (Ed.). *Handbook of industrial and organizational psychology.* Chicago: Rand McNally.

McCormick, E. J., Jeanneret, P. R., and Mecham, R. C. (1972). A study of job dimensions as based on the Position Analysis Questionnaire. *Journal of Applied Psychology, 56,* 347–368.

McCormick, E. J., and Ilgen, D. R. (1980). *Industrial psychology.* Englewood Cliffs, NJ: Prentice-Hall.

McGregor, D. M. (1960). *The human side of enterprise.* New York: McGraw-Hill.

Mobley, W. H., and Ramsey, R. S. (1973). Hierarchical clustering on the basis of inter-job similarity as a tool in validity generalization. *Personnel Psychology, 26,* 213–226.

Morsh, J. E., and Archer, W. B. (1967, September). *Procedural guide for conducting occupational surveys in the United States Air Force.* Lackland Air Force Base,

TX: Personnel Research Laboratory, Aerospace Medical Division, PRL–TR–67 –11.

O'Donnell, R. J. (1953). The development and evaluation of a test for prediction of dental student performance. *University of Pittsburgh Bulletin, 49,* 240–245.

Pearlman, K. (1980). Job families: A review and discussion of their implications for personnel selection. *Psychological Bulletin, 87,* 1–28.

Peters, L. H., and O'Connor, E. J. (1980). Situational constraints and work outcomes: The influences of a frequently overlooked construct. *Academy of Management Review, 5,* 391–397.

Porter, L. W., and Lawler, E. E., III. (1968). *Managerial attitudes and performance.* Homewood, IL: Irwin.

Prien, E. P. (1977). The function of job analysis in content validation. *Personnel Psychology, 30,* 167–174.

Primoff, E. S. (1975). *How to prepare and conduct job-element examinations* (TS– 75–1). Washington, DC: U. S. Civil Service Commission, Personnel Research and Development Center.

Roberts, K. H., and Glick, W. (1981). The job characteristics approach to task design: A critical review. *Journal of Applied Psychology, 66,* 193–217.

Schein, E. H. (1980). *Organizational psychology.* Englewood Cliffs, NJ: Prenctice-Hall.

Schmidt, F. L., Caplan, J. R., Bemis, S. E., Decuir, R., Dunn, L., and Antone, L. (1979). *The behavioral consistency method of unassembled examining.* Washington, DC: U. S. Office of Personnel Management.

Schmidt, F. L., Hunter, J. E., and Pearlman, L. (1981). Task differences as moderators of aptitude test validity in selection: A red herring. *Journal of Applied Psychology, 66,* 166–185.

Schneider, B. (1978). Implications of the conference: A personal view. *Personnel Psychology, 31,* 299–304.

Schneider, B., Parkington, J. J., and Buxton, V. (1980). Employee and customer perceptions of service in banks. *Administrative Science Quarterly, 25,* 252–267.

Selected Characteristics of Occupations Defined in the Dictionary of Occupational Titles. (1981). U. S. Department of Labor, Washington, DC.

Smith, P., and Kendall, L. M. (1963). Retranslation of expectations: An approach to the construction of unambiguous anchors for rating scales. *Journal of Applied Psychology, 47,* 149–155.

Thompson, D. E., and Thompson, T. A. (1982). Court standards for job analysis in test validation. *Personnel Psychology, 35,* 865–874.

Thorndike, R. L. (1949). *Personnel selection.* New York: Wiley.

Turner, A. M., and Lawrence, P. R. (1965). *Industrial jobs and the worker: An investigation of response to task attributes.* Boston, MA: Harvard.

Vroom, V. H. (1964). *Work and motivation.* New York: Wiley.

3

STAFF APPRAISAL
Conceptualization, Development, and Measurement of Criteria

AIMS OF THE CHAPTER

THE IMPORTANCE OF ORGANIZATIONAL GOALS

THE CRITERION DEFINED

DESIRABLE ASPECTS OF CRITERIA
    Relevance
    Reliability
    Practicality
    Discriminability
    Summary

CRITERION ISSUES
    Criterion Dimensionality and Combination
    Criterion Change
        Individual change
        Organization change
        Changes in criterion dimensionality
    Criterion Contamination
    Summary

ACTUAL CRITERION MEASURES
    Production of Output
    Quality of Work Products
    Trainability: Training Time, Training Cost, and Training
        Success
    Personnel Data as Criteria
        Absenteeism
        Tenure
        Rate of advancement

AIMS OF THE CHAPTER

Whereas job and organizational analyses are not directly concerned with people, staff appraisal is people-oriented. Staff appraisal is concerned with the analysis of how well people do their jobs and how satisfied they are in their work setting. More generally, staff appraisal is the process of gaining information about what individual workers do and feel. This information is collected so that organizations can make improved decisions regarding:

1. *Evaluation:* to enable the organization to share the money, promotions, and perquisites "fairly"
2. *Auditing:* discover the work potential, both present and future, of individuals and departments
3. *Constructing succession plans:* for manpower, departmental, and corporate planning
4. *Discovering training needs:* by exposing inadequacies and deficiencies that could be remedied by training
5. *Motivating staff:* to reach organizational standards and objectives

6. *Developing individuals:* by advice, information, and attempts at shaping their behavior by praise or punishment
7. *Checking:* the effectiveness of personnel procedures and practices (Randell et al., 1974, pp. 16–17)*

We can see that just as job and organizational analyses are useful for multiple purposes, so is staff appraisal. Staff appraisal issues must be considered before hiring the staff; organizations must decide on what bases, and how, they will assess staff before meaningful programs for staffing, training, or motivation can be developed. Without knowing the standards against which people will be evaluated, procedures for getting people who will meet those standards are only guesswork. This chapter is about the different kinds of standards against which people are evaluated.

It is also about how important specifying standards and goals is for understanding why people behave the way they do in organizations. A number of issues connected with how organizations go about conducting staff appraisals and on what issues the organization focuses serve as clues to employees about what their organization stands for, what is important to it, and where their efforts are required. If the organization involves employees in the design of the appraisal process, it tells employees that their opinions are valued; this is especially true if the organization also evaluates how satisfied employees are and holds managers responsible for taking action on this kind of information. If the organization evaluates employees regarding their rejects and faulty products, then employees have one kind of feeling about the organization. Contrast that organization with another that focuses exclusively on employees' total quantity of productivity. Because we think the nature of organizational goal emphasis is so important for understanding behavior in organizations, we turn to this topic before discussing the details of staff appraisal.

THE IMPORTANCE OF ORGANIZATIONAL GOALS

Most organizations do not consciously choose but, rather, passively embrace their goals. Thus, the procedures for accomplishing those goals, and jobs as well, are often poorly defined and designed. As a result, the standards of excellence against which employees are evaluated are also poorly defined. The end result is that the staff fails to apply itself to the accomplishment of crucial organizational objectives because they are unsure about what

---

*From *Staff Appraisal*, rev. ed. by G. A. Randell, P. M. A. Packard, R. L. Shaw, and A. J. Slater. Copyright 1974 by the Institute of Personnel Management. Used with permission.

those goals are. It is clear that if organizations do not know what their goals are, then the staffing process itself cannot be integrated effectively into other personnel systems; we won't know exactly what is effective.

Evidence in industrial and organizational psychology now clearly shows that poorly defined goals and poorly designed procedures for accomplishing goals both have a negative impact on employee motivation and performance (cf. Locke and Latham, 1984). Failure to specify or poor definition of goals affects motivation and performance because people behave on the basis of the goals they have. When these goals are specific and when people receive feedback regarding their progress toward goal accomplishment, they perform better than when goals are left poorly defined (Locke and Latham, 1984).

But even in the most goal-oriented system people do more than work toward specific, carefully defined goals. They interact with each other, they help each other, they get in each other's way, they argue, they play politics. As Katz and Kahn (1978, pp. 403–404) noted:

> No organizational plan can foresee all contingencies within its own operations, can anticipate with perfect accuracy all environmental changes, or can control perfectly all human variability. The resources of people for innovation, for spontaneous cooperation, for protective and creative behavior are thus vital to organizational survival and effectiveness. An organization that depends solely on its blueprints of prescribed behavior is a very fragile social system.

If what Katz and Kahn said is true, we can ask the following question: What kinds of information do people depend on as a basis for making decisions to behave in ways that enhance effectiveness?

People decide what the general or guiding practices and procedures of an organization are based on many little events they witness, the hundreds of work experiences they have, and what practices and procedures the organization seems to emphasize. In a sense, they form concepts of what their organization is all about; they sense the "climates" of the setting (Schneider, 1975).

People form concepts about the climates that exist in their organization with reference to many issues. Thus, Tom Smith may have concepts about the organization he works for with respect to what its goals are, how it rewards people, the kind of supervisors it promotes, its policies on accidents and safety, and how it relates to the world external to the organization. A single climate does not exist in an organization; many climates are created by the various practices and procedures in which an organization engages (Schneider, 1980).

The important thing about organizational climates is that employees use them as benchmarks or guidelines for behavior. Each of us has had the experience of trying to decide how, or whether or not, to do something. How does the decision get made? It is made on the basis of what we sense is most appropriate for the situation.

Think of people weighing how to best accomplish a particular work task. On what basis do they decide how to accomplish their objective? They try to "fix" where they are, try to locate themselves in the larger environment, and, after locating themselves, they chart the course necessary to achieve the goal. Employees use their concepts of the organization as a frame of reference for locating themselves and deciding how to behave.

If the concepts people have of their organization help guide their behavior, then the stated goals and the subsequent standards of excellence an organization establishes give employees clear cues about what is important and where their efforts are required. When translated into specific standards for evaluating employees, the goals or objectives of an organization lead to particular employee behavior.

The question of organizational or company policy (goals) is important for reasons beyond gaining an understanding of the bases of behavior among employees. That is, if company policy determines the definition of what a superior employee is, then the organization's staffing procedures will be targeted toward those same goals and objectives. Company policy, because it dictates standards for evaluating employees, *actually dictates the entire staffing process.* Particular kinds of employees will be attracted to the organization, recruited and selected for the organization, stay in the organization, be evaluated highly by the organization, and be promoted within the organization.

Another point needs to be made at the beginning of this chapter. The goals and standards of excellence adopted by an organization can serve both *administrative* and *developmental* purposes as they get translated into actual measures of employee performance. If these measures serve as aids in decision-making (deciding whom to promote or whether a selection procedure is effective), then they are administrative. If the data collected about people's performance are used to counsel them about strengths, weaknesses, and possible behavioral change, then they are developmental. While the various measures of individual performance discussed in this chapter may be used for both purposes, there are differences in how effective different types of data are in meeting administrative and developmental purposes and in the amount of detail in the information collected.

We will begin our chapter discussing performance standards or *criteria;* in general, what it is we want in a performance measure, and what major issues confront an organization as it defines its goals and attempts to develop measures of the degree to which goals are met. A large portion of the chapter is devoted to a discussion of various actual measures. Finally, we discuss several special issues dealing with performance measurement, and we provide some guidelines as to how organizations can feed back performance information to employees in an effective manner.

THE CRITERION DEFINED

It becomes awkward discussing "standards of excellence," "goals and objectives," and so forth. Staffing researchers simply speak of a criterion, or, plural, *criteria.* A simple definition of a criterion is *something you are interested in.* A definition closer to the use of the word in the staffing literature is a *standard of excellence.* The definition we find most suitable for our purposes is the following: **Criteria are those behaviors and outcomes at work that competent observers can agree constitute necessary standards of excellence to be achieved in order for the individual and the organization to both accomplish their goals.** Criteria are those behaviors and outcomes at work that we try to predict with our staffing procedures. Criteria are the behaviors against which employees are judged, and on which organizations base various administrative decisions vis-a-vis employees (promotion, wages and salaries, training, etc.). Criteria are those factors that constitute "doing the job well."

Traditionally, industrial/organizational psychologists spoke of ultimate and actual criteria. Definition and articulation of organizational goals as discussed here provide the ultimate criteria. For example, an organization's ultimate goals might include (1) investor confidence that allows them to generate money in the amounts and at the time it is needed; (2) having a reputation for honesty and integrity; and (3) satisfied and motivated customers. At the personal level, the ultimate goal may be to feel that we are living satisfying productive lives both in work and non-work spheres. Clearly, these are desirable objectives, but they are often, if not always, difficult to measure. Our actual measures of the degree to which we meet these ultimate criteria represent proxies to some extent and have been labeled actual criteria. They include measures of production, absenteeism, accidents, performance ratings, and employee attitudes. The goal of criterion development efforts is to increase the degree to which actual and ultimate criteria overlap. While this distinction, and the discussion in general, may sound abstract, it is

FIGURE 3–1. *RELATIONSHIP BETWEEN THE ULTIMATE CRITERION AND AN ACTUAL CRITERION.*

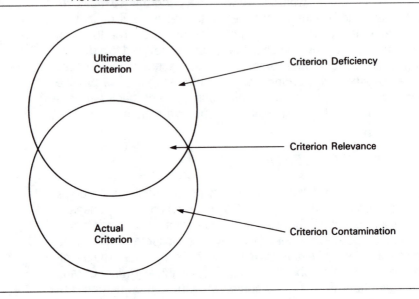

extremely useful in describing the type of problems staffing researchers are interested in and discuss when they speak of "the criterion problem."

Consider the Venn diagram (Figure 3–1) which depicts the relationship between an actual and ultimate criterion. The degree to which the actual and ultimate criterion overlap is the degree to which we say that the actual criterion is *relevant*. The portion of the ultimate criterion that does not overlap with the actual criterion is referred to as criterion *deficiency*. (We are not measuring aspects of job performance which we should be including.) It is through systematic job and organizational analyses such as those described in Chapter 2 that we hope to minimize criterion deficiency and maximize criterion relevance. The third area in the diagram, called criterion *contamination,* represents variance in the actual criterion which has nothing to do with the ultimate criterion. Both deficiency and contamination represent significant problems to the staffing researcher or practitioner who wants to use measurements of job performance when making the various personnel decisions cited at the beginning of this chapter. Because we rarely, if ever, have data on any ultimate criteria, we must rely on the judgments of "experts" concerning the appropriateness of the actual criteria we measure. In the next section we discuss desirable aspects of criteria and how we develop acceptable criteria. In terms of Figure

3–1, we describe what is important as we try to maximize criterion relevance and minimize deficiency. In the section after, we consider issues regarding the minimization of criterion contamination.

DESIRABLE ASPECTS OF CRITERIA

When listing aspects of criteria that are particularly desirable, most authors usually state that criteria be relevant, reliable, practical, and allow for discriminability.

Relevance

Of these four criteria for criteria, relevance is, of course, indispensable. Researchers used two major approaches in developing criteria that are maximally relevant. Muchinsky (1983) refers to these two approaches as inductive and deductive; other writers have referred to them as objective and subjective. Both sets of labels are less than satisfactory in a descriptive sense, so we will offer a couple of examples that illustrate the two approaches.

Muchinsky (1975) used an inductive (or objective) approach to the study of the criteria used to determine the characteristics of a person who was a poor consumer credit risk. Starting with no prior theoretical notions as to the behaviors or issues that defined people judged to be poor credit risks, he obtained the financial records of 250 people who were labled poor credit risks and 250 people who were considered good credit risks and who had been extended loans. After comparing these two groups of people on the basis of how well they repaid their loans, he found two dimensions that distinguished those persons considered good risks from those considered bad risks. Poor risk people were characterized by delinquency in making monthly payments and by missing payments completely. So there were two criteria for defining a poor credit risk: missed payments and late payments. These criteria were derived from an empirical analysis.

In a deductive (or subjective) approach to criterion development, the researcher *begins* with a careful and rational identification of the possible criterion variables of interest. This is usually accomplished through job analyses, literature reviews, review of training program goals, or even a review of organizational goals. The relative importance of these various criteria is best deduced by rational judgments of a panel of judges. As we saw in the chapter on job analysis, several subject matter experts can be interviewed in groups to generate a list of issues on which staff performance can be judged. These issues are then grouped into major dimensions and their relative importance is judged by the same or a different group of experts. Once the important dimensions are identified, then actual measures of each are developed.

Whether one employs an inductive or deductive approach to the identification of criteria, remember that, as a cluster or set, they define effectiveness for us. We use measures of these criteria to decide training issues, or to initiate special counseling efforts. Or, as in selection, we use criteria as the standard(s) against which we evaluate the usefulness of hiring procedures. What this discussion of objective and subjective criterion development shows is that the relevant issues or facets of criteria that need to be assessed are identifiable through empirical analysis and/or informed judgments. When feasible, it would be useful to employ both strategies—it is very important to use at least *one* strategy for the development of criteria, or the criteria against which staffing procedures are validated may not be *relevant*. The prediction and/or understanding of non-relevant criteria is a useless exercise, to say the least!

Reliability

A more complete discussion of the general topic of reliability is contained in Chapter 5. But, at this point, note that if criteria are to be useful, they must be measurable in a consistent manner. Several types of reliability can be assessed and determining which is appropriate depends on the actual measure itself and the use to which we want to adapt the criterion.

Whenever we measure people, we are usually interested in whether we get the same values for a group of people when measurements of their performance are made on two occasions; this is called *stability* or *rate-rerate reliability*. For ratings criteria, it is often most essential that we have high *interrater reliability;* that is, two or more raters agree on how a group of ratees are performing. Occasionally, we may have several kinds of measures of a single dimension of the criterion; in this case, those separate measures should yield similar information. In this case, *internal consistency estimates of reliability* are important. We should also note that high internal consistency is desirable only when we want to make the case that various indices are measures of the same aspect of performance. When the actual measures are perceived of as measures of different performance dimensions, then they ought to yield different values for a person's performance and ought to rank order people differently.

Internal consistency estimates of reliability are interesting because they focus on the many different ways of analyzing particular facets of performance. For example, suppose we wanted to assess

the *quality* of bank tellers' performance at work. We could do one
or more of the following:

1. Ask their coworkers about the quality of their performance
2. Track their balances at the end of the day, (i.e., are they consistently over or under?)
3. Ask their customers about the quality of their performance
4. Ask their managers to rate their quality.

What we would hope is that the different kinds of measures of
quality across a group of tellers would yield similar data allowing
us to rank order the tellers in terms of the quality of their performance. When the different kinds of measures yield similar rank orderings, we can infer we have internal consistency reliability—the
different kinds of measures of quality are *consistent* with each
other.

As noted in the introduction to the topic of criterion reliability,
a more complete discussion of it is presented in Chapter 5. For now
it needs to be clear that:

1. Reliability is an important criterion attribute;
2. Depending on the situation, one or more kinds of reliability are
   important: stability, interrater, and/or internal consistency.

Finally, while reliability of criteria is an important issue, *it should
always be secondary to relevance.* This has not always been true,
and it has led to the problem of emphasizing what we *can* measure
rather than what we *should* measure.

Practicality

Obviously, an actual measure of any criterion must be available (or
collection must be possible) and generalizable across units of an
organization. It must be a criterion which organizational members
accept as an appropriate measuring index. Most organizations are
interested in the dollar contribution of employees to the organization. This remains a difficult criterion to measure, particularly for
complex managerial and technical jobs, though some new me-
thodological advances described in Chapter 7 are allowing estimates of dollar worth. Or, for people in service industries, we are
probably most interested in how satisfied clients or customers are
and how often they return for service (or how often they don't
return) because of the way they have been helped. The practical
problems in collecting these types of data can be significant. If a
criterion is judged relevant, however, effort must be made to overcome practicality problems.

Discriminability

The final desirable aspect of criteria is that they be useful in discriminating among staff members. In Chapter 5 we make the point that the purpose of measurement is discrimination; this applies to job performance measurement as well. It may be very important that workers come to work. Yet, if all employees in a company are absent the full amount of time allowed under union contract, or if none of them misses any work, then absenteeism does not differentiate among employees and is of no use in making decisions about them. It may be desirable to introduce programs to cut down the general level of absenteeism when all are missing a large constant amount, but no basis for differential treatment of staff is justified. Some research indicates that the variability in various performance measures changes as a function of tenure on the job. (See the following discussion of dynamic criteria.) This means that a criterion that discriminates well among new employees may not discriminate that well later on as workers all tend to attain satisfactory performance levels (or more technically, this criterion has a ceiling effect). The point is that, for measures to be useful as criteria in personnel selection, there must be differences in individual performance levels.

Discriminability is important as a criterion for criteria in personnel selection but it may not be important when raising the issue of overall unit or overall organizational effectiveness. That is, if we can assume that no one individual's poor performance will bury a unit or the organization, then for most practical purposes it is how well people, *in the aggregate,* are performing that is the question of interest. In other words, in general, are employees performing effectively?

However, any time a decision needs to be made about a *particular* employee—send to training, promote, dismiss, give a raise —then a procedure for measuring performance that has good discriminability is critical.

Summary

Four aspects of a good criterion, in rank order, are:

- relevance
- discriminability
- reliability
- practicality

And shun practicality as a major determinant whenever it interferes with any of the other three!

CRITERION ISSUES

In this section, we outline three major problems staffing personnel confront when developing or measuring criteria. First, how do we combine information on various aspects of performance? Second, do criteria change over time? Third, how do we identify and deal with criterion contaminants? In a sense, all three involve the problem of including irrelevant information in our criterion measure; hence, all are aspects of the contamination problem depicted in Figure 3–1.

Criterion Dimensionality and Combination

For most jobs we can identify several different important aspects of job performance that are relatively independent of each other. To say that aspects of job performance are relatively independent means we can have secretaries who are slow but accurate or faculty members who have excellent research credentials but mediocre teaching skills. Among industrial psychologists, a controversy has waged for years between those who maintain that measures of different aspects of job performance should be combined into a single overall composite measure and those who feel that measures of performance should be kept separate and used independently of each other. Typical of the latter position is this citation from Dunnette (1963):

> Most selection and validation [staffing] research has gone astray because of an overzealous worshiping of the criterion with an accompanying will-o-the-wisp searching for the best single measure of job success. The result has been an oversimplification of the complexities involved in test validation and the prediction of employee success. Investigators have been reluctant to consider the many facets of success and the concomitant investigation of the prediction of many success measures and instead persist in an unfruitful effort to predict the criterion. Thus, I say: junk the criterion! (p. 254).

Dunnette was saying that effective job performance is made up of many kinds of behaviors, that successful employees are not necessarily the ones who can produce the most widgets, and that short-term effectiveness is not a guarantee of long-term success. He was arguing for criteria dealing with the job behaviors necessary to accomplish the multiple, sometimes relatively independent, objectives of a job. And we all know that it takes many kinds of behavior, behavior along many dimensions, to do a job—witness the Data, People, Things categories of behavior from the Department of Labor job analysis procedure, or the five clearly different

TABLE 3-1. *INTERCORRELATIONS AMONG FIVE CRITERION VARIABLES FOR 975 DELIVERYMEN.*

	1	2	3	4	5
Effectiveness (1)					
Productivity (2)	.28				
Accidents (3)	-.02	.12			
Absences (4)	-.08	-.01	.03		
Errors (5)	-.32	-.26	-.18	.15	

From Seashore et al., (1960).

kinds of behaviors McCormick identified in his research with the Position Analysis Questionnaire, or the satisfaction/satisfactoriness distinction made in Chapter 1 of this book.

Typical of the research cited by people who hold Dunnette's position (1963) is a study by Seashore, Indik, and Georgopoulos (1960). Seashore et al. studied 975 deliverymen on whom five job performance criteria were available. These criteria included: productivity (objectively measured by time standards), effectiveness (subjective ratings based on quality of performance), accidents, unexcused absences, and errors (based on the number of packages not delivered). Correlations among these five variables are shown in Table 3-1. These data show that the five criteria are relatively independent of each other (correlations of .00 indicate complete independence, while correlations of 1.00 indicate complete redundancy). The largest correlations were among the variables of productivity, effectiveness, and errors (.28, −.26, and −.32). For this job, then, there does not appear to be a single overall performance index; rather, each criterion measures a different relatively independent facet of performance.

For a commonsense illustration of this problem, consider a secretary's job. Secretaries must type accurately and quickly, take shorthand accurately and quickly, answer telephones promptly and courteously, dress neatly and cleanly, make appointments correctly and politely, file papers efficiently and precisely, appear for work on time, cooperate with colleagues cheerfully and tactfully, get to know important people quickly, and unobtrusively, keep up with company changes, keep the office neat, order supplies, and on and on. It is clear that most jobs require a great variety of behaviors from the people working at them. This variety of behavior must be predicted by staffing processes and must be the source of dimensions against which staff are evaluated.

The controversy between advocates of a single composite criterion and those who believe multiple criterion measures ought to be considered has been summarized by Schmidt and Kaplan

(1971). Their solution to this controversy is that the selection of multiple or composite criteria should depend on the intended use. If the goal is to make practical decisions about staff members (as in making salary recommendations), then computation of some weighted composite is essential. Weights are determined by considering the contribution of each performance facet to the total contribution of the job to the organization. These weights are multiplied by the measured performance of people on corresponding job dimensions to come to a value which represents the overall worth of a worker. However, if the goal is to understand the dimensions of job performance and how they contribute to job success or how they are determined by various job experiences, training, or employee attitudes, then multiple criteria should be used.

The basis for resolution of the controversy lies in the use we intend to make of the criteria. If the interest is in promoting the best person from a group, then a composite criterion is essential. If we want to train or counsel staff people concerning their job performance, then multiple criteria are most useful. The composite criterion notion, however, is not useful when high job performance on one dimension cannot compensate for high job performance on another job facet. Consider our previous example. The secretary can type rapidly but has dyslexia which means that he or she cannot recognize letter reversals. Therefore, those mistakes will go unrecognized and uncorrected. Clearly, speed of typing could not make up for large numbers of undetected errors in final manuscripts. The idea that lack of good performance in one dimension can be compensated for by high performance in other dimensions works for most, but not all, jobs. To add to the problems in considering what constitutes overall effectiveness, there is some evidence that the dimensionality of job performance changes as a function of job tenure. This possibility is referred to as the dynamic nature of the criterion.

Criterion Change

When a person is hired for a job in which promotion is an important consideration, then changes in the criteria the person must meet must be specified. If only early criteria are a part of the staffing process, then decisions about hiring will be useful only in predicting early achievement. But because people develop in a job, understanding their stages of development helps pinpoint the appropriate standards against which they should be evaluated at different times.

For example, in management jobs the standards against which people will be evaluated change over time. The criteria are not static; they are dynamic. The criteria for evaluating the success of a new management trainee may concentrate on promotability, while at a later time the standards may concentrate more on the manager's effectiveness in achieving outcomes. Promotability may be assessed with reference to such traits as "willingness to learn," "ability to assume responsibility," and other traits thought to be necessary for promotion.

Individual change.   Changes that occur in people over time have not typically been a criterion of interest in staffing research except when considering the selection of managers (Campbell et al., 1970). The idea of dynamic criteria, however, seems important whenever the degree or rate of development and change is an important job feature. For example, transition time from level of training proficiency to acceptable job proficiency might be an important criterion in some organizations. The point, of course, is that process as well as outcome—how behavior occurs as well as whether it occurs—may be an important criterion.

Suppose you wish to recruit, select, and train sales representatives. What is an obvious criterion of job proficiency? Sales? True, sales are very important, but they are outcomes of some process of behavior. It is obvious that early in a sales representative's career we want to predict the behavior that eventually will result in sales. If we understood what behaviors resulted in sales, then we would be in a position not only to predict sales but (1) to predict the behaviors that are necessary precursors of sales; (2) not incidentally, to train workers in those behaviors; and (3) to create reward contingencies for those behaviors. By focusing only on end-states rather than on means we may be very diligent but very ignorant (Wherry, 1957), and we will never understand why our staffing procedures either are effective or ineffective (Wallace, 1965). Both goals and processes are important for staff analysis.

Organization change.   Another way in which criteria are dynamic concerns changes in organizational policy. For example, as noted earlier, an organization's policy concentration may shift from the quality market to the mass-production market. Such a change will result in different criteria for evaluating people and will, of course, affect the entire staffing process. Consider what happened to many companies when the U.S. government ended its massive support of space exploration and turned its focus instead to ecological issues. Companies had to reevaluate their goals—those that had not anticipated change found their staffs unable to cope with the new criteria.

Prien (1966) proposes that changes in organizational goals

over time may lead to changes in the relative importance of functions making up a given job. He cites the example that over time a company may change its primary goal from growth to the development of existing client accounts. The function "acquisition of new clients and accounts" would then decline in importance over time, while the development function increased in importance. What this means is that the weights assigned to various job performance facets in any combination of these criterion elements would change over time.

By raising this issue we hope to show that establishing criteria is a continuing responsibility of management rather than something accomplished once and then forgotten. As organizations and people grow and develop, the goals of the organization, and thus the standards for evaluating employees, should be adjusted accordingly.

Continual re-evaluation of an organization's goals can serve many more functions than merely updating the standards for evaluating employees. Etzioni (1964) and others (e.g., Argyris, 1957) note that organizations frequently lose sight of their original goals and purposes. That is, instead of pursuing the development and accomplishment of original goals, after a number of years organizations expend their greatest efforts in simply maintaining themselves. An example is provided by Crozier's (1964) description of those French civil servants who expend great effort in consolidating their bases of power and influence but little time in being of service to the general public. We should also note that changes in criteria are important administratively only if they result in different orderings of people—for example, in selection or promotion. If not, then, there is little with which to concern ourselves in those situations; though the changes would still be important when these criteria are to be used developmentally.

Changes in criterion dimensionality. While the above changes refer to changes in the criterion itself, other authors have used the phrase *dynamic criteria* to refer to the fact that different staffing procedures predict a different criterion at different stages in employees' tenure on the job (Ghiselli, 1956; Ghiselli & Haire, 1960). Researchers have gathered two types of evidence for this proposition: (1) relationships among performance dimensions from one time period with performance at another time period decline over time, indicating changes in the rank order of those whose performance is measured; (2) the relationships among criterion measures as evidenced by correlational and factor analyses (a statistical technique used to group dimensions) change over time. This type of change has not been frequently reported.

Recently, Rambo, Chomiak, and Price (1983) reviewed the literature on the stability of correlations among job performance dimensions across time. In a study of taxicab drivers, Ghiselli and Haire (1960) reported a correlation of .19 (indicating almost no relationship) between performance measures taken eighteen weeks apart. The taxicab driver subjects were new to the job and, hence, the correlation between performance at Time 1 and performance eighteen weeks later would have been maximally influenced by factors associated with adjustment to a new job. Rambo et al. (1983) collected data from a group of women sewing machine operators and a group of women working in packaging and folding jobs. Over 3 1/2 years, the relationships from one week to the next were consistently high (correlations above .80), though slightly less for the more complex sewing machine operator's job. Over longer periods of time, correlations for the sewing machine group leveled off at around .65; for the more routine packaging and folding jobs, correlations leveled off at about .85. Correlations will be explained in Chapter 5, but it is enough for now to know that these results indicate two things. First of all, output rates in highly specialized and routine jobs that had little or no variation in the essential details of the work and that were linked to a wage-incentive system that appeared to be an effective motivator of performance were highly consistent. Secondly, consistency of output rates appears to be a function of the complexity of the job. The latter finding could mean that there is some change (although minor in the Rambo et al. data) in the relative importance of criterion elements.

Relative to changes in the relationship among various aspects of job performance, the most systematic data has been collected by Fleishman and his colleagues (Fleishman & Fruchter, 1960; Fleishman & Hempel, 1954; 1955). They report findings of changes in the relationships among performance measures over time for work on psychomotor and visual discrimination tasks, such as learning Morse Code. The authors are aware of no similar work on more complex tasks.

In yet another view of the dynamic nature of criteria, Weitz advanced the notion that "difficult" and "easy" criterion measures will differentiate individuals on performance maximally at different points in time (Weitz, 1961; 1964; 1966; Levine and Weitz, 1971). Specifically, he proposed that easy measures will discriminate optimally early in task performance, while difficult measures will work best later in performance. This is another way of saying that criteria should have discriminability. What is useful as a criterion on which to make discriminations among workers is determined by the degree to which incumbents have learned their jobs.

We believe two conclusions concerning the dynamic criterion issue are warranted. First, on a practical level, one should be sensitive to changes in *variability* of various criterion measures over time. These changes will cause changes in the relationships among different criterion measures as well as changes in the usefulness of tests that are designed to measure performance at a certain point. Second, we believe questions concerning changes, or lack thereof, in criterion structure have important theoretical and practical implications and that the current knowledge concerning this issue is woefully inadequate.

Criterion Contamination

The framework of staff behavior presented in Chapter 1 suggests a number of possible contaminants of employee behavior.* For example, the nature of the task itself may affect employee behavior and make it unpredictable. Tasks can be made more or less interesting to employees. Suppose a factory decides to change some jobs in order to make them more interesting. The results will be that some employees have more interesting jobs than others, although all were hired to do the same work. In evaluating the performance of these employees, it is important to know which ones worked on the "enlarged" or "enriched" tasks. Evidence suggests that task enrichment results in decreased waste, decreased absenteeism, and decreased turnover (Hackman & Oldham, 1980) and if these are criteria against which the effectiveness of staffing procedures are judged, then the criteria will be unreliable. Workers who were previously absent a great deal but who were given more interesting tasks will no longer be absent. If workers were ordered by frequency of absences at Time 1 and then some underwent job enrichment while others did not, an ordering of workers at Time 2 would be contaminated by change (see Ronan and Prien, 1971, pp. 87–91).

A second consideration in the way tasks affect the ordering of workers on effectiveness indices deals with the breakdown of machinery. It can be necessary to ask such questions as: is my secretary a poor worker or does the typewriter frequently break down? Since most of the staffing literature has been generated by psychologists, there has been a tendency to attribute the cause of poor performance to individual shortcomings. However, considering events external to the individual, such as one worker having a

---

*By contaminants here we simply mean events, conditions, and so forth that affect employee job performance but about which they have no control. Issues like those mentioned in Chapter 2 in discussing Organizational Analysis are examples.

better typewriter than another, can help us better understand the adequacy of our criteria.

A different example of contamination is represented by the experience of one of the authors as a young lieutenant in the military. He was the supervisor of an enlistment unit that included an office supervisor and nine typists. The typists prepared all enlistment papers. Occasionally he needed something of a special nature typed and requested a specific typist to do it for him. One such time he required that something be done immediately, gave the work to the typist, and waited for it to be accomplished. The employee began to work. She stumbled over keys, made overstrikes, and typed errors in almost every word. When asked what was wrong she broke down and indicated that she could not type! The other typists, it turned out, were covering for this one employee and had been doing so for months—more and more all the time. While these employees may have been deriving some sense of intrinsic reward from helping their colleague, their action created havoc for those in a position requiring adequate performance from all individuals.

Finally, conditions outside the organization may affect the behavior of employees—for example, the state of the economy. An unstable economic picture results in unstable patterns of organizational turnover; therefore, if turnover is a criterion of interest, it will be difficult to predict (Staw, 1984). All kinds of influences, both extra- and intra-organizational, may affect behavior and cause it to be inconsistent, thus compounding the problems encountered in predicting behavior.

Traditionally, discussions of criterion contamination (also called criterion bias) include a distinction among three major kinds of bias. *Opportunity bias* occurs when some employees have advantages that are not available to other workers. Our job enrichment and machinery breakdown examples represent potential criterion contamination due to differences in employee opportunity. Group characteristic bias occurs when measures of an individual's job performance are partly a function of the work or social group to which they belong. The non-typing secretary example is a good example of *group characteristic bias* (the secretary's coworkers had artificially maintained the satisfactory level of her performance) and so would the performance of individuals artificially restricted by group norms concerning how much work should be done in a given period of time. Also cited as a source of criterion contamination is *knowledge of predictor* bias. This type of bias occurs when a supervisor knows the skill levels of persons whom she or he employs

KINDS OF CRITERION MEASURE	PERCENTAGE
OBJECTIVE MEASURES (Total = 28.3%)	
Production Records	3.6
Work Samples	.5
Achievement Tests	12.4
Tenure	3.5
Advancement	5.8
Turnover	1.2
Wages	1.3
JUDGMENT BY OTHERS (Total = 63%)	
Supervisory Evaluations	58.4
Peer Evaluations	4.6
	100.0

Adapted from Lent, Aurbach, and Levin, (1971).

either through standardized tests or the recommendations (formal or informal) of colleagues. Such knowledge can translate into special opportunities or challenges for certain people. In fact, it is quite clear now that when supervisors have high expectations of subordinates and/or teachers have high expectations of students, then the performance of subordinates on the one hand and students on the other is significantly improved (Eden and Shani, 1979). Finally, if the supervisor *also* supplies the criteria in the form of performance ratings, such knowledge may directly affect her or his ratings of certain individuals, compounding the bias or criterion contamination.

Finally, several kinds of contamination or bias are unique to performance rating:

1. *Leniency* error refers to the fact that some raters give higher ratings than do others. Most students are familiar with faculty members who have a reputation for giving all As and Bs while others rarely give grades above a C. Leniency error becomes a problem when performance ratings are compared across raters or when students who took similar courses from different professors are to be compared.

2. *Central tendency* error occurs when raters are reluctant to use the extreme points on a rating scale. Such a rater would be giving ratings that are biased against the truly superior performers and unfairly advantageous to those employees whose performance is really inadequate.

3. *Halo error* refers to the fact that a rater does not discrimi-

nate among the different facets of performance. A rater who is impressed by an employee's punctuality gives that person high ratings on other dimensions of performance such as the quality of work, the amount she or he gets done, and the degree to which the person's behavior contributes to the social atmosphere of work in spite of evidence that her or his performance on these latter dimensions is not as superior as their punctuality.

Summary

Up to this point we discussed issues related to criteria in a general fashion. We noted the nature of criterion deficiency, relevance, and contamination. Desirable aspects of criteria were listed. We discussed the development of criteria, the dimensionality of job performance measures and how they can be combined, the possibility that criterion dimensions change over time, and the various types of criterion contamination, and we showed how contamination may be due to situational conditions and/or facets of the appraisal itself. In the following section we will discuss the various types of actual criteria—their relative advantages and limitations.

ACTUAL CRITERION MEASURES

The types of criterion measures typically used and the proportionate use of these in one set of published studies involving the validation of staff selection procedures is presented in Table 3–2. Another more detailed list from Cascio (1982) is presented in Table 3–3. As can be seen from Table 3–2, judgmental criteria were most frequently used while objective measures such as production records are infrequently used. In this section, we will detail the various objective measures of criteria while we reserve discussion of judgmental criteria for the following section. A review of validity studies published in two journals (*Journal of Applied Psychology* and *Personnel Psychology*) between 1964 and 1983 by Schmitt, Gooding, Noe, and Kirsch (1984) indicated that 38 percent of 366 studies used judgmental criteria. Approximately 13 percent used turnover, achievement, and status change, 8 percent used productivity and wages, and 7 percent used work sample criteria. The studies published in validity information exchange (Table 3–2) are probably more representative of validity studies in general than are those studies summarized by Schmitt et al. (1984). The latter are publications in journals that only print papers that have been reviewed for technical competency. These papers should be methodologically superior to what is typically being done.

TABLE 3–3.

Output measures
  Units produced
  Number of items sold
  Dollar volume of sales
  Number of letters typed
  Commission earnings
  Number of candidates attracted (recruitment program)
  Readership of an advertisement
Quality measures
  Number of errors (coding, filing, bookkeeping, typing, diagnosing)
  Number of errors detected (inspector, troubleshooter, service person)
  Number of policy renewals (insurance sales)
  Number of complaints and dissatisfied persons (clients, customers,
    subordinates, colleagues)
  Rate of scrap, reworks, or breakage
  Cost of spoiled or rejected work
Lost time
  Number of occasions (or days) absent
  Number of times tardy
  Length and frequency of unauthorized pauses
Personnel turnover
  Number of discharges for cause
  Number of voluntary quits
  Number of transfers due to unsatisfactory performance
  Length of service
Trainability and promotability
  Time to reach standard performance
  Level of proficiency reached in a given time
  Rate of salary increase
  Number of promotions in a specified time period
  Number of times considered for promotion
  Length of time between promotions
Ratings of performance
  Ratings of personal traits or characteristics
  Ratings of behavioral expectations
  Ratings of performance in work samples

From Wayne F. Cascio, *Applied Psychology in Personnel Management*, 2nd Ed., © 1982, p. 103. Reprinted by permission of Prentice-Hall, Inc., Englewood Cliffs, NJ.

Production of Output

Measures of the amount produced appear to have obvious relevance. The amount of life insurance sold, the amount of machinings
per day, the number of letters typed, the number of legal briefs
written—all these measures seem at first glance to have undeniable
utility. And, indeed, they sometimes do. But all too often problems
of contamination essentially invalidate production indices as criterion measures. Some salespeople by chance have "richer" sales
territories than others. One machinist appropriates the newest lathe
for himself and another must do his work on an outmoded heap that
operates slowly, if at all. One secretary is assigned difficult letters

and papers because of her reputation for quality work; another receives simpler material. Thus, the production figures do not really reflect individual differences in value to the organization. Sometimes it is possible to make statistical corrections for contaminants of this sort. That is, one can assess the contaminating factors and remove them from the criterion. Nicholson (1958), for example, adjusted his measure of amount of life insurance sold for differences in quality of sales territories. But such adjustments can be fairly difficult and are sometimes made impossible by the unavailability of the information necessary to make the corrections.

Quality of Work Products

For any job, the old adage that quality is more important than quantity is almost certainly true. One important patented invention by a research engineer is apt to be more valuable to the organization than a number of minor ones. A smaller number of automobiles properly repaired by a mechanic may contribute more to shop success than a larger number improperly "repaired." Quality of output may often be difficult to assess, but it can be assessed in many situations. Illustrative indices include percentage of work products that pass (or fail) inspection, the percent of insurance policies sold that are later renewed, the number of legal clients who later return for further services, the error rate in mail sorting or in punching computer cards. Like measures of quantity, quality measures must be closely scrutinized for contamination. The quality of machinings, for example, will not accurately reflect individual differences in employee contributions if there are wide variations in the condition of machines used. Likewise, the secretary who is assigned the more difficult papers may have more errors per paper despite her superior value to the organization. Furthermore, if the best secretaries are assigned the most difficult material, contamination of this latter kind may result in the following paradox: If the test is valid, the best secretaries will tend to have the highest test scores and the lowest quality of work scores. This produces a negative relationship between test scores and performance that is entirely spurious!

Quality and quantity indices can sometimes be combined into a composite. For example, suppose the amount of time a mechanic needs to redo an unsatisfactory repair job is equal to 3/4 the time required for a satisfactory repair job. The overall criterion index might then be number of jobs completed minus .75 times the number of unsatisfactory jobs. If contaminating factors can be avoided or controlled, such a composite provides a criterion measure that is high in relevance. Such an index directly reflects difference between employees in value to the organization.

What about the problem of potential criterion deficiency in quantity and quality of output measures? Won't such measures typically be deficient in that they do not reflect, for example, the employee's impact on group morale, on the production of other workers, and on a whole host of relevant variables in the work setting? Such deficiency is a possibility, and it is an obvious problem if our focus is performance counseling or training. If we are using the criteria to evaluate selection procedures, this deficiency may or may not be a serious problem. If the criterion components that have been left out correlate positively with the tests, then the selection program operates to increase worker standing on these variables. If the missing components correlate zero with the selection battery, the selection program will have no effect on average levels of social competency among incumbents. Only if the missing criterion components have a true *negative* relationship with the selection battery will worker standing on these variables be adversely affected by the use of the selection battery. Few studies have examined the relationships among these different types of criteria, and when they do, the results indicate low positive or zero correlations between quantity and quality of performance and the social impact types of criteria suggested above.

Trainability: Training Time, Training Cost, and Training Success

Trainability, as defined by Wexley (1984), is a person's ability to acquire the skills, knowledge, or behavior necessary to perform a job at a given level and to achieve these outcomes in a given time. Use of training criteria in personnel selection work is attractive for several reasons. First, training time and cost can usually be calculated fairly objectively, and savings from a selection program that reduces training time and cost can be fairly easily documented. This, in turn, makes it easy to promote a good selection program to management. Measures of training success are often more easily developed than measures of job performance because they can be directly related to training content.

Ghiselli (1966) found that measures of amount learned in training were relatively well predicted from cognitive tests. Further, training criteria were usually better predicted than were subsequent job performance measures. Prediction of training success has continued to interest staffing researchers. For example, Williams, Sauser, and Kemery (1982) found that success in early combat training was predicted best by scores on a test of general intelligence and a measure of physical fitness (two-mile run time) for over 800 individuals in entry-level training.

Recently, Siegel (1983) has developed an interesting new approach to the prediction of trainability. He has shown that classification of naval personnel could be improved by using a technique called *miniature training and evaluation testing*. This concept involves training a person on a sample of the tasks she or he will be expected to perform on the job and then testing the person's ability to perform these tasks. The concept holds that a recruit who demonstrates an ability to learn a sample of the tasks in a Navy job will be able to learn and perform satisfactorily all of the tasks if given appropriate on-the-job training.

An objection sometimes raised against using training performance as a staffing criterion is that among those who complete training there may be no relationship between success in training or time to complete training and later job performance. Indeed, the computed relationship can be low. Severin (1952), in a review of such data, found a median correlation of .24 between grades in training and later job performance measures. But, even when the true correlation between trainability and job performance is zero, ultimate job performance will, on the average, be the same whether tests to predict trainability are used or not. If the test is related to training performance, then use of the test can be justified on the basis of training savings relative to the cost of testing. Only when the relationship between job performance criteria and training criteria is negative does the use of training criteria for personnel decisions result in hiring less capable persons. This issue is related to the previous discussion concerning the overlap between actual and ultimate criteria. If both training and performance criteria are relevant, the overlap between the two will be substantial and both sets of criteria will be predicted equally well by the same types of predictors. As more training programs are evaluated as to their validity (Goldstein, 1978), training performance may be found to have meaningful relationships to on-the-job performance.

Personnel Data as Criteria

Personnel data criteria of various kinds fall under the general rubric of objective criteria. Personnel data measures include absenteeism, turnover (tenure), promotion rate, and salary increase rate.

Absenteeism. Typically, absenteeism is a relevant criterion because it is costly to the organization. Often it can be predicted from scores on empirically derived biographical data blanks. As would be expected, absenteeism seems to depend more on personality or "character" factors than on abilities and skills, although low work ability or skill could conceivably lead to low job satisfaction, and the latter could lead to increased absenteeism. The association of low job satisfaction with above average absence rates has repeatedly been confirmed (Mowday, Porter, & Steers, 1981). Recently, Steers and Rhodes (1978) have questioned the assertion that absenteeism is only caused by job dissatisfaction. The complexity of the absenteeism issue is reflected in Figure 3–2. This figure shows that differing levels of ability to be at work (family responsibilities, transportation problems) and pressure to attend (work group norms, organizational commitment) combine with job satisfaction to predict absenteeism. So, in trying to predict absenteeism through some selection system, a host of issues may serve to contaminate the absenteeism criterion. Contaminants of this sort probably are neither predictor-correlated nor particularly reliable. Thus, they probably function essentially as random error; that is, they lower reliability. Lowered reliability means, as we will see in Chapter 5, that the true size of relationships among variables is higher than the ones we observe.

Different indices of absenteeism apparently differ in reliability. Huse and Taylor (1962) examined the reliability of four different measures over a one-year period for 393 truck drivers. They found that "attitudinal absences" (frequency of one day absences) were correlated .52 over a one-year time period. "Absence frequency" (the total number of *times* absent) had slightly higher reliability, .61. The other two absence measures were much lower in reliability. "Absence severity" (total number of *days* absent) and "medical absences" (total number of three days or longer absences) had reliabilities of .23 and .19 respectively. For selection purposes, attitudinal absence or absence frequency would then be the most appropriate. The Huse and Taylor results indicate these measures may have only moderate reliability. Higher reliabilities may require measurement over even longer time periods.

Tenure. Like absenteeism, turnover can also be costly to the employing organization. Schmidt and Hoffman (1973) found that the cost to a large hospital of hiring and training a replacement for a nurse's aide who had quit was $1650. This is a relatively low-level occupation, and one would expect higher costs for many other occupations, especially those with longer training periods. This study also serves to illustrate the prediction of turnover from empirically weighted biographical data blanks. A weighted blank composed of 16 items produced a cross-validated point biserial correlation of .49 with turnover. Given the number of nurses aides

FIGURE 3–2.   MAJOR INFLUENCES ON EMPLOYEE ATTENDANCE.

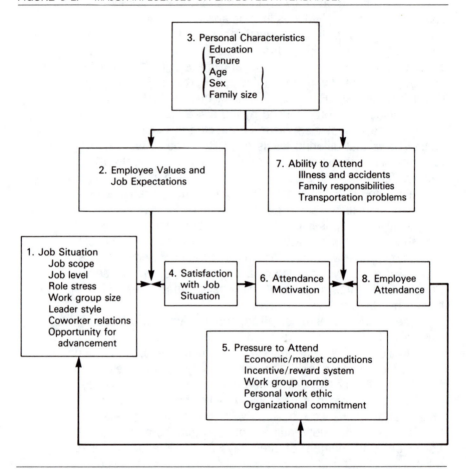

From Steers and Rhodes, (1978).

hired and their turnover rate, use of this instrument led to an estimated reduction in employment and training costs of $80,600 per year. In addition, this study was conducted nearly fifteen years ago; inflation has certainly doubled or tripled their dollar estimates.

Turnover and absenteeism are not independent criteria. Lyons (1972) reviewed eleven studies and found that, in each one, employees who quit their jobs showed higher absence rates for the time period preceding their quitting. The Lyons data are consistent with a model of turnover proposed by Mobley, Horner, and Hollingsworth (1978). This model is depicted in Figure 3–3 and its main message is that turnover may be a gradual process (people begin to think about it and evaluate options some time before they actually

A SIMPLIFIED REPRESENTATION OF INTERMEDIATE LINKAGES   FIGURE 3-3.
IN THE EMPLOYEE WITHDRAWAL DECISION PROCESS.

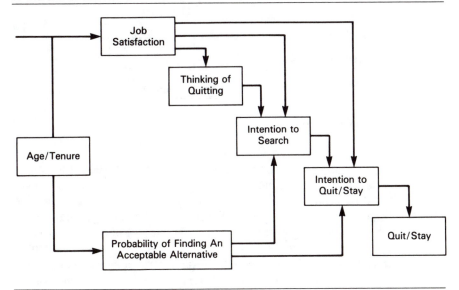

From Mobley, Horner, and Hollingsworth, (1978).

quit) and that turnover is also determined by individuals' assessment of their ability to secure other employment. One major result
of the publication of the Mobley et al. (1978) model is that turnover
research has begun to focus on intent to turnover rather than actual
turnover. Turnover, itself, has been hard to predict, probably because of its dichotomous nature (people either quit or stay) and the
fact that longitudinal research is difficult because of the necessity
to wait long periods of time till sufficient numbers of people quit.
Further, as the Mobley et al. model indicates, turnover may be
contingent on alternate job opportunities. Research examining the
relationship between turnover and intent to quit indicates a consistent, but modest correlation between .40 and .60.

Focus on turnover and its reduction may also backfire. In the
study cited above concerning the turnover of nurses aides, the
scored biographical data blank was extremely useful in eliminating
turnover. However, several years later, the personnel director of
this hospital complained that the hospital administration would have
preferred more turnover among these aides so that they could hire
more competent and well-motivated aides! Again, the short-term
interest in reduction of turnover apparently was not consistent with
potentially more important long-term objectives of the hospital.

Perhaps, then, turnover itself is not the appropriate criterion of

FIGURE 3–4. *FUNCTIONAL AND NON-FUNCTIONAL TURNOVER.*

<table>
<tr><td rowspan="3"></td><td rowspan="3"></td><td colspan="2">Organization's Desires
for Employee to stay</td></tr>
<tr><td>+</td><td>−</td></tr>
<tr><td>non-functional
turnover</td><td>functional
turnover</td></tr>
</table>

		+	−
Individual's desires	+	non-functional turnover	functional turnover
to stay in organization	−	non-functional turnover	functional turnover

Adapted from Dalton, (1981).

interest; turnover of *competent* or *effective* employees is the more relevant criterion (Dalton, 1981). In fact, if we consider the possibilities involved, turnover may be functional for organizations. For example, consider Figure 3–4. It shows that employees may desire to stay in an organization (+) or leave it (−) and the employing organization may desire to keep the employee (+) or see him or her leave (−). Except where the organization desires the employee to remain (+), *from the organization's standpoint,* turnover will be functional (Abelson & Baysinger, 1984; Dalton, 1981). So, the variable to be predicted is not "turnover" but a reduction in the number of *competent* people who leave. Of course, if the staffing system is working optimally, the number of incompetents will be relatively low, but since our systems fail to work optimally, it is important to remember *who* we want to retain. The issue of retaining competent employees will emerge again in Chapter 4, Recruitment.

Rate of advancement. Rate of promotion can be taken as a reflection of the value the organization places on the services of the individual. If those promoted faster have more organizational value, it is logical to attempt to increase the number of selectees capable of rapid advancement. The relevance of this criterion, as of all others, is based ultimately on judgment. In addition to number of promotions per time period, measures of rate of salary increase and time to first promotion have also been used. Contamination in the form of opportunity bias is obviously a potential problem and should be carefully watched for.

On a practical level, longitudinal studies of the rate of advancement necessitate a long time perspective because of the relative infrequency of advancements in most organizations and jobs. Rate of advancement is most frequently used as a criterion in studies of managerial or management trainee selection. At least two major programs of selection research have used promotions or salary increases or both as measures of job performance. Standard Oil (now Exxon) researchers used biographical data and paper and pencil tests in the early identification of managerial talent (Exxon Company, U.S.A., 1976), and AT&T researchers (Bray, Campbell & Grant, 1974) have explored the use of assessment centers (see Chapter 7) as predictors of rate of advancement.

Personnel and production criteria are frequently referred to as "hard" criteria while ratings criteria such as those discussed in our next section have been termed "soft" criteria because of their judgmental basis. As should be evident, various hard criteria are not necessarily free of contamination, nor are they more relevant or necessarily more reliable than soft criteria. Further, it can frequently be the case that "hard" criteria themselves are the result of some supervisory judgment. For example, success in training can be measured by a trainer's grade or rating, while promotions are usually partly the result of some supervisor's recommendation.

JUDGMENTS AS CRITERIA: METHODS

As we saw earlier, the majority of criterion-related validity studies employ measures of job performance that are based on judgments, usually those of supervisors. In the vast majority of these studies, the instrument used in making these evaluations is some form of graphic rating scale. Graphic rating scales require the rater to *evaluate* ratees along trait or performance dimensions in an *absolute* sense. Unlike graphic rating scales, checklists of various kinds require that the rater *describe* rather than evaluate the ratees. For example, the rater may merely indicate which of a series of statements is descriptive of the ratee. As we shall see, this distinction, while useful, is sometimes not always clear. Employee comparison systems differ from both rating scales and checklists in that they are based on *relative* rather than absolute judgments. That is, they require the rater to compare workers to each other rather than evaluating them or describing them in the abstract. In this section, we will review the various types of judgmental criteria and outline their relative advantages and disadvantages.

Methods Requiring Absolute Judgments

Graphic rating scales. Formats differ widely among graphic rating scales. Figure 3–5, taken from Guion (1965), is an illustration of some of the many variations. At first glance it would appear that the most important dimension—in terms of information provided—the formats in Figure 3–5 vary along is degree of structure provided to the rater. The formats at the top of the page provide little information to the rater on the dimension to be rated and no definition of the meaning of different points on the scale. At the other extreme, the formats at the bottom of the page attempt to define the dimension being rated and give some idea of what different points on the scale along the dimension mean. It seems reasonable that the formats providing more information should produce "better" ratings, that is, ratings with higher reliabilities and fewer rating errors. The surprising finding, however, is that this is often not the case. Indeed, newer rating formats providing even more information than any in Figure 3–5 do not, in general, produce better ratings (Wexley and Klimoski, 1984).

The formats in Figure 3–5 also differ in number of rating categories. That is, they differ in the fineness of discriminations required. Little research has been done to determine the optimum number of categories for graphic rating scales, but research results are available for scales with a Likert format (like those in Figure 3–5). The best and most recent of the studies on this question found no relationship between the numbers of scale points and either validity or reliability of the scales (Matell and Jacoby, 1972) as long as the number of scale points is five or greater.

Recall that in our discussion of criterion contamination we cited problems of halo, leniency, and central tendency as ones that were particularly important or unique to ratings. In the last two decades, much effort has been directed toward the development of rating formats which minimize these errors. The most thoroughly discussed and researched of the new rating formats has been the *behaviorally anchored rating scales* (BARS) first proposed by Smith and Kendall (1963). An example of a BARS scale is presented as Figure 3–6.

Behaviorally anchored rating scales. The idea behind BARS was that there were two primary reasons graphic rating scales typically showed low reliability and high halo and leniency errors. The first was that the performance dimensions included in the scales were vague and lacked meaning to raters. It was thought that dimensions like "Overall Performance," "Quality of Output," "Human Relations Ability," etc., which were chosen by psychologists or other personnel researchers, were not the dimensions used by supervisors when they viewed job performance. As a result, different supervisors read different meanings and intentions into the same dimension. The second reason was that scale points on the dimensions were vague and undefined, again leading to different interpretations by different raters. For example, does "Satisfacto-

FIGURE 3–5.

VARIATIONS ON A GRAPHIC RATING SCALE. EACH LINE
REPRESENTS ONE WAY IN WHICH A JUDGMENT OF THE
QUALITY OF A PERSON'S WORK MAY BE GIVEN.

a. Quality   High |_____|___✔___|_____|_____| Low

b. Quality   High |_____|___✔___|_____|_____| Low
                 5   4   3   2   1

c. Quality |_____|___✔___|_____|_____|
             Exceptionally Work usually Quality is   Work contains Work is
             high-quality   done in a   average for frequent   seldom
             workmanship   superior-way this job   flaws   satisfactory

d. Quality |_____|_____|_____|__✔__|_____|
             Too many   About   Occasional   Almost never
             errors   average   errors   makes mistakes

e. Quality   5   ④   3   2   1

Performance Factors	Performance Grade			
	Consistently superior	Sometimes superior	Consistently average	Consistently unsatisfactory
f. Quality Accuracy Economy Neatness	☐	☒	☐	☐

1 2 3 4 5	6 7 8 9 10	11 12 13 14 15	16 17 18 19 20	21 22 23 24 25
			☒	
g. Quality Poor	Below average	Average	Above average	Excellent

h. Quality of Work
      15   13   ⑪   9   7   5   3   1
   Rejects and errors   Work usually OK;   Work passable;   Frequent errors
   consistently rare   errors seldom   needs to be   and scrap: careless
                         made   checked often

i. Quality of Work   Judge the amount of scrap; consider the
                      general care and accuracy of his work;
                      also consider inspection record.
                      Poor: 1–6; Average: 7–18; Good: 19–25.   20

ry" mean "About Average," or does it mean something closer to
"In the Top Two-Thirds?"

In an attempt to overcome these two perceived deficiencies,
Smith and Kendall (1963) proposed that the dimensions to be used
be derived by raters who would actually use the scale, and that
different points on each dimension be anchored by statements
describing actual job behavior which would illustrate specific levels
of performance. There are variations in how these two concepts are

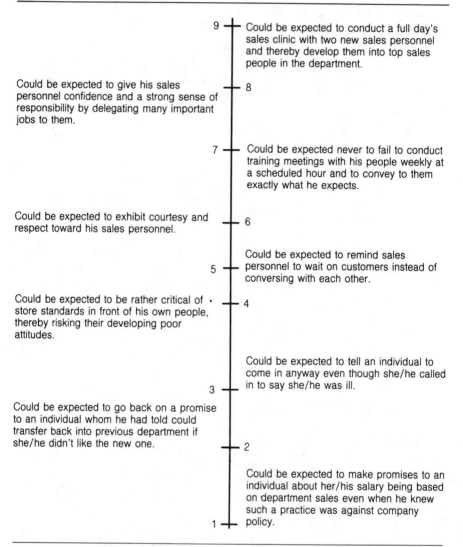

FIGURE 3–6. *BARS SCALE FOR EFFECTIVENESS OF SUPERVISION OF SALES PERSONNEL BY DEPARTMENT MANAGERS IN A LARGE RETAIL STORE.*

9 — Could be expected to conduct a full day's sales clinic with two new sales personnel and thereby develop them into top sales people in the department.

Could be expected to give his sales personnel confidence and a strong sense of responsibility by delegating many important jobs to them. — 8

7 — Could be expected never to fail to conduct training meetings with his people weekly at a scheduled hour and to convey to them exactly what he expects.

Could be expected to exhibit courtesy and respect toward his sales personnel. — 6

Could be expected to remind sales personnel to wait on customers instead of conversing with each other. — 5

Could be expected to be rather critical of · store standards in front of his own people, thereby risking their developing poor attitudes. — 4

Could be expected to tell an individual to come in anyway even though she/he called in to say she/he was ill. — 3

Could be expected to go back on a promise to an individual whom he had told could transfer back into previous department if she/he didn't like the new one. — 2

Could be expected to make promises to an individual about her/his salary being based on department sales even when he knew such a practice was against company policy. — 1

From Campbell, Dunnette, Arvey, and Hellernik, (1973).

applied in developing BARS, but typically at least five steps are included.

1. *Generation of Descriptive Statements.* Persons with a thorough knowledge of the job, (typically supervisors or job incumbents) are assembled in a group and asked to describe specific

behaviors that indicate effective or ineffective job performance. What is really done is close to a critical incidents job analysis as described in Chapter 2. The following are two examples taken from a study of department store managers (Campbell, et al. 1973):

> Conducts a full day's sales clinic with two new sales personnel, thereby developing them into top sales people.
>
> Makes promises to an individual about her or his salary based on department sales even when he knew such a practice was against company policy.

2. *Determination of Performance Dimensions.* The same expert group is asked to define the major dimensions of job performance. Actually, this step can be carried out first but has been moved to second in a number of studies in order to focus the experts on specific job behaviors before moving to the broader dimensions.

3. *Assignment of Behaviors to Dimensions.* Members of the group then independently assign each of the behaviors from step 1 to the various dimensions from step 2.

4. *"Retranslation" of Behavior Statements.* A new group of job-knowledgeable judges then "retranslates" or reallocates each behavioral statement to the performance dimension to which they think it belongs. If a certain specified percentage (usually 50–80%) of the judges in this group reallocate a statement to its dimension as established in step 3, the statement is retained.

5. *Scaling of Behavior Statements.* This group or another similar group then rates each statement as to the level of performance it represents on its performance dimension. The statements finally chosen to anchor each performance dimension are those showing low standard deviations across judges on these ratings (indicating good rater agreement) and covering the performance dimension as evenly as possible.

6. *Final Rating Scale.* The final instrument consists of 5–10 performance dimensions, each anchored by about 5–7 behavioral statements. An example of one such anchored performance dimension—effectiveness of supervision given by a department store manager to his sales personnel—is shown in Figure 3–6 (from Campbell et al. 1973).

While BARS require much effort and time to construct, they typically do not result in scales with better measurement properties (for example, Borman & Dunnette, 1975; Keaveny & McGann, 1975; Bernardin, Alvarez, & Cranny, 1976; Schwab, Heneman, & Decotiis, 1975). However, there are other advantages which may make BARS attractive. There is some evidence that the greater participation that workers and supervisors have in developing these scales leads to all employees taking the rating process much

INTERACTIONS WITH SUBORDINATES

1. Communicates objectives of SPG to the people he/she works with

   Almost Never 0 1 2 3 4 5 Almost Always

2. Requires managers to engage in planning and forecasting

   Almost Never 0 1 2 3 4 5 Almost Always

3. Encourages key managers to consider the value of team building activity for their respective departments

   Almost Never 0 1 2 3 4 5 Almost Always

4. Clearly defines the role responsibilities of the key managers

   Almost Never 0 1 2 3 4 5 Almost Always

5. Communicates measurable standards against which people will be evaluated

   Almost Never 0 1 2 3 4 5 Almost Always

6. Solicits divergence of thinking on issues

   Almost Never 0 1 2 3 4 5 Almost Always

7. Sends key people to seminars for developmental purposes

   Almost Never 0 1 2 3 4 5 Almost Always

8. Attracts and trains people necessary to perform functions that will be critical within the next 3 to 5 years

   Almost Never 0 1 2 3 4 5 Almost Always

9. Changes the organization to fit the people who are reluctant to transfer, retire, be promoted, etc. (rather than insisting upon an organization that is designed to accomplish the work that is expected of it)

   Almost Always 0 1 2 3 4 5 Almost Never

10. Procrastinates in dealing with poor performers

   Almost Always 0 1 2 3 4 5 Almost Never

11. Encourages subordinates to express their ideas in written form on 1 to 2 pages

   Almost Never 0 1 2 3 4 5 Almost Always

From Latham and Wexley, (1981).

more seriously, and this, in turn, generates positive motivational outcomes. This result may occur with greater employee participation no matter what type of scale is used (Friedman & Cornelius, 1976). A second possible advantage may be that the BARS themselves communicate performance expectations more explicitly than do other formats. Finally, the BARS format is much more acceptable from a legal standpoint (Ashe, 1980), even though there may be no scientific psychometric basis for this preference.

Behavioral observation scales. An approach to rating format that represents something of a blend between graphic rating and a checklist as defined here is the *behavioral observation scale* or BOS (Latham & Wexley, 1981). An example of these scales is given in Figure 3–7. BOS retain the behavioral specificity of BARS but require the rater to indicate how often each behavior occurred; no

1. He/she is a self-starter. Always takes the initiative. Superior never has to stimulate.
2. While generally he/she shows initiative, occasionally superior has to prod to get work done.
3. He/She has a tendency to sit around and wait for directions.

Scoring Mixed Standard Scale Triads

1. Assign numerical values to the statements in a triad:
   1, 2, 3 according to their favorability.
2. Assign similar values to the response options; that is,
   Better than = 3, Equal to = 2, Worse than = 3.
3. The response to each statement is then scored as the product of the statement and response values as follows:

	Response Value		
	Worse than	Equal to	Better than
Statement Value	(1)	(2)	(3)
Low (1)	1	2	3
Medium (2)	2	4	6
High (3)	3	6	9

4. The resulting scale value for the triads range from 6–18 because the total sum for the triad is the sum of the Response Value—Statement Value product for each of the three items.

---

evaluation of the behavior or the person is required, though in developing these scales some behaviors are recognized as effective and others as ineffective regarding their contribution to total job performance. The major advantage of BOS relative to BARS may be that BOS provides more data for performance feedback and counseling. Memory requirements of BOS, however, may be such that the frequency ratings become evaluations (Murphy, Martin, & Garcia, 1982) rather than reports of the frequency of particular behaviors.

Mixed standard scales. Another attempt to construct rating scales with a behavioral format is the *mixed standard scale* (MSS) proposed by Blanz and Ghiselli (1972). Mixed standard scales also are like checklists in that the rater checks which one of three statements in a set is most like the person rated. One of several of these triads that might be used in a rating instrument is presented in Figure 3–8. Triad statements are developed from critical incidents describing especially effective and ineffective behavior. Within each triad, the three statements describe good, average, or poor performance along a single dimension. These statements are then randomly ordered on the form, and for each statement the rater indicates whether the ratee's performance is better than, worse than, or equal to, that described by the statements. Scoring procedures for each of these triads are described at the bottom of Figure 3–8.

Research to explore differences among rating scale formats in their ability to eliminate halo, central tendency, and leniency indicates that these more modern attempts (BARS, BOS, MSS) yield little improvement in measurement (Wexley & Klimoski, 1984). However, in terms of performance feedback and counseling, communicating the importance of high standards of performance and performance appraisal, and communicating to employees what aspects of performance are most relevant, we believe behaviorally based ratings represent a significant improvement.

Some research was also done on the reduction of rating errors through rater training (Wexley, Sanders, & Yukl, 1973). These training programs involve instructing raters in the major types of rating errors, practicing ratings, demonstrating the errors, and discussing performance dimensions and levels. While there is consistent evidence that this rater error training effectively reduces rating errors, there are two problems. First, the reduction of these errors is not large even when statistically significant. Second, in the absence of information about actual performance levels (Schmitt & Lappin, 1980), we do not know whether reduction in these errors (as defined in the experimental studies) results in more accurate ratings or not (Borman, 1978). In other words, raters can agree with each other and be wrong; or all employees in a group can be excellent performers, in which case all the ratings in that group should be good. Accurate ratings for such a group may, in fact, look like leniency errors have occurred. Some research (Pulakos, 1984) suggests that training to reduce errors may have no effect on accuracy even though ratings seem to have improved.

The main conclusion to be drawn from this research on rating errors is that ratings should be monitored for evidence of possible errors. Rater training should familiarize raters with possible errors, the meaning of the rating dimensions, and the defined levels of effective and ineffective performance. It should also give them practice at rating and use that practice to demonstrate errors and ways to correct those errors. Finally, raters must believe that the organization places importance on securing accurate and carefully documented performance appraisals.

Methods Requiring Employee Comparisons

Judgments about performance that require the rater simply to compare various employees are called *employee comparisons* and consist of three types: rank ordering, paired comparison, and forced distribution. Employee comparisons are highly reliable; apparently comparative judgments are easier to make than absolute judgments are (Guilford, 1954). Of the rating errors, central tendency and leniency cannot occur because in an ordering system someone must be highest and someone else lowest. Further, halo is not usually a problem because, for practical reasons, employee comparison systems are limited to assessing only overall performance. (Comparing large numbers of employees only once is tedious; comparisons along several dimensions would be extremely time-consuming.) One of your authors once required the supervisors of a group of prison guards to pair-compare their subordinates along three performance dimensions. The resulting correlations among performance dimensions exceeded .80, indicating employees were rank ordered almost identically on all three dimensions. Finally, rank ordering people in separate supervisory groups and comparing those rank orders across groups assumes equal performance across groups. So, a person working in a group in which all employees are above average would be at a disadvantage when compared with another person working in a group in which all employees were below average.

Methods of rank order. One of the simplest approaches to job performance measurement is to have supervisors rank order their employees. The ranking can be on overall job performance only or on separate dimensions of job performance. Ranking becomes more difficult as the number to be ranked increases; a technique called alternate ranking can be helpful in this connection. The supervisor is given a stack of cards, each one containing the name of an employee. He sorts through the stack and picks out the two individuals who are highest and lowest on the dimension being ranked. He then goes through the remaining cards and selects the highest and the lowest. This process continues until the ranking is complete.

Method of paired comparisons. In using this method, one first constructs all possible pairings of employee names. For each pair of names, the rater then chooses the one he or she feels is highest on the dimension being evaluated. For each ratee, we then compute the percentage of comparisons in which that ratee was preferred over the other person in the pair. These percentages are then converted into their corresponding standard scores. Tables are available for converting to standard scores (see Chapter 5) directly from frequency data; the information needed is the number of times the ratee was preferred over others and the total number of ratees (Lawshe, Kephart & McCormick, 1949). These standard scores are most useful if one is interested in making cross-group comparisons of individuals.

The paired comparison technique is capable of producing highly reliable ratings with a minimal number of judges. The major drawback is the fact that the number of pairs of judgments one must make increases rapidly as *n*, the number rated, increases. The number of pairs of employees to be compared can be computed by the following formula:

$$\text{Number of comparisons} = (n(n-1))/2$$

So, to pair compare 20 employees, one must make 190 comparisons; with 30 employees, this number becomes 435.

Forced distribution method.   This employee comparison system is actually an approximate ranking method which allows numerous ties. Typically there are five categories (and thus five "ranks") into which raters must sort ratees in specified proportions. These proportions are usually chosen to approximate frequencies in the normal distribution. As an aid to the rater, the number as well as the percentage of individuals to be assigned to each category is given. The scale might appear as follows:

Highest 10%	Next 20%	Middle 40%	Next 20%	Lowest 10%
5 names	10 names	20 names	10 names	5 names

Typically, a list of names of ratees is presented along with the above information. The forced distribution method is usually used to measure along a single dimension of overall performance, but this need not be the case. The forced distribution method is often useful when the number to be rated is large—making ranking and pair comparison difficult—and when there are at least several raters, which insures the reliability of the final composite. When the added condition holds that the raters would find it difficult to make fine differentiations between the ratees, we have the ideal set of circumstances for use of forced distribution. In combining ratings across judges, the five categories can be assigned numbers (ranging from 1 through 5, for example) and values averaged across judges. In one recent study, ratees were evaluated by an average of 7.5 judges (peers in this case) and the composite ratings had an average reliability of .80 (Schmidt & Johnson, 1973). Incidentally, if raters are equal in their ability to rate, it is always better to have more raters, since the reliability of their composite rating increases. We will elaborate on this point in Chapter 5.

Forced distribution ratings are superior to graphic rating scales in that there can be no leniency or central tendency errors. Halo, however, is not necessarily reduced; in the study mentioned above the average correlation between the two dimensions assessed ("drive and aggressiveness" and "predicted future success as a foreman") was .66. Reliability of forced distribution ratings, while usually superior to that of graphic rating scales, will typically be lower than that of pair comparisons or ranking, given the number of raters is constant. Differences in reliability will be greater the smaller the number of raters; conversely, differences should be negligible with large numbers of raters.

All three employee comparison methods discussed are highly reliable and have worked well when a researcher is interested only in a unidimensional judgment of employees' overall organizational contribution. This might be the case when we want to determine pay raises, promotions, or when the judgments are to be used as standards against which to evaluate some personnel staffing function, such as selection. There are two distinct limitations. These systems are of no use for performance feedback or counseling and may be most difficult to explain or justify to questioning employees. Further, the use of employee comparisons for pay raises or promotions will most certainly increase competition among the members of a work group which may produce significant negative long-term outcomes (see Schein, 1980).

Methods Requiring Reports of Behavior

Checklists. The idea behind checklists is that the quality of information obtained from supervisors about employee work performance can be improved by eliminating the evaluative function and turning the supervisor into a mere describer or reporter of observed behavior. This distinction often appears somewhat strained. For example, a rater reporting the frequency with which the ratee displays a desirable work behavior (on a scale where, say, 5 = "always" and 1 = "never") is likely making an evaluative judgment. For this reason, we included our discussion of BOS and mixed standard scales with our discussion of graphic ratings. However, one checklist technique, forced choice, may be more truly descriptive than others.

The forced choice technique. This method was developed by Wherry in the late 1940s for use in rating officers in the Army. The major purpose in substituting forced choice scales for the older graphic rating scales was reduction in leniency: military personnel people consistently found that the vast majority of ratees were landing in the top two rating categories. Although they felt their officer corp was good, they knew it was not that good. The forced choice procedure was designed to reduce leniency by making it difficult, if not impossible, for a rater to deliberately assign a high rating to an undeserving ratee. In this method, the rater—who, it will be remembered, is cast as an observer-reporter rather than an evaluator—is typically presented with blocks of two or more (usually four) statements, each statement within a block having been carefully equated with the others on some "attractiveness" index. All statements within a block thus look equally flattering, but they differ in ability to differentiate high from low employees. Only those that differentiate the high from the low are counted when the form is scored. The rater-reporter's task is to select the statements in each block that are most (and sometimes least) descriptive of the ratee. The theory is that even a rater who would like to fake will not be able to do so under these circumstances. Since this first military application, forced choice rating scales have been used in evaluating highway patrolmen and police officers (Peres, 1959), engineers (Lepkowski, 1963), teachers (Toole & Murray, 1958), and medical doctors (Newman & Howell, 1961; Newman, Howell & Harris, 1957).

A number of research studies have been done on the appropriate format of forced choice scales. The conclusion of these studies is that the attractiveness of items should be judged on the basis of "importance to the job," that forced choice items should be arranged in groups of four equally attractive items, and that the rater-reporter be asked to pick the two most descriptive of a ratee. An example of forced choice blocks developed for rating of Michigan State Troopers is presented as Figure 3–9.

There are three potential problems with the use of forced choice techniques. First, in developing these scales, we frequently find the discrimination index (the ability of the item to separate high from low performing individuals) and the job importance index (or attractiveness index) computed for each item highly correlated. This means that it is impossible to arrange items in groups of four equally attractive items—two of which discriminate between good and poor workers, and two others which fail to discriminate. Second, the technique is not popular with supervisors who want to know what rating they are giving subordinates. Third, the scales cannot be used for feedback because once one tells supervisors/subordinates what the scored items are, the scale is no longer useful in eliminating leniency—the reason for its development. The latter two reasons were instrumental in deciding to discontinue using a forced choice scale for evaluating Michigan State Troopers.

Select two phrases which best describe the trooper.
Remember to treat each set of statements independently.

1

1. He makes good contacts with both the general public and public officials.
2. He leaves a very good impression of the department with the younger generation.
3. He does not accept or solicit gifts or services from the public.
4. He knows the criminal element in the post area.

2

1. His attitude toward the job is one of sincerity and belief that the job is important.
2. He has pride in the department and himself.
3. He keeps the firearms that he carries clean and in proper working order.
4. He never compromises a principle or writes a ticket just to be number one on the activity sheet.

3

1. He seems to know when the letter of the law should be discarded in favor of the spirit of the law.
2. He practices good first aid.
3. He takes advantage of resource materials department-wide.
4. His reports convey meaning without the use of superficial and excessive language.

4

1. He does not present a false front to command officers and fellow workers.
2. He is diplomatic with the public.
3. He knows his limitations.
4. He knows the trouble areas in traffic and he works them.

If the latter two concerns are organizationally relevant, we would not recommend using forced choice rating scales.

ISSUES IN EMPLOYEE APPRAISALS

Up to this point we have discussed the definition and mechanics of criterion measurement. In this last section, we raise a number of special issues regarding employee performance appraisal, among them the fairness of employee appraisals, how raters make ratings, and how to conduct performance appraisal interviews. Finally, we draw attention to the importance of the criterion issues discussed in this chapter as they relate to use of a predictor in selection.

Fairness of Performance Ratings

Another important consideration for those staffing researchers who use ratings for any organization is the legal constraint placed on using performance appraisals. Fair employment complaints reflect a dramatic increase in those cases in which the relevance of job

TABLE 3–4. CHECKLIST OF CHARACTERISTICS OF LEGALLY DEFENSIBLE PERFORMANCE APPRAISALS.

1. Clear written instructions to raters.
2. Relevant training for raters.
3. Documented rater familiarity with the nature and importance of the various job duties on which the employee is rated (with the actual job analysis or position description being incorporated by the reference) and with the ratee's actual performance of those duties.
4. Design and use of a performance appraisal form as job-related and easily understood as the circumstances allow.
5. Reasonable precaution against improper rater bias of any kind.
6. At least two level rater review and signoff.
7. Central monitoring to insure use of uniform rating standards.
8. Strenuous efforts to achieve accuracy rather than the more typical excessive leniency.
9. Employee review and right to comment.
10. Employee concurrence (or specified disagreement) with the listing of major duties on which performance was rated.
11. Employee signoff to signify having read the review, but not necessarily having concurred in the rating received.
12. Right of employee appeal within a reasonable time.
13. Statistical checks for adverse impact and for any unusual rating pattern requiring specific investigation.
14. Specific and mutually acceptable goals.

From Ashe and Lawrence, (1980).

performance appraisals is the central issue. Examples include promotional disputes, merit-based layoff decisions, terminations of older employees, and the employment of the handicapped, as well as selection decisions. Maximum feasible objectivity and demonstrable accuracy and fairness will be the key to successful defense. Ashe (1980) writing in *EEO Today* provided a checklist of important performance appraisal characteristics, many of which we discussed previously. This checklist is reproduced as Table 3–4. Interestingly, Ashe (1983) used a BARS Scale as an example of a legally acceptable rating format.

Of most relevance for legal considerations are racial issues, and in this area we, perhaps, have the largest body of literature. A comprehensive review of literature on ratee race effects in performance ratings was done by Kraiger and Ford (1985). In their paper, Kraiger and Ford reported on 74 studies involving 17159 ratees in which the rater was white, and 14 studies involving 2420 ratees in which the rater was black. They found that white raters assigned significantly higher ratings to white ratees than black ratees, and that black raters similarly favored black ratees over white ratees. Race effects were more pronounced in field research than in laboratory settings and were also more likely when the proportion of blacks in the workforce was small. Kraiger and Ford point out that, in the absence of objective performance data, we cannot necessarily conclude that ratings are biased in favor of whites or against blacks. What is needed, of course, are studies in which objective and subjective data are available for groups of black and white ratees. Needless to say, these data are difficult to produce except in controlled laboratory settings (Schmitt & Lappin, 1980). This problem is related to our discussion of the rater training research in which the distinction between rating errors and rating accuracy was made. In many situations, we have only expert judgment to distinguish rating errors from relevant individual differences in job performance.

The Performance Appraisal Process

As noted earlier in this chapter, The Performance Appraisal Process research efforts aimed at improving ratings through rater training and format changes have not produced marked improvements in ratings. Recently, various authors have noted both the complexity of the organizational environment in which ratings take place (Landy & Farr, 1980; Wexley & Klimoski, 1984) and the complexity of the cognitive process involved in making a rating (Ilgen & Feldman, 1983; Wexley & Klimoski, 1984).

Wexley and Klimoski (1984) drew attention to the variety of cognitive processing demands made on the rater. For example, the rater must be attentive to employee performance if he or she is to encode the relevant performance information and remember it when appraisals are made. We said earlier that the more behaviorally based rating formats inform the rater or draw her or his attention to relevant job behaviors. They also acknowledge a stage in which information must be integrated over a number of instances (or across ratees) in order to make a rating. Quality of performance ratings could suffer as a result of factors affecting any of the stages in this process. For example, when it comes to observing, interpreting, or evaluating behavior, a failure could occur in the way behavior is categorized, in the opportunity for sampling ratee behavior, in the way instances of behavior are encoded in memory, or in the way all of the information about a worker is put together to make some rating. Research on these various stages of gaining and processing information may tell us why ratings are good or bad. The conceptual models are available, but there is little information on what occurs in the various cognitive stages in the rating context.

The Landy and Farr model (1980) of the rating process is broader in that it includes the context in which the rating takes place: rater and ratee characteristics, characteristics of the position a ratee holds, and the organization in which the rating is made. Their model is presented as Figure 3–10. If one remembers that the

FIGURE 3-10.   *PROCESS MODEL OF PERFORMANCE RATING.*

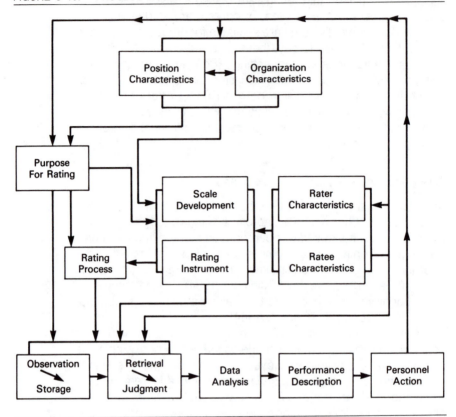

From Landy and Farr, (1980).

goal of performance rating is to give an accurate performance description of the person in question, we can see that there are many potential obstacles, all of which may serve to make ratings less relevant or more susceptible to criterion deficiency or contamination. Landy and Farr (1980) conclude that little is known about the effect of position or organizational characteristics, the rating process as outlined by Wexley and Klimoski (1984), or past personnel practices on the accuracy of performance ratings.

Non-Traditional Criteria of Worker Success

This issue of translating goals into criteria involves organizational policy toward both achieving production criteria (satisfactoriness) and also facilitating the attainment of the objectives of its human resources (satisfaction).

With reference to organizational philosophy, the emphasis on individual performance alone is "an unworkable model for social organization":

> . . . extreme emphasis on performance as a criterion [of status] may foster an atmosphere of raw striving that results in brutal treatment of the less able, or less vigorous, or less aggressive; it may wantonly injure those whose temperament or whose values make them unwilling to engage in performance rivalries; it may penalize those whose undeniable excellences do not add up to the kinds of performance that society at any given moment chooses to reward (Gardner, 1961, p. 18).

Worker satisfaction has served as an important criterion for evaluating the effectiveness of vocational counseling, organizational change, human relations training, and task redesign, but it is difficult to find satisfaction used as a criterion of staffing procedures. Indeed, worker attitudes of any kind have rarely been used as criteria for evaluating the effectiveness of staffing procedures. The selection of workers who will have more positive job attitudes (be more satisfied, be more committed, experience less alienation) has not been a goal of staffing researchers (Schneider, Hall, & Nygren, 1972), although Bass suggested that:

> Instead of evaluating the success of programs for improving selection, placement, training, job methods, and human relations in an industrial organization solely in terms of the extent to which they serve to increase the company's productivity, profits and efficiency, [1] propose that they also be evaluated on the extent to which they increase the worth of the organization to its members and society as a whole (1952, p. 156).

Recently, Pulakos and Schmitt (1983) and Schmitt and Pulakos (1985) have shown that job satisfaction is predictable over a period of up to two years. In the first study cited above, pre-employment expectations concerning the degree to which a job would meet or delay certain needs were significantly related to the job satisfaction of newly hired high school graduates in a wide variety of occupations. In the second study, pre-employment measures of general life satisfaction predicted subsequent levels of job satisfaction. It seems that satisfaction may be a relatively stable and general aspect of certain individuals which is a function of particular personality characteristics and/or an inclination toward interpreting various situations in a favorable manner. The results of these two studies suggest that some portion of the differences in individual job satisfaction is likely to be independent of any effort to make a particular job more rewarding or satisfying. Locke (1969) pointed out that whether or not the determinants of satisfaction reside with the worker or the job itself has not been resolved; more work on this question clearly should be undertaken.

While we maintain that job satisfaction should be an important organizational goal in its own right, Schmitt and Pulakos (1985) have cited a number of studies that indicate the effect of job satisfaction on a variety of individual and organizational effectiveness variables. For example, job satisfaction plays a significant role in absenteeism and turnover (Mobley, Horner, & Hollingsworth, 1978; Porter & Steers, 1973; Steers & Rhodes, 1978). Also, work dissatisfaction contributes to unionization activity (e.g., Hammer & Smith, 1978; Hammer & Berman, 1981). On an individual level, job satisfaction has been related to physical health (Burke, 1970), mental health (Kornhauser, 1965), life satisfaction (Iris & Barrett), and longevity (Palmore, 1969).

A similar argument that individual and organizational goals need not conflict is made by Etzioni as follows:

> At this point we must confront a major misunderstanding. Not all that enhances [organizational] rationality reduces happiness, and not all that increases [human] happiness reduces efficiency. Thus, to a degree, organizational rationality and human happiness go hand in hand (Etzioni, 1964, p. 2).

In support of Etzioni's concept of reciprocity in employee satisfaction and positive organizational outcomes, note that more satisfied employees may produce indirect but important organizational benefits:

1. *Commitment to the organization.* When the crunch comes, who will stay and help the organization? Mowday, Porter, and Steers (1980) reviewed the literature and showed that relationships exist between job satisfaction, commitment to the organization, and employee turnover. Indeed, they showed (see Schneider et al., 1972) that both personal characteristics and job characteristics may contribute to an individual's sense of job satisfaction and organizational commitment. Further discussion of job satisfaction and commitment as they relate to staffing, particularly the recruitment and turnover of employees, occurs in Chapter 4.

2. *Customer satisfaction.* Employees of service organizations may be the entire organization to the customers (Schneider, 1980). Perhaps some questions to be asked by service organizations should be: is my climate showing? What effect does employee

satisfaction have on repeat business in a bank, hospital, department store, and so forth? (Schneider, 1972) If it has no effect, why do companies try to create (and indeed put a price on) good will? The lack of research in and on service organizations is startling given that 70 percent of American workers are engaged in service to the public. Will an employee who is not being satisfied by his or her organization perceive the necessity to in turn satisfy the needs of those being served? One index of the importance of employee satisfaction in service organizations is the recent adoption of programs to increase the job satisfaction in such service-oriented companies as AT&T, IBM, and Sears. Another index of the importance of customer satisfaction to organizational effectiveness is the popularity of the book *In Search of Excellence* by Peters and Waterman (1982).

3. *Future employees.* What effect does a satisfied work force have on the kinds of employees who seek work in a particular organization? How much of a role do the opinion leaders in a community have on who works where? It seems reasonable to assume that the satisfied employees will tell their acquaintances about the company for which they work. The corporate image or organizational reputation will in turn have an effect on who applies for work (Katz and Kahn, 1978). Indeed, research on the turnover of employees who come from various recruiting sources shows that employees who are recruited through *current* employees have the lowest eventual turnover rates—lower than, for example, responses to advertisements or referrals from employment agencies (LIMRA, 1982).

There are, then, a number of good reasons for organizations to evaluate employees on how satisfied they are in addition to evaluating their behavior and the outcomes from their behavior. Company policy regarding employee satisfaction surely determines the degree to which employees will be committed, not be absent or quit, encourage new employees to seek work in the organization, and create a favorable image of the company in the community at large.

However, using satisfaction as a standard of excellence cannot be justified by research on the relationship between individual employee satisfaction and individual employee productivity. There is a remarkably consistent body of literature that suggests that if we assess how satisfied individual employees in a company are and how well they perform on the job, we probably will find a negligible relationship. A recent meta-analytic review (Iaffaldano and Muchinsky, 1985) reaffirmed this lack of relationship in that the average correlation across 217 estimates was only .17 (note .00 indicates no relationship and 1.00 is a perfect relationship). That is, satisfied employees today may not be higher producing employees tomorrow. Neither are they likely to be the lower producing employees; there just is no reliable relationship between the two indices.

However, most, if not all research exploring the satisfaction-performance relationship has been done on individuals within an organization—all of whom are likely to be similar in satisfaction and performance. As we shall see in Chapter 5, this homogeneity of individuals makes it unlikely that we can document any relationship. What might prove more useful is to do a study in which *organizations* are subjects and address the following question: Are organizations which have more satisfied employees more likely to be more productive and profitable than organizations whose employees are less happy (Schneider, 1985)? The importance of examining organizations as opposed to individuals as subjects is illustrated in a paper by Schmitt, Colligan, and Fitzgerald (1980). In examining the relationship between job attitudes and job stress, they found little evidence of a relationship at the individual level but they found meaningful differences among organizations. Attitude-stress relationships were much stronger when organizations were treated as subjects.

However, even in the absence of a significant or sizable satisfaction-performance relationship, Bass argues that:

> . . . the success with which a psychologist matches employees to jobs may not be gauged merely by the serviceability of the employees to the organization in which they are performing these jobs but also on the basis of the satisfaction that accrues to the employees by being placed on the given job—not because this increased satisfaction necessarily will lead to increased productivity and lower turnover within the organization, but because worker satisfaction is considered an intrinsic value—desirable in its own right (1952, p. 166.)

We are not arguing for the demise of productivity, that is, the satisfactoriness of the individual to the organization, as an important criteria, nor that employee satisfaction become *predominant* as a criterion. What is being argued is that job satisfaction is an *inherently* worthwhile criterion against which the effectiveness of staffing procedures can be evaluated. Because people are humans and humans have feelings, how they feel about the circumstances and outcomes from work is of necessity tied in with their general mental health and general life satisfaction (Rappaport, Rappaport, and Wilmott, 1971).

Improvement of Employee Performance

The analysis procedures discussed here are primarily useful, as noted, for monitoring purposes. They are devices for generating data against which the validity of various personnel practices can be checked. But they serve an important function and may also be useful in evaluating employee performance for the purpose of improving performance.

Whether the appraisal is done primarily for monitoring purposes or not, employees will want to know how they are doing and what information is being collected and retained about their performance. It seems performance appraisal very often means the obligation to feed back information to the person appraised. This latter purpose requires a different kind of philosophy. For staff improvement, analyses must be conducted with the heart and mind of a counselor rather than treated as an accounting problem. *Staff analysis for improvement purposes must involve the person whose performance is being analyzed.* While such a requirement seems obvious, research suggests that companies often feel that they have involved their staff in an appraisal, while the staff may not even be aware of the fact that they have been appraised. Hall and Lawler (1969) refer to this phenomenon as the "vanishing performance appraisal."

The performance appraisal that most involves the appraised person focuses on the development of the individual and goal-setting for his or her specific needs. A joint appraiser-appraisee conference may be held aside from a more traditional evaluation session. Both conferences may utilize the same data as input to discussion, but in one session the appraiser plays the role of *evaluator,* in the other the role of *developer.* While the motivation of employees is not the primary focus of interest here, we should note the importance of the motivational potential underlying the usually haphazard annual appraisal.

An entire motivation theory has developed around a paper titled "An Uneasy Look at Performance Appraisal" (McGregor, 1957). A few years later, in his now classic book, *The Human Side of Enterprise* (1960), McGregor further detailed the typical appraisal session and contrasted it to the "potential" appraisal.

McGregor's approach to management suggests using appraisal as a joint superior-subordinate effort toward attaining individual and organizational goals. This orientation, Theory Y, presupposes that workers will contribute to organizational effectiveness and growth when the organization provides the conditions for individual effectiveness and growth. As Schein (1980) noted, the organizational condition to strive for is one in which there is a psychological contract between the individual and the organization that substantiates a philosophy of mutual growth and effectiveness.

In a recent look at performance feedback, Wexley and Klimoski (1984) have identified four alternative approaches to feedback: tell and sell, tell and listen, problem-solving, and the mixed model.

In the *tell and sell* approach, the supervisor's role is to communicate the employee's appraisal as accurately as possible and to persuade the worker to follow a plan outlined for her or his improvement. The manager's persuasive power, the manager's control over incentives, and the manager-subordinate interpersonal relationship will all serve to determine the success of the tell and sell approach.

The *tell and listen* approach is characterized by the communication of the manager's evaluation to the employee and the employee's response to the evaluation. In the *problem-solving* approach, the emphasis is on employee development. The manager's role is more that of a helper than a judge. Together the manager and subordinate try to generate solutions to problems and agree on the steps to be taken as in the management by objectives approach detailed above. The *mixed model* begins with an open-ended discussion and exploration of problems, with the employee leading the discussion and the manager listening. Then, there is the problem-solving discussion with the manager assuming a stronger role; they both agree on performance problems and a plan to solve them. Finally, the manager ends the interview by giving her or his views and final evaluation.

Wexley and Klimoski (1984) do not advocate any one of these approaches; rather, they propose that a manager might use any one of them in a given situation. The important situational determinants of which approach is best include characteristics of the employee and the manager, the manager-employee relationship, and the organizational environment. Wexley (1982) provides advice on how to make performance appraisal interviews more effective in general. Before the interview, the manager must have clearly assessed the employee's job performance, prepared the assessment to include information on examples of the employee's behavior which were especially good or bad, and prepared suggestions as to how the subordinate might change her or his behavior. Wexley (1982) also maintains that the employee should be asked to prepare a self assessment and to consider work and career goals in anticipation of the interview. During the interview, Wexley (1982) provides several suggestions which may be more appropriate for the problem-solving or mixed model interviews described above, but some may be appropriate in all four types of interviews. We reproduce them as Table 3–5.

1. Start the interview by getting your employee talking. This can be accomplished by asking open-ended questions such as "How do you feel things are going on your job?" and "What goals do you feel you've accomplished since we met last?"

2. To avoid defensive reactions you should avoid making general statements (e.g., "You're always late getting your reports to me"), attributing motives to behavior (e.g., "You're not committed to our team"), or comparing one employee to another (e.g., "You're not nearly as innovative as Sam").

3. Allow the employee to do the majority of the talking by remaining silent, especially during the early part of the interview. Stimulate conversation by periodically "reflecting" an employee's *feelings*. For example:
   E: The most miserable part of my job is having to attend those boring meetings each month.
   M: You really despise them.
   E: That's for sure!

4. Your feelings can be conveyed nonverbally as well as verbally (Wexley, Fugita, and Malone, 1975). You might say that you are satisfied with an employee's work, but your facial expressions, gestures, posture, and lack of eye contact communicate something quite different to the individual. It is therefore important to be consciously aware of one's nonverbal behaviors.

5. Negative feedback should be tactfully given by being *specific* about behaviors you have observed on the part of the employee. Keep your comments at the behavioral level. This will minimize attacks on the employee's self-esteem which will likely be perceived as criticism. This is where BOS can be a great help to the manager.

6. Encourage the employee to suggest performance goals which you can then modify and expand. By letting the employee lead the way, you can also reduce defensiveness as compared with your assigning goals unilaterally.

7. Avoid what has come to be known as the "sandwich approach." Here, the manager provides negative feedback between heavy doses of positive feedback. The manager begins the interview on a positive note, but the employee barely listens for fear of what is coming next.

8. Avoid providing your employees with a "vanishing performance appraisal." Here, managers report having given their employees individual feedback, but the employees report that no such session had been held. To combat this, do not conduct your interviews on an airplane or in the company diningroom. Make it visible by meeting in either your office or your employee's office.

9. Be sure to distinguish between your assessment of the employee's performance on his or her current job and his or her potential for promotion. These are two distinct issues that are often incorrectly intertwined.

10. Close the session with a follow-up meeting with the employee to insure that progress is being made toward the goals you have both established.

From Wexley, (1982).

The Criterion-Predictor Relationship

At the beginning of this chapter we used a diagram of the relationship between the actual and ultimate criterion to define criterion deficiency, contamination, and relevance. Now that we have seen

FIGURE 3–11.   *RELATIONSHIP AMONG ACTUAL AND ULTIMATE CRITERION AND
A PREDICTOR VARIABLE.*

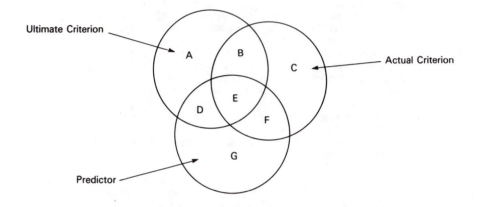

A: Criterion *deficiency* which is uncorrelated with the predictor.
B: Criterion *relevance* which is uncorrelated with the predictor.
C: Criterion *contamination* which is uncorrelated with the predictor.
D: Criterion *deficiency* which is correlated with the predictor.
E: Criterion *relevance* which is correlated with the predictor.
F: Criterion *contamination* which is correlated with the predictor.
G: Portion of predictor which is uncorrelated with either actual or
   ultimate criterion.

Adapted from Blum and Naylor, (1968).

some of the strengths and potential limitations of various actual
criteria, let's return to that diagram but with an added complexity
so as to point out the importance of criterion measurement as it
relates to employee selection. In Figure 3–11, we illustrate the
actual-ultimate criterion relationship and add to that figure a predictor of job performance (as we said at the beginning of the chapter,
a major purpose of criterion measurement is to assess the appropriateness of staffing decisions). Theoretically, at least, this produces seven different areas as identified at the bottom of the figure.
We have no knowledge of the ultimate criteria, so the relative sizes
of A, B, D, and E are unknown. In an actual study performed to
evaluate the relationship between a test or some other selection
instrument, Areas E and F represent the validity of the test as
estimated in the study (see Chapter 6 for a definition and discussion
of validity issues), while Areas D and E represent the "true" validity
of the test as measured against the ultimate criterion. Since we do
not know the relative sizes of Areas D and F, we do not know
whether our actual study validity over or underestimates the "true"
validity of our predictor.

Perhaps the area of most concern in the diagram is Area F which is that part of the actual criterion we can predict *that is unrelated to the ultimate criterion.* If this area is large, then our selection instrument is actually predicting *contamination* or *bias.* Our validity study will yield high-validity estimates, but certainly not for the right reason. An example of this kind of bias may occur in the following fashion. If we use supervisory ratings as a criterion and those ratings produce artificial or *non-relevant* differences in the measured job performance of black and white employees (Ford and Kraiger, 1985) and our predictor is a paper-and-pencil test of some cognitive ability on which large black/white differences in scores usually are observed, then the study estimate of validity will be an overestimate; we will be predicting the bias in supervisory ratings. Because of professional, legal, and social concerns, industrial/organizational psychologists have spent considerable effort in studies of potential bias. A book by Arvey (1979) provides a comprehensive review of much of this literature.

If Area D, on the other hand, is very large, then a potentially useful predictor will be discarded or its utility seriously underestimated. The size of Area E, then, is what one wants to maximize. Unfortunately, in practice one has no way of knowing whether the actual estimate of a test's validity is an overestimate or underestimate because the relative size of Areas D and F are unknown. However, the entire chapter on job analysis and this chapter on criterion measurement are devoted to minimizing the problems of criterion deficiency and contamination and maximizing relevance and, hence, Area E in Figure 3–11.

SUMMARY

We began this chapter discussing the role of staff appraisal in organizations and how organizational goals are translated into measures of individual excellence called criteria. We noted the problems that can occur when this translation is imperfect. We said a desirable criterion should be relevant, reliable, practical, and show discriminability. We discussed alternative ways of developing criteria and provided some examples. Problems in the contamination of criteria were noted. Methods for the combination of various measures of job performance into composites were described. We noted the potential for change in the criterion dimensions as a function of individual and organizational change.

In discussing actual criterion measures, we noted that the most frequently used criterion was a performance judgment of some kind. Ratings, various forms of employee comparisons, and checklists were described. Each was discussed in terms of their susceptibility to rating errors. Production records and personnel records (absenteeism, turnover, etc.) were enumerated as useful criteria. A case was also made for the inclusion of job satisfaction and employee commitment as criteria in evaluating the effectiveness of staffing procedures. We also briefly reviewed approaches to the performance appraisal process and finally, we outlined the implications of criterion problems when we estimate the validity of selection procedures.

This chapter can most usefully be concluded by producing a summary of the standards for performance appraisal outlined by Cascio and Bernardin (1981). They reviewed court cases to see the kinds of violations of appropriate staff appraisal procedures that various court decisions had shown were injurious to an organization as a defendant. That is, they asked the question "What should a staff appraisal system be like if it is going to be well-respected both legally and professionally?" They answered the question like this:

1. Appraisals of job performance need to be based on a job analysis that details the behavioral requirements of the job in question.
2. Staff appraisals should focus on the behaviors that make up the various dimensions of performance rather than on undefined global measures.
3. Staff appraisals should be psychometrically sound—relevant, reliable, and as uncontaminated as possible.
4. The standards of performance (criteria) against which employees will be evaluated should be communicated to them.

REFERENCES

Abelson, M. A., and Baysinger, B. D. (1984). Optimal and dysfunctional turnover: Toward an organizational level model. *Academy of Management Review, 9,* 331–341.

Argyris, C. (1957). *Personality and Organization.* New York: Harper.

Arvey, R. D. (1979). *Fairness in Selecting Employees.* Reading, MA: Addison-Wesley.

Ashe, E. L., Jr. (1980). How do your performance appraisals perform? *EEO Today, 7,* 30–36.

Ashe, L. R. (1983). EEO issues in the 80s. Address to the Michigan Association of I/O Psychologists, Detroit, MI.

Bass, B. M. (1952). Ultimate criteria of organizational worth. *Personnel Psychology, 5,* 156–173.

Bernardin, H. J., Alvarez, K. M., and Cranny, C. J. (1976). A recomparison of behavioral expectation scales to summated scales. *Journal of Applied Psychology, 61,* 554–560.

Blanz, F. and Ghiselli, E. E. (1972). The mixed standard scale: A new rating system. *Personnel Psychology, 25,* 185–200.

Blum, M. L. and Naylor, J. C. (1968). *Industrial Psychology: Its Theoretical and Social Foundations.* New York: Harper & Row.

Borman, W. C. (1978). Exploring the upper limits of reliability and validity in job performance ratings. *Journal of Applied Psychology, 63,* 135–144.

Borman, W. C. and Dunnette, M. D. (1975). Behavior-based versus trial-oriented performance ratings: An empirical study. *Journal of Applied Psychology, 60,* 561–565.

Bray, D. W., Campbell, R. J. and Grant, D. L. (1974). *Formative Years in Business.* New York: Wiley.

Burke, R. J. (1969/1970). Occupational and life strains, satisfaction, and mental health. *Journal of Business Administration, 1,* 35–41.

Campbell, J. P., Dunnette, M. D., Arvey, R. D., and Hellervik, L. W. (1973). The development and evaluation of behaviorally based rating scales. *Journal of Applied Psychology, 57,* 15–22.

Campbell, J. P., Dunnette, M. D., Lawler, E. E., III, and Weick, K. E., Jr. (1970). *Managerial behavior, performance, and effectiveness.* New York: McGraw-Hill.

Cascio, W. F. (1982). *Applied psychology in personnel management.* Reston, VA: Reston Publishing Co.

Cascio, W. F. and Bernardin, H. J. (1981). Implications of performance appraisal litigation for personnel decisions. *Personnel Psychology, 34,* 211–226.

Crozier, M. (1964). *The bureaucratic phenomenon.* Chicago: University of Chicago Press.

Dalton, D. R. (1981). Personnel and human resource management perspectives on turnover and absenteeism. In R. S. Schuler and S. A. Youngblood (Eds.). *Readings in Personnel and Human Resources Management.* New York: West.

Dunnette, M. D. (1963). A note on the criterion. *Journal of Applied Psychology, 47,* 251–254.

Eden, D., and Shani, A. B. (1979). *Pygmalion goes to boot camp: Expectancy, leadership and trainee performance.* New York City: APA.

Etzioni, A. (1964). *Modern organizations.* Englewood Cliffs, NJ: Prentice-Hall.

Exxon Company, U.S.A. (1976). *The personnel development series and success of managerial-professional-technical personnel.*

Fleishman, E. A. and Fruchter, B. (1960). Factor structure and predictability of successive stages of learning Morse code. *Journal of Applied Psychology, 44,* 97–101.

Fleishman, E. A. and Hempel, W. E. (1954). A factor analysis of dexterity tests. *Personnel Psychology, 7,* 15–32.

Fleishman, E. A. and Hempel, W. E. (1955). The relation between abilities and improvement with practice in a visual discrimination reaction task. *Journal of Experimental Psychology, 49,* 301–312.

Ford, J. K. and Kraiger, K. (1986). The study of race effects in objective indices and subjective evaluations of performance: A meta-analysis of performance criteria. *Psychological Bulletin.*

Friedman, B. A. and Cornelius, E. T., III. (1976). Effect of rater participation in scale construction on two psychometric characteristics of two rating scale formats. *Journal of Applied Psychology, 61,* 210–216.

Gardner, J. N. (1961). *Excellence: Can we be equal and excellent too?* New York: Harper.

Ghiselli, E. E. (1956). Dimensional problems of criteria. *Journal of Applied Psychology, 40,* 1–4.

Ghiselli, E. E. (1966). *The validity of occupational aptitude tests.* New York: Wiley.

Ghiselli, E. E. and Haire, M. (1960). The validation of selection tests in light of the dynamic character of criteria. *Personnel Psychology, 13,* 225–232.

Goldstein, I. L. (1978). The pursuit of validity in the evaluation of training programs. *Human Factors, 20,* 131–144.

Guion, R. M. (1965). *Personnel testing.* New York: McMillan.

Guilford, J. P. (1954). *Psychometric methods.* New York: McGraw-Hill.

Hackman, J. R., and Oldham, G. R. (1980). *Work redesign.* Reading, MA: Addison-Wesley.

Hall, D. T. and Lawler, E. E., III. (1969). Unused potential in research and development organizations. *Research Management, 12,* 339–354.

Hammer, T. H. and Berman, M. (1981). The role of non-economic factors in faculty union voting. *Journal of Applied Psychology, 66,* 415–421.

Hammer, W. C. and Smith, F. J. (1978). Work attitudes as predictors of unionization activity. *Journal of Applied Psychology, 63,* 415–421.

Huse, E. F. and Taylor, E. K. (1962). Reliability of absence measures. *Journal of Applied Psychology, 46,* 159–160.

Iaffaldano, M. T. and Muchinsky, P. M. (1985). Job satisfaction and job performance: A meta-analysis. *Psychological Bulletin, 97,* 251–273.

Ilgen, D. R., and Feldman, J. M. (1983). Performance appraisal: A process focus. *Research in Organizational Behavior, 5,* 141–197.

Iris, B. and Barrett, G. V. (1972). Some relations between job and life satisfaction and job importance. *Journal of Applied Psychology, 56,* 301–304.

Katz, D. and Kahn, R. L. (1978). *The Social Psychology of Organizations, 2nd Ed.* New York: Wiley.

Keaveny, T. J. and McGann, A. F. (1975). A comparison of behavioral expectation scales and graphic rating scales. *Journal of Applied Psychology, 60,* 695–703.

Kornhauser, A. W. (1965). *Mental health of the industrial worker: A Detroit study.* New York: Wiley.

Kraiger, K. and Ford, J. K. (1985). A meta-analysis of ratee race effects in performance ratings. *Journal of Applied Psychology, 69,* 56–65.

Landy, F. J. and Farr, J. L. (1980). A process model of performance rating. *Psychological Bulletin, 87,* 72–107.

Latham, G. P. and Wexley, K. N. (1981). *Increasing productivity through performance appraisal.* Reading, MA: Addison-Wesley.

Lawshe, C. H., Kephart, N. C. and McCormick, E. J. (1949). The paired comparison technique for rating performance of industrial employees. *Journal of Applied Psychology, 33,* 69–77.

Lent, R. H., Aurbach, H. A., and Levin, L. S. (1971). Predictors, criteria, and significant results. *Personnel Psychology, 24,* 519–533.

Lepkowski, J. (1963). Development of a forced-choice rating scale for engineer evaluation. *Journal of Applied Psychology, 47,* 87–88.

Levine, E. L. and Weitz, J. (1971). Relationship between task difficulty and the criterion: Should we measure early or late? *Journal of Applied Psychology, 55,* 512–520.

LIMRA, (1962). "Source mix" and "Source performance." Hartford, CT: Life Insurance Marketing and Research Association.

Locke, E. A. (1969). What is job satisfaction? *Organizational Behavior and Human Performance, 4,* 309–336.

Locke, E. A., and Latham, G. P. (1984). *Goal setting: A motivational technique that works!* Englewood Cliffs, NJ: Prentice-Hall.

Lyons, T. F. (1972). Turnover and absenteeism: A review of relationships and shared correlates. *Personnel Psychology, 25,* 271–281.

Matell, M. S. and Jacoby, J. (1972). Is there an optimal number of alternatives for Likert-scale items? Effects of testing time and scale properties. *Journal of Applied Psychology, 56,* 506–509.

McGregor, D. M. (1957). An uneasy look at performance appraisal. *Harvard Business Review, 35,* 89–94.

McGregor, D. M. (1960). *The human side of enterprise.* New York: McGraw-Hill.

Mobley, W. H., Horner, S. O., and Hollingsworth, A. T. (1978). An evaluation of precursors of hospital employee turnover. *Journal of Applied Psychology, 63,* 408–414.

Mowday, R. T., Porter, L. W., and Steers, R. M. (1982). *Employee-organizational linkages: The psychology of commitment, absenteeism and turnover.* New York: Academic Press.

Muchinsky, P. M. (1975). Consumer installment credit risk: A need for criterion refinement and validation. *Journal of Applied Psychology, 60,* 87–93.

Muchinsky, P. M. (1983). *Psychology Applied to Work.* Homewood, IL: Irwin.

Murphy, K. R., Martin, C., and Garcia, M. (1982). Do behavioral observation scales measure observations? *Journal of Applied Psychology, 67,* 562–567.

Newman, S. H., and Howell, M. A. (1961). Validity of forced choice items for obtaining references on physicians. *Psychological Reports, 8,* 367.

Newman, S. H., Howell, M. A., and Harris, F. J. (1957). Forced-choice and other methods of evaluating professional health personnel. *Psychological Monographs, 71,* (10, Whole No. 439).

Nicholson, J. R. (1958). A study of the relationship between response consistency on a personality test and success as a life insurance agent. Unpublished master's thesis. Bowling Green State University, Bowling Green, OH.

Palmore, E. (1969). Predicting longevity: A follow-up controlling for age. *The Gerontologist, 9,* 247–250.

Peres, S. H. (1959). A diagnostic forced-choice evaluation of highway patrolmen. *Dissertation Abstract, 19,* 3013.

Peters, L. H., and O'Connor, E. J. (1980). Situational constraints and work outcomes: The influences of a frequently overlooked construct. *Academy of Management Review, 5,* 391–397.

Peters, T. J., and Waterman, R. H. (1982). *In search of excellence.* New York: Harper & Row.

Porter, L. W. and Steers, R. M. (1973). Organizational, work, and personal factors in employee turnover and absenteeism. *Psychological Bulletin, 80,* 151–176.

Prien, E. P. (1966). Dynamic character of criteria: organization change. *Journal of Applied Psychology, 50,* 501–504.

Pulakos, E. D. (1984). A comparison of two rater training programs: Error training versus accuracy training. *Journal of Applied Psychology, 69,* 581–588.

Pulakos, E. D. and Schmitt, N. (1983). A longitudinal study of a valence model approach for the prediction of job satisfaction of new employees. *Journal of Applied Psychology, 68,* 307–312.

Rambo, W. W., Chomiak, A. M. and Price, J. M. (1983). Consistency of performance under stable conditions of work. *Journal of Applied Psychology, 68,* 78–87.

Randell, G. A., Packard, P. M. A., Shaw, R. L., and Slater, A. M. (1974). *Staff appraisal.* London: Institute of Personnel Management.

Rappaport, R., Rappaport, R. N., and Wilmott, P. (1971). *Human Relations* (Special Issue on Family and Work) *24,* (Whole No. 6).

Ronan, W. W. and Prien, E. P. (Eds.). (1971). *Perspectives on the measurement of human performance.* New York: Appleton-Century-Crofts.

Schein, E. H. (1980). *Organizational Psychology.* Englewood Cliffs, NJ: Prentice-Hall.

Schmidt, F. L. and Hoffman, B. (1973). Empirical comparison of three methods of assessing utility of a selection device. *Journal of Industrial and Organizational Psychology, 1,* 13–22.

Schmidt, F. L., and Johnson, R. H. (1973). Effect of race on peer ratings in an industrial situation. *Journal of Applied Psychology, 57,* 237–241.

Schmidt, F. L. and Kaplan, L. B. (1971). Composite vs. multiple criteria: A review and resolution of the controversy. *Personnel Psychology, 24,* 419–434.

Schmitt, N., Colligan, M. J., and Fitzgerald, M. (1980). Unexplained physical symptoms in eight organizations: Individual and organizational analyses. *Journal of Occupational Psychology, 53,* 305–317.

Schmitt, N., Gooding, R. Z., Noe, R. A. and Kirsch, M. (1984). Meta-analyses of validity studies published between 1964 and 1982 and the investigation of study characteristics. *Personnel Psychology, 37,* 407–422.

Schmitt, N. and Lappin, M. (1980). Race and sex as determinants of mean and variance of performance ratings. *Journal of Applied Psychology, 65,* 428–435.

Schmitt, N. and Pulakos, E. D. (1985). Predicting job satisfaction from life satisfaction: Is there a general satisfaction factor? *International Journal of Psychology, 20,* 155–168.

Schneider, B. (1972). Organizational climate: Individual preferences and organizational realities. *Journal of Applied Psychology, 56,* 211–217.

Schneider, B. (1975). Organizational climate: Individual preferences and organizational realities revisited. *Journal of Applied Psychology, 61,* 459–465.

Schneider, B. (1980). The service organization: Climate is crucial. *Organizational Dynamics,* Autumn, 52–65.

Schneider, B. (1985). Organizational behavior. *Annual Review of Psychology, 36,* 573–611.

Schneider, B., Hall, D. T., and Nygren, H. T. (1972). Self-image and job characteristics as correlates of changing organizational identification. *Human Relations, 24,* 397–416.

Schwab, D. P., Heneman, H. G., III, and Decotiis, T. A. (1975). Behaviorally anchored rating scales: A review of the literature. *Personnel Psychology, 28,* 549–562.

Seashore, S. E., Indik, B. P., and Georgeopoulos, B. S. (1960). Relationships among criteria of job performance. *Journal of Applied Psychology, 44,* 195–202.

Severin, D. (1952). The predictability of various kinds of criteria. *Personnel Psychology, 5,* 93–104.

Siegel, A. I. (1983). The miniature job training and evaluation approach: Additional findings. *Personnel Psychology, 36,* 41–56.

Smith, F. J. (1977). Work attitudes as predictors of attendance on a specific day. *Journal of Applied Psychology, 62,* 16–19.

Smith, P. C. and Kendall, L. M. (1963). Retranslation of expectations: An approach to the construction of unambiguous anchors for rating scales. *Journal of Applied Psychology, 47,* 149–155.

Staw, B. M. (1984). Organizational behavior: A review and reformulation of the field's outcome variables. *Annual Review of Psychology, 35,* 627–666.

Steers, R. M. and Rhodes, S. R. (1978). Major influences on employee attendance: A process model. *Journal of Applied Psychology, 63,* 391–407.

Toole, E. R. and Murray, W. I. (1958). Forced-choice: An improvement in teacher rating. *Journal of Educational Research, 51,* 680–685.

Vroom, V. H. (1964). *Work and motivation.* New York: Wiley.

Wallace, S. R. (1965). Criteria for what? *American Psychologist, 20,* 411–417.

Weitz, J. (1961). Criteria for criteria. *American Psychologist, 16,* 228–231.

Weitz, J. (1964). The use of criterion measures. *Psychological Reports, 17,* 803–817.

Weitz, J. (1966). Criteria and transfer of training. *Psychological Reports, 19,* 195–210.

Wexley, K. N. (1982). The performance appraisal interview. Paper presented at Fourth Johns Hopkins University National Symposium on Educational Research. Washington, DC.

Wexley, K. N. (1984). Personnel training. *Annual Review of Psychology, 35,* in press.

Wexley, K. N., Fugita, S. S., and Malone, M. P. (1975). An applicant's nonverbal behavior and student-evaluators' judgments in a structured interview setting. *Psychological Reports, 36,* 391–394.

Wexley, K. N. and Klimoski, R. (1984). Performance appraisal: An update. In Rowland, K. M. and Ferris, G. D. (Eds.) *Research in Personnel and Human Resources, 2.* Greenwich, CT: JAI Press, Inc.

Wexley, K. N., Sanders, R. E., and Yukl, G. A. (1973). Training interviewers to eliminate contrast effects in employment interview. *Journal of Applied Psychology, 57,* 233–236.

Wherry, R. J. (1957). The past and future of criterion evaluation. *Personnel Psychology, 10,* 1–5.

Williams, B. B., Sauser, W. I., Jr., and Kemery, E. R. (1982). Intelligence and physical fitness as predictors of success in early infantry training. Presented at Annual Meeting of the Southeastern Psychological Association Meeting, New Orleans.

4

RECRUITING

AIMS OF THE CHAPTER

In the last two chapters we were concerned with a description of the organization and job that confront a worker, the knowledge, skills, and abilities required of workers (Chapter 2) and the standards by which we judge how effectively individuals and organizations perform (Chapter 3). In this chapter, we turn our attention to considering how organizations attract and keep employees.

The chapter begins with a discussion of the role of internal recruitment (filling positions with current employees). In this context, we discuss the role of job satisfaction and organizational commitment in retaining a pool of competent internal recruits. We present a brief review of the determinants of satisfaction, commitment, and turnover. Then we describe procedures for internal recruitment such as job posting and career pathing.

In discussing external recruitment, a central thesis is that both the organization and the individual are making choices. From the individual's point of view, we discuss career and occupational choice. From the organization's point of view, we discuss what individuals want in an organization, how best to present the organization and job to prospective employees, and the availability and effectiveness of various techniques.

Before we begin, it is important to elaborate two important premises that are reflected here and throughout this chapter.

1. Most openings in companies are filled with internal persons; entry jobs are the ones most likely to be filled from the outside. The two major sections in this chapter, then, deal with *internal* recruitment and *external* recruitment. For internal recruitment, the central issue is employee retention and the focus is on understanding the job and organizational conditions that individuals find attractive enough in their current organization to want to be a candidate for available jobs. For external recruitment, the concern is for the ways people and organizations become attractive to, and seek out, each other.

2. Recruitment really is a two-way street, with both the individual and the organization having a series of decisions to make. Many organizations tend to focus on their decisions and forget about applicant decisions. In this chapter, a great deal of our discussion deals with applicants' decisions: what they want to join, and remain in, an organization.

INTERNAL RECRUITMENT

If the organization is not an attractive place to work, internal recruits will not be available for job openings as they occur. More importantly, if the organization is not attractive to the *best* current employees, the only incumbents available for new openings are the least desirable, and the organization must go outside of the company for candidates. A brief review of the correlates of employee job satisfaction, commitment, and turnover is presented as relevant background information regarding what makes an organization attractive.

Employee Job Satisfaction, Commitment, and Turnover

There are many models and conceptualizations of employee turnover, and they have been reviewed in a number of places (see Mobley, 1982 for a comprehensive review). In all of the models of turnover, five major categories of issues emerge as important elements in turnover decisions (Baysinger and Mobley, 1983):

1. Attraction of the present job. The issue of job satisfaction captures most of the research on the attraction of the present job. Since that is the major issue for this chapter, a summary of the job satisfaction literature is presented below.

2. Future attraction of the present job. While Baysinger and Mobley (1983) include this as a separate category, our review of the job satisfaction literature suggests that this is an issue incumbents include in their thinking when evaluating present job satisfaction. In fact, the most frequently used measure of job satisfaction, the *Job Descriptive Index* (JDI: Smith, Kendall and Hulin, 1969), includes an assessment of promotion *opportunities.*

3. External alternatives. Many models of turnover include the issue of alternative possibilities as an important component in understanding why, or under what circumstances, incumbents are likely to leave. In tight labor markets, where jobs are scarce, turnover is lower than when the economy is booming. At the individual level, what this means is that the more an employee feels there are alternatives that are more attractive than the present job, the more likely he or she is to leave. March and Simon (1958), who provided an early conceptual discussion of turnover in organizations, gave this perception the commonsense label of "perceived ease of movement."

4. Investments. In discussing employee investments, Baysinger and Mobley refer to both monetary-related and psychologi-

cal investments. Monetary investments include issues like being "vested" in a retirement plan. Employees who are vested are those who have stayed long enough with a company so that, when they retire, they will be able to collect on the company's retirement package. Most companies require that employees work some period of time before they are vested—anywhere from 6 months to 10 years. Vesting refers to all kinds of benefits, not just retirement. Sample benefits include participation in bonus plans, life insurance policies, stock ownership, and so forth. Sometimes these packages can be very lucrative and leaving them, therefore, can be very costly. When employees choose to remain with a company because of the monetary benefits to which they are entitled *only if they stay,* these benefits are called "golden handcuffs."

On the psychological side, investments can take the form of commitment to the organization. For example, someone who has been with an organization since its beginning can become psychologically committed to the organization. Leaving it would be emotionally painful even when it looks like the "rational" thing to do. The issue of commitment will be reviewed in more detail later.

5. Non-job factors. This category includes issues like family responsibilities and the compatability of job and perceived non-job responsibilities (March and Simon, 1958). For example, being a member of a religious community or a country club or even being a member of a volunteer organization to which one is committed can all influence a decision to terminate an employment relationship.

The two issues that have received the most attention in the study of turnover are *job satisfaction* and *organizational commitment,* listed above as the attraction of one's present job and investments (monetary and psychological), respectively.

What is job satisfaction? Job satisfaction is individuals' attitudes about the work and work setting that reflect their feelings about what happens to them and around them. It is most frequently thought of as some comparison people make between what they desired/expected/valued/wanted/hoped for/was important to them (alone or in various combinations, see Locke, 1976) and what they perceive actually is happening to and around them.

There have been literally thousands of studies of job satisfaction, and these studies have been conducted from a variety of theoretical vantage points. These studies have yielded a complex and interesting set of findings:

1. *Job satisfaction is a multifaceted construct.* What this statement means is that many elements make up job satisfaction,

so sometimes it is not very useful to speak about "job satisfaction" in a general sense (Scarpello & Campbell, 1983). It is more useful to speak about satisfaction *with* something. The "somethings" that seem to recur most frequently in the studies of job satisfaction are satisfaction with pay, the opportunities for promotion, supervision, coworkers, and the work itself (Smith, Kendall and Hulin, 1969). Other facets of the work setting that have received some attention are: fringe benefits, working conditions, and recognition (Locke, 1976).

2. *There is an intimate relationship between job satisfaction and the quality of work life experienced by employees.* In recent years, particularly since the late 1960s, the manner in which organizational members have reacted to their work and work settings has been expressed in *quality of work life* (QWL) terms. The issue of QWL became prominent towards the end of the Viet Nam era when there was a general alienation from authority and from demands made on people by powers beyond individual control. In addition, this era was characterized by the enormous influx of the post-World War II baby boom into the workplace—a workplace dominated by management that had lived through the Great Depression of the 1930s. The generation gap that emerged took many forms, but in the work setting it seemed to focus on an unwillingness of organizational members to be afraid of supervisors and managers and/or afraid of the consequences of losing a job. Further, individuals demanded more from their worklife than a paycheck. They wanted to enjoy their work, insisted on increased involvement in organizational decision-making, etc. The economy was extremely healthy and jobs were readily available for anyone with some skills.

QWL is important because it is the result of a management philosophy that values humans and permeates *everything* that happens in the organization (Beer, 1980). So, in addition to the isolated facets of satisfaction, perceived QWL is a function of the thousands of everyday actions and behaviors that occur in organizations to people.

3. *Job satisfaction and productivity are usually not strongly related.* Up until the middle 1950s, it was assumed by both researchers and managers that a satisfied worker was a productive worker. In 1955 a series of reviews of this assumption began to appear (e.g., Brayfield & Crockett, 1955; Vroom, 1964; Locke, 1976) and each of them indicated that the assumption was tenuous at best.

We think that the assumption of a relationship between satisfaction and productivity was derived from observations of researchers and managers that in organizations which were efficient and effective, morale of the workers (the sum of job satisfaction scores from all workers) seemed to be higher than in ineffective and inefficient organizations. The conclusion that this observation held for individual measures of job satisfaction and appraisals of individual job productivity appears to have been an error. It was an error because efficient and effective organizations have low turnover, high work quality, good customer relationships, and so on—in other words, individual productivity is but one element in overall organizational effectiveness.

4. *Job satisfaction is a function of personal variables as well as the result of what organizations do to people.* For the most part, job satisfaction has been studied as if its only determinant is what happens to people after they get on the job. This approach makes the assumption that all people tend to be satisfied or dissatisfied by the same things, but this assumption is not necessarily true. Of course there is a core of organizational conditions that are generally satisfying to a broad cross-section of workers, but at least one of these conditions appears to be the worker's own self-esteem. Locke (1976), in his comprehensive summary of the literature on job satisfaction, presented the list of conditions conducive to job satisfaction as follows:

1. mentally challenging work with which the individual can cope successfully;
2. personal interests in the work itself;
3. work which is not too physically tiring;
4. rewards for performance which are just, informative, and in line with the person's aspirations;
5. working conditions which are compatible with the individual's physical needs and which facilitate the accomplishment of his work goals;
6. high self-esteem on the part of the employee;
7. agents in the work place who help the employee to attain job values such as interesting work, pay, and promotions, whose basic values are similar to his own, and who minimize role conflict and ambiguity (p. 1328).

This listing by Locke shows that, for virtually each condition, an interaction of both a personal and a situational condition accounts for the satisfaction the person will derive. So, for mentally challenging work, the person needs to be able to cope, that is, have the skills and abilities required by the job; in addition, for satisfaction, interests are also required. What an individual brings to a setting in the way of needs, values, interests, abilities and self-esteem will also determine the degree to which he or she will experience satisfaction there.

5. *A person's job satisfaction is dependent on the ages and life stages of him/herself, family, and parents.* Frequently we forget that how satisfied a particular person is will depend upon the satisfaction of those around him or her. For example, Joan may have a job with intrinsically interesting work, very good pay, and considerate supervision. But she must travel extensively, and if her husband gives her grief because she is not home enough, Joan is likely to be dissatisfied. Alternatively, Sue has a job that was quite challenging when she first took it straight out of college, but now it is a bore because nothing new ever happens—she is likely to be dissatisfied not because of a change in the job but because of a change in her. Pay satisfaction seems to be susceptible to similar issues, especially as children appear, thus increasing financial obligations, and again later when they go to college. A significant issue for many married couples today is how to coordinate two careers and child-rearing responsibilities. Frequently, organizations find themselves recruiting a couple rather than a single job applicant. Thus, the age and stage of the family affect specific facets of family members' job satisfaction.

6. *Job satisfaction is an important correlate of physical and mental well-being.* The relationship between job satisfaction and both physical and mental well-being has been extensively studied for many years. In a series of studies, French (e.g., 1974) has tested a common theme in job satisfaction research, that is, that the goodness of fit between the individual's desires and the environment is the major determinant of job satisfaction. But French went one step further, showing that dissatisfaction as the result of a poor individual-environment fit was causally related to depression, physiological strain, and other indices of poor health.

7. *Assessments of job satisfaction yield useful information for organizations, especially when accomplished on a continuing basis.* When broadly conceptualized as QWL, the assessment of job satisfaction is becoming as important for organizations as other kinds of resource or expense audits. A useful way to think about assessing job satisfaction is to picture it as an audit of the feelings of human resources about the various facets of organizational life. Many organizations have ongoing programs of assessment, utilizing the data as diagnostic information and as input into corporate and managerial decision-making. Indeed, some companies such as Sears, Roebuck and Co. and IBM hold supervisors accountable for the data generated by the work units. In this kind of assessment model, supervisors have as much responsibility for the quality of work life of employees as they do for unit performance of the more traditional kind. At Sears, every employee is surveyed every third year; one-third of the entire company is surveyed every year. Thus, it is possible to study the level of job satisfaction in each unit over

a period of years. Within a particular year, it is possible to compare the total score on each item of job satisfaction *within each unit* to the *combined total scores* on each item for *all* sub-units. Typically, the questionnaire uses a seven-point scale of agreement-disagreement, as shown in Figure 4–1.

The measurement of job satisfaction is both a science and an art. The science concerns developing reliable and valid procedures for questioning organizational members; the art deals with tapping into the issues to be assessed in ways that make organizational members feel that they are contributing to their own benefit as well as to the organization's interests. One just does not put together a few questions and send them out to employees as a way of assessing the general feelings of employees about the work setting. Just as with the development of tests for assessing skills and abilities for making personnel-selection decisions, the development of measures of QWL is best left to professionals.

Summary. We have tried to summarize an unbelievably voluminous amount of literature with a few summary statements. Research on job satisfaction in the past 10 or 15 years has been one of the two most frequent objects of study in the organizational sciences (the other is leadership) (Campbell, Daft & Hulin, 1982). In a real sense it may be presumptuous of us to detail so much of the relevant findings in a few subcategories, yet the complexity of the issue seems to come through when it is presented this way. The message is that the work experiences of employees with respect to how satisfied they feel in their jobs is multi-determined and multi-faceted. Therefore, when attempting to influence employee job satisfaction, remember that no one facet of the situation can be expected to affect employee feelings of job satisfaction. *Entire* systems and procedures regarding the multi-facets of organizational life must be used to obtain significant effects on some global idea such as *satisfaction.*

In Chapter 2 we said that an organization must analyze the reward characteristics of the jobs in the organizations. The role of job satisfaction (presumably a response to those characteristics) as one organizational criterion was described in Chapter 3. In this section we have argued that job satisfaction is important because it is one determinant of continued accessibility to competent internal recruits.

What is organizational commitment? Organizational scientists, it must be observed, speak a convoluted language. By this we mean that a literal interpretation of the title of this section is that organizations are committed; of the last section, it is that jobs are

FIGURE 4–1. EXAMPLE OF JOB SATISFACTION ITEMS.

THE FOLLOWING ARE SOME STATEMENTS ABOUT YOU AND YOUR JOB. PLEASE CHECK THE NUMBER THAT INDICATES HOW MUCH YOU AGREE OR DISAGREE WITH EACH STATEMENT. PLEASE READ EACH STATEMENT CAREFULLY.

STRONGLY DISAGREE *DISAGREE* *SLIGHTLY DISAGREE* *NEITHER AGREE NOR DISAGREE* *SLIGHTLY AGREE* *AGREE* *STRONGLY AGREE*

1. All in all, I am satisfied with my job............. [1] [2] [3] [4] [5] [6] [7]
2. _____ rewards those who do their jobs well.. [1] [2] [3] [4] [5] [6] [7]
3. I get a feeling of personal satisfaction from doing my job well. .... [1] [2] [3] [4] [5] [6] [7]
4. In the next few months, I am likely to look for a job outside of_____. .... [1] [2] [3] [4] [5] [6] [7]
5. The organization cares more about money and machines than people. .... [1] [2] [3] [4] [5] [6] [7]
6. I don't care what happens to this organization as long as I get a paycheck. .... [1] [2] [3] [4] [5] [6] [7]
7. I feel free to tell people higher up what I really think. .... [1] [2] [3] [4] [5] [6] [7]
8. Decisions are made around here without ever asking the people who have to live with them. .... [1] [2] [3] [4] [5] [6] [7]
9. What happens at _____ is really important to me. .... [1] [2] [3] [4] [5] [6] [7]
10. My supervisor encourages subordinates to participate in important decisions that concern them. .... [1] [2] [3] [4] [5] [6] [7]
11. All in all, I am satisfied with the quality of my supervision. .... [1] [2] [3] [4] [5] [6] [7]
12. The team concept is working in my department. .... [1] [2] [3] [4] [5] [6] [7]
13. My coworkers are afraid to express their real views. .... [1] [2] [3] [4] [5] [6] [7]
14. It is easy to get other people in this department to help me when I need it............ [1] [2] [3] [4] [5] [6] [7]
15. All in all, I am satisfied with my shift hours. .... [1] [2] [3] [4] [5] [6] [7]
16. I have difficulty getting the tools and supplies I need on my job. .... [1] [2] [3] [4] [5] [6] [7]
17. My pay is fair considering what other places in this area pay. .... [1] [2] [3] [4] [5] [6] [7]
18. My work group knows exactly what things it has to get done. .... [1] [2] [3] [4] [5] [6] [7]
19. I understand the Problems and Complaints Procedures. .... [1] [2] [3] [4] [5] [6] [7]
20. I feel I can get help for my problems using the Problems and Complaints Procedures....... [1] [2] [3] [4] [5] [6] [7]

From Survey Research Center, *Michigan Organizational Assessment Package, Progress Report II*, August, 1975. Ann Arbor, MI: Institute for Social Research, The University of Michigan.

satisfied. The real purpose of this section, however, is to understand the commitment of people to their employing organization. Commitment is an important concept because it says something about what people are likely to do when the chips are down, when there is not an obvious reward for doing something, or when no one really asks them to behave a particular way. Katz and Kahn (1978) speak of this kind of behavior as "Innovative and spontaneous behavior: performance beyond role requirements for accomplishment of organizational functions:

1. Cooperative activities with fellow members
2. Actions protective of system or subsystem
3. Creative suggestions for organizational improvement
4. Self-training for additional organizational responsibility
5. Creation of favorable climate for organization in the external environment" (1978, p. 403).

Katz and Kahn are quite explicit about the need for these kinds of behaviors in organizations, behaviors not usually addressed by either theories of work motivation or theories of job satisfaction:

> The organizational need for actions of an innovative, relatively spontaneous sort is inevitable and unending. No organizational plan can foresee all contingencies within its own operations, or can control perfectly all human variability. The resources of people for innovation, for spontaneous cooperation, for protective and creative behavior are thus vital to organizational survival and effectiveness. An organization that depends solely on its blueprint of prescribed behavior is a very fragile social system. (pp. 403–404)

The kinds of behaviors described by Katz and Kahn as exemplifying the organizationally committed person have many important components. One component is obviously of a motivational origin because the behaviors are directed at particular kinds of activities, and the desired outcome seems to be more valuable to the organization than to the individual. So, Katz and Kahn are really speaking about behaviors that are indicative of commitment to the organization.

Another way to think about commitment is from the perspective of the individual. Most frequently this concerns some variant of the theme that the goals of the individual and the organization are congruent (Morrow, 1983). That is, the individual who views the organization as sharing goals and outcomes with him or herself will be the one who will behave as Katz and Kahn describe (Bateman & Organ, 1983).

When the behaviors specified by Katz and Kahn are viewed as the outcome of a congruence between individual and organizational goals, commitment becomes a *process*.

FIGURE 4–2. *AN INTEGRATED MODEL OF ORGANIZATIONAL COMMITMENT.*

New employee arrives with tenuous levels of compliance and attachment commitment	+ Organization reveals its commitment to new employees by providing for job satisfaction	= Cycle of attitude and behavioral commitment yielding people who want the organization to exist and prosper and want to continue to be part of the organization. Their behavior will exceed standard job descriptions.

Figure 4–2 presents an integrated model of the kinds of behaviors organizations require from employees that go beyond their formal job descriptions. First, organizations require some form of *compliance* on the part of employees—to come to work, to follow some basic rules and procedures, and so forth. Without some basic compliance like this, individual employees won't be around to be spontaneous! Second, the *attachment* of people to organizations begins to occur when they make a decision to join an organization. By the very act of deciding, they eliminated other alternatives in favor of the position available in the employing organization. This act of choice indicates a personal investment in the organization, leading to a desire to see the organization survive. But it also leads to a high value being placed on the organization itself. The attachment models of commitment, then, hold that the first act of commitment is the choice, and the compliance model argues that the choice will be followed by adherence to certain powerful other people and their rules and procedures. Putting these two ideas together yields the concept that people will be compliant because they like the organization and that they like the organization because they chose it!

Our hypothesis is that organizational employees begin their tenure in an organization with relatively high levels of commitment because of the process we just described. But we think that this high commitment is very tenuous because it has not been tested through actual participation in the organization and because it has not been reinforced by the organization or the individual through many cycles of behavior and attitudes. This suggests that, as far as commitment is concerned, early experiences with the organization are absolutely critical—critical because of the very tenuousness of the commitment new employees bring with them to the organization. In our discussion of external recruitment, this issue of early experiences will receive more attention.

We hypothesize that these feelings and behaviors on the part of new employees will only be maintained if the organization, in turn, displays its commitment to the employee, literally organizational commitment. Organizations display their commitment to employees in many ways, and these ways are neatly summarized by the facets of job satisfaction already discussed earlier in this chapter. In other words, in order for the typical employee to be committed in both attitudes and behavior, he or she must have behavioral evidence that the organization is committed, too. Without this behavioral evidence, the attitude-behavior cycle will not begin nor be maintained, and the early levels of commitment with which employees arrive will dissipate.

At this point it is important to introduce the concept of the *psychological contract* (Schein, 1965) in order to understand the reciprocal interaction of the individual and the organization and the role of mutual commitment in facilitating the integration of the individual and the organization. The psychological contract is the set of mutual, implicit agreements between employees and employing organizations that govern the expectations each has of the other. So, for example, the employee expects that for coming to work and working, the organization will provide pay, good supervision, worthwhile work and opportunities for bettering oneself. In turn, the organization expects the worker to come to work on time, to work hard during the day, to exercise initiative for the organization and to be loyal to it. But what are the factors that can disrupt this psychological contract?

The commitment of the parties to each other, then, is the critical issue in maintaining a beneficial psychological contract; the idea of mutual commitment summarizes our conceptualization of commitment very well. It must be emphasized, prior to leaving this topic, that supporting and maintaining a mutually beneficial psychological contract requires continual attention by both parties. This is true because the expectations of each party will constantly evolve as they work together in achieving organizational goals. It is important to view the psychological contract as being in a kind of constant renegotiation, for today's committed employee may be tomorrow's alienated employee because of a change in expectations. Similarly, employees to whom the organization is committed may lose this status because of a failure to identify any new ground rules for behavior that may be associated with changes in the organization, such as those due to new supervisors, new technology, mergers, and so forth.

Summary.   What is important about this summary of the literature on job satisfaction and organizational commitment is that people who are more satisfied and committed are those who will be available for openings that emerge throughout the organization. Of equal importance is the discovery that many of the issues that seem to be associated with improved levels of employee job satisfaction are the kinds of issues addressed in Chapter 2. That is, the reward attributes in tasks and the general human resources climate of the organization (including Quality of Working Life) are reflected in employee job satisfaction and, ultimately, employee retention. Also important is noting the relevance of Chapter 3 as we begin to think about how we know who should be internally recruited for jobs that do open up. That is, it is only by having a systematic means for appraising current staff that a company is able to maximally capitalize on its internal human resources for filling openings. This latter issue, the one of knowing who is available, will be addressed in more detail when we discuss human resources planning and career pathing. Before doing that, however, it is important to make explicit the assumption that it is better to retain than to (externally) recruit.

The Benefits of Internal Recruitment

We have been writing about the importance of job satisfaction and commitment as correlates of turnover under the assumption that it is better to retain than recruit (from outside). One of the reasons behind this assumption is that current employees do not have to go through the kinds of socialization experiences new employees require before they can feel adjusted to the (new) job. So, as will be noted in the section on external recruitment, an important element in recruiting new employees is concern for the entire new employee entry process.

This does not mean that internal recruitment allows organizations to ignore socialization issues. It only means that the problems of adjustment are likely to be less severe for a move involving a current employee than for one involving a brand new employee. Some of the "problems" we are addressing here are:

1. *Start-up time.* Current employees, especially in smaller organizations, know a lot about the organization and how it functions, so they do not have to go through this learning process. They know about how and when they are paid, what their fringe benefits are, what the goals and objectives of the company are, who holds the power and who wields it, who to avoid and who to try and become friends with, and so forth. These kinds of informal, get-along issues will not require so much time and, therefore, fewer surprises will exist than would be true for a newcomer (Louis, 1980). Fewer surprises that require attention permits getting up to speed faster.

2. *Probability of success.* An organization that has a satisfactory staff appraisal process bases the choice of an internal candidate on much more information than we have in choosing someone from the outside. There is no substitute for living with a person to know them, and working with someone requires living with them. If the best predictor of future performance is past performance, then observations of persons *today* provides a lot of the information required for predicting their performance *tomorrow.* However, this all depends on the appropriateness of the performance appraisal information available at the time internal candidates are recruited, especially with respect to the similarity of the present job to the future job. This means that we can take an excellent salesperson and make him a terrible manager because the past performance, used as the predictor, does not fit the job to which he is moved.

3. *Cost.* It is certainly less costly to the organization to recruit internally than to go outside for people. This would be especially true in management and professional ranks where the costs of recruitment can be very high indeed (see section on Executive Recruitment). The costs not only include the actual costs of recruitment but also costs associated with selection, training, start-up time (see Cascio, 1982) and the psychological advantage organizations can gain from having a promotion-from-within policy. That is, if one of the issues that is important to employees as they make turnover decisions is the future they may have in the company, then a way for a company to reduce turnover would be to promote from within!

It is useful to note here that internal recruitment is not entirely a bed of roses. *If* everything is going well on the retention of the best people for the jobs that open, then all is well. However, as noted earlier, people can stay in an organization for many reasons, and some of those are not as healthy for the company as others. For example, consider the case of the "golden handcuffs." If people are staying only or primarily because of monetary incentives, then they are likely not those who are most committed to the goals and objectives of the organization. Also they probably won't display those kinds of commitment behaviors companies desire as people who stay because they love their job and the organization in which they work. More subtle, but perhaps equally important, are people who are so committed to the organization that they derive all of their social and emotional support from it. Such people can become a burden on the organization, especially in higher ranks, because their entire being is wrapped up in the organization, and they can become unwilling to take any risks that might jeopardize their job! Price (1977), for example, has shown that organizations with lower turnover rates tend to be less innovative. When people are unwilling to take risks that might jeopardize their job, a company that re-quires people to take risks can be in a great deal of trouble. The point here, and the caution, is that as in all things behavioral and psychological, too much of a seemingly good thing (like organiza-tional commitment) needs to be carefully monitored for potential unintended negative consequences.

Internal recruitment also puts significant demands on the orga-nization's performance appraisal process. Employees must per-ceive the fairness of internal recruitment; hence, the organization's methods of promotion must be accepted by the employees. Per-sons who feel they are unfairly passed over for promotion can create significant problems in the organization and/or leave.

Finally, an organization that promotes from within must be con-cerned about career planning and pathing. It cannot generate ex-pectations for promotion that are impossible to meet, and it must plan realistically with employees what opportunities will be avail-able and how the employee will be best prepared to take advantage of those opportunities.

Conducting Internal Recruitment

As strange as it seems, there is not much research literature avail-able on internal recruitment. It is clear from what we have presented that if employees are not satisfied and committed, we are in trouble because employees provide the potential supply of candidates. Beyond that, however, the mechanics of internal recruitment do not seem to be well specified.

Job posting. Our own experience in various kinds of orga-nizations indicates that the most frequently used method of internal recruitment is the bulletin board. The personnel department (or person) serves as a clearinghouse for receiving notices of open-ings from all over the company. The openings are posted on one or more bulletin boards along with other information about the job (e.g., the KSAs required, salary, hours, and so forth). Schneider (1984) reports that more than 50 percent of all companies an-nounce openings using a job-posting system. About 15 percent of companies circulate memoranda to supervisors that describe openings so that nominations can be made. And 15 percent also put announcements of openings in company newsletters or news-papers.

Various formal mechanisms for announcing job openings may be good for employee morale because they are fair, they provide opportunity and they may do a good job of matching skills to openings. However, there are also some potential drawbacks to formal posting (Schuler, 1984):

1. Time—posting can increase the time from having an opening to filling it.
2. Conflict—a person who thought she would get the job does not because a more qualified person, from another unit, for example, posts for the opening.
3. Stress—the supervisor who must make the decision can be confronted with two or three equally attractive candidates.
4. Turmoil—subordinates in a unit who constantly bid on any job opening that arises may be viewed by their supervisor in a negative way. This can result in turmoil between superior and subordinate.

For these reasons, 25 percent of organizations (Schuler, 1984) seem to do no publicizing of openings. They use an informal system, one based on personal contact. For example, organizations with norms that encourage the most internal progress for their employees sanction direct contact with potential promotable employees. On the other hand, organizations that treat employees as personal possessions demand prior permission to talk with the potential recruit, much like recruiting an already-employed coach or manager in sports.

While the informal network may work effectively in small organizations, the larger organizations require more sophisticated human resources information systems. These systems maintain the kinds of data generated by the job analysis and staff appraisal processes. By maintaining the data according to competencies, requests for persons can come in specifying the desired attributes in the new person, and a computer search can turn up the most appropriate candidates. In today's world of sophisticated information processing and data retrieval systems, there is no good reason why an organization's human resources capabilities should not be as well documented as are other features (like investments, production capabilities, and so on). Some companies have designed sophisticated systems for working with people's *careers* rather than just worrying about getting the right person into each job as the need arises.

Career pathing and planning. When recruitment is thought about as internal recruitment, and when recruitment includes long-term issues like job satisfaction and organizational commitment, then recruitment naturally involves the care and monitoring of employee career experiences. This is true because careers are made

FIGURE 4–3. CAREER PATH FOR A GROUP MANAGER.

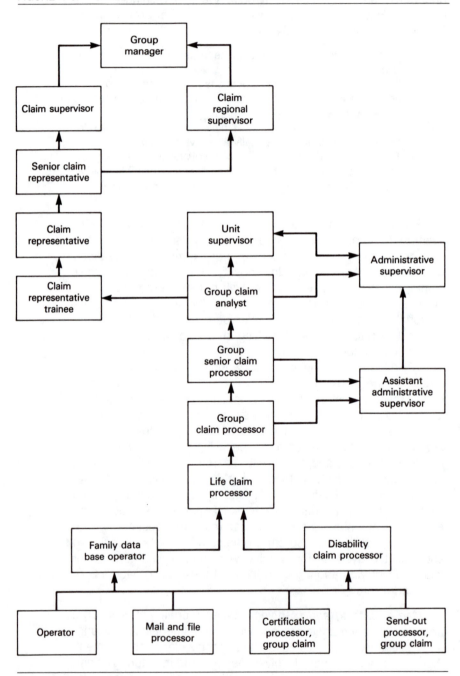

From London and Stumpf, (1982).

INDIVIDUAL AND ORGANIZATIONAL CAREER
PLANNING ACTIVITIES.

FIGURE 4–4.

ACTIVITY	PRIMARY RESPONSIBILITY
Self-assessment and obtaining others' perceptions of one's skills, interests, and values.	Individual
Setting career objectives and goals.	Individual
Skill assessment exercises.	Organization
Collecting and providing information on organizational practices, policies, and opportunities.	Organization
Preliminary career and life planning.	Individual/Organization
Sharing relevant information with supervisors, family, and relevant others.	Individual/Organization
Developing a personal career development plan and work preferences.	Individual/Organization
Routine examination and re-evaluation of career plans and progress.	Individual/Organization

From Stumpf and Hanrahan, (1984).

up of a series of work-related experiences (Hall, 1976). As one example of what this means, look at the experiences of a person who becomes a group manager, as shown in Figure 4–4. Organizations can either facilitate these work-related experiences or they can inhibit them. They facilitate them by doing a number of very specific things, as shown in Figure 4–3 (Stumpf and Hanrahan, 1983).

Figure 4–4 is a list of the issues for which individuals and organizations are responsible in career planning. The issues for which organizations bear responsibility appear to be very important to employees, especially with respect to turnover. This was shown in a study by Mitchell and Schneider (1984) in which a number of facets of organizational functioning, including career planning, were correlated with employee turnover intentions and actual turnover.

Mitchell and Schneider (1984) studied the relationship between each of five issues and turnover across fourteen organizations; their results indicate that the consistently strongest correlate of turnover concerned Career Facilitation. That is, the less attention an organization paid to Career Facilitation, the greater was their turnover. Many organizations are implementing career planning and pathing for employees because employees seem to want this kind of information and help and because organizations need data on their human resources for their own planning.

For example, London and Stumpf (1982) have provided a summary of what is going on in business with respect to the management of careers. Companies such as General Electric, Bell of Pennsylvania, and Polaroid all have implemented these kinds of programs, the general structure of which is presented in Figure 4–4. As is clear from this figure, these companies put emphasis not only on their own responsibilities for career planning, but also on the employee him or herself. This issue of individual and organizational responsibility characterizes all of the careers literature (see Hall, 1976; Schein, 1978).

The data collected on employees through these kinds of career planning programs, combined with the information obtained through the staff appraisal process, provides organizations with the potential to understand the nature of their *internal* human resources, including what their talents and desires are, as well as the kinds of *external* persons they may have to recruit. The nature of the external recruits needed is obtained by comparing projections of the positions to be filled with the kinds of internal persons who will be available.

Projections of the kinds of positions that will have to be filled is the job of the human resources planner. Human resources planning is a problem that we will not present in detail because the mathematics involved are somewhat complex. In the abstract, the problem is one of tracking past experiences regarding the movement of people into, through, and out of the various positions in the organization combined with projections for growth of the organization and changes in the way the organization functions (due to technological changes, for example). Early models of human resources planning were deficient because they failed to consider strategic issues like the last two noted above. More recently, human resources planners have engaged in strategic human resources planning, i.e., they have included long range corporate strategy in their projections *and* corporate strategists have included human resources issues in their own planning (Stumpf and Hanrahan, 1983).

SUMMARY

Our goal in the extensive discussion of internal recruitment was to insure that we adequately expressed the idea that in order to *have* internal recruits, the organization needs to gain employee commitment. The model of commitment that was developed integrated the literature on job satisfaction with the literature on commitment and showed that organizations can gain employee commitment by providing satisfaction to employees.

A second major emphasis in the section was the repeated message that organizations must retain adequate information on the available pool of internal recruits in order to make wise internal choices. Such information is most useful if it is based on a carefully developed staff appraisal and career management system.

EXTERNAL RECRUITMENT

An organization decides to pursue recruits from the outside when it decides that no qualified people inside are available. That is, when specification of the openings available and the KSAs required fails to yield a match among job incumbents, then a search begins for an appropriate recruit.

Actually, at the same time an organization decides to go outside, people outside are looking, exploring, and choosing. In fact, then, potential candidates for jobs are doing the same things organizations are doing—they are looking for a match.

In this section of the chapter, we first examine some of the research on what job candidates are looking for and how they developed their interests in particular kinds of occupations and jobs. Then we present a description of some of the ways organizations actually go about recruiting suitable job applicants.

Career Development and Choice

This brief section reviews some theories and literature that indicate that people do not just walk into an organization through some random selection and ask to join the staff. This is an important idea because it confirms that the people who comprise the working staff of an organization have prior histories, lives outside of their organization, and futures that may not include the organization. To understand the behavior of people at work requires that we place those people in their larger context.

The evidence suggests that particular kinds of people choose certain careers or vocations and even specific occupations within those careers.* There is less evidence regarding the circumstances and conditions governing organizational choice, but we will explore some hypotheses about the conditions by which people choose one organization over another.

---

*The terms *vocation* and *career* will be used interchangeably. The word *occupation* will be used in a more specific sense to designate a set of similar working tasks; a career or vocation is a chain of interrelated occupations.

Like jobs, people do not spring fullblown and ready to go. Like jobs, particular kinds of people exist in organizations as a function of the larger environment, the conditions that exist in the world around them, and the nature of the goals they may be trying to achieve. Unlike jobs, people can choose whether or not they want to be a part of an organization. Also unlike jobs, people go through different stages as they develop their career plans and aspirations. Choosing a career and an organization is part of a continuum whereby a person first works through the stages of career development, then makes his or her career decision, then searches for the appropriate context in which the career should be carried out, then chooses the organization.*

More than thirty years ago Super (1953) stated the following ten propositions as a theory of career development:

1. People differ in their abilities, interests, and personalities.
2. They are qualified, by virtue of these characteristics, each for a number of occupations.
3. Each of these occupations requires a characteristic pattern of abilities, interests, and personality traits, with tolerances wide enough, however, to allow both some variety of occupations for each individual and some variety of individuals in each occupation.
4. Vocational preferences and competencies, the situations in which people live and work, and, hence, their self-concepts, change with time and experience (although self-concepts are generally fairly stable from later adolescence until late maturity), making choice and adjustment a continuous process.
5. This process may be summed up in a series of life stages characterized as those of growth, exploration, establishment, maintenance, and decline, and these stages may in turn be subdivided into (a) the fantasy, tentative, and realistic phases of the exploratory stage, and (b) the trial and stable phases of the establishment stage.
6. The nature of the career pattern (that is, the occupational level attained and the sequence, frequency, and duration of trial and stable jobs) is determined by the individual's parental socioeconomic level, mental ability, and personality characteristics, and by the opportunities to which he is exposed.
7. Development through the life stages can be guided, partly by facilitating the process of maturation of abilities and interests and partly by aiding in reality testing and in the development of the self-concept.
8. The process of vocational development is essentially that of developing and implementing a self-concept: it is a compromise

---

*Of course development of the person occurs after organizational choice, but in this section we emphasize what happens up to the time the person enters an organization.

process in which the self-concept is a product of the interaction of inherited aptitudes, neural and endocrine makeup, opportunity to play various roles, and evaluations of the extent to which the results of role playing meet with the approval of superiors and fellows.

9. The process of compromise between individual and social factors, between self-concept and reality, is one of role playing, whether the role is played in fantasy, in the counseling interview, or in real life activities such as school classes, clubs, part-time work, and entry jobs.

10. Work satisfactions and life satisfactions depend upon the extent to which the individual finds adequate outlets for his abilities, interests, personality traits, and values; they depend upon his establishment in a type of work, a work situation, and a way of life in which he can play the kind of role which his growth and exploratory experiences have led him to consider congenial and appropriate. (pp. 189–90)*

Between the time of this statement and the present, considerable research evidence and more detailed theoretical positions have appeared regarding vocational development and choice (see Hall, 1976; Holland, 1976; Schein, 1978). However, while Super's (1953) position was quite general, it indicated areas in which more specific information should be collected if we are to understand eventual career decisions. For example, Super noted that the socioeconomic level of parents, and an individual's opportunity to obtain occupational information both have an effect on career development. In addition, more personal attributes such as mental ability and interests seem to be related to vocational development and choice.

Figure 4–5 can help summarize the various effects on career development and occupational choice. The figure is also a convenient beginning for our discussion of how an individual decides to choose an organization in which to carry out her or his occupational choice.

Conceptually, socioeconomic status, race, sex, environment, and intelligence/aptitudes serve as limitations to the range of occupations available to individuals. Interests operate to focus preferences. Although not previously discussed, interests also have antecedents, most probably in the psychosocial upbringing of the individual (Roe, 1957).

The successful resolution of conflicts between an individual's perception of available alternatives and his or her preference for

*From D. E. Super, "A Theory of Vocational Development," *American Psychologist, 8* (1953), 185–90. Copyright 1953 by the American Psychological Association. Reprinted by permission.

FIGURE 4–5. A WAY OF THINKING ABOUT ORGANIZATIONAL CHOICE.

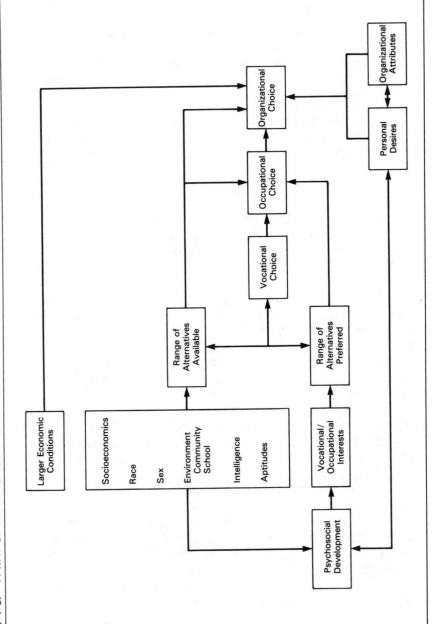

alternatives results in a vocational choice. More specific alternatives lead to a clearer specification of choice—i.e., the occupation within the career. This further specification necessarily limits the range of organizations in which the occupation exists. A comparison of specific desires and what potential organizations offer results in an organizational choice.

Note that this conceptualization places the heavy emphasis of a person's eventual career/occupation/organization choice on pre-existing conditions in the person's larger environment. Indeed, one may speak realistically of these choices as being, in many cases, the result of a series of externally imposed compromises. That is, the fewer the alternatives available, the more choice is directed or imposed by what is available rather than by what is preferred (cf. Blau et al., 1956; March & Simon, 1958; Mobley, 1982).

Perhaps the phrase "externally imposed compromise" requires some elaboration. An individual's vocational maturity may be a composite of her or his knowledge and ability: (1) the ability to resolve conflicts between the factors in vocational choice; (2) the ability to plan the steps to vocational choice; (3) knowledge about occupations and careers; (4) self-knowledge; and (5) the ability to make realistic vocational choices given appropriate information (Crites, 1978). Vocational maturity then signifies the ability of the individual to synthesize career-relevant knowledge with self-knowledge. The range of alternatives available to some people is restricted by many externally imposed conditions. These people have fewer opportunities to test the world and discover their true capabilities and interests. That is, a career decision will be immature to the extent that a person's environment limits his career-relevant knowledge and self-knowledge.

Note that we are not suggesting a "womb to tomb" approach to occupations and careers, where the individual does not experience tension or the need to make the kinds of compromises most people's lives realistically require. Nor do we espouse an approach which suggests that every job be available to every person. Compromise and choice should be the person's responsibility, but people should have opportunities to make choices in a free and open marketplace.

It would seem reasonable, although shortsighted, for organizations to be more concerned with organizational than occupational or vocation choice. After all, one might say, an organization should be concerned with who works for it. However, as was shown in Figure 4–5, artificial limitations on people's occupational alternatives also limit the kinds of people the organization may ultimately attract.

Motivation and Organizational Choice

Let us suppose for the moment that organizational choice is not terribly constrained by environmental limitations of alternatives. If this were true, an interesting question to ask ourselves would be: what motivates an individual to choose one organization over another? In answering this question, we will give some attention to three of the more prominent theories of motivated work behavior. These theories are introduced here for two reasons: (1) they help us understand why people make choices the way they do; and (2) these same theories will be useful later in our discussion of hiring procedures (see Chapter 10).

Three major theories that are useful in understanding organizational choices dominate recent thinking in the study of motivated work-related behavior: *need theory, instrumentality theory,* and *social reference theory.* Need theories suggest the kinds of things people desire from life or work. Some theories stress money (i.e., the so-called Scientific Management theories represented by Taylor, 1911), others stress the social rewards to be derived from participation in groups (for instance, the Hawthorne studies: Roethlisberger & Dickson, 1939; Maier, 1952; Trist & Bamforth, 1951), and a third group emphasizes the need for individuals to fulfill themselves as people ("self-actualization"—Argyris, 1957; McGregor, 1960; Herzberg, 1968).

One position incorporates something from each of these types of theories and has been very popular in the management literature. This is the orientation proposed by Maslow (1943, 1954) as a general theory of personality development. He hypothesized that people develop through stages, first being concerned with satisfying their physiological needs, then with security needs, then social or interpersonal needs, esteem needs, and finally self-actualization needs. Needs, he hypothesized, are arranged in a "hierarchy of prepotency" through which individuals must pass in order to reach a point where the need for self-actualization predominates. While evidence for this prepotency notion is lacking at least in the work setting, Maslow's list of needs is reasonably representative of those that seem to motivate work behavior.

A second group of theories, social reference theories, suggest not only that people need and seek the company of others, but also indicate why they do so. Two major ideas follow from social reference theories. The first position holds that people seek others in order to better evaluate themselves, particularly their skills, abilities, ideas, and opinions (Festinger, 1954). While height, weight, hair color, and other physiological characteristics can be assessed with reference to a nonhuman standard, we can only assess psychological characteristics with reference to other people. Thus, people may gain some self knowledge locating themselves in the larger fabric of their social contacts. This social reference theory suggests the importance of having a wide range of social comparison opportunities as we develop. The theory also predicts that people will seek to locate themselves in situations where their abilities and opinions are similar to those of others.

The other major idea with regard to social comparison theories stems naturally from the first and was presented by Adams (1963, 1965). Adams noted that if Festinger's comparison thesis was correct, then, in the industrial situation—as in any situation—people would compare themselves to each other. Adams hypothesized that workers compare themselves on the basis of *perceived equitable rewards;* his theory has been called "equity theory." Adams hypothesized that people perceive the contribution they make to their organization vis-a-vis the contributions others make. They also compare the rewards others receive to the rewards they receive. When the contribution/reward (what Adams calls input/outcome) ratio of others is thought to be more favorable than one's own ratio, then the person is dissatisfied and tries to reduce the imbalance in ratios. Being dissatisfied, the person may leave the situation, reduce effort, change the quality of performance, etc., but will seek to avoid the situation in which the *dissonance* exists (Festinger, 1954).

A third class of theoretical knowledge includes what are variously called expectancy, instrumentality, path-goal, performance-reward, or valence theories of motivation; we shall use the term *instrumentality* here. These theories do not specify *what* people desire; they show how people's desires motivate the direction and level of their behavior. Need theories then, tell us that different things energize people to do *something*—the theories do not indicate *what* people will do. The same is true (but to a lesser extent) for social reference theories. But instrumentality theories, on the other hand, are very practical. They do not postulate the kinds of needs all people have in general. Instrumentality theories concentrate on the thought processes that enable people to decide what they must do in order to obtain the things—whatever they are—that they desire. Instrumentality theories suggest that people ask themselves a series of questions: (1) What do I desire? (2) What do I have to do to obtain what I desire? (3) Can I do what I have to do in order to get what I desire? Effort, or motivated behavior, is thereby directed at obtaining specific, manifest, desired rewards—whether money, prestige, early retirement, equity, or whatever the person desires and perceives he can attain.

Instrumentality theory has frequently been used to explain career and organizational choice (for example see Sheard, 1970; Muchinsky & Taylor, 1975; Schmitt & Son, 1981). These studies have found impressive evidence that the degree to which individuals value certain outcomes and the degree to which an organization or career is perceived as useful in obtaining those outcomes is related to individuals' choices.

Instrumentality theories view people as rational beings, as thinking humans who are able to make decisions. A person's desires might be considered irrational by some standards, yet the theory would still accurately predict the "irrational" behavior. Instrumentality is then, a very functional concept, stressing the movement of individuals toward objects they desire when they perceive the objectives to be (1) available and (2) attainable.

A proposed synthesis. Motivation theories may be synthesized by recognizing that:

1. Different people have different needs—some need the kinds of feelings that money can provide, others need the kinds of feelings that people provide, others seek self-actualization, and some want a little of everything.
2. People are more comfortable in situations where they are treated equitably. This means that organizations must not only provide what people desire, but must also reward them—with *all* kinds of rewards, not just pay (Telly, French, & Scott, 1971)—in a way that will be perceived as equitable.
3. In choosing their organization, people will choose one in which (a) they perceive they have the ability to perform satisfactorily in order to obtain rewards, and (b) the rewards that are offered are those they desire.

Of course, this integration of motivation theories supposes that people make decisions about where they work. *Given* this assumption, then, the decision can only be as good as the information on which it is based. It follows that withholding or giving misleading information to prospective employees leads to poor decisions, a concept we shall turn to in discussing recruitment. This theory also takes a "free-market" approach, which makes (for some) the false assumptions that (1) more than one alternative exists, and (2) the attractive alternatives are also the available alternatives. Our discussion of career choice has suggested this may not necessarily be true (see Figure 4–5).

Having discussed some theoretical notions about how individuals choose careers and what motivates their choice of an organization, we now turn to a discussion of how organizations can and do attempt to recruit applicants.

External Recruitment:
Overview of Approaches

The flypaper approach. As noted earlier, recruitment should be concerned with the dual problem of *securing* people the company needs and *insuring* that they will remain. The latter concern has been neglected. Recruitment policy is too often based on what organizations need and what will attract people to fill the need. Organizations have tended not to delve deeper into the recruitment process to ask what will keep people. This can be called the *flypaper* approach to recruiting: if you can attract people, they will get stuck and stay. Of course, if flies (people) knew the gooey stuff was just a come-on, they would not get stuck. Organizations seem to think they should only give out information that makes them look attractive initially.

One argument against "telling it like it is" can be that *it* is so bad that no one would be attracted. The solution here, of course, is to change the job/organization matrix of rewards offered, not to lie about it. All the research evidence (cf. Wanous, 1980) suggests that when people are given realistic information about the job, (1) there is no decrease in the number of people who apply for a job, and (2) there is a marked improvement in turnover rates. Obviously, job analyses and organizational diagnoses provide one source of information for sketching out the organization/job for potential employees.

Note that the emphasis should not only be to describe the job but also to describe the organization. It must be assumed that people desire to work for a particular organization as well as on a particular job. Further, the person-organization relationship will probably last longer than the person-job relationship. This factor re-emphasizes the importance of giving people adequate information on which to base their organizational choices.

A study by Taylor and Sniezek (1984) revealed that applicants interviewed during campus recruiting trips were favorably impressed by a recruiter who provided and asked for job-relevant information. Perhaps more importantly, Taylor and Sniezek found in their study of 58 campus recruiters that:

1. Recruiters failed to agree with each other on the topics they should cover in an interview.
2. Recruiters consistently failed to cover topics they believed *were* important.
3. Applicants report that recruiters most often want to discuss non-academic issues of university life and extracurricular activities.

Is this the appropriate way to begin an employee-employer relationship? Does it provide the information job applicants want and does it project the desired image of the organization?

What individuals want. Earlier in this chapter we discussed career and organizational choice in order to show how various personal and external forces lead individuals to seek out specific occupations and organizations. We suggested that money may not be the sole determinant of a person's decision. In addition to monetary rewards, people seeking employment consider these factors:

1. The *intrinsic rewards* available in an environment; i.e., the job/ organization potential for satisfying many of the kinds of feelings an individual desires to experience (social, esteem, self-actualization, etc).
2. The status *image* of an organization; i.e., the impact that the fact of working in a particular organization has in the larger life of the individual.
3. The *supervisory style* typical of an organization; i.e., the dominant mode—supportive or democratic versus task-oriented or authoritarian—the individual perceives to exist.
4. The dominant *values* of an organization; i.e., whether the organization's goals stress a more Social orientation than an Enterprising one. Or is it a Conventional or Realistic kind of organization? Some jobs (e.g., welfare work) automatically seem to fit into a particular value orientation (e.g., Social) more so than other occupations. But even within a certain system of interests, say Enterprising, the range of applicable organizations is exceedingly large. Again we must stress the importance of organizational goals.

As a side note, it is worth summarizing research on the question of the job preferences of men and women; the data show they are very similar (Lacy, Bokemeier, & Shepard, 1983). Lacy et al. studied about 7,000 people, equally split by sex, and discovered that there was essential agreement that important and meaningful work is their most preferred characteristic. This was followed by income and promotion and, lastly, by job security or working hours. While other studies indicate that pay levels are most directly associated with the acceptance of job offers, it may be likely that job applicants get accurate information only about their starting pay level. As the Sniezek and Taylor study (1984) indicated, recruiters tend to ignore applicants' needs for job-relevant information.

Keeping in mind the many things people desire from an organization, we must ask: (1) What can organizations offer people? (2) How can organizations convince people that they can provide certain benefits? Careful job and organizational analyses answer the first question. The second question should be answered with reference to the idea proposed in Chapter 3 that an organization's behavior manifests its philosophy. What exactly does this mean?

Ivancevich and Donnelly (1971) present an example of organizational recruitment behavior structured to meet individual needs. They took as the basis for their study one of the major problems in recruitment, the number of people who accept job offers and then back out of their acceptance. The rate of such behavior is between 10 and 15 percent for management jobs. Ivancevich and Donnelly hypothesized that if people who accept a job offer are given some social reinforcement of their acceptance, they are less likely to back out than those whose acceptance is treated with a typical impersonal acknowledgement. One half of a group of prospective managers (N = 196) were telephoned immediately upon their acceptance of a job offer. In the following weeks they were telephoned twice more. The other half of the group (N = 196) were sent some literature and a confirmation of receipt of their acceptance. (Incidentally, the average number of offers each person received was three.) Of those receiving the personalized treatment, 2.6 percent backed out; 12.5 percent of those receiving the usual treatment backed out. Of course, the concern for people displayed by this "special touch" must be consistent with the organization's subsequent treatment of the employee, or the telephone calls will represent one form of the "sticky goo" that attracts unsuspecting "flies" (people).

When it is realized that recruits are choosing among various alternatives, corporate attention to them may pay important dividends. As Soelberg (1967) points out, people who are seeking a job consider a *mix* of alternatives in making their decisions, not one alternative in isolation from all other possibilities. If this is true, then as Power and Aldag (1985) note, the nature of recruit desires and goals is of great importance to organizations if they are going to be able to recruit effectively. Since recruit self-esteem is also related to recruit desirability to organizations (Ellis and Taylor, 1983), the importance of paying attention to the particular characteristics of attractive recruits is clear.

An interesting study supporting this idea concerns Type A people. Type A people are characterized by such factors as high ambition, competitiveness, high needs for achievement, time urgency, and working frenetically at more than one thing at a time (Friedman & Rosenman, 1974; Chesney & Rosenman, 1980). Research on Type A people reveals they tend to experience some significant physiological disorders (heart disease, ulcers) but, at the same time, they tend to be effective and successful. The question Burke and Descza (1982) asked was would Type A persons prefer (be more satisfied with, successful, and more likely to join) some organizations more than others? To answer this question, they gave 188 people a measure of preferred organizational climate and a measure of their Type A behavior (the Jenkins Activity Survey; Jenkins, Rosenman & Friedman, 1967). The data showed that people with higher Type A scores preferred climates characterized by high performance standards, spontaneity, ambiguity, and toughness.

Realistic Job Previews. An approach to recruitment that concurrently takes into account the attributes of persons and of organizations is the *realistic job preview* (RJP). Over the past 15 years, Wanous and his colleagues (e.g., Wanous, 1973; 1977; 1980; Popovich & Wanous, 1982; Premack & Wanous, 1985) have shown that a small dose of organizational reality presented prior to organizational entry can have major positive consequences. For the individual, the consequence is increased job satisfaction, a perception of the climate of the organization as supportive, trustworthy, honest or candid, and self-confidence on the part of recruits that they can cope with the organization and job. For the organization, the major consequences are increased retention, commitment, and performance.

What is an RJP? It is either, or a combination of, booklets, films, conversations, and job-site visits that provide a potential job candidate with realistic information about the job and the organization, typically prior to the time a job offer is made. In one small organization in which one of your authors worked, recruits were taken on a tour of the facility and were presented with explanations of the work to be done and the equipment to be used *prior* to their formal selection interview and tests. Some companies fear that providing the RJP prior to a job offer will turn off candidates; the data indicate this is somewhat true. In fact, not only is the candidate who receives realistic information somewhat less likely to accept a job offer, persons who do get the RJP have significantly less inflated expectations about how wonderful the job and organization will be when they go to work. So, what the RJP seems to do is literally inoculate the applicant* against having inflated expectations. Obviously, since we already know that unfulfilled expectations are a major source of dissatisfaction and turnover, it looks like some of the unrealistic expectations candidates bring to jobs can be handled with the RJP. Further, and perhaps most significantly, persons who

---

*RJPs should work effectively for internal recruitment, too, but we are not aware of research on this use.

SOURCE	OCCUPATION				
	Office/ Clerical	Plant/ Service	Sales	Professional/ Technical	Management
Employee Referrals	92	94	74	68	65
Walk-ins	87	92	46	46	40
Newspaper Advertising	68	88	75	89	82
Local High Schools or Trade Schools	66	61	6	27	7
U.S. Employment Service (USES)	63	72	34	41	27
Community Agencies	55	57	22	34	28
Private Employment Agencies (company pays fee)	44 (31)	11 (5)	63 (49)	71 (48)	75 (65)
Career Conferences/ Job Fairs	19	16	19	37	17
Colleges/Universities	17	9	48	74	50
Advertising in Special Publications	12	6	43	75	57
Professional Societies	5	19	17	52	36
Radio-TV Advertising	5	8	2	7	4
Search Firms	1	2	2	31	54
Unions	1	12	0	3	0

Figures are percentages of companies providing data for each employee group.

Reprinted by special permission from *Personnel Policies Forum,* Copyright © 1979, by the Bureau of National Affairs, Inc., Washington, D.C.

do not want to put up with the reality to which they have been introduced self-select themselves out of the process. This not only saves later turnover, but it may save organizations costs associated with training persons who will leave when "reality shock" hits. All of the other negative consequences of turnover are also potentially avoided.

It is reasonable to ask how much the procedure can reduce turnover for an organization. Premack and Wanous (1985) calculate that savings in replacement costs due to turnover vary depending upon the turnover rate that exists at the time the RJP is put into effect. Across twenty experiments in which RJP was compared to some traditional process, they showed that organizations where 20, 50, and 80 percent of hires survive, the savings in replacement costs attributable to only using the RJP are 24, 12, and 6 percent, respectively. In other words, the higher the current turnover rate, the more an organization has to gain from instituting the RJP process. Parenthetically, remember that this principle of an effect (savings in replacement costs) being greater the more severe the problem (turnover) is a central issue in calculating the utility of all kinds of selection procedures (see Chapter 7).

In this section, then, we have said that the external recruitment

TABLE 4–2.   EFFECTIVENESS OF RECRUITING SOURCE BY OCCUPATION.

SOURCE	OCCUPATION				
	Office/ Clerical	Plant/ Service	Sales	Professional/ Technical	Management
Newspaper Advertising	39	30	30	38	35
Walk-ins	24	37	5	7	2
Employee Referrals	20	5	17	7	7
Private Employment Agencies	10	2	23	25	27
U.S. Employment Service (USES)	5	6	0	1	1
Local High Schools or Trade Schools	2	2	0	0	0
Colleges/Universities	1	1	8	15	2
Community Agencies	1	3	0	1	2
Unions	0	2	0	0	0
Career Conferences/ Job Fairs	0	1	2	2	1
Professional Societies	0	1	1	0	2
Search Firms	0	0	2	5	17
Radio-TV Advertising	0	1	0	0	1
Advertising in Special Publications	0	0	3	5	8

Figures are percentages of companies providing data for each employee group. Columns may add to more than 100 percent because of multiple responses or less than 100 percent because of nonresponses. These percentages are votes for effectiveness.
Reprinted by special permission from *Personnel Policies Forum*, Survey No. 126. Recruiting Policies & Practice, pp 4–5. Copyright © 1979, by the Bureau of National Affairs, Inc., Washington, D.C.

of employees should be realistic; that is, the organization should provide the employee with accurate information about the job *and* the organization in which he or she may work.

Conducting External Recruitment

Our attention now turns to a review of some of the practices actually used by organizations to do their external recruitment. Table 4–1 shows a listing of the 14 most frequent sources of recruits for different kinds of occupations; the figures in the table refer to the percentage of companies who report that they use the procedure. Table 4–2 shows some differences in source of recruits as a function of the type of job being filled. For example:

1. At the extremes, Office/Clerical and Plant/Service people are recruited predominantly via employee referrals, walk-ins and newspaper advertisements. Management persons, however, are located from private employment agencies rather than walk-ins, as well as through newspaper ads and employee referrals.

2. Professional/Technical persons tend to be located through ads in specialized publications far more frequently than are people for other occupations.

3. Search firms, a topic we will spend some time on later, are used primarily for Management occupations; however, they are also used by some firms for finding Professional/Technical candidates, as well.

Most of the strategies listed in Table 4-1 are fairly obvious to anyone who has looked for a job. But a few of them warrant some additional attention. *Community Agencies* are formal sources of job information other than the United States Employment Service and affiliated state employment services. The latter two agencies have access to all manner of jobs for all kinds of interests and ability levels. Community agencies tend to specialize in particular kinds of persons based on such characteristics as sex, race, religion, handicap (physically or emotionally disabled, for example), or occupational history (some agencies specialize in working with the chronically unemployed). Some examples of these agencies would be the Catholic Youth Organization (CYO), the Urban League, and Alcoholics Anonymous.

Career Conferences/Job Fairs are programs set up by community groups, schools (high schools and colleges/universities) to which many companies, governments (Federal, state and local) and the military (for armed services) may come to present information about themselves. These large job marketplaces are used by organizations to publicize what they do, what they have to offer, and the kinds of persons in which they may have interest. The analogy to a fair is appropriate in that typically these events have a wide variety of opportunities—and a wide variety of risks! In other words, such fairs can be slick in the extreme—the flypaper approach to recruitment typified. This is not always true, but it is worth remembering when seeking a job.

In Table 4-1, *Colleges/Universities* refers to what is also called *campus recruitment.* Numerous large companies and large colleges/universities have an annual recruiting season (spring) that occupies graduating seniors for a number of months. It works something like this: The university has a staff of people, usually in a Counseling, Placement or Job Center. These people maintain two lists, one of candidates and the other of companies that will be visiting. Companies place notices about the kinds of people they are looking for, and candidates file a document summarizing their interests and accomplishments. A match is made, sometimes by the placement center but more often by the companies looking over the paperwork filed by interested candidates. It is important to note here that the quality of the paperwork filed may have a bearing on whether an interview is obtained! We will discuss at length the nature of the interview that occurs in Chapter 6.

The fact that some companies that do campus recruitment have teams of people traveling from campus to campus during "the season" reveals the magnitude of the investment companies make in attempting to attract the kinds of people they want. Some companies, like AT&T or the various telecommunications firms formed after divestiture of AT&T, IBM, General Electric, and so on, will have numerous teams made up of professional personnel/recruiting persons as well as people who actually do the kind of work for which the team is seeking recruits. These teams may travel for six or eight weeks to campuses, conducting interviews and living as a group.

Search Firms are specialized employment agencies that work only from requests made by companies. That is, in contrast to Employment Agencies, candidates do not contact search firms; search firms contact people in whom their client may have an interest. For example, imagine that a company wishes to hire a new comptroller. Comptrollers are typically responsible for all accounting/financial issues in a corporation. As such they are very well paid, critical to the company and difficult to hire. So the company might call a search firm (sometimes called an *executive search firm* and sometimes called a *head hunter*). For example, the head hunter may be asked to find a comptroller with five years experience in a real estate firm to be paid $70,000 in salary, $20,000 in other compensation (moving expenses, purchase of the current home, reduced mortgage rates on a move, stock options and bonuses, etc.), plus additional help as required (finding a job for a spouse, a school for the children, etc.)

Executive search firms are a post World War II phenomenon, the first being founded in 1946 (Wareham, 1980); now there are about 2500 such firms ranging from one-person operations to firms with billings in excess of $15 million (*Business Week,* 1980). For finding a comptroller as described above, the head hunter would be paid about one-third of the comptroller's first year salary. In return, the search firm would agree to:

1. Confidentiality—in exchange for the opportunity to search for a comptroller, the search firm agrees to not divulge its mission. Search firms are frequently used to find likely successors for people who do not know they are about to be succeeded.
2. Off limits—search firms generally agree to leave placed recruits in the new job at least 2 years before trying to recruit them again for another job.
3. Retention—search firms also usually agree to help the company locate another recruit if one that is placed fails to last a year—and they do this for no additional fee. So, recruiters have a stake in

making placements that last. Indeed some search firms have very extensive questionnaires for both the corporate client and the recruit to try and arrange the most effective match (Zippo, 1980).

Most search firms belong to the Association of Executive Search Consultants (AERC). The Association has a code of ethics, does some research on the industry, and publishes statistics of use to companies seeking executive search information. The most important facet of executive or technical search, however, is *names.* Search firms must maintain elaborate systems replete with thousands of biographies because when a client needs someone, time is usually very important. And clients want more than one name— they want to make a choice. To keep the file up to date, search firms retain or develop "clipping" services which track news articles about particular people and/or particular industries. Biographical files in the best firms are continuously updated—not a bad model for organizations themselves.

Prior to leaving this topic, the issue of employee relocation deserves brief comment. Regardless of whether internal or external recruitment is involved, employees frequently have to be relocated. Just as there are search firms there are also relocation firms. These firms, most of which are members of the Employee Relocation Council (ERC), handle *everything* connected with a move: mortgages, storage of household goods, temporary living arrangements, househunting trips (with the whole family), redecorating of new home, repurchase of old home, and so on (ERC, 1983). At least 20 companies in the U.S. relocated more than 1,000 current employees each in 1981 (ERC, 1983), so relocation represents a significant personnel problem.

There is not much research on relocation. One study showed that, contrary to the popular press image of resistance and hardship, executives and their families are generally willing to move for career enhancement and job challenge and that adjustment to the new location does not present great hardship (Brett, 1980).

The Validity of External Recruiting Methods

It may be one thing to know about different methods of recruiting people for jobs and another to know which methods work best. By work best here we refer back to all of the different kinds of criteria of success discussed in Chapter 3: productivity, absenteeism, turnover, job satisfaction, etc.

There have been a number of different ways this question has been studied. Table 4-2 presents the impressions of corporate personnel about which of the different sources of candidates has

TABLE 4-3. PERCENTAGE OF WORKERS WHO SURVIVE USING DIFFERENT RECRUITMENT SOURCES.

Researcher/ Occupation	Employee Referrals	Walk-Ins	Newspaper Advertisements	Private Employment Agencies
Decker and Cornelius (1979)				
Bank Employees (non-management)	69%	57%	67%	52%
Insurance Agents	70%	64%	57%	62%
Abstract Service	96%	90%	79%	94%
Gannon (1971)				
Bank Employees (non-management)	74%	71%	61%	61%
Reid (1972)				
Engineering and Metal Trades	39	25	16	—
Taylor and Schmidt (1983)				
Packers (Food packing)	51	45	37	—
Ullman (1966)				
Clerical, Company 1	25	—	12	—
Clerical, Company 2	72	—	26	38

All but Taylor and Schmidt based on Schwab, (1982).

been most effective for them in finding qualified persons for different occupations. Since this study was done by the Bureau of National Affairs, the same research company that accomplished the study in Table 4–1, the same methods and occupations are listed. These data are probably very impressionistic, since no company either of us has worked with actually maintains data on the effectiveness of different sources of referrals.

A number of researchers have been more systematic in attempts to discover which of the sources of candidates are more effective. In the typical study (see studies listed in Table 4–3), all of the recruits hired for a year are identified with regard to source and then are monitored with respect to various criteria including absenteeism, performance, and turnover. After each person hired has been on the job for a year, the data on the criteria are tabulated and statistical analyses are carried out to see if some sources produce superior people. If it is discovered that some sources of recruits are significantly better than others, then the implications for recruitment are clear.

Table 4–3 summarizes some of the studies that shed some light on the question of the validity of different recruit sources. As is clear in the table, employee referrals generally yield superior people in terms of survival. In an innovative study, Taylor and Schmidt (1983) attempted to figure out why referrals by employees tend to yield such positive outcomes. They hypothesized that one explanation for effectiveness could be that current employees provide potential employees with realistic information about the job and organization. Thus, they thought that employee referrals might be equivalent to the RJP. They also hypothesized however, that maybe what is really important is not so much the *source* of the recruit as the kind of *person* recruited. In other words, they tested the following question: is it more important to focus on recruiting people through particular *sources* of recruits or to try to find particular kinds of *people.*

Taylor and Schmidt tracked 300 people hired by a food-packing plant (the job was seasonal—packing Christmas gift boxes) to see which hypothesis seemed correct. They discovered the data shown in Table 4–3 but also turned up some other interesting findings. First, they showed that one source not much researched, employees rehired or *rehires,* were best of all in terms of their various criteria (absenteeism, turnover, and performance). Rehires, of course, should have the most realistic picture of a job. More interestingly, however, they discovered that the plant was paying current employees a bonus for referring a person who was subsequently hired. Taylor and Schmidt suspect that paying bonuses like this might defeat the RJP idea behind employee referrals since incumbents may end up using the flypaper approach themselves!

Their second interesting finding has potentially important consequences for recruitment efforts in organizations. They found that it was more important to identify the kinds of *people* who would be successful than to focus on a particular *source* of recruits. This means that companies should know what kinds of people are going to succeed and then they should go and find them. It may be that particular *sources* of recruits provide more *able* recruits, so that this finding by Taylor and Schmidt is not inconsistent with the findings of the studies reported in Table 4–3. Of course, the remainder of the book is all about ways of identifying the kinds of people likely to meet organizational requirements; the link between recruitment and selection has been made very explicit in the Taylor and Schmidt research.

SUMMARY

In this chapter we have presented the argument that recruiting has two facets, internal recruitment and external recruitment. The reason for this somewhat artificial, but important, distinction was to focus on organizational conditions that will keep competent employees so that when future needs emerge, already socialized, trained, and experienced persons will be available. As became clear, organizations must create conditions that will satisfy employees and gain employee commitment to the organization if competent persons are to be retained. The importance of this issue cannot be overstressed because many organizations view turnover as an employee problem when, in fact, turnover can be attributed to inappropriate recruitment processes, poor selection processes, and a poor work environment—all of which are organizational responsibilities.

The second part of the chapter, external recruitment, emphasized the dual ideas that people are looking for certain organizational characteristics at the same time organizations try to find people. The *realistic job preview* (RJP) was presented as a possible mechanism for helping organizations and individuals create a match. Some support for the RJP approach was summarized, including more than 20 experiments revealing success in improving retention, job satisfaction, and even performance. In addition, research on the effectiveness of recruiting practices was summarized showing that employee referrals and, perhaps, rehires of former employees may yield more effective recruits. Finally, an innovative study by Taylor and Schmidt (1983) suggested that the key to effectiveness in external recruiting may be knowledge of the kind of persons that should be recruited.

Effective recruitment, then, depends on adequate information about the job and organization acquired using techniques discussed in Chapter 2. Realizing that satisfaction and commitment are important organizational criteria as was argued in Chapter 3, this chapter should lead to better internal recruitment and, as the reputation of the organization spreads, better external recruitment as well. The connection between *internal* human resources practices and *external* recruitment deserves special emphasis. The companies that are the most satisfying to work for are also the companies that have the least trouble getting good applicants. So positive human resources practices may be yielding another (unintended) benefit: superior applicants for jobs at lower costs (see Chapter 7).

REFERENCES

Adams, J. S. (1963). Toward an understanding of inequity. *Journal of Abnormal and Social Psychology, 67,* 422–436.

Adams, J. S. (1965). Injustice in social exchange. In L. Berkowitz (Ed.). *Advances in experimental social psychology,* Vol. 2. New York: Academic Press.

Argyris, C. (1957). *Personality and organization.* New York: Harper.

Bateman, T. S., and Organ, D. W. (1983). Job satisfaction and the good soldier: The relationship between effort and employee "citizenship." *Academy of Management Journal, 26,* 887–895.

Baysinger, B. D., and Mobley, W. H. (1983). Turnover. In K. M. Rowland and G. Ferris (Eds.). *Research in personnel and human resources,* Vol. 2. Greenwich, CT: JAI Press.

Beer, M. (1980). *Organization change and development: a systems view.* Santa Monica, CA: Goodyear.

Blau, P. M., Gustad, J. W., Jesson, R., Parnes, H. R., and Wilcox, R. C. (1956). Occupational choice: A conceptual framework. *Industrial and Labor Relations Review, 9,* 531–543.

Brayfield, A. H., and Crockett, W. H. (1955). Employee attitudes and employee performance. *Psychological Bulletin, 52,* 415–422.

Brett, J. M. (1980). The effects of job transfer on employees and their families. In C. L. Cooper and R. Payne (Eds.). *Current concerns in occupational stress.* New York: Wiley.

Bureau of National Affairs (1979). Recruiting policies and practice. *Personnel policies forum,* Survey No. 126. Washington, DC.

Burke, R. J., and Deszca, E. (1982). Preferred organizational climates of Type A individuals. *Journal of Vocational Behavior, 21,* 50–59.

Business Week (1980). Billings in executive recruiting. May 5, 66–69.

Campbell, J. P., Daft, R. L., and Hulin, C. L. (1982). *What to study: Generating and developing research questions.* Beverly Hills, CA: Sage.

Cascio, W. F. (1982). *Costing human resources: The financial impact of behavior in organizations.* Boston: Kent.

Chesney, M. A., and Rosenman, R.H. (1980). Type A behavior in the work setting. In C. L. Cooper and R. Payne (Eds.). *Current concerns in occupational stress.* New York: Wiley.

Crites, J. O. (1978). *Career maturity inventory* (rev. ed.). Monterey, CA: MTB/McGraw-Hill.

Decker, P. J., and Cornelius, E. T. (1979). A note on recruiting sources and job survival rates. *Journal of Applied Psychology, 64,* 463–464.

Ellis, R. A., and Taylor, M. S. (1983). Role of self-esteem within the job search process. *Journal of Applied Psychology, 68,* 632–640.

Employee Relocations Council (1983). *Relocation assistance: Transferred employees.* Washington, DC.

Festinger, L. (1954). A theory of social comparison processes. *Human Relations, 7,* 117–140.

French, J. R. P., Jr. (1974). Person-role fit. In A. McLean (Ed.). *Occupational Stress,* Springfield, IL: Thomas.

Friedman, M., and Rosenman, R. H. (1974). *Type A behavior and your heart.* New York: Knopf.

Gannon, M. J. (1971). Sources of referral and employee turnover. *Journal of Applied Psychology, 55,* 226–228.

Hackman, J. R., and Oldham, G. R. (1980). *Work redesign.* Reading, MA: Addison-Wesley.

Hall, D. T. (1976). *Careers in organizations.* Santa Monica, CA: Goodyear.

Herzberg, F. (1968). One more time: How do you motivate employees? *Harvard Business Review, 46,* 53–62.

Holland, J. L. (1973). *Making vocational choices: A theory of careers.* Englewood Cliffs, NJ: Prentice-Hall.

Holland, J. L. (1976). Vocational preferences. In M. D. Dunnette (Ed.). *Handbook of industrial and organizational psychology.* Chicago: Rand McNally.

Ivancevich, J. M., and Donnelly, J. M. (1971). Job offers acceptance behavior and reinforcement. *Journal of Applied Psychology, 55,* 119–122.

Jenkins, C. D., Rosenman, R. H., and Friedman, M. (1967). Development of objective psychological tests for the determination of the coronary-prone behavior pattern in employed men. *Journal of Chronic Diseases, 20,* 371–379.

Katz, D., and Kahn, R. L. (1978). *The social psychology of organizations, 2nd ed.* New York: Wiley.

Lacy, W. B., Bokemeier, J. L., and Shepard, J. M. (1983). Job attribute preferences and work commitment of men and women in the United States. *Personnel Psychology, 36,* 315–330.

Locke, E. A. (1976). The nature and causes of job satisfaction. In M. D. Dunnette (Ed.). *Handbook of industrial and organizational psychology.* Chicago: Rand McNally.

London, M., and Stumpf, S. A. (1982). *Managing careers.* Reading, MA: Addison-Wesley.

Louis, M. (1980). Surprise and sense-making: What newcomers experience in entering unfamiliar organizational settings. *Administrative Science Quarterly, 25,* 226–251.

Maier, N. R. F. (1952). *Principles of human relations: Applications to management.* New York: Wiley.

March, J. G., and Simon, H. A. (1958). *Organizations.* New York: Wiley.

Maslow, A. H. (1943). A theory of human motivation. *Psychological Review, 50,* 390–396.

Maslow, A. H. (1954). *Motivation and personality.* New York: Harper, 1957.

McGregor, D. M. (1960). *The human side of enterprise.* New York: McGraw-Hill.

Mitchell, T. M., and Schneider, B. (1984). *Development of the turnover diagnostic.* College Park, MD: Department of Psychology, University of Maryland. Unpublished Technical Report.

Mobley, W. H. (1982). *Employee turnover: Causes, consequences and control.* Reading, MA: Addison-Wesley.

Morrow, P. C. (1983). Concept redundancy in organizational research: The case of work commitment. *Academy of Management Review, 8,* 486–500.

Muchinsky, P. M., and Taylor, M. S. (1976). Intrasubject predictions of occupational preference: The effect of manipulating components of the valence model. *Journal of Vocational Behavior, 8,* 185–195.

Popovich, P. M., and Wanous, J. P. (1982). The realistic job preview as a persuasive communication. *Academy of Management Review, 7,* 570–578.

Power, D. J., and Aldag, R. J. (1985). Soelberg's job search and choice model: A clarification, review and critique. *Academy of Management Review, 10,* 48–58.

Premack, S. L., and Wanous, J. P. (1985). A meta-analysis of realistic job preview experiments. Columbus, OH: College of Administrative Sciences, The Ohio State University.

Price, J. L. (1977). *The study of turnover.* Ames: Iowa State University Press.

Reid, G. L. (1972). Job search and the effectiveness of job-finding methods. *Industrial and Labor Relations Review, 25,* 479–495.

Roe, A. (1957). Early determinants of vocational choice. *Journal of Counseling Psychology, 4,* 212–217.

Roethlisberger, F. J., and Dickson, W. J. (1939). *Management and the worker.* Cambridge, MA: Harvard University Press.

Rosen, C., Klein, D. J., and Young, K. M. (1986). *Employee ownership in America.* Lexington, MA: Lexington Books.

Salancik, G. R. (1977). Commitment and the control of organizational behavior and belief. In B. M. Staw and G. R. Salancik (Eds.). *New directions in organizational behavior.* Chicago: St. Clair Press.

Scarpello, V., and Campbell, J. P. (1983). Job satisfaction: Are all the parts there? *Personnel Psychology, 36,* 577–600.

Schein, E. A. (1965). *Organizational psychology.* Englewood Cliffs, NJ: Prentice-Hall.

Schein, E. A. (1970). *Organizational psychology,* 2nd ed. Englewood Cliffs, NJ: Prentice-Hall.

Schein, E. A. (1978). *Career dynamics.* Reading, MA: Addison-Wesley.

Schmitt, N., and Son, L. (1981). An evaluation of valence models of motivation to pursue various post high school alternatives. *Organizational Behavior and Human Performance, 27,* 135–150.

Schneider, B., and Alderfer, C. P. (1973). Three studies of need satisfaction in organizations. *Administrative Science Quarterly, 18,* 489–509.

Schuler, R. A. (1984). *Personnel and human resource management,* 2nd ed. St. Paul, MN: West.

Schwab, D. P. (1982). Organizational recruiting and the decision to participate. In K. Rowland and G. Ferris (Eds.). *Personnel management: new perspectives.* Boston: Allyn, Bacon.

Sheard, J. L. (1970). Intrasubject prediction of preferences for organization types. *Journal of Applied Psychology, 54,* 248–252.

Smith, P. C., Kendall, L. M., and Hulin, C. L. (1969). *The measurement of satisfaction in work and retirement.* Chicago: Rand McNally.

Soelberg, P. O. (1967). Unprogrammed decision-making. *Industrial Management Review, 8,* 19–29.

Stumpf, S. A., and Hanrahan, N. M. (1984). Designing organizational career management practices to fit strategic management objectives. In R. S. Schuler and S. A. Youngblood (Eds.). *Readings in personnel and human resource management,* 2nd ed. St. Paul, MN: West.

Super, D. E. (1953). A theory of vocational development. *American Psychologist, 8,* 185–190.

Taylor, F. W. (1911). *The principles of scientific management.* New York: Harper.

Taylor, M. S., and Schmidt, D. W. (1983). A process-oriented investigation of recruitment source effectiveness. *Personnel Psychology, 36,* 343–354.

Taylor, M. S., and Sniezek, J. A. (1984). The college recruitment interview: Topical content and applicant reactions. *Journal of Occupational Psychology, 57,* 157–168.

Telly, C. S., French, W. L., and Scott, W. G. (1971). The relationship of inequity to turnover among hourly workers. *Administrative Science Quarterly, 16,* 164–172.

Trist, E. L., and Bamforth, K. W. (1951). Some social and psychological consequences of the long-wall method of coal-getting. *Human Relations, 4,* 1–38.

Ullman, J. C. (1966). Employee referrals: Prime tools for recruiting workers. *Personnel, 43,* 30–35.

Vroom, V. H. (1964). *Work and motivation.* New York: Wiley.

Wanous, J. P. (1973). Effects of a realistic job preview on job acceptance, job attitudes, and job survival. *Journal of Applied Psychology, 58,* 327–332.

Wanous, J. P. (1977). Organizational entry: Newcomer moving from outside to inside. *Psychological Bulletin, 84,* 601–618.

Wanous, J. P. (1980). *Organizational entry: Recruitment, selection and socialization of newcomers.* Reading, MA: Addison-Wesley.

Wareham, J. (1980). *Secrets of an executive headhunter.* New York: Athenum.

Zippo, M. (1980). Getting the most out of an executive search firm. *Personnel, 57,* 47–48.

MEASUREMENT CONCEPTS AND TOOLS

Perhaps the single most important contribution American psychology has made to the Western world is the pragmatic approach to understanding and predicting behavior. As in other sciences, Americans have not been consistently superior in developing psychological theories, but they have excelled in applying and evaluating theories and procedures. A major contribution of American psychologists to organizational functioning and effectiveness has been the development and application of sophisticated measurement procedures for evaluating the validity and usefulness of staffing programs.

This chapter is concerned with some of the concepts and methods useful in evaluating the procedures used to staff organizations. Specifically, the chapter presents some basic methods of measurement (measures of central tendency, variation, and covariation) and measurement/evaluation concepts (reliability and validity). These topics will prove very useful in later chapters as we explore ways to calculate the dollar benefits of staffing programs (Chapter 7) and ways to evaluate the relative effectiveness of different staffing procedures (Chapters 8, 9, and 10).

AIMS OF THE CHAPTER

Personnel selection is rooted in the psychology of individual differences. The basis of this area of psychology is obviously the fact that people do differ along a wide variety of dimensions. We all have eyes, but we vary considerably in our capacity to see the world around us.

Obviously, if a measurement is documenting a real individual difference, then another measurement of the same phenomenon should yield a similar result or, as social scientists say, the measurement should be *reliable*. Further, if the score resulting from the measurement has some practical consequence for the person measured, or for society, we say it is *valid*. Various phenomena are measured with varying degrees of validity and reliability. We also know that some human attributes psychologists have tried to measure have more important work consequences than others. For example, cognitive ability tests are generally more valid than personality tests for predicting productivity kinds of performance.

In this chapter we intend to describe:

1. the nature of measurement in psychology in general, and selection in particular;
2. methods of summarizing our measurements; and

3. ways of quantifying or operationalizing the relationships among measures, and the reliability and validity of our staffing procedures.

In chapter 6, we will explore the issue of validity in detail.

NATURE OF MEASUREMENT

Measurement has been defined as the assignment of numbers to objects or events (Stevens, 1946). Sometimes measurement more precisely involves assigning numbers to *properties* of things or to events. In other words, the thing itself is not measured but some sign or indicant of it is. A person who continually tries to win at every pursuit he or she undertakes is said to possess a great deal of competitiveness. This person's behavior in interactions with others is a *sign* of competitiveness. This is true of physical as well as psychological measurement, though in the case of height and weight, as opposed to intelligence and creativity, the properties are more directly tied to direct observation and less dependent on our inference.

The assignment of numbers to objects or events was a phenomenal intellectual accomplishment. Prior to the development of measurement, no scientific progress was possible. It was impossible because of the wide variety of non-specific (loose) ways of describing nature. Even with the advent of language, even written language that had some precision, specification of the properties of objects, events or their indicants was extremely cumbersome until the advent of measurement.

Since we assign numbers to properties of things, it is necessary to know the features of numbers. There are three important features of the real number series:

1. *Numbers are ordered.* This means that when we assign numbers to properties of things, we can order the things, for example, rank them according to the numbers. If it makes sense only to order things after assigning numbers to them, we say that our scale is *ordinal*.

2. *Differences between numbers are ordered.* This means that when numbers are assigned to properties of things, not only can the things be ordered, but the size of the differences between things is known and can also be ordered. This type of measurement is called *interval* measurement because the size of the differences or intervals among ordered objects is known and càn also be ordered.

3. *The number series has a unique origin.* When the assignment of numbers to properties of things allows the assignment of zero (such as zero weight or height), we say that we have *ratio scales* of measurement. Not only can the size of the difference between numbers be ordered, but numbers can also be presented as ratios of each other. If we can reasonably multiply or divide numbers to obtain ratios like "half as cold" or "twice as heavy," we have ratio measurement.

In addition to ordinal, interval, and ratio forms of measurement, when we simply assign a number to something as a way to identify it, we say we have a *nominal* scale. Nominal scales include numbers on football jerseys or baseball uniforms. The numbers do not signify any ordering of uniforms or players, hence no higher level of measurement.

Sex and race are measured at a nominal level. That is, we can reliably classify individuals as black or white, male or female, but we do not typically order racial subgroups or sex subgroups. The color of hair of a group of individuals can be ordered from light to dark, so we would say that the lightness-darkness of one's hair color is an ordinal variable. The order requirement means that if Person A's hair is darker than B's hair, and B's hair in turn is darker than C's hair, then A's hair must be darker than C's. If we assigned the number 10 to A's hair color, 6 to B's, and 2 to C's, then our scale would be an interval scale only if we can establish that the difference between A and B and C or any other difference of 4 on our scale was equivalent. Finally, if the property we are measuring satisfies the order and interval rules and also has a meaningful zero point we say we are measuring that property with a ratio scale. Height, weight, distance, and temperature measured on the Celsius (Centigrade) scale are examples of variables in which 0 is meaningful. The zero point makes it possible to make ratio statements in comparing individuals. If Person A weighs 200 pounds and B 100 pounds then we can say that A weighs twice as much as B. However, if 200 and 100 were scores on an intelligence test, it would not be useful or correct to say that A was twice as intelligent as B since zero intelligence has no operational meaning.

The level of measurement with which we index variables has practical consequences when we start summarizing our measurements or performing arithmetic operations on the numbers we use to represent the objects of interest. For example, we can transform nominal data in any way at all that maintains the identity implied by the original assignment of numbers. So, for example, we could multiply all of the baseball uniform numbers by 2 and each player would still have a unique identity or number. (It would, however, mess up the sports announcer!) Numbers assigned to objects using an *ordinal* scale may be added, subtracted, multiplied, divided, squared, or transformed in any way that preserves the original order of the objects. Transformations of interval data must preserve both the order and relative size of the scale intervals; that is, multiplying, dividing, adding, or subtracting by a constant is fine, but taking the square root or squaring would change the size of the intervals between or among the numbers, so those transformations are not permissible. Finally, the ratio properties of a scale would be preserved only by multiplication or division by a constant; addition or subtraction of a constant would change the zero point.

Most psychological variables are measured close to an interval scale. So we almost invariably use statistics such as the mean, standard deviation, and Pearson product-moment correlation (explained later) which are appropriate when we have interval data. There are two reasons for using these statistics even with data whose interval nature may be questionable. The first argument involves the observation that variables with known interval and/or ratio properties such as height and weight are normally distributed. Typically, the measures we use in staffing programs, especially those we use as predictors, yield a normal distribution of measurements (see Figure 5–1 for a normal distribution), so we make the inference that they have interval properties. We do not claim ratio properties, however, because we do not have knowledge of a zero point. Because our psychological variables are assumed to be normally distributed and our scale yields scores which are normally distributed, we believe our scales possess interval properties (Magnusson, 1966, Ch. 1). In fact, psychological measures can be constructed in such a manner that they yield a normal distribution, or we can transform the data in a way that yields a normal distribution. Of course, both methods rely on the implicit assumption that individual differences on psychological variables are indeed distributed normally, but since so many of the measures of natural characteristics (tree size, fish speed, amount of rain) take this form, it is perfectly reasonable to make the same assumption for our measures. Some scholars (e.g., Baker, Hardyck, & Petrinovich, 1966) have even shown that the kinds of statistics we use in staffing, when computed on distributions of non-interval data, yield essentially the same decisions as did statistics based on distributions of interval data.

In summary, we have explained that a number does not always mean the same thing; *what* it means depends upon the kind of measurement from which it was derived. The number 100, then, can mean nothing more than a football jersey, or it can mean something as numerically useful as the temperature at which water boils. Most personnel selection measurement is neither nominal nor ratio in form; it is usually somewhere between ordinal and interval and we treat it as interval. For practical purposes, this means we can rank order people from high to low on various measures of individual differences and that we can summarize many persons' scores using various descriptive statistics. In the remainder of this chapter, we will from time to time mention the importance of level of measurement when we describe individual differences or use information about individual differences on one variable to predict behavior on another dimension.

SUMMARIZING MEASUREMENTS OF INDIVIDUAL DIFFERENCES

When we gather a set of measurements, we usually report, in addition to the raw (actually obtained) scores, some summary indices of the total set of scores. These summary indices include measures of *central tendency* and *variability.* At times we are also interested in the relationship of scores, say some test scores, to other variables of interest—for example, the relationship between scores on job attitude measures and scores on job performance measures. In the latter case, our summary measure is called a *correlation.*

Central Tendency Measures

When we receive a score on an exam, we have little or no idea of what that score means until we have some framework for understanding it. So a common question is, what was the class average or *mean.*

Formally: Mean $= \Sigma \; X/N$

     Where Σ = the sum of all Xs

           X = each raw score

           N = the number of persons, objects, items, etc. in the set.

This measure of central tendency allows us to make some sense of our score; that is, we are either above or below the mean. The mean is strictly appropriate only when data with interval properties have been collected. If we have only ordinal data, we correctly report the *median* which is the middle score in a distribution of scores. The median of income statistics is commonly reported as the measure of central tendency because a few millionaires in a group of people, most of whom have salaries around $20,000,

	SCORES				
1.	13	Mean =	$\dfrac{\text{Sum of Scores}}{\text{Number of Scores}}$	$= \dfrac{400}{20} = 20$	
2.	15				
3.	17				
4.	17	Median =	Middle score in the = 20.0		
5.	18		ranked distribution		
6.	18				
7.	18	Mode =	the most frequently occurring score = 20.0		
8.	19	Range =	13 – 27		
9.	20				
10.	20	Standard Deviation =	$\sqrt{\dfrac{\Sigma(X_i - M)^2}{N}}$	$= \sqrt{\dfrac{214}{20}} = 3.27$	
11.	20				
12.	20				
13.	21	where X_i is an individual score, M is the mean,			
14.	21	N is the number of scores, and Σ indicates the sum			
15.	22	of $X_i - M$ values.			
16.	22				
17.	23				
18.	24				
19.	25				
20.	27				
Total	400				

Very rarely are the mean, median, and mode of a score distribution precisely equal. We made them equal to provide a simple example. They will also be equal when the distribution of scores is normal as in Figure 5–1.

would significantly distort the average. The *mode* is the appropriate index of central tendency when one has only nominal data. In Table 5–1* we present a distribution of scores and the computed mean, median, and mode. It should be noted that the mean, median, and mode are identical when the distribution of scores is normal (see Figure 5–1).

Variability Measures

In receiving feedback on an exam we take in some course we are first interested in our score. Our next concern is the average score or mean of the group or class. Then, we are likely to ask what the highest and/or lowest scores were. In other words, we are asking what the variability of the score distribution is. We know intuitively that a score 2 points above the mean is more impressive when the range of scores is 6–10 than when the range of scores is 0–16. A simple measure of variability—the range or difference between the

---

*In the following figures we will represent the distribution of scores by curved lines like those in Figure 5–1. The frequency of people obtaining each score is indicated under this line. This bell-shaped curve, usually called the *normal curve* (when it is normal) always reflects a set of people (objects, things) that have been counted, measured, or assessed on some trait or attribute and then ordered by the attribute according to the frequency or number of people who obtained each score. Since attributes of people typically distribute themselves in a curve of this shape it is also called a *normal distribution.*

FIGURE 5-1. *EXAMPLE OF DISTRIBUTION OF TEST SCORES.*

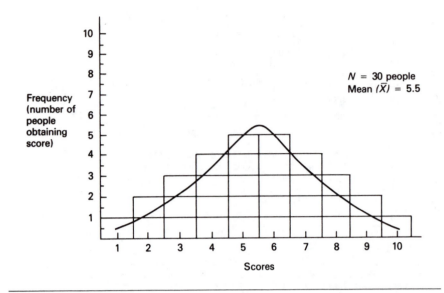

highest and lowest score—is appropriate when we have ordinal data. An arithmetically more complex measure of variability, the standard deviation, is used as the measure of variability when we have interval data. The standard deviation is commonly used in staffing research.

The standard deviation is computed for the set of data presented in Table 5-1 and is particularly useful because of its relationship to the normal distribution or normal curve pictured in Figure 5-1. The percentage of cases falling in any portion of the normal curve are known and presented in tabular form in statistics books. For example, we know that a person whose score is one standard deviation above the mean score lies above approximately 84% of the people represented by the distribution. Most cases (approximately 96%) are found within plus or minus two standard deviations of the mean. In Table 5-1 this would mean most scores lie between 26.54 and 13.46 (20.00 $\pm$ 2(3.27)). Some scores will obviously fall outside these figures, but the probability of this occurring is rather low. When behavioral scientists are interested in determining whether or not they have produced a real change, or whether two variables are really related, or the conclusions from a set of observations can be explained by chance alone, they use a form of the standard deviation called the standard error to form confidence intervals around a particular score beyond which it is unlikely to observe scores. This procedure will be described later.

Standard Deviations and Standard Scores

When a person applies for a job, we may administer a battery of tests. Since tests are man-made, the possible range of scores on any test is decided by each test-maker. Suppose our job applicant scores:

> 40 on a numerical reasoning test
>
> 100 on a sales inventory
>
> 2.0 on a test of initiative
>
> 100 on a sociability scale

We want to know two things: (1) how well, relative to others, did the applicant do on each of the tests, and (2) is the applicant better at sales than at numerical reasoning? How well have others done on these tests—i.e., what is the average performance? Say average scores are:

> $\bar{X}$ numerical reasoning $= 35$
>
> $\bar{X}$ sales inventory $= 85$
>
> $\bar{X}$ initiative $= 3$
>
> $\bar{X}$ sociability $= 85$

Such information demonstrates our knowledge that a score or number does not have inherent meaning. A number only has meaning *in some context.*

Unscrupulous test publishers capitalize on people's assumptions about the context of numbers. A score of 100 is always better than a score of 80, right? Wrong. A score of 100 is always the same as another score of 100, right? Wrong. Given two scores of 100 on two different tests, and given that 85 is the average performance on those two tests, then the two scores are the same, right? Wrong. *Test users must know how to interpret scores; this requires that they know the scores' contexts.*

Average performance on a test, as we learned from the classroom example cited above, demonstrates only one piece of contextual information. The mean gives us some idea about where our applicant stands, but not a very good picture. The mean alone provides no information about the relative spread of the distributions on tests. But now, referring back to the tests our applicant took, we find that:

> S.D. numerical reasoning $= 5$
>
> S.D. sales inventory $= 30$
>
> S.D. initiative $= .5$
>
> S.D. sociability $= 15$

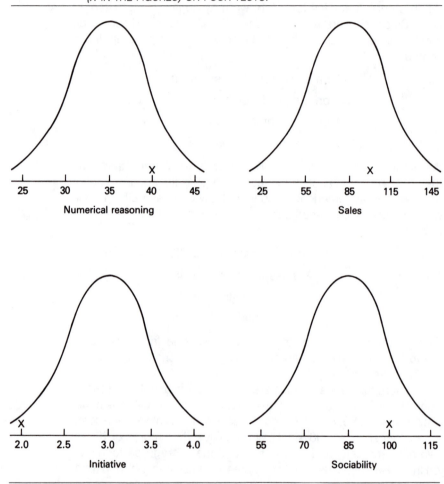

FIGURE 5-2. MEANS, STANDARD DEVIATIONS, AND APPLICANT SCORES (X IN THE FIGURES) ON FOUR TESTS.

Figure 5–2 shows distributions for the four tests above, along with the respective mean, standard deviation, and our hypothetical applicant's scores. Note that our applicant achieved the same numerical score on the sales inventory and the sociability scale. Also note that the average performance on these two tests is the same in the general population. However, the standard deviations are different. An examination of the standard deviation indicates that on sociability our applicant is one standard deviation above the mean ($\bar{X} = 85$, S.D. $= 15$, $X = 100$). On the sales inventory,

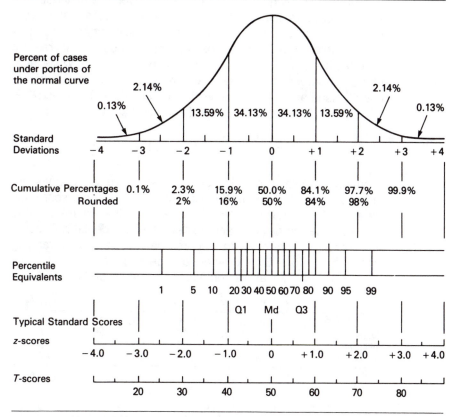

Percent of cases under portions of the normal curve

2.14%   2.14%

0.13%   13.59% | 34.13% | 34.13% | 13.59%   0.13%

Standard Deviations: −4   −3   −2   −1   0   +1   +2   +3   +4

Cumulative Percentages: 0.1%   2.3%   15.9%   50.0%   84.1%   97.7%   99.9%
Rounded: 2%   16%   50%   84%   98%

Percentile Equivalents:
1   5   10   20 30 40 50 60 70 80   90   95   99

Typical Standard Scores   Q1   Md   Q3

z-scores
−4.0   −3.0   −2.0   −1.0   0   +1.0   +2.0   +3.0   +4.0

T-scores
20   30   40   50   60   70   80

Reprinted from The Psychological Corporation, Test Service Bulletin Number 48, January 1955.

however, our applicant is one-half standard deviation above the mean ($\bar{X} = 85$, S.D. $= 30$, $X = 100$).

The concept of standard deviation indeed implies a standard. The standard deviation tells something about the degree of variation around the mean. This permits us to locate how far above or below the mean any score lies. Indeed, given the mean, the standard deviation, and a particular score, we can tell from the distribution *precisely* how far above or below the mean the score is—"how far" indicating percentage of people when the distribution of scores is normal. Figure 5–3 presents these percentiles schematically. Note in Figure 5–3 that the standard deviations are presented as +1 S.D., +2 S.D., −1 S.D., and so forth. Note also that the mean of the distribution is zero (0). Given the mean and standard deviation of a distribution of scores, we may convert the distribution to a common score unit called a standard score. Standard scores are useful because, as we will see, they allow us to compare the scores people obtain on different measures when those measures are reported in different raw score form (as in Figure 5–2). While there exists a number of potential standard scores, the two most frequently used are z-scores ($\bar{X} = 0$, S.D. $= 1$) and T-scores ($\bar{X} = 50$, S.D. $= 10$). The formula for these scores are:

$$z = \frac{X - \bar{X}}{S.D._x} \text{ and } T = 10z + 50$$

From this formula, it should be clear that we can express any score in units which are standard units. That is, a person's score has meaning if we know how others typically did (the mean), and the spread of the scores (the standard deviation). Incidentally, T-scores are sometimes preferred to z-scores because z-scores, ranging from -5 to $+5$ at the extremes, can be negative.

Let us apply the above formulas to our applicant's test scores.

	X	$\bar{X}$	S.D.	z	T	Percentile*
Numerical Reasoning	40	35	5	1.00	60	84
Sales Inventory	100	85	30	0.50	55	70
Initiative	2	3	.5	−2.00	30	2
Sociability Scale	100	85	15	1.00	60	84

$$z = \frac{X - \bar{X}}{S.D._x} = \frac{40 - 35}{5} \quad \frac{5}{5} = 1.00 \text{ (Numerical Reasoning)}$$

$$= \frac{100 - 85}{30} \quad \frac{15}{30} = .50 \text{ (Sales Inventory)}$$

$$= \frac{2 - 3}{.5} \quad \frac{-1}{.5} = -2.00 \text{ (Initiative)}$$

$$= \frac{100 - 85}{15} \quad \frac{15}{15} = 1.00 \text{ (Sociability)}$$

Now we can see that on numerical reasoning and sociability our applicant is one S.D. above the mean ($z = 1.00$, $T = 60$, percentile $= 84$). Her strongest traits relative to others are numerical reasoning and sociability; her weakest, initiative, on which she

---

*When the distribution of scores is normal

stands in approximately the second percentile. The percentiles are derived from Figure 5–3.

Transforming scores to standard scores is a linear transformation which preserves the original distribution of scores. If the raw score distribution is not normal, then our scores are not distributed symmetrically around the mean as in Figure 5–1. Standardized scores will also not be normally distributed but will retain their original distribution. Standardized scores from distributions with very different shapes are not directly comparable; hence, we occasionally apply a more complex nonlinear transformation called *normalization*. For most score distributions this is probably not necessary, but we can easily observe serious departures from the normal distribution if the distribution of scores is plotted as in Figure 5–1.

COVARIATION

Two Predictor Scores

We really want, however, to be able to make predictions about applicants. That is, given test scores like those above, and given the scores of a particular person's performance on tests, we want to make some statements about the person in regard to a certain criterion or criteria of effectiveness. Are different scores on these tests related to different levels of effectiveness? Do test scores covary with criterion scores? To deal with these questions requires extending the concepts of means and standard deviations.

Suppose for a moment that you administered some predictor (test, interview, etc.) to a group of applicants. Suppose further that for some reason the applicants scored either X_1, or X_2, on the predictor.

You then follow up those who scored X_1 and those who scored X_2 to see how effective they are on the job. You find that those who scored X_1 on the predictor tend to score lower on the criterion than those who scored X_2. You note, however, that for both those who scored X_1 and those who scored X_2 on the predictor, there are distributions of criterion scores. That is, not all who scored X_1 on the predictor were equally effective on the job. The situation is portrayed in Figure 5–4.

Obviously, the criterion performance of a person scoring X_1 would be best characterized by $\bar{Y}_1$, the average performance of all those who scored X_1. We would hope, of course, that the deviation around $\bar{Y}_1$ was small, because as the size of the standard deviation increases relative to the mean, our estimate of the mean is more likely to be in error as a measure of central tendency.

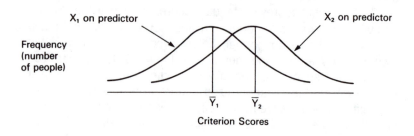

X_1 on predictor

X_2 on predictor

Frequency
(number
of people)

$\bar{Y}_1$ $\bar{Y}_2$

Criterion Scores

Multiple Predictor Scores

Deviation around the mean of criterion scores becomes clearer when there are more than two possible scores on the predictor. When there are many predictor scores, there is theoretically a corresponding distribution of criterion scores for each predictor score. In Figure 5–5 the hypothetical distribution of criterion scores for eight of forty predictor scores is presented; another set of analogous distributions is presented in Figure 5–6. For any predictor score in Figure 5–5 the range of criterion scores is lower than for the same predictor score in Figure 5–6.

Figure 5–5 represents a more accurate prediction than Figure 5–6 because Figure 5–5 shows less deviation from the means of criterion distributions for each predictor score than does Figure 5–6. While the same overall range of criterion and predictor scores (from 1 to 40) is observed in both figures, the deviation from the mean of each of the distributions of criterion scores is smaller in Figure 5–5; the mean of each of the criterion distributions in Figure 5–5 would be a better estimate of criterion performance for its predictor score than would be true in Figure 5–6.

In both figures, the best estimate of criterion behavior for any predictor score is the mean of the criterion distribution for that predictor score. Once again, as when we discussed standard deviations, if one were putting money on a particular criterion score, one would bet on the situation pictured in Figure 5–5.

Now think about the following: if the best estimate of *criterion* behavior for any predictor score is the mean of the criterion distribution for that predictor score, *the reverse is also true.* Not only is there a distribution of criterion scores for each predictor score but *there is a distribution of predictor scores for each criterion score.* Figures 5–7 and 5–8 show this schematically. Figures 5–5 and 5–6 are reproduced in Figures 5–7 and 5–8 respectively and overlaid

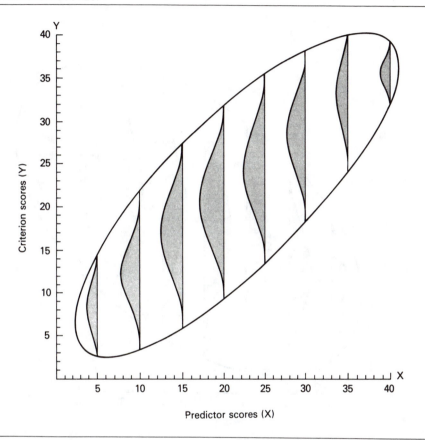

It is a convention to label the horizontal (X) axis as the predictor and the vertical axis (Y) as the criterion.

with a graph of the predictor score distributions for each criterion score. In addition, a line passes through the means of the distributions, from X (predictor) to Y (criterion). This is because the best estimate of a distribution of scores is the mean.

Let us take stock. For every predictor score there is a set of criterion scores for all the people with that predictor score. This means that for a person's score of, say, 15 on a test, although we do not know exactly what the criterion score will be, our best estimate is the mean of the criterion scores of all others who also scored 15 on the predictor. The probability of being right by guessing the mean is a function of the standard deviation of the distribution from which the mean comes. The same would hold true in estimating the mean of the *predictor* scores for all those scoring,

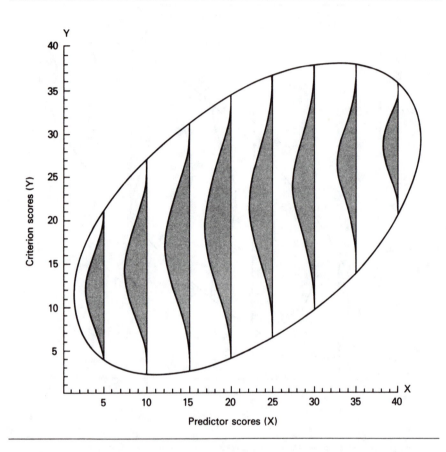

say, 5 on the *criterion;* predictions from *Y* to *X* are more accurate when the distribution of possible predictor scores has a small standard deviation.

To summarize all of this information we can only say that the degree of relationship between predictor and criterion yields a statistic called the *correlation coefficient.* This statistic summarizes the degree of linear relationship between two variables.

THE PEARSON PRODUCT-MOMENT CORRELATION COEFFICIENT (r)

Like the mean and the standard deviation, the correlation coefficient represented by *r* is a convention. Staffing researchers have used *r* as their index of relationship because of (1) its parsimony—

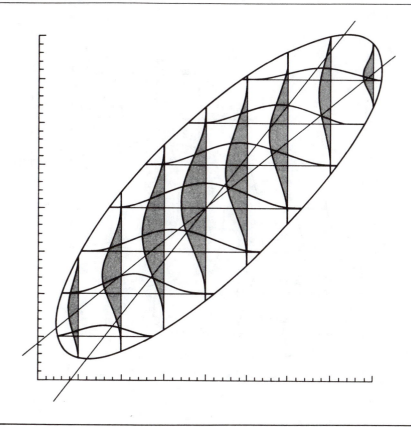

the result is only one number, and (2) it meets the same criterion
as the $\bar{X}$ and σ (S.D.)—it is an index of relationship which is a
mean.*

The technicalities of the arguments underlying the use of r
need not concern us here. What is important, though, because of
the extensive use of correlation coefficients in staffing work, is to
begin to grasp the concepts of (1) the range of r, (2) the wonder

---

*It is a mean in the sense that it is the mean of the cross products of standard scores:

$$r_{xy} = \Sigma Z_x Z_y / N$$

The spread of the distributions of both the predictor and criterion scores affects the size of the
correlations, which makes sense because the correlation is between X and Y. Note also that
the correlation is the average sum of the z-score values of X times the z-score values of Y. Since
z-scores are being multiplied it is clear that the units of measurement for test and predictor need
not be the same; the raw score formula for calculating the correlation coefficient converts them
both to z-scores.

FIGURE 5–8. *DIFFERENT PREDICTOR SCORE DISTRIBUTIONS FOR SELECTED CRITERION SCORES.*

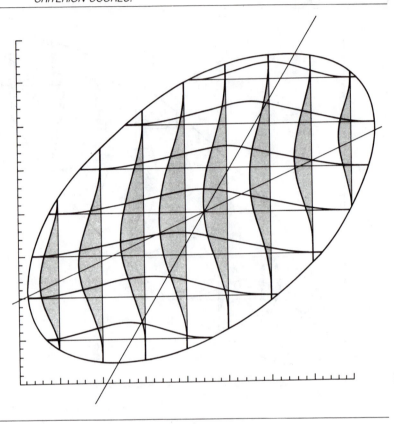

of *r*, (3) the limitations of *r*, (4) the uses of *r* in reliability and validity analyses, and (5) alternatives to *r*.

The Range of r

The correlation coefficient may range in size from +1.00 through 0 to −1.00. We rarely observe correlations above .90, and then generally only in relation to reliability (i.e., consistency or reproducibility). Typical observed predictive validity coefficients range between .20 and .40.

A correlation of 1.00, positive or negative, indicates that information about an individual regarding *X* also yields perfect information regarding *Y*; it provides an "if . . . , then . . ." situation. For instance, in Figures 5–7 and 5–8 this circumstance would be in-dicated by one straight line, rather than by an elipse. You need not worry about this problem as far as staffing procedures are con-cerned!

The "positiveness" or "negativeness" of a correlation refers to the covariance of scores in X and Y. No "goodness" or "badness" is implied. If scores on a predictor go up as scores on the criterion go up, we speak of positive relationships. For example, we know that higher scores on mechanical aptitude tests are related to high-er automotive mechanic performance; a case of positive correla-tion. We also know that high job satisfaction is related to low turnover and absenteeism; a case of the negative correlation. Both cases are, in fact, "good," if we are interested in predicted job performance or turnover and absenteeism.

The correlation coefficient, r, being a summary statistic, repre-sents a picture of how two variables covary. You should be able to picture what an r of a particular level portrays. For example, go back and re-examine Figures 5–7 and 5–8. Figure 5–7 shows the relationship between a relatively accurate predictor and criterion behavior; Figure 5–8 indicates a weaker relationship between pre-dictor and criterion. Because the distribution of criterion scores for each predictor score has greater variability in Figure 5–8, an elipse enclosing the set of distributions in Figure 5–8 is more circular or wider than an elipse enclosing the set of distributions in Figure 5–7. The less spread there is—that is, the more the elipse is cigar-shaped rather than circular—the stronger the relationship between the two variables.

Figure 5–9 presents three *bivariate scatterplots* for correla-tions, positive and negative, of different sizes. A bivariate scatter-plot is a pictorial presentation of the scores of a group of people (organizations, products, etc.) on *two variables* (bivariate). The two scores for each person are plotted on paper as one point. This is called a scatterplot because the points are usually pretty well scat-tered!

Look at Figure 5–9a. This figure presents test scores and crite-rion data for ten people.* Each person was scored on the predictor variable X, and on the criterion variable Y. For each person, then, there are two scores, X and Y, which are plotted from the data presented for Figure 5–9a. The correlation between X and Y is + .76 in Figure 5–9a.

---

*Usually data would be collected on a much larger number of people before calculating a correlation. The data in Figure 5–9 are just for illustrative purposes.

FIGURE 5–9. *CORRELATION COEFFICIENTS OF DIFFERENT SIZES PLOTTED AS BIVARIATE SCATTERPLOTS.*

Data for (a)

	X Score	Y Score
Pete	13	4
Jack	12	3
Bob	16	7
Chris	15	3
Joe	17	5
Ed	13	6
Tim	15	5
Matt	14	4
Rog	11	1
Irv	13	2

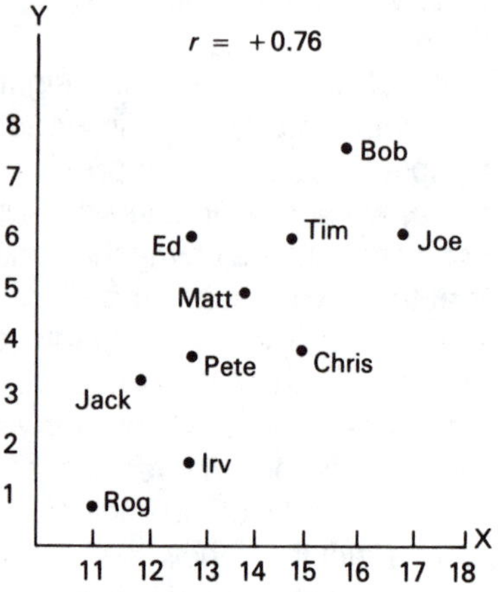

(a)

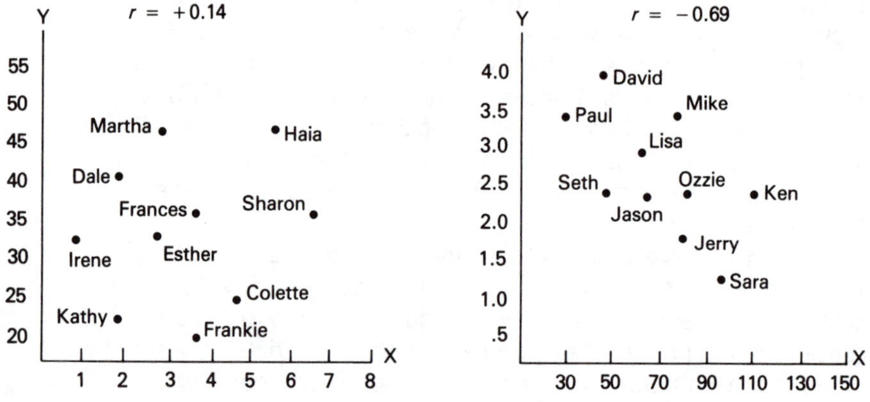

(b)

(c)

Any relationship between these names and actual people is purely *intentional*. The shape of the figures was suggested by J. P. Guilford, *Fundamental Statistics in Psychology and Education*, 2nd ed. (New York: McGraw-Hill, 1950), pp. 156–57. Used with permission.

The Wonder of r

It is difficult to convey the wonder of *r* because it is a truly creative statistic. Think of it. In one number the magnitude of the relationship between two sets of data can be summarized regardless of the scale units on which one or both sets of data are measured and regardless of the number of people (objects, things) that have been assessed.

Because of its simplicity (one number), statistical and mathematical purity, and the fact that it subsumes the mean and standard deviation, *r* is the major statistic of interest in all of psychological measurement, including staffing. As we will see, reliability and validity are both assessed using *r*. In addition, advanced concepts in measurement like *factor analysis* (a procedure useful in grouping or clustering issues that are related to each other) and *multiple regression* (a procedure for combining measures to help understand a phenomenon of interest) are also based on *r*. All of these uses of *r* are described below.

The Limitations of r

The correlation coefficient is technically called the Pearson product-moment coefficient of correlation. It is named after Karl Pearson, the British statistician, who solved the problem of presenting the extent of a linear relationship between two variables in one number. *Linear relationship* means that the trend of relationship between two variables is a straight, rather than a curved line. As with any summary, *r* may not be an adequate summary of the actual state of affairs; if the relationship between two variables is non-linear, then the *correlation ratio* or *eta* is a more appropriate statistic.* While the primary limitation of *r* is that it is not always the appropriate index to use to show the relationship between two variables, the overwhelming proportion of situations encountered in staffing is adequately described by *r*.

For our purposes it is important to note that: (1) eta may be a more appropriate index of relationship than *r* when one or both of the variables to be correlated deviates markedly from the normal bell-shaped distribution; (2) eta varies from − 1.00 through 0 to + 1.00 and is interpreted in the same way as *r*; and (3) eta is a summary index that can be applied to any bivariate distribution—if *r* and eta yield markedly different results, eta is the more appropriate statistic.

Both a wonder and a limitation of *r* is that *r* yields only one number; this fact makes people think it easy to interpret. It is obvious that we had to present some background information so you

---

*Eta summarizes extent of non-linear relationship between two variables.

could understand the concepts underlying *r*; *r* is quite mathematically sophisticated. Simple explanations of *r* are difficult to make and would be quite misleading. Some things to remember are that:

1. An *r* of .50 does not mean 50 percent of this or half of that.
2. Under some circumstances (in addition to those described in discussing eta) *r* cannot be legitimately calculated.
3. In validity analyses, *r* is difficult to describe to the statistically unsophisticated and alternative procedures are required to explain relationships.

Alternatives to r

Procedures generally called *expectancy charts* are very good substitutions for *r* when explaining correlations to unsophisticated people. The principle underlying expectancy charts is as follows: with any criterion it is possible to say that below a certain point, performance on that criterion is unacceptable. With reference to Figure 5–10a, we can see that when such a performance criterion is set, the proportion of people who meet or exceed the criterion given any predictor score increases as one moves from left to right on the predictor axis. Translating the bivariate scatterplot to an expectancy chart is a simple matter. The percent of persons above the point on the criterion which separates successful and unsuccessful employees is calculated and then graphed as in Figure 5–10b. In this graph, the likelihood of success increases as test scores increase, indicating a high degree of correlation. The point on the job performance criterion at which we decide people are successful or unsuccessful is, of course, arbitrary, but this should not be a problem if we remember that this is a standard against which we judge potential improvements in the work force selected with the procedures we've evaluated. Figure 5–10b, incidentally, can be contrasted with a simple "*r* = .50" to see how really remarkable the Pearson *r* is!

PREDICTIONS BASED ON CORRELATION

The reader should now see the relationship between correlation and probability statements using an expectancy chart. The important point to remember is that, the higher the calculated correlation, the more certain the probability statement. The higher the correlation is, the more cigar-shaped the elipse encircling the bivariate scatterplot; i.e., the less deviation there is of points in the scatterplot

EXPECTANCY CHART SHOWING PERCENT WHO SUCCEED FOR
EACH OF SEVEN DIFFERENT PREDICTOR SCORE RANGES.

FIGURE 5–10.

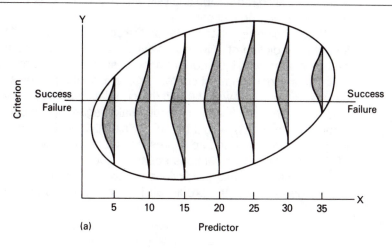

(a)   Predictor

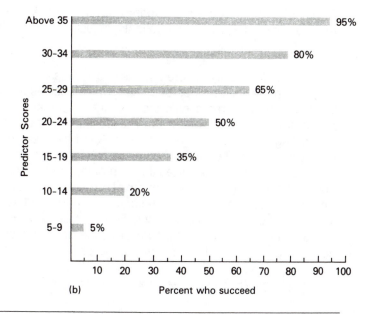

(b)   Percent who succeed

An excellent discussion of the preparation and use of expectancy charts is provided by Lawshe and Balma (1966).

from a line passed through the means of distributions (see Figures 5–7 and 5–8). Using the correlation coefficient between job performance and predictor scores and the knowledge of a person's score on the predictor, we can also make exact predictions of a person's job performance.* To make these predictions, we use a technique called regression analysis which gives us an equation by which we make predictions.

When the predictor and criterion are both in standardized form, then the prediction of Y from X is simply $Z\hat{Y} = r_{XY} Z_X$ where $Z\hat{Y}$ represents predicted job performance in standard score form and Z_X is the standardized test score. For example, if a person's standard score on a test was .50 and the correlation between X and Y was .3, the best prediction one could make regarding the person's standard score on Y would be .15, or slightly above the mean of the group, since all standard scores in z-score form have averages of .00 and standard deviations equal to 1.00.

If we want to make predictions in raw score terms, as would usually be the case, the prediction formula becomes more complicated:

$$\hat{Y} = r_{XY} \frac{SD_Y}{SD_X}(X) + A_{YX}$$

Where SD_Y and SD_X are the standard deviations of X and Y and A_{YX} is a constant which is used to make adjustments for the difference between the means of X and Y. The $r_{XY} \frac{SD_Y}{SD_X}$ term in the equation is frequently referred to as the regression coefficient (b_{YX}). It represents the slope of the line which best fits the data in the scattergram. It represents the amount of increase in Y that results from unit increases in X. The constant is calculated by subtracting from the mean of Y the product of the mean of X and the regression coefficient. This equation describes the line of best fit in the sense that it minimizes the sum of the squared distances from the regression line in the scatterplot. An illustration of a regression line and its components is presented in Figure 5–11. Consider a person whose score on the test is 50. The test has a validity of .50, a mean of 50, and a standard deviation of 20; the standard deviation of Y is 30 and Y's mean is 65. The regression coefficient is $.50\left(\dfrac{30}{20}\right)$ or .75. The constant for the equation is 65 $-.75$ (50), or 27.5. These calculations yield the following regression equation:

$$\hat{Y} = .75\,(X) + 27.5$$

and the best prediction concerning the job performance of a person

---

*However, just because we make *exact* predictions does not mean those predictions are *correct* (see Figure 5–11).

DEMONSTRATION OF CALCULATION OF A REGRESSION
EQUATION, THE PLOT OF A REGRESSION LINE AND THE
STANDARD ERROR OF ESTIMATE.

FIGURE 5-11.

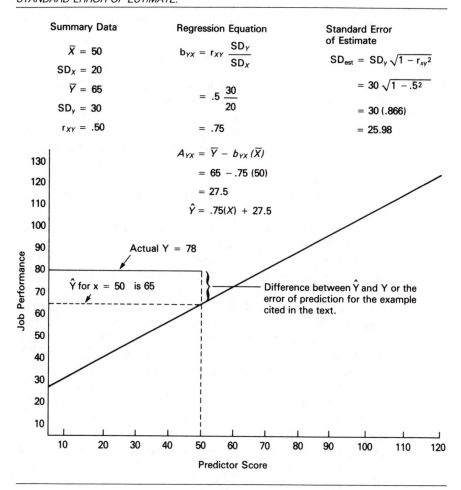

Summary Data

$$\bar{X} = 50$$
$$SD_X = 20$$
$$\bar{Y} = 65$$
$$SD_y = 30$$
$$r_{XY} = .50$$

Regression Equation

$$b_{YX} = r_{XY} \frac{SD_Y}{SD_X}$$
$$= .5 \frac{30}{20}$$
$$= .75$$
$$A_{YX} = \bar{Y} - b_{YX}(\bar{X})$$
$$= 65 - .75(50)$$
$$= 27.5$$
$$\hat{Y} = .75(X) + 27.5$$

Standard Error
of Estimate

$$SD_{est} = SD_y \sqrt{1 - r_{xy}^2}$$
$$= 30 \sqrt{1 - .5^2}$$
$$= 30 (.866)$$
$$= 25.98$$

Actual Y = 78

$\hat{Y}$ for x = 50 is 65

Difference between $\hat{Y}$ and Y or the error of prediction for the example cited in the text.

Job Performance

Predictor Score

with a score of 50 is .75(50) + 27.5 or 65.0. But if this person's actual job performance score equaled 78, we would be wrong by 13 (78 − 65).

The scatter in a scatterplot represents these errors in prediction. That is, the more scatter there is in the criterion scores for each predictor score, the more errors in prediction we would make. The nice feature of the *regression line* is that it is the one line that will minimize the total amount of errors we will make. In other words, using the regression line as our basis for prediction, the sum of squared errors will be smaller than using any other basis for predicting a criterion score for a particular predictor score.

If we were to examine all our mistakes in prediction and compute the standard deviation of those mistakes, they would be equal to the *standard error* of *estimate* (SD$_{est}$); computationally:

$$SD_{est} = SD_Y \sqrt{1 - r_{XY}^2}$$

From this formula we see that if r_{XY} is equal to 1.00, the standard error of estimate is .00. This is another way of saying two things; first, we are making no errors of prediction, and second, the scatter plot is reduced to a straight line. Alternately, if r_{XY} is .0 then the standard error of estimate is equal to the standard deviation of Y.

Since the worst case in terms of making errors of prediction is that their standard deviation would be equal to SD$_Y$, psychometricians frequently use the percent reduction in the size of the SD$_{est}$ relative to SD$_Y$ as a measure of the usefulness of a test. In this case, the regression coefficient reduces to 0 and the constant is equal to the mean of Y. (The reader can confirm this is true by using the formula for the regression coefficient and the constant presented above.) So, for all values of the predictor variable, we would predict the mean of Y and the deviations ($\hat{Y} - Y$) would be the same as those we calculate when we find the standard deviation of Y (because $\hat{Y}$ is the mean) (see Table 5–1). As r_{XY} increases, of course, the standard error of estimate decreases indicating better prediction and more confidence in the results we obtain. Using the standard error of estimate, we can place confidence intervals around our predictions of any given person's score. For example, in the case cited above, the standard error of estimate is equal to $30 \sqrt{1 - .5^2}$ or almost 26. So, we are 68% confident that the person whose test score is 50 has a Y-score somewhere between 65 ± 26 (recall 68% of the cases fall within 1 standard deviation of the mean in the normal curve).

Clearly, prediction of single cases may not be as accurate as we would like, given such a large standard error of estimate. In the chapter on utility of testing, we will discuss the standard error of estimate as a utility measure and show how it is an unnecessarily pessimistic view of the total worth of a selection procedure. It is useful, however, to remember the size of the standard error of estimate when we are trying to make decisions in individual cases or when we encounter a single case in which use of a valid selection instrument resulted in an error. Obviously, errors are certainly possible and inevitable but, as will become clear in Chapter 7, the procedures we have developed are quite useful, and it makes sense to use them even in the presence of imperfect prediction.

We should also discuss the degree of confidence we have in the validity coefficient itself; that is, whether or not the estimated relationship between X and Y is really nonzero. The degree of confidence we have is related to the size of the sample upon which the correlation is calculated, as well as the size of the validity coefficient itself. If our correlation coefficient is based on two cases, it will always be equal to 1.00 because the line we would draw between the two points on a scatterplot would always allow perfect prediction for these two cases. As the sample size (N) increases, we will no longer be able to draw such a perfectly fitting line, but the question remains as to whether our estimate of r_{XY} is dependent on the particular sample we have drawn. Obviously, as N increases, we have more confidence that our results are not just flukes, but that there is a relationship of some magnitude between X and Y. The degree to which our estimate of r_{XY} varies from sample to sample can be estimated from the standard error associated with r_{XY} (the standard error of the correlation) which is equal to $1/\sqrt{N-1}$. If our estimate of r_{XY} is more than two standard errors (1.96 precisely) above zero, then we say we are 95% confident that our validity is above zero.

We can see from the standard error of the correlation that we can expect much variability in our estimates of correlation even when they come from relatively large samples. For example, r_{XY} estimated from samples equal to 101 has a standard error of .10. If the true population coefficient is .30, we can expect about 32% of the coefficients based on samples of 100 to be less than .21 or greater than .39.* We will return to this point in the next chapter when we discuss criterion related validity and its feasibility. It is also important to remember in our later discussion of validity generalization because this predictable sample variability is in large part responsible for the mistaken notion that the validity of tests depends on the organizational circumstances in which they are used or that test validities are situationally specific.

PREDICTIONS USING MULTIPLE PREDICTORS

When we introduced the regression equation and issues concerning the prediction of criterion performance, one question that may have occurred to you is what happens when we want to use two

---

*For values of r greater than .00, the standard error is $(1-r^2)/\sqrt{N-1}$, hence as r increases, the standard error decreases. We use $1/\sqrt{N-1}$ because we are testing the hypothesis that r equals zero.

or more predictors? It would seem that if we can predict a criterion with one predictor, then using two or more predictors should permit even better prediction of the criterion of interest. This is a good question and staffing researchers have grappled with the problem and arrived at a number of conclusions about it.

First, it is important to try and weight predictors when using two or more predictors. To weight predictors means to derive the relative importance of two or more predictors in helping to predict a criterion. The weight a predictor will receive is dependent upon:

- how well it correlates with the criterion
- how well it correlates with the other predictor(s)

Next, it is important to estimate the correlation of the combinations of predictors with the criterion. Whenever we combine predictors to correlate with a criterion we speak of a *multiple correlation* or *multiple regression* situation, called a "multiple *r*" and symbolized by *R*.

Calculating Weights

The multiple regression formula for two predictors is:

$$\hat{Y} = b_1 X_1 + b_2 X_2 + A_{Y12}$$

where b_1 and b_2 are the derived weights for predictors 1 and 2

where A_{Y12} is the constant in the two predictor regression equation

The idea, then, is to calculate b_1 and b_2 so we know how much to weight each of the predictors; this calculation works out so that the multiple *R* is as high as possible. In other words, the weights that are calculated are *optimal weights;* no other weights will yield as high a multiple *R*. As noted above, the weights will depend upon how much each predictor correlates with the criterion and how much it correlates with the other predictor(s).

Various possible multiple predictor-criterion relationships are illustrated in Figure 5–12. In Situation 1, we have two valid predictors which are moderately intercorrelated (represented by the overlap in the circles or Venn diagrams). Each of these two predictors is somewhat related to the criterion *and* somewhat related to a portion of the criterion that the other is unrelated to; there is also a portion where all three overlap. If our goal is the best possible

Situation 1	Situation 2	Situation 3
X_1 = valid	X_1 = valid	X_1 = valid
X_2 = valid	X_2 = valid	X_2 = not valid
X_1X_2 = correlated	X_1X_2 = uncorrelated	X_1X_2 = correlated

prediction of the criterion, then we want to minimize this overlap in predictors while maximizing overlap with the criterion (validity).

In Situation 2, we have pictured such a case: both predictors are valid and they overlap with different portions of y. You can see that in both Situation 1 and Situation 2, the predictors overlap (correlate) with the criterion to the same extent. However, because in Situation 2 the predictors do not overlap (correlate) with *each other,* when the two predictors are used together they explain more of the criterion in Situation 2 than they do in Situation 1. The rule to follow, then, is that when decisions are made about the composition of a test battery, they should be made in light of the intercorrelations among the various predictors as well as in terms of their independent validity.

Situation 3 is more difficult to interpret. In Situation 3, X_2 will add to predictability when used in combination with X_1 even though it is not valid by itself. This occurs because X_2 accounts for some of the variance in X_1 which is not related to y. Or, if we examine the formula for R (given below), we see that the term in the numerator which is subtracted will be zero because r_{Y2} is zero; the denominator, however, will be substantially lower because r_{12} is high. This combination of predictor-criterion relationships is called a *suppressor effect* and results in a negative regression coefficient for X_2. Just for your information, we present below the formulae for calculation of the weights b_1 and b_2 for the two-prediction case. We will present only the two-predictor case partly because of this complexity but also because the method of dealing with additional predictors is identical to that which allows an optimal combination of two predictors. Equations for the regression coefficients, or the optimal predictive weights, in the two-predictor case read as follows:

$$b_1 = \left(\frac{r_{y1} - r_{y2}\, r_{12}}{\sqrt{(1-r^2_{y2})\,(1-r^2_{12})}} \right) \left(\frac{SD_y \sqrt{1-r^2_{y2}}}{SD_1 \sqrt{1-r^2_{12}}} \right)$$

$$b_2 = \left(\frac{r_{y2} - r_{y1}\, r_{12}}{\sqrt{(1-r^2_{y1})\,(1-r^2_{12})}} \right) \left(\frac{SD_y \sqrt{1-r^2_{y1}}}{SD_2 \sqrt{1-r^2_{12}}} \right)$$

where r_{y1} and r_{y2} are the validities of the two predictors; r_{12} is the correlation of the two predictors with each other and SD_y, SD_1, and SD_2 are the standard deviations of the criterion and the two predictors. The equation for the constant in the two predictor regression is as follows:

$$A_{y12} = \bar{y} - b_1\,\bar{x}_1 - b_2\,\bar{x}_2$$

where A_{y12} is the constant and $\bar{y}$, $\bar{x}_1$, and $\bar{x}_2$ are the means of the criterion and the two predictors.

The formula for multiple R is:

$$R_{y12} = \sqrt{ \frac{r^2_{y1} + r^2_{y2} - 2r_{y1}\, r_{y2}\, r_{12}}{1 - r^2_{12}} }$$

It is easy to see that the complexity of these equations is due to the intercorrelation of the two predictors, r_{12}, and the fact that all three variables overlap. In other words, x_1 and x_2 may predict the same portion of the variability in job performance. If they do not overlap (i.e., $r_{12} = .00$), then the equations above become very simple.

One question that may have occurred to you as we have discussed the prediction of job performance is why we are interested in predicting something if we already have it. (All the computations described above are based on data collected in a study of predictor-job performance relationships.) The answer is that we are only interested in making an estimate of the utility of the regression equation in the available sample as justification for use of the selection instrument in subsequent samples. Since the R we obtain in a sample is the best possible description of the data, we then should be concerned about what will happen in a new sample. Figuring out how large R will be in a new sample is called *cross-validation*. That is, since the original R estimate includes idiosyncrasies (error) associated with the particular sample on which it is calculated, we need some way to judge how R is going to behave in a new set of data.

Cross-Validation of Multiple Regression

There are two procedures to use to estimate cross-validated R (how well our prediction equation works in a new sample). The more traditional proposal (Mosier, 1951), called *double cross-validation*, involves the following steps:

1. Randomly split the validation sample into two equal groups.
2. Compute R and regression weights in both samples.
3. Use the regression equation computed in each sample to predict job performance values in the other sample.
4. Estimate cross-validated R by correlating these predicted values with actual values of Y.
5. Average the two resulting Rs to obtain an estimate of the R one can expect in subsequent samples.

If one has not preselected predictors (based on earlier evidence) prior to estimating R, a much more desirable method of estimating cross-validated R is to use the formula provided by Cattin (1980) presented below:

$$\rho_c^2 = \frac{(N - k - 3)\, \rho^4 + \rho^2}{(N - 2k - 2)\rho^2 + k}$$

where ρ_c^2 = estimated population cross-validity

N = number of people in the sample

k = number of predictors in the regression equation

ρ = population multiple correlation

To get ρ in this equation one must use the Wherry formula:

$$\rho^2 = 1 - \left(\frac{N - 1}{N - k - 1}\right)(1 - R^2)$$

where R^2 is the observed multiple correlation.

The population cross-validity is the value of R we would expect if we cross-validated a prediction equation in an infinite number of new samples. An example of the use of these equations is presented in Table 5–2. As can be seen, significant shrinkage of the R obtained in the original sample is predicted when the regression equation is used to make predictions in subsequent samples. The role of the N/K ratio in these equations is obvious and critical. If this ratio is close to one, then a great deal of shrinkage will occur; if it is much larger than one, then little shrinkage will be predicted. The lesson for validation research is obvious: large sample sizes

TABLE 5–2. *DEMONSTRATION OF ESTIMATION OF CROSS-VALIDITY.*

Sample Statistics

$N = 80$

$K = 12$

$R = .40$

Wherry Estimate of Population Multiple Correlation

$$\rho = \sqrt{1 - \frac{80\text{-}1}{80\text{-}12\text{-}1}} \;\; (1 - .4^2)$$

$$= \sqrt{1 - \frac{79}{67}} \;\; (.84)$$

$$= \;\; .10$$

Cattin Estimate of Population Cross-Validity

$$\rho_c = \sqrt{\frac{(80 - 12 - 3)\,.0001 + .01}{(80 - 24 - 2)\,.01 + 12}}$$

$$= \sqrt{\frac{.0065 + .01}{.54 + 12}}$$

$$= \;\; .036$$

---

are important, but it is also important to choose predictors judiciously—not use just whatever is available. Estimates of cross-validity based on the entire sample (as in formula estimation) are more accurate than estimates from the double cross-validation procedures (Schmitt, Coyle, & Rauschenberger, 1977). This general statement may not hold if predictors are chosen with *a priori* evidence of their validity (evidence from earlier work) or if N/K ratios are very low (less than 3).

MULTIPLE REGRESSION AS A COMPENSATORY MODEL

It is clear from the multiple regression formula and the calculation of weights that a relatively high score on one predictor can compensate for a low score on others. Assume, for example, that the following regression equation is appropriate:

$$\hat{Y} = 2 + 5\,X_1 + 3\,X_2.$$

Applied to three individuals with different predictor scores, the results might look as follows:

Person X_1 X_2 $\hat{Y}$

A 3 2 23 $(2 + (5 \times 3) + (3 \times 2))$

B 4 1 25 $(2 + (5 \times 4) + (3 \times 1))$

C 0 7 23 $(2 + (5 \times 0) + (3 \times 7))$

Clearly, the predicted performance of these three persons is not very different, yet their pattern of scores on the two tests *is* very different. Person C's lack of ability on X_1 is *compensated for* by a high level of skill on X_2; a very different compensating effect is evident for Person B. For this reason, multiple regression is called a *compensatory model*.

While there appear to be few human abilities that are noncompensatory, some are likely to be critical in some jobs; for example, eyesight, color vision, or in some form, many physical abilities. In cases where a minimal amount of some ability is critical, the compensatory regression model is inappropriate and should be replaced by some use of *noncompensatory* or *multiple cutoff* models. In a *noncompensatory model,* minimal necessary levels of ability are determined and no one is selected who lacks those levels.

PRACTICAL USES OF CORRELATION AND REGRESSION

There are three very practical uses of correlation coefficients: (1) reliability estimates; (2) examination of the underlying dimensions which may account for the correlations among our measures; and (3) estimates of the relationships between job performance and predictor data. In the following section, we will discuss various ways of estimating reliability and determining the underlying structure of our measures. We will define validity, but will defer discussion of the concept of validity and various validation designs for presentation in Chapter 6.

Reliability

In both Chapters 2 and 3 the topic of reliability was covered conceptually; here we give procedures for actually calculating the different kinds of reliability only mentioned earlier. That is, now that we know something about correlation coefficients, procedures for computing reliability in its different forms can be described.

Reliability of measurement is necessary if the measure is to be useful in making any type of decision, including selection decisions. Reliability can be assessed in several ways, all of which depend on the computation of correlations among different measures. Each of these estimates of reliability differ in terms of what is treated as error, i.e., measurement of something other than was intended.

The most commonsense notion of reliability is that of the *stability* of measurement. To calculate the stability of a measure we correlate scores of persons on the same measure given at two different points in time. Sometimes this is called *retest reliability.* Implicit in this treatment of reliability is the notion that any changes in the scores of persons over time are errors; perfect reliability of measurement in this sense would mean that individuals would be ordered in identical fashion both times the test was given.

A second estimate of reliability can be obtained by correlating scores derived from parallel forms of a test. Parallel forms of a test are supposed to measure the same concept with different items, hence the content of the items is treated as error. Arithmetically, parallel forms are also assumed to have equal means and standard deviations and item intercorrelations. (Some models of *parallel forms reliability* relax these assumptions.) Occasionally, a test is given for which no alternate form is available. In this case, the test may be split in half (randomly assigning items to halves) and *split-half* reliability may be calculated.

Whenever we calculate the reliability of a test based only on an analysis of that test at one point in time, we are calculating what is called *internal consistency reliability.* There are different forms of internal consistency reliability only one of which is the split-half procedure. In this procedure, each individual taking the test is given a score on both halves and the two sets of half scores are correlated across all test takers. However, reliability is related to test length and the correlation between half scores represents the reliability of a test half as long as the one on which we will make decisions. Assuming items in the two halves are equivalent in the sense defined above we can use the Spearman Brown correction formula to estimate the reliability of the full length test. This formula reads as follows:

$$r_f = \frac{2\ r}{1+r}$$

where r_f represents the reliability of the full-length test; and r is the correlation between the two sets of half scores. For example, if the half scores on a test are correlated .6, the reliability of the full-length test would be

$$(2 \times .6)/(1 + .6) \text{ or } .75.$$

The notion of a split half reliability led to development of what is perhaps the most popular single way to estimate internal consistency reliability: *coefficient alpha*. Coefficient alpha rests on the assumption that a test can be split in many different ways. If we split a test in all these ways, compute the correlations between all pairs of splits, and average the correlations, we have coefficient alpha. Fortunately, this involved process is not necessary. A relatively simple formula exists:

$$\alpha = \frac{n^2 \; \overline{cov}_{ij}}{SD^2_{test}}$$

where n equals the number of items in the test

$\overline{cov}_{ij}$ is the average covariance among the items;

and SD^2_{test} is the squared standard deviation of the test, or the test variance.

The covariance is an unstandardized correlation or the correlation between items multiplied by both items' standard deviation.

All three of these measures of reliability—parallel forms, corrected split half, and coefficient alpha, are reliability estimates that treat content differences in items on the measure as error. Since all three involve administration of a measure or two forms of a measure at a single point in time, stability, or lack thereof, is not treated as error.

Incidentally, the general form of the Spearman Brown formula is extremely useful. It reads as follows:

$$r_f = \frac{Kr}{1+(K-1)r}$$

where r_f is a full-length test as before

r is the reliability of the original set of items

K is the number of times by which a test's length is multiplied.

Assume, for example, that we have a three-item measure which has an internal consistency reliability of .50 and that we can develop six new equally good items (their intercorrelations or covariances are the same as those of the original three) to measure the concept. This nine-item measure will be three times as long as the original, and we want to estimate its reliability. Applying the Spearman Brown formula gives the following numbers:

$$r_f = \frac{3 \times 5}{1+(3-1).5} = \frac{1.5}{2.0} = .75$$

The nine-item test should have a reliability of .75. Or, alternatively, we have a 30-item test with a reliability of .90 and we would like to shorten this measure to 12 items. What would its reliability be? In this case, $n = 12/30$ or .4.

$$r_f = \frac{.4 \times .9}{1 + (.4 - 1).9} = \frac{.36}{.46} = .78$$

The short test has a reliability of .78 and we have saved time and space associated with 18 items.

These examples reveal a very interesting characteristic of these kinds of estimates of the internal reliability of a test or measure: the incremental reliability gained from adding items to a test or measure falls off rather quickly.

To see this, think for a moment of how many questions you would want to have on your final exam so that you would feel comfortable that the exam was reliable. One question, five questions, 25 questions, 125 questions? Five questions is certainly better than one, and 15 would be better than 10; 20 is better than 15, and 25 better than 20. But notice that we know intuitively that the incremental reliability in going from

1 to 5 is greater than going from

5 to 10 which is greater than going from

10 to 15 which is greater than going from

15 to 20.

Thus, while length always does increase internal consistency reliability (when the added length is at least as reliable as what exists) more and more length must be added after a certain point to obtain equivalent benefits.

A third approach to reliability is to assess it with *parallel forms with a time interval* between administration of the forms. The correlation of the two resulting sets of scores will be the lowest estimate of reliability because both stability and content differences can produce differences across scores for the individuals taking the test. This approach is particularly appropriate when we want to assess performance rating criteria used to validate a selection instrument. Since we are interested in *predicting* the criterion, we must be certain that the criterion itself can be measured with some degree of stability. We also hope the performance rating is consistent across raters, which is similar to saying that the employee's performance is not dependent on the particular test or test item presented.

The last statement suggests that interrater reliability (particularly important in many predictor and criterion assessments) can be viewed as the internal consistency of a test. Interrater reliability is the correlation of the ratings from two raters; if we use the composite of those two ratings as our criterion, then we can correct the intercorrelation of the ratings with the Spearman Brown correction to estimate the reliability of the composite. Likewise, coefficient alpha can be computed for three or more raters.

An appropriate applied question at this point would be: what form of reliability should we use? The answer is that it depends on our intended use of an instrument or, as Cronbach, Gleser, Nanda, and Rajaratnam (1972) indicate, we must decide to what situations we intend to generalize. We indicated earlier and in Chapter 3, for example, that an appropriate reliability estimate for a performance rating criterion is interrater reliability with an "appropriate time interval" between ratings. The appropriate time interval depends on the period of time over which predictions about the criterion are to be made. For managers this could be three to five years; for short-order cooks, two weeks. When our primary interest is if our test measures a given set of content, then an internal consistency measure is required.

As we said at the beginning of the discussion of reliability, we are interested in reliability because it places limits on validity—the correlation of our measure with other measures or phenomena of interest. We can use our reliability estimates to estimate what the correlation among various measures would be if they were measured with perfect reliability. This estimate for two variables x and y is given as follows:

$$\hat{r}_{xy} = \frac{r_{xy}}{\sqrt{r_{xx}} \sqrt{r_{yy}}}$$

where $\hat{r}_{xy}$ is the estimated correlation for error-free measures, r_{xy} is the observed correlation, and r_{xx} and r_{yy} are the reliabilities of the two measures. Note that theoretically the true intercorrelation between two variables ought to be 1.00, but it will not be because of imperfectly reliable measures. For example, the highest correlation between two measures both of which are measured with a reliability of .80 would be .80. Hence, we say observed correlations are *attenuated* and the formula above is referred to as the *correction for attenuation.* Observed validity coefficients are typically corrected for unreliability of measurement in the criterion to estimate true validity. Corrections for lack of reliability in the predictor are not made because in using the predictor in any other situations, we will still have its unreliability.

Reliability can be used in still another way to examine the

FIGURE 5–13. *AN ILLUSTRATION OF THE METHOD OF ESTABLISHING A CONFIDENCE LIMIT AROUND AN OBSERVED SCORE BY MEANS OF ERROR DISTRIBUTIONS FOR TWO GIVEN TRUE SCORES.*

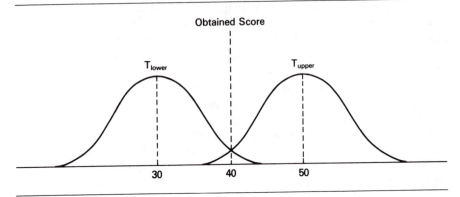

precision or confidence we can place in the fact that our test scores represent an individual's true level on some measurement. Theoretically, if it were possible to repeatedly give a test to some person and make each observation independently, not all measured values would be the same but they would distribute themselves around the true value of this person's tested ability. The standard deviation of this distribution is called the *standard error of measurement* and is given by the following formula:

$$\text{SEM} = \text{SD}_{\text{test}} \ \sqrt{1 - r_{xx}}$$

An interpretation of the standard error of measurement is given in Figure 5–13. Assume we have a person whose score on some test is 40 and the standard error of measurement is 5.00. The obtained score of 40 could be part of a distribution of scores for true values as different as 30 and 50 (given four standard errors would encompass about 96 percent of the cases). So we could say that an obtained score of 40 could be a result of a true score anywhere between 30 and 50. Examination of similar confidence limits for tests with very high reliabilities will usually indicate that any given score can be evidence of relatively different levels of true score on the part of a given person. The lesson of the standard error of measurement is that we exercise caution in statements about the scores we get on a particular individual and that we are cautious when we make comparisons of persons or scores. These cautionary statements are facilitated by many of the better test manuals now published in that they give confidence limits for various score levels.

Dimension Definition

Frequently, a personnel researcher collects or has available information on a large number of variables for which he or she might want a much more parsimonious explanation. Or, to put it another way, the researcher is interested in identifying a relatively small number of factors or dimensions that explain the correlations among a large number of variables. This might be true when we are working with a new selection instrument and have multiple items measuring four or five major definitions (we think) or when a variety of criterion data have been collected and we're interested in understanding the major dimensions of job performance. We often resort to a technique called *factor analysis* to define empirical dimensions that account for the correlations among our variables. In this section, we explain a relatively simple procedure using only correlations by which we can examine the dimensionality of a set of variables. Whether we use our approach or some more sophisticated approach, we feel the following discussion is instructive because it represents a combination of rational definitions of dimensions/scales with their empirical verification.

First, we recommend beginning by content analyzing the items —defining ahead of data analysis what we feel are the major dimensions. (If we are responsible for writing the items, they should be written to reflect the major dimensions of interest.) We then add up scores on the variables we believe define each of the hypothesized categories. Next we compute the following correlations: (1) coefficient alpha for each group of items; (2) the intercorrelation among the groups of items; (3) correlations between each item and all of the groups of items; and (4) correlations of each item with various demographics. An example of the type of analysis proposed is presented in Table 5–3.

In this hypothetical example, the researcher had available nine biographical items and four demographics—gender, age, job level, and job experience. Prior to the data analysis, the researcher decided the first three items indicated something about "Motivation" to work—items concerned the number of hours worked in high school, number of household chores performed at home, etc. The second set of three items dealt with the number of clubs/social organizations joined and the number of parties attended and the number of close friends the respondent reported having. These items were tentatively labeled "Sociability." The third set of items dealt with various leadership activities in which the respondent reported being engaged in so they were labeled "Leadership."

We indicated that coefficient alpha for each set of items should be computed as well as the intercorrelations of each of the item

TABLE 5–3. CONFIRMATORY ANALYSIS OF BIOGRAPHICAL INVENTORY.

	M1	M2	M3	S1	S2	S3	L1	L2	L3	M	S	L
M1	1.0											
M2	.4	1.0										
M3	.3	.5	1.0									
S1	.1	.2	.2	1.0								
S2	−.1	.0	.3	.5	1.0							
S3	−.2	.0	.1	.6	.3	1.0						
L1	.2	.2	1	.2	.3	.3	1.0					
L2	.3	.2	.1	.2	.1	.0	.4	1.0				
L3	.0	.2	.2	.3	.2	.1	.6	.5	1.0			
Motivation (M)[b]	.3	.4	.2	.1	.2	.0	.2	.3	.2	.67[a]		
Sociability (S)	.0	.1	.1	.4	.3	.4	.3	.2	.2	.11	.73[a]	
Leadership (L)	.1	.2	.2	.3	.2	.3	.4	.5	.4	.27	.30	.75[a]
Gender	.2	.3	.4	.0	−.01	.1	.3	.4	.3	.4	.0	.5
Age	.1	.2	.2	.0	−.1	.1	.3	.2	.2	.2	.0	.3
Job Level	−.1	−.1	.0	.3	.2	.3	.4	.3	.3	.0	.4	.4
Job Experience	.0	.1	.1	.3	.3	.3	.1	.1	.2	.1	.4	.1

[a]Coefficient alpha for motivation, sociability and leadership
[b]Those item-scale correlations which involve an item's correlation with itself are corrected for this overlap with the scale (see Magnusson, 1966, p.212).

sets. Alphas were .67, .73, and .75, and the scale intercorrelations of the three dimensions with each other were .11, .27, and .30. The relatively high alpha values and the low scale intercorrelations indicate that correlations among items within a set were high relative to item intercorrelations among items from different sets. In other words, our content definition of these items seems to be confirmed. Each item's correlations with the three dimensions is available in the rectangle in Table 5–3. Items belonging to a given group ought to correlate most highly with the dimension to which they belong. If not, we should reexamine the item content; perhaps the item should be included in a different dimension. In this set of data only one item's correlation (the third motivation item, M3) is questionable. It correlates .2 with Motivation but also .2 with Leadership.

Correlations of each item with the four demographics are examined to see if the items exhibit what has been termed *external parallelism.* This means that, for this example, the pattern of correlations of each of the Motivation items with the demographics should be similar. In our example, this is relatively true in that correlations with gender are relatively high, those with age are moderate, those with job level are low negative, and those with job experience are low positive. Examining the demographic correlations for both Sociability and Leadership items also reveals that some *external parallelism* exists.

If this type of analysis revealed any inconsistencies—low coefficient alphas and high intercorrelations among scales, item-scale correlations indicating misplacement of an item, or lack of external parallelism—item and dimension content should be reexamined. This may lead to regrouping items and a second analysis to examine whether the new item grouping better fits the observed data. Content and meaning should always guide the data analysis and the actual items should always be reported in written reports of this type of analysis. While our labels for the three scales may seem reasonable to us, some other investigator may provide a different interpretation.

Analyses such as those described in this section can be extremely helpful in a number of ways. First, they allow simplification; we can speak of major dimensions rather than individual items. But, more importantly, the grouping of items and our empirical verification of these groupings provide understanding about what is being measured that can frequently be used in personnel practices unrelated to the immediate staffing problem such as career planning and training.

Validity

Validity is the degree to which the inferences we draw about our test scores are correct. Correlation and regression analysis are used extensively in examining the relationship between the test scores on our instruments and measures of job performance. This approach to validity is called *criterion-related validity,* and we've already seen how correlation and regression can be used to make job performance predictions. In the next chapter, we extend our discussion of the concept of validity and identify various strategies by which personnel researchers attempt to establish the validity of their procedures.

SUMMARY

We began this chapter with a discussion of the levels of measurement with which we can assign numbers to persons or objects. Ways of summarizing measurements on many objects and methods of describing the degree of relationship between two or more measured variables (correlation) were described. Regression analysis with a single predictor and multiple predictors were outlined briefly.

Next we discussed reliability and its relationship to validity of measurement. Various types of reliability information as well as uses of reliability information were detailed. Finally, we described how we could use a relatively simple examination of correlations among scales and items to better describe and understand the measures we take. Throughout, we became aware of the absolutely central role of the correlation coefficient, r, in understanding the relationships *between* measures and the characteristics (reliability) of measures. It is critical that the reader grasp the origins of r in data, the degree to which r follows from means and standard deviations in terms of underlying mathematics, and its use as a foundation for much of the discussion in the rest of this book.

REFERENCES

Baker, B. O., Hardyck, C. D., and Petrinovich, L. F. (1966). Weak measurement vs. strong statistics: An empirical critique of S. S. Stevens' proscriptions on statistics. *Educational and Psychological Measurement, 26,* 291–309.

Cattin, P. (1980). Estimation of the predictive power of a regression model. *Journal of Applied Psychology, 65,* 407–414.

Conover, W. J. (1971). *Practical nonparametric statistics.* New York: Wiley.

Cronbach, L. J., Gleser, G. C., Nanda, H., and Rajaratnam, N. (1972). *The dependability of behavioral measurements: Theory of generalizability for scores and profiles.* New York: Wiley.

Hays, W. L. (1973). *Statistics for the social sciences.* New York: Holt, Rinehart, & Winston.

Lawshe, C. H., and Balma, M. J. (1966). *Principles of personnel testing, 2nd. ed.* New York: McGraw-Hill.

Magnusson, D. (1966). *Test theory.* New York: Addison-Wesley.

Mosier, C. I. (1951). Problems and design of cross-validation. *Educational and Psychological Measurement, 11,* 5–11.

Schmitt, N., Coyle, B. W., and Rauschenberger, J. M. (1977). A Monte Carlo evaluation of three formula estimates of cross-validated multiple correlation. *Psychological Bulletin, 84,* 751–758.

Stevens, S. S. (1946). On the theory of scales of measurement. *Science, 103,* 677–680.

6

VALIDATION STRATEGIES

AIMS OF THE CHAPTER

As we stated in the previous chapter, *validity* refers to the degree to which inferences made from predictor scores or other selection procedures are correct or accurate. For example, knowing the content of the Graduate Record Examination (GRE) and the demands of graduate school, one might look at students' scores on the GRE and infer for each student that he or she would do well in graduate school. If such inferences are correct (relatively speaking) more often than expected by chance alone, we would say that the GRE yields valid inferences about subsequent performance in graduate school.

Most books in measurement and industrial psychology and the Standards for Educational and Psychological Tests (APA, 1974) indicate that there are three "types" of validity: criterion-related, content, and construct validity. *Criterion-related* validity refers to the extent that scores on selection instruments are related to job performance measures. *Content* validity is the degree to which the responses required by the test items are a representative sample of the behaviors to be exhibited in some area of job performance about which we want to make inferences. *Construct* validity represents the degree to which test scores are consistent with our theoretical notions about what the test measures. For several reasons, this categorization of the different kinds of validity has produced considerable problems when psychologists attempted to explain validity to people not trained in test construction and validation. It has also been the source of considerable confusion among professionals themselves. Recently there has been recognition that the distinctions themselves are artificial.

We organized this chapter in the traditional manner by discussing, in turn, criterion-related, content, and construct validity. However, we argue that all validation work is really an aspect of construct validity; that is, a criterion-related validation study provides one piece of evidence concerning the construct validity of a test. Further, content validity, as usually defined, is not validity but an evaluation of the adequacy of test construction (Guion, 1977; Tenopyr, 1977). We also believe that care in insuring content validity, as traditionally defined, is a necessary precondition for construct validity. Because of the centrality of content validity to validity *per se* and because many organizations must rely on content validity when designing and using selection instruments, we discuss methods of test construction which are designed to insure content validity. We also discuss the legal status of the use of tests that have no

FIGURE 6-1.

	TIME ₁	TIME ₂
Concurrent validity	−Collect test data −Collect criterion data −Correlate test and criterion data (Study participants are job incumbents.)	
Predictive validity	−Collect test data from job applicants but do not use it to make hiring decisions.*	−Collect criterion data −Correlate test and criterion data

*Frequently, organizations employ a predictive design to evaluate criterion-related validity, but employ the test in making decisions, thereby producing a restriction in the range of predictor scores and, to the degree that the test is valid, in the criterion as well. The correlation computed between predictor and criterion in these instances will be an underestimate of criterion-related validity.

evidence of criterion-related validity; that is, using only evidence that the test behavior measured was important to job performance. Third, we outline the kinds of information used to assess the construct validity of a measure.

CRITERION-RELATED VALIDITY

Criterion-related validity applies when we want to infer from some measure of a person's attributes her or his standing on a criterion. The criterion in industrial applications is usually some measure of job performance. We are interested in predicting an individual's future level on the criterion from his or her current standing on a test. Even in the case of "job samples," the reason for using the job sample in hiring people is not that we are interested in their scores on the job sample but that we believe those scores are indicative of job performance later. It follows that when we intend to measure ability or aptitude, we are hypothesizing a relationship of ability to job performance, and in a criterion-related validity study, we are investigating the validity of that hypothesis, not the validity of the test (Guion, 1976). This would seem simple enough to establish: collect scores on the predictors to be evaluated, measure job performance, and correlate the two sets of measures. However, there are significant problems associated with criterion-related validity studies which make their feasibility problematic in many situations.

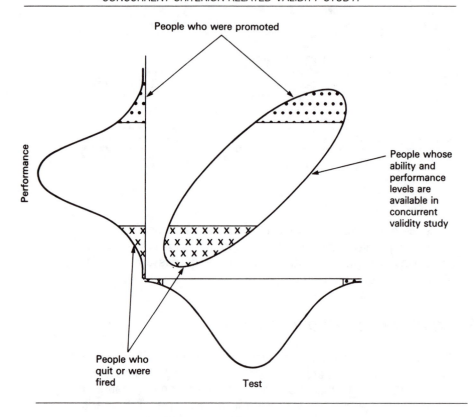

FIGURE 6–2. *RESTRICTION OF RANGE CAUSED BY LOW PERFORMING WORKERS BEING FIRED OR LEAVING (X X X X) AND HIGH PERFORMING WORKERS BEING PROMOTED (• • •) IN A CONCURRENT CRITERION-RELATED VALIDITY STUDY.*

People who were promoted

People whose ability and performance levels are available in concurrent validity study

Performance

People who quit or were fired

Test

Concurrent and Predictive Validity

There are two basic designs by which industrial psychologists have sought to establish the criterion-related validity of their instruments: *concurrent* and *predictive*. In a *concurrent validity* study, predictor and criterion data are collected at the same time from current employees. In a *predictive validity* study, selection data are collected on a group of applicants but not used for selection decisions. When it is possible to measure their subsequent job performance, the job performance data are correlated with the original scores on the selection procedures being evaluated. The difference between concurrent and predictive criterion-related validity studies is shown in Figure 6–1.

Industrial psychologists have nearly always preferred the predictive design if it is feasible. Concurrent studies were criticized because experience on the job might affect test scores and present employees would not approach the test with the same motivation or anxiety as would a job applicant. Further, problems result when (a) low-performing employees have left the firm and (b) the best-performing employees have been promoted, resulting in the collection of data on a group of employees whose job performance and test scores are much less variable than they would be for an unselected group. The latter problem scientists assumed should produce underestimates of the validity of tests through what is called a *restriction of range* problem (see Figure 6–2). However, actual empirical comparisons of validity coefficients derived from concurrent and predictive studies indicate they yield virtually identical estimates (Barrett, Phillips, & Alexander, 1981; Bemis, 1968; Schmitt, Gooding, Noe, & Kirsch, 1984).

Feasibility of Criterion-Related Validity Studies

Industrial psychologists have long preferred the use of criterion-related studies whether concurrent or predictive over the more judgmental approaches we will be discussing. However, in the last decade we've recognized that criterion-related studies are infeasible in many situations. Furthermore, we now recognize that judgment is also basic to criterion-related validity in that someone must decide what data will serve as criteria. If the criteria with which tests are correlated are not relevant (that is, contaminated or deficient in some manner as discussed in Chapter 3), then our estimates of the validity of the tests are also not appropriate.

In an excellent analysis of the feasibility of criterion-related validation studies, Schmidt, Hunter, and Urry (1976) examined the implications of both lack of criterion reliability and restriction of range in test validation research. Their basic point was that, given (a) the sample size available in most criterion-related studies, and (b) the modest usual level of validity, criterion reliability, and range restriction, the probability that we will find a statistically significant validity coefficient is very low. Their analyses were based on two formulae which quantify the problems of range restriction and criterion unreliability.

Above we noted that use of a predictor to make selection decisions means we can't evaluate the predictor-criterion relationship for the full range of individual differences. As shown in Figure 6–2, this was true because job performance scores of those persons with low test scores as well as those with high test scores will be unavailable. The portion of the scatterplot that is available for study is more nearly circular (recall from Chapter 5 that a circular scatterplot represents a correlation of zero), hence the estimate of validity in this situation will be lower than is actually the case. The diagram is intended to depict a concurrent study, but similar restriction very likely occurs in predictive studies as well. Organizations frequently use a predictive validation design but do not hire low-scoring persons or hire based on other criteria which are correlated with the predictor being studied.

As an example of the effect of restriction of range, consider a situation in which the true validity of a prediction for a population is .60, the standard deviation of scores of the applicant group on some test is 20, and the standard deviation of the test score of those selected is 10 (which would be true if the top 30 percent of all applicants were selected). The expected observed validity in this case can be estimated by modification of a formula provided by Thorndike (1949) for correction of range restriction:

$$r_{xy} = \frac{(s_r/s_u) R_{xy}}{\sqrt{(s_r/s_u)^2 R_{xy}^2 - R_{xy}^2 + 1}} = \frac{(10/20).60}{\sqrt{(10/20)^2.60^2 - .60^2 + 1}}$$

$$= .35 \qquad\qquad [6.1]$$

where:

s_r = standard deviation on the test for those selected

s_u = standard deviation on the test for all applicants

r_{xy} = observed validity of the test

R_{xy} = true validity of the test if calculated on the basis of hiring all applicants.

The formula and computations indicate that even though the true validity of the test is .60, a study conducted in this situation would yield an estimate of .35.

In addition, the validity of the test could be underestimated because the criterion against which the test is evaluated is not measured with perfect reliability. Assume a criterion reliability of .81. The correction for attenuation due to lack of reliability (recall our discussion of this issue in Chapter 5) and the calculation for our hypothetical situation is as follows:

$$r_{xy} = \sqrt{r_{yy}}\, r_{xyc} = \sqrt{.81}(.35) = .315 \qquad\qquad [6.2]$$

where:

r_{xy} = observed validity

r_{yy} = criterion reliability

r_{xyc} = validity after the correction for restriction of range.

These calculations, then, suggest that the actual observed validity given this relatively realistic set of data would be only .31. The problem with the expectation that our observed validity coefficient is going to be .31 as opposed to .60 is that a much larger sample size will be required for us to conclude that the coefficient is statistically significant. In tests of criterion-related validity, we are testing the hypothesis that the validity is greater than chance ($r = .00$). If we fail to find a coefficient significant (see Chapter 5), as is more likely with a small sample size, we falsely conclude that the test is not predictive of job performance.

It is possible to calculate the sample sizes required in order to be reasonably confident of concluding that a validity coefficient of typical magnitude would be statistically significant (Schmidt, Hunter, & Urry; 1976). The results are often quite discouraging. For example, if we estimate the true validity coefficient to be 0.35, and we want a 90 percent probability of finding a significant result, our criterion measure has a reliability of 0.70, and we are selecting the top 30 percent of the applicants, the required sample size would be 428. It is also important to note that, aside from the issue of finding statistical significance, the underestimates of validity that result from range restriction and lack of criterion reliability lower our estimates of the utility of selection instruments (see Chapter 7 for a full discussion of utility).

Without going into the details, the conclusion of the Schmidt et al. work is straightforward: with the sample sizes we usually encounter (less than 100, see Lent, Aurbach, & Levin, 1971; Schmitt et al., 1984), researchers conducting a criterion-related validity study will have little chance of observing a significant validity coefficient. From their paper we can also derive a set of rules to use when deciding whether or not a criterion-related validity study is feasible.

1. Decide on the alpha-level. This is the probability that we conclude that a test is valid when it really is not. An alpha-level of .05 is the level most frequently used. However, if we are willing to increase this probability, say to 0.10, we will be able to reduce the necessary sample size.

2. Read the literature to decide what level of validity you can expect to find or make a determination of the level of validity you need to make the whole selection procedure worthwhile (see the utility discussion in Chapter 7).

3. Decide on an acceptable level of probability that you will conclude the test has no validity. That is, what is a reasonable probability that you will decide not to use a potentially worthwhile selection instrument?

4. Apply the following formula to determine the necessary sample size:

where:
$$N = \frac{(Z_1 - Z_2)^2}{E(F_z)^2} + 3 \qquad [6.3]$$

N = sample size

Z_1 = standard normal deviate corresponding to the alpha probability

Z_2 = standard normal deviate corresponding to the probability that we will not find a significant validity coefficient

$E(F_z)$ = Fisher Z equivalent of the expected validity coefficient after correction as above for restriction of range and criterion unreliability.

Fisher Z equivalents of correlations can be found in tables in most measurement books.

For example, assume the estimate of observed validity calculated above; namely, .315. Its Fisher Z equivalent is .326. Also assume the alpha-level is .05; Z is then 1.96. Finally, assume that we must be 90 per cent certain that we will detect a significant validity; Z is then -1.28. Solving for N in the equation above yields the following:

$$N = \frac{(1.96 - (-1.28))^2}{.326^2} + 3 = 102$$

So, we must have a sample of 102 or more to conclude that the criterion-related validity study is feasible within the levels of probability set above. Even when feasible, it may be more desirable to rely on the results of validity generalization studies outlined below to get the most accurate assessment of validity.

Given the implications of the Schmidt, Hunter, and Urry analysis, different strategies of test validation (content and construct) have become increasingly popular. Indeed, work on validity generalization (which is summarized in Chapter 8) should make it less obligatory to conduct criterion-related validation studies of tests that have been frequently validated for the same job for which some new test usage is proposed. Where existing validity evidence is substantial, it should be sufficient to show that use of a test to select people for a particular job is similar to the jobs and the criteria for which validity data are available.

There is another approach that solves the problem of small sample sizes. Some companies within a single industry (e.g., banking, electric utilities, and life insurance) cooperate in validation studies for jobs which are similar across the companies. Such consortium studies substantially increase the sample size available for any given job (see Schmidt, Hunter, & Caplan, (1981) as one example).

We do not believe, however, that criterion-related validation will, or ought to, be abandoned. We have sufficient evidence for validity generalization for only a few types of tests. Continued criterion-related validation of novel testing strategies with larger sample sizes, perhaps multi-organizational cooperative validation efforts, are needed and are currently being conducted.

Why Are Predictors that Should Be Valid Not Valid

Another issue requiring attention here conerns attempts to understand why predictors that *should* work don't, even when sample size, criterion reliability, and range restriction problems are minimal or nonexistent. Contextual factors may (a) permit a correlation between predictor and criterion but suppress preformance levels or (b) prevent a predictor from revealing a strong relationship to a criterion. The kind of investigation which represents the issue being presented here is what is called *process validation* by training researchers.

In the training literature, process validation refers to a focus on the process by which learning takes place as well as the outcomes the training is designed to achieve. Goldstein (1986), for example, reports on the learning experiment in which a particular pigeon's level of obtaining reinforcement was much lower than other pigeons in the cohort. The researcher observed the pigeon and discovered that, rather than pecking the key, the pigeon was running into the wall that held the key, and the crash into the wall was triggering the food dispensing mechanism.

It is clear that if pigeon strength is assessed as a predictor of reward attainment, then stronger pigeons can achieve higher levels of reward by running into walls than weaker pigeons can. It is also clear that stronger pigeons can outperform weaker pigeons by directly pecking the key and that, as a group, key-pecking pigeons will outperform the pigeons that run into walls. Finally, it is also clear that if wall-banging and key-pecking pigeons are undifferentiated in analysis, the relationship between pigeon strength and attainment of rewards is likely to be weak. The moral of the story is clear: it is possible that weak predictor-criterion relationships may be due to some individuals' running into walls (of various kinds), keeping them from performing up to their actual potential. This is precisely

FIGURE 6–3. *HOW RELATIONSHIPS BETWEEN PREDICTORS AND CRITERIA CAN BE THE SAME IN TWO OR MORE GROUPS WITH DIFFERING LEVELS OF PERFORMANCE BETWEEN GROUPS. NOTE THE DOTTED LINE AROUND THE SCATTERPLOTS FOR BOTH KEY-PECKING PIGEONS AND WALL-BANGING PIGEONS IS REPRESENTATIVE OF WHAT WE WOULD OBTAIN IF THE TWO GROUPS WERE UNDIFFERENTIATED. THIS DOTTED SCATTERPLOT IS MORE CIRCULAR, INDICATING A LOWER VALIDITY COEFFICIENT.*

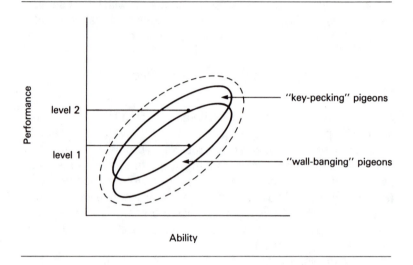

what we meant in Chapter 4 when we discussed constraints on performance (Peters and O'Connor, 1980). While in appropriate subgroups validities may be equal, studies conducted *across* groups (departments, organizations) may yield lower validities. When overall unit or organizational performance is of interest, equal validities may be a relatively unimportant index of the relative effectiveness of personnel selection practices. This phenomenon is shown in Figure 6–3.

The search for contextual factors that moderate predictor-criterion relationships has been a failure; there seem to be none (Schneider, 1978a; 1978b; 1983). But the reasons these factors don't exist is that it was assumed that the effect of contextual issues was to suppress correlations. That is, true moderators were sought wherein it was expected that the predictor-criterion relationship in one context would be shown to be significantly different from the relationship in another context. In fact, the more likely outcome was that the relationships (slopes) were the same in the two contexts, but the levels of performance on the criteria differed, as shown in Figure 6–3. So when we remove barriers to employee performance, we can expect *all* employees to perform better, not just some subgroup or organization.

Test Fairness Issues

Since the passage of the Civil Rights Act of 1964 and the increased frequency with which hiring decisions are challenged in the courts, there has been a rapid accumulation of research on possible ethnic differences in the predictive meaning of test scores. The large majority of such studies have dealt with black Americans (see Schmidt, Berner, & Hunter, 1973) though an increasing number of studies on other ethnic groups (Schmidt, Pearlman, & Hunter, 1980) as well as male-female differences are now available (Reilly, Zedeck, & Tenopyr, 1979; Schmitt, Mellon, & Bylenga, 1978). The problems investigated are generally subsumed under the heading of *test bias.* The main questions raised regarding test bias pertain to validity coefficients (referred to as *slope bias*) and to the relationship between group means on the test and the criterion (referred to as *intercept bias*). Current examination of these questions treats them as part of a general "differential prediction" problem (Linn, 1978).

Studies of differential prediction involve examining the regression equations computed separately for ethnic groups. Using this approach we subgroup study participants on the basis of sex, race, or ethnic group and then compute and compare regression slopes, intercepts, and standard errors of estimate (see Chapter 5 for an example of these computations). According to Cleary (1968):

> A test is biased for members of a subgroup of the population if, in the prediction of a criterion for which the test was designed, consistent non-zero errors of prediction are made for members of the subgroup. In other words, the test is biased if the criterion score predicted from the common regression line is consistently too high or too low for members of the subgroup. With this definition of bias, there may be a connotation of "unfair," particularly if the use of the test produces a prediction that is too low. If the test is used for selection, members of a subgroup may be rejected when they were capable of adequate performance (p. 115).

While other definitions of bias exist (Schmidt & Hunter, 1974; Cascio, 1982), most professionals, as well as the Uniform Guidelines on Employee Selection Procedures, endorse the Cleary model (Ledvinka, 1979).

When prediction systems are compared in this fashion, the most frequently occurring difference is in intercepts—the differences between "wall-banging" and "key-pecking" pigeons in Figure 6–3 are intercept differences. In one review, researchers found significant intercept differences in about 18 percent of 1190 racial group comparisons and slope differences in 5 percent of the comparisons (Bartlett, Bobke, Mosier, & Hannan, 1978). In the few instances in which differences are observed, we commonly find that the prediction system for the nonminority group slightly overpredicts minority group performance. That is, minorities would tend to do less well on the job than their test scores indicate.

In Figure 6–4 we illustrate the regression approach to examining the possibility of differential prediction given the usual research findings, namely, overprediction of minority job performance using a common regression line (in which a single regression equation is computed for all study participants). Note that use of the minority regression equation to predict minority job performance for the one test score level illustrated would yield a predicted value of P_{min}. If we used a common regression line or the majority regression equation to make predictions for the same test score, we would obtain higher predicted performance values; in this case, P_c or P_{maj}. The differences between P_c and P_{min} and P_{maj} and P_{min} represent overprediction. Similar analyses for other possibilities of subgroup differential prediction are available in Anastasi (1982) and Cascio (1982) and an excellent analysis of actual subgroup differences in prediction is represented in a paper by Gael, Grant, and Ritchie (1975).

While it is reassuring to know that differential prediction does not occur often when subgroups are compared, few data are really available for other than black-white comparisons. Continued examination of the possibility of differential prediction given substantial subgroup sample sizes may be appropriate. Remember also that the Cleary definition of test bias places a heavy burden on the fairness of criterion measurement. The definition indicates a test is fair if test score differences are reflected in differences in job performance. If the job performance measure is itself biased, and the predictor similarly biased, then we may simply be predicting criterion bias. In Chapter 3 we also identified this problem and labeled it predictor-related bias.

The Courts and Test Use

In this section we outline briefly some of the impact the legal system has had on employment decisions and the way criterion-related validation studies are evaluated by the courts. A later section in this chapter outlines legal considerations relevant to content validation *per se;* though similar issues, for example, the adequacy of job analyses, are relevant in both types of validation efforts. We also

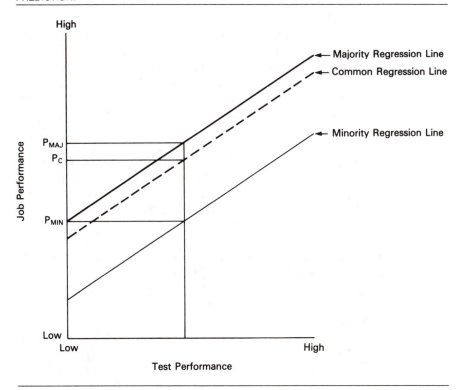

think it is important to note at the outset of this section that many of the court decisions and/or legal "guidelines" are not necessarily consistent with good professional practice. In 1964, President Johnson signed the Civil Rights Act which was further amended in 1972. The Act includes several "titles" which forbid discrimination in various sectors of our society such as education, federally assist- ed programs, and the right to vote. Title VII deals with discrimination in employment making it illegal for an organization with more than fifteen employees or a labor union or an employment agency "to fail, refuse to hire, discharge any individual, or otherwise to dis- criminate against any individual with respect to his compensation terms, conditions, or privileges of employment because of the in- dividual's race, color, religion, sex, or national origin." Title VII also established the Equal Employment Opportunity Commission (EEOC) to investigate and bring about conciliation between parties. The 1972 amendment extended coverage of Title VII to state and governmental institutions and to educational institutions, and it gave the EEOC authority to bring direct action in U.S. district courts against organizations. The latter had the effect of giving the EEOC some real power.

By itself, Title VII may have done little to change employment practices. However, several other events or series of events brought about significant change in the way personnel procedures are enacted in organizations. First, in 1965, President Johnson issued Executive Order 11246 which imposed obligations on governmental contractors to insure nondiscrimination of the type provided for in Title VII. Specifically, this order stated that the contractor will not discriminate against any employee or applicant for employment because of race, color, religion, sex, or national origin. The contractor will take affirmative action to insure that applicants are employed, and that applicants are treated during employment without regard to race, color, religion, or national origin. The directive applied to all federal contractors supplying a service to a governmental agency with payment in excess of $10,000. The directive not only prohibited discrimination but also required affirmative action efforts as well. The Office of Federal Contract Compliance (OFCC), which was established by the Johnson directive, proceeded to issue guidelines and timetables designed to increase minority hiring.

A second important event was the publication by EEOC of guidelines on employee selection procedures, the last revision of which is called the Uniform Guidelines on Employee Selection Procedures (1978). While this document carries the title "guideline", it has been given extraordinarily careful attention by organizations because courts have alluded to the Guidelines in deciding employment discrimination cases. In this context, the Uniform Guidelines have nearly become laws. To explain why this is so, we turn next to the concept of case law and its development in the area of employment testing.

Cases in which alleged discrimination occurs are first tried in district courts. (We describe only the federal court system; similar systems apply in most states. A case decided in a state supreme court can be appealed to a federal district court). Employment discrimination cases are tried and evidence is presented before a single federal judge who writes the decision. Either party in the case has the right of appeal to a circuit court consisting of three judges. Finally, a case can be appealed to the U.S. Supreme Court where nine justices make a decision on cases they consider most important. This court structure is illustrated in Figure 6–5, taken from Arvey (1979).

Obviously, Title VII did not and could not specify all the possibilities and problems in any given employment discrimination

FIGURE 6-5. *FEDERAL COURT SYSTEM.*

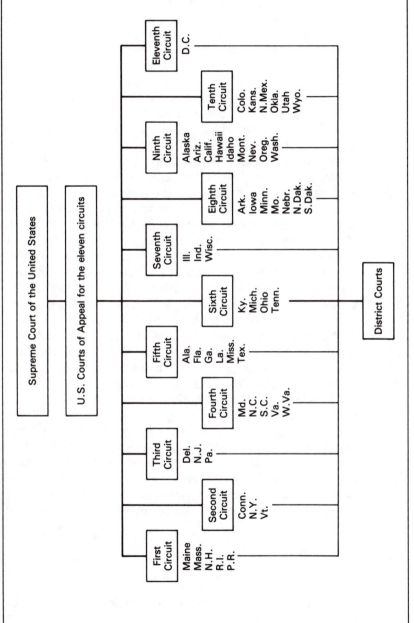

From Arvey, (1979).

case, so much of the implication of Title VII was left for the courts to develop as they decided specific cases. Once a judgment is made on a specific case, however, an attempt is made in subsequent judgments on similar cases in that district, or in other districts when the decision is reached at the Circuit level, to be consistent. Hence, different *case laws* may develop in different Circuit Courts. Until the Supreme Court decides a significant number of these cases dealing with different issues, the potential for a lack of uniformity in the way Title VII is, or was, enacted exists.

In court cases involving employment discrimination, a fairly typical sequence of events occurs. The plaintiff who brings the charge of discrimination has the responsibility of establishing *adverse impact*. To demonstrate adverse impact, one must demonstrate that a protected class is being treated in some fashion that places that class in an unfavorable position compared to the majority group, for example, being denied employment at a more frequent rate than the majority is denied employment. One important issue in determining adverse impact is how different the rates of hiring from majority and minority groups must be for the court to conclude that adverse impact has occurred. Several different ways of presenting this evidence have been provided but possibly the most consistently applied criterion is the *four-fifths rule*. As stated in the Uniform Guidelines, adverse impact is defined as "a selection rate for any race, sex, or ethnic group which is less than four-fifths (4/5) (or eighty percent) of the rate for the group with the highest rate" (Uniform Guidelines, p. 38297). In Table 6–1 we give a computational example of data that would and would not be taken as adverse impact under the four-fifths rule.

A second problem in establishing the presence or absence of adverse impact is in determining what comparisons should be made in computing the four-fifths rule. If a company has a history or reputation for discriminatory hiring practices, it is likely that few minority persons will apply, so it has been argued that the number hired/number of applicants ratio in adverse impact calculations be replaced by a proportion of the minority group available in the local job market. In this context, a number of issues have been argued:

1. the definition of the "relevant" qualified labor market;
2. the proper geographical scope;
3. the proper time frame;
4. the sample size necessary to establish a case.

Assuming adverse impact exists, the defendant must provide evidence concerning the job relatedness or business necessity of the selection techniques used. It is interesting to note that in the presence of adverse impact, the defendant must prove its inno-

A. Adverse Impact by Four-Fifth Rule

	Majority Statistics	Minority Statistics
Number of Job Applicants	200	75
Number Hired	80	15
Hiring Rate	80/200 = .40	15/75 = .20

Ratio of Minority Rate to Majority Rate = .20/.40 = .50

B. Lack of Adverse Impact as Defined by Four-Fifths Rule

	Majority Statistics	Minority Statistics
Number of Job Applicants	200	50
Number Hired	80	18
Hiring Rate	80/200 = .40	18/50 = .36

Ratio of Minority Rate to Majority Rate = .36/.40 = .90

cence in the discrimination charge, the exact opposite of what is true in other legal situations in our system. In the absence of adverse impact, an organization could, theoretically, use a coin toss to select employees without violating case law or the Uniform Guidelines. Most of the argument in employment discrimination cases and most of the text in the Uniform Guidelines is directed toward a discussion of what is or is not job related. While it is clearly beyond the scope of this book to review case law in this area, we will describe the Supreme Court cases on employment discrimination. Given the primacy of the Supreme Court in the development of case law, this will provide both an illustration of the issues and cases the courts have dealt with and the type of "guidelines" case law provides.

The first Supreme Court case involving employment discrimination was decided in 1971 and has become known as the Griggs vs. Duke Power case. Prior to the passage of the Civil Rights Act, Duke Power had used a high school diploma as a prerequisite for transfer from the general labor pool to other organizational departments. When Title VII became effective, Duke Power began to use the Wonderlic Personnel Test and the Bennett Mechanical Comprehension Test to select people for such transfers. To "pass" these two tests, employees had to score at or above the median of high school graduates nationwide. The district court and the circuit court found in favor of Duke Power on the ground that the high school diploma and test score requirements were applied in the same manner to both whites and blacks. However, the Supreme Court reversed the lower courts' findings and in their written decision made several points which were extremely important in all subsequent employment discrimination cases:

1. The Court noted that intent to discriminate was irrelevant, that the Civil Rights Act referred to overt discrimination. Congress, the Court stated, had meant the Act to apply to the consequences of employment practices, not simply their motivation.
2. Employment practices which operated to exclude black persons must be shown to be job related, otherwise they are in violation of Title VII.
3. The Court stipulated that the employer has the burden of showing that employment practices are job related. Given the resource requirements necessary to conduct an adequate validation study, this finding was of significant practical importance.
4. Finally, the Court gave special credibility to the EEOC guidelines mentioned above. The Court stated that the administrative interpretations of the Act by EEOC were entitled to "great deference." Subsequent lower court cases frequently used the Guidelines as standards by which to judge employment procedures.

In the next case involving employment discrimination, the Supreme Court dealt primarily with what the employer must show to establish that tests with adverse impact are sufficiently job related so as to survive a Title VII challenge. In the Albemarle vs. Moody (1975) case, the plaintiffs challenged the company's use of a verbal intelligence test and the Wonderlic Personnel Test in making promotions. The company had employed an industrial psychologist who conducted a concurrent validation study in which relationships were established between test scores and supervisors' judgments of job performance for job groupings in the middle and top of the plant's skilled promotional ladders. The tests were used in 13 different lines of progression. Significant correlations were found for the verbal intelligence test for three of 13 job groupings and in seven job groupings for the Wonderlic test and for two job groupings for the battery consisting of both tests. While the district court found in favor of the company, the Circuit Court and the Supreme Court ruled with the plaintiffs. In writing their decision, the Supreme Court made the following important points:

1. The tests were not equally valid for all jobs. Even if the study were adequate, the Court, quoting from the guidelines, noted

that a test may be used in jobs other than those for which it has been professionally validated only if there are no significant differences among the jobs. Since no systematic job analysis had been done, there was no basis on which to make statements about the similarity or dissimilarity of the jobs.

2. The Court questioned the supervisory performance ratings used as criteria in the validation study. The Court felt that there was no way of knowing precisely what criteria of job performance the supervisors were considering or whether any of the supervisors applied a "focused and stable body of criteria of any kind."

3. The study focussed on jobs at the top of the career ladder while the tests were used to select for entry-level jobs.

4. The study participants were white, experienced workers while the tests were given to young, inexperienced applicants who were frequently black. Further, the company did not show that it was technically infeasible to study whether the tests were differentially valid for whites and blacks.

5. Finally, throughout its written decision the Court quoted from the EEOC guidelines. In fact, Chief Justice Burger expressed his reservation concerning the degree to which the Court had relied on the Guidelines, in this case the 1970 version.

Several aspects of this decision were not consistent with the results of scientific research cited in various parts of this book, though it was likely true that the organization's validation study in this case was not well done. For example, the jobs for which the tests were validated were similar; therefore, one would expect the same validity. Some or all of the differences in validities across jobs were likely due to sampling error. Also, there is substantial evidence indicating no difference among ethnic groups in the validity of tests; therefore, the demand that differential validity be examined was not appropriate. Further, the court seemed to object to performance ratings as criteria. While industrial psychologists recognize the limitations of ratings, they are the criterion of choice in most situations. Unfortunately, while criticisms of individual validation efforts may be appropriate, the logic of case law is such that inappropriate generalizations to *all* use of tests or criteria are sometimes made.

A third case, Washington vs. Davis, was decided in 1976. Use of a verbal ability test to select police recruits was challenged. The Police Department provided a validation study which showed that scores on the test were related to the average score recruits received in the department's training school. The Supreme Court found in favor of the Police Department; their most important statement in their decision was that use of training success as a criterion in a validation study was acceptable provided the training program itself had been validated in some way.

Two Supreme Court decisions, Bakke vs. California and Weber vs. Kaiser Aluminum, have investigated allegations of reverse discrimination. That is, white persons were challenging an organization's alleged favored treatment of minority individuals. In Bakke, the Court decided in favor of the plaintiff who was granted admission to medical school, but in Weber, the Court decided in favor of the organization's special training to provide accelerated promotional opportunities to minorities.

In the final case to be discussed, Connecticut vs. Teal, the Court ruled that all steps of a selection process are open to scrutiny and that examination of the final result of the hiring process (the bottom-line) is not sufficient. Previously, organizations might have found that certain aspects of a hiring process (for example, use of standardized tests) produced adverse impact. In those cases, subsequent steps were taken to remove any adverse impact in terms of those individuals who were actually hired. In Connecticut vs. Teal the Court ruled that each step of the hiring process could be examined for evidence of adverse impact. If adverse impact were present, then the employer would need to show evidence of validity.

In summary, these cases have established some principles. A finding that adverse impact has occurred is the first step and represents a *prima facie* case of discriminatory practice. Second, in the presence of adverse impact, employers must show test procedures are job related. In showing job relatedness, special attention should be given to the EEOC Guidelines, though there is recent evidence that courts are paying more attention to professional guidelines on testing such as the *Principles on Test Validation and Use* published by the Society for Industrial/Organizational Psychology of the American Psychological Association. Very few other general statements concerning right and wrong practices including those involving issues of possible reverse discrimination are possible.

Summary

In this section on criterion-related validity, we learned that, generally speaking, predictive and concurrent validity studies tend to yield similar results. However, based on a considerable amount of research and theory, it turns out that good criterion-related validity studies are less feasibly conducted than was once thought. For the most part, lack of feasibility is a function of the small sample sizes typically available for such studies. But other factors, like criterion unreliability and restriction of range, may be important as well. Also, pooling data from similar jobs in similar industries, through consortium studies or validity generalization work, might be a solution to small sample problems.

An extensive discussion of fairness and legal issues in testing revealed that the courts tend to be first concerned with adverse impact and then appropriateness of the selection process a company uses. As will be emphasized in the next section, the courts have been particularly concerned with the job relevance of selection procedures when considering the issue of appropriateness.

CONTENT VALIDITY

The APA Standards (1974) state that evidence of content validity is required when the test user wishes to estimate how a person performs in the universe of situations the measure (test or criterion) is intended to represent. This universe of situations in the employment context must include job behaviors. Content validity is usually a concern when people construct knowledge or achievement tests. However, a similar concern should guide the construction of personality and aptitude tests as well as the criteria of job performance that staffing researchers use as standards to evaluate tests in criterion-related validity studies. In all cases, *content validity refers to the degree to which the test items are a representative sample of behaviors to be exhibited in some performance domain.* Consequently:

1. The performance domain must be carefully specified,
2. The objectives of the test user must be clearly formulated,
3. The method of sampling from the possible performance domain must be adequate.

The importance of these steps is underscored by Ebel's position (1977) that content validity is essential to the basic intrinsic meaning of any measure. Following Ebel's position, it must be restated that not only predictor but also criterion measures must possess content validity. This makes content validity concerns important in every criterion-related validation effort.

An outline of the steps involved in the construction of predictors is presented below and follows closely that presented by Lindvall and Nitko (1975).

Test Construction to Insure Content Validity

Procedures designed to insure the content validity of tests have been detailed most adequately for achievement and knowledge tests in education. The characteristics necessary to insure the content validity of educational achievement tests are:

1. The classes of behaviors that define different achievement levels are specified as clearly as possible before the test is constructed.
2. Each behavior class is defined by a set of test situations (that is, test items or test tasks) in which the behaviors and all their important nuances can be displayed.
3. Given that the classes of behavior have been specified and that the test situations have been defined, a representative sampling plan is designed and used to select the test tasks that will appear on any form of the test.
4. The obtained score must be capable of being referenced objectively and meaningfully to the individual's performance characteristics in these classes of behavior (Lindvall & Nitko, 1975, p. 76).

The application of content validation procedures to educational tests has been relatively straightforward. The educational curriculum identifies a body of knowledge and instructional objectives, and in educational circles it is generally agreed that asking a question about specific knowledge is an adequate way to measure that knowledge. When the entire set of possible questions is asked, the sum of the correct answers is taken as the level of people's knowledge. When using samples of the entire set of possible items as a test, we infer something about the proportion of the total set of possible items people would have answered correctly. Further, educational researchers have a valuable tool in the Taxonomy of Educational Objectives (Bloom, 1956) which is intended to describe and classify all possible educational objectives. These objectives can be combined with specific course content to construct tests by making decisions about the varying importance of the different objectives and the different content areas. An example of this procedure is best presented in tabular form as in Figure 6–6. In this particular plan for an achievement test on measurement concepts and tools, the concepts of validity and reliability are shown to be equally important (both are assessed with 40 test items). Application of these concepts is the most important educational objective in this plan, while Analysis, Synthesis, and Evaluation are relatively unimportant.

In applications of content validation to personnel selection, however, this approach is more ambiguous because performance domains have not been as clearly specified for many jobs. It is

TEST PLAN FOR A COURSE IN MEASUREMENT. [a]   FIGURE 6–6.

TEST CONTENT

Educational Objective[b]	Reliability	Validity	Item Analysis	Total
Knowledge	10	10	5	25
Comprehension	10	10	2	22
Application	15	20	12	47
Analysis	2	0	1	3
Synthesis	2	0	0	2
Evaluation	1	0	0	1
Total	40	40	20	

[a]Provided as an example only. An actual plan may involve more detail in both content and objectives. The numbers in the blocks of the table represent the number of test items and, assuming equal item variability, are indices of the importance of particular content areas.

[b]The objectives listed are from the *Taxonomy of Educational Objectives* (Bloom, 1956). These objectives are universal in that they cover all potential objectives of achievement tests.

necessary, then, to be more creative in constructing tests and test items.

Mussio and Smith (1973) have indicated the five components necessary for adequate content validation of personnel selection instruments. Because of their importance, we present an extended discussion of each.

1. *Thorough and reliable job analysis.* This job analysis is conducted with individuals who have considerable knowledge about the position under study and is designed to identify the knowledge and skills and/or tasks required for satisfactory job performance and their relative importance within the position.

In Mussio and Smith's (1973) own work, they used a combination of three of the job analysis methods discussed in Chapter 3: the critical incident approach, the functional job analysis approach, and Primoff's job element approach. While the first two approaches focus on a description of what the worker does on the job or what the job calls for in terms of worker behavior, the job element approach involves a direct listing of the knowledge, skills, and abilities. The purposes of the job analysis in content validation work are to: (a) identify and describe the primary tasks performed on the job; (b) determine the knowledge, skills, abilities, and personal characteristics required of the worker performing these specific tasks, and their relative importance; and (c) the substantiation of the required knowledge, skills, abilities, and personal characteristics by collecting descriptions of actual occurrences of effective and ineffective behavior resulting from the possession or lack of a particular knowledge, skill, ability, or personal characteristic.

Task statements are developed from existing job descriptions, manuals, training materials, observations of people performing the job, and interviews with job incumbents and supervisors. A meeting with a group of job experts can then be held to review the accuracy and completeness of the task statements and to list the knowledge, skills, abilities, and personal characteristics needed to carry out each task. In listing each new requirement the group is asked to justify the requirement in terms of an incident which resulted from the relative possession or lack of the knowledge, skill, or ability requirement.

After job analysts have had an opportunity to review the lists of tasks to be performed and the requirements in the form of knowledge, skills, and abilities for completeness and clarity, another group meeting is called for purposes of final review and modification, if any is required. The list of knowledge, skill, and ability requirements are then reviewed against three criteria: (a) Is it essential that newly hired employees have the particular requirement; (b) Can this particular requirement be quantified and how; and (c) Do varying amounts of the requirement result in varying degrees of performance effectiveness? If the answer to the first two questions is "Yes" but the answer to the third question is "No," as might be the case if we were considering the requirement for color vision in reading color-coded information, then the element is used only on a pass-fail basis. The remaining knowledge, skills, and abilities are arranged in major categories using a "bids" system. Specifically, raters are asked to distribute 100 points among the major categories to indicate their relative importance. The same procedure is used to weight sub-elements in each major category. In effect, the job incumbents are drawing up test specifications using a procedure similar to that illustrated in Figure 6–6. It is now clear why we paid so much attention to job analysis in Chapter 3; not only does it provide the foundation for performance appraisal but it also is the basis for content validation of proposed predictors of performance.

2. *Construction of the examination.* The second phase of a content validation strategy is the actual construction of the predictor. The results of the weighting exercise outlined above determine the content areas which should be examined. In constructing the test, we must be concerned whether the examination format conforms as closely as possible to the job task. The more closely the actual performance required on the job is to the behavior actually tested, the more likely it is that the required knowledges, skills, and abilities are being measured. An example of the presumed content validity of several possible test formats to measure the "ability to relate verbally to persons of varied socioeconomic levels" is graphed in Figure 6–7. One problem in developing actual job samples or using previous work experience as a basis for assuming

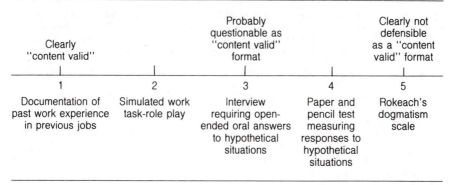

THE "CONTENT VALIDITY" OF VARIOUS TEST FORMATS AS POSSIBLE MEASURES OF THE ABILITY TO RELATE TO MEMBERS OF VARIED SOCIOECONOMIC LEVELS.

FIGURE 6-7.

Clearly "content valid"		Probably questionable as "content valid" format		Clearly not defensible as a "content valid" format
1	2	3	4	5
Documentation of past work experience in previous jobs	Simulated work task-role play	Interview requiring open-ended oral answers to hypothetical situations	Paper and pencil test measuring responses to hypothetical situations	Rokeach's dogmatism scale

From Campbell, (1973).

content validity is that some candidates—usually young or minority applicants—may not have the requisite experience. Simulations have been employed in tests defined as content valid and the courts have generally dealt favorably with their use and the content validity defense (Perticone & Wiesen, 1979). Probably the most common use of simulations as content valid instruments is their use in the assessment center (see Chapter 8), an extensive simulation of management tasks used in evaluating potential managers. Oral interviews in which questions are carefully prepared to reflect and elicit candidate reports of job relevant behavior are perhaps the last point on our graph at which it would seem defensible to say that the procedure has content validity. In some cases, answers to hypothetical situations may be useful in measuring job knowledge and predicting job behavior (Latham, Saari, Pursell, & Campion, 1980). More details on these kinds of predictors are presented in Chapters 9 and 10.

As well as matching the format of a predictor to the performance requirements of the job, the test constructor must also use communication devices or techniques that are consistent with the requirements of the job. For example, when written tests are used, the reading requirements should match those necessary to read job-related manuals or instructions. When the intent of a test is to measure the ability to perform physical aspects of a job, then the instructions should be clearly understood by all examinees. Reading ease formulas are available to make appropriate assessments of reading difficulty (Flesch, 1949; McLaughlin, 1969) and are easily applied as shown in Table 6-2.

TABLE 6–2. *APPLICATION OF FLESCH READING EASE FORMULA TO A SHORT TEXT.*

Text

After its purchase, the corporate management of the Weldon Company was taken over by Harwood, but the plant manager and the managerial and supervisory staffs in the Weldon plant were retained. A few additional supervisors were appointed subsequently. The Weldon plant is located in Williamsport, Pennsylvania and employs approximately 800 employees.

1. Count the word length in syllables and compute an average word length, then multiply by 100.

   Total Number of Syllables = 102
   Total Number of Words   = 51
   Average Word Length   =   2.0
   Multiply by 100   = 200.0

2. Compute the average number of words in each sentence.

   Total Number of Words   = 51
   Total Number of Sentences = 3
   Average Sentence Length   = 17.0

3. Compute the Reading Ease Formula as Follows:

   R.E. = 206.835 − .846 (100 × Average Word Length) − 1.05 (Average Sentence Length)
        = 206.835 − 169.2 − 17.85
        = 19.785

4. Refer to the table below to determine the level of reading difficulty represented by this text.

PATTERN OF "READING EASE" SCORES

"Reading Ease" Score	Description of Style	Typical Magazine	Syllables per 100 Words	Average Sentence Length in Words
0 to 30	Very difficult	Scientific	192 or more	29 or more
30 to 50	Difficult	Academic	167	25
50 to 60	Fairly difficult	Quality	155	21
60 to 70	Standard	Digests	147	17
70 to 80	Fairly easy	Slick-fiction	139	14
80 to 90	Easy	Pulp-fiction	131	11
90 to 100	Very easy	Comics	123 or fewer	8 or fewer

Of course, examinations should represent good test construction principles as outlined by such publications as Adkins-Wood (1961) and Thorndike (1971). One list of do's and don'ts in multiple choice item writing for paper and pencil tests is included as Table 6–3. Many of these guidelines apply to paper and pencil items not written in multiple choice format as well. The guidelines for constructing simulations, interviews, and exercises have not been as clearly specified.

Generally speaking, this discussion of the construction of predictors has emphasized two issues: (1) the criticality of the job analysis and (2) the relationship between the actual job behaviors and the behaviors measured by the proposed predictor of job

1. Make sure the stem and each alternative are grammatically correct and consistent with each other.
2. Make the question as simple and specific as possible.
3. Avoid technical terms unless the job analysis specifically indicates a need for it.
4. Make each of the alternatives about equal in length.
5. Insure that the stem and each alternative have equal reading levels.
6. Avoid negatives, both in the stem and the alternatives—if you use negatives, underline them to draw attention to that part of the item.
7. Be sure only one of the alternatives is right.
8. Make each of the incorrect alternatives believable.
9. Avoid repeating words in the alternatives—include them in the stem.
10. Do not give answers to questions as a part of other questions.
11. Do not give clues to the correct answer within the stem.
12. Make each of the wrong alternatives separate and distinct. Do not offer the wrong alternative in different forms in different alternatives.
13. Make sure the wrong answers do not overlap with another.
14. Try to construct all the alternatives so they differ from the correct answer in about the same way.
15. As a general rule, do not construct wrong answers that are direct opposites of the correct answer.

performance. In general, we can state that the more the predictor is psychologically similar to the criterion, the more the predictor is content valid. By "psychologically similar" we mean that the predictor makes the same kinds of psychological demands on an applicant as the job will make on a worker. Trainers refer to psychological similarity as *psychological fidelity*—the overlap of the training with the requirements of on-the-job performance (Goldstein, 1986). We can use the same analogy for the overlap of a predictor with on-the-job requirements. In the next section, we present a strategy for quantifying this overlap.

   3. *Calculating the job relevance of a test: the Lawshe procedure.* After content selection and examination construction, the items on the exam should be reviewed by a panel of experts in the content area represented by the test. Mussio and Smith (1973) provide scales by which these judges can evaluate the job relevancy, accuracy (of the situation presented and the alternative answers if a multiple choice question), and the fairness of the item (manner of presentation). Of most importance of course is job relevance.

   Lawshe (1975) proposed that a *content validity ratio* (CVR) be calculated from the independent relevancy ratings of the expert judges. Each judge is asked to indicate whether the knowledge, skill, or ability measured by the item is essential, useful but not essential, or not necessary to the performance of the job. The CVR for each item is then computed using the following formula:

FIGURE 6–8. *JOB ANALYSIS AND CONTENT VALIDITY.*

IMPORTANCE OF KSAs TO JOB PERFORMANCE
(FROM JOB ANALYSIS)

		Not Important	Important
REPRESENTATION IN SELECTION INSTRUMENT	Not Represented	A	B
	Represented	C	D

$$CVR = \frac{(n_e - N/2)}{N/2} \qquad [6.4]$$

where n_e equals the number of judges indicating the item was essential and N is the total number of judges. Items are then eliminated if most of the judges do not indicate the item is essential. Lawshe (1975) presents a table of significant values. A *content validity index* can also be computed for the test as a whole by averaging the CVRs for the items remaining. The content validity index, then, represents the extent to which the judges perceive overlap between the ability to function in the job performance domain and the test performance domain.

Prien and Goldstein (1984) have summarized the possibilities of this type of review and the goal of content validation in Figure 6–8. The goal of content validation is to maximize the representation of KSAs that are considered important to job performance in the selection instrument (Area D in the figure). Items in the selection instrument representing KSAs that are not demonstrably important to job performance (Area C) must be removed. KSAs that are important to job performance but not included in the selection instrument (Area B) must be added.

4. *Establishing cutoff scores for content valid tests.* This may be the most difficult task of all. The reason for this difficulty lies in the fact that most abilities are continuously, not dichotomously distributed. The ability to distinguish colors may be a minimal requirement for an interior decorator, but it would be less easy to say what minimal level of interpersonal skill is essential. The solution is again judgmental. A panel of judges is asked to categorize the test tasks or content into those which require skills or knowledge that all employees must possess and those test tasks which discriminate between average and superior employees. The rating scales

discussed in connection with several of the job analysis methodologies (see Chapter 3) provide this information. More complicated procedures for establishing cutoff scores have been developed by educational psychologists and are detailed in a short manual by Livingston and Zieky (1982). Establishment of minimal cutoff scores while intending to choose randomly above some point is not the optimal way to use a test. Selecting the most qualified applicants from the top down in rank order almost always results in higher expected job performance than other strategies do.

5. *Selecting the raters for conducting content validity analyses.* Content validation of tests requires informed judgments from people who know about the job and its knowledge and ability requirements as well as the test content. These judges must be carefully selected and instructed and, for legal reasons, their credentials must be documented. Some personnel psychologists are reluctant to use a content validation strategy as the sole legal defense for use of tests. This is because content validity involves inferences about test construction rather than the accuracy of the inferences drawn from test scores (Tenopyr, 1977). However, many may have been reluctant to employ content validation strategies because, prior to the availability of the Lawshe (CVR) index, there was no quantifiable index of the estimated relationship between test scores and job performance. Ebel (1977), in stressing the centrality of content validity, made the following statement with which we agree:

> Some would say that content validity is inferior to, or less scientifically respectable than criterion related validity. . . . Content validity is the only basic foundation for any kind of validity. If the test does not have it, the criterion measures used to validate the test must have it. And one should never apologize for having to exercise judgment in validating a test. Data should never substitute for good judgment'' (p. 59).

Quantification of those judgments, whether directly through a procedure such as Lawshe's or indirectly by computation of a correlation coefficient, may allow comparisons of tests or testing situations, but it does not remove the necessity for human judgment.

Administering and scoring a content valid exam is no different than administering or scoring any other exam. Examinees should be informed of the test content, perhaps employing sample items; efforts should be made to minimize extraneous variables such as test anxiety, lighting and noise problems, etc. Above all, standardization of the testing situation for all applicants must be assured. Finally, item analyses and reliability estimates (appropriate estimates may include test-retest, inter-coder, or internal consistency) of the test should be made following test administration. Given this information, the tests may be further revised for future administration.

Fairness of Content Valid Tests

Earlier in this chapter we discussed the fairness of the use of psychological tests in making inferences about job performance. Research evidence indicates less difference between minority and majority groups when using tests developed with content validity in mind (Campion, 1972; Schmidt, Greenthal, Berner, Hunter, & Seaton, 1977). However, Guion (1978) has pointed out that there are at least four ways in which "content-valid" tests may be unfair:

1. The job content may differ for different subgroups of incumbents. Cases in which the job content is partially defined by the person holding the job may be judged unfairly. Guion cites the example in which some managers use participative techniques in assigning goals where others who accomplish the same amount of work use a more directive style. A simulation requiring the use of participative techniques will be unfair if there are large individual differences in the use of equally effective approaches.

2. Content valid tests may be unfair in terms of item and incumbent subgroup interactions. This means that subgroups of persons differ in their responses to certain items. The presence of these interactions in test development would be a clue to possible unfairness.

3. A "content valid" test in many Civil Service units consists of an on-the-job probationary period. But performance on this job must be evaluated, usually by means of supervisory ratings. If these ratings are significantly related to sex or ethnicity of the person on probation, we have no way of knowing whether any reported differences are due to bias or to real differences in performance. Or, if there are no subgroup differences on the ratings, perhaps raters have given members of the protected groups a compensatory edge. Similar questions, of course, are applicable to the criterion in criterion-related studies. In those cases where performance outcomes are relatively clearly specified, such bias is less likely. In one laboratory study (Schmitt & Lappin, 1980), for example, 60 to 80 percent of the variance in performance ratings was accounted for by objective differences in performance. More field studies should be conducted to determine under what conditions bias is likely.

4. Bias may occur in the scoring of content valid tests. Where

outcomes of work such as the number of parts assembled, the conductivity of a solder connection, or the weight of produce collected in a given period of time are accepted as salient outcomes by a panel of qualified judges, the test could be accepted as job related. However, in those cases where the outcome is judged by raters who know the sex or race of the examinee or those cases in which the process of the work is scored, bias in scoring the items may occur even though the items themselves may be representative of the job performance domain or content valid.

Content Validity in the Courts

Since the use of tests involves the inference that test scores tell us something about subsequent job performance, and since a content validation design tells us nothing directly about the accuracy of those inferences, the legal status of content validity has been problematic. Suppose, for example, that a content validity approach is taken to construct a test of the knowledge necessary to be a successful patrol officer. This test might not have criterion-related validity because possessing knowledge does not mean that that knowledge will be adequately utilized in a given situation. This is the gist of the argument used by plaintiffs in most court cases involving content validity. It is important to note that the defense of predictors as possessing content validity is that there is no inference involved or that the inference is minimal *because the "test" is the "job."*

Early court cases in which content validity was an issue (Vulcan Society of New York City Fire Department Inc. vs. Civil Service Commission, 490 F2d 387, Second Circuit, 1973, and Kirkland vs. New York State Department of Correctional Services, 520 F2d 420, Second Circuit, 1975) involved tests which had not been designed in compliance with EEOC guidelines; hence, there was little documentation of test preparation other than job description forms. The court found it easy to strike down these tests on the grounds of sloppy or inadequate test preparation without tackling the more difficult problem of deciding whether individual items in the test were content valid.

When the Second Circuit Court encountered a case in which the job-analysis-test preparation phase of the content validity claim was well documented (Guardians Association of New York City vs. Civil Service Commission, 431 F Supp 526, 1977), the judge examined the plaintiff's complaints that some questions were irrelevant to job performance, inappropriately difficult, or too abstract. The judge claimed familiarity with the detective jobs in question and used his judgment in revising the imperfect test. Very few tests will meet all professional or judgmental criteria, but the conclusion of the Second Circuit's analysis was that there must be adequate test preparation and that that preparation should be reflected in the test content. The latter conclusion was reinforced by an Eighth Circuit Court case (Firefighters' Institute for Racial Equality vs. City of St. Louis, 549 F 2d 506, SONY, 1977).

Several points seem to be critical in the design of tests for successful defense of content valid examinations:

1. Everything one does in job analysis and test preparation—interviews, questionnaires, observations, etc.—should be documented.

2. The successful test designers accumulate all the information about the job from subject matter experts and from materials and records relating to the job (Jackson vs. Nassau County Civil Service Commission, 424 F Supp 526, SONY, 1976; Bridgeport, supra; United States vs. South Carolina, 15 FEP 1198). This information includes the job tasks or behaviors and a determination of the relevant knowledge, skills, and abilities (KSAs) for the job.

3. The test designer must eliminate all those tasks or KSAs which can "be acquired in a brief orientation to the job." While this issue has not been subjected to much legal analysis, there is an obvious trade-off between the employer's concern for training costs and safety and the applicant's or court's concern that individuals who lack an adequate level of some KSAs but who could "quickly" become proficient not be eliminated. To determine KSAs which meet this criteria involves a judgment on the part of the test designer and the subject matter experts he or she consults.

4. A substantial amount of the KSAs required by the job must be represented in some portion of the examination procedure. The court ruled against the test designer in Firefighters' Institute because the examination procedure for a fire captain's position did not include supervisory skills which the job analysis indicated comprised 40 percent of the job.

5. The use of abstract knowledge questions, such as items testing civic awareness in the Bridgeport case, is normally unacceptable.

6. Cutoff scores must be based on competence to perform a job rather than customary practice or state law.

In summary, content validation that is thoroughly documented and carefully undertaken appears to be a legally defensible method to establish selection procedures. With the increased awareness of the infeasibility of criterion-related studies in many situations, content validation will certainly be used more frequently.

CONSTRUCT VALIDATION OF PREDICTORS

Construct validity is evaluated by investigating the qualities a test measures to determine the degree to which certain explanatory psychological concepts or constructs account for performance on a test. A psychological construct is an idea which is used to organize or integrate existing knowledge about some phenomenon. For example, a researcher might observe that some people move about more frequently than others while waiting for an examination to begin. Because of the circumstances and the researcher's previous experience with examinations, she or he might infer that the individuals who move about more are experiencing more *anxiety.* Anxiety itself is not observable, but the movement which is an hypothesized correlate of anxiety is observable and is the basis for the inference. Anxiety might also be associated with certain body changes and oral reports of being worried. In fact, investigators interested in studying anxiety have developed measures of it, such as paper-and-pencil questionnaires or the galvanic skin response (which assesses minute changes in bodily functions).

Information on the construct validity of these anxiety measures takes many forms. First, the different measures themselves (the questionnaires and the galvanic skin response, for example) should yield the same information about people's anxiety states; that is, they should correlate highly. Second, the measures should be sensitive to situations in which the experience of anxiety is logically high or low. That is, people engaged in a competitive sporting event, taking an important licensing exam, getting married, or caught in a severe storm should get high scores on the anxiety measure. People relaxing at home should get low scores. Third, individuals who typically appear excitable or nervous to others should get high scores while those seen by others as always calm should receive low scores.

The complexity of construct validation as well as its inherently time-consuming nature make it an infrequently used procedure in the selection context. In a sense, construct validation is an ongoing process. For example, while we know a great deal about the implications of scores on intelligence tests, scientific work extending the understanding of these instruments and the IQ construct itself continues. It is also true, as we stated earlier, that criterion-related validity studies provide information concerning the construct validity of instruments used for selection purposes.

Approaches which represent construct validation of selection tests are, however, becoming more frequent. In a study done for Armco Steel, for example, Guion directed a construct validation of tests of physical ability (Arnold, Rauschenberger, Soubel, & Guion, 1982). These tests were relatively simple measures of the ability to grip or lift material. Evidence of the construct validity of the physical tests consisted of the correlation between scores on these simple, inexpensive, and easy to administer tests and scores on relatively elaborate job simulations. The job simulations were difficult to administer in various locations to many job applicants, but correlations of substantial magnitude between the simple tests and the complex simulations indicated that the simpler tests were measuring the same underlying abilities (constructs) required for successful job performance that the more elaborate job simulations measured.

The Multitrait-Multimethod Matrix

The most frequently employed approach to construct validity involves comparing correlations in a *multitrait-multimethod matrix* (MTMM) (Campbell & Fiske, 1959). This method is most frequently used to examine the meaning of scores on new measures in light of people's scores on other measures about which more is known. Or, it can be usefully employed to help understand the dimensionality of multiple performance measures in a criterion-related study (e.g., Lawler, 1967; Schmidt & Johnson, 1973). Basic to the use of the multitrait-multimethod matrix is the idea that a measure of some phenomenon should correlate highly with other measures of the same phenomenon *and* that it should not correlate with measures of different phenomena from which it should theoretically differ. When a measure of a phenomenon correlates highly with other measures of the same phenomenon as it theoretically should, this indicates *convergent validity;* when the test predictably does not correlate with measures of other phenomena, this indicates *discriminant validity.*

A hypothetical MTMM matrix is illustrated in the top half of Table 6–4. The triangles on the diagonal are referred to as heterotrait-monomethod (many traits, one method) triangles. The three heterotrait-monomethod triangles represent the correlations among Traits A, B, and C when each is measured respectively by Methods 1, 2, and 3. The off-diagonal boxes, called heterotrait-heteromethod blocks (many traits, many methods), portray the cor-

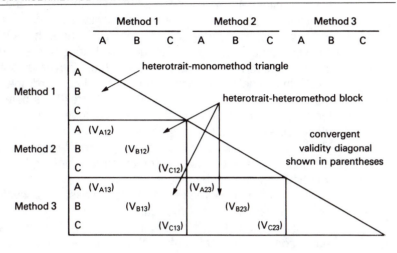

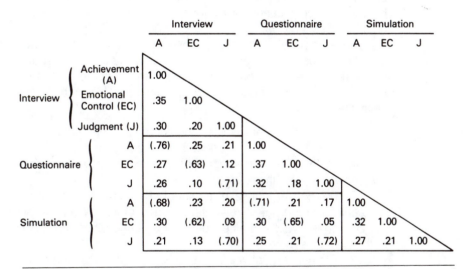

aA, B, and C represent different traits, V_{A12}, V_{B12}, etc. are the validities or the correlations between different measures of the same trait.

relations among traits measured by different methods. The diagonal values in these heterotrait-heteromethod blocks (labeled as V in Table 6-4) are the correlations between different measures of the same trait and are termed validities.

Four criteria have been suggested by Campbell and Fiske (1959) for evaluating the MTMM matrix. First, the correlations between similar traits measured by different methods (i.e., the convergent validities) should be both statistically significant and high enough to warrant further consideration. Second, the convergent validities should be higher than the correlations between different traits measured by different methods (i.e., the off-diagonal elements in the heterotrait-heteromethod blocks). Third, the convergent validities should be higher than the correlations between different traits measured by the same method (i.e., the validity diagonals should be higher than the heterotrait-monomethod triangles). Finally, a similar pattern of trait intercorrelations should be apparent in the heterotrait-monomethod triangles and the heterotrait-heteromethod submatrices.

We can see that when a new test or measure is developed to assess a particular construct called a trait in MTMM language, determining how it correlates with other known measures of the same construct is useful information. That is, if convergent and discriminant validity are evident, this leads to confidence in the construct validity of the new measure. In the bottom half of Table 6-4, we present a set of correlations that meet the Campbell-Fiske criteria reasonably well.

The bottom half of Table 6-4 shows three methods (Interviews, Questionnaires, and Simulation) for assessing three constructs (Achievement, A; Emotional Control, EC; and Judgment, J). If we take the four issues suggested for examining MTMM, it becomes clear that:

1. The convergent validities should be strong enough to warrant further consideration. We note that the convergent validities in the three heterotrait-heteromethod blocks are all above .60 (these are shown in parentheses in the table).

2. The convergent validities should be higher than the other correlations in the heterotrait-heteromethod blocks. We note that the convergent validities all exceed .60 while no other correlation in these blocks exceeds .30.

3. The convergent validities should be higher than the correlations in the heterotrait-heteromethod triangles. Again, the convergent validities all exceed .60, yet the strongest correlation in the heterotrait-monomethod triangle is .37.

4. The heterotrait-monomethod triangles should have a similar pattern to the off-diagonal entries in the heterotrait-heteromethod blocks. This means, for example, that the interview assessments of A, EC, and J should be intercorrelated similarly to the way the questionnaire and simulation measures of these three variables are intercorrelated. As can be seen in the bottom half of Table 6-4, the patterns are similar.

Construct Validity Conference

Recently, a number of psychologists met to discuss their understanding of construct validity and to present methods by which this understanding has been operationalized. At least four of the papers (Carroll, 1979; Frederiksen, 1979; Hunter, 1979; and Sternberg, 1979) which were produced as a result of this conference are relevant to a discussion of the appropriateness of construct validity in personnel selection.

Better and more systematic use of item analysis and test score distribution data might yield information about the construct validity of a test and this information may be readily understood by lay consumers of tests (Carroll, 1979). Carroll's method involves comparing test items that differ in difficulty and then making inferences about the increased demands on mental processing, knowledge, or problem-solving ability that more difficult items demand. He presented an example of 15 vocabulary items taken from the verbal portion of the SAT test, a widely used college entrance examination, and showed that the difficulty level of these items is highly correlated with the frequency of their use in written English. Similarly, he presented analysis of other "scholastic aptitude" tests showing that a careful analysis of the difficulty and content of the items revealed that the tests measured vocabulary knowledge, ability to notice relationships in verbal analogies, and the ability to perform arithmetic, algebraic, or geometric manipulations.

The approach seems simple, yet it yields information about which professionals can talk to consumers and about the scientific information relevant to a test's construct validity.

In a design similar to that described above, Frederiksen (1979) detailed the development of a test for admission of medical students to medical school. Frederiksen and his collaborators began by constructing a criterion measure to assess a doctor's ability to solve "patient management problems." The test simulates, on paper, a situation that might be encountered by a resident on duty in the emergency ward of a hospital. At first the examinees are given a small amount of information about a patient and are asked to indicate what diagnosis comes to mind. Then, they are allowed to seek further information, which is provided, and they start a new cycle of information-gathering and hypothesis-testing concerning diagnosis.

Assuming that the best way to predict performance on this criterion test was to use a test similar to it, the selection tests were constructed using problems requiring similar information-gathering strategies and hypothesis-generation components, *but not requiring medical knowledge* (which a medical school *applicant* would not have). A third set of variables, which Frederiksen termed *pro-cess variables,* was included to investigate the construct validity of both the selection and criterion measures. These are called pro-cess variables because they represent hypotheses concerning what might be happening of an internal or process nature that would account for success on either or both the criterion and pre-dictor variables. These tests included tests of medical knowledge, medical school grades, and ratings, as well as cognitive and per-sonality tests. All three sets of measures—the criterion tests, the selection measures, and the process measures—were adminis-tered to fourth-year medical students in a concurrent validity strate-gy.

Frederiksen and his colleagues then assessed validity in sever-al different ways. First, the correlations between criterion and selec-tion tests represent concurrent validity assuming the job relevance of the criterion measures. Second, future evidence of predictive validity can be gathered by correlating scores of incoming students on the selection tests with their subsequent performance in medical school. By correlating criterion measures with the process varia-bles mentioned above and examining the correlations in light of reasonable hypotheses about diagnostic problem solving, informa-tion about the construct validity of the criterion measures will ac-cumulate.

Similarly, we can examine the construct validity of the selection tests and other more traditional medical school entrance exams. The pattern of correlations between the selection tests and process variables on the one hand, and the criterion tests and process measures on the other, should be similar if the criteria and predic-tors involve similar constructs. Finally, comparisons of fourth-year and first-year medical students with respect to the relationships between selection tests and process measures would provide evi-dence of the effect of medical training on the constructs measured.

The implications of the work on validity generalization for con-struct validity were outlined by Hunter (1979). Hunter's major point was that job performance is predictable on the basis of currently available constructs and measures and that if one removes me-thodological artifacts from the thousands of validity coefficients already reported, the ability-job performance relationship is simple and extremely stable across a relatively wide variety of jobs. More recently, Hunter and Hunter (1984) argue that three ability factors (cognitive, perceptual and psychomotor) account for job perform-ance across virtually all jobs (see Chapter 8 for more detail on this work). They contend that which of these three factors is most im-portant in the performance of any given job is a function of job complexity and that cognitive ability tests increase in validity as job complexity increases, while psychomotor ability measures increase in validity as complexity decreases. They present evidence to show, for example, that psychomotor ability is a valid predictor of job performance on all but a few high-complexity jobs.

Recently, cognitive psychologists have begun work which may also provide information on what underlying constructs are measured by cognitive ability tests. Pellegrino and Glaser (1979) identify a "cognitive correlates" approach in which psychologists compare the performance of high and low ability groups (defined by scores on tests of verbal and quantitative skills) on various elementary cognitive tasks such as choice-reaction tasks, short-term memory tasks, and the "Posner task" (which requires the subject to indicate whether two alphabetic characters presented tachistoscopically are similar or different with respect to physical or name identity). The "cognitive components" approach represented by Sternberg's work (1977; 1979) delineates the separate processes underlying reading behavior and assesses their relative importance in performance on conventional standardized tests of reading comprehension.

The construct validity of aptitude tests has received increasing attention and the results are encouraging, but construct validation in employment settings is rare. Use of construct validation procedures, while sanctioned in the 1978 Uniform Guidelines, has not been frequently tested in court and companies or personnel researchers are not likely to risk a construct validation of selection procedures. However, continued scientific effort aimed at construct validation will certainly yield significant practical and scientific outcomes.

SUMMARY

In this chapter we defined *validity* in general and outlined the three strategies by which industrial/organizational psychologists seek to establish the validity of selection procedures. We argued that all validity is construct validity in which we seek to confirm hypotheses about concepts that we feel explain or organize human behavior. A criterion-related validation effort seeks to empirically establish that we are correct in the inferences we draw from test scores about the way that persons will perform their jobs. We discussed the two major research designs, concurrent and predictive, used to assess criterion-related validity, and the feasibility of conducting criterion-related validity studies. The issue of feasibility led to a discussion of content validation, a strategy of test development designed to insure that tests and measures represent significant portions of actual job behavior. Construct validation, on the other hand, is theoretical and involves a series of studies in which efforts are made to understand a concept that is hypothesized to account for a variety of human behaviors.

Finally, we presented a relatively detailed description of current legal and fairness issues related to personnel selection. Case law and the typical sequence of events in an unemployment discrimination case were briefly described. An important conclusion of this review was the critical role job analysis plays in the development of job relevant predictors.

REFERENCES

Adkins-Wood, D. (1961). *Test construction.* New York: Merrill.

Albemarle v. Moody Paper Company. (1975). 10 FEP 1181.

American Psychological Association. (1985). *Standards for educational and psychological tests.* Washington, DC: American Psychological Association.

Anastasi, A. (1982). *Psychological testing.* New York: McGraw-Hill.

Arnold, J. D., Rauschenberger, J. M., Soubel, W. G., and Guion, R. M. (1982). Validation and utility of a strength test for selecting steelworkers. *Journal of Applied Psychology, 67,* 588–604.

Arvey, R. D. (1979). *Fairness in selecting employees.* Reading, MA: Addison-Wesley.

Barrett, G. V., Phillips, J. S., and Alexander, R. A. (1981). Concurrent and predictive validity designs: A critical reanalysis. *Journal of Applied Psychology, 66,* 1–6.

Bartlett, C. J., Bobko, P., Mosier, S. B., and Hannan, R. (1978). Testing for fairness with a moderated multiple regression strategy: An alternative to differential analysis. *Personnel Psychology, 31,* 233–241.

Bemis, S. E. (1968). Occupational validity of the General Aptitude Test Battery. *Journal of Applied Psychology, 52,* 240–249.

Bloom, B. S. (1956). *Taxonomy of educational objectives.* New York: McKay.

Campbell, D. T., and Fiske, D. W. (1959). Convergent and discriminant validation by the multitrait-multimethod matrix. *Psychological Bulletin, 56,* 81–105.

Campbell, J. P. (1973). *Comments on Content Validity: A Procedural Manual.* Unpublished report prepared for Minneapolis Civil Service Commission.

Campion, J. E. (1972). Work sampling for personnel selection. *Journal of Applied Psychology, 56,* 40–44.

Carroll, J. B. (1979). Measurement of abilities constructs. In *Construct validity in psychological measurement.* Proceedings of a colloquium on theory and application in education and employment. Princeton, NJ: Educational Testing Service.

Cascio, W. F. (1982). *Applied psychology in personnel management.* Reston, VA: Reston Publishing Co.

Cleary, T. A. (1968). Test bias: Prediction of grades of Negro and white students in integrated colleges. *Journal of Educational Measurement, 5,* 115–124.

Ebel, R. L. (1977). Prediction? Validation? Construct validity? *Personnel Psychology, 30,* 55-63.

Flesch, R. (1949). *The art of readable writing.* New York: Collier.

Frederiksen, N. (1979). Research models for exploring constructs. In *Construct validity in psychological measurement.* Proceedings of a colloquium on theory and application in education and employment. Princeton, NJ: Educational Testing Service.

Gael, S., Grant, D. L., and Ritchie, R. L. (1975). Employment test validation for minority and nonminority clerks with work sample criteria. *Journal of Applied Psychology, 60,* 420–426.

Goldstein, I. L. (1986). *Training: Program development and evaluation.* Belmont, CA: Brooks/Cole.

Griggs v. Duke Power Company. (1971). 3 FEP 175.

Guion, R. M. (1976). Recruiting, selection and job placement. In M. D. Dunnette (Ed.). *Handbook of industrial and organizational psychology.* Chicago, IL: Rand-McNally.

Guion, R. M. (1977). Content validity—the source of my discontent. *Applied Psychological Measurement, 1,* 1–10.

Guion, R. M. (1978). Content validity in moderation. *Personnel Psychology, 31,* 205–214.

Guion, R. M. (1978). Scoring of content domain samples: The problem of fairness. *Journal of Applied Psychology, 63,* 499–506.

Hunter, J. E. (1979). Construct validity and validity generalization. In *Construct validity in psychological measurement.* Proceedings of a colloquium on theory and application in education. Princeton, NJ: Educational Testing Service.

Hunter, J. E., and Hunter, R. F. (1984). Validity and utility of alternative predictors of job performance. *Psychological Bulletin, 96,* 72–98.

Latham, G. P., Saari, L. M., Pursell, E. D., and Campion, M. A. (1980). The situational interview. *Journal of Applied Psychology, 65,* 422–427.

Lawler, E. E., III. (1967). The multitrait-multirater approach to measuring managerial job performance. *Journal of Applied Psychology, 51,* 369–381.

Lawshe, C. H. (1975). A quantitative approach to content validity. *Personnel Psychology, 28,* 563–575.

Ledvinka, J. (1979). The statistical definition of fairness in the federal selection guidelines and its implications for minority employment. *Personnel Psychology, 32,* 551–562.

Lent, R. H., Aurbach, H. A., and Levin, L. S. (1971). Predictors, criteria, and significant results. *Personnel Psychology, 24,* 519–533.

Lindvall, C. M., and Nitko, A. J. (1975). *Measuring pupil achievement and aptitude, 2nd. ed.* New York: Harcourt, Brace, and Jovanovich.

Linn, R. L. (1978). Single-group validity, differential validity, and differential prediction. *Journal of Applied Psychology, 63,* 507–512.

Livingston, S. A., and Zieky, M. J. (1982). *Passing scores.* Princeton, NJ: Educational Testing Scores.

McLaughlin, G. H. (1969). SMOG grading—a new readability formula. *Journal of Reading, 12,* 639–646.

Mussio, S. J., and Smith, M. K. (1973). *Content validity: A procedural manual.* Minneapolis, MN: Civil Service Commission.

Pellegrino, J. W., and Galser, R. (1979). Cognitive correlates and components in the analysis of individual differences. *Intelligence, 3,* 187–214.

Perticone, J., and Wiesen, J. P. (1979). *Content validity studies in the courts.* Massachusetts Division of Personnel Administration, Test Development and Validation Unit, Publication # 11357-28-125-5-79-C.R.

Peters, L. H., and O'Connor, E. J. (1980). Situation constraints and work outcomes: The influences of a frequently overlooked construct. *Academy of Management Review, 5,* 391-397.

Prien, E. P., and Goldstein, I. L. (1984). *Validation research: Some models and design considerations.* Presented at Content Validity III Conference. Bowling Green State University, Bowling Green, OH.

Regents of the University of California v. Bakke. (1978). 17 FEP 1000.

Reilly, R. R., Zedeck, S., and Tenopyr, M. L. (1979). Validity and fairness of physical ability tests for predicting performance in craft jobs. *Journal of Applied Psychology, 64,* 262-274.

Schmidt, F. L., Berner, J. G., and Hunter, J. E. (1973). Racial differences in validity of employment tests: Reality or illusion? *Journal of Applied Psychology, 58,* 5-9.

Schmidt, F. L., Greenthal, A. L., Berner, J. G., Hunter, J. E., and Seaton, F. W. (1977). Job sample vs. paper-and-pencil trades and technical tests: Adverse impact and employee attitudes. *Personnel Psychology, 30,* 187-198.

Schmidt, F. L., and Hunter, J. E. (1974). Racial and ethnic bias in psychological tests: Divergent implications of two definitions of test bias. *American Psychologist, 29,* 1-8.

Schmidt, F. L., Hunter, J. E., and Caplan, J. R. (1981). Validity generalization results for two jobs in the petroleum industry. *Journal of Applied Psychology, 66,* 261-273.

Schmidt, F. L., Hunter, J. E., and Urry, V. W. (1976). Statistical power in criterion-related validation studies. *Journal of Applied Psychology, 61,* 473-485.

Schmidt, F. L., and Johnson, R. H. (1973). Effect of race on peer ratings in an industrial situation. *Journal of Applied Psychology, 37,* 237-241.

Schmidt, F. L., Pearlman, K., and Hunter, J. E. (1980). The validity and fairness of employment and educational tests for Hispanic Americans. *Personnel Psychology, 33,* 705-724.

Schmitt, N., Gooding, R., Noe, R. A., and Kirsch, M. (1984). Meta-analyses of validity studies published between 1964 and 1982, and the investigation of study characteristics. *Personnel Psychology, 37,* 407-422.

Schmitt, N., and Lappin, M. (1980). Race and sex as determinants of the mean and variance of performance ratings. *Journal of Applied Psychology, 65,* 428-435.

Schmitt, N., Mellon, P. M., and Bylenga, C. (1978). Sex differences in validity for academic and employment criteria and different types of predictors. *Journal of Applied Psychology, 63,* 145-150.

Schneider, B. (1978a). Person-situation selection: A review of some ability-situation interaction research. *Personnel Psychology, 31,* 281-298.

Schneider, B. (1978b). Implications of the conference: A personal view. *Personnel Psychology, 31,* 299-304.

Schneider, B. (1983). Interactional psychology and organizational behavior. In L. L. Cummings and B. M. Staw (Eds.). *Research in organizational behavior.* Greenwich, CT: JAI Press.

Sternberg, R. J. (1977). *Intelligence information processing, and analogical reasoning: The componential analysis of human abilities.* Hillsdale, NJ: Erlbaum.

Sternberg, R. J. (1979). The construct validity of aptitude tests: An information processing assessment. In *Construct validity in psychological measurement.*

Proceedings of a colloquium on theory and application in education and employment. Princeton, NJ: Educational Testing Service.

Tenopyr, M. L. (1977). Content-construct confusion. *Personnel Psychology, 30,* 47–54.

Thorndike, R. L. (1949). *Personnel selection.* New York: Wiley.

Thorndike, R. L. (1971). *Educational measurement, 2nd. ed.* Washington, DC: American Council on Education.

Uniform Guidelines on Employee Selection Procedures. (1978). *Federal Register, 43,* 38290–38315.

United Steelworkers of America v. Weber. (1979). 99 S. Ct. 2721.

Washington v. Davis. (1976). 12 FEP 1415.

7

THE UTILITY OF PERSONNEL SELECTION PRACTICES

AIMS OF THE CHAPTER

Industrial/organizational psychologists have acted as though the presentation of a significant validity coefficient (relating scores on some selection procedure to some measure(s) of employee performance) was proof of the test's usefulness and should convince an enlightened management of the great importance of our work. Occasionally, we assert that our procedures are content valid and leave the management decision-makers the chore of comparing our assertions with those of others who may document their claims and requests in much more meaningful terms. Those meaningful terms usually are monetary and almost always are directly related to the company's continued survival, at least as far as management is concerned.

For example, when a production manager comes with a request for new machinery, he supports this request with projected increases in productivity and resultant decreases in unit cost of production. The sales manager supports her request for a centralized computer system to process orders with figures concerning the amount of salesperson time saved and estimates of the increased amount of sales that could be generated during this time. The maintenance manager supports his request to hire three new people with figures concerning the amount of down-time due to equipment malfunction that could be reduced and the resulting savings that could be achieved by the addition of three new persons working at the same rate as his current maintenance people. The point is if a personnel manager does not compete for scarce organizational resources in the same way as her or his colleagues, the chances of *successfully* competing are small.

A plea that psychologists learn and use the language of economists has been voiced repeatedly in the last five years (Cascio, 1982; Dunnette & Borman, 1979; Schmidt, Hunter, McKenzie, & Muldrow, 1979; Tenopyr, 1981; 1983). These authors maintain that the terminology of economists cannot be ignored by industrial and organizational psychologists. Unless we have the means for measuring and tracking productivity and showing how our personnel techniques relate to productivity, we cannot know the short- or long-term effects of our contributions. In short we must be able to translate our validity coefficients into dollar and cents values, however crude those translations may be. This translation is called *utility analysis.* As we gain experience with these translations, we may be surprised to find that the utility of various personnel programs far exceeds even our expectations.

There are at least three reasons why utility analyses are important. The first we have alluded to above—namely, as a means to strengthen and support the human resources practices we espouse vis-à-vis other claims for organizational resources. The second reason is certainly implicit in the first: we should have better information *ourselves* concerning the relative cost/benefit of various human resource efforts such as training, selection, recruitment, career development programs, etc. For example, is it more cost-beneficial to invest in sophisticated selection procedures or training programs when preparing to open a fast-food restaurant? Or, more specifically relevant to selection, how much money should be invested in the selection of the manager of a nuclear facility or the hiring of an airplane pilot? What *are* the costs of a failure when making these hiring decisions? The third reason is that, on a societal level, it is more important to provide information concerning the relative costs and benefits of making different kinds of choices when confronted with conflicting goals regarding human resource allocation. A good example is the apparent conflict between productivity and affirmative action goals. Hiring those persons whose predicted performance is greatest may result in the nearly total exclusion of minority individuals. The work of Hunter, Schmidt, and Rauschenberger (1977) and Cronbach and his colleagues (Cronbach and Schaeffer, 1981; Cronbach, Yalow, and Schaeffer, 1980) has delineated the circumstances in which these two goals are most in conflict and the hiring strategies which would maximize the realization of both goals. The implications of their analyses are that quotas be set for both minority and majority groups and that the best qualified persons be selected in rank order fashion in both groups. Negative effects on productivity are minimized relative to rank order selection without identification of ethnic status (i.e., purely on the basis of qualifications) and are far superior to a strategy which selects individuals randomly with quotas above some minimal cutoff.

A final point concerning utility estimation should be mentioned now. Many psychologists object to the estimation of human outcomes in dollar terms; such calculations may be in conflict with the set of values that brought them to careers in psychology. However, refusal to express our contributions in these terms ignores the reality of the language of business and assures maintenance of the status quo. That is, by failing to consider utility issues, we say that the bases for decisions that are currently being made are fine and that the values which guide those decisions are also fine. By refusing to speak the language of business, we lack influence on decision-makers and, thus, ensure that potentially valuable human resource programs are not fully utilized. The result of wearing such blinders is a loss to both individuals and organizations.

We hope we have been convincing in our statement of the importance and appropriateness of converting our procedures and their outcomes into economic terms—of performing utility analysis. In the remainder of this chapter we trace the development of ideas and methodology in utility analyses and present techniques which have been found useful in various contexts. The numerical examples we provide should stimulate similar computations by practitioners in organizations.* Finally, we present some refinements, questions, and complications to which more research attention should be directed.

HISTORY OF THE DEVELOPMENT OF SELECTION UTILITY MODELS

Early Estimates Based on the Magnitude of Prediction Errors

The question of the utility of selection procedures has been of long-term interest to some industrial psychologists. Most early attempts focused on psychometric considerations rather than dollars. For example, one procedure examined the relative size of the errors of prediction (Hull, 1928) or the percent of variance in the job performance measure which is accounted for by knowledge of predictor scores. This estimate, called the *index of forecasting efficiency* is equal to $1 - \sqrt{1 - r_{xy}^2}$ where r_{xy} is the validity coefficient. The index of forecasting efficiency compares the standard deviation of the errors we make in predicting job performance scores using test information with the standard deviation of the errors that would result from the use of random selection or nonvalid information.

For example, the index of forecasting efficiency for a test of .60 validity would show that the predictor does only 20 percent better than chance:

$$\text{Efficiency} = 1 - \sqrt{1 - .36}$$
$$= 1 - \sqrt{.64}$$
$$= 1 - .8 = .20$$

---

*Our examples and computations will be presented for personnel selection programs but this is only a convenience for this book. The procedures are useful for *any* situation where *any* intervention (e.g., training, job redesign, organizational change) is made and the validity of the intervention is established.

FIGURE 7-1.

PROPORTION OF EMPLOYEES CONSIDERED SATISFACTORY = .50
SELECTION RATIO

r	.05	.10	.20	.30	.40	.50	.60	.70	.80	.90	.95
.00	.50	.50	.50	.50	.50	.50	.50	.50	.50	.50	.50
.05	.54	.54	.53	.52	.52	.52	.51	.51	.51	.50	.50
.10	.58	.57	.56	.55	.54	.53	.53	.52	.51	.51	.50
.15	.63	.61	.58	.57	.56	.55	.54	.53	.52	.51	.51
.20	.67	.64	.61	.59	.58	.56	.55	.54	.53	.52	.51
.25	.70	.67	.64	.62	.60	.58	.56	.55	.54	.52	.51
.30	.74	.71	.67	.64	.62	.60	.58	.56	.54	.52	.51
.35	.78	.74	.70	.66	.64	.61	.59	.57	.55	.53	.51
.40	.82	.78	.73	.69	.66	.63	.61	.58	.56	.53	.52
.45	.85	.81	.75	.71	.68	.65	.62	.59	.56	.53	.52
.50	.88	.84	.78	.74	.70	.67	.63	.60	.57	.54	.52
.55	.91	.87	.81	.76	.72	.69	.65	.61	.58	.54	.52
.60	.94	.90	.84	.79	.75	.70	.66	.62	.59	.54	.52
.65	.96	.92	.87	.82	.77	.73	.68	.64	.59	.55	.52
.70	.98	.95	.90	.85	.80	.75	.70	.65	.60	.55	.53
.75	.99	.97	.92	.87	.82	.77	.72	.66	.61	.55	.53
.80	1.00	.99	.95	.90	.85	.80	.73	.67	.61	.55	.53
.85	1.00	.99	.97	.94	.88	.82	.76	.69	.62	.55	.53
.90	1.00	1.00	.99	.97	.92	.86	.78	.70	.62	.56	.53
.95	1.00	1.00	1.00	.99	.96	.90	.81	.71	.63	.56	.53
1.00	1.00	1.00	1.00	1.00	1.00	1.00	.83	.71	.63	.56	.53

If a validity of .30 is placed into the formula, the result shows it would only do about 5 percent better than chance. These are not very positive interpretations of validity

The coefficient of determination, r_{xy}^2, became popular in the 1930's and 1940's and continues to be cited by some industrial psychologists as a measure of utility. This coefficient is the amount of variance in the job performance measure that is accounted for by the selection procedure. A test with validity equal to .60 would be described as a measure which accounts for 36 percent of the criterion variance; likewise, a test with validity of .3 would account for 9 percent of the variance.

Neither the index of forecasting efficiency nor the coefficient of determination bear any direct relationship to the actual economic value of a selection instrument. In addition, neither recognizes that the value of a test varies as a function of various situational parameters (for example, the current level of work force performance). Both lead to the conclusion that validities must be very high before a test has much economic value. As we shall see below, this is false. Various authors have shown that the validity coefficient itself is an inappropriate index of the utility of a selection device (Brogden, 1946; Cronbach and Gleser, 1965; Taylor and Russell, 1939).

PROPORTION OF EMPLOYEES CONSIDERED SATISFACTORY = 0.10 SELECTION RATIO										
r	0.05	0.10	0.20	0.30	0.40	0.50	0.60	0.70	0.80	0.90	0.95
0.00	0.10	0.10	0.10	0.10	0.10	0.10	0.10	0.10	0.10	0.10	0.10
0.05	0.12	0.12	0.11	0.11	0.11	0.11	0.11	0.10	0.10	0.10	0.10
0.10	0.14	0.13	0.13	0.12	0.12	0.11	0.11	0.11	0.11	0.10	0.10
0.15	0.16	0.15	0.14	0.13	0.13	0.12	0.12	0.11	0.11	0.10	0.10
0.20	0.19	0.17	0.15	0.14	0.14	0.13	0.12	0.12	0.11	0.11	0.10
0.25	0.22	0.19	0.17	0.16	0.14	0.13	0.13	0.12	0.11	0.11	0.10
0.30	0.25	0.22	0.19	0.17	0.15	0.14	0.13	0.12	0.12	0.11	0.10
0.35	0.28	0.24	0.20	0.18	0.16	0.15	0.14	0.13	0.12	0.11	0.10
0.40	0.31	0.27	0.22	0.19	0.17	0.16	0.14	0.13	0.12	0.11	0.10
0.45	0.35	0.29	0.24	0.20	0.18	0.16	0.15	0.13	0.12	0.11	0.10
0.50	0.39	0.32	0.26	0.22	0.19	0.17	0.15	0.13	0.12	0.11	0.11
0.55	0.43	0.36	0.28	0.23	0.20	0.17	0.15	0.14	0.12	0.11	0.11
0.60	0.48	0.39	0.30	0.25	0.21	0.18	0.16	0.14	0.12	0.11	0.11
0.65	0.53	0.43	0.32	0.26	0.22	0.18	0.16	0.14	0.12	0.11	0.11
0.70	0.58	0.47	0.35	0.27	0.22	0.19	0.16	0.14	0.12	0.11	0.11
0.75	0.64	0.51	0.37	0.29	0.23	0.19	0.16	0.14	0.12	0.11	0.11
0.80	0.71	0.56	0.40	0.30	0.24	0.20	0.17	0.14	0.12	0.11	0.11
0.85	0.78	0.62	0.43	0.31	0.25	0.20	0.17	0.14	0.12	0.11	0.11
0.90	0.86	0.69	0.46	0.33	0.25	0.20	0.17	0.14	0.12	0.11	0.11
0.95	0.95	0.78	0.49	0.33	0.25	0.20	0.17	0.14	0.12	0.11	0.11
1.00	1.00	1.00	0.50	0.33	0.25	0.20	0.17	0.14	0.13	0.11	0.11

More Complex Utility Estimates

A more widely used and well-known approach to utility is that described by Taylor and Russell (1939). Their approach took into account not only the validity coefficient but also the *selection ratio* (the proportion of applicants who actually get hired) and the *base rate* (the percentage of employees considered successful prior to the introduction of a new selection procedure*) to make estimates of the value of the selection instrument. Estimates of the utility of a procedure are made in terms of the proportion of successful candidates hired using the new procedure. One portion of the tables they developed as an aid in utility estimation is presented in Figure 7–1. This table indicates the percent of all employees who will be successful after introducing a test with varying levels of validity and various selection ratios when half of the current work force is already considered successful (i.e., without using the *new* procedure, 50 percent are already performing successfully).** Thus, using the first half of Figure 7–1, a procedure with validity (*r* in the

---

*The current procedure might be none at all, or one with zero validity, or one with lower validity than the new procedure.
**Taylor and Russell (1939) provided similar tables for other base rates as well.

Table) of .50 used in a situation in which the selection ratio is .50 produces a work force which is now 67 percent successful as opposed to 50 percent successful. This represents a 34 percent $\left(\frac{67-50}{50}\right)$ increase in the percent of successful employees or an absolute increase of 17 percent. Similarly, a selection ratio of .20 and validity of .50 would yield 78 percent successful employees, an increase of 56 percent in the proportion of successful employees or an absolute increase of 28 percent successful employees. An examination of the rows in the first half of Figure 7–1 will indicate the "percent successful" (1) is always greatest when selection ratios are low, and that (2) tests of quite low validity can be useful if the selection ratio is low. We can see how the organization's attractiveness to prospective employees can pay the organization back in unexpected ways: increased attractiveness should increase the number of applicants, lowering the selection ratio, and raising the value associated with the use of any selection device of any validity.

We can also see by examining figures for various base rates (percent of current employees considered successful) that we achieve maximal increases in absolute percent successful when the base rate is close to .50 given both constant validity and constant selection ratio. At low base rates there will be small changes in absolute percent successful but large relative changes. For example, when the base rate equals .10 (the second half of Figure 7–1), the selection ratio is .50, the validity of the test is .40, the percent successful when employing the test is 16. This represents a 6 percent increase in successful employees (16–10), but 60 percent improvement (16–10/10). An examination for a similar situation (same validity and selection ratio) in which the base rate is .50 indicates that 63 percent of the selected persons would be successful. This is a 13 percent increase (63–50) in successful employees but only a 26 percent (63–50/50) improvement. The principle is that the poorer the present base rate, the more the potential relative gain.

While the Taylor-Russell tables represented a significant improvement in utility estimation by showing the benefits of using selection procedures under different circumstances, there are two distinct disadvantages associated with their use:

1. The Taylor-Russell approach neglects any consideration of (a) the *cost* of gathering information concerning applicants (that is, testing, interviewing, checking references, etc.) and (b) the cost of recruiting an applicant pool that is of similar quality but much larger. Recall that the utility of a test is greatly influenced by the

selection ratio and that to maintain a low selection ratio one must recruit and test many applicants.

2. Perhaps the more important limitation is that workers are either put in a "successful" or a "not successful" group. Splitting employees into two performance groups is called *dichotomizing the criterion*. When we dichotomize the criterion we are forced to treat all employees in the "successful" group as *equally* successful; similarly, in the "unsuccessful" group, all employees are treated as *equally* unsuccessful. Obviously this does not reflect reality because employees perform at more than two different levels of effectiveness and the contributions of those different levels are lost when we dichotomize the criterion (Cronbach & Gleser, 1965, Pp. 123–124).

Subsequent treatments of utility have solved both of these problems. Brogden (1946) showed that the validity coefficient is a direct index of utility. Assuming the predictor and criterion are continuous and have identical distributions, and that the predictor and criterion are linearly related, a test with validity of .50 could be expected to produce 50 percent of the gain in utility that would result if we had a test of perfect validity. So, if an organization has turnover costs of $200,000 annually, a test battery that predicts turnover with a validity of .50 would save the company half of the $200,000, or $100,000 per year.

Brogden also showed how the selection ratio and the standard deviation of job performance in dollars (SD_y) influence the utility of a selection procedure. Mathematically:

$$\Delta \bar{u}/\text{person selected} = r_{xy} \bar{z}_x SD_y$$

where $\Delta \bar{u}$ = the average per person gain in utility in dollars;

$\bar{z}_x$ = the mean standard score on the test of those persons selected (standard scores are based on the applicant distribution).

Note the lower the selection ratio, the higher $\bar{z}_x$ will be assuming the highest scoring people are selected; SD_y = the SD of job performance *in dollars* among employees hired without use of the test. Determination of SD_y in dollar terms is discussed below.

The product of the validity and the mean standard score ($r_{xy} \bar{z}_x$) is equal to the mean standard score of the criterion ($\bar{z}_y$) for those selected. So, the Brogden formula reduces to an important formula: $\Delta \bar{u}/\text{person selected} = \bar{z}_y SD_y$. As stated below, figures for $\bar{z}_y$ for various levels of validity and selection ratio are given in Figure

7-2. Utility per selectee is the mean standard score on the criterion for those selected × the standard deviation of the performance criterion in dollar form. Multiplying this figure by the number selected gives the total dollar gain of the selection procedure.

The implications of these mathematics are worked out for various levels of validity and selection ratios by Brown and Ghiselli (1953) and are reproduced here as Figure 7-2. The values in this table are the mean standard criterion score of those selected ($\bar{z}_y$). Using the table for the situation in which predictor validity is .50 and the selection ratio is .20 yields the information that the average standard criterion score of those selected is .70. By comparison, the average standard criterion score of a randomly selected group or one selected with a nonvalid test would be .00. If we also have information that indicates the standard deviation of job performance in dollar terms per year is $1,000, then the average gain *per person selected* with a predictor with validity (r_{xy}) equal to .50 is $700 (.7 × $1,000). Further, if 10 are selected, the test procedure would result in a net gain of $7,000 (10 × $700) *in the first year* these people would be employed.

Obviously a critical feature of this analysis is the standard deviation in dollar terms of the performance criterion (SD_y). For jobs in which the contribution of individual employees to the organization is widely different, valid testing will result in large dollar gains; in those situations in which individual contributions are relatively similar (e.g., for jobs that are essentially machine paced), a valid testing procedure and a low selection ratio will not result in large dollar gains.

Both Figures 7-1 and 7-2 indicate that utility increases without limit as the selection ratio decreases. Brogden (1949) showed, however, that at the extremes selection ratio and utility are curvilinearly related. This is because for very low selection ratios we incur relatively large testing costs, since we test many applicants to make few selections. Hence the cost of testing per selectee can become large. To make up for the cost of testing, the SD_y must be large or the net gain in utility becomes negative (i.e., the costs outweigh the benefits). Notice that Brogden successfully addressed the two major problems with the Taylor-Russell work: (1) the necessity to dichotomize the criterion, and (2) the failure to consider the costs in recruiting and testing.

In 1965, Cronbach and Gleser published a book titled *Psychological Tests and Personnel Decisions.* It presented detailed and sophisticated formulations about utility when employing various placement, classification, and sequential selection strategies as well as strategies involving the simple hire/reject decisions we discussed. In classification, an employer has multiple jobs and the

FIGURE 7-2. MEAN STANDARD CRITERION SCORE ($\bar{z}_y$) OF SELECTED CASES IN RELATION TO TEST VALIDITY AND SELECTION RATIO.

Selection Ratio	VALIDITY COEFFICIENT																				
	.00	.05	.10	.15	.20	.25	.30	.35	.40	.45	.50	.55	.60	.65	.70	.75	.80	.85	.90	.95	1.00
.05	.00	.10	.21	.31	.42	.52	.62	.73	.83	.94	1.04	1.14	1.25	1.35	1.46	1.56	1.66	1.77	1.87	1.98	2.08
.10	.00	.09	.18	.26	.35	.44	.53	.62	.70	.79	.88	.97	1.05	1.14	1.23	1.32	1.41	1.49	1.58	1.67	1.76
.15	.00	.08	.15	.23	.31	.39	.46	.54	.62	.70	.77	.85	.93	1.01	1.08	1.16	1.24	1.32	1.39	1.47	1.55
.20	.00	.07	.14	.21	.28	.35	.42	.49	.56	.63	.70	.77	.84	.91	.98	1.05	1.12	1.19	1.26	1.33	1.40
.25	.00	.06	.13	.19	.25	.32	.38	.44	.51	.57	.63	.70	.76	.82	.89	.95	1.01	1.08	1.14	1.20	1.27
.30	.00	.06	.12	.17	.23	.29	.35	.40	.46	.52	.58	.64	.69	.75	.81	.87	.92	.98	1.04	1.10	1.16
.35	.00	.05	.11	.16	.21	.26	.32	.37	.42	.48	.53	.58	.63	.69	.74	.79	.84	.90	.95	1.00	1.06
.40	.00	.05	.10	.15	.19	.24	.29	.34	.39	.44	.48	.53	.58	.63	.68	.73	.77	.82	.87	.92	.97
.45	.00	.04	.09	.13	.18	.22	.26	.31	.35	.40	.44	.48	.53	.57	.62	.66	.70	.75	.79	.84	.88
.50	.00	.04	.08	.12	.16	.20	.24	.28	.32	.36	.40	.44	.48	.52	.56	.60	.64	.68	.72	.76	.80
.55	.00	.04	.07	.11	.14	.18	.22	.25	.29	.32	.36	.40	.43	.47	.50	.54	.58	.61	.65	.68	.72
.60	.00	.03	.06	.10	.13	.16	.19	.23	.26	.29	.32	.35	.39	.42	.45	.48	.52	.55	.58	.61	.64
.65	.00	.03	.06	.09	.11	.14	.17	.20	.23	.26	.28	.31	.34	.37	.40	.43	.46	.48	.51	.54	.57
.70	.00	.02	.05	.07	.10	.12	.15	.17	.20	.22	.25	.27	.30	.32	.35	.37	.40	.42	.45	.47	.50
.75	.00	.02	.04	.06	.08	.11	.13	.15	.17	.19	.21	.23	.25	.27	.30	.32	.33	.36	.38	.40	.42
.80	.00	.02	.04	.05	.07	.09	.11	.12	.14	.16	.18	.19	.21	.22	.25	.26	.28	.30	.32	.33	.35
.85	.00	.01	.03	.04	.05	.07	.08	.10	.11	.12	.14	.15	.16	.18	.19	.20	.22	.23	.25	.26	.27
.90	.00	.01	.02	.03	.04	.05	.06	.07	.08	.09	.10	.11	.12	.13	.14	.15	.16	.17	.18	.19	.20
.95	.00	.01	.01	.02	.02	.03	.03	.04	.04	.05	.05	.06	.07	.07	.08	.08	.09	.09	.10	.10	.11

(From Brown and Ghiselli, 1953, p. 342)

task involves assigning individuals to jobs in such a way as to maximize productivity while insuring that each job receives the required number of workers. Classification usually involves multiple predictors and a separate prediction equation for each job. The case in which there is only a single predictor and multiple jobs is called placement.

We will not discuss the classification and placement models except to point out that classification can produce gains in utility over selection because classification systems automatically decrease the selection ratio. That is, when we can consider each applicant as an applicant for all jobs, the selection ratio becomes smaller for all jobs. The gain in utility which may result from classification as opposed to selection also depends on the differences in prediction equations and the standard deviation of the contribution of persons in different jobs to the organization (SD_y). If our prediction equations are similar, then we predict that the same set of persons be hired for all jobs. If we predict the same value for the performance of a given person on two jobs, and if the jobs do not differ in SD_y, the expected gain in utility resulting from the separate consideration of these two jobs would be zero. On the other hand, if there are large differences in SD_y for the two jobs, the most appropriate assignment of a person with identical predicted job performance for the two jobs would be to the job that has the greatest SD_y.

With some simplifying assumptions, Brogden (1951; 1959) provided examples and tables expressing the gain that could be realized by the use of classification over selection. Because of the complexity of the mathematics and the relatively rare applicability of classification strategies (the military being a notable exception), very little attention has been directed to classification problems.

A MAJOR BREAKTHROUGH: CALCULATING SD_y

Brogden's work in the 1940's and Cronbach and Gleser's (1965) formal introduction of cost of testing in utility formulations provided the mathematical solution to problems of estimation of utility. But until recently, almost no application of these formulations has occurred. Perhaps because of social and economic pressure, it is now essential that we consider the productivity implications of all programs, including those of a human resource nature. But equally important, only recently have industrial psychologists provided a methodology for the calculation of SD_y, the standard deviation of individuals' dollar contribution to the organization. Previously, only very complex cost accounting procedures could be used to provide such estimates and in most cases, human performance differences would not lend themselves to such analyses. In the next two sections, we present recent work that has stimulated renewed interest in utility estimation.

Schmidt-Hunter Estimates of Dollar Worth

In 1979, Schmidt et al. reported a pilot study in which they derived estimates of SD_y for budget analysts. Supervisors were used as judges of the worth of their budget analysts because they were thought to have had the best opportunities to observe actual performance and output differences among employees. Schmidt et al.'s method was based on the following reasoning: if job performance in dollar terms is normally distributed (see Chapter 5 for a description of the normal curve), then the difference between the value to the organization of the products and services produced by the average employee and those produced by an employee at the 85th percentile (one whose performance is as good as or better than 85 percent of the employees) is equal to SD_y. Similarly, the estimated difference between the average performer and the person who performs at the 15th percentile (as good as or better than only 15 percent of the employees) ought to be equal to SD_y. Further, those two separate estimates ought to be equal to each other and also to the difference between the 85th and 97th percentile values if the normality assumption is correct (see Bobko, Karren, and Parkington (1983) for an evaluation of this assumption).

Budget analyst supervisors in the pilot study (Schmidt et al., 1979) were asked to estimate the contribution of employees at both the 50th (average) and 85th percentile and these values were averaged over 62 supervisors. The average SD_y was $11,327 for the budget analyst position. Since the instructions to the judges who make SD_y estimates are a critical element of the procedure, we reproduce the Schmidt et al. instructions in Figure 7–3.

Schmidt et al. (1979) cite two advantages for their procedure. First, the mental standard provided for the supervisor-judges in the instructions is the estimated cost to the organization of having an outside consulting firm provide the same products/services. This appears to be a relatively concrete and meaningful standard for most judges, since Schmidt et al. report that very few questions or

FIGURE 7-3. *INSTRUCTIONS FOR THE ESTIMATION OF SDy.*

The instructions to the supervisors were as follows:

The dollar utility estimates we are asking you to make are critical in estimating the relative dollar value to the government of different selection methods. In answering these questions, you will have to make some very *difficult judgments.* We realize they are difficult and that they are judgments or estimates. You will have to ponder for some time before giving each estimate, and there is probably no way you can be absolutely certain your estimate is accurate when you do reach a decision. But keep in mind three things:

1. The alternative to estimates of this kind is application of cost accounting procedures to the evaluation of job performance. Such applications are *usually* prohibitively expensive. And in the end, they produce only imperfect estimates, like this estimation procedure.
2. Your estimates will be averaged in with those of other supervisors of computer programmers. Thus errors produced by too high and too low estimates will tend to be averaged out, providing more accurate final estimates.
3. The decisions that must be made about selection methods do not require that all estimates be accurate down to the last dollar. Substantially accurate estimates will lead to the same decisions as perfectly accurate estimates.

Based on your experience with agency programmers, we would like for you to estimate the yearly value to your agency of the products and services produced by the average GS 9–11 computer programmer. Consider the quality and quantity of output typical of the *average programmer* and the value of this output. In placing an overall dollar value on this output, it may help to consider what the cost would be of having an outside firm provide these products and services.

Based on my experience, I estimate the value to my agency of the average GS 9–11 computer programmer at _____ dollars per year.

We would now like for you to consider the *"superior"* programmer. Let us define a superior performer as a programmer who is at the 85th percentile. That is, his or her performance is better than that of 85 percent of his or her fellow GS 9–11 programmers, and only 15 percent turn in better performances. Consider the quality and quantity of the output typical of the superior programmer. Then estimate the value of these products and services. In placing an overall dollar value on this output, it may again help to consider what the cost would be of having an outside firm provide these products and services.

Based on my experience, I estimate the value to my agency of a superior GS 9–11 computer programmer to be _____ dollars per year.

Finally, we would like you to consider the *"low-performing"* computer *programmer.* Let us define a low-performing programmer as one who is at the 15th percentile. That is, 85 percent of all GS 9–11 computer programmers turn in performances better than the low-performing programmer, and only 15 percent turn in worse performances. Consider the quality and quantity of the output typical of the low-performing programmer. Then estimate the value of these products and services. In placing an overall dollar value on this output, it may again help to consider what the cost would be of having an outside firm provide these products and services.

Based on my experience, I estimate the value to my agency of the low-performing GS 9–11 computer programmer at _____ dollars per year.

Reproduced with permission from Schmidt, Hunter, McKenzie, and Muldrow, 1979, Page 621.

objections are raised. Second, idiosyncratic tendencies, biases, and random errors of the judges can be minimized by averaging across a large number of judges. For example, estimates for the budget analyst position were averaged over 62 supervisors; the resultant standard error of the mean was $1,120, which means that in approximately 90 percent of similar samples, the judges should give estimates between $9,480 and $13,175. A conservative esti- mate of SD_y then would be the lower bound of this estimate, which was $9,480 for the budget analyst position.

Examples of the Application of the Schmidt et al. Analyses

Now suppose we as personnel administrators or consultants are interested in the utility that would accrue to our organization if we institute a new selection procedure. The job is that of secretary. Job incumbents perform a variety of duties: answering telephone calls, typing papers and letters, filing, and answering client or customer questions and complaints. Thirty supervisory personnel, following the Schmidt et al. (1979) procedure provide a mean estimate of SD_y equal to $5,000 (average earnings in this position are $15,000 annually). The standard error of this estimate is $1,000. The true validity (corrected for attenuation due to unreliability in the criterion —see Chapter 5) of the selection procedure is found to be .40. The cost of testing associated with the new procedure is shown to total $100 per applicant. We want to estimate what the utility of this selection procedure would be for various selection ratios. Current- ly, you have 200 applicants for the 100 positions you must fill annually, so the selection ratio is .50. An estimate of current recruit- ing and job advertising costs is approximately $50.00 per appli- cant. Using the Brogden formula and Figure 7–2 which produces $\bar{z}_y$, which is the product $r_{xy}\bar{z}_x$, we can estimate utility:

$$\Delta \bar{u}/\text{person selected} = \bar{z}_y \, SD_y$$

$\bar{z}_y$ from Figure 7–2 with $r_{xy} = .40$ and a selection ratio of .50 is equal to .32.

SD_y is $5,000.00 as stated.

So,

$$\Delta \bar{u}/\text{person selected} = .32 \times \$5,000$$
$$= \$1,600 \text{ per person selected}$$

Multiplying this figure by 100, the number of persons selected in a given year, yields a total value of $160,000. However, the use of the selection tests costs us $100 per applicant, or $20,000 (200 × $100) for the total applicant pool, and recruiting costs are equal to $50 × 200 or $10,000. So the net gain for the year would be equal to *$130,000.*

Now suppose we can, with an increased recruiting effort, reduce the selection ratio to .40. This increased emphasis on recruiting increases our per applicant recruiting cost to $75.00. For a selection ratio of .40, we have the following figures. First, the benefit in dollar terms would be equal to .39 (mean standard criterion score of selected persons from Figure 7-2) × $5,000 ($SD_y$) × 100 (the number selected), or $195,000. Costs of testing would be equal to $100 × 250 (the number of applicants needed to achieve SR = .40) or $25,000. Cost of recruiting would be $75 × 250 or $18,750. Net gain for the year would be $195,000 − $25,000 − $18,750 or **$151,250.**

If further emphasis on recruiting produces a selection ratio of .20 and per applicant recruiting costs of $200, we have the following computations. Our dollar benefit would be .56 (mean standard criterion score from Figure 7-2) × $5000 ($SD_y$) × 100 (the number selected), or $280,000. Costs of testing would be $100 × 500 (the number needed to achieve SR = .20) or $50,000 and the cost of recruiting would be 500 × $200, or $100,000. So, the net gain for one year would be $280,000 − $100,000 − $50,000 or **$130,000.**

In this particular example, we can see that all three approaches to the use of the selection battery indicate that it has substantial organizational worth. The best strategy in terms of overall utility ($151,250) would be to increase recruiting efforts nominally so as to achieve a selection ratio of .40. At a selection ratio of .20, the added costs of recruiting offset the gain realized by the opportunity to raise the average standard score performance of the people selected. However, it is important to point out that if the gains associated with a more competent work force are projected beyond the first year of employment, the analysis would certainly favor a selection ratio of .20, since recruiting and testing costs occur only at the time of hire. The more competent group of employees hired with a selection ratio of .20 will likely add to organizational productivity for more than a single year. Also, our analysis assumes an organization can recruit equally competent persons to lower the selection ratio. This may not be the case as Murphy (1986) has noted, and the utility gains will not be as great as would be estimated by the procedures outlined above. Boudreau (1983a; 1983b) has detailed some of the complexities of projecting gains beyond the first year of employment.

1. Curriculum and Instructional Leadership
2. Coordination of Student Activities
3. Direction of Support Services
4. Staff Selection, Evaluation, and Development
5. Development and Maintenance of Community Relations
6. Coordination with District Offices and Other Schools
7. Fiscal Management
8. Maintenance of School Plant
9. Structures Communication to Facilitate Cooperation Among Various Groups
   in School

Cascio-Ramos Method for Computation of SD_y

Cascio (1982) describes a more complex method to compute the standard deviation of job performance. The Cascio-Ramos approach assumes an organization's compensation program reflects current market rates for jobs and that the economic value of each employee's labor is best reflected in his or her annual wage or salary. Each employee's job is broken down into its principal activities and a proportional amount of the annual salary is assigned to each principal activity. Supervisors then rate each employee's job performance on each principal activity. These ratings are then translated into estimates of dollar value for each activity. The sum of these dollar values associated with each principal activity equals the economic value of each employee's job performance and the standard deviation of the individuals' economic values represents the standard deviation of job performance, SD_y.

1. *Principal activities must be derived.* These data are usually available from job analyses; if not, the methods described in Chapter 3 can be used to generate principal activities. One such list compiled for a school administrator's job by one of your authors is reproduced as Table 7-1.

2. *Each principal activity is rated* numerically for time/frequency, importance, consequence of error, and level of difficulty. Each of these scales is anchored with a zero point so that a judge could indicate that one or more properties of a principal activity is absent. Rating scales for each dimension are presented in Cascio (1982); similar scales and dimensions were described in Chapter 3 of this text.

3. *Multiply the numerical ratings* for time/frequency, importance, consequence of error, and level of difficulty for each principal activity. From this product, relative weights for each principal

TABLE 7-2. *EXAMPLE OF COMPUTATION OF RELATIVE WEIGHTS FOR PRINCIPAL ACTIVITIES OF A SCHOOL ADMINISTRATOR'S JOB.*

PRINCIPAL ACTIVITY	TIME/ FREQUENCY	IMPORTANCE	CONSEQUENCE OF ERROR	LEVEL OF DIFFICULTY	PRODUCT	RELATIVE WEIGHT (%)
1	10	5	5	6	1500	8.4
2	0	3	2	1	0	0.0
3	5	3	4	2	120	0.7
4	20	6	6	6	4320	24.2
5	25	6	6	6	5400	30.2
6	5	2	3	2	60	0.3
7	0	2	2	1	0	0.0
8	10	3	2	3	180	1.0
9	25	6	7	6	6300	35.2
					17880	100.0

PRINCIPAL ACTIVITY	RELATIVE WEIGHT	DOLLAR VALUE
1	8.4	3360
2	0.0	0
3	0.7	280
4	24.2	9680
5	30.2	12080
6	0.3	120
7	0.0	0
8	1.0	400
9	35.2	14080
		40000

activity are derived. After the products for each principal activity are obtained, they are summed to produce a grand total. The product for each principal activity is then divided by the grand total to obtain the relative weight for each principal activity. An example of such a derivation for the nine activities listed in Table 7–1 is given in Table 7–2.

4. *Dollar values are assigned to each principal activity.* Take an average annual rate of pay for job incumbents and allocate it across principal activities. Assume our school administrators receive an average pay of $40,000. Allocation across principal activities using the relative weights derived in Table 7–2 is presented in Table 7–3.

5. *Job performance on each principal activity must be rated.* Cascio suggests a 0–200 scale for ease of computation, though transformations from other rating scales would be possible. On the Cascio scale, 100 is defined as an average employee, and supervisors are asked to make comparisons relative to this value. An example of a performance appraisal form useful for this kind of rating is presented as Figure 7–4.

6. *Multiply the rating for each principal activity expressed as a decimal by the activity's dollar value.* An example for a hypothetical school administrator is presented in Table 7–4.

7. *Compute the overall economic value* for each employee's job performance by adding the results of Step 6. In our example, the economic worth of the school administrator is $47,144 or $7,144 more than the average administrator is paid.

8. *For all employees, compute the mean and standard deviation of dollar-valued job performance.* The mean should be approximately equal to the actual average salary of job incumbents. The standard deviation is the index required for all utility analyses.

Name of principal being rated _____

For each major category of activities listed below, rate how the principal is performing. To do this, use the rating scale below. That is, relative to other principals, how many points (0–200) would you give *this* principal for *each* major category of activities he or she performs.

Principal Activity	*Points*
1. Curriculum and Instructional Leadership	_____
2. Coordination of Student Activities	_____
3. Direction of Support Services	_____
4. Staff Selection, Evaluation, and Development	_____
5. Development and Maintenance of Community Relations	_____
6. Coordination with District Offices and Other Schools	_____
7. Fiscal Management	_____
8. Maintenance of School Plant	_____
9. Structures Communication to Facilitate for Cooperation Among Various Groups in School	_____

From a practical or feasibility point of view, it is important to note that only two sets of ratings are required of the supervisor: (1) a rating of the principal activities on the four scales; and (2) a rating of subordinate's performance on each principal activity. All other steps would be carried out by a staffing specialist.

At this point, we hope that the reader has the tools to develop information concerning the economic implications of various human resource activities and alternatives. In the following section, we will draw upon a recent analysis of utility formulations by Boudreau (1983a) to discuss the possibility of utility analyses that include employee flows in and out of an organization. We also make some suggestions concerning additional research, but we assert that the methods presented above provide reasonable estimates of utility and ought to be used much more widely by industrial/organizational psychologists generally and staffing researchers in particular (Schneider, 1985).

RESEARCH AND RESERVATIONS CONCERNING UTILITY ANALYSES

The research stimulated by the Schmidt et al. (1979) paper as well as their proposed methodology are extremely important developments in utility research and industrial/organizational psychology, in general. It is equally important, however, for the continued credi-

COMPUTATION OF A SCHOOL ADMINISTRATOR'S ECONOMIC
CONTRIBUTION.

TABLE 7–4.

PRINCIPAL ACTIVITY	POINTS ASSIGNED*	DOLLAR VALUE OF ACTIVITY	NET DOLLAR VALUE
1	1.30	3360	4368
2	0.80	0	0
3	0.60	280	168
4	1.20	9680	11616
5	1.25	12080	15100
6	0.70	120	84
7	0.50	0	0
8	0.80	400	320
9	1.10	14080	15488
		Total	47144

*On the 0–200 scale, each of the ratings has been divided by 100. For example, a value of 1.30 reflects a rating of 130.

bility of economic figures generated by these techniques that re-search continue and that necessary refinements to these measurement methods be made. In this section, we detail some of the problems, refinements, and research on utility models that we believe are particularly important.

Dreher and Sackett (1983) have provided several reservations concerning the Schmidt et al. rational estimates of SD_y. They argued that there is no evidence that the rational estimates are valid in the sense that they approximate the true value of SD_y. The Dreher and Sackett comment was made prior to the presentation of some indirect supporting evidence by Schmidt and Hunter (1983). Schmidt and Hunter (1983) noted that their rational estimates of the standard deviation of dollar output are usually about 40 to 60 percent of the average salary employees receive. In the United States economy as a whole, wages and salaries make up about 57 percent of the total value of goods and services produced. So it follows that a worker's output should be about 57 percent of the actual value of the goods and services he produces. Consequently, the standard deviations of actual output should range from 23 percent (.57 × .40) to 34 percent (.57 × .60) of their mean output.

Schmidt and Hunter (1983) calculated the average productivity figures and the average standard deviations in productivity from available studies which reported averages and standard deviations (or information from which they could be calculated). They showed that the average standard deviation of productivity from studies involving employees under piecerate pay systems was 15 percent of their mean output, the average standard deviation of non-piece-rate systems was 20 percent of their mean output, and the average standard deviation of nonspecified compensation systems was 22 percent of their mean output. This suggests that individual differences in productivity tend to be lower under piecerate pay systems. While these figures are somewhat lower than the 23 to 34 percent estimates provided by the rational estimates procedure, they do provide evidence that estimating the degree of individual differences in productivity agrees well with individual differences in productivity reported in the literature. This is indirect evidence of the validity of rational estimates. Of course, it would be helpful if we had studies in which productivity data, or traditional cost accounting data, and rational estimates of dollar productivity were used to compute SD_y for the same sets of employees or organizations. Substantial correlations among these various measures of SD_y would provide the type of construct validity evidence industrial/organizational psychologists demand of other measures.

As Schmidt and Hunter (1983) have recognized, their analysis assumes all people who receive a job offer accept it. If this is not true (i.e., more applicants need to be generated in order to actually hire a given number of people), the selection ratio changes. Further, it is assumed that the organization's applicant pool is a representative sample of the potential applicant pool (i.e., that improved recruiting procedures will not improve or decrease the quality of the applicants). Maintenance of a favorable selection ratio and an applicant pool which possesses the requisite skills obviously depends in part on the success of the organization's recruiting efforts. In the examples above, we assumed that it became increasingly costly to recruit applicants as the selection ratio decreased. Our figures are illustrative only; some research should be done which addresses the relationship between selection and recruiting costs for various occupations. We can expect that this relationship would vary across occupations and with changes in the general economy.

In late 1984 and early 1985 when we were completing our work on the book, there were very large geographic differences in the costs associated with recruiting candidates for job openings. These differences were attributable to unemployment rate differences. For example, around Durham, North Carolina, the unemployment rate was under 5 percent compared to Detroit's almost 15 percent. In Durham, companies were offering higher starting salaries, free child care, flexible working hours, and so forth in their competition for employees. It is important to take these kinds of costs into account when calculating the utility of selection procedures.

These issues become even more important when one attempts to assess the utility of a selection procedure for the national economy. The Taylor-Russell approach, the Brogden formulation, and the Schmidt et al. treatment of utility all consider only the value of the performance of selected applicants for a particular organization.

For the national economy, the rejected applicant represents an expense if their education or training costs are lost when they cannot find employment in a job for which they were trained, if there are costs associated with retraining if they choose that route plus costs associated with their lack of a productive role while being educated, and there is the potential for costs related to physical and mental health problems which result from unemployment or underemployment. It is important that these costs be recognized for several reasons. First, few would deny their reality. Second, the costs associated with unused or unsuccessful education and training and medical care certainly affect our economy in general, and the individual firm through increased taxation. Finally, the use and promotion of simplistic models of the utility of selection devices will certainly destroy the credibility of industrial/organizational psychologists among the very people it is important that we influence.

For example, Boudreau (1983a; 1983b) has cited three economic reasons why the value of productivity "as sold" or the sales value of productivity may misrepresent the institutional benefits of productivity increases. First, where variable costs (like wages) rise or fall with productivity (e.g., with incentive or commission-based pay or variable production overhead), then the portion of the gain in utility to be expected from a selection procedure changes with productivity levels. Second, when the organization faces tax liabilities, a portion of the organization's profit (sometimes an increasing portion) goes to pay taxes. As with individual wage earners, then, increases are not always profitable. Third, when costs and benefits accrue over time, the value of future costs and benefits must be discounted to reflect inflation. While adjustments of the sort suggested by Boudreau usually would serve to suggest a more modest estimate of utility than those presented by Hunter and Schmidt (1982), Boudreau showed that when we consider using selection procedures over a number of years with several cohorts of employees, the Schmidt et al. (1979) utility estimates are conservative. Our point is that industrial/organizational psychologists must learn the language and techniques of economists and accountants not only to increase the accuracy of our utility estimates but also to maximize our credibility.

EMPLOYEE SATISFACTION AND UTILITY

At various places in this text (see especially Chapters 3 and 4), we asserted that individual or employee satisfaction is also an appropriate concern for those interested in selection. While we are not suggesting that attempts be made to express degrees of satisfac-

FIGURE 7–5. A HEURISTIC MODEL OF THE CONSEQUENCES OF A NEGATIVE EMPLOYMENT DECISION.

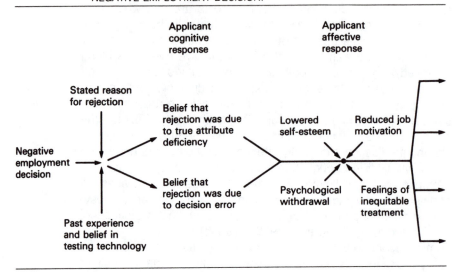

tion in terms of dollar output, it is important that we recognize that we have been discussing only one possible outcome of selection—namely, the positive outcomes that accrue to an organization selecting the most competent applicants.* Dreher and Sackett (1983) have drawn out the personal and societal outcomes generated by false negative (a person is rejected who should have been selected) and true negative (a person who did not possess the requisite skills is rejected) employment decisions. Their model of the consequences of a negative employment decision is presented as Figure 7–5.

The model in Figure 7–5 suggests possible cognitive responses to rejection—either the belief that one is truly deficient or that the organization was wrong in its decision to reject. Possible affective responses include lowered self-esteem and job motivation, psychological withdrawal, and feelings of inequitable treatment. Behaviorally, applicants may respond in a variety of ways depending on their cognitive responses. Their responses also have a variety of individual and societal outcomes. Some attention should be directed toward evaluating the linkages hypothesized in

---

*Obviously, since individual satisfaction is related to individual absenteeism and turnover, predictions of satisfaction (and absenteeism and turnover) can be converted to utility estimates as well (cf. Mirvis and Lawler, 1977). The point here, however, is that there are other foci requiring consideration in addition to the benefits that accrue to an organization.

Applicant behavioral response	Societal outcome		
	If false negative		If true negative
Seek developmental activities ⟶	Wasted personnel and training resources	or	Attribute increment, increased employability
Seek job not requiring attribute ⟶	Manpower underutilization	or	Increased likelihood of proper person-job match
Seek same or similar employment ⟶	Likelihood of proper person-job fit	or	Wasted resources due to recurring application process
Abandon job search ⟶	Long-term unemployment	or	Long-term unemployment

Dreher and Sackett, (1983).

this model. Certainly it is essential that these outcomes be recognized when evaluating organizational outcomes. Frequently there are trade-offs to be made, and these cannot be made intelligently unless the implications of our actions are as clearly specified as possible. Very little work has been done which even specifies what nonorganizational outcomes are relevant or possible or what values are implicit in the decisions we make.

SUMMARY

In this chapter, we have stated our position that utility analyses are essential even using imperfect technology. We have traced the history of utility analyses beginning with the development of purely psychometric definitions of utility. Taylor-Russell tables represented an advance in that they focused attention on the organizational consequences of a selection and the situation (base rate and selection ratio) in which the selections are made. Brogden developed a utility formulation that eliminated the necessity to dichotomize the criterion (a problem with Taylor-Russell tables) and began work which incorporated the cost of testing. Cronbach and Gleser extended the Brogden formulations to placement and classification problems.

The Brogden and Cronbach-Gleser formulations were used rarely until methodology was developed to estimate SD_y. The Schmidt et al. (1979) work as well as that of Cascio (1982) has generated renewed interest, use, and research on utility. Research on utility is needed in several areas: (1) refinements of a cost accounting nature; (2) the construct validity of measures of SD_y; (3) the implications of classification models for utility analyses of the economy; (4) the degree to which practical and statistical assumptions of utility models are met as well as the importance of their violation; and (5) the importance of outcomes associated with applicant rejection.

REFERENCES

Bobko, P., Karren, R., and Parkington, J. J. (1983). Estimation of standard deviations in utility analyses: An empirical test. *Journal of Applied Psychology, 68,* 170–176.

Boudreau, J. (1983a). Effects of employee flows on utility analysis of human resource productivity improvement programs. *Journal of Applied Psychology, 68,* 396–406.

Boudreau, J. W. (1983b). Economic considerations in estimating the utility of human resource productivity improvement programs. *Personnel Psychology, 36,* 551 –576.

Brogden, H. E. (1946). On the interpretation of the correlation coefficient as a measure of predictive efficiency. *Journal of Educational Psychology, 37,* 65–76.

Brogden, H. E. (1949). When testing pays off. *Personnel Psychology, 2,* 171–183.

Brogden, H. E. (1951). Increased efficiency of selection resulting from replacement of a single predictor with several differential predictors. *Educational and Psychological Measurement, 11,* 173–196.

Brogden, H. E. (1959). Efficiency of classification as a function of number of jobs, percent rejected, and the validity and intercorrelation of job performance estimates. *Educational and Psychological Measurement, 19,* 181–190.

Brown, C. W., and Ghiselli, E. E. (1953). Percent increase in proficiency resulting from use of selective devices. *Journal of Applied Psychology, 37,* 341–345.

Cascio, W. F. (1982). *Costing human resources: The financial impact of behavior in organizations.* Boston: Kent.

Cronbach, L. J., and Gleser, G. C. (1965). *Psychological tests and personnel decisions.* Urbana, IL: University of Illinois Press.

Cronbach, L. J., and Schaeffer, G. A. (1981). Extensions of personnel selection theory to aspects of minority hirings. Stanford University Project Report No. 81–A2.

Cronbach, L. J., Yalow, E., and Schaeffer, G. A. (1980). A mathematical structure for analyzing fairness in selection. *Personnel Psychology, 33,* 693–704.

Dreher, G. F., and Sackett, P. R. (1983). *Perspectives on employee staffing and selection: Readings and commentary.* Homewood, IL: Irwin.

Dunnette, M. D., and Borman, W. C. (1979). Personnel selection and classification systems. *Annual Review of Psychology, 30,* 477–525.

Hull, C. L. (1928). *Aptitude testing.* Yonkers, NY: World Book Co.

Hunter, J. E., Schmidt, F. L. and Rauschenberger, J. M. (1977). Fairness of psychological tests: Implication of four definitions for selection utility and minority hiring. *Journal of Applied Psychology, 62,* 245–260.

Hunter, J. E., and Schmidt, F. L. (1982). Fitting people to jobs: The impact of personnel selection on national productivity. In M. D. Dunnette and E. A. Fleishman (Eds.). *Human Performance and Productivity.*

Mirvis, P. H., and Lawler, E. E., III (1977). Measuring the financial impact of employee attitudes. *Journal of Applied Psychology, 62,* 1–8.

Murphy, K. A. (1986). When your top choice turns you down: Effect of rejected job offers on the utility of selection tests. *Psychological Bulletin, 99,* 133–138.

Schmidt, F. L., Hunter, J. E., McKenzie, R., and Muldrow, T. (1979). Impact of valid selection procedures on workforce productivity. *Journal of Applied Psychology, 64,* 609–626.

Schmidt, F. L., and Hunter, J. E. (1983). Individual differences in productivity: An empirical test of estimates derived from studies of selection procedure utility. *Journal of Applied Psychology, 68,* 407–414.

Schneider, B. (1985). Organizational behavior. *Annual Review of Psychology, 36,* 573–611.

Taylor, H. C., and Russell, J. T. (1939). The relationship of validity coefficients to the practical effectiveness of tests in selection. *Journal of Applied Psychology, 23,* 565–578.

Tenopyr, M. L. (1981). Trifling he stands. *Personnel Psychology, 34,* 1–18.

Tenopyr, M. L. (1983). Comments on Symposium: Cost Analyses of Human Resource Interventions: Are they worth it? Anaheim, CA: American Psychological Association.

8

HIRING PROCEDURES I
Overview and Cognitive Ability Testing

AIMS OF THE CHAPTER

In previous chapters you have been exposed to some principles underlying the history of staffing (Chapter 1), procedures and rationale for conducting job and organizational analyses (Chapter 2), staff analysis (Chapter 3), factors determining the supply of applicants to an organization (Chapter 4), methods for interrelating variables (Chapters 5 and 6), and procedures for calculating the utility of using personnel selection procedures (Chapter 7). In Chapters 8, 9 and 10 we will discuss the various procedures psychologists have devised as aids to making predictions about individual behavior. These procedures include different kinds of paper and pencil tests, interviews, and simulations.

The next three chapters, then, restate ways to predict the behavior of individuals through assessments of their individual characteristics. They are based largely on the idea that individuals' attributes are among the most important determinants of their success.

This chapter has two major sections. First we present an overview of issues related to assessing individuals for employment: how applicants are treated, the current levels of the use of selection procedures, and thoughts on the three facets of behavior usually assessed (aptitude, training, and motivation). The second section focuses on paper and pencil tests of aptitudes and the validity of aptitude tests. In the latter section, we discuss the very important topic of validity generalization.

OVERVIEW OF ISSUES IN THE HIRING PROCESS

Chapters 8, 9 and 10 are concerned with the relative effectiveness of different ways of identifying people who are (1) most likely to meet various criteria (2) under particular organizational conditions (3) on a specific job. However, the hiring process is in fact a two-way process. It does not simply involve a single point in time when an organization makes a decision. As a two-way process, the hiring process is a situation in which both the organization and the individual have mutual needs and something to offer each other. The problem is to create a match that will satisfy both parties. Through job and organizational analysis we can identify what the organization wants, but how many organizations ask their potential new hires that question?

The hiring process has typically been one in which only the

organization expresses its needs and relates them to what applicants offer. We asked in Chapter 4: do individuals have the opportunity to find out what organizations have to offer? If organizations desire to create the kind of implicit, or psychological, contract (Schein, 1980) with their employees that will have mutual long-term benefits, then the hiring process that follows the recruiting process should also reflect the organization's commitment to its human resources.

Certainly the work reviewed in Chapter 4 by Wanous and his colleagues on the effect of realistic job previews is evidence of the behavioral and attitudinal impact of information given to employees before hiring. A study by Schmitt and Coyle (1976) is also evidence of the fact that participants in the hiring process form important perceptions of the company during that process. Schmitt and Coyle asked college graduates for their perceptions of a college recruitment interview and their appraisals of the interviewer, the organization she or he represented and the likelihood of their accepting a job if one was offered. The respondents' perceptions that the interviewer was "a nice person" and that she or he supplied job-relevant information during the interview were significantly related to their impressions of organizations and the feeling that they would be likely to accept a job offer.

The early interactions between individual and organization may be crucial. An individual's first contact with an organization is especially important when the individual has no prior work history. For such people everything is new, and the impressions they form of an organization fill an information-hungry vacuum. For more experienced people, the initial contact with an organization represents their first opportunity to determine the tone or philosophy under which it operates. Of course, for experienced people, their previously reinforced views about organizational life will persist for a period of time, but, with *behavioral* evidence, people *can* change their attitudes and opinions.

Just as during recruitment, everything that occurs in the formal hiring process clues people in about the working conditions that prevail in an organization. Guion (1965), although speaking of testing per se, supported this view when he noted that:

> Organizational policies decide many of the details of personnel testing in any given setting. Attitudes toward the whole idea of testing held by major organizational officers may determine whether any tests at all will be used and, if so, the degree of importance attached to them . . . . But there are other elements to be considered as well: the community, as a source of applicants and as a judge of the organization and its treatment of people, and the broader spirit of the times that

says that human dignity must not be compromised with unethical ends or shoddy means (p. 512).

Guion (1965, p. 485) also provides a review of the kinds of factors that may influence the effectiveness of a hiring program.

1. *General Personnel Policies*—including beliefs about selection, placement and development, discrimination, etc., which affect the kinds of hiring procedures utilized.
2. *The Environment of the Organization*—which affects production and marketing policies that in turn impact on the kinds of employees required and the speed with which they must be hired.
3. *Organizational Characteristics*—including centralization or decentralization, which may affect the design of hiring processes and procedures and the management philosophy regarding the value of human resources.
4. *Written Policies Governing the Hiring Process*—including the presence or absence of clear objectives, the qualifications of the people running the hiring process, who has the responsibility for making decisions, and so forth (see Albright, 1974, for a comprehensive sample of corporate policy statements on staffing issues).
5. *Administration of the Hiring Program*—including the care with which hiring procedures are evaluated, the administration of tests, the conduct of interviews, the availability of facilities for conducting testing and interviewing, and the integration of hiring procedures with recruiting, training, and evaluation.
6. *Researching the Hiring Process*—the extent to which there is a continuing investment of time and money in improving the understanding and predictability of human behavior at work.

In the terminology used in Chapter 2, Guion has put forth a list of behaviors that create the "climate" of the hiring process. All of these variables suggest to those involved in hiring personnel—and, obviously, to those going through the hiring process—the organization's care and concern for its human resources. Two clear ways in which an organization can demonstrate its concern for what happens in the hiring process are to provide information to applicants and to utilize staffing specialists.

The Life Insurance Marketing and Research Association (LIMRA) has prepared a pamphlet, which presents information in a constructive manner, for those taking the test used in selecting life insurance sales representatives. It also presents to test takers *their* responsibilities for decision-making as they go through the hiring process. This is to stress the two-way nature of the decision to be made. Of course, each company must insure that what it says about the role of testing represents the facts about the role of testing in its particular organization. The pamphlet used by LIMRA member companies is reproduced as Figure 8–1.

With regard to the use of staffing specialists, remember that hiring procedures are diagnostic processes, and diagnosis requires expertise. Just as we would not trust an assessment of the physical health of employees to an untrained person, assessment of the psychological attributes of employees should also be under the direction of trained staffing specialists.

Such specialists are trained, not born, and simply because people call themselves consultants does not make them experts. There is evidence to suggest, for example, that corporations are likely to believe what consultants tell them without attempting to validate the consultant (Campbell et al., 1970); someone who claims expertise should prove it just as a test should be validated before it can legitimately be used as a basis for hiring decisions.

The amount of confidence we place in staffing specialists should be governed by their answers to questions like, where were they trained and in what?

1. *Generally* speaking, people trained in psychology departments in clinical, counseling, or industrial-personnel psychology at the M.A. level or above will have some competence in the use of various hiring procedures. However, someone without a Ph.D., unless they have *verifiable* prior experience, should probably not be permitted to direct a hiring program.
2. People who work for a consulting firm under the direction of a Diplomate in Psychology or a Fellow of a relevant Division of the American Psychological Association (APA) can generally be relied on. The Diplomate in Psychology is awarded to psychologists in Clinical, School, and Organizational-Industrial psychology and certifies that they are competent practitioners. The Fellowship in APA is awarded only to acknowledged contributors to the science and profession after a lengthy evaluation of credentials. Diplomates and Fellows are listed by the APA.
3. One should not rely, in any case, on the enthusiastic endorsement of consultants by other people who are unaware of what constitutes acceptable practices in hiring employees.

The point here is that, after recruitment, the next contact people have with the prospective employing organization takes place during the hiring process. How this process is handled, the care taken to insure that it is directed by competent people, and the treatment and concern shown to applicants, provide information that applicants use as they also make their decisions. The impact of such carelessness cannot be underestimated because, as noted in Chapter 4, the applicant, as well as the organization, has an information void at the time of the initial contact. Both are anxious for

FIGURE 8-1. INFORMATION SUPPLIED TO LIMRA EXAMINEES.

Now That You've Taken the AIB

You've just completed the *Aptitude Index Battery* (AIB)

The AIB will probably have been mailed to Hartford, Connecticut, by the time you read this. It will be scored by machine within a few hours of its receipt at the Life Insurance Marketing and Research Association headquarters, and the results will be mailed direct to the office where the AIB was administered to you. As soon as the results arrive, you will be notified.

As you may already know, this is but one step in a complex selection process. No selection tool, no matter how good, can substitute for a thorough exploration of the job and of the individual, and how they match up. This statement is true of any job, but it is especially true of a job as involved and as challenging as that of an insurance agent.

The Role of the AIB

Before going futher, however, let's be sure that you understand the role of the AIB in the selection process. The AIB is designed to determine your aptitude for selling. It was developed by the Life Insurance Marketing and Research Association, an international, cooperative research organization. The questionnaire has been polished and sharpened by continuous research over a period of 40 years.

The precision of the AIB is in part based on the fact that it has one purpose only: *to determine your odds of succeeding as a sales representative.* It says *nothing* about your aptitude for other types of jobs in the insurance business or in any other industry.

The Meaning of the Results

Your AIB rating may indicate that your chances of succeeding as a sales representative are very low. You should be glad to know this early in the process before you or the people with whom you have talked have invested a lot of time—and before you have committed yourself by severing present occupational ties. The risks to you and to the organization for which you completed the questionnaire would be great if you proceeded further. But, *you can be sure that the results say nothing about your career potential in other areas.*

On the other hand, don't feel that a high rating is a guarantee of success. It merely means that you have passed the first hurdle toward a favorable recommendation to look into a career as a sales representative. There is much more to be considered before the final decision is made. Because this job is complex, there are two major steps to take before reaching a final decision.

Further Steps

First, you must provide as much information about yourself as possible. Only in this way can you be advised properly. Those talking to you should know all about your past accomplishments—and the things that you like and don't like to do. You can expect a number of interviews in order to examine your background fully.

In addition to the interviews, several other steps will be taken. These steps are essential not only to help you make your decision but also to help the company decide whether it is justified in making the substantial investment necessary to start you in the business.

Have a Clear Picture of the Job

Another important step to take if you receive a favorable AIB rating is to ask questions that will give you a picture of exactly what the insurance business is all about.

For the right person, it can be the finest opportunity ever encountered. It represents one of the few opportunities for individual enterpreneurship

without substantial personal investment. It offers one of the few opportunities in our economy in which income is totally dependent on the competence of the individual. It represents one of the few opportunities that you may ever find where eventual total independence is possible. For the wrong person, however, it can be a very short path to frustration and failure. For that reason, it's very important that you find out exactly what kind of job you are looking at.

The organization giving you the AIB will expect careful scrutinizing on your part and will assume that you will accept a careful examination of your potential through the additional steps in the selection process. There will be a systematic schedule that will provide for opportunities to explore the career. You will have a chance later in the process to find out exactly what it is that you will be doing, how you will spend your days, how you will spend your evenings, and where you will go to obtain your prospects.

You may have a chance to experience certain parts of the job before either you or the organization makes a commitment. You may be given training assignments similar to those that you will have in the future, and your may be taken into the field to see what actually happens during sales calls.

Just as the organization that gave you the AIB will not be satisfied with less than a clear picture of you and your potential, you should not be satisfied until you have a clear picture of the kind of work that you will be asked to do. *Don't be satisfied until you feel that you completely understand the kinds of satisfactions—and frustrations—that you will find.*

After you have this clear picture of the business and the company has a clear picture of you, then you are ready for a decision—not before.

So, if you do not obtain a high *Aptitude Index Battery* rating, forget about this position; it is not for you. But if the rating is satisfactory, then realize that from the point of view of both the company and you, the selection procedures have just begun.

From *Now that You've Taken the Test.* Hartford, Conn: LIMRA, undated. Used by permission.

TABLE 8-1.   SELECTION PROCEDURES USED IN HIRING AND PROMOTING.

	PERCENT OF COMPANIES (n=437)	
	Procedures for Outside Applicants	Procedures for Candidates for Promotion
Reference/record check	97% (426)	67% (292)
Unstructured interview	81 (355)	70 (305)
Skill performance test/work sample	75 (329)	40 (176)
Medical examination	52 (229)	8 (34)
Structured interview	47 (206)	32 (142)
Investigation by outside agency	26 (112)	3 (14)
Job knowledge test	22 (94)	15 (64)
Mental ability test	20 (89)	10 (44)
Weighted application blank	11 (49)	7 (30)
Personality test	9 (39)	4 (18)
Assessment center	6 (28)	7 (30)
Physical abilities test	6 (27)	4 (16)
Polygraph test/written honesty test	6 (27)	1 (4)
Other	3 (13)	2 (9)

From ASPA, (1983).

information to use as a basis for decision-making. In the next section, we will review how organizations obtain information on job applicants.

Extent of Use of Selection Procedures

In 1961, figures indicated that from 150 to 250 million standardized tests were administered yearly (Goslin, 1963). Although many of these were used in schools, a large number were also used in employment. The Psychological Corporation, a major test publisher, reported in the late 1960s that 90 percent of the 500 largest U.S. companies purchased tests from their firm during a five-year period. The Equal Employment Opportunity Commission contended that the extent of employment test usage increased markedly in the 1960s. There is some evidence that the use of psychological tests declined in the 1970s because of the increased litigation resulting from the alleged unfair use of tests (Prentice-Hall, 1975). Recently, survey responses from 437 personnel executives randomly selected from among the members of American Society for Personnel Administration (ASPA, 1983), also indicated a move away from traditional paper and pencil tests to procedures that have less frequently been the subject of legal challenges. Table 8–1 is a summary of these responses.

Selection techniques most frequently used by companies to

screen outside job applicants were reference checks, unstructured interviews, skill performance tests and medical examinations. Generally, the same selection methods are used for all outside applicants, regardless of the position being filled. The one exception is for office/clerical job applicants who faced skill tests in 73 percent of the firms surveyed, whereas only 20 percent of the skilled non-office workers were selected by skill tests and less than 10 percent in other occupations. Approximately one third of the companies used commercially prepared tests. Of those 132 firms, 80 percent use tests developed for office/clerical positions and 30 percent use standard tests for professional/technical applicants such as computer programmers, police officers, and firefighters.

Changes in use of employee selection procedures are equally interesting. According to the ASPA report, 26 percent of the companies surveyed discontinued some aspect of their employee selection program. Thirteen companies discontinued all testing between 1977–1982. Mental ability tests which include math, grammar, and spelling tests were eliminated in 17 companies during the same years. Fifteen companies indicated that clerical testing in general, or specifically, typing, shorthand, or mental ability tests for office/clerical applicants have been stopped. Personal questions were removed from application blanks in nine companies and medical exams have been dropped by seven companies. Other procedures that have been cut from selection programs include informal interviews, personality tests, polygraph tests, credit checks, reference or record checks and dexterity tests. Reasons for stopping the use of these procedures were usually related to fear of legal action or inability to validate the measures.

New or revised selection techniques were introduced by 32 percent of the companies during the same five year period. The largest number of these (38 firms) have implemented structured interviews and/or interviewer training. Tests were added by 19 companies and more emphasis was placed on reference checking in 11 firms and revised application blanks in 10. Respondents also mentioned incorporating assessment centers, skills tests, job knowledge tests, and increased reliance on outside consulting and testing services.

A General Portrait of Human Behavior

The whole idea of collecting information on job candidates is to make some statement about *future job behavior.* If job behaviors are our criteria, then we have to ask ourselves: what are the characteristics of people that should be related to their future behavior? One important characteristic of work behavior is *motivation.* People apparently work for certain reasons. They come to work or fail to come to work, do good or poor work, stay or leave because their behavior results in the attainment of something they desire. People are motivated, and this motivation in part determines the behavior we observe.

A second factor in work behavior is *experience* associated with formal *education and training.* The behavior of people is quite reliable over time because their training and education today in part determine their behavior tomorrow. The quality and quantity of training people bring with them to an organization, and the training an organization provides them, should be related to their behavior.

A third characteristic of people that is important for us to identify is *aptitude.* Generally speaking, we think of people's motivation and experience as tied to their environment, and their aptitude as more strongly related to hereditary factors or the sum total of their cultural or general life experiences (as compared to experiences from formal education and training). In any event, aptitude seems less changeable than either motivation or experience although it should be noted parenthetically that motivation and the results of education and training are also frequently difficult to broaden or change.

If a person's motivation, experience, and aptitude are not relevant for being effective on a particular job, then we cannot expect him to perform appropriately. And not one of these personal attributes seems to be both necessary *and* sufficient for effective behavior; in *combination* they yield effective behavior.

Thus, while aptitudes are probably the most fundamental requirement, without motivation and an appropriate response repertoire, effective job behavior will not be displayed. So, aptitude gets reflected in job-relevant behavior when the environment provides the right conditions in the form of rewards (and training, if needed).

Note that for each issue (aptitude, motivation, and training/experience) it is the fit or match of the individual and the job/organization that is important. The person's aptitudes need to fit the job requirements; the job/organization rewards need to fit the individual's desires; and the match between job requirements and individual experience must either exist or be created through training. When all of these matches are present, both individuals and organizations should be successful.

Unfortunately, not all people have the appropriate aptitudes for a task, and the desires they have may be incompatible with the rewards an organization has to offer. In addition, an organization may not be able (may not have the time) to provide the training necessary for effective performance, so individuals must come to them with the training or not be employed. All varieties of such situations exist; simply using high (H) or low (L) categories to rate aptitude, training and individual desire-organization reward congruence, we can obtain eight possible combinations; only one, HHH, is clearly a case in which there is a high probability of success.

APTITUDE	TRAINING	DESIRE-REWARD CONGRUENCE
H	H	H
H	H	L
H	L	L
H	L	H
L	L	L
L	L	H
L	H	H
L	H	L

Adequate job and organization analysis can tell us the KSAs required for task performance, the reward characteristics of the job and organization, and the background required to accomplish the task. Given such analysis, the development of adequate predictors is possible. By assessing Aptitude and Training, we assess what a person *can* do; when we assess Desire-Reward Congruence, we assess what they *will* do.

A distinction among types of predictors that captures the difference between *can* and *will* do has been referred to by Cronbach (1970) as the difference between *maximum* performance and *typical* performance predictors. The former includes measures of physical capabilities, general mental ability, proficiency in some job task, or specific knowledge and skills. Measures of *typical* performance include procedures designed to assess character, personality, interests, attitudes, and motivation.

In the remainder of this chapter and the next two we will discuss different procedures for assessing maximum and typical performance as predictors of success. These procedures include paper and pencil tests, interviews, situational experiences and the assessment of biographical information. The greatest attention will be given to paper and pencil tests (hereafter simply "tests"), specifically aptitude tests, as predictors. There are two reasons for this. First, since tests are objectively scored, the chances of their being reliable and fair are greater than for other assessment procedures; this is particularly true of tests of aptitude and achievement. Second, an organization has less opportunity to influence the aptitude of its work force than it does to influence the motivation and experience of its people. Aptitude assessment, in turn, permits organizations to make decisions about what experiences employees need.

PAPER AND PENCIL APTITUDE TESTS

General Intelligence

In Chapter 1 we placed considerable emphasis on the concept of individual differences and on the late nineteenth-century attempts of Binet and Simon to diagnose children who were most likely to benefit from the typical school curriculum. The items for their tests were developed on the basis of observation of the kinds of knowledge, skills, and abilities required for success at school and validated against teacher judgments of whether the students were fast or slow learners.

Note that because Binet and Simon selected the actual items for their test based on the item's validity, a person's score on the test would be a simple sum of the items answered correctly. That is, the score would be a single number. Note also that the situation for which the test would be valid was the classroom, a fairly well-standardized situation—a single teacher in the front of the room, rows of desks, about twenty children, and so forth. In addition, since the items selected for the test were those that correlated with school performance as judged by teachers, adaptations and translations of the test into many languages (in the United States by Lewis Terman at Stanford University, resulting in what is called the Stanford-Binet) created a tidal wave of testing in Western countries. Subsequently, adult forms of the Stanford-Binet were developed and a competing test, the Wechsler-Bellevue (Wechsler, 1944), subsequently the *Wechsler Adult Intelligence Scale* or WAIS, was produced for assessing adult intelligence. And, while the Stanford-Binet and WAIS required one tester for each examinee (*individually administered tests*), other tests were produced (e.g., Otis Quick-Scoring Mental Abilities) that were suited to group administration (*group administered tests*).

Tests of general mental ability have been shown to be valid in many industrial studies, especially in the selection of first line supervisors (Ghiselli, 1966; 1973; Schmidt, Hunter, Pearlman, & Shane, 1979). One of the more frequently used tests of this sort is the Wonderlic Personnel Test (Wonderlic, 1984). This 12-minute test contains 50 items that are quite varied in content, covering vocabulary, arithmetic reasoning, spatial visualization, number series, and other areas. The Wonderlic has more parallel (or equivalent or alternate) forms available for use than any other test in this category that we are aware of—nine different forms. Wonderlic has provided extensive norms on this test, broken down by region of the country, sex, age, race, and education. This allows the comparison of any applicant's score to scores made by others of the same region, race, educational level, etc. This may sound at first like a real advantage, and it is of some value. But norms are usually not very important in employment because people should be hired on the basis (at least in part) of the magnitude of their test score, not their standing in a norm group. The critical question is how *valid* the test had been in past applications. Various studies of the Wonderlic suggest validity for a wide range of jobs. The Wonderlic and other tests like it, however, often show majority-minority differences in average scores, and the Equal Employment Opportunity Commission has come to react negatively to the use of tests like it even before the validity evidence is examined. This is an example of a situation in which scientific support for validity is in conflict with court decisions regarding employment discrimination.

Multidimensional Concepts of General Intellectual Aptitude

Thurstone (1941) thought that the idea of general intelligence was an oversimplification. He was intrigued by a technique Spearman (1904) had developed called factor analysis (see Chapter 5). Spearman had used factor analysis to show that whenever a set of tests was given to a group of people, the intercorrelations of the tests always revealed something in common—that is, there was always some overlap or relationship between the tests. He interpreted this as support for his concept of "G" or General Intelligence. "Thurstone . . . turned the question around and asked *how many* and *what kinds* of factors are needed to account for the observed correlations among tests of ability." (Nunnally, 1978).

To make a very long, very systematic, very original set of research efforts short, the following intellectual abilities were identified as being primary (see Thurstone, 1941):

1. Verbal Comprehension—found in tests of vocabulary, antonyms and synonyms, completion tests, and various reading comprehension tests.
2. Word Fluency—found in tests of anagrams, rhyming, and producing words with a given initial letter, prefix, or suffix.
3. Space—any test in which the task of the subject is to manipulate an object imaginally in a two or three dimensional space.
4. Number—tests which require the subject to rapidly and accurately do relatively simple calculations; *not* problem solving.
5. Memory—test of the ability to memorize quickly.

6. Reasoning—tests requiring the subject to discover rules or principles covering the material of a test. (Two such factors seemed to emerge, one for deductive and another for inductive reasoning.)

Guilford (1967) made another major effort to identify factors of intellect. He attempted not only to identify ability factors but also to conceptualize the structure of intellect. That is, given existing factors he asked the question: how can I organize what already exists so I can know what is still to be discovered? In reviewing the research of other scholars, and by conducting his own research over a number of years, Guilford (1967) presented a three-factor, or three-faces, of intellect model:

1. The kind of process or *operation* the abilities represent: What the individual must do to respond appropriately to the item.
   a. Cognition—to know or be aware or be able to discover information
   b. Memory—retention of information
   c. Convergent thinking—use of information to achieve one best answer
   d. Divergent thinking—use of information to develop many possible answers
   e. Evaluation—judging the quality ("goodness") of information
2. The *content* of the ability. That is, the nature of the kinds of information the individual is required to *operate* on.
   a. Figural—information coming through the various sense modalities (smell, touch, etc.)
   b. Symbolic—information coming in the form of symbols (numbers, letters, etc.)
   c. Semantic—verbal meanings or ideas
   d. Behavioral—pertaining to the behavior of other people
3. The *product* or outcome of the operation of the ability on any kind of content.
   a. Units
   b. Classes
   c. Relations
   d. Systems
   e. Transformations
   f. Implications

Multidimensional Concepts of Potentially Job-Related Aptitudes

There are single measures of aptitude for specific occupations (e.g., clerical, sales) and *multi-aptitude batteries.* The latter are sets of tests, administered as a package, that yield aptitude scores on anywhere from eight to fourteen potentially job-relevant dimensions.

Of course, since these batteries are commercially available, the tests are not specific to a particular job. The tests are designed to be applicable to a wide variety of jobs and settings. On the other hand, the care taken in developing the measures to insure their generality, reliability, and *potential* validity make them useful in approximating the contribution more specific tests can make to predicting effective job performance.

In the larger scheme of things, including the use of tests for *promotion* as well as for hiring, the multi-aptitude batteries provide the most information on job candidates in the least amount of time. Furthermore, profiles of aptitude scores can be used to evaluate individuals from a multi- rather than uni-dimensional viewpoint. Such a view may be a step toward conceptualizing personnel selection decisions in terms of complex humans. However, one additional note: multi-aptitude batteries do not assess all of the important job aptitudes. In each situation job analyses should reveal the salient aspects of the job situation, thereby pinpointing which characteristics of potential employees should be assessed. Further, we shouldn't expect that all aptitudes are best assessed by "paper and pencil" tests; this is a point we shall consider later in this chapter.

Four of the better known multi-aptitude batteries are:

1. Differential Aptitude Tests (DAT)
2. Flanagan Aptitude Classification Tests (FACT)
3. General Aptitude Test Battery (GATB)
4. Employee Aptitude Survey (EAS)

Table 8–2 presents the subtests offered in each. It can be noted that there is considerable overlap in content among the tests and between multi-aptitude batteries and tests of more general intellectual factors. While there is overlap in content between EAS and the other batteries, the EAS (besides having considerable validity evidence) takes about one hour to complete; the DAT, on the other hand, required four hours, and FACT a comparable period. The GATB is not available for in-house use; applicants are generally tested only at State Employment Services.

In Chapter 2 we suggested that the GATB factors could be used as categories by which aptitude requirements could be estimated during job analysis. It should be clear now that any one of the batteries we have mentioned, or some locally developed battery, can serve as a system for categorizing the kinds of ability requirements that predominate in a particular organizational situation.

Another point regarding Table 8–2 is that two of the batteries, GATB and EAS, include tests of fine motor abilities, while the DAT and FACT do not. These "eye-hand" kinds of abilities, along with the "pure" sensory tests of vision (including color blindness) and hearing, represent some of the earliest and most continually valid measures we have for tasks involving a high sensorimotor component. Measurement of physical abilities is so important that we shall discuss the topic in a special section in Chapter 9.

You may think that the aptitudes listed in Table 8–2 are very general in that they appear somewhat abstract and somewhat removed from the kinds of activities people engage in at work. This perception is accurate because the general kinds of aptitude batteries discussed so far emphasize basic or primary abilities, and it may require expert judgment to make the inference about which of these aptitudes is most likely to be valid for a particular job.

Some test publishers have also seen the potential for problems here, and they have presented batteries of tests more clearly related to the kinds of abilities and skills required at work. Thus, they have reasoned that the basic or primary aptitude tests can be useful for making general assessments of people's basic abilities, but that more specificity in assessment could be valuable for the prediction of effectiveness at a specific job.

Table 8–3, for example, presents the 20 subtests available in one battery of specific aptitude tests (Psychological Services, *Basic Skills Tests,* 1982). The titles and descriptions suggest that these tests may have more work relevance. This is true even though a factor analysis of the 20 tests yields clusters of the tests with familiar names like:

- Verbal Ability
- Quantitative Ability
- Reasoning Ability
- Perceptual Speed

It is always likely that similar analyses of any set of tests will yield factors similar to those labeled primary mental abilities by Thurstone, but tests can be developed that appear more directly job content relevant.

Some interesting characteristics of the Basic Skills Tests are:

- No test requires more than 10 minutes and most (14 of them) take only 5 minutes;
- A technical report is available (Ruch & Dye, 1982) that documents the results of a consortium study of the validity of these tests for clerical jobs including the job analysis procedures, and information about the validation sample, criteria, and testing procedures.

TABLE 8-2. SOME MULTI-APTITUDE BATTERIES AND WHAT THEY TEST.

DAT	FACT	GATB	EAS*
1. Verbal Reasoning	1. Inspection	1. General Intelligence	1. Verbal Comprehension
2. Numerical Ability	2. Coding	2. Verbal	2. Numerical Ability
3. Abstract Reasoning	3. Memory	3. Numerical	3. Visual Pursuit
4. Space Relations	4. Precision	4. Spatial	4. Visual Speed and Accuracy
5. Mechanical Reasoning	5. Assembly	5. Form Perception	5. Space Visualization
6. Clerical Speed and Accuracy	6. Scales	6. Clerical Perception	6. Numerical Reasoning
7. Language Usage (Spelling)	7. Coordination	7. Motor Coordination	7. Verbal Reasoning
8. Language Usage (Sentences)	8. Judgment and Comprehension	8. Finger Dexterity	8. Word Fluency
	9. Arithmetic	9. Manual Dexterity	9. Manual Speed and Accuracy
	10. Patterns		10. Symbolic Reasoning
	11. Components		
	12. Tables		
	13. Mechanics		
	14. Expression		

*Designed specifically for the industrial situation with considerable validity data (Grimsley and Jarrett, 1973; Ruch and Ruch, 1980)

TABLE 8–3. *SPECIFIC APTITUDES TESTED BY THE PSI BASIC SKILLS TESTS.*

1. Language Skills—ability to recognize correct spelling, punctuation, capitalization, grammar, and usage.
2. Reading Comprehension—ability to read a passage and answer literal and inferential questions about it.
3. Vocabulary—ability to identify the correct meanings of words.
4. Computation—ability to solve arithmetic problems involving operations with whole numbers, decimals, percents, and simple fractions.
5. Problem Solving—ability to solve "story" problems requiring the application of arithmetic operations.
6. Decision-Making—ability to read a set of procedures and apply them to new situations.
7. Following Oral Directions—ability to listen to information and instructions presented orally, taking notes if desired, and to answer questions about the content.
8. Following Written Directions—ability to read and follow a set of rules.
9. Forms Checking—ability to verify the accuracy of completed forms by comparison to written information.
10. Reasoning—ability to analyze facts and to make valid judgments on the basis of the logical implications of such facts.
11. Classifying—ability to place information into predetermined categories.
12. Coding—ability to code information according to prescribed system.
13. Filing Names—ability to insert names in a list in alphabetical order.
14. Filing Numbers—ability to insert numbers in a list in numerical order.
15. Visual Speed and Accuracy—ability to see differences in small detail.
16. Memory—ability to recall information after having a chance to study it.
17. Typing-Practice copy—a preparatory typing test to Tests 18, 19, and 20. Test 18 assesses typing of straight copy; Test 19 the typing from copy that has been revised in handwriting; and, Test 20 measures the ability to set up and type tables according to specific directions.

From Psychological Services, Inc. (1982).

The Validity of Aptitude Tests: Validity Generalization

Most of the manuals for the tests discussed above report data on the validity of the tests in various situations for different groups of people. Additional information concerning many of these tests is available in the Mental Measurements Yearbook (Buros, 1978). This book publishes critical reviews of tests by one or more expert reviewers and is now undergoing its ninth revision, the first occurring in 1938. These yearbooks cover nearly all commercially available psychological, educational, and vocational tests published in English.

A number of psychological and educational journals represent additional sources of current information about tests. New tests are regularly abstracted in *Psychological Abstracts,* as are articles about tests. *Educational and Psychological Measurement* and *Personnel Psychology* have, in the past, included a section dealing with the construction, use and evaluation of tests, particularly articles on test validity.

OCCUPATION	INTELLECTUAL ABILITIES	SPATIAL AND MECHANICAL ABILITIES	PERCEPTUAL ACCURACY	MOTOR ABILITIES
Managerial	.25(.20– .30)	.23(.18–.24)	.19(.00–.32)	
Clerical	.27(.21– .36)	.20(.05–.30)	.27(–.17–.46)	.15(–.11– .42)
Sales (Clerks)	–.10(–.16– .08)		–.05(–.15–.02)	
Sales	.31(.26– .33)	.07(–.02–.16)	.21(.21)	
Protective Service	.23(.08– .26)	.16(.08–.23)	.17(.16–.17)	.19(.19)
Personal Service	.03(–.11– .07)		–.10(–.27–.14)	–.05(–.09—.01)
Vehicle Operator	.14(.04– .14)	.20(.18–.21)	.36(.36)	.30(.28– .32)
Trades and Crafts	.19(–.17– .34)	.23(.04–.44)	.22(–.12–.53)	.19(.01– .57)
Industrial	.16(–.01– .34)	.16(.11–.42)	.18(–.11–.36)	.17(–.02– .43)

Adapted from Edwin E. Ghiselli, *The Validity of Occupational Aptitude Tests* (New York, Wiley, 1966). pp. 34, 37, 41, 44, 46, 48, 50, 56. Reprinted with permission.

Perhaps the most comprehensive reviews of the use of tests in personnel selection have been conducted by Ghiselli (1966, 1973). His reviews included summaries of studies done on the validity of maximum and typical performance tests for different occupations. His work provides a starting point for clues regarding the kinds of assessments most likely to be valid in a particular occupation. In Table 8–4, Ghiselli has summarized some of these data by type of test and for various occupations. While Ghiselli (1966) included the validity of each kind of test for both proficiency criteria and training criteria, Table 8–4 contains only the *proficiency* data. Note that the levels of validity coefficients include both predictive and concurrent studies, averaged together. Note further that for any one type of test according to Ghiselli's system of classification, a large number of different tests may have actually been used; the same caution applies to the notions of proficiency (it includes many different criteria) and occupations (each occupation includes studies for many different jobs). The fact that the tests show any validity after all of this averaging and collapsing of categories, attests to their potential usefulness in particular situations. For information about specific occupations, the reader should consult Ghiselli (1966). In his book he reports coefficients for some 21 different occupations as coded by the General Occupational Classification system, and 45 occupations according to coding by the Dictionary of Occupational Titles.

However, the fact that observed validity coefficients vary considerably from study to study even when jobs and tests appear to be similar or essentially identical has been taken as evidence that test validity is specific to a given situation and that to justify the use of a test, even a thoroughly researched test, a selection expert must conduct a validation study whenever the test is used in a different situation or company or with a different group of employees. This difficult problem has been cited widely and identified as the most serious shortcoming in selection psychology (Guion, 1976).

However, beginning in 1977, Frank Schmidt and John Hunter attacked this *situation specificity hypothesis* in a series of papers (Schmidt & Hunter, 1977; 1981a; 1981b; Schmidt, Hunter, Pearlman, & Shane, 1979). Schmidt and Hunter argued that true validity does generalize across situations and that differences observed in validity coefficients are statistical artifacts due to various defects in the validity studies such as small sample sizes, range restriction, and criterion unreliability—problems we discussed in Chapters 5 and 6. Schmidt and Hunter pooled the results of validity studies for a given test type and a given job grouping, and proceeded to determine how much of the variability in validity coefficients could be accounted for by these statistical sources of error. If most of the variation in validities can be accounted for by these statistical errors, Schmidt and Hunter maintain it is difficult to see how the situational specificity hypothesis holds, and the conclusion that validity is generalizable across situations is appropriate.

The procedure employed by Schmidt, Hunter, and their colleagues as well as others (Callender and Osburn, 1980) is detailed in their various papers as well as a book (Hunter, Schmidt, & Jackson, 1982). Most of this work has involved reviews of cognitive paper and pencil measures. In a wide variety of jobs, the major cognitive and perceptual tests always exhibited potentially useful validities (Pearlman, 1980; Schmidt, Hunter, & Pearlman, 1981). Recently, Hunter (1983) has extended this work by broadening the job base to include virtually the entire job spectrum and to include psychomotor abilities (see our discussion of measures of psychomotor abilities in Chapter 9). In the following several paragraphs and tables we present some of Hunter's results as an example of this very important work.

The data in the Hunter and Hunter (1984) analysis came from 515 validation studies conducted by the United States Employment Service for jobs encompassing the entire job spectrum covered by the Dictionary of Occupational Titles. Of the 515 validation studies, 425 used a criterion of job performance, while 90 used a criterion of training success. The average sample size in the 515 studies was 75. The test battery being validated was the General Aptitude Test Battery.

Table 8–5 presents the results of the 515 validity studies in a

DISTRIBUTION OF OBSERVED AND TRUE VALIDITY FOR **TABLE 8–5.**
COGNITIVE ABILITY (GVN), PERCEPTUAL ABILITY (SPQ),
AND KFM (PSYCHOMOTOR ABILITY) FOR ALL JOBS.

A. Distribution of Observed Validity Coefficients Across All Jobs

	GVN	SPQ	KFM
Mean Observed Correlation	.25	.25	.25
Observed Standard Deviation	.15	.15	.17
Observed 10th Percentile	.05	.05	.03
Observed 90th Percentile	.45	.45	.47

B. Distribution of Observed Validity Coefficients Corrected for Sampling Error

	GVN	SPQ	KFM
Mean Observed Correlation	.25	.25	.25
Corrected Standard Deviation	.08	.07	.11
Corrected 10th Percentile	.15	.16	.11
Corrected 90th Percentile	.35	.34	.39

C. Distribution of True Validity Across All Jobs (Validity Corrected for Unreliability
in the Job Performance Measure and Restriction of Range of Test Scores for
Study Participants)

	GVN	SPQ	KFM
Mean True Validity	.47	.38	.35
Standard Deviation of True Validity	.12	.09	.14
10th Percentile of True Validity	.31	.26	.17
90th Percentile of True Validity	.63	.50	.53

Adapted from Hunter and Hunter, (1984). GVN refers to the first three subtests of the Genral Aptitude Test
Battery, SPQ to the second set of three, KFM to the last three GATB subtests. See Table 8–2 for their labels.

number of different ways. Section A in Table 8–5 is a summary of
what Hunter found when he looked at the 515 validity studies. That
is, he found that (1) on the average, the validity of the different
subtests of the GATB was .25 (Mean observed correlation in the
table); (2) the standard deviation of the distribution of validity coefficients was about .15; (3) about 90 percent of the observed validities exceeded .05; and (4) about 10 percent exceeded .45.

Section A in Table 8–5, then, is a summary of what the actual
distribution of validity coefficients looked like when Hunter found
them. Like any distribution, the mean and standard deviation can
be calculated, even when the "scores" being distributed are 515
validity coefficients.

By displaying not only the mean of the distribution but the
standard deviations and 10th and 90th percentiles, Hunter was
showing us that there is a great deal of variability in the distribution.
In fact, the variability in the coefficients is comparable to those of
Ghiselli summarized in Table 8–4.

However, Hunter and Hunter go on to statistically remove the
variability due to sample size differences in Section B of Table 8–5.

We can now see that much of the variability in validity coefficients was due to differences in the sample sizes in the various validity studies. That is, the tenth and ninetieth percentiles indicate a much smaller range of validity coefficients around the mean once the validities are corrected for sample size. Moreover, subtracting two standard deviations from the mean observed validity coefficients for the psychomotor tests (.25 − (2 × .11)) indicates there is little likelihood that these tests will have zero validity for *any* job. Recall from our discussion of the normal curve in Chapter 5 that plus or minus two standard deviations from the mean includes over 96 percent of the cases.

Finally in Section C of Table 8–5, Hunter and Hunter correct the mean observed validity coefficients for lack of reliability in the criterion and for restriction of range of test scores in the study population (only those applicants who were selected were study participants). With those corrections, the observed validity coefficients shown in Section A turned out to be considerable *underestimates* of the true validity; the logic and nature of both corrections is explained in Chapters 5 and 6. These corrections produce substantial changes in mean validity. Also, the tenth percentiles of the true validity distributions are all substantially above .00, indicating that the GATB ability composites are valid in predicting performance in virtually all Dictionary of Occupational Titles jobs.

While Hunter and his colleagues repeatedly present evidence that cognitive ability tests are valid for virtually all jobs, the primary purpose of the Hunter and Hunter paper was to show that the type of test which is most valid for a given job depends on the complexity of the job. In Table 8–6 we present some of the data for an analysis of the effect of job complexity as indexed by a derivation of the Data and Things categories of the Dictionary of Occupational Titles (see Chapter 2). Cognitive ability tests (GVN) increase in validity as job complexity increases, while psychomotor ability increases in validity as job complexity (KFM) decreases. The pattern of validities for perceptual ability tests (SPQ) is similar to that of the cognitive ability tests.

The primary conclusion that should be drawn from the Schmidt-Hunter work is that paper and pencil cognitive ability tests are indeed valid and that there is no empirical basis for requiring separate validity studies for each job; tests can be validated at the level of job families. Further, while these tests can be used in many, if not all, contexts, the data in Table 8–6 indicate that there are substantial differences among validities for jobs which vary in complexity. After 85 years of aptitude testing and validation work, it seems that aptitude tests are valid for virtually all jobs. An identifica-

| | OBSERVED VALIDITY | | | |
Complexity Level	GVN	SPQ	KFM	Number of Jobs
1. Set up	34	35	19	21
2. Synthesize/Coordinate	30	21	13	60
3. Analyze/Compile/Compute	28	27	24	205
4. Copy/Compare	22	24	30	209
5. Feeding/Offbearing	13	16	35	20

Adapted from Hunter and Hunter, (1984).

GVN referes to the first three subtests of the General Aptitude Test Battery, SPQ to the second set of three, and KFM to the last three GATB subtests. See Table 8–2 for their labels.

tion of the job family to which a particular job belongs should adequately identify appropriate paper and pencil predictors of job performance.

Another conclusion from the validity generalization work is that research results should be described as fully as possible to allow for appropriate meta-analytic (validity generalization) computations and to produce maximally useful results for practitioners and scientists alike. Validation studies should include the following data:

1. Firm: the sponsor of the study and the organization or firm with which the study was done (or the type of firm when this information is proprietary).
2. Problem and setting: the problem to which the study was addressed and the social, economic, organizational elements of the setting.
3. Job title and code: the title and code of the job performed as taken from the *Dictionary of Occupational Titles.*
4. Job description: a description supplementing the DOT description when necessary.
5. Sample: the sample size and the characteristics of the people studied, i.e., their sex, age, education, ethnic status, job level, job experience, proportion of the total population represented in the sample and applicant versus study participant characteristics.
6. Predictors: the kinds of data being investigated for their usefulness in guiding personnel actions are described to include appropriate reliability estimates and the intercorrelations among predictors.
7. Criteria: detailed description of the criterion data collected (including their reliability) and a discussion of their relevance. If ratings were used, some estimate of the amount of contact the

rater had with the employee should be reported; if production records were used, the duration of the data collection period and whether any unusual events occurred during that period should be reported.

8. Data reported: the means, variances, and intercorrelations of variables for applicant and employee groups should be reported as fully as possible. The methods used to analyze the data, that is, regression, analysis of variance, contingency tables, etc., should be reported in detail.

Care in reporting the results of expensive, time-consuming studies will insure that future researchers can cumulate data in an informed manner and draw appropriate conclusions.

SUMMARY

We have reported on the history and concepts that underlie paper and pencil aptitude testing. From early assessments of scholastic aptitude to contemporary (seemingly) job relevant specific ability tests, a huge investment has been made in the development of reliable and efficient procedures for assessing cognitive competence. Schmidt and Hunter's work suggests this investment has been worthwhile in two senses:

- From an individual's standpoint, paper and pencil tests of cognitive ability are a great equalizer because objective scoring ignores all attributes of persons but their marks on an answer sheet. Such objectivity in scoring, we believe, has literally opened thousands of doors that would otherwise have been closed due to prejudice, stereotype, ignorance, bias, etc.
- Organizations have a potentially efficient method for making wise selection decisions based on professionally developed, job-relevant paper and pencil cognitive ability tests. As shown in Chapter 7, the utility of these tests can be very high indeed.

REFERENCES

ASPA (1983). ASPA-BNA Survey no. 45: Employee selection procedures. Washington, DC: Bureau of National Affairs.

Buros, O. K. (1978). The ninth mental measurements yearbook. Highland Park, NJ: The Gryphon Press.

Callender, J. C., and Osburn, H. G. (1980). Development and test of a new model for generalization of validity. Journal of Applied Psychology, 65, 543–558.

Campbell, J. P., Dunnette, M. D., Lawler, E. E., III, and Weick, K. E., Jr. (1970). Managerial behavior performance and effectiveness, New York: McGraw-Hill.

Cronbach, L. J. (1970). Essentials of psychological testing. New York: Harper & Row.

Ghiselli, E. E. (1966). The validity of occupational aptitude tests. New York: Wiley.

Ghiselli, E. E. (1973). The validity of aptitude tests in personnel selection. *Personnel Psychology, 26,* 461–478.

Goslin, D. A. (1963). *The search for ability.* New York: Russel Sage Foundation.

Grimsley, G., and Jarett, H. F. (1973). The relation of past managerial achievement to test measures obtained in the employment situation: Methodology and results. *Personnel Psychology, 26,* 31–48.

Guilford, J. P. (1967). *The nature of human intelligence.* New York: McGraw-Hill.

Guion, R. M. (1965). *Personnel testing.* New York: McGraw-Hill.

Guion, R. M. (1976). Recruiting, selection, and job placement. In M. D. Dunnette (Ed.). *Handbook of industrial and organizational psychology.* Chicago: Rand McNally.

Hunter, J. E., and Hunter, R. F. (1984). Validity and utility of alternative predictors of job performance. *Psychological Bulletin, 96,* 72–95.

Hunter, J. E., Schmidt, F. L., and Jackson, G. B. (1982). *Metaanalysis: Cumulating research findings across studies.* Beverly Hills, CA: Sage.

Nunnally, J. C. (1978). *Psychometric Theory.* New York: McGraw-Hill.

Pearlman, K. (1980). Job families: A review and discussion of their implications for personnel selection. *Psychological Bulletin, 87,* 1–28.

Prentice-Hall, Inc. (1975). P-H/ASPA survey: Employee testing procedures—where are they headed? *Personnel Management: Policies and Practices.*

Psychological Services, Inc. (1982). *Administrator's guide to the PSI basic skills tests.* Los Angeles: Psychological Services, Inc.

Ruch, W. W. and Dye, D. A. (1982). *Cooperative clerical study validation report, Volume 1.* Los Angeles: Psychological Services, Inc.

Ruch, F. L. and Ruch, W. W. (1980). *Employee aptitude survey: Technical report.* Los Angeles: Psychological Services, Inc.

Schein, E. H. (1980). *Organizational psychology.* Englewood Ciffs, NJ: Prentice-Hall.

Schmidt, F. L., and Hunter, J. E. (1977). Development of a general solution to the problem of validity generalization. *Journal of Applied Psychology, 62,* 529–540.

Schmidt, F. L., and Hunter, J. E. (1981a). Employment testing: Old theories and new research findings. *American Psychologist, 36,* 1128–1137.

Schmidt, F. L., and Hunter, J. E. (1981b). The future of criterion-related validity. *Personnel Psychology, 33,* 41–60.

Schmidt, F. L., Hunter, J. E., and Pearlman, K. (1981). Task differences as moderators of aptitude test validity in selection: A red herring. *Journal of Applied Psychology, 66,* 166–185.

Schmidt, F. L., Hunter, J. E., Pearlman, K., and Shane, G. S. (1979). Further tests of the Schmidt-Hunter Bayesian validity generalization procedure. *Personnel Psychology, 32,* 259–282.

Schmitt, N., and Coyle, B. W. (1976). Applicant decisions in the employment interview. *Journal of Applied Psychology, 61,* 184–192.

Spearman, C. (1904). General-intelligence, objectively determined and measured. *American Journal of Psychology, 15,* 201–292.

Thurstone, L. L. (1941). Primary mental abilities of children. *Educational and Psychological Measurement, 1,* 105–116.

Wechsler, D. (1984). *Measurement of adult intelligence.* Baltimore: Williams and Wilkins.

Wonderlic, E. F. and Assoc. (1984). *Wonderlic personnel test manual.* Northfield, IL: E. F. Wonderlic & Associates, Inc.

9

HIRING PROCEDURES II
Performance and
Simulation Testing

AIMS OF THE CHAPTER

In this chapter, the focus shifts from paper and pencil testing for assessing primarily cognitive aptitudes (Chapter 8) to an emphasis on the assessment of behavioral skills. The concern in this chapter, then, is the assessment of actual behavior compared to the assessment of cognitive processes.

It is important to remember that our overt job (and most other) behavior is controlled by cognitive processes. This is important to remember because overt and observable behavior constitutes a very seductive basis for estimating the job relevance of particular assessment procedures. The point here is that a lot of important job-relevant behavior is not directly observable; it is behavior that occurs in the cortex. The paper and pencil cognitive ability tests discussed in Chapter 8 constitute attempts to make inferences about cortex behavior and to use those inferences to make predictions of eventual job performance. As Hunter and Hunter (1984) showed, the more complex the cognitive demands of a job, the more valid are cognitive ability tests—but cognitive ability tests are at least somewhat valid for *all* jobs because all job behaviors require cognitive skills.

The bottom line, so to speak, is that as we explore more behavioral assessment strategies for evaluating the KSAs of people, we need to remember that the kinds of mental processes necessary for job performance can be assessed efficiently with paper and pencil tests. In fact, selection programs will frequently use paper and pencil tests of job relevant cognitive aptitudes as screening procedures (hurdles) for "admission" to the more time-consuming and expensive behavioral assessment procedures. We will have more to say about this throughout the chapter.

This chapter is presented in three major sections. First, tests of sensory (e.g., color vision) and motor (e.g., strength) skills are discussed. Second, a variety of actual job simulations are reviewed, including simulations that actually ask people to try to *learn* the job as a basis for making a hiring decision. Third, a relatively new topic for books on selection—licensing exams—will be reviewed.

PERFORMANCE TESTING

Psychomotor abilities typically include the senses (vision, hearing), reaction time, dexterity (eye-hand, finger), control, and precision. Physical abilities are usually thought of as strength, flexibility, stamina, and gross body movement.

As with any other human characteristic, there are individual differences in psychomotor and physical abilities and, as Hunter and Hunter (1984) have shown, these differences are reflected in job performance. Given the Hunter findings, which in fact summarize many years of research, it is useful to describe some procedures that have been used for assessment.

Prior to doing that, however, it is necessary to underscore the issue of individual differences. So much of the modern world is designed so that "everyone" can use the everyday equipment and machinery that we forget that some can use it better than others. McCormick (1976, p. 15), a psychologist concerned with the design of equipment and machinery, put it this way:

> In the design of physical systems and accoutrements in terms of human considerations there is an easy reference to the "typical" or "average" human being. However, three words of caution are in order in conceptualizing the "model" of human beings for whom the designer is designing whatever he is designing: (1) Human beings come in assorted sizes, shapes and varieties . . .; (2) Some things are to be designed for special groups, such as infants, children, teenagers, the elderly or the infirm . . .; (3) When certain things or facilities are to be designed for "the public," the designer should provide for almost the entire gamut of human beings . . .

Precisely because "things" (machinery and equipment) are typically designed for "the entire gamut of human beings," it is critical that we identify where in the gamut the particular human beings applying for a specific job lie. Obviously, job analysis is a first step. Then, given that particular basic human performance abilities have been identified as required for effective performance, various testing procedures can be employed to assess job applicants for the KSAs required for effective performance.

Psychomotor Abilities

As a class, psychomotor abilities tests are often of two major types —sensory tests and dexterity tests.

*Sensory tests.** Reliable and useful sensory tests of visual acuity, hearing, and color vision are available, and as a grammar school child you probably encountered them all. The chart you had to read from when you took your "eye test" is called a Snellen chart. In this test, examinees stand 20 feet from the chart and read

---

*Based on Aiken (1982).

off that series of letters they can see. When the letters they can read are those a normal person can read at 20 feet, then their vision is said to be 20/20. When they can read only those letters a normal person could read at 40 feet, their vision is said to be 20/40. Usually this is done for each eye and for both eyes combined.

Audiometers are used to measure auditory acuity. These instruments present pure tones of varying intensities and frequencies to the listener. The typical examining sequence is to do one ear at a time, starting above the examinee's auditory level, moving to below acuity and then coming back up to the level of audition. By doing this for various frequencies, we obtain a person's auditory acuity for different frequencies; jobs in which information is presented through the ears at particular frequencies are obviously good candidates for this procedure.

Color vision is assessed in various ways, most often with the Ishihara Test for Color Blindness. This test presents a person with a series of cards and each card is made up of colored dots. Depending upon the level and kind of color blindness, different numbers embedded in the dots are reported. Some people are said to be color weak, not color blind because, like all kinds of acuity, color "blindness" is a matter of the degree of deficiency, rather than an all-or-none phenomenon. Also, as in tests of audition where people can vary based on the frequencies they can hear, color blindness exists for different color combinations. Red-green confusion is most frequent, females rarely are color blind, and some people can see no colors at all. These people, called monochromates (one color), see only different shades of gray.

There are some multipurpose sensory tests, especially for visual abilities, for use when sophisticated assessment of complex visual abilities are required. One such test, the Frostig Developmental Test of Visual Perception, permits assessment of eye-motor coordination, perception of figure-ground relationships, and spatial relationships, among others. In addition, Bausch & Lomb and the American Optical Company have very quick tests (about five minutes) that permit assessment of visual acuity (near and far) and color discrimination as well as eye muscle control for pursuing objects both horizontally and vertically. The Bausch & Lomb procedure has a booklet that comes with the test that includes norms for *visual job families.*

It is too easy to forget about these basic sensory issues in selection. Perhaps one reason for this is the tendency to forget about them in *job analysis.* The point is that whenever vision, audition, and color perception are important abilities for performance they should be so identified because testing for them is quick and reliable.

*Dexterity tests.** Basically, dexterity tests are tests of *manipulation*—using tweezers, fingers, and hands in a coordinated way to move, place or put together objects or things. For example, the Crawford Small Parts Dexterity Test has two parts. In Part I, examinees use tweezers to insert pins in close-fitting holes and then they place a small collar over each pin. In Part II, small screws are screwed into threaded holes with a screwdriver. There are similar small parts dexterity tests in which only fingers are used and others in which larger tools are required.

One popular test requiring tools is the Bennett Hand-Tool Dexterity Test. The Bennett test uses a three-sided open wood frame. Two sides have holes in them into which large screws and bolts can be inserted. Then, using screw driver, pliers, and wrench, washers and nuts are placed on the screws. The test requires disassembling the screws, bolts, washers, and nuts and then reassembling them.

The fine and moderate dexterity tests have a reaction time and precision component as well as a dexterity component, because time-to-completion is critical and actually doing the task as prescribed is required. Since many jobs, especially in the recent explosion of high-technology electronics, require fine dexterity/precision, these tests, or similar ones, will be useful. In our discussion of job sample tests later in the chapter, tests designed specifically for certain jobs will be discussed.

Physical Ability Performance Testing

Tests of physical abilities have only recently been of interest to personnel selection specialists. The interest in the last fifteen years has been spurred primarily by equal employment opportunity considerations especially as they relate to women entering nontraditional jobs, and possibly, even more recently, because of concern for handicapped persons. When physical ability was assessed previously, it was usually done by a physician who made a judgment concerning the possibility that a person would experience risk to her or his health as a result of employment. The research by Fleishman (Fleishman, 1964; 1975) on physical ability measurement began twenty-five years ago, but only recently has his work been used as a basis for developing selection procedures (see Reilly, Zedeck, & Tenopyr, 1979; Arnold, Rauschenberger, Soubel, & Guion, 1982; and Cooper and Schemmer, 1983 as examples). The importance of physical ability measurement to staffing personnel is underscored by the review of personnel selection for physically demanding jobs recently written by Campion (1983).

Traditionally, organizations have used height and weight requirements as indices of strength. However, these standards were

*Based on Aiken (1982).

typically set arbitrarily and their job relatedness was not demonstrated; hence, in most cases they have been ruled illegal (for example, see Blake v. City of Los Angeles, 1979). Given their expected adverse impact against females and some ethnic groups, the need to validate physical abilities selection procedures against job performance is especially important. In this section, we will discuss methods of assessing physical abilities and the physical requirements of jobs and then describe an example of the use of physical abilities testing for selection purposes.

Concepts and models. Campion (1983) distinguished among three types of physical abilities tests: endurance tests, strength, and overall physical fitness. In an endurance test, actual expired air is measured, or heart rate is used as an indirect assessment of oxygen use. The three most common exercises are the bicycle ergometer, the treadmill, and the step test. Strength tests include tests of static strength (involving no movement) and dynamic strength. Chaffin (1975) provides a useful guide to available strength measurement techniques. The third approach to the measurement of physical abilities has been provided by Fleishman (1978; Hogan and Fleishman, 1979; Hogan, Ogden, Gebhardt, and Fleishman, 1980). A series of experimental and correlational studies of the actual performance of participants on a wide range of physical tasks yielded eleven physical abilities. These physical abilities included endurance, strength, flexibility, coordination, and balance. The tests that measure these abilities require little instrumentation or administrator training which makes them easy to adapt to a variety of applied settings. A list and description of the eleven physical abilities generated from the Fleishman research is presented in Table 9–1. The Fleishman abilities have been the basis of most selection research on physical abilities.

As we have noted elsewhere in this text, use of tests to assess abilities must be preceded by a demonstration that the job requires those abilities. In this connection efforts have been made to assess oxygen consumption and heart rate during work (Astrand and Rodahl, 1977). The work load/heart rate ratio for each person must be established, the same muscle groups must be used, and the same environmental conditions must be present for the heart rate to be a useful index of work load. Further, one must be aware of the intermittent versus continuous nature of the work load on a job.

Perhaps the most complicated measures of the strength requirements of jobs have been made by Chaffin, Herrin, Keyserling and Garg (1977). They developed a biomechanical strength model which included body angles, weights, load locations, and normative population strength statistics. This model was then used to predict the proportion of men and women who could be expected

TABLE 9–1. *PHYSICAL ABILITIES FACTORS DEFINED BY PHYSICAL ABILITIES ANALYSIS (PAA).*

EQUILIBRIUM:

The ability to maintain or regain one's balance or stay upright when in an unstable position. It is required to maintain balances while moving or standing still, particularly when external forces act against stability.

FLEXIBILITY:

The ability to bend, stretch, twist or reach out with the body or its appendages. It includes extending the limbs through a range of motion at the joints and making rapid, repeated flexing movements.

UPPER BODY STATIC STRENGTH:

The ability to use muscle force in the shoulder, upper back, arms, and hands to lift, push, pull, or carry objects for a brief period of time.

LOWER BODY STATIC STRENGTH:

The ability to use muscle force in the legs and feet to lift, push, pull, or carry objects for a brief period of time.

UPPER BODY DYNAMIC STRENGTH:

The ability of the muscles in the shoulder, upper back, arms, and hands to support, hold up, or move the body or external objects repeatedly or for prolonged periods. It represents muscular endurance and emphasizes the resistance of the muscles to fatigue.

LOWER BODY DYNAMIC STRENGTH:

The ability of the muscles in the legs and feet to support, hold up, or move the body or external objects repeatedly or for prolonged periods. It represents muscular endurance and emphasizes the resistance of the muscles to fatigue.

UPPER BODY EXPLOSIVE STRENGTH:

The ability to use muscle force in the shoulder, upper back, arms, and hands to propel one's own body weight or external objects in one or a series of explosive acts or short bursts of effort.

LOWER BODY EXPLOSIVE STRENGTH:

The ability to use muscle force in the legs and feet to propel one's own body weight or external objects in one or a series of explosive acts or short bursts of effort.

TRUNK STRENGTH:

The ability to use the muscles in the trunk area, i.e., the abdominal and lower back muscles, to support part of the body repeatedly or continuously over time. It is characterized by resistance of the trunk muscles to fatigue.

STAMINA:

The ability of the cardiovascular and respiratory body systems to perform effectively over long periods of time.

COORDINATION:

Frequently referenced as agility, this is the ability to coordinate the actions of different parts of the body simultaneously while the whole body is in movement.

From Fleishman, (1977).

FLEXIBILITY

This is the ability to bend, stretch, twist, or reach out with the body, arms, or legs.

HOW FLEXIBILITY IS DIFFERENT FROM OTHER ABILITIES:

FLEXIBILITY: *vs.*   STRETCH FACTORS:

Involves the ability of the arms,   The ability of the muscles
legs, and back to move in all   to exert a force.
directions without feeling "tight" or
being able to move to a desired
position (e.g., toe-touching,
reaching high above one's head,
crawling through a very small
space).

Requires a high degree of
bending, stretching, twisting, or
reaching out into unusual
positions.

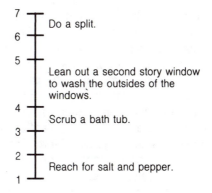

7

6   Do a split.

5

           Lean out a second story window
           to wash the outsides of the
           windows.

4

           Scrub a bath tub.

3

2

           Reach for salt and pepper.

1

Requires a low degree of
bending, stretching, twisting, or
reaching out.

From Fleishman, (1977)

to do the task. Chaffin and his associates have reported at least three validation efforts in which they have used their tests of physical strength and the standards they apply to measure job requirements (Chaffin, 1974; Chaffin, Herrin, & Keyserling, 1978; Keyserling, Herrin, & Chaffin, 1980). In all three studies strength tests were correlated with the incidence of lower back injuries.

Fleishman's approach to the measurement of human physical ability has also resulted in a method to measure the physical requirements of jobs called the Physical Abilities Analysis (Fleishman, 1978). Behaviorally anchored rating scales are constructed to assess the job requirements along each of the physical ability dimensions identified in his earlier research plus measures for upper and lower body strength. One such behaviorally anchored scale used to assess flexibility requirements is illustrated in Figure 9–1. Note the definition of flexibility and the behavioral anchors describing various points on the scale of flexibility. Also note the behavioral anchors describing various points on the scale of flexibility requirements. The scales are easy to use in a field setting, they cover a broad range of physical ability requirements, these requirements are linked to job tasks, and they relate to abilities for which specific tests are available.

Cooper-Schemmer study of physical abilities tests. An example of the application of the work by Fleishman is represented by a study reported by Cooper and Schemmer (1983) on employees of 45 investor-owned utilities which were members of Edison Electric Institute (a consortium of electric companies). The purpose of the study was to develop and validate pre-employment tests for three classes of jobs: Electrical/Mechanical Plant Maintenance, Substation Maintenance and Construction, and Overhead/ Underground Linework. A job analysis included a review of job descriptions, career path charts, training material, observation, and actual work participation by the job analysts as well as group interviews with job incumbents. On the basis of the analysis, task lists were generated. Groups of workers then rated these tasks on three scales: Physical Effort, Frequency of Performance, and Consequence of Poor Performance. These ratings were used to select physically demanding tasks (defined as those with high Consequence of Poor Performance ratings or high Frequency ratings). Ten job categories were then formed on the basis of the degree to which the same set of tasks were deemed critical in job performance.

The next step involved the use of *Physical Abilities Analysis* (PAA) for each of the critical tasks. A group of knowledgeable trained raters from each of the participating companies provided ratings of physical ability requirements using PAA (as shown in Table 9–1 and Figure 9–1). Ratings on the PAA scales over 4.00 were used to determine which tests were to be used in a selection battery. Five abilities were indicated for the various job groups: Upper Body Static Strength, Upper Body Dynamic Strength, Trunk Strength, Equilibrium, and Flexibility. Four of the eight tests selected to measure these abilities are pictured in Figure 9–2. As can be seen in the figure, these tests are all relatively simple, require little in the way of equipment or administrator training, and little in the way of examinee time. Concurrent validation of these tests against supervisor ratings of physical job performance indicated four tests were the best predictors: Arm Lift, Arm Ergometer, Stabilometer, and the Sit and Reach Test. The multiple correlation between the four tests and the criterion was .54. While the tests were nearly equally valid for all jobs and all companies and for various subgroups, including men and women, there were large mean differences between men and women. Differences between men and women on physical ability tests are large and generalizable (though usually less so for measures of lower body strength); hence, use of these tests will result in adverse impact on women and evidence of the job-relatedness/validity of these measures is critical.

Of course, it is difficult to say how large the differences between men and women will be in the future given the physical fitness emphasis (at least in Western countries). Contrary to popular opinion, however, if men and women train equally, the gap in physical abilities will get *larger,* not smaller. This is true because training usually has the effect of increasing, not decreasing, individual differences (Goldstein, 1986).

SIMULATION TESTING

One objective method of gathering job-relevant information on applicants that has been gaining in popularity in recent years is the job sample or job simulation test. A job or work sample test is one in which the applicant performs a selected set of actual tasks which are psychologically and, occasionally, physically similar to those performed on the job. Job analysis and other techniques are used to insure that the tasks selected are representative of important tasks or problems actually encountered on the job. Procedures are standardized and scoring systems are worked out with the aid of experts in the occupation in question. A job sample test for electricians, for example, might involve, among other things, the wiring of a switch box for a standard house.

Increased interest in job sample tests is partly due to an article by two industrial psychologists who criticized the assumptions of conventional paper and pencil aptitude testing. Wernimont and Campbell (1968) argued that "samples" of the kinds of behaviors or performances actually required on the job will be better predictors of future job performance than scores on aptitude or ability tests. Scores on aptitude and ability tests, they argued, are merely "signs" of potential which are statistically but imperfectly related to

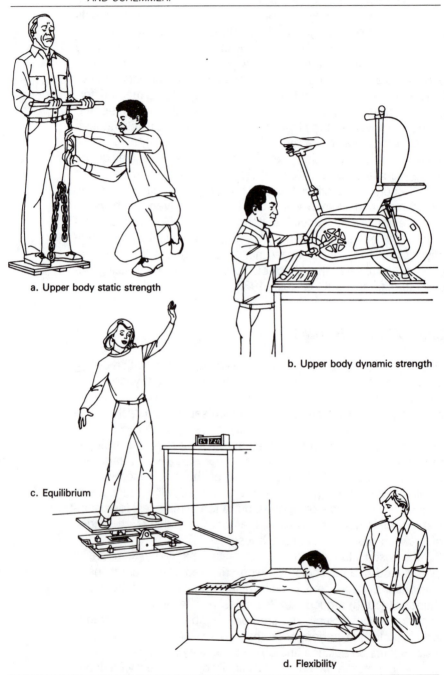

a. Upper body static strength

b. Upper body dynamic strength

c. Equilibrium

d. Flexibility

Adapted from Cooper, M., et al. (1982).

future job performance. They recommended that we strive to make the performances sampled by our tests as similar as possible to the performances required on the job. Written knowledge and achievement tests come closer to meeting this stipulation than aptitude and ability tests. Job sample tests come even closer.

This recommendation has received support in a review of validity research (Asher & Sciarrino, 1974) which shows that only biographical data has a better record of validity than work sample tests. That is, work sample tests generally show higher validity than ability, aptitude, or personality tests. The recent validity generalization work, however, suggests that for some jobs, paper and pencil aptitude tests are at least as valid as other types of predictors (see Campion, 1972, and Dreher & Sackett, 1983, for a comparison and discussion of the two procedures).

But there is a more important reason for the increasing emphasis on job sample tests—the increasing level of public criticism of the paper and pencil aptitude and ability tests in recent years. Much of this criticism is based on the fact that the content of paper and pencil aptitude and ability tests often appears to have little to do with the content of the jobs on which performance is being predicted. Job sample tests, on the other hand, are not subject to this criticism and selection psychologists and personnel workers must frequently justify their techniques to the general public and courts who have had little appreciation for statistical arguments related to validity. In other words, "signs" require more of an inference about psychological fidelity than "samples;" samples appear to be more content relevant.*

Another reason for increased interest in job sample tests is that they may increase employment opportunities for minorities and the disadvantaged. Research in the area of selection has repeatedly shown that the difference between majority and minority group members is typically smaller on appraisals of actual job performance than on tests. This is true for valid tests as well as invalid tests, and for racially fair as well as unfair tests. Now, the content of job sample tests is psychologically more like the content of the job itself. Therefore we would expect majority-minority differences on the simulation test to be closer in size to those observed on the job—and smaller than on paper and pencil tests. Obviously, this would lead to more minority group members being hired.

This is what was found in a recent study by Schmidt, Greenthal,

---

*Not only are they valid from a content validity perspective, but they are "face" valid. *Face validity* refers to how the applicant taking the test or simulation feels with respect to whether job relevant skills are being assessed. Indeed, Sackett and Dreher (1982) have shown that face validity *is* correlated with a test's perceived fairness and appropriateness.

Hunter, Berner, and Seaton (1977). A job sample test of apprentice skills in the machine trades was carefully constructed and administered to a group of white and black apprentices. Paper and pencil tests were also administered. All of the paper and pencil tests—including a well-constructed achievement test in the metal trades—showed large and significant differences between minority and majority. But two of the three scores on the work sample test ("tolerance" scores and "finish" scores, measured on the completed workpieces) showed no differences between white and black apprentices. The third score was a measure of amount of time taken to complete the work sample; this did show a difference. The minority apprentices took considerably more time. But the total scores on the job sample test (tolerance score + finish score + time taken) showed smaller differences between minority and majority groups than total scores on the written tests. Thus, using the job sample test as a selection device would have resulted in the hiring of more minority group members.

This does not mean the written achievement test, for example, was invalid or unfair. The achievement test was probably valid. It was well-constructed and, further, those who scored higher on it took significantly less time to finish the performance test than those who scored lower on it. The point is that there are a large number of factors that go into determining job performance. On some of these, differences between the white and black apprentices were small or zero. On others, the differences were larger. The achievement test apparently tapped more of those dimensions that show differences favoring the majority apprentices. The job sample test, on the other hand, tapped both kinds of factors determining performance—those on which there are differences and those on which there are no differences.

Many times the use of job sample tests requires observers to rate the *performance* of applicants rather than the *results* of the job sample (e.g., the finished product in the Schmidt et al. study). When this is the case, the job sample ratings may be subject to various kinds of rater bias as discussed in Chapter 3 (Guion, 1978; Hamner, Kim, Baird, & Bigoness, 1974; Schmitt & Lappin, 1980).

Recently, Brugnoli, Campion, and Basen (1979) conducted a careful study to see if they could obtain ratings of job sample performance that did not reveal racial bias. In their project, 56 maintenance mechanics evaluated the videotaped performance of black and white job applicants performing both a job relevant task and an irrelevant task. In evaluating applicants the maintenance mechanics used a highly specific behavioral recording form, similar to the Behavioral Observation Scale discussed in Chapter 3, a global rating scale, or both. Racial bias was not found when the mechanics used the behavioral recording form or in global evaluations made following the behavioral recording. Only when global evaluations of irrelevant job behavior were required did the experimenters report any evidence of racial bias. Brugnoli et al. (1979) concluded that if one uses careful selection and development procedures and provides assistance to observers in focusing on and recording relevant behavior, there is little potential for rater bias in the use of job samples.

Job sample testing has been used for years, and studies going back to the first quarter of this century can be found (see Asher & Sciarrino, 1974). One of the more interesting tests is that used by the U.S. Public Health Service in selecting dentists (Newman, Howell, & Cliff, 1959). One of the tasks in this test is preparing and filling a cavity in a synthetic tooth, and another involves constructing a gold inlay. Job sample tests have been common for many years in clerical areas. Among the available tests are the Seashore-Bennett Stenographic Proficiency tests (Bennett & Seashore, 1946), the Blackstone Stenographic Proficiency tests (1932) and the Thurstone Examination in Typing (Thurstone, 1922).

The rather elaborate program of job sample testing at the New Jersey Civil Service Commission merits special mention. A number of state civil service organizations have recently been moving into job sample testing, but the New Jersey program is by far the largest and most successful. Job sample tests have been constructed for a wide variety of semi-skilled and skilled occupations—carpentry, electrical work, plumbing, general maintenance and many others (Schener, 1970). These tests are regularly administered to groups of applicants in a specially modified building devoted solely to performance testing. Several groups of applicants applying for different jobs are tested simultaneously in different parts of the building. Workpieces and end products are scored immediately, giving the examinee very fast feedback. In some tests, work behavior or processes are also observed. A few moments after the completion of any test, all materials are disassembled and replaced for the next examinee.

Assessment Centers: Simulation for Management Selection

The assessment center, another type of job sample, is widely used for selecting managerial personnel. Like other job samples, assessment centers are based on the basic behavior sampling assumption that the best predictor of future behavior or performance is present or past behavior or performance of the same kind.

TABLE 9-2. *BRIEF DESCRIPTIONS OF THREE ASSESSMENT CENTERS.*

	School Administrator	First-line Supervisor	Middle Manager
		POSITION FOR WHICH CANDIDATES ARE EVALUATED	
Length of Time for Candidate Evaluation	2 days	1 day	3 days
Length of Time for Assessor Integration Meetings	2 days	1 day	2 days
Assessor/Candidate Ratio	1 : 2	1 : 3	1 : 4
Exercises	• In-basket • Personal interview • Leaderless group discussion of case • Assigned role group discussion • Fact-finding exercise with oral presentation	• In-basket • Interview • Group exercise involving human relations problem • Problem-solving group exercise • Biographical questionnaire • Mechanical test • Situational questionnaire	• Intelligence test • Projective test • In-basket • Group discussion of case study • Assigned role exercise • Self-report • Personality tests • Oral report
Sample of Rated Dimensions	• Problem analysis • Judgment • Organizational ability • Sensitivity • Personal motivation • Oral and written communication	• Organizing and planning • Analyzing • Decision-making • Controlling • Influencing • Oral communications • Interpersonal relations • Flexibility	• Judgment • Initiative • Adaptability • Planning and organizing • Originality • Abstract reasoning • Interpersonal sensitivity • Impact • Technical expertise • Oral and written communication

EAGLETOWN HIGH SCHOOL

TO: Joe
FROM: Bill Smith
RE: Sex Education Classes
DATE: January 25

As you know, a few of the counselors and Mary Brown, our Home Economics teacher, have been tossing around the idea of completely revamping our sex ed. classes. We have researched the curriculum content with several Class A communities and feel confident it will be a plus to all involved. We're ready to move on it but realize we've got some convincing ahead—it's still controversial in some parts of the community. What do you suggest be the first step?

Dear Mr. Heckle:

As you know, I take pride in my students' ability to achieve. Having to deal with behavioral problems decreases my effectiveness in assisting the rest of the class successfully.

Perhaps you haven't heard of what a troublemaker Tom Miller is. He continually disrupts the class during student participation in delivering oral book reports (an area by the way, which I emphasize for building reading comprehension and communication skills). He has never given a report and when I asked him to read aloud a passage from our text, he barely could get through one sentence.

I want Tom to be reassigned to a different class—anything but mine. I'm bringing this to your attention first, because the sooner the better.

Sincerely,

Viola Twig

Viola Twig

A typical assessment center works something like this. Potential candidates for a management job, either workers recruited to the organization or workers chosen based on nominations by their immediate supervisors, are sent in groups of 10–12 participants to a central facility. For two or three days they take part in exercises specially developed to reveal important management behaviors. One such exercise is the leaderless group discussion in which a group of participants is presented with a problem—for example, a production scheduling problem—and told to solve it. The group is watched carefully and the contributions of each individual to the solution are assessed. Other exercises include business games and the in-basket test. An in-basket test consists of letters, memos, reports, etc. that might appear in a job incumbent's in-basket. The examinee is asked to act on these items as though she were on the job. These actions are scored as a test. Traditional paper and pencil tests are also used, as are structured, in-depth interviews.

In most assessment centers, the evaluators are not psychologists but managers who are thoroughly trained to be assessors. These assessors spend two or more days after the center exercises are over preparing final evaluations of the participants, describing their strengths and weaknesses as future managers and making recommendations for future training and development. In addition, some overall recommendations concerning candidates' promotability are usually made. Assessment center participants are also provided with the opportunity to receive feedback on their performance. A brief description of three assessment centers is shown in Table 9–2. Two examples of items in an in-basket used to evaluate school administrators are pictured in Figure 9–3.

Validity.   The best research on the validity of the assessment center has been done at AT&T (Bray & Grant, 1966). In one study, for example, 123 newly hired college graduates and 144 non-college first level supervisors were assessed, but the assessment center reports were filed away and not used. Eight years later, it was found that 82 percent of the college graduate assessees and 75 percent of the non-college assessees who had been promoted to middle management had been correctly identified by the assessment center as persons likely to be promoted to middle management. The ability of the assessment center to identify those who would not be promoted was even greater. Eighty-eight percent of the "unsuccessful" college graduates and 95 percent of the "unsuccessful" non-college assessees were correctly identified.

Notice that the critical feature of this particular study was that the results of the assessment center were not used in any way to make the promotion decision. In some studies of the assessment center, this has not been true. Thus results of these studies are "contaminated." Obviously, if a report is used in making promotion decisions, it will probably correlate with those decisions whether it is valid or not. Another important fact about this study is that sufficient time—eight years—was allowed for the managerial abilities of the assessees to emerge. A twenty-year followup of these managers has also been published and the results are similar. It may be critical to the validity of such studies to include a long time period. While managerial ability may pay off in the long run in a large organization, it may not in the short run. For one thing, it takes some time for positions appropriate for promotion to become "open."

There is considerable evidence for the validity of assessment centers; the most recent reviews reveal that the typical validity for them is about .40 (Schmitt, Gooding, Noe, & Kirsch, 1984; Hunter & Hunter, 1984). Many studies use salary level achieved or promotion as the criterion of interest, though studies using other criteria are also available. Jaffee, Bender, and Calvert (1978) reported that subordinates' grievances, absences, and visits to the infirmary were also predicted by assessment center ratings. A thorough review of assessment center validity data by Thornton, Gaugler, Rosenthal, and Bentson (1985) indicated that validities were comparable across different types of criteria.

Other advantages. Assessment centers have a number of advantages in addition to the considerable evidence supporting their validity. High "face validity" is one such advantage. Assessment center reports and the assessment process itself have been favorably accepted by large numbers of managers. The fact that some of these managers have served as assessors has aided this process, of course, but this factor alone probably does not explain the high level of acceptance. Responses of assessees have been equally positive—even those who do not do well feel the assessment process has value. From the viewpoint of assessees, the assessment center experience often stimulates self-development efforts by focusing attention on their training and development needs. Assessees might learn, for example, that their major weakness is a tendency to jump to decisions before gathering adequate information. As a result, they might develop a well thought out plan for changing their behavior.

Another positive point is the fact that serving as assessors provides valuable training and experience to managers. They learn how to systematically observe and evaluate management behavior —something they might typically have been too busy to learn before.

About half of all assessment centers are used to identify potential first line supervisors. At this level, detailed feedback on assessment center performance is provided to each assessee. At higher management levels, training and development programs, in addition to feedback, are often provided. A final positive point is the fact that assessment centers have usually been favorably reviewed by courts concerned with violations of equal employment opportunity. In fact, the courts have, in one case, required that assessment centers be used to eliminate possible bias against women and to increase their movement into managerial positions. A consent decree involving AT&T, the EEOC, and the Department of Labor resulted in the evaluation of 1,634 women over a 15 month period and the judgment that 42 percent possessed the requisite management skills. Validity evidence generalized from other studies and the contention that assessment center exercises are content valid have been enough to save even the centers that have not been validated from challenge.

Moreover, studies concerning the internal validity of the assessment center (Huck, 1976; Mitchel, 1975; Schmitt, 1977; Schmitt & Hill, 1977; Thornton & Byham, 1982) indicate that inter-rater reliability is high and that overall assessment judgments are indeed more highly correlated with performance on individual assessment dimensions than are test scores or other available information.

Critiques. Assessment centers are not without critics, however. Klimoski and Strickland (1977) have questioned the use of promotions as criteria, stating that those criteria have less to do with managerial effectiveness than they do with survival and adaptation. Klimoski and Strickland contend that assessment center raters are rating those people who can maneuver their way upward in the organization, not necessarily those who are the most effective. The criteria used have been those that will insure a status quo organization if we used them to validate our tests (Schneider, 1983). The Klimoski-Strickland hypothesis may have some validity but it is important to note that they assume that company promotions have little or nothing to do with performance and that company promotions are totally explained by the manager's ability to manipulate upward. They further assume that this ability is not, in fact, useful when these managers perform their jobs.

Recently, Schmitt, Noe, Meritt, and Fitzgerald (1984) conducted a study in which performance criteria were used to assess the validity of an assessment center used to predict the potential of school administrators to lead a school. Ratings on behaviorally anchored rating scales were collected from the supervisors of these principals and assistant principals as well as the teachers and support staff in their schools. Most correlations among the fifteen performance dimensions and the assessment center ratings were statistically significant and ranged from .20 to .30. It could still be argued that the supervisory ratings were subject to the same sort of bias Klimoski and Strickland attribute to promotion and salary criteria; however, the rating scales' behavioral nature should make that bias less severe. Further, it is much less likely that teacher and support staff rating criteria would be similarly affected.

Assessment centers have other potential practical disadvantages. They can be costly, and as we documented in Chapter 7, the cost compared with the gain obtained from its validity relative to validity using other techniques must be evaluated. Another possibility is that those not nominated by their supervisors to attend the center may become demoralized. Not being selected may lead to reduced motivation. The same applies to those who are selected to attend but who do not do well. In addition, the assessment process might be very threatening to some assessees and result in such high levels of anxiety that assessment results have little validity. Most programs attempt to keep stress at acceptable levels and thus minimize this possible effect. But stress is often an important part of the managerial job, and those who can not handle reasonable levels of stress and anxiety during assessment may not be able to handle it on the job. Thus it would not be desirable to eliminate all stress from the assessment setting. Many of these concerns are reflected in the publication of ethical standards for assessment center operations by a special committee of industrial/ organizational psychologists (Moses, 1977).

Finally, some authors have questioned the content validity of assessment centers, and they have provided evidence to support their reservations (Sackett & Dreher, 1982b, Sackett & Harris, 1983; Turnage & Muchinsky, 1982). The evidence presented suggests that ratings of assessees on a given dimension of behavior (say Flexibility) in one part of the assessment center (say the In-Basket) do not tend to correlate well with ratings made of Flexibility in the Leaderless Group Discussion. These kinds of findings suggest that the internal consistency reliability of the behavioral dimension ratings may not be adequate to defend the use of Flexibility as a behavioral dimension that has content validity. That is, it has been argued (Dreher & Sackett, 1981; Sackett & Dreher, 1981) that a defense of assessment centers on content validity grounds implies that the dimensions being assessed are assessed with a common metric across opportunities for assessment. If dimension assessments are uncorrelated across opportunities, then the dimensions do not have content validity.

These are potentially serious arguments and would be particularly damaging in the absence of consistent predictive validity for the assessment center procedure. As Dreher and Sackett (1981) suggest, the predictive validity studies are strong evidence for use of assessment centers, but the very usefulness of them needs to be better understood. From the standpoint of *understanding,* the data provided by Dreher and Sackett (1981) are not reassuring.

Summary. The British and the Germans, during World War II, were the first to use something like our current assessment centers —for the selection of spies. Potential spies were placed in realistic situations requiring them to cope, reason, solve, and work under the stress of fear and time deadlines. The last 25 years have seen an explosion in the use of these job simulation techniques, strategies that permit assessors to observe many facets of behavior in a variety of contexts—contexts thought to simulate the psychological requirements of the job. Today, assessment centers are used by most large companies (AT&T, GE, IBM, SOHIO); some consultant groups exist that do nothing but develop centers for clients. And the procedure is apparently not only useful for managers. As with other simulations, any job is amenable to this procedure.

Miniaturized Training Tests

Another relatively new approach to test development which incorporates the job sample notions is an approach described by Siegel as *mini job training and evaluation* (Siegel & Bergman, 1972). The miniaturized training test also presents a possible solution to a problem with content validation strategies we noted in Chapter 6. Content validation, or the use of work sample tests, is difficult, if not impossible, for entry level or low skill jobs when on-the-job experience is critical in learning the job and subsequent job performance. The miniaturized training test is based on the hypothesis that people who can show their ability to learn and perform a job *sample* will also be able to learn and perform on the *whole job*. Job seekers are trained to perform a sample of tasks involved in the job they are applying for. Following the training, they are tested on their ability to perform these tasks. During training, applicants are allowed to proceed at different rates, they are given "hands-on" experience, and literacy requirements are minimized.

A description of three miniature job training and evaluation exercises developed by Siegel and Wiesen (1977) is presented in Figure 9–4. Each of the tests was individually administered to job applicants. Recently a study was conducted to demonstrate the possibility of developing a miniaturized training test that could be administered to many individual candidates simultaneously (Siegel, 1983). In this study, data were collected to provide validation of miniaturized training tests that corrected deficiencies in the earliest research (Siegel & Bergman, 1972). Cohen and Penner (1976) detailed some of these problems, though they lauded the careful attention to test construction in the earlier Siegel and Bergman work.

One thousand thirty-four male enlisted personnel at the Naval Training Center in San Diego were evaluated using nine miniaturized tests. These Navy seamen, airmen, and firemen were then subsequently evaluated by their commanding officers nine months after assignment and eighteen months after initial assignment. While only 39 percent were available in the first follow-up and 29 percent in the second, attrition and mobility account for most of the loss of criterion data. Further, no differences were found between

Computation and Projection (CAP)

In the training aspect of the Computation and Projection (CAP) miniature training and evaluation situation, intercept course projection was taught. This included instruction about how to read a simplified plot diagram of the positions of two ships, their headings and speeds, and how to: (1) extrapolate the new position of each ship after one hour, and (2) evaluate the danger of collision. Simple addition, subtraction, and ruler measurement were required to perform the work. After a training and a practice session, problems were administered in a group session. Three subscores (projection, collision identification, and course change direction) were summed to derive a total subtest score.

Conceptual Integration and Application (CIA)

In the Conceptual Integration and Application (CIA) training session, the operation of an elementary, simulated electromechanical pumping system was explained and demonstrated. Potential malfunctions were diagnosed and the cause-effect relationships behind each diagnosis were explained. This ability to integrate facts and system relationships and to derive a conclusion about the cause of a malfunction is commonly termed "trouble-shooting." After the training session and a set of practice problems, 10 problems involving system malfunctions symptoms were group administered. The task was to state the cause of each malfunction. Score on the subtest was right minus wrong.

Dual Task (DT)

The ability to share time between the performance of two or more different tasks is required for many Navy jobs. Watch keeping and equipment operation are examples. The simultaneous performance of two tasks was consolidated into the Dual Task (DT) exercise: (1) simulated watch standing, and (2) fabricating a pipe assembly. In the watch standing aspect, the persons under evaluation attended to series of "alarm" lights and recorded their time of occurrence. The pipe assembly task included assembly of a set of pipes inaccordance with a schematic diagram.

During the training aspect of the exercise, schematic diagram interpretation and how to make the required measurements for completing the pipe assembly task were taught. In the evaluation aspect, the recruits were required to fabricate the pipe assembly while simultaneously monitoring the "alarm" lights and entering their time of activation on a simulated log form. The total score for the subtest was the sum of the pipe assembly and the alarm reaction scores.

From Siegel, (1983).

the group for whom performance data were available and the group for whom criterion data were not collected on the usual Navy paper and pencil tests or in terms of duty assignments.

Correlations between total scores on the miniaturized training test and performance ratings ranged between .30 and .42 for all three jobs with the exception of the first follow-up for the airmen's job ($r = .04$). Further, rate-rerate criterion reliabilities were low (in the .40's) and corrections for attenuation due to criterion unreliability yielded validities for the total miniaturized training test between .45 and .61 with the exception noted above. In comparison, validities for the more frequently administered Armed Services Vocational Aptitude Battery (a series of 12 paper and pencil tests of quantitative, verbal, and general knowledge components) yielded validities which were substantially lower and in many cases near zero or negative. Validities for both traditional tests as well as the miniaturized training tests were likely lower because only very low aptitude persons were included in the study.

The miniature training test has several advantages. Job applicants unanimously agreed that the test was fair and that it was preferred to paper and pencil measures. Second, the job analytic and work sampling techniques employed in developing the miniature training and evaluation situations conform to current legal guidelines and standards for developing content valid measures. The initial research by Siegel and his colleagues indicates substantial validity, perhaps in excess of paper and pencil measures. Several factors make this approach to testing more costly than traditional approaches: (1) smaller numbers of persons can be tested by a single examiner or at a single time; (2) testing time may be greater; and (3) the cost of equipment used in the tests may be substantial. Finally, further research on applicants who include the entire range of ability should be conducted.

The Behavioral Consistency Approach to Selection

The Office of Personnel Management published a technical report in which the researchers (Schmidt, Caplan, Bemis, DeCuir, Dunn, & Antone, 1979) described a *behavioral consistency* method of selecting new employees. The basic assumption (by now, a familiar one) in this approach to selection is "that past behaviors are the best predictors of future behaviors. And the more similar the past behaviors are to future behaviors, the better they should be as predictors" (Schmidt et al., 1979, p. 7). The emphasis in the new procedure was on the documentation and reliable rating of actual past achievements, rather than simple exposure or education and experience credentials.

Briefly, the development of the procedure involves the following steps:

1. A group of eight or more subject matter experts are convened. These people are asked to list those knowledge, skills, abilities, and other characteristics (KSAOs) which best differentiate between superior employees and those who are minimally acceptable.
2. This KSAO information is used to construct an application form usually with five to seven major achievement dimensions. The applicant will be asked to describe at least two achievements per dimension and to supply:

a. information concerning the nature of the problem,
b. what he or she actually did,
c. what the outcome was,
d. what percentage of the outcome he or she believes was due to his or her efforts, and
e. the name of someone who can verify the achievement.
3. This preliminary form is reviewed by the subject matter experts.
4. Data are collected from a group of applicants and the subject matter experts judge the quality of the achievements so that they can be used as benchmarks for the construction of achievement scales.
5. The procedure is used operationally to construct lists of people to fill jobs. In Figure 9–5, we present two items in the behavioral consistency form developed for the positions of budget analyst by Schmidt et al. (1979).

Schmidt et al. (1979) report that average interrater reliabilities concerning the ratings of achievements using this procedure were above .80. Further, this procedure correlated near zero with other more traditional methods which only documented the fact that people held a particular job or achieved an educational degree. While the investigators were unable to collect criterion-related validity data in their preliminary study, they noted that the procedure may be defensible on the basis of its content validity. The logic is that behaviors sampled for each of the achievement dimensions are those required in the performance of the job—those judged most critical by the subject matter experts.

While a potential disadvantage of the procedure is the tremendous effort required on the part of applicants, research done subsequent to Schmidt et al. (1979) suggests this behavioral consistency approach to prediction is not only conceptually sound but valid as well. In one concurrent validity study, for example, correlations between an "Accomplishment Record" and rated job performance for 329 attorneys was .25 (Hough, 1984). This study used procedures adapted from Schmidt et al., collecting attorneys' self-reported accomplishments on job relevant behavioral dimensions. Again, good interrater agreement on scoring past accomplishment was obtained on all dimensions rated:

DIMENSION	RATER AGREEMENT
Researching/Investigating	.75
Using Knowledge	.76
Planning and Organizing	.79
Writing	.76
Oral Communication and Assertive Advocacy	.79
Working Independently	.77
Hard Work, Dedication	.80
Overall Evaluation	.82

1. Analytical and Quantitative Reasoning Abilities

Budget Analysts must analyze complex technical data and other information, using logic and quantitative reasoning abilities. In doing this, they must be able to distinguish essential from nonessential information. On a separate sheet of paper, give examples of your past achievements demonstrating these abilities.

DO NOT COMPLETE the following rating until after you have described your achievements relevant to this factor. Remember to use a separate sheet of paper to describe these achievements. Do not forget to include, *for each achievement;*

1. What the problem or objective was.
2. What yo: actually did, and when (approximate date).
3. What the outcome or result was.
4. The estimated percentage of this achievement which you claim credit for.
5. The name, address, and telephone number of somebody who can verify the achievement.

The statements I have provided on this factor are accurate descriptions of my own achievements and the above rating reflects what I believe to be a fair evaluation of the achievements described.

Signature: _____ Date: _____

2. Interpersonal and Organizational Skills

Budget Analysts must be able to work with all kinds of people—different ethnic groups, personalities, age groups and occupational levels. In addition, they must be able to determine where to go within their organization for needed information and to judge what information should be passed on to different levels of management. They must also be sensitive to the needs and requirements of people at different organizational levels and realize the extent to which they can aggressively promote their own ideas. On a separate sheet of paper, give examples of your past achievements which demonstrate that you possess these skills.

DO NOT COMPLETE the following rating until after you have described your achievements relevant to this factor. Remember to use a separate sheet of paper to describe these achievements. Do no forget to include, for each achievement:

1. What the problem or objective was.
2. What you actually did, and when (approximate date).
3. What the outcome or result was.
4. The estimated percentage of this achievement which you claim credit for.
5. The name, address, and telephone number of somebody who can verify the achievement.

The statements I have provided on this factor are accurate descriptions of my own achievements and the above rating reflects what I believe to be a fair evaluation of the achievements described.

Signature: _____ Date: _____

From Schmidt, F. L., et al (1979).

While other potential predictor data correlated more strongly with attorney performance (e.g., bio-data $r = 43$; Law School Admissions Test, $r = .29$), this early work using the behavioral consistency framework appears promising (Hough, Dunnette, & Keyes, 1983).

The assumptions upon which the behavioral consistency approach are based are those guiding the research into the use of biographical data which are quite valid in the prediction of job success across a wide variety of jobs (see Chapter 10). The major disadvantage with respect to the use of bio-data is its lack of conceptual base and the resultant brute empiricism of the validation of biographical items. This has often meant that there is a rather large "validity decay" over time. The behavioral consistency methodology does not collect biographical data on a "shotgun" basis, but rather collects that information which is directly relevant to performance of the job in question. Hence, it should be more acceptable to applicants and the courts, and the validities obtained using the procedure should be more stable.

LICENSING EXAMS: TESTS OF TRAINING

Perhaps the single most frequent use of tests of ability and training in our country is for licensing purposes. Shimberg (1981) estimated that approximately 800 occupations in the United States are regulated by state governments. Most people are familiar with bar exams or licensing for physicians and nurses, but licensing laws also exist in some states for occupations such as clock repair persons, landscape architects, travel agents, and even horseshoers and lightning rod installers.

Licensure allows people to engage in a given occupation when they demonstrate minimal competency necessary to insure public safety and health. Shimberg makes a useful distinction between exams used for licensing and exams used for predicting job success. In predicting job success, we are interested in identifying those persons whose performance will be the best. This difference in purpose may lead to differences in the knowledge, skills, and abilities assessed as well as the way decisions are made based on the tests.

For example, a friendly, empathic physician or nurse may be more instrumental in producing patient satisfaction with health care and even perhaps physical health. However, licensing exams exist to protect public safety and health, so a licensing exam would not likely include measures of interpersonal skills. The emphasis would be on diagnostic skills, knowledge of health problems and appropriate care, and, perhaps, performance of critical tasks.

The second major difference is the way a test score is used to make decisions. If the aim is to predict job success, the optimal use of test scores is to pick in rank order those individuals who do best. For licensing purposes, the goal is to deny access of individuals to a profession when there is a possibility that the individual's incompetence would result in client harm. So, a minimal cutoff is usually established.

Setting cutoffs is always judgmental. Livingston (1980) points out that standards exist in people's minds but not in a manner that is easily transformed into an objective decision rule. Methods of choosing a cutoff score are actually ways of expressing people's personal standards in terms of the test score. Livingston suggests three approaches to setting a cutoff score on a test, each of which employs a different type of judgment. In the first, judgments are made about some reference group. For example, we arbitrarily decide that ten percent of those graduating from a course on real estate are incompetent. The cutoff score is then set so as to deny licensure to the bottom ten percent. In the second approach to setting cutoff scores, we look at those practitioners or recent trainees who are clearly competent, assess their performance on the proposed exam, and decide on the cutoff score accordingly. Finally, what seems to be the most logically defensible method is to examine the test items themselves (Ebel, 1972). Must a person answer the item correctly to certify that she or he possesses appropriate knowledge or skill? Does lack of correct response indicate that the person would be a danger to society? Whatever the basis for judgment, Livingston (1980) recommends four criteria to apply in setting the passing score:

1. The judgments must be made by qualified subject matter experts.
2. The judgments must be made in a way that is meaningful to those experts.
3. The decision process must take into account the purpose for which the test is being used.
4. Both types of decision errors (denying a qualified person and accepting an unqualified individual) must be considered.

The most frequently used type of test in the licensing situation is the multiple-choice test, though many occupations also use performance (job sample) tests and oral examinations. Problems of bias in administering and grading performance exams for licensure are similar to those encountered in the selection situation. Because examiners are observed directly in most instances, rater biases are certainly possible. Because of this concern, the dental examining board in California instituted a testing procedure in which the candidates completed their work alone and the examiner then inspected and graded the product. Shimberg points out that this procedure precludes from consideration any information as to how the work was accomplished. For example, the dental candidate may produce an acceptable filling in a patient, but may have caused unnecessary discomfort. The use of multiple choice tests to assess job knowledge on the theory that this relates to job performance has, of course, been criticized frequently. An example of such criticism is this quote from Ryans and Fredericksen (1971):

> From the standpoint of validity one of the most serious errors committed in the field of human measurement has been that which assumes the high correlation of knowledge of facts and principles on the one hand and performance on the other. Nevertheless, examinations for admission to the bar, for medical practice, for teaching and even tests of ability to cook and sew, are predominantly verbal tests of fact and principle in the respective fields. Relatively little attention has been paid to the testing of performance as such (p. 195).

The validity and reliability of licensing exams represent somewhat different problems than selection tests do. Since the major decision is a pass-fail one, we should be interested in the consistency of pass-fail decisions on repeated administration of the licensing exam. Hence, reliability estimates should be made in a manner consistent with this pass-fail criterion. (For a detailed discussion of these reliability estimates for what are called criterion-referenced exams, see Livingston & Wingersky, 1979).

The only validation evidence presented for most licensing exams is content in nature. The questions addressed in our discussion of content validity in Chapter 6 are relevant here as well. In addition, we must ask whether the knowledge, skills, and abilities assessed are represented at a level of complexity and in proportions consistent with the goal of protecting the public health, safety, and welfare. A criterion-related validity study of licensing exams would seem especially difficult. Shimberg (1981) points to the fact that licensees work in widely different organizations, frequently with different job performance goals. Further, it seems the appropriate criterion ought to be a *dual* criterion. On the one hand it should be demonstrated that persons who did not pass a licensing exam are incompetent and in some way would harm the clients they served. On the other hand, it should be shown that those who passed did *not* harm the client. Clearly, we do not have information concerning the job performance of those rejected. Indirect evidence of criterion-related validity might consist of changes in malpractice occurrences before and after the passage of licensing legislation, but the authors know of no such work.

The legal liability of licensing agencies is unclear. The Uniform Guidelines on Employee Selection Procedures published by the Equal Employment Opportunity Commission (1978) state:

> Whenever an employer, labor organization, or employment agency is required by law to restrict recruitment for any occupation to those applicants who have met licensing or certification requirements, the licensing or certifying authority, to the extent it may be covered by Federal Equal Employment law, will be considered the user with respect to those licensing and certification requirements (p. 38308).

In a set of questions and answers later published by the EEOC (1979) the following question and answer appeared:

> Q. Do the Guidelines apply to licensing and certification functions of state and local governments?
> A. The courts are divided on the issue of such coverage. The government has taken the position that at least some kinds of licensing and certification which deny persons access to employment opportunity may be enjoined in an action pursuant to Section 707 of the Civil Rights Act of 1964, as amended (p. 11997).

The Supreme Court has not ruled on this issue, although most federal circuit courts have held that Title VII of the Civil Rights Act does *not* apply to licensing agencies. Whether because of legal threat or a desire to serve the public, there has been consistent improvement in test construction and validation efforts on the part of licensing bodies (Shimberg, 1980).

SUMMARY

This chapter discussed various alternatives to traditional paper and pencil tests. Rationale for the use of these alternatives is usually that they represent actual job samples (as opposed to signs) or that they measure past behavior of the type required in a new situation on the hypothesis that past behavior is the best predictor of future behavior. In this context, we described and reviewed performance testing, job sample research, assessment center studies, the behavioral consistency approach, miniaturized training tests, and licensing exams. For most of these latter approaches, with the possible exception of the assessment center, relatively few validity studies have been conducted.

This has been a lengthy chapter and it contains a lot of information. Sometimes length and detail leads to a failure on our part to emphasize the main point: *The level of ability of the people hired by a company will have long-term consequences for productivity there.* There is *no* substitute for competence. By this we mean that job-relevant aptitude, the ability to learn to do a job, is a minimum requirement for effectiveness on a job.

In the next chapter we will review selection procedures which assess whether a job applicant is *willing* to do the work required by the job. As the reader will undoubtedly find, some of the procedures discussed in the following chapter can also be used to assess whether a job applicant *can* perform a job. For example, biographical information indicating previous successful employment in a job similar to the one for which an applicant is now applying could indicate both her or his ability *and* motivation.

REFERENCES

Aiken, L. R. (1982). *Psychological Testing and Assessment, 4th ed.* Boston: Allyn and Bacon.

Arnold, J. D., Rauschenberger, J. M., Soubel, W. G., and Guion, R. M. (1982). Validation and utility of a strength test for selecting steelworkers. *Journal of Applied Psychology, 67,* 588–604.

Asher, J. J., and Sciarrino, J. A. (1974). Realistic work sample tests: A review. *Personnel Psychology, 27,* 519–538.

Astrand, P. O., and Rodahl, K. (1977). A nomogram for calculation of aerobic capacity from pulse rate during submaximal work. *Journal of Applied Physiology, 7,* 218–221.

Bennett, G. K., and Seashore, H. G. (1946). *The Seashore-Bennett Stenographic Proficiency.* New York: Psychological Corporation.

Blackstone Stenographic Proficiency Tests. (1932). New York: Harcourt, Brace, and World.

Blake v. City of Los Angeles. 19 FEP 1441 (9th Cir., 1979).

Bray, D. W., and Grant, D. L. (1966). The assessment center in the measurement of potential for business management. *Psychological Monographs, 80,* Whole No. 625.

Bray, D. W., and Campbell, R. J. (1968). Selection of salesmen by means of an assessment center. *Journal of Applied Psychology, 52,* 36–41.

Brugnoli, G. A., Campion, J. E., and Basen, J. A. (1979). Racial bias in the use of work samples for personnel selection. *Journal of Applied Psychology, 64,* 119–123.

Byham, W. C. (1977). Application of the assessment center method. In J. L. Moses and W. C. Byham (Eds.). *Applying the assessment center method.* New York: Pergamon.

Byham, W. C. (1980a). *Review of legal cases and opinion dealing with assessment centers and content validity.* Pittsburgh: Development Dimensions International.

Byham, W. C. (1980b). Starting an assessment center the correct way. *Personnel Administrator,* pp. 27–32.

Campbell, R. J., and Bray, D. W. (1967). Assessment centers: An aid in management selection. *Personnel Administration, 30,* 6–13.

Campion, J. E. (1972). Work sampling for personnel selection. *Journal of Applied Psychology, 56,* 40–44.

Campion, M. A. (1983). Personnel selection for physically demanding jobs: Review and recommendations. *Personnel Psychology, 36,* 527–550.

Carleton, F. O. (1970). *Relationships between follow-up evaluations and information developed in an assessment center.* Paper presented at the 78th Annual Convention of the American Psychological Association, Miami Beach.

Chaffin, D. B. (1974). Human strength capability and low back pain. *Journal of Occupational Medicine, 16,* 248–254.

Chaffin, D. B. (1975). Ergonomics guide for the assessment of human static strength. *American Industrial Hygiene Association Journal, 36,* 505–511.

Chaffin, D. B., Herrin, G. D., Keyserling, M., and Garg, A. (1977). A method for evaluating the biomechanical stresses resulting from manual materials handling jobs. *American Industrial Hygiene Association Journal, 38,* 662–675.

Chaffin, D. B., Herrin, G. D., and Keyserling, W. M. (1978). Pre-employment strength testing: An updated position. *Journal of Occupational Medicine, 20,* 403–408.

Cohen, S. L., and Penner, L. A. (1976). The rigors of predictive validation: Some comments on "a job learning approach to performance prediction." *Personnel Psychology, 29,* 595–600.

Cooper, M. and Schemmer, F. M. (1983). The development of physical ability tests for industry-wide use. Paper presented at the national convention of the American Psychological Association, Anaheim, CA.

Cronbach, L. J., and Gleser, G. C. (1965). *Psychological tests and personnel decisions.* Urbana, IL: University of Illinois Press.

Dreher, G. F., and Sackett, P. R. (1983). *Perspectives on employee staffing and selection: Readings and commentary.* Homewood, IL: Irwin.

Dreher, G. F., and Sackett, P. R. (1981). Some problems with the applicability of content validity to assessment centers. *Academy of Management Review, 6,* 551–560.

Dunnette, M. D. (1967). Predictors of executive success. In Wickert, R. R., & McFarland, D. E. (Eds.). *Measuring executive effectiveness.* New York: Appleton-Century-Crofts.

Ebel, R. L. (1972). *Essentials of educational measurement.* Englewood Cliffs, NJ: Prentice-Hall.

Equal Employment Opportunity Commission, Civil Service Commission, Department of Labor and Department of Justice (1978). Adoption by four agencies of Uniform Guidelines on Employee Selection Procedures. *Federal Register, 43,* 38290–382315.

Equal Employment Opportunity Commission, Office of Personnel Management, Department of Justice, Department of Labor and Department of the Treasury. (1979). Adoption of questions and answers to clarify and provide a common interpretation of the Uniform Guidelines on Employee Selection Procedures. *Federal Register, 44,* 11966–12009.

Fleishman, E. A. (1964). *The structure and measurement of physical fitness.* Englewood Cliffs, NJ: Prentice-Hall.

Fleishman, E. A. (1975). Toward a taxonomy of human performance. *American Psychologist, 30,* 1127–1149.

Fleishman, E. A. (1978). *Physical abilities analysis manual.* Washington, D.C.: Advanced Resources Research Organization.

Fleishman, E. A. (1979). Evaluating physical abilities required by jobs. *Personnel Administrator, 24,* 82–91.

Ginsberg, L. R., and Silverman, A. (1972). The leaders of tomorrow: Their identification and development. *Personnel Journal, 51,* 662–666.

Goldstein, I. L. (1986). *Training: Program development and evaluation, Rev. ed.* Belmont, CA: Brooks, Cole.

Guion, R. M. (1976). Recruiting, selection, and job placement. In Dunnette, M. D. (Ed.). *Handbook of industrial and organization psychology.* Chicago: Rand-McNally.

Guion, R. M. (1978). Scoring of content domain samples: The problem of fairness. *Journal of Applied Psychology, 63,* 499–506.

Hamner, C. W., Kim, J. S., Baird, L., and Bigoness, W. J. (1974). Race and sex as determinants of ratings by potential employers in a simulated work sample task. *Journal of Applied Psychology, 59,* 705–711.

Hinrichs, J. R. (1969). Comparison of "real life" assessments of management potential with situational exercises, paper and pencil ability tests, and personality inventories. *Journal of Applied Psychology, 53,* 425–432.

Hinrichs, J. R. (1978). An eight year follow-up of a management assessment center. *Journal of Applied Psychology, 63,* 596–601.

Hogan, J. C., and Fleishman, E. A. (1979). An index of physical effort required in human task performance. *Journal of Applied Psychology, 64,* 197–204.

Hogan, J. C., Ogden, G. D., Gebhardt, D. L., and Fleishman, E. A. (1980). Reliability and validity of methods for evaluating perceived physical effort. *Journal of Applied Psychology, 65,* 672–679.

Hough, L. M. (1984). Development and evaluation of the "Accomplishment Record" method of selecting and promoting professionals. *Journal of Applied Psychology, 69,* 135–146.

Hough, L. M., Dunnette, M. D., and Keyes, M. A. (1983). An evaluation of three "alternative" selection procedures. *Personnel Psychology, 36,* 261–276.

Huck, J. R. (1976). The research base. In Moses, J. L., & Byham, W. C. (Eds.). *Applying the assessment center method.* New York: Pergamon.

Hunter, J. E., and Hunter, R. F. (1984). Validity and utility of alternative predictors of job performance. *Psychological Bulletin, 96,* 72–95.

Jaffee, C. L., Bender, J., and Calvert, O. L. (1978). The assessment center technique: A validation study. *Management of Personnel Quarterly, 9,* 9–14.

Jaffee, C. L., and Sefcik, J. T. (1980). What is an assessment center? *Personnel Administrator,* February, 40–43.

Keyserling, W. M., Herrin, G. D., and Chaffin, D. B. (1980). Isometric strength testing as a means of controlling medical incidents on strenuous jobs. *Journal of Occupational Medicine, 22,* 332–336.

Klimoski, R. J., and Strickland, W. J. (1977). Assessment centers—valid or merely prescient. *Personnel Psychology, 30,* 353–361.

Kraut, A. I., and Scott, G. J. (1972). Validity of an operational management assessment program. *Journal of Applied Psychology, 56,* 124–129.

Linn, R. L. (1978). Single-group validity, differential validity, and differential prediction. *Journal of Applied Psychology, 63,* 507–512.

Livingston, S. A. (1980). Comments on criterion-referenced testing. *Applied Psychological Measurement, 4,* 575–581.

Livingston, S. A., and Wingersky, M. S. (1979). Assessing the reliability of tests used to make pass/fail decisions. *Journal of Educational Measurement, 16,* 247–260.

McCormick, E. J. (1976). *Human factors in engineering design, 4th ed.* New York: McGraw-Hill.

Mitchel, J. O. (1975). Assessment center validity: A longitudinal study. *Journal of Applied Psychology, 60,* 573–579.

Moses, J. L. (1977). Standards and ethical considerations for assessment center operations. *The Industrial Psychologist, 14,*(3), 1–15.

Moses, J. L., and Boehm, V. R. (1975). Relationship of assessment center performance to management progress of women. *Journal of Applied Psychology, 60,* 527–529.

Newman, S. H., Howell, M. A., and Cliff, N. (1959). The analysis and prediction of a practical examination in dentistry. *Educational and Psychological Measurement, 19,* 557–568.

Norton, S. D. (1977). The empirical and content validity of assessment centers vs. traditional methods for predicting managerial success. *Academy of Management Review, 2,* 442–453.

Norton, S. D. (1981). The assessment center process and content validity: A reply to Dreher and Sackett. *Academy of Management Review, 6,* 561–566.

Nunnally, J.C. (1978). *Psychometric Theory.* New York: McGraw-Hill.

Reilly, R. R., Zedeck, S., and Tenopyr, M. L. (1979). Validity and fairness of physical ability tests for predicting performance in craft jobs. *Journal of Applied Psychology, 64,* 262–274.

Ruch, W. W. and Dye, D. A. (1982). *Cooperative clerical study validation report, Volume 1.* Los Angeles: Psychological Services, Inc.

Ryans, D. G., and Frederickson, N. (1971). Performance tests of educational achievement. In Ronan, W. W. and Prien, E. P. (Eds.). *Perspectives on the measurement of human performance.* New York: Appleton-Century-Crofts.

Sackett, P. R., and Dreher, G. F. (1981). Some misconceptions about content-oriented validation: A rejoinder to Norton. *Academy of Management Review, 6,* 567–568.

Sackett, P. R., and Dreher, G. F. (1982a). Face validity and empirical validity as determinants of selection decisions. Paper presented at the national meeting of the American Psychological Association, Washington, DC.

Sackett, P. R., and Dreher, G. F. (1982b). Constructs and assessment center dimensions: Some troubling empirical findings. *Journal of Applied Psychology, 67,* 401–410.

Sackett, P. R., and Harris, M. (1983). A further examination of the constructs underlying assessment center ratings. Paper presented at the national meeting of the American Psychological Association, Anaheim, CA.

Schener, N. (1970). Performance Testing in New Jersey. *Good Government, 87,* 5–15.

Schmidt, F. L., Caplan, J. R., Bemis, S. E., Decuin, R., Dunn, L., and Antone, L. (1979). *The behavioral consistency method of unassembled examining.* Washington, DC: U.S. Office of Personnel Management.

Schmidt, F. L., Greenthal, A. L., Hunter, J. E., Berner, J. G., and Seaton, F. W. (1977). Job samples vs. paper-and-pencil trades and technical tests: Adverse impact and examinee attitudes. *Personnel Psychology, 30,* 187–197.

Schmitt, N. (1977). Interrater agreement in dimensionality and combination of assessment center judgments. *Journal of Applied Psychology, 62,* 171–176.

Schmitt, N., Gooding, R. Z., Noe, R. A., and Kirsch, M. (1984). Meta-analyses of validity studies published between 1964 and 1982 and the investigation of study characteristics. *Personnel Psychology, 37,* 407–422.

Schmitt, N., and Hill, T. E. (1977). Sex and race composition of assessment center groups as a determinant of peer and assessor ratings. *Journal of Applied Psychology, 62,* 261–264.

Schmitt, N., and Lappin, M. (1980). Race and sex as determinants of the mean and variance of performance ratings. *Journal of Applied Psychology, 65,* 428–435.

Schmitt, N., Noe, R. A., Merritt, R., and Fitzgerald, M. P. (1984). Validity of assessment center ratings for the prediction of performance ratings and school climate of school administrators. *Journal of Applied Psychology, 69,* 207–213.

Schneider, B. (1983). An interactionist perspective on organizational effectiveness. In K. Cameron and D. Whetten (Eds.). *Organizational effectiveness.* New York: Academic Press.

Shimberg, B. (1981). Testing for licensure and certification. *American Psychologist, 36,* 1138–1146.

Siegel, A. I. (1983). The miniature job training and evaluation approach: Additional findings. *Personnel Psychology, 36,* 41–56.

Siegel, A. I., and Bergman, B. A. (1972). Nonverbal and culture fair performance prediction procedures. I. Background, test development. Wayne, PA: Applied Psychological Services.

Siegel, A. I., and Weisen, J. P. (1977). *Experimental procedures for the classification of Naval personnel* (NPRDC TR 77–3). San Diego: Navy Personnel Research and Development Center.

Thompson, H. A. (1970). Comparison of predictor and criterion judgments of managerial performance using the multitrait-multimethod approach. *Journal of Applied Psychology, 54,* 496–502.

Thornton, G. C., III., and Byham, W. C. (1982). *Assessment centers and managerial performance.* New York: Academic Press.

Thornton, G. C., III, Gaugler, B. B., Rosenthal, D. B., and Bentson, C. (1985). Meta-analysis of assessment center validity. Paper presented at the 93rd Annual Convention of the American Psychological Association. Los Angeles, CA.

Thurstone, L. L. (1922). *Thurstone Employment Tests: Examination in Typing.* New York: Harcourt, Brace and World.

Turnage, J. J., and Muchinsky, P. M. (1982). Transsituational variability in human performance within assessment centers. *Organizational Behavior and Human Performance, 30,* 174–200.

Uniform guidelines on employee selection procedures. (1978). *Federal Register, 43,* 38290–38309.

Wechsler, D. (1944). *Measurement of adult intelligence.* Baltimore: Williams and Williams.

Wernimont, P. R., and Campbell, J. P. (1968). Signs, samples, and criteria. *Journal of Applied Psychology, 52,* 372–376.

Wollowick, H. B. and McNamara, W. J. (1969). Relationship of the components of an assessment center to management success. *Journal of Applied Psychology, 53,* 348–352.

Worbois, G. M. (1975). Validation of externally developed assessment procedures for identification of supervisory potential. *Personnel Psychology, 28,* 77–91.

10

HIRING PROCEDURES III
Personality Tests, Biodata, and Interviews

APPLICATION BLANKS AND BIOGRAPHICAL DATA
  Application Blank
  Biographical Information Blanks
  Validity of Biographical Data
  Adverse Impact with Biodata
  Reference Checks
  Employee Honesty: A Critical Reference Issue

THE EMPLOYMENT INTERVIEW
  Bias in the Interview
  Interview Validity
  Interviewer Validity
  Summary

PEER EVALUATIONS

SELF ASSESSMENTS

SUMMARY

AIMS OF THE CHAPTER

This chapter continues our discussion of different kinds of hiring procedures. As stated in the previous chapters, measures discussed in this chapter should be measures that indicate an employee's motivation or willingness to do the work required by a particular job. Consequently, we discuss here personality and interest measures, application blanks and biographical data, interviews, self-assessments, and peer nominations. We also recognize that some of these measures can be used to assess the degree of ability job applicants possess.

PERSONALITY AND INTEREST TESTS

We described a few of the prominent motivation theories for the work setting in Chapter 4. However, there is little resemblance between these theories and the types of personality and interest tests used to predict job behavior. The major tests of personality and interest were not developed for use in the industrial setting; therefore, their generally unimpressive validity in distinguishing successful from unsuccessful employees is not surprising. Stogdill's (1948) early review of the predictability of leadership effectiveness from trait measures of personality discouraged researcher attention in these measures. Reviews of personality tests used for

TABLE 10–1. *GHISELLI'S SUMMARY OF THE VALIDITY OF PERSONALITY AND INTEREST MEASURES[a]*

OCCUPATION	PERSONALITY	INTEREST
Managerial	.17 (15–27)	.22 (.15–.31)
Clerical	.24 (.17–.30)	.12 (–.01–.23)
Sales (Clerks)	.35	.34
Salesmen	.24	.31
Protective Services	.24	–.01
Vehicle Operators	—b	–.26
Trades and Crafts	—b	—b
Industrial	—b	—b

[a]The range of validity coefficients is presented to show the average validity, not the coefficient for a particular measure correlated with a particular performance criterion for a particular occupation or job.

[b]Very small samples or no data.

Adapted from Edwin E. Ghiselli, *The Validity of Occupational Aptitude Tests* (New York, Wiley, 1966). Reprinted with permission.

other work roles were equally discouraging (Guion & Gottier, 1965; Ghiselli, 1973). Attacks on these types of tests are commonplace in the industrial psychology literature and textbooks (Campbell, Dunnette, Lawler, & Weick, 1970; Korman, 1977; Landy & Trumbo, 1984; Muchinsky, 1983b). More recent reviews continue to be discouraging (Schmitt, Gooding, Noe, & Kirsch, 1984). A review published in 1966 (Ghiselli) was similarly discouraging, as shown in Table 10–1.

However, some useful relationships between personality/motivation-type measures and various indices of individual and organizational effectiveness have been reported. For example, the *Thematic Apperception Test* (TAT) measures of *need for Achievement* (nAch) and *need for Power* (nPow) predict leadership accession and effectiveness at work (Yukl, 1981); Miner's Sentence Completion Scale predicts managerial success (Miner, 1978); the Thematic Apperception Test (TAT) appears to predict long-term management success (McClelland & Boyatzis, 1982); Type A behavior is reflected in academicians' productivity (Taylor, Locke, Lee, & Grist, 1985) and recently, Cornelius (1983) has provided a sympathetic review of projective personality measures as correlates of work behavior. We will first provide a description of some of these tests and the research summaries and then give some examples of successful and valid use of personality tests.

TYPES OF PERSONALITY TESTS

Just as there are general intelligence and specific aptitude tests, so are there global personality measures and assessments of specific personality traits.

Global Personality: Projective Tests

A projective personality measure is one which is composed of one or more relatively ambiguous stimuli, usually pictures of persons or scenes. Respondents are asked to relate what they see or what is happening in the picture. The respondents are assumed to project their own personalities onto the ambiguous stimulus and by reporting what they experience, think, or feel, to reveal the kind of people they are. Prominent examples of this procedure are the Rorschach Ink Blot Test, the Holtzman Ink Blot Test, and the Thematic Apperception Test (TAT).

The task of the test administrator is to ascertain, on the basis of such global responses, the personality dynamics of the respondents. Usually there is no a priori scoring system, but if there is, considerable disagreement exists over which system is best (cf. various scoring systems for the Rorschach).

The TAT used in the assessment of need for Achievement (nAch), is an exception to the scoring dilemma. (See McClelland et al., 1953; Atkinson, 1958; McClelland, 1961). In the TAT assessment of nAch, a person is shown a series of relatively ambiguous pictures and asked to write a story about each picture containing information on:

1. What is happening? Who is involved?
2. What has led up to this situation? (That is, what has happened in the past?)
3. What is being thought? What is wanted? By whom?
4. What will happen? What will be done?

The stories are then scored for their *achievement imagery;* for *themes* that suggest that a person strives for accomplishment, ego enhancement, and recognition, or toward surmounting obstacles in the face of potential failure. Not only written themes resulting from TAT stimuli, but the folk tales of different societies, the pottery designs of different ages and societies, etc. are all amenable to scoring for achievement content (e.g., McClelland, 1961). To briefly describe a very long, fruitful research project, in an impressively large number of instances, high achievement imagery is associated with high performance on both the individual and the societal level.

We can raise the question: are high nAch scores a social response to situations or a stable personality trait, invariant over situation? Research evidence points to an interaction—people with higher achievement motivation will display it in achievement-oriented situations (Litwin & Stringer, 1968; Schneider, 1983a). Therefore, nAch scores should be most useful as predictors of success under these organizational conditions (Yukl, 1981):

1. Effectiveness at work depends on a person's own effort, persistence and ability rather than luck or chance or other issues outside the person's control.
2. The tasks or goals to be accomplished are challenging and moderately risky rather than easy or totally impossible. By risky we mean success is not a certainty.
3. There is feedback available in the work process and in progress toward goal accomplishment and the feedback is concrete/specific.
4. The nAch person wants to be able to initiate action rather than (a) only follow others' directions or (b) only react to immediate problems.

One would not expect nAch to predict the success of the assembly line worker, but would expect a prediction for the executive in an entrepreneurial setting; in the latter case the TAT measure of nAch is an effective predictor for men (Campbell et al., 1970).

There has not been a great deal of research on nAch with women (Bowen, 1973), and the research that does exist is equivocal. A very complete review of the literature on the achievement orientation of women (Stein & Bailey, 1973) indicates that early conclusions about women having lower nAch might have been due to an over-interpretation of data. As Stein and Bailey note, it seems that women have tended to focus their nAch on social or *affiliative situations,* and not, as had been thought, that women have a high need for *affiliation* (nAff, another score obtainable from TAT protocols).

We might easily mistake social imagery in a theme as a score of nAff rather than as *nAch through affiliative processes.* Stein and Bailey suggest that it has been primarily through social situations that women have been able to express their achievement motive. In the testing situation this has led women to focus on a similar sex-typed strategy of expression. The problems of women coping with expression of their needs through work is an area only recently researched (cf. Hall and Gordon, 1973).

Cornelius (1983) pointed out that positive evidence concerning the use of projective tests was noted in several reviews. Guion's (1965) Table 2, for example, included eleven validity studies on projective tests, eight of which contained significant results. The 17 validity coefficients ranged from .17 to .73, seven of which exceeded .50. While Kinslinger (1966) decries the generally poor quality of studies on projectives, he does cite 20 "fairly rigorous studies" of which 16 report positive findings. In particular, Kinslinger (1966) mentions a sentence completion test which predicted sales success in various jobs with validities between .53 and .73. Similarly, the Tomkins-Horn Picture Arrangement Test yielded validity coefficients in the high .50s for sales positions and from .58 to .82 for tabulating equipment operators (Cornelius, 1983, p. 137). Finally, in a review of predictors of managerial performance, Korman (1968) expressed surprise at the consistently positive predictive validity of the *Miner Sentence Completion Scale* (MSCS).

The MSCS deserves special mention. Along with the TAT, it is the most frequently used projective device in the selection of managers, and validity evidence is quite impressive (Miner, 1978). Further, its scoring and the theory underlying the use of the test relate directly to managerial work; this is the purpose for which the test was developed. Respondents to the MSCS (Miner, 1960) must complete sentences which may begin with words such as:

My family doctor . . .
Police officers . . .
Running for political office . . .
Wearing a necktie . . .
Presenting a report at a staff meeting . . .

Theoretically, Miner (1978) hypothesizes that managers must competently fill six different roles, and the motivation to act in each of these roles is scored using the responses to sentences in the MSCS. These six managerial role prescriptions are described by Miner (1978, pp. 741–742) as follows:

1. Managers must be in a position to obtain support for their actions at higher levels. This requires a good relationship with superiors. It follows that managers should have a generally positive attitude toward those holding positions of authority over them. Any tendency to generalize hatred, distaste, or anxiety in dealing with people in positions of authority will make it extremely difficult to meet job demands.
2. There is a strong competitive element built into managerial work. Managers must strive to win for themselves and their subordinates and accept such challenges as other managers may offer. In order to meet this role requirement managers should be favorably disposed toward engaging in competition. If they are unwilling to compete for position, status, advancement, and their ideas, they are unlikely to succeed.
3. Although the behaviors expected of a parent and those expected of a manager are not identical, both are supposed to take charge, to make decisions, to take such disciplinary actions as may be necessary, and to protect other members of a group. Thus, one of the common role requirements of the managerial job is that the incumbent behave in an active and assertive manner. Those who prefer more passive behavior patterns, no matter what their sex and those who become upset or disturbed at the prospect of

behaving in an assertive manner would not be expected to possess the type of motivation needed.

4. Managers must exercise power over subordinates and direct their behavior. They must tell others what to do and enforce their words through appropriate use of positive and negative sanctions. Individuals who find such behavior difficult and emotionally disturbing, who do not wish to impose their wishes on others or believe it is wrong to do so, would not be expected to meet this particular role requirement.

5. The managerial job requires people to stand out from the group and assume a position of high visibility. They must deviate from the immediate subordinate group and do things which inevitably invite attention, discussion, and perhaps criticism from those reporting to them. When this idea of standing out from the group elicits feelings of unpleasantness, then behavior appropriate to the role will occur much less often than would otherwise be the case.

6. There are administrative requirements such as constructing budget estimates, serving on committees, talking on the telephone, filling out forms, and so on in all managerial work, although the specific activities will vary. To meet these prescriptions a manager must at least be willing to face this type of routine and ideally gain some satisfaction from it. If such behavior is consistently viewed with apprehension or loathing, a person's chances of success are low.

Scores for each of these roles (two scores are computed for desire to compete) as well as a total score are computed. In 21 studies of the MSCS reviewed by Miner (1978), all yielded significant results for the MSCS total score. Those subscale scores having to do with attitudes toward authority and the desire to exercise power were valid in over half of the studies, while motives to be assertive, stand out, and perform administrative duties were valid in about one-third of the studies.

In his review of criterion-related validity studies for projectives published in *Journal of Applied Psychology* and *Personnel Psychology* between 1960 and 1981, Cornelius (1983) reported that 10 of 14 studies (excluding the studies on the MSCS reviewed by Miner in 1978) yielded significant validity coefficients. Five of these studies used the TAT described above. One (Edel, 1968) used a Selective Word Memory Test in which respondents' ability to remember "success," "failure," and "neutral" words is assessed. One study used a sentence completion task (Hundel, 1971), and another used a word association test (Gough, 1976). After the Cornelius review was completed, a study by McClelland and Boyatzis (1982) reported significant correlations between TAT scores and promotion progress of managers after eight and sixteen years.

Clearly, a variety of projective devices for assessing general personality can produce significant predictions of job performance and the generally negative image they have with some selection researchers seems unwarranted.

We emphasize that the projective tests described here are not for use by untrained persons. Projective test scoring requires a thorough immersion in the constructs underlying the particular measure, rigorous training in applying existing scoring guidelines, and supervised practice.

Personality Inventories

Personality inventories (surveys, blanks, scales, profiles, or schedules) are multi-dimensional in nature. As such, they, like aptitude batteries, attempt to define and assess sets of specific aspects or traits of the person. Also, like aptitude tests, these inventories are of the paper and pencil test variety.

Also, like aptitude batteries, they are developed through internal consistency analyses such as factor or cluster analysis. In this procedure a hypothetical trait is defined by a set of questions or items in a test. Certain items are written to provoke or "tap" the trait cluster, and if responses to the items across a large number of people are strongly correlated the items are said to assess the trait. This procedure, or one similar to it, has been used to develop the personality inventories most frequently utilized in the employment setting.

1. Edwards Personal Preference Schedule (EPPS)
2. California Psychological Inventory (CPI)
3. Gordon Personal Profile (GPP)
4. Thurstone Temperament Survey (TTS)
5. Guilford-Zimmerman Temperament Survey (G-ZTS)

Usually, the problem with these measures is that their relevance to the work setting is unknown. Therefore, the traits the test assesses are even of unknown *potential* validity (for an exception see Ghiselli's (1971) monograph on personality predictions of management effectiveness). A second significant problem is the fact that these measures can be faked, and in the employment setting there certainly exists the motivation to do so (Dunnette, McCartney, Carlson, & Kirschner, 1962).

Personality inventories differ from projective devices in that the response format is structured; that is, respondents indicate whether they agree or disagree with a statement, or the statement is true or false, and so on. Given this structured response format, these tests can be mechanically or objectively scored.

Another possible explanation for the reports of lack of personality-behavior correlation has been offered by Mischel (1973) who argues that behavior is situationally determined and that the trait measurement approach is inherently incorrect. Mischel's is a radical situationalist position, and it is likely that a more moderate view represents reality. Schneider (1983a) believes that both the situation and the person's ability/personality are determinants of behavior but that there is little evidence of the interaction or moderator effects suggested by Mischel. What Schneider is saying is that a person who is inherently "calm" will appear less perturbed in a stressful situation than others, but that he or she will act differently while reading a book than when he or she has a car accident. So, situations have some effects on people, but they do not totally determine people's behavior. The Mischel argument is important in another respect, however. Most structured personality inventories have not been developed with the expectation that they will be used in an employment situation; hence, it is not surprising to find their general lack of validity when used to predict work behavior.

Industrial psychologists are often amazed and disconcerted by the attitudes of managers toward personality tests. The same manager who is hard-nosed and skeptical in evaluating production or inventory techniques will very often be a soft touch for a charleton peddling a panacea personality test. One study demonstrated this gullibility quite dramatically. Ross Stagner (1958), an industrial psychologist, gave a group of personnel managers attending a convention a published personality test. As feedback, each manager received not his actual score but a list of thirteen statements indicated as descriptive of his personality. The managers did not know it, but they all received the same description; all statements had been taken from horoscopes, astrology books, and similar sources. Managers were asked to rate the accuracy of their scores. Eighty percent felt that their profile was either an "amazingly accurate" or a "rather good" description of them. Here are some examples of the 13 statements each manager received and agreed were descriptive:

> While you have some personality weaknesses, you are generally able to compensate for them.
> At times you are extroverted, affable, and sociable, while at other times you are introverted, wary, and reserved.
> Security is one of your major goals in life.

Results like these help explain the continued heavy use of already existing personality inventories in industry. Add to this gullibility a tendency for managers to want a "quick fix" to a problem, and we have the purchase and use of potentially non-valid personality inventories.

As we will show with some case studies, personality inventories *can* be valid in employment situations when they are tailored to the setting, when they are used to predict global criteria of success (e.g., promotion), and/or when personality constructs relevant for job performance constructs are the bases for choosing the personality measure used. Prior to turning to these studies, however, it is important to point out that this discussion of personality testing now, cognitive ability testing earlier, or interviewing later, must be part of a comprehensive assessment package. This means that because the criteria of effectiveness at work are multi-dimensional, we may very well need a number of different procedures for assessing job applicants. In *combination,* the data these procedures yield may help us make more valid predictions of the future behavior of employees. So, keep in mind that perhaps cognitive skills, achievement motivation, and sales orientation are three hypothesized correlates of job performance and that these require paper and pencil ability measures, a projective test, and an interview for adequate assessment.

Finally, it may be that personality-type measures may be most appropriate for predicting how well people will "fit in" a setting, regardless of how well they can do the technical facets of the work. While this is an appealing hypothesis (Schneider, 1983b) to our knowledge there is no research to support it.

Tests Developed for a Particular Setting: The Standard Oil Studies

What about the adaptation of personality inventories to a specific work setting? One such study, carried out by *Standard Oil of New Jersey* (SONJ), was part of an attempt to identify management potential at the time of hire. Such studies, under the title *Early Identification of Management Potential* (EIMP), have been underway for a number of years (see Laurent, 1968, 1970). The research staff at SONJ, aware of the "gloom" in personality testing but convinced of the potential for developing job-relevant inventories, followed these steps:

1. They utilized careful criterion development. They identified three important facets of success and combined them for an overall success index:
   a. Position level attained
   b. Salary history
   c. Effectiveness ranking

2. They administered the *Guilford-Zimmerman Temperament Survey* (G-ZTS) (and other measures) to a sample of 443 managers in many different SONJ functions. Because people with different years of experience and age were included in the sample, these variables were statistically controlled in developing the success index. (The perceptive reader will note that this was a *concurrent validity* study.)
3. They correlated the ten G-ZTS scores with the success index and found correlations with success ranging from −.08 to .14.
4. Using the scores of one-half of the sample of 443 men, they examined all of the test items in the G-ZTS for significant correlations with the success index. The valid items were then combined into an organizationally relevant personality test.
5. The items found to be valid on the first half of the sample were checked against the second half of the sample. This procedure replicates the item validities and gives the researcher confidence that the validity was not due to chance.
6. The correlation between the special keys developed from the G-ZTS and the success index in both samples was found to be about .32.
7. The studies were repeated many times on samples of different functional roles, in different companies, and in different countries (Laurent, 1970). These studies showed the measure to have predictive validity.
8. The specially developed G-ZTS keys, combined with other tests and measures, yielded correlations of about .60 to .70 between the EIMP prediction and success. (A biographical information blank was shown to be the consistently best single correlate of success—we shall discuss this subject further later on in this chapter.)

Few studies have been revalidated as frequently as those conducted at SONJ, and few have been as carefully tailored to the specific job situation in which they were used as was true at SONJ.

The Mills-Bohannon Study

A study reported by Mills and Bohannon (1980) using the *California Psychological Inventory* (CPI) illustrates well our point that personality inventories must be tailored to the job on which performance is to be predicted. The CPI yields eighteen scales which are listed in Table 10–2. This self-report inventory was given to 49 police cadets, and performance ratings were obtained on those people on leadership and overall suitability for police work after one year on the job. A special formula providing a general leadership score developed by Gough (1969) was also computed. Finally, a leadership formula for police officers developed nearly a decade before (Hogan, 1971) allowed computation of a police performance score.

CPI SCALE/EQUATION	CORRELATION WITH RATINGS OF	
	LEADERSHIP	SUITABILITY
Dominance	.02	–.02
Capacity for Status	.15	.01
Sociability	–.02	–.14
Social Presence	.24	.16
Self-Acceptance	–.01	–.07
Well-Being	.24	.14
Responsibility	.07	.05
Socialization	.17	.26*
Self-Control	.23	.08
Tolerance	.33*	.26*
Good Impression	.02	–.12
Communicability	.19	.32*
Achievement via Conformity	.07	–.03
Achievement via Independence	.32*	.31*
Intellectual Efficiency	.43*	.27*
Psychological Mindedness	.01	–.02
Flexibility	.25	.39*
Feminity	.20	–.09
General Leadership (Gough, 1969)	.15	.20
Police Performance (Hogan, 1971)	.43*	.45*

*p <.05.
From Mills and Bohannon, (1980).

The validities for all eighteen scales as well as the generalized leadership score and the specific police performance score are given in Table 10–2. The most valid subscales of the CPI included the Tolerance, Achievement via Independence, Flexibility, and Socialization Scales. Most importantly for our argument, however, was the superior validity of the police performance equation developed ten years before by Hogan (1971).

The Borman-Rosse-Abrahams Study

In a complex effort directed toward the establishment of the construct validity of personality and interest inventory items, Borman, Rosse, and Abrahams (1980) conducted a study of Navy recruiters that involved the following steps:

1. Job analyses and factor analyses of measures of job performance indicated the importance of three major dimensions (selling skills, human relations skills, and organizing skills) plus an overall performance dimension.

TABLE 10–3. *RELATIONSHIPS BETWEEN OLD AND NEW PERSONALITY ITEM COMPOSITES AND VALIDITIES OF THOSE COMPOSITES AGAINST RECRUITER PERFORMANCE.*

		VALIDITIES*		
Performance Category (Overall Performance)	Correlations Between Old and New Items	Old Items in First Sample	Old Items in Second Sample	New Items in Second Sample
Working Hard	.51	.28	.05	.16
Impulsive	.61	.15	.05	.07
Leading & Influencing	.64	.28	.26	.31
Good Impression	.62	.25	.12	−.02
People-Oriented	.57	.26	.07	−.04

*Correlations above .14 are statistically significant (p<.05)

From Borman et al., (1980).

2. Based on the author's understanding of the Navy recruiter's job, 310 items were selected from various personality instruments. In addition, the entire Strong-Campbell Interest Inventory (see below) was administered. Those items formed a trial inventory.

3. Responses to each of these items were correlated with ratings on the four major performance categories listed in # 1 above. Using only those items whose validity was highest, the researchers selected four sets of personality items and four sets of interest items.

4. Factor analyses of each of these sets of "valid" items were conducted.

5. Investigators then wrote or found new items that reflected the same factors which were discovered in the factor analyses of the valid items.

6. The items generated in # 5 above were then correlated with measures of recruiter performance. Note that if these latter items correlate with performance, they reflect the investigator's ability to understand the factors underlying personality and interest items and the investigator's ability to write new items reflecting the same factors.

In Table 10–3, we reproduce a portion of the results regarding personality items from the Borman, Rosse, Abrahams (1980) study. Similar results were obtained for the interest inventory items. Correlations between old and new items represent the degree to which the two sets of items measure the same construct and could be considered convergent validities. Validities of old items in the second sample are equivalent to cross-validated correlations (see Chapter 6). Finally, in the last column, we have validities for new items in a second sample. The validity of these items represents the degree to which the researchers captured a similar job-relevant construct in their new items. While these correlations are not high, this methodology represents an extremely stringent test of the understanding of personality and interest dimensions important in the job of the Navy recruiter.

INTEREST MEASURES

In this next section, we turn to interest measures which can be similar to personality inventories both in terms of the content they attempt to measure and the format of items (Jackson, 1977). However, whereas personality tests focus on generic typical behavior (e.g., self-confidence), interest inventories are used to diagnose work and career orientations. In fact, the impetus for the construction of interest inventories came from vocational guidance and this is still the locus of much of the research with such procedures (Muchinsky, 1983b).

The Strong-Campbell Interest Inventory (SCII)

The SCII (formerly the *Strong Vocational Interest Blank* or SVIB) was developed through a process known as *criterion keying*. In this procedure, a test item is retained for use on a test only when the item reveals significant validity for a particular criterion. In the SCII case, scoring was supposed to differentiate the interests of people in different occupations (there are now 162 occupational scales) from each other and from other people in general. Since the scoring keys were developed to separate the kinds of interests people in one occupation have from the kinds of interests people in other occupations have, the SCII will not separate one individual from another on some performance or turnover criterion on a particular job. It does predict the occupation people enter, and it does this with commendable accuracy.

In the Strong-Campbell Interest Inventory (SCII), the 1981 edition of the Strong Vocational Interest Blank (SVIB), the person is given a list of 325 items regarding a wide range of occupations, occupational activities, hobbies, amusements, school subjects and types of people (see Campbell and Hansen, 1981, for the SCII research manual). The person is asked to respond "Like," "Indifferent," or "Dislike" to each of them. It typically takes about 30 minutes to respond to the 325 items.

The respondent's answers are analyzed, usually by computer, to identify (1) general overall interest trends; (2) consistency of response to 23 Basic Interest areas, and (3) the degree of similarity

FIGURE 10–1. MEAN TEST-RETEST PROFILES FOR A SAMPLE OF 37 PSYCHOLOGISTS.

PROFILE – STRONG VOCATIONAL INTEREST BLANK FOR MEN

FOR USE WITH STD. FORM T399 OR T399R, HAND-SCORED ANSWER SHEET, AND HAND-SCORING STENCILS

LETTER RATINGS AND STANDARD SCORES

Group	Scale	Test M	Test SD	1948 Retest M	1948 Retest SD	1968 Retest M	1968 Retest SD
I	DENTIST	29	9.6	29	10.7	32	9.9
	OSTEOPATH	28	8.1	28	7.9	31	7.7
	VETERINARIAN	16	8.5	19	6.7	18	7.5
	PHYSICIAN	35	10.2	37	9.7	43	9.5
	PSYCHIATRIST	44	9.7	45	8.5	47	9.9
	PSYCHOLOGIST	50	10.1	51	9.8	52	9.1
	BIOLOGIST	44	10.7	45	11.0	50	9.8
II	ARCHITECT	32	8.9	33	10.7	35	10.1
	MATHEMATICIAN	37	11.7	38	11.4	44	10.8
	PHYSICIST	34	10.1	35	13.0	38	11.9
	CHEMIST	42	10.5	41	12.4	43	13.4
	ENGINEER	33	8.7	35	10.9	35	11.1
III	PRODUCTION MGR.	26	7.2	26	9.1	23	10.1
	ARMY OFFICER	18	13.4	20	13.1	14	12.8
	AIR FORCE OFFICER	28	11.7	27	10.9	23	10.8
IV	CARPENTER	15	11.2	15	10.5	13	10.7
	FOREST SERVICE MAN	12	11.4	12	11.2	9	11.8
	FARMER	26	8.3	26	7.9	25	8.8
	MATH-SCIENCE TEACHER	37	9.0	32	9.1	32	8.9
	PRINTER	25	8.6	22	6.7	21	8.6
	POLICEMAN	11	10.5	11	9.9	6	7.5
V	PERSONNEL DIRECTOR	29	12.8	29	12.9	25	11.0
	PUBLIC ADMINISTRATOR	38	11.7	39	11.5	36	10.7
	REHAB COUNSELOR	32	11.3	32	9.9	33	10.0
	YMCA SECRETARY	16	11.8	15	11.9	11	10.7
	SOCIAL WORKER	32	11.9	34	12.4	32	11.7
	SOCIAL SCIENCE TEACHER	25	8.3	23	9.8	22	11.5
	SCHOOL SUPERINTENDENT	26	11.5	28	10.9	30	11.6
	MINISTER	26	11.4	25	11.8	30	13.3
VI	LIBRARIAN	37	11.2	37	10.6	41	11.3
	ARTIST	32	8.2	32	9.4	34	9.6
	MUSICIAN PERFORMER	37	8.4	38	8.2	38	9.1
	MUSIC TEACHER	27	9.0	28	9.8	29	11.9
VII	CPA OWNER	27	10.5	27	8.4	30	9.4
VIII	SENIOR CPA	20	8.1	18	10.0	19	10.6
	ACCOUNTANT	20	9.0	17	9.6	16	9.1
	OFFICE WORKER	17	7.7	13	8.6	12	8.6
	PURCHASING AGENT	19	8.0	19	8.2	18	7.7
	BANKER	14	7.8	15	7.0	15	6.9
	PHARMACIST	21	9.2	20	9.0	20	8.0
	MORTICIAN	18	5.8	19	5.8	17	4.8
IX	SALES MANAGER	19	8.6	18	8.7	15	6.6
	REAL ESTATE SALESMAN	25	7.1	25	7.0	25	5.7
	LIFE INSURANCE SALESMAN	20	8.6	20	8.9	20	8.6
X	ADVERTISING MAN	28	8.3	28	7.7	30	8.9
	LAWYER	33	10.3	31	8.5	37	10.0
	AUTHOR-JOURNALIST	35	8.5	36	8.8	38	9.5
XI	PRES., MFG. CONCERN	23	9.0	22	8.1	21	7.4

Suppl. Occup. Scales

	Scale	M	SD	M	SD	M	SD
	CREDIT MANAGER	21	10.2	21	11.5	17	10.2
	CHAMBER OF COMM. EXEC.	26	10.2	27	10.0	25	9.3
	PHYSICAL THERAPIST	29	12.3	28	9.9	26	8.3
	COMPUTER PROGRAMMER	36	10.2	35	11.6	31	12.9
	BUSINESS EDUC. TEACHER	23	9.7	22	9.1	20	9.1
	COMMUNITY RECR. ADMIN.	15	12.2	17	12.4	14	10.2

Legend:
● ● 1927, '35 Test
– – – – 1948 Retest
○—○ 1968 Retest

Nonoccupational Scales
AACH 61 61 67 · AR 52 59 62 · DIV 55 51 49 · MFII 49 49 46
MO 39 39 36 · OIE 51 51 52 · OL 60 61 63 · SL 55 56 55

From M. Vinitsky, "A Forty-Year Follow-Up on the Vocational Interests of Psychologists and Their Relationship to Career Development," *American Psychologist*, 28(1973), p.1001.

TABLE 10–4.

| Study | N | Study Span (Yrs) | PERCENT OF PEOPLE WHO WERE IN PREDICTED OCCUPATION | | |
			Good Hits	Poor Hits	Clean Misses
Strong	524	18	48	18	34
McArthur (total sample)	60	14	45	20	35
McArthur (public school)	31	14	61	13	26
Trimble (total sample)	177	10	44	15	41
Trimble (special scale sample)	120	10	49	17	34
Brand & Hood (total sample)	259	7	47	20	33
Brand & Hood (MMPI-deviant sample)	129	7	56	16	28
Dolliver et al.	130	12	42	12	46

Adapted from Dolliver, Irwin, and Bigley, (1972).

between the person's responses and the characteristic responses of men and women employed in 162 occupations. The results are reported on a sheet called a profile that presents the scores on a number of scales and offers interpretive advice. The retest reliability of the SVIB scores across long periods is impressive. The results of one such study (Vinitsky, 1973) are illustrated graphically in Figure 10–1. These data represent the interest profiles of 37 psychologists tested in 1927, 1948, and finally in 1968.

The various editions of the Strong Interest Inventories were developed, and are used, primarily in counseling situations. Some evidence of the predictive validity of the SVIB as presented by various investigators is shown in Table 10–4. The column labeled Good Hits contains the percentages of people who were in an occupation for which they had received a standard score of 45 or more (mean of people in the occupation equals 50, standard deviation equals 10), while Poor Hits contains those persons who had standard scores of 40–44. Clean Misses contains those who were in an occupation for which their standard score was 39 or below. Dolliver et al. (1972) summarize their results as follows: the chances are about 1:1 that a person getting a score of 45 or more will end up in that occupation; chances that a person with a score

FIGURE 10-2. *OCCUPATIONS SCORING HIGH AND LOW ON SIX OCCUPATIONAL THEMES*

REALISTIC	INVESTIGATIVE	ARTISTIC
	High Scores	
Agribusiness	Astronomers	Actors
managers	Biologists	Advertising
Carpenters	Chemists	executives
Cartographers	College professors	Architects
Engineers	Geologists	Art teachers
Farmers	Mathematicians	Artists
Foresters	Medical technologists	Broadcasters
Highway patrol	Physicians	Interior decorators
officers	Physicists	Ministers
Industrial arts	Psychologists	Musicians
teachers		Music teachers
Military officers		Photographers
Police officers		Public relations
Veterinarians		directors
Vocational agricul-		Reporters
ture teachers		
	Low Scores	
Advertising	Bankers	Agribusiness
executives	Beauticians	managers
Artists	Business education	Bankers
Broadcasters	teachers	Correctional officers
Florists	Buyers	Farmers
Foreign language	Carpenters	Foresters
teachers	Chamber of Com-	Industrial arts
Interior decorators	merce executives	teachers
Life insurance agents	Correctional officers	Military officers
Poets	Farmers	Physical education
Political scientists	Florists	teachers
Psychologists	Interior decorators	Sales personnel
Public relations	Realtors	Skilled trades
directors	Writers	Veterinarians
Writers		Vocational agricul-
		ture teachers

From Campbell and Hansen, (1981).

of 39 or below are 8:1 that the person will *not* end up in that occupation.

Of considerable theoretical interest in the work using the SCII has been the discovery that types of general vocational interest themes characterize occupations. Thus, just as general aptitude test batteries provide evidence of the basic or primary mental abilities, we can ask the question: are there fundamental themes that characterize vocations?

To answer this question, researchers on the SVIB and SCII adopted Holland's (1973) scheme for characterizing occupations. Holland proposed that occupations are usefully clustered into six

SOCIAL	ENTERPRISING	CONVENTIONAL
	High Scores	
Flight attendants	Agribusiness	Accountants
Guidance counselors	managers	Auto sales dealers
Mental health	Auto sales dealers	Bankers
workers	Business education	Business education
Ministers	teachers	teachers
Physical education	Buyers	Credit managers
teachers	Chamber of Com-	Department store
Recreation leaders	merce executives	managers
Rehabilitation	Computer sales	Executive
counselors	Department store	housekeepers
School administrators	managers	Farmers
Social science	Food service	IRS agents
teachers	managers	Nursing home
Social workers	Life insurance agents	administrators
Special education	Realtors	Office workers
teachers	Retail clerks	Purchasing agents
YMCA/YWCA	Sales managers	
directors	Stockbrokers	
	Low Scores	
Architects	Actors	Actors
Artists	Anthropologists	Anthropologists
Carpenters	Artists	Art teachers
Engineers	Astronomers	Artists
Farmers	Biologists	Broadcasters
Florists	Economists	Florists
Geologists	Geologists	Interior decorators
Geographers	Mathematicians	Musicians
Marketing executives	Physicists	Occupational
Mathematicians	Psychologists	therapists
Musicians	Writers	Reporters
Photographers		
Physicists		

categories. In addition, he noted that because people with certain interests join occupations that fit them, and because occupations tend to be industry and organization-specific, that the environments in which occupations exist can also be described by these six categories. The names of these categories, with representative occupations, are shown in Figures 10–2 and 10–3; also shown are occupations that have the *lowest* scores for the six themes.

Figure 10–3 presents the hexagonal form of Holland's perspective showing the relationship between different kinds of occupations and occupational environments. It shows that, for example, Intellectual and Artistic interests are closer in type than are Intellectual and Enterprising interests. Thus, adjacent occupations share

FIGURE 10–3. *HEXAGONAL MODEL OF VACATIONAL INTERESTS.*

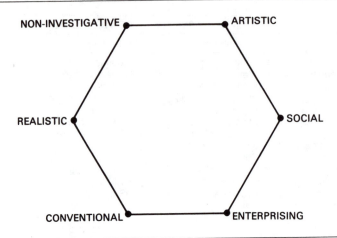

From Holland, J. L. (1985).

some similar interests while occupations further apart share few to no common interests. There is a very large body of evidence to support the Holland classification scheme (cf. Campbell & Hansen, 1981).

This scheme for classifying occupations has potentially important implications for understanding how particular organizations, because of the people in them, tend to develop particular kinds of climates or cultures—why hospitals "feel" different from auto assembly plants (Schneider, 1983b). By implication, we might think that people who do not fit a particular climate would be unhappy there and tend to leave, but research on this issue is not clear. What *is* clear is that when people expect a particular kind of organization but do not find it, they will tend to be dissatisfied and leave (Wanous, 1980).

More relevant to our present discussion is the validity of the interest inventory to predict job success. Some data concerning this question were presented in Table 10–1 and we return to this question again after discussing a second popular interest inventory.

The Kuder Preference Records
(Occupational and Vocational)

The Kuder interest inventories (Occupational, O; Vocational, V) represent two different procedures for developing a measure; internal consistency analysis served as the technique in the development of the Kuder V, while the criterion-key approach was used for the Kuder O.

The Kuder V, developed first, concentrates on activities. Each item in the inventory consists of three activities (a triad) and respondents must choose which of the three activities they would like to do most and which they would like to do least. For example, a triad might be:

1. Go for a long hike in the woods
2. Go to a symphony concert
3. Go to an exhibit of new inventions

By internal consistency analysis, items were assigned to one of ten vocational groupings: Outdoor, Mechanical, Computational, Scientific, Persuasive, Artistic, Literary, Musical, Social Service, Clerical. Some evidence for the validity of the Kuder V is provided in a study conducted by McCully (1954). McCully followed up a group of men who had been given the Kuder V as part of a counseling program run by the Veterans Administration after World War II. He tabulated the occupations these men entered and examined their Kuder V scores; the data in Table 10–5 reveal his findings and suggest the kinds of occupational groupings among which the Kuder V discriminates.

The Kuder O was developed through the criterion-key method, the same procedure used with the SCII. The Kuder O yields scores on forty or so occupational scales but has not received as much attention as the SCII.

Are They All the Same?

Cole and Hanson have noted:

> The several inventories of vocational interest used in this country were constructed in different ways, scored by different methods, and reported scores on different numbers of scales with different names. However, the similarity of scale names across instruments raises the question of the degree to which the different inventories measure the same or similar interests (1971, p. 478).

Indeed, Cole and Hanson (1971) show that if we take the SVIB, Kuder, and other interest inventories, the different scales can be easily sorted into Holland's six-factor scheme and the factors will retain the same hexagonal shape Holland proposed as shown in Figure 10–3. Interests close to each other in the hexagon are more similar than those farther apart. Research supporting this idea of clustering occupations into a few categories is also presented by

TABLE 10-5. AVERAGE KUDER V STANDARD SCORES OF DIFFERENT OCCUPATIONAL GROUPS*

	Mechanical	Computational	Scientific	Persuasive	Artistic	Literary	Musical	Social Service	Clerical
Accounting (and related)	*-78*	*152*	-32	37	-82	19	2	-14	*118*
Engineering (and related)	*56*	45	*82*	-16	7	1	-21	-46	-41
Managerial	-28	44	-18	*56*	-27	19	-15	- 2	42
Clerical-Computing and Recording	-27	*67*	- 9	9	-50	4	3	-14	*68*
General Clerical	-19	- 3	-31	- 9	-14	22	3	17	30
Sales-Higher	-65	-14	-40	*111*	-54	38	17	18	30
Sales-Lower	-19	-12	-25	79	-32	10	6	15	16
General Farming	22	-25	-16	-37	- 4	-49	-42	12	-10
Mechanical Repairing	*81*	-21	3	-40	28	-28	-30	-40	-29
Electrical Repairing	*66*	- 3	27	-35	5	-41	-13	-19	-29
Bench Crafting (Fine)	*63*	- 5	12	-24	38	-23	-20	-33	- 2

Based on a mean of 0 and a standard deviation of 100 for the reference group of 2,797 employed veterans. Italicized scores represent high correspondence
Based on McCully (1954) from R.L. Thorndike and E.P. Hagen. *Measurement and Evaluation in Psychology and Education* 3rd ed. (New York, Wiley, 1969). p 397. Reprinted by permission.

Harrington, Lynch, and O'Shea (1971), and by Lee and Hedahl (1971), and, as noted above and shown in Figure 10–2, it is incorporated into the current version of the SCII.

Research with a newly developed interest inventory, the *Jackson Vocational Interest Survey* (JVIS, Jackson, 1977) also suggests that scores from different inventories are consistent and sometimes strongly related. The fact that the JVIS interest scales are intercorrelated with SCII scales is not particularly surprising— just as GATB tests correlate well with EAS tests of aptitudes. Perhaps of more interest is the fact that JVIS scales are composed of items that are more activity-oriented than the SCII items tend to be. In some cases the increased activity orientation of JVIS might improve the potential for its use as an individual predictor, but that has not yet been established.

The Validity of Interest Inventories in Work Settings

The simple fact is that, while conceptually and from a vocational choice point of view it is good to understand the underlying structure of people's career interests, from the organization's point of view it is necessary to know only if the person has interests similar to those of successful people holding the job under consideration (whatever the criterion or criteria of success are). In this regard, given that we have the job of "engineer" to fill, the chances of the SCII, Kuder, or JVIS predicting success on our *particular* engineering job is not very strong (Dunnette and Aylward, 1956). However, a special scoring key for one of these inventories that portrays the interest profile of one particular engineering job enhances the chances for successful prediction based on interests (Dunnette, Wernimont, & Abrahams, 1964).

Specially constructed scoring keys can work in particular instances because the only items in the inventory that actually get scored are those that are shown to be statistically related to the criterion or criteria of interest. We know that the only items that can relate to the success criteria are items on which people *differ*. That is, the only personality or interest traits that have a chance of correlating with the way people differ on the *criteria* are those *traits* on which people differ.

The evidence we presented above suggests that people doing a similar job in a similar setting may, in fact, have similar interests. Indeed, Jackson (1977) has presented convincing evidence to show that people who share occupational interests are likely to share personality characteristics as well.

It follows that in any one setting it will be difficult to establish a relationship between individual differences in personality/interest and effectiveness criteria *because there are likely to be few individual differences in personality/interest* (Schneider, 1983a). Care must be taken to find those differences that do exist, as shown in the studies reviewed earlier and the biographical data studies to be reviewed later, if validity in a setting is going to be found.

Finally, it may be that discouraging validity for personality and interest measures derives from the way they are scored. Many of these inventories are scored so that one person's highest score may actually be lower than another person's average score. This happens when the test-taker must make a choice on every item they encounter on the inventory such that the very choosing of one alternative means a non-choice of some other alternative(s). When this situation exists, one person can have some very strong trait (personality or interest) scores and some weak scores while another person can have a very flat distribution of trait scores. Regardless, the two people may both have the same "score" if, for both, the same trait is highest for them.

When scores are assigned to individuals based on their own relatively highest trait, the scoring is called *ipsative scoring,* where *ipse* refers to *self.* Such scoring causes problems for our statistical analyses and, more importantly, for the potential validity of these scales.

ORGANIZATIONALLY RELEVANT MOTIVATION INVENTORIES: AN ALTERNATIVE

Motivation

The fundamental idea underlying personality and interest testing is motivation. As noted at the beginning of Chapter 8, motivation means aroused and directed behavior. We suggested earlier that what arouses people in the work setting is the work and work setting itself. What directs people's behavior is their perception that a particular behavior will enable them to obtain the kinds of rewards and outcomes they desire.

In the work setting, motivation is a function of what the organization offers the individual and what the individual desires in terms of rewards. However, our review of personality testing showed that, unlike the aptitude and job sample testing literatures, the use of personality and interest tests reveals little concern for tailoring tests to a specific job and job situation.

In order to make personality-type measures more relevant to the work setting, we should ask some of the same questions applicable to organizational choice (see Chapter 4):

1. What are the prevailing individual differences between people's desires to obtain certain kinds of feelings at work? Do some people want to feel secure while others want a sense of belonging and still others want a feeling of self-esteem? Are there what Alderfer (1972) calls "chronic individual differences" in the desire to experience particular kinds of feelings at work?

Considerable evidence suggests that measures taken of people after they are employed reveal meaningful, individual differences in such desires (Alderfer, 1972; Porter, 1964). Do these differences exist at the time of hire and, if so, will they be related to such criteria as job satisfaction, attendance, and turnover?

2. What outcomes do people desire from work in the tangible sense of money, fringe benefits, retirement plans, stock options, and so forth? (cf. Nealy, 1964).

There may be a relationship between the tangible desires people have and the feelings they want to experience (Lawler, 1973), but there is neither a necessary connection nor any connection specifying which tangible rewards satisfy which desires.

Taking as an example one of the motivation theories discussed in Chapter 4—instrumentality theory—let us see how we might design a work-relevant personality test.

Instrumentality Theory

Instrumentality theory assumes that people will be more satisfied when they perceive that they can attain desired rewards for their efforts.

To test this idea we have to develop two sets of measures: one for assessing how much people desire particular rewards, and one for assessing the kinds of rewards available in a particular organization (remember the job rewards form of job analysis from Chapter 2). There are sufficient theories about what people desire from work to generate a categorized list of potential rewards (e.g., Alderfer, 1972; Herzberg, Mausner, & Snyderman, 1959; Maslow, 1954). Indeed, this is precisely what the Work Adjustment Group at the University of Minnesota has done (Gay et al., 1971).

This group developed two measures for evaluating motivation, the *Minnesota Importance Questionnaire* (MIQ) and the *Occupational Reinforcer Pattern* (ORP). Both measures assess twenty features of the work situation; the MIQ assesses the importance (i.e., desirability) of these twenty features to people, while the ORP describes the reward characteristics of the work situation. Both measures have good reliability; the MIQ reveals good internal consistency reliability, and the ORP shows good interjudge reliability when different people rate the reward characteristics of the work situation (this is also true of the Hackman and Oldham, 1980, research on task rewards).

One study by Betz (1969) indicates some predictive validity for relating high person/job congruence (personal desires/work situation reward) to individual satisfaction. More research with this measure and this idea is clearly warranted. The construct validity of the measure is denoted by the fact that a factor analysis of the twenty reward characteristics represents six factors, which are closely related to categories from other work-related motivation theories; this is shown in Table 10–6. Clearly the MIQ fits other work-related theoretical positions and operationalizes the instrumentality theory idea of assessing the desirability of different rewards for different people.

In Conclusion

Note that in Table 10–6 the different motivation theories emphasize the interplay of personal and organizational characteristics in the prediction of individual behavior. Note especially the importance of organizational features in influencing the motivation of individuals. This is far from the traditional way of thinking about "personality" testing. Need for achievement theory, the desire for intrinsic motivation theory proposed by Hackman and Oldham (1975), Instrumentality theory, Equity theory—all these stress the relationship of the person to the organization that provides for, supports, and rewards its employees as individual humans with human needs and desires. For some reason, while job analysis has been the *sine qua non* of ability measures in employment, job and especially organizational analysis has not been employed as a basis for developing personality tests. It seems that:

> Most prediction studies of personality have been guided by trait and state theory with the assumptions that behavioral signs can reveal enduring generalized personality structures that serve as broad behavioral predispositions, and that future behavior is chiefly determined by these predispositions. These two basic assumptions focus

WORK-RELATED DESIRES (VOCATIONAL NEEDS) ACCORDING TO TABLE 10-6.
DIFFERENT THEORIES.

GAY ET AL. (1971)	MASLOW (1954)	ALDERFER (1972)	HERZBERG (1968)
MANAGEMENT			
Supervision—Human Relations	} Social	} Relatedness	
Supervision—Technical			
Company Policies and Practice			} Hygiene
Compensation	Security		
Working Conditions	Safety/Security	} Existence	
Security	Security		
AUTONOMY			
Responsibility	} Self-Actualization	} Growth	} Motivator
Creativity			
Authority	Social/Esteem	Relatedness	
CONDITIONS OF WORK			
Activity	} Self-Actualization	} Growth	} Motivator
Independence			
Variety			
Security	Security	} Existence	} Hygiene
Working Conditions	Safety-Security		
ALTRUISM			
Social Service			
Moral Values	} Social	} Relatedness	} Hygiene
Co-Workers			
ACHIEVEMENT			
Ability Utilization			
Achievement	} Self-Actualization	} Growth	} Motivator
Advancement			
RECOGNITION			
Social Status			Hygiene
Recognition	} Esteem	} Relatedness	} Motivator
Authority	Social Esteem		Hygiene

on stable individual difference or personality variables as the key determinants of behavior; they largely ignore the role of environmental conditions or stimulus situations in the regulation of behavior. . . . What a person does cannot be isolated meaningfully from the conditions in which he does it (Mischel, 1968, p. 293).

But, that:

It is, of course, self-evident that there would be no human behavior without persons, and while stimuli or situations come to evoke and maintain behavior patterns they do not respond by themselves. No one challenges the fact that response potentiality resides in persons; situations may evoke behavior but they do not perform it (Mischel, 1968, p. 295).

The point is that, *especially* with personality variables, we must be aware of the situation in which the personality will behave.

DILEMMAS AND PROBLEMS IN MOTIVATION TESTING

Dilemmas

A major dilemma in motivation testing is whether to develop general measures or measures specific to particular jobs; this is the same dilemma encountered in ability testing. If we think about testing as an operation performed only at the time of hire and for only one job, then the specific job approach advocated in this book is the relevant strategy. However, there is no real reason to restrict the use of personality and interest testing to the initial employment situation, and it is wasteful to test for only one particular job at a given time.

A solution to this dilemma is to administer general measures and score them in the traditional ways and also to develop keys specific to the particular job under consideration. Sears, Roebuck and AT&T, for example, have successfully adopted this strategy. Engineers being hired for an engineering job, for example, may be groomed for a management job tomorrow. Their qualifications should therefore be scored both with a key designed specifically for the engineering job, and with several keys evaluating their profiles in terms of management and executive positions. And, today's managers being considered for promotion can be similarly evaluated. At companies like AT&T, for example, assessment centers are run to help evaluate the promotability of managers to higher levels and part of the data used as input for these decisions are the results of personality and interest-type testing.

A second dilemma concerns the problem of *fostering* behavior. That is, even if we could identify people who would have the kinds of motivation we wanted, would they be so motivated? Thus, we want to offer a thought about the necessity for the organization to *support* the kinds of personality/interest/motive patterns that are likely to yield both personal and organizational effectiveness. In short, no person is an island; his or her characteristics and traits, along with the characteristics and traits of the organization, are what will determine effectiveness. A good, and important, example of this phenomenon concerns creativity in the work place.

Research on creativity has identified five major characteristics of creative people (Barron, 1972; Mackinnon, 1962):

1. Creative people have strong self images—they believe they are competent.
2. Creative people are not the "brightest" people although they are smart; IQ above a certain level is unrelated to creative production.
3. Creative people tend to have slightly but consistently different personality from less creative people: they are more in tune with

their emotions and feelings and more self-aware; they have very wide ranging interests including, for males, more interests in traditionally female ideas.

4. Creative people tend to be intuitive rather than rational: they avoid detail for the sake of detail; their occupational interests tend toward arts and sciences rather than business and engineering; they are contemplative and slow to make decisions; and, they will include their feelings and emotions as data when reaching a decision.

5. Creative persons tend to have more unusual mental associations. For example, on word association tests, creative people tend to give more unusual associations.

Our point here is not so much to address creativity, an important topic in its own right, but to note that evidence suggests that people like those described here are likely to be most creative in particular kinds of settings. That is, it is one problem to select creative people and it is another to have them *be* creative. If we return to the idea of *work facilitation* introduced in Chapter 2, we can ask: what kinds of conditions facilitate creativity?

In fact, there have been a number of classical studies of this question. Perhaps McCall (1979) puts the issue most starkly when he notes that the usual reaction to creativity in business is to isolate it, control it, judge it, and, if at all possible, eliminate it. An alternative perspective on creativity is that it should be nurtured, fostered, rewarded, identified and encouraged—but how to do this?

One solution is to ask what kinds of situations have produced people who are creative? That is, from what kinds of background environments have creative people come? One summary of this literature is presented by Solano (undated). She shows that the childhood environments of creative adults are characterized by:

1. Experiencing multiple perspectives. They move more frequently, they are confronted with more ideas and more cultural diversity, and they come from homes where reading and wide interests were encouraged.

2. Being challenged. Parents set standards early on for children to meet, give children early responsibilities, and provide supportive expectations.

3. Goal accomplishment being the reward. Parents emphasize the joy of accomplishing a challenging goal rather than extrinsic rewards (money, movies, etc.).

4. Development of self-confidence. The child is given opportunities to perform independently at play and at school but the parents try to insure successful experiences rather than let the child overreach.

5. Mothers working rather than being full-time homemakers.

Solano (undated) concludes that a work environment charac- terized by these elements will be one in which creativity is likely to be observed. Incidentally, Solano suggests that the reason creativi- ty is associated with having had a working mother is due to relaxed supervision of the child.

Problems

Six problems with motivation testing are as follows:

1. Motivation testing should be done by motivation testing experts. Administering and interpreting personality and interest tests are jobs for people explicitly trained in the field. This is not a suggestion, it is a warning, and the warning applies not only to developing such measures (which would "obviously" require a trained person), but to administering, scoring, and interpreting the results of such tests as well.

2. Motivation testing makes sense to executives and person- nel managers because people consider themselves to be experts in diagnosing the personality of others. Thus we often hear people say "I can read him like a book," or, "I got where I am because I can tell what a person is like after talking to her for five minutes." While such people may exist, there is no evidence yet that one has been found.

3. Another reason personality and interest (especially per- sonality) testing may be attractive to executives is that it sounds so mysterious, "psychological," and "Freudian." We have recounted in this chapter how Stagner (1958) demonstrated this gullibility among personnel managers.

4. The potential "fakability" of motivation tests is another possible problem. When people think about faking personality in- ventories, they usually think of "faking good." In the language of testing, this is called giving a response high on "social desirability" (Edwards, 1957; 1966). Social desirability is a facade or an attempt (not necessarily a conscious one) to put up a good front. In a job applicant, it would be an attempt to try and appear like the stereo- type held of the successful job incumbent.

The evidence on the fakability of personality and interest tests shows clearly that they can be successfully distorted; the evidence about job applicants distorting such tests points to the finding that they do not. As McCormick and Ilgen note: "This is not to say that some individuals would not fake, nor that in certain circumstances faking would not occur more generally. But it does suggest that faking may not be as great a factor in the use of personality and interest inventories as has been generally suspected" (1980, p. 176).

Various procedures have been developed to reduce the possibility of faking (e.g., forced-choice inventories), and to aid in identifying fakers. In the latter case a separate score is developed for a measure that indicates respondents who choose items that people who are asked to fake also choose. Of course, the best method for alleviating this particular problem is to conduct a predictive validity study in which the personality measure (or interest measure) is administered prior to hiring a group of people but is not used in selecting the people. A valid test would then incorporate at least some of the tendency of any applicants for jobs to fake the measure.

5. The "square American" (Gross, 1962) and "organization man" (Whyte, 1957) allegations provoke another problem of motivation testing. The argument Gross and Whyte use against personality testing is that the use of such measures in the hiring process leads to conformity in the kinds of people (especially professional managers) who are hired. Their argument makes considerable sense when (1) the tests used to select employees have not been validated, and/or (2) the criterion or criteria against which the tests are validated indicate that successful people will be conformist.

The evidence against the conformist-as-effective-manager is impressive; the interested reader need only review the literature prepared by Campbell et al. (1970). It shows the effective manager as one who has "dispositions towards interpersonal relationships, hard work, being active, and taking risks; and temperamental qualities such as dominance, confidence, straightforwardness, low anxiety, and autonomy (Campbell et al., 1970, pp. 195–96). More recently, Bentz (1984) summarized more than 30 years of success in using personality inventories as valid predictors at Sears, Roebuck and with a similar conclusion. Consistent predictors of management success are mental alertness, dominance, self-confidence, emotional strength (optimism, emotional control, composure), social competence, and social leadership. This description hardly fits the "square American" or "organization man" image.

6. A final problem has been the resistance of people to taking personality tests. This resistance seems to be based on two interrelated issues: invasion of privacy and the nature of the testing philosophy. Invasion of privacy is an absolutely legitimate criticism of personality testing in the world of work when tests designed for clinical purposes are used. However, the invasion of privacy idea stems more from the apparent lack of any obvious relationship between some questions asked and job performance, rather than

from an unwillingness of people to answer the questions (see Rosenbaum, 1973, for some data on invasion of privacy). Thus in jobs that clearly require a complete examination of an applicant's personality (for example, FBI agent or astronaut) because of potential possible harm to the person and others, few people would forbid the use of our best diagnostic procedures. However, the relevance of some very personal questions to performance on most jobs is difficult to understand; as noted earlier, low content validity in test development can be interpreted as low face validity by candidates and may spark resistance to test-taking.

Regarding the nature of the philosophy underlying testing, one may hypothesize (and it is only an hypothesis) that if an organization's philosophy or orientation toward its work force is one of suspicion, coercion, the man-is-a-machine idea, then the testing process (and the hiring process) will be handled in a mechanistic style. Let us suppose that some very personal questions are relevant for some jobs. Should we not indicate to respondents that although some of the questions asked may seem irrelevant for job performance to them, they have been shown to differentiate between those who succeed and those who fail? Instead respondents are usually told "There is no right or wrong answer," when, if this were true, the test would not be given!

The faking issue may similarly stem from a certain orientation on the part of test-givers. Frequently in psychological experiments, subjects are misled into believing something is true when in fact it is not. This is done to "manipulate" the subjects in order to test some hypothesis. Now, if psychologists "fake" subjects, is it not reasonable to assume that subjects will "fake" psychologists? Argyris (1968) has presented some very interesting analogies between organizational practices vis-à-vis employees, and experimental psychologists' behavior vis-à-vis their subjects.

In Conclusion

It is difficult to argue with the logic of assessing motivation as an important component in the prediction of performance and satisfaction at work. However, it seems clear that personality tests (designed to separate "normal" individuals from non-normals) and interest tests (designed to make predictions of vocational or occupational choice) have not been very effective in predicting individual differences in performance in the work setting. When such tests are essentially re-designed to fit the needs of a particular organization for predicting performance on particular jobs, they can be effective.

An alternative approach to motivation testing builds on the

organizational relevance theme. This alternative also stems from the idea that motivation is the result of some interaction or "fit" of personal desires and organizational reward characteristics. There is, however, little research to indicate the predictive validity of this alternative, although it seems worthwhile from a construct validity standpoint.

We have also offered some dilemmas and problems with motivation testing. These included questions about: (1) how job-specific testing should be; (2) how to support particular individual motivations; (3) the necessity to use specialists in personality testing; (4) the "seductiveness" of personality testing to executives; (5) the potential fakability of such tests; (6) the view that personality tests lead to the selection of conformists; (7) the question of invasion of privacy; and (8) the frequent manipulative use of testing and test administration.

APPLICATION BLANKS AND BIOGRAPHICAL DATA

Application Blanks

The usual first step in the employment process is to fill out an application blank. Application blanks typically request information about previous jobs held, educational level and type, and any special skills. (See Table 10–7 for examples of biographical items.) The information about jobs held will include job title, a description of duties and responsibilities, period of employment, salary, name/ telephone number of the organization and immediate supervisor, and reason for leaving or thinking of leaving. With respect to education, similar kinds of information are collected—schools attended and dates (including schools in the military and other training courses), major (for college) or program (such as college preparatory, commercial, or vocational if only a high school graduate), and, where specific training is important (e.g., engineering, accounting, plumbing, or auto repair), details about such courses.

Some application blanks also include requests for information about job-related hobbies and interests as well as accomplishments the applicant thinks are relevant to the job being applied for. Examples of this kind of information include athletic team and/or club participation and offices held, volunteer work (sometimes especially important to have for homemakers returning to paid employment), awards and prizes, and so forth. Responses to these kinds of additional information on the application blank should be voluntary since, as in testing, job relevance is an important issue

TABLE 10–7. *EXAMPLES OF BIOGRAPHICAL ITEMS USED IN BIODATA RESEARCH.*

PERSONAL	SOCIOECONOMIC LEVEL-FINANCIAL STATUS
Age	Minimum current living expense
Marital Status	Debts
Number of years married	Real estate owned
Number of dependents	Expected earnings
GENERAL BACKGROUND	INTERESTS
Occupation	Hobbies
Occupation of relatives	Sports activities
Military service/rank	Prefer outside to inside labor
Parental family adjustment	Most important leisure activity
EDUCATION	PERSONAL CHARACTERISTICS/ATTITUDES
Level	Willingness to relocate
Spouse's education	Confidence
Subjects liked	Basic expressed personality needs
Grades	Stated job preferences
EMPLOYMENT EXPERIENCE	MISCELLANEOUS
Previous occupations	Source of references
Tenure on previous jobs	Number of references
Number of previous jobs	Relatives working in company
Reason for quitting other jobs	Availability

From England, (1971).

on the application blank. For example, a statement such as the following might be used:

After listing your previous positions you may, if you wish, include in this space any pertinent civic, welfare, or organizational activity which you have performed, either with or without compensation.

Table 10–8 reproduces some information from the Michigan Department of Civil Rights regarding lawful and unlawful questions applicants can be asked. The legal issues noted in Table 10–8 apply to interview questions as well as the application blank. So, questions that were previously (say, pre-1967) asked on applications regarding issues such as sex, marital status, and age, are now illegal.

Making such issues illegal creates somewhat of a Catch-22 situation because organizations need to know whether they are meeting legal requirements regarding discrimination. If they do not collect such information on the application blank, how can they track their hiring practices? The issue here is one of *when* the information is collected and the *purpose* for collecting it. Data on age, race, and sex can be collected after an employment decision has been made (hire or not hire), and this information can be

EXAMPLES OF LAWFUL AND UNLAWFUL PRE-EMPLOYMENT
INQUIRIES AS SPECIFIED BY THE MICHIGAN DEPARTMENT OF
CIVIL RIGHTS.

TABLE 10–8.

SUBJECT	LAWFUL PRE-EMPLOYMENT INQUIRIES	UNLAWFUL PRE-EMPLOYMENT INQUIRIES
Name	Applicant's full name. Have you ever worked for this company under a different name? Is any additional information relative to a different name necessary to check work record?	Original name of an applicant whose name has been changed by court order or otherwise. Applicant's maiden name
Age	Are you 18 years old or older?	How old are you? What is your date of birth?
Marital Status		Requirement that an applicant provide any information regarding marital status or children. Are you single or married? Is your spouse employed? What is your spouse's name?
Sex		Mr., Miss, or Mrs. or an inquiry regarding sex. Inquiry as to ability to reproduce or advocacy of any form of birth control
Organizations	Inquiry into the organizations of which an applicant is a member excluding organizations, the name or character of which indicates the race, color, religion, national origin, or ancestry of its members	List all clubs, societies, and lodges to which you belong
Arrests	Have you ever been convicted of a crime? If so, when, where, and nature of offense? Are there any felony charges pending against you?	Inquiry regarding arrests

maintained in a separate file from actual application materials. Thus, the purpose for maintaining age, sex, and race data is to track decisions in the *aggregate,* that is, across *all* hiring decisions, so the information need not be maintained in a *particular* candidate's file.

On the surface, it is sensible to have an application blank because the information collected should be useful in screening candidates. However, we've found that application blanks are used quite subjectively and haphazardly by many organizations. By this we mean that the people who review application blanks as a way of screening for candidates are rarely provided with specific guidelines about what they should be looking for. Is length of time on previous jobs important? Is why they left jobs important? Are the job duties previously performed critical in the new job? Or, how about majors or school programs?

Research shows, in fact, that people who screen application blanks *think* they know what they are looking for because they *think* they know what is important. What a reviewer thinks is important will be the issue he or she assigns the most weight to. The weight given to the various pieces of information are *implicit weights* if no guidelines are provided. *Explicit* weights are contained in a set of guidelines or rules for evaluating application blanks.

Selection researchers have devised procedures for weighting application blank information. When these procedures are used, we have a *weighted application blank* or WAB. These systems allow staffing people to literally score an application blank. Indeed, researchers have developed even more sophisticated ways of collecting and weighting background information on applicants. These procedures are called *biographical information blanks* or BIB. Based on the premise that the best predictor of future performance is past performance (Chapter 9), these weighted application blanks (WAB) or biographical information blanks (BIB) have proven to be one of the most valid alternatives to standardized tests (see Reilly and Chao, 1982; and Schmitt, Gooding, Noe, & Kirsch, 1984). Examples of the kinds of questions asked on BIBs are presented above in Table 10–7.

Biographical Information Blanks

A number of techniques are available for statistically weighting biographical items. Perhaps the most popular is the technique described by England (1971). An illustration of the technique using sample data from a study by Schmitt and Pulakos (1983) is presented in Table 10–9. The development of scoring keys was begun by separating the BIB responses of 192 transport drivers (persons who deliver gas to local gas stations) into high and low accident groups on four different measures of accident behavior. The data in Table 10–9 represent transport drivers who had a high or low record of having made the error of blending two or more types of gas. Table 10–9 shows that persons in the low accident group are most likely to indicate option 1, 2, or 3 in answering this particular item. Hence, the scoring key for this item indicates that persons picking Options 4 or 5 in response to this item get 0 points, those picking 1, 2, or 3 get 1 point. All items in the inventory are similarly keyed and the persons' scores on all items are summed to produce a total score, which is used to predict a criterion; in the case of the example described in Table 10–9, the criterion is accidents involving gasoline blends. Obviously, this procedure will score items

EXAMPLE OF SCORING KEY DEVELOPMENT.   TABLE 10–9.
(ITEM 33—TRANSPORT DRIVER INVENTORY)

RESPONSE* OPTIONS	# ENDORSING OPTIONS IN LOW ACCIDENT GROUP	# ENDORSING OPTIONS IN HIGH ACCIDENT GROUP	SCORING KEY
1	13	4	1
2	11	5	1
3	14	7	1
4	12	21	0
5	2	20	0
Total	52	57	

*Note that for response options 1, 2, and 3, persons in the high accident group were less likely to endorse the option than those in the low accident group. The reverse was true for response options 4 and 5. Hence, those persons responding 1, 2, or 3, are scored 1 and those responding 4 or 5 are scored 0.

optimally and result in keys which produce significant relationships between total BIB scores and criteria in the sample upon which the keys are developed. Hence, these keys must be evaluated, or cross-validated, in another sample.

Cascio (1982) summarized the necessary steps in choosing biodata items and their weights:

1. Choose an appropriate criterion (e.g., tenure, proficiency).
2. Identify criterion groups (low vs. high performing individuals).
3. Select the application blank items to be analyzed.
4. Specify the item response categories to be used in the analysis.
5. Determine item weights and/or scoring weights for each response option.
6. Apply the weights to a holdout group (cross-validation sample) and correlate total scores with criteria.
7. Set cutting scores for selection.

Validity of Biographical Data

A number of rather comprehensive validity studies have been conducted on the use of biographical data as a selection device. Although inconsistent validity evidence has been found, most reviews report mean criterion-related validities in the range of .30 to .50, e.g., .50 (Asher, 1972), .42 (England, 1971), .33 (Holberg & Pugh, 1978), and .35 (Reilly & Chao, 1982).

The review by Reilly and Chao (1982) is the most recent comprehensive validity review of biodata and is essentially an update and extension of earlier validity studies. Reilly and Chao included only cross-validated findings and both verifiable and unverifiable data in their review. Their results indicate that biodata is a valid predictor for military occupations (mean $r = .30$), clerical workers (mean $r = .52$), management (mean $r = .38$), sales (mean $r = .50$), and scientific/engineering occupations (mean $r = .41$). The authors located only two coefficients for non-management jobs other than clerical, and these yielded the low average validity of .14. Reilly and Chao found that biodata successfully predicted a number of different measures of job success, including tenure (mean $r = .32$), performance in training (mean $r = .39$), performance ratings (mean $r = .36$), productivity (mean $r = .46$), and salary progress (mean $r = .34$).

While the overall results of validity studies are very favorable, unsuccessful validity studies have been reported. Schmidt, Hunter, and Caplan (1981) reported no validity (mean $r = -.03$) across eight studies attempting to use biodata to predict the performance of maintenance workers, and Korman (1968) found biodata to have lower mean validities than other predictors for predicting managerial performance. Rather than indicating that biodata cannot and generally does not validly predict measures of job performance, these two reviews indicate that biographical data, like any other prediction data, is fallible. Cascio summarizes current validations of biographical data by stating, "Compelling evidence exists that where appropriate procedures are followed, the accuracy of personal history data as predictors of future work behavior may be superior to any known alternative" (1982, p. 195–196).

Hopefully, the reason for the effectiveness of biodata is clear: the items that are scored are items determined to be correlated with the criterion or criteria of interest. As noted earlier, when tailored scoring (also known as criterion keying) is used, substantial validity is attainable.

Adverse Impact Problems with Biodata

Reilly and Chao (1982) also reported a comprehensive review of the available research on adverse impact of biodata and concluded that the use of empirical keying of biographical data has strengths and weaknesses. Cross-validated empirical keying indicates that the data is job related. However, because the keying is not necessarily done on a rational basis, the data can lack face validity (which can lead courts to question the job relatedness of the data) and can have adverse impact against some subgroups. Both of these results will lead to serious problems for the organization when it defends the use of the data in an Equal Employment Opportunity Commission (EEOC) suit.

There are two conclusions drawn from Reilly and Chao's review of eighteen studies on this issue:

1. Adverse impact will result when criterion mean differences are large; and
2. The validity and fairness of biodata can be demonstrated when comparing ethnic groups, but different scoring keys are necessary for men and women.

Dreher and Sackett (1983) concluded that the use of biodata is "relatively likely" to produce adverse impact. It seems clear that we should choose and use biodata items carefully. We agree with Pace and Schoenfeldt (1977), who recommended that the most reasonable and justifiable approach is to base the choice of biodata items on a well done job analysis, matching items to the knowledge, skill, and ability requirements of the job description. In other words, a move away from a strictly empirical approach toward a more rational approach may be necessary for a legal defense of the use of biodata information for personnel selection. We also contend that rational selection of biodata items provides dividends in terms of greater understanding of the predictor and criterion measures used.

The issue of face validity can also be a problem, as Dreher and Sackett (1983) have reported. They developed and validated a selection battery, commissioned by an industry consortium, for a particular job. When the validated battery was presented to the member organizations, some of the participants refused to use the device because some of the items didn't seem to make sense— they lacked face validity. A rational approach to biodata item selection could eliminate problems with face validity.

Owens and his colleagues (e.g., Brush & Owens, 1979; Schoenfeldt, 1974; Owens & Schoenfeldt, 1979) conducted the most sophisticated research on biodata. Their assessment-classification model uses scores on empirically derived biodata factors to form life-history subgroups which represent different life experience patterns. Membership in these life history subgroups is then related to performance and satisfaction with different kinds of work. For selection, we find out which life history subgroups perform well and are satisfied with the work involved; then we select members of those subgroups. This approach clearly goes beyond the usual simplistic empirical keying of application blank responses. While we believe that rational keying may be more appropriate than empirical keying for scientific and legal reasons, our discussion would not be balanced if we neglected to mention a study by Mitchell and Klimoski (1982). In their study, they found that scoring keys developed with empirical keying were superior to those developed with rational methods. Most of the relatively impressive validation evidence concerning biodata also derives from empirical keying.

Finally, we should note that various state laws prohibit asking certain questions in pre-employment inquiries. As an example, a portion of a pre-employment inquiry guide published by the Michigan Department of Civil Rights was presented in Table 10–7. Staffing personnel should consider the legal ramifications of the use of biodata.

Reference Checks

Frequently, one outcome of the application blank is a series of potential sources of additional job-relevant information—the people the candidate lists as references and/or prior supervisors. Reference checks can serve two major purposes:

1. To verify the accuracy of information provided by job applicants.
2. To provide new data to use as a basis for predicting job success.

The verification process is especially critical since the incidence of false information on application blanks is sometimes mind-boggling; we are all aware of the M.D. who never went to medical school! So, verification of claimed prior education, licensure, and experience makes sense. If applicant claims are not substantiated, this may be a signal that the applicant is not who he or she claims to be. Thus, failure to verify can lead to rejection.

As far as collecting new data is concerned, we can interview references or prior supervisors about any important job-relevant information—e.g., punctuality, honesty, alcohol or drug abuse, getting along with coworkers, or whatever. As with any kind of interview (to be discussed next), the questions asked should be well-structured and, after the interview is over, a series of judgments (ratings) should be made. As with the employment interview, it is important to ask questions about behavior(s) that are important for the job.

Sometimes it is not possible to contact a potential reference by telephone (or in person, as for a promotion). In that case it is possible to write a letter to the referee containing the questions that require answers. In fact, this can even be in the form of a questionnaire or checklist. Nash and Carroll (1970) report that a one-page questionnaire sent to former employers of clerical applicants yielded an 85 percent response rate. However, telephone reference checks typically yield these good response rates and they appear to be favored by staffing personnel for the following reasons (Nash & Carroll, 1970; Pyron, 1970):

1. On the telephone, the reference can be probed for completeness of answers.

2. Apparently references are more easily obtained over the telephone; i.e., referees are more open and honest on the phone.
3. The information is more speedily obtained since there is no mail delay.
4. Answers on the telephone may contain hesitancies and voice inflections that can be probed for meaning.
5. It is more personal than a letter.

Perhaps the worst kind of reference is an unsolicited letter of reference. Such letters depend upon the subjective inferences of the letter-writer; unless the letter *writer* is known to be reliable in his or her judgments, the only inference we should probably draw from an unsolicited letter, or a response to an unstructured request, is that if it contains negative information, beware.

Do letters of reference and/or reference checks contribute to selection validity? Not many studies exist to answer the validity question. However, the research does suggest the following criteria in order for the reference to contribute to validity (McCormick & Ilgen, 1980, p. 190):

1. The person must have had a chance to observe the applicant on the job, i.e., to actually watch him or her perform.
2. The person must have the competence—technical or otherwise—to accurately judge that performance. For example, a manager with no training in chemistry probably is not competent to judge the performance of research chemists.
3. The person must be *able* to express his or her evaluations in a clear manner. The person must be able to write clearly.
4. The person must be willing to give his or her frank opinion and evaluations.

In perhaps the majority of cases, one or more of these conditions are not met, and the result is that letters of reference tend to be of only limited usefulness. Although all of these four conditions frequently contribute to lowered validity, we have observed that the fourth usually creates the most serious problems. As a general rule, then, and as noted above, most people are reluctant to say unfaltering things about past employees, especially in writing.

Recently, Muchinsky (1979) reviewed the literature on reference reports and confirmed their widespread use. Very few studies report either reliability data (Mosel and Goheen, 1959) or validity data. Validity tends to be best when the rater is well acquainted with the person rated (see #1 above) or the rater is the ratee's supervisor. The low validity (an average of .13 was reported by Muchinsky) may be partially attributable to low interrater reliability; 80 percent of the reliabilities reported by Mosel and Goheen were less than .40. Muchinsky also cites the restriction of range problem resulting from the unwillingness of referees to say anything bad about the people they are writing about.

Another problem with the use of reference checks may be their legal status. Miner and Miner (1977) state that various laws and court decisions are likely to constrain the use of references and background investigations in order to protect individual privacy rights. The possibility of legal entanglements exists, but a survey of major American employers indicated that few had encountered any legal problems as a result of reference-checking practices (Levine & Randolph, 1977). Another legal guideline that may have an effect on what referees are willing to say is that the applicant may have access to letters under freedom of information guidelines. A person writing a letter may be much more reluctant to write anything negative if she or he knows that the person who is the subject of the letter will have access to it. Perhaps the best use that can be made of letters of recommendation is to be especially wary of an applicant whose letters are not positive.

Employee Honesty: A Critical Reference Issue

The theory underlying the reference check (like the BIB) is the theory of behavioral consistency, i.e., the idea that the best predictor of future behavior is past behavior. By now it should be clear that this maxim is at the heart of a potentially valid selection system.

Perhaps nowhere else is the maxim more important than on the issue of honesty; it is *very* difficult to "test" for honesty (Sackett & Harris, 1984). Because of the difficulty of identifying dishonest persons at the hiring interview, information obtained about prior instances of dishonesty are critical. Since many jobs require a judgment about honesty (bank tellers, custodians, guards, truck drivers, cashiers, and so on), any information source is important. And a conscientious solicitation of information from references can prove very useful.

The reference check is particularly helpful for checking on honesty because other forms of collecting data are suspect and/or costly. For example, a current "hot topic" is the polygraph, also called a "lie-detector." The polygraph has low esteem in the scientific community (Sackett and Harris, 1984) as a technique for detecting honesty. Yet polygraphers, companies, and government security agencies find that job applicants confronted with a polygraph test will admit to prior crimes. It seems, then, that the *threat* of the polygraph test results in confessions rather than the test itself detecting dishonesty. Unfortunately, at least in crime detection cases, the polygraph also mistakenly identifies a high proportion of innocent people as suspicious.

Sackett and Harris (1984) presented an extensive review of about a dozen paper and pencil surveys designed to detect dishonesty. Their review suggests some potential validity for a number of measures against some actual indices of honesty (see their Table 3, pp. 229–230). For example, the London House Personnel Selection Inventory significantly predicted those caught stealing or disciplined for cash shortages as well as persons discharged for theft; the Milby Profile predicted gas station attendants' cash shortages; and, the Personal Outlook Inventory correlated about $r = .40$ with department store discharges for theft of cash or merchandise.

While these results are encouraging, we feel that there should be *at least* a reference check whenever honesty emerges as a critical employment issue.

THE EMPLOYMENT INTERVIEW

It is highly unlikely that anyone applying for a job will be able to escape the interviewing process. The employment interview is probably more widely used than any other selection tool. In one survey of 852 organizations (Ulrich and Trumbo, 1965), 99 percent of the firms reported using interviews. More recently Heneman, Schwab, Fossum, and Dyer (1980) reported that the interview was the most commonly used selection technique. As we might suspect from the widespread use of interviews, most managers and personnel workers—especially those who actually are interviewers— have a great deal of faith in the usefulness and validity of the selection interview. Hundreds of "how to" books have been written on the interview, purporting to tell the interviewer or potential interviewer how best to conduct interviews. Though still substantial there is much less *research* material on the interview. Industrial psychologists have been interested in the interview since the early part of this century and have carried out numerous studies to determine both the typical validity of the interview and the decision processes of the interviewer.

During the last 30 years, eight separate reviews of research on the interview have been published: Arvey and Campion, 1982; Hakel, 1982; Mayfield, 1964; Schmitt, 1976; Ulrich and Trumbo, 1965; Wagner, 1949; Webster, 1982; and Wright, 1969. Wagner (1949) located 106 articles dealing with the validity and/or reliability of the interview but only 25 of those articles reported any quantitative data. Reliability coefficients for 174 sets of ratings and 96 different traits ranged from .23 to .97 for ratings of specific traits and $-.20$ to .85 for ratings of overall ability. Intelligence was the only trait consistently rated with high reliability. Validity and reliability was satisfactory for only one area—that of sociability. As subsequent reviews reconfirmed the finding that the validity of the employment interview was low, attention turned to understanding the reasons why.

Webster's (1964) research on decision processes within the interview has been especially instrumental in bringing about this change in focus. In his review of the literature, Schmitt (1976) found that nearly all studies on the employment interview focused on factors which determined interview decisions rather than the outcomes resulting from those decisions. While evidence gathered on the decision-making process in the interview does not necessarily have implications for validity, Schmitt (1976, p. 97) did provide the first nine of the following suggestions for practicing personnel interviewers (we have added the last two).

1. Use of a structured interview guide will improve interviewer reliability. Simply recording information and then returning to it later to make ratings or recommendations may remove some of the order effects, over-weighting of negative information, and contrast effects which may act to diminish the relevance of interview outcomes.
2. Knowing the requirements of the job you are interviewing for should help focus on relevant information.
3. Interviewer training to avoid bias in ratings may be appropriate, though not much effort has been directed toward this problem or the evaluation of such training.
4. The interviewee is also forming an impression of the interviewer, and even when he or she is not an acceptable candidate, the interview may be employed effectively as a public relations vehicle.
5. Interpersonal skills and motivation are perhaps best evaluated by the interview; consequently, the interview will likely be an effective selection device when these elements are also required for effective job performance.
6. Allowing the applicant time to talk will make rapid first impressions less likely and provide a larger behavior sample.
7. The training of interviewers especially with possible applicants of different race or sex may increase their "ability to relate," though if such training exists, it has not been evaluated. At any rate, periodic checks on the number of minorities hired or recommended along with the jobs they are recommended for may alert us to possible bias.
8. Attention should be directed to evaluating the purpose of the interview, i.e., whether it is intended to select on a given number of variables, whether it is an initial screening device, or whether it is primarily education.

9. It is certainly repetitious to state this, but research should still be directed to determining what variables are reliably, validly and uniquely assessed in the selection interview and that research can best be conducted with the cooperation of personnel interviewers.

10. The typical interview, even when it is structured and requires the interviewer to make a series of ratings, may not be useful for predicting productivity criteria (units produced, sales made, programs written, and so on). In the most optimistic case, interviews are useful for assessing applicant interests, motivation, or affinity for particular jobs which in turn may predict job satisfaction, attendance, and retention. We recommend the latter criteria as the foci of the typical interview process.

11. Supervisors of interviewers should try to control the organizational conditions under which decisions need to be made. The evidence is quite clear that the following conditions lead to poor decision-making (Webster, 1982):

    a. The *physical environment* of the interview is noisy, too hot, or too cold.

    b. The *contrast effect:* A mediocre candidate who follows two or three poor candidates will be rated very highly.

    c. The *pressure to hire:* If a training class is starting up and two people are required to fill it, it is remarkable how quickly two qualified applicants can be found!

One of the problems with the employment interview is that its inherently subjective nature leaves it subject to interviewer bias of various types. Recently, Arvey (1979) has provided an excellent review of the employment interview and the legal and psychological nature of unfair discrimination in the interview. Arvey found three basic strategies of research on the problem of bias in the interview. In the *résumé study,* subjects (students, managers, recruiters, etc.) are asked to review a series of job resumes (in interview research these are called "paper people") and to determine the suitability of each of the candidates for employment. Each of these resumes contains information concerning the candidate's age, sex, handicaps, job experience, education, and often a photograph. The independent variable of interest, for example, sex or race, is manipulated while education, experience, and other variables are controlled (remain the same across candidates). In the *in-basket study,* participants are asked to play the role of a personnel manager who takes action on a series of memoranda or letters. These in-baskets typically contain information about the organization and require the subject to make decisions about personnel. As in the résumé study, various independent variables are manipulated by writing two or more versions of the in-basket items changing the characters in the problem. There have also been three *video-tape* or *actual field experiments* in which job candidates have been evaluated by subjects who act as personnel decision-makers.

Arvey's summary of these studies indicates that some biases do exist. Evidence from the résumé research indicates women are evaluated more poorly than men particularly when they are being considered for typically masculine jobs. When the qualifications and sex of candidates were available to interviewer judges, sex accounted for a small portion of the variance in interviewer judgments. Physical attractiveness of candidates seems to be an important factor but independent of applicant gender. Interview ratings do not seem to be a function of applicant race, but applicant age exerts a strong effect on ratings. While not many studies have been reported on the effect of handicaps, there is some indication that a handicapped person is judged to be more highly motivated than persons without handicaps.

Arvey (1979) also reviewed those instances in which the interview was the subject of litigation when minority group persons alleged discriminatory action on the part of employers. While relatively few lawsuits have occurred, Arvey indicates that interviews are clearly vulnerable. Further, he predicts an increase in such suits and warns that organizations are likely to be ill-equipped to defend the interview because of the little attention given to quantifying and validating interview judgments.

We could argue that Arvey might be incorrect here about the potential for litigation on the interview. That is, since *all* interviewers believe the interview is valid and believe they are great interviewers no one would make the claim that the interview is not valid. Would you hire anyone without interviewing him or her? Would a judge hire an assistant without interviewing him or her? The point is that its very general acceptance by the public may make the interview less susceptible to legal battle.

In addition to the kinds of bias discussed by Arvey, there are other biases that may affect interview judgments. Some of these are the same problems discussed in Chapter 3 on Staff Analysis (halo, leniency, and central tendency). This is not surprising since performance appraisals of people after they are on the job are judgments just as decisions about applicants are judgments. Indeed, performance appraisal data probably "hire" more people than do interviews because performance appraisals are a basis for most promotion decisions.

The following biases have been studied primarily in the interview:

1. *Stereotyping*—a kind of halo effect wherein a person is judged based on his or her group membership rather than on the

basis of his or her unique characteristics. For example, as in Arvey's work reviewed above, sex, race, age, or handicap can become the issue rather than job-relevant experience. Interviewers can learn their biases and confront themselves with them; structured interviews both in the form of questions and judgments may help.

2. *Similar-to-me phenomenon*—I am wonderful and I have the following attitudes and opinions, so if candidates I interview have the same attitudes and opinions, they must also be wonderful. When combined with stereotyping, the similar-to-me phenomenon can be a potent determinant of interviewer decision-making.

Interview Validity

Arvey and Campion (1982) cite several recent studies which indicate that interview judgments can be valid indicators of subsequent job performance. Two studies assessed the validity of a "board" interview in which several interviewers assess candidates but make independent judgments of candidates' qualifications which are pooled for purposes of an overall candidate appraisal. Conducted this way, the interview becomes more like the assessment center. Landy (1976) gathered data on 150 police officer candidates on three interview factors and correlated scores on these three factors with ratings on four job performance factors collected one year later. Four of the twelve validity coefficients were statistically significant and of modest magnitude (.26, .29, .33, and .34) after correction for restriction of range in the predictor variables (the 150 selected were a subset of 399 evaluated).

A more positive outcome was reported by Anstey (1977) in a 30-year follow-up of the British Civil Service Selection Board procedure. Using Civil Service ranks obtained 30 years after the board interview data were collected as a criterion, he found the validity coefficient for the interview was .35 for a sample of 301 employees. With appropriate range restriction corrections, the validity coefficient was .66.

A study by Latham, Saari, Purcell, and Campion (1980) represents an innovative and, apparently, valid development in the employment interview. These investigators used the critical incident technique to develop what they refer to as a *situational interview*. Recall that critical incidents are reports by job incumbents or supervisors of situations in which especially effective or ineffective behavior was displayed. These critical incidents were converted into situational interview questions by posing the situation to applicants (with no previous job experience) and asking them to indicate how they would behave. Each answer was rated independently by

TABLE 10–10. *EXAMPLES OF SITUATIONAL INTERVIEW QUESTIONS AND THEIR CORRESPONDING CRITICAL INCIDENTS USED FOR SELECTION OF EMERGENCY TELEPHONE OPERATORS.*

INTERVIEW QUESTION	CRITICAL INCIDENT
1. Imagine that you tried to help a stranger, for example, with traffic directions or to get up after a fall, and that person blamed you for their misfortune or yelled at you. How would you respond?	1. Telephone operator tries to verify address information for an ambulance call. The caller yells at them for being stupid and slow. The operator quietly assures the caller an ambulance is on the way and that she is merely reaffirming the address.
2. Suppose a friend calls you and is extremely upset? Apparently, her child has been injured. She begins to tell you, in a hysterical manner, all about her difficulty in getting babysitters, what the child is wearing, what words the child can speak, etc. What would you do?	2. A caller is hysterical because her infant is dead. She yells incoherently about the incident. The operator talks in a clear calm voice and manages to secure the woman's address, dispatches the call, and then tries to secure more information about the child's status.
3. How would you react if you were a salesclerk, waitress, or gas station attendant and one of your customers talked back to you, indicated you should have known something you did not, or told you that you were not waiting on them fast enough?	3. A clearly angry caller calls for the third time in an hour complaining about the 911 service because no one has arrived to investigate a busted water pipe. The operator tells the caller to go to _____ and hangs up.

two or more interviewers on a five-point scale with anchors provided by job experts to facilitate objective scoring. Interrater reliability was acceptable and concurrent validities against performance appraisal criteria for foremen and hourly workers were .30 and .46 respectively. In another predictive study, validities of .33 and .39 were observed for women and blacks respectively. The important point concerning this study is the careful linking of interview questions to job analysis and performance criterion data. One of your authors developed a situational interview for the selection of emergency telephone operators. Examples of the interview questions and the critical incidents from which they were derived are given in Table 10–10.

Interviewer Validity

Because the validity of the interview is a direct function of interviewers' ratings of applicants, we can ask: are some interviewers more valid than others? That is, are some people better judges of candi-

HYPOTHESIZED MODEL OF INTERVIEWER INFORMATION
SEEKING RECEIPT AND PROCESSING.

FIGURE 10–4.

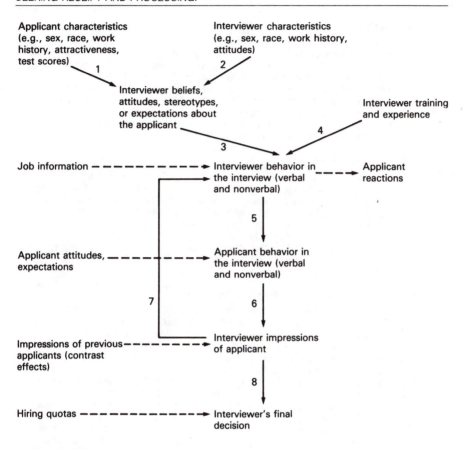

From Dreher and Sackett, (1983).

dates? Unfortunately, there is not much research on this question.
What would be required to investigate this issue?

1. More than one interviewer, preferably four or five, all of whom interview the same variety of applicants and each of whom interviews many candidates.

2. Each interviewer's judgments about applicants should be arrayed against how well the person actually performed/behaved/stayed on the job/did on the criterion of interest.

3. For each interviewer, correlate the end-of-interview rating with criterion behavior for all the interviewees. The resulting correlations will provide evidence about the relative validity of different interviewers.

TABLE 10–11. *AN ABBREVIATED INTERVIEW GUIDE FOR USE IN EVALUATING SELECTION INTERVIEWER APPLICANTS.*

Opening

- Give a warm, friendly greeting—smile.
- Names are important—yours and the applicant's. Pronounce it correctly and use first and last names consistently. Tell the applicant what to call you and then ask the applicant for his or her preferred form of address.
- Talk briefly about yourself (your position in the company and then your personal background, hobbies, interests, etc.) to put the applicant at ease so that she or he might reciprocate with personal information.
- Ask the applicant about hobbies, activities, or some other topic that you believe will be of interest to "break the ice."

Structure the Interview

- State the purpose of interview: "The purpose of this interview is to discuss your qualifications and to see whether they match the skills needed to work as a selection interviewer. First, let's talk about your work experience and next your education and training. Then I will give you a preview of what the interviewer's job is really like. Finally, there will be a chance to ask about anything you want. How's that?
- Since you plan to take notes, mention this to the applicant: "By the way, I will be taking some notes during the interview so that I don't miss any pertinent information that may come from our discussion. Okay?"

Work Experience: Most Relevant Job

- Use this comprehensive opening question: "Let's talk about your work experience. How about starting with the job that you feel gave you the best preparation for working as a selection interviewer. Tell me all about the job: how you got it, why you chose it, your actual job duties, what you learned on the job, the hours and your attendance record, the pay, why you left (or are leaving), and things like that."
- Probe and follow up to cover each of these items thoroughly: how the applicant got the job, reasons for choosing it, job duties, etc.
- Summarize the major facts and findings from the applicant's most relevant job. For example: "Let me summarize what we have covered to make sure that I've got it right. You worked as a _____ where most of your time was spent doing _____ and _____ , and you used these skills, _____ and _____ . You chose the job because of _____ and your reasons for leaving it are _____ and _____. Anything else to add?"

Other Work Experience

- If time is available, discuss other jobs the applicant has held that might be pertinent. Get a brief overview of each job the applicant has held. Emphasize jobs held in the last five years or less, since older experience is less likely to be relevant for your decision.
- Ask the work experience questions you specifically prepared for this applicant when you planned the interview.
- Summarize your major findings about all jobs. When the summary is satisfactory to the applicant, go on to discuss education and training.

Education and Training

- Use this question to start the discussion: "Now let's talk about your education and training—schools, courses, likes and dislikes, things like that. Let's start

with this: What did you learn in school that might be helpful for you in working as a selection interviewer?''
- Probe to get specific answers to these questions: "What training have you had in interviewing techniques? What courses have you had in psychology or personnel management?" and so on.
- Ask the education and training questions you specifically prepared for this applicant when you planned the interview.
- Summarize the applicant's education and training, just as you summarized work experience. When the applicant is satisfied with your summary, go on to discuss the Job Preview List.

Job Preview List

- Introduce the Job Preview List: "As a selection interviewer, you have many responsibilities and duties. Here is a list of some major factors."
- Give the applicant the Job Preview List. Discuss it point by point. Be sure that you describe the job realistically. Don't "paint a rosy picture."

SELECTION INTERVIEWER JOB PREVIEW LIST

1. Conduct screening and final evaluation interviews with all applicants for nonexempt factory and clerical positions.
2. Administer and score screening tests and weighted application blanks.
3. Maintain records and compile reports on all applicants for Affirmative Action purposes.

  •

  •

  •

10. Recommend two candidates for each position for interviews by the hiring manager.

Applicant's Questions

- Turn the interview over to the applicant: "As I mentioned at the start, you would have a chance to ask anything you would like. We've just had a short preview of what the job would be like, but here is a chance to ask anything you want about the company, training, and so on."
- Respond fully and frankly to all of the applicant's questions, and note any further information that the applicant volunteers that will aid you in making your evaluation.

Closing the Interview

- Conclude with a warm, friendly close—smile.
- Outline the next steps in the decision process.
- Tell the applicant when to expect a decision.
- Thank the applicant.

After the Interview

- Take time to write summary notes immediately. Describe the applicant's behavior and the impressions he or she created. Cite facts and specific incidents from the interview or from the person's work or educational history.
- Wait a day and then complete the Evaluation Form.

From Hakel, (1982).

One study similar to that described here was accomplished using 10 interviewers of 412 people, 131 of whom were actually placed on the job. Each interviewer's judgments were subsequently analyzed and it was shown (Zedeck, Tziner, & Middlestadt, 1983) that: (a) interviewers used different *kinds* of applicant information as a basis for making the end-of-interview ratings; (b) interviewers based their overall judgment of applicants on different *combinations* of the ratings they made at the end of the interview; and (c) some interviewers appeared to be more valid than others and those who were most valid used the same combination of ratings for their decisions.

There will be individual differences in interviewer competence just as there are individual differences in other human characteristics. Most organizations probably have more than one person conducting hiring interviews. If any records are kept, it should be possible to identify who is doing the best job; go back and see which interviewer had the best percentage of "hits" (good people hired); which was best at identifying people who would meet the criterion of interest. The major requirement for this analysis is meeting the assumption that each interviewer was assigned candidates randomly. If the hypothesis of randomness is not tenable, then comparisons of interviewers will be biased.

It has become customary for reviewers of the interview literature to present models of the interview process (Arvey and Campion, 1982; Dreher and Sackett, 1983; Schmitt, 1976). These models are useful in that they underscore the complexity of the interview situation, although they have not been useful in generating coordinated research programs. The Dreher-Sackett model, presented as Figure 10–4, and the accompanying discussion, suggests a set of causal hypotheses concerning interviewer information processing. Dreher and Sackett argue convincingly on the reasonableness of their model from already published research, and we believe that models like these should direct research on the interview. The result would be greater understanding than is offered by the myriad of "micro-analytic" studies and a more practically useful set of guidelines for the staffing specialist who uses interviews to make employment decisions.

One such set of guidelines, based on a very comprehensive review of the interviewing literature, is presented as Table 10–11 (Hakel, 1982). While the suggested format is an interview for selecting *employment interviewers,* we think it is easily adaptable to interviews for other kinds of jobs. Note in Table 10–11 that Hakel uses the interview as an information collecting *and* an information sharing opportunity. In the latter case, he takes full advantage of the literature we reviewed in Chapter 4 on the realistic job preview (RJP).

In summary, staffing specialists should heed Arvey and Campion's (1982) advice that employment interview use be preceded by a thorough analysis of the target job, the development of a structured set of questions based on the job analysis, and the development of behaviorally specific rating instruments by which to evaluate applicants. Even with carefully developed interviews, validities have rarely exceeded those using other predictors.

PEER EVALUATIONS

In some organizations, particularly in the military, a simple technique has proven to be an extremely valid predictor of future job success, particularly leadership effectiveness. This technique involves asking coworkers to judge each other on various rating dimensions. In other words, instead of asking an *interviewer* to rate an applicant, we ask peers, such as other workers, to do the rating.

Three types of peer evaluations have been used, and they are all subject to the problems connected with ratings introduced in Chapter 3. One procedure is to have peers *rank order* each other on all major performance dimensions. Obviously, this can become confusing and we must equate rank ordering across groups with different numbers of people. The second type of procedure is to have peers *rate* each other on one or more performance dimensions. This can be extremely time-consuming if the group contains a large number of persons, but perhaps is the easiest method from a data analysis point of view.

The peer *nomination* method requires the rater to list a specified number of coworkers as being the highest or best people in the group on some particular dimension of job performance. Occasionally, raters are also asked to designate the worst performers on each dimension as well. Usually a person's score is calculated by dividing the number of nominations received by the total number possible. Nomination scoring can become troublesome if negative nominations have been received. The usual solution is to subtract the number of negative nominations from the positive nominations and divide by the total number of possible positive nominations (Downey, Medland, & Yates, 1976). Furthermore, it is necessary to correct for group size if several groups of varying membership are to be compared. Willingham (1959) points out that large groups will have more spread for the number of people being nominated than will small groups, and he provides a scale transformation correcting for group size to deal with this problem.

The validity information on peer ratings is summarized in the reviews of the literature by Lewin and Zwamy (1976; see also Kane and Lawler, 1978). These reviews reveal that peer evaluations are valid tools for predicting future success; moreover, in those studies in which other selection instruments were also used, peer ratings were superior to those other techniques.

One possible problem with peer ratings is that people will rate their friends highest. Studies by Hollander (1956) and Waters and Waters (1970) have indicated that peer evaluations do correlate with friendship choices but that the predictive validity of the nominations does not appear to be affected. Cox and Krumboltz (1958) and DeJung and Kaplan (1962) reported that racial prejudice affects peer ratings with both whites and blacks rating same-race peers higher. In these two studies, blacks were a small percentage of the total; in a study by Schmidt and Johnson (1973) using an industrial sample of approximately equal numbers of blacks and whites, this effect did not occur.

Another factor that may influence peer rating is the degree of prior acquaintance. This variable and the degree of interaction with those to be rated seems to be important only when they are necessary to allow the observation of relevant behaviors. Finally, peer evaluations seem to be remarkably consistent over time even when the composition of the peer group changes. While there is little dispute concerning the validity of peer nominations, several authors (see Korman, 1968; Lewin and Zwamy, 1976) have decried the lack of any attempt to understand why peer ratings are valid. To the authors, it seems probable that peers can predict better because they have had more opportunity to observe the behavior of the people they are rating. This is inconsistent, however, with the Passini and Norman (1966) data which indicate that degree of acquaintanceship has little to do with validity of peer ratings. Another explanation is that peers know the job that is to be required of the subjects better than anyone else—an analysis not yet evaluated to our knowledge. Whatever the explanation, peer ratings could be very useful if we are interested in promoting staff members.

If peer evaluations are so valid, why aren't they more frequently used? One reason may be that people resist judging their peers—a role they associate with supervisory personnel. Or, alternatively, supervisory personnel are unwilling to relinquish control over the promotion process which would likely result if peer ratings were used. There is also the danger that peer ratings used repeatedly can and will be manipulated when people "learn the system."

Finally, peer evaluations have been used as criteria in recent studies (see Siegel, 1982; Zammuto, London, & Rowland, 1982). However very little recent research has been conducted on the relevance of peer ratings.

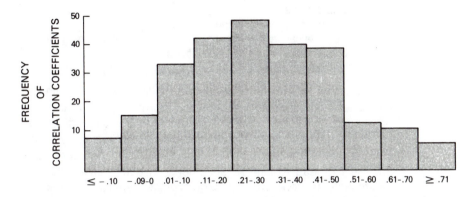

MAGNITUDE OF CORRELATION COEFFICIENTS

From Mabe and West, (1982).

SELF ASSESSMENTS

In contrast to peer evaluation, research on, and use of, self evaluations of competency to perform a given job is relatively recent. In
self assessment, neither an interviewer nor a peer is required.
Although self reports have been regarded as important in various
applied contexts such as attitude surveys, therapy outcome research, and personnel selection, use of self evaluations to assess
ability is relatively rare. Mabe and West (1982) provided an excellent review of the validity of self evaluations of ability. Their review
of 55 studies including 267 coefficients indicated a mean correlation of .29 between self-reported ability and other ability/perform-
ance measures including tests, grades, supervisory ratings, and,
less frequently, performance output. Their meta-analysis yielded a
highly variable set of validities (see Figure 10–5 for a frequency
distribution of the observed validities), and this variability was not
accounted for by differences in sample size as is usually the case
in the validity generalization work on cognitive aptitude tests (see
Chapter 8).

Mabe and West (1982) then attempted to account for this variability by examining the measurement conditions of the various
studies yielding data for their meta-analysis. Conditions most relat-

ed to increases in the validity of self evaluations were the following four:

1. Expectation on the part of the respondent that self evaluations would be validated.
2. The rater's previous experience with self evaluation.
3. Self evaluation instructions emphasizing that the rater should compare him or herself with others.
4. Instructions guaranteeing the anonymity of the self rating.

Note that several of these actors make it difficult to use self evaluations for selection purposes. Thornton (1980) also expressed caution in the use of self appraisals for selection, diagnosis of training needs, and other administrative decision-making. When used for gathering information at time of selection, self appraisals are likely to lead to inflated statements of qualification and little differentiation among applicants. Most of the research summarized in Thornton (1980) and Mabe and West (1982) was not predictive. In addition, Heneman (1980) points to two additional troublesome aspects of self appraisals. The first is whether or not the dimensions a job applicant would be asked to rate are meaningful to him or her. The second problem relates to the fact that self evaluations are typically justified because they correlate with tests which in turn correlate with job performance. This is true of a large number of the studies summarized by Mabe and West (1982). The lack of congruence between test and job performance allows for a widely different correlation between self appraisals and job performance. Hence, it is difficult to recommend self appraisals in a selection context until the necessary predictive validation work is done. Self appraisals must be collected in the context of hiring and correlated with subsequent measures of job performance.

Levine (1980) provided a number of hypotheses about the appropriateness of self appraisal based on Bandura's (1978) description of the self system. Self ratings ought to be appropriate for four reasons:

1. We directly experience the effects of our actions in a number of real-world settings.
2. We gain information about things in the world around us by observing others.
3. We have also received others' judgments of our performance.
4. We have had a good deal of time to verify feelings about ourselves and our performance.

However, Bandura's theory also suggests a number of reasons why self appraisals may be deficient:

1. The self-observation process is, according to Bandura, very complex. He maintains that individuals monitor their behavior on as many as eight dimensions.
2. The judgment of an individual's self performance can be influenced by a number of factors including personal standards, reference groups, whether the activity is a valued one, or whether or not the person attributes performance to her or his ability.
3. The individual may never have evaluated his or her ability along the required dimensions.

While a staffing specialist's focus must be on outcome measures, use of theoretical notions may provide greater knowledge of the process of self ratings. In any event, it would seem reasonable to require additional research and more data on self appraisal before recommending its use.

In the context of theory and validity, recall our discussion in Chapter 8 of the Behavior Consistency concept in predicting performance (Schmidt et al., 1979). This approach is very much a self-assessment process in which applicants literally sign off on their task relevant prior accomplishments. Indeed, Hough's (1984) work used the title Accomplishment Record. If we add to the behavior consistency research the validity already established for Biographical Information Blanks (BIBs) (which frequently focus on people's prior accomplishments), we note that self assessments have, perhaps, more consistent validity than we would suspect by only examining "self assessment" research.

In fact, one of your authors is in the process of validating a self-assessment process that focuses on the skills and abilities required for job performance in a telephone sales job. The first step was to conduct a job analysis and specify the kinds of skills and abilities the organization felt applicants should have in order to be hired. The result of this analysis was the specification of nine clusters of skills and abilities. For each cluster 3, 4, or 5, specific tasks like those performed on the job are presented to applicants and they are asked to indicate with a five-point scale where they see themselves in terms of ability for doing that task. Specifically, they are told:

You have probably had several full-time and part-time jobs. If not, you may have been involved in various voluntary groups and organizations. As you think back over all of these work and organization experiences, how would you rate your ability to do each of the activities listed below? Use the following alternatives to rate yourself on each activity:

1 = far below average

2 = below average

3 = average

4 = above average

5 = far above average

The items rated for Social Sensitivity, for example, are:

1. Knowing the right thing to say to someone who is feeling low.
2. Maintaining a friendly attitude even when others are upset or disagree.
3. Adjusting my conversation to the level of the person I'm talking to.
4. Controlling how a conversation is going without aggravating the other person.
5. Figuring out how other people are going to react so that I can ask a question the right way.

We obviously hope this *self assessment of skills* (SAS) procedure will prove valid, at least as a correlate of tested performance. In the organization trying the process, SAS is administered concurrently with an application blank. SAS is scored while the candidate is tested and the SAS scores are used as input into the interview process where details can be obtained about the circumstances or situations in which the applicant did the activities on the SAS and why he or she felt they are above/below average.

SUMMARY

This chapter summarized evidence showing significant validity can be achieved using carefully developed personality and interest tests as well as background information, interviews, peer and self assessments. Surprisingly the data show that the typically *least* valid procedure is the interview. The caution is to use these *other* methods, these multiple methods, for gaining additional information about job applicants. The key to validity appears to be a careful job analysis, followed by careful choice of an appropriate criterion, and then the development of Tests/BIBs/Reference Checks/Interviews/Peer Ratings/Self Assessments that measure prior experience in situations or circumstances with psychological fidelity. The objective, as in Chapters 8 and 9, should be to make the hiring procedure as relevant as possible for the job and criterion of interest.

Of course, given that various procedures may yield practically meaningful validity coefficients, choice will depend upon administrative cost, face validity and/or utility. The best choice of selection procedure should be *multiple* procedures whose intercorrelations are minimal. In combination, the chances for useful levels of validity will be enhanced.

REFERENCES

Alderfer, C. P. (1972). *Human needs in organizational settings*. New York: Free Press.

Anstey, E. A. (1977). A 30-year followup of the CSSB procedure, with lessons for the future. *Journal of Occupational Psychology, 50,* 49–159.

Argyris, C. (1968). Some unintended consequences of rigorous research. *Psychological Bulletin, 70,* 185–197.

Arvey, R. D. (1979). Unfair discrimination in the employment interview: Legal and psychological aspects. *Psychological Bulletin, 86,* 736–765.

Arvey, R. D., and Campion, J. E. (1982). The employment interview: A summary and review of recent research. *Personnel Psychology, 35,* 281–322.

Asher, J. J. (1972). The biographical item: Can it be improved? *Personnel Psychology, 25,* 251–269.

Atkinson, J. W. (Ed.). (1958). *Motives in fantasy, action, and society*. Princeton, NJ: Van Nostrand.

Bandura, A. (1978). The self system in reciprocal determinism. *American Psychologist, 33,* 344–358.

Barron, F. (1972). *Artists in the making*. New York: Seminar Press.

Bentz, V. J. (1984). *Research findings from personality assessment of executives.* Detroit: Michigan Association of Industrial and Organizational Psychologists.

Betz, E. (1969). Need-reinforcer correspondence as a predictor of job satisfaction. *Personnel and Guidance Journal, 47,* 878–883.

Borman, W. C., Rosse, R. L., and Abrahams, N. M. (1980). An empirical construct validity approach to studying predictor-job performance links. *Journal of Applied Psychology, 65,* 662–671.

Bowen, D. D. (1973). Reported patterns in TAT measures of need achievement, affiliation and power. *Journal of Personality Assessment, 37,* 424–430.

Brush, D. H., and Owens, W. A. (1979). Implementation and evaluation for an assessment classification model for manpower utilization. *Personnel Psychology, 32,* 369–383.

Campbell, D. P., and Hansen, J. C. (1981). *Manual for the SVIB-SCII*. Stanford, CA: Stanford University Press.

Campbell, J. P., Dunnette, M. D., Lawler, E. E., III, and Weick, K. E., Jr. (1970). *Managerial Behavior, Performance, and Effectiveness*. New York: McGraw-Hill.

Cascio, W. F. (1982). *Applied psychology in personnel management*. Reston, VA: Reston Publishing Co.

Cole, N. S., and Hanson, G. R. (1971). An analysis of the structure of vocational interests. *Journal of Counseling Psychology, 18,* 478–486.

Cornelius, E. T., III. (1983). The use of projective techniques in personnel selection. In Rowland, K. M., and Ferris, G. R. (Eds.). *Research in personnel and human resources management.* Greenwich, CT: JAI Press.

Cox, J. A., and Krumboltz, J. D. (1958). Racial bias in peer ratings of basic airmen. *Sociometry, 21,* 292–299.

DeJung, J. E., and Kaplan, H. (1962). Some differential effects of race of rater and ratee on early peer ratings of combat aptitude. *Journal of Applied Psychology, 46,* 370–374.

Dolliver, R. H., Irvin, J. A., and Bigley, S. E. (1972). Twelve-year followup of the Strong Vocational Interest Blank. *Journal of Counseling Psychology, 19,* 212–217.

Downey, R. G., Medland, F. F., and Yates, L. G. (1976). Evaluation of a peer rating system for predicting subsequent promotion of senior military officers. *Journal of Applied Psychology, 61,* 206–209.

Dreher, G. F. and Sackett, P. R. (1983). *Perspectives on staffing and selection* Homewood, IL: Irwin.

Dunnette, M. D., and Aylward, M. S. (1956). Validity Information Exchange, No. 9–21. *Personnel Psychology, 9,* 245–247.

Dunnette, M. D., McCartney, J., Carlson, H. C., and Kirschner, W. K. (1962). A study of faking behavior on a forced-choice self-description checklist. *Personnel Psychology, 15,* 13–24.

Dunnette, M. D., Wernimont, P., and Abrahams, N. (1964). Further research on vocational interest differences among several types of engineers. *Personnel and Guidance Journal, 42,* 484–493.

Edel, E. C. (1968). "Need for success" as a predictor of managerial performance. *Personnel Psychology, 21,* 231–240.

Edwards, A. L. (1957). *The social desirability variable in personality assessment and research.* New York: Dryden.

Edwards, A. L. (1966). Relationship between probability of endorsement and social desirability scale value for a set of 2824 personality statements. *Journal of Applied Psychology, 50,* 238–239.

England, G. W. (1971). *Development and use of weighted application blanks.* Dubuque, IA: Brown.

Gay, E. G., Weiss, D. J., Hendel, D. D., and Lofquist, L. H. (1971). Manual for the Minnesota Importance Questionnaire. *Minnesota Studies in Vocational Rehabilitation: XXVIII.*

Ghiselli, E. E. (1966). *The validity of occupational aptitude tests.* New York: Wiley.

Ghiselli, E. E. (1971). *Explorations in managerial talent.* Santa Monica, CA: Goodyear.

Ghiselli, E. E. (1973). The validity of aptitude tests in personnel selection. *Personnel Psychology, 26,* 461–478.

Goldstein, I. L. (1971). The application blank: How honest are the responses? *Journal of Applied Psychology, 55,* 491–492.

Gough, H. G. (1969). A leadership index on the California Psychological Inventory. *Journal of Counseling Psychology, 16,* 283–289.

Gough, H. G. (1976). Studying creativity by means of word association tests. *Journal of Applied Psychology, 61,* 348–353.

Gross, M. L. (1962). *The brain watchers.* New York: Random House.

Guion R. M. (1965). *Personnel testing.* New York: McGraw-Hill.

Guion, R. M., and Gottier, R. F. (1965). Validity of personality measures in personnel selection. *Personnel Psychology, 18,* 49–65.

Hackman, J. R., and Oldham, G. R. (1975). Development of the job diagnostic survey. *Journal of Applied Psychology, 60,* 159–170.

Hakel, M. D. (1982). Employment interviewing. In K. M. Rowland and G. R. Ferris (Eds.), *Personnel management.* Boston: Allyn and Bacon.

Hall, D. T., and Gordon, F. E. (1973). Career choices of married women: Effects on conflict, role behavior, and satisfaction. *Journal of Applied Psychology, 58,* 42–48.

Harrington, T. F., Lynch, M. D., and O'Shea, A. J. (1971). Factor analyses of twenty-seven similarly named scales of the SVIB and the Kuder OIS, Form DD. *Journal of Counseling Psychology, 18,* 229–233.

Heneman, H. G. III. (1980). Self assessment: A critical analysis. *Personnel Psychology, 33,* 297–300.

Heneman, H. G., III, Schwab, D. P., Fossum, J. A., and Dyer, L. D. (1980). *Personnel/Human Resource Management.* Homewood, IL: Irwin.

Herzberg, F. H., Mausner, B., and Snyderman, B. (1959). *The motivation to work.* New York: Wiley.

Hogan, R. (1971). Personality characteristics of highly rated policemen. *Personnel Psychology, 24,* 679–686.

Holberg, A., and Pugh, W. M. (1978). Predicting navy effectiveness: Expectations, motivation, personality, aptitude, and background variables. *Personnel Psychology, 31,* 841–852.

Holland, J. L. (1985). *Making vocational choices: A theory of careers.* Englewood Cliffs, NJ: Prentice-Hall.

Hollander, E. P. (1956). The friendship factor in peer nominations. *Personnel Psychology, 1,* 435–447.

Hollander, E. P. (1965). Validity of peer nominations in predicting a distant performance criterion. *Journal of Applied Psychology, 49,* 434–438.

Hough, L. M. (1984). Development and evaluation of the "accomplishment record" method of selecting and promoting professionals. *Journal of Applied Psychology, 69,* 135–146.

Hough, L. M., Dunnette, M. D., and Keyes, M. A. (1983). An evaluation of three "alternative" selection procedures. *Personnel Psychology, 36,* 261–276.

Hundel, P. S. (1971). A study of entrepreneurial motivation: A comparison of fast and slow progressing small scale industrial entrepreneurs in Punjab, India. *Journal of Applied Psychology, 55,* 317–323.

Jackson, D. N. (1977). *Jackson vocational interest survey manual.* Port Huron, MI: Research Psychologists Press.

Johnson, J. A., and Hogan, R. (1981). Vocational interests, personality, and effective police performance. *Personnel Psychology, 34,* 49–54.

Kane, J., and Lawler, E. E., III. (1978). Methods of peer assessment. *Psychological Bulletin, 35,* 555–586.

Kinslinger, H. J. (1966). Application of projective techniques in personnel psychology since 1940. *Psychological Bulletin, 66,* 134–149.

Korman, A. K. (1968). The prediction of managerial performance: A review. *Personnel Psychology, 21,* 295–322.

Korman, A. K. (1977). *Organizational behavior.* Englewood Cliffs, NJ: Prentice-Hall.

Landy, F. J. (1976). The validity of the interview in police officer selection. *Journal of Applied Psychology, 61,* 193–198.

Landy, F. J., and Trumbo, D. A. (1984). *Psychology of work behavior.* Homewood, IL: Irwin.

Latham, G. P., Saari, L. M., Pursell, E. D., and Campion, M. A. (1980). The situational interview. *Journal of Applied Psychology, 65,* 422–427.

Laurent, H. (1968). Research on the identification of managerial potential. In J. A. Myers, Jr. (Ed.). *Predicting managerial success.* Ann Arbor, MI: Foundation for Research on Human Behavior.

Laurent, H. (1970). Cross-cultural cross-validation of empirically validated keys. *Journal of Applied Psychology, 54,* 417–423.

Lawler, E. E. III (1973). *Motivation in work organizations.* Monterey, CA: Brooks/Cole

Lee, D. L., and Hadahl, B. (1971). Holland's personality types applied to the SVIB basic interest scales. *Journal of Vocational Behavior, 3,* 61–68.

Levine, E. L. (1980). Introductory remarks for the symposium "Organizational Applications of Self Appraisal and Self-Assessment: Another Look." *Personnel Psychology, 33,* 259–262.

Levine, E. L., and Randolph, S. M. (1977). *Reference checking for personnel selection: The state of the art.* Berea, OH: American Society for Personnel Administration.

Lewin, A. Y., and Zwamy, A. (1976). Peer nominations: A model literature critique, and a paradigm for research. *Personnel Psychology, 29,* 423–447.

Litwin, G. H., and Stringer, R. A. (1968). *Motivation and organizational climate.* Boston: Harvard Business School, Division of Research.

Mabe, P. A., and West, S. G. (1982). Validity of self-evaluation of ability: A review and meta-analysis. *Journal of Applied Psychology, 67,* 280–296.

Mackinnon, D. W. (1962). The nature and nurture of creative talent. *American Psychologist, 17,* 484–495.

Maslow, A. H. (1954). *Motivation and personality.* New York: Harper.

Mayfield, E. C. (1964). The selection interview: A reevaluation of published research. *Personnel Psychology, 17,* 239–260.

McCall, M. W., Jr. (1979). Conjecturing about creative leaders. *The Journal of Creative Behavior, 14,* 225–234.

McClelland, D. C. (1961). *The achieving society.* Princeton, NJ: Van Nostrand.

McClelland, D. C., Atkinson, J. W., Clark, R. A., and Lowell, E. L. (1953). *The achievement motive.* New York: Appleton-Century Crofts.

McClelland, D. C., and Boyatzis, R. E. (1982). Leadership motive pattern and long-term success in management. *Journal of Applied Psychology, 67,* 737–743.

McCormick, E. J., and Ilgen, D. R. (1980). *Industrial psychology.* Englewood Cliffs, NJ: Prentice-Hall.

McCully, C. H. (1954). *The validity of the Kuder Preference Record.* Unpublished doctoral dissertation. George Washington University.

Mills, C. J., and Bohannon, W. E. (1980). Personality characteristics of effective state police officers. *Journal of Applied Psychology, 65,* 680–684.

Miner, J. B. (1960). The effect of a course in psychology on the attitudes of research and development supervisors. *Journal of Applied Psychology, 44,* 224–232.

Miner, J. B. (1978). Twenty years of research on role motivation theory of managerial effectiveness. *Personnel Psychology, 31,* 739–760.

Miner, J. B., and Miner, M. G. (1977). *Personnel and industrial relations.* New York: MacMillan.

Mischel, W. (1968). *Personality and assessment.* New York: Wiley.

Mischel, W. (1973). Toward a cognitive social learning reconceptualization of personality. *Psychological Review, 80,* 252–283.

Mitchell, T. W., and Klimoski, R. J. (1982). Is it rational to be empirical? A test of methods for scoring biographical data. *Journal of Applied Psychology, 67,* 411–418.

Mosel, J. N., and Goheen, H. W. (1959). The employment recommendation questionnaire: III. Validity of different types of references. *Personnel Psychology, 12,* 469–477.

Muchinsky, P. M. (1979). The use of reference reports in personnel selection: A review and evaluation. *Journal of Occupational Psychology, 52,* 287–297.

Muchinsky, P. M. (1983a). Vocational behavior and career development, 1982: A review. *Journal of Vocational Behavior, 23,* 123–178.

Muchinsky, P. M. (1983b). *Psychology applied to work.* Homewood, IL: Irwin.

Nash, A. N., and Carroll, S. J., Jr. (1970). A hard look at the reference check: Its modest worth can be improved. *Business Horizons, 13,* 43–49.

Nealy, S. M. (1964). Determining worker preferences among employee benefit programs. *Journal of Applied Psychology, 48,* 7–12.

Owens, W. A., and Schoenfeldt, L. F. (1979). Toward a classification of persons. *Journal of Applied Psychology, 46,* 329–332.

Pace, L. A., and Schoenfeldt, L. F. (1977). Legal concerns in the use of weighted applications. *Personnel Psychology, 30,* 159–166.

Passini, F. T., and Norman, W. T. (1966). A universal conception of personality structure. *Journal of Personality and Social Psychology, 4,* 44–49.

Porter, L. W. (1964). *Organizational patterns of managerial job attitudes.* New York: American Foundation for Management Research.

Pyron, H. C. (1970). The use and misuse of previous employer references in hiring. *Management of Personnel Quarterly, 9,* 15–22.

Reilly, R. R., and Chao, G. T. (1982). Validity and fairness of some alternative employee selection procedures. *Personnel Psychology, 35,* 1–62.

Rosenbaum, B. L. (1973). Attitude toward invasion of privacy in the personnel selection process and job applicant demographics and personality character- istics. *Journal of Applied Psychology, 58,* 333–338.

Sackett, P. R., and Harris, M. M. (1984). Honesty testing for personnel selection: A review and critique. *Personnel Psychology, 37,* 221–245.

Schmidt, F. L., Caplan, J. R., Bemis, S. E., DeCuin, R., Dunn, L., and Antone, L. (1979). *The behavioral consistency method of unassembled examining.* Wash- ington, DC: U. S. Office of Personnel Management.

Schmidt, F. L., Hunter, J. E., and Caplan, J. R. (1981). Validity generalization results for two job groups in the petroleum industry. *Journal of Applied Psychology, 66,* 261–273.

Schmidt, F. L., and Johnson, R. H. (1973). Effect of race on peer ratings in an industrial situation. *Journal of Applied Psychology, 57,* 237–241.

Schmitt, N. (1976). Social and situational determinants of interview decisions: Im- plications for the employment interview. *Personnel Psychology, 29,* 79–101.

Schmitt, N., Gooding, R. Z., Noe, R. A., and Kirsch, M. (1984). Meta-analyses of validity studies published between 1964 and 1982 and the investigation of study characteristics. *Personnel Psychology, 37,* 407–422.

Schmitt, N., and Pulakos, E. D. (1983). Evaluation of tests for the selection of transport drivers. Reported submitted to Marathon Oil Company, Findlay, Ohio.

Schneider, B. (1983a). Interactional psychology and organizational behavior. In L. L. Cummings and B. L. Staw (Eds.). *Research in organizational behavior, 5.* Greenwich, CT: JAI Press.

Schneider, B. (1983b). An interactionist perspective on organizational effective- ness. In K. Cameron and D. Whetten, (Eds.). *Organizational Effectiveness.* New York: Academic Press.

Schoenfeldt, L. F. (1974). Utilization of manpower: Development and evaluation of an assessment-classification model for matching individuals with jobs. *Journal of Applied Psychology, 59,* 583–594.

Siegel, L. (1982). Paired comparison evaluations of managerial effectiveness by peers and supervisor. *Personnel Psychology, 35,* 843–852.

Solano, C. (undated). Social climates that encourage the creative performance of managers. In S. G. Gryskiewicz, J. T. Shields, and W. H. Drath (Eds.). *Selected readings in creativity, Vol. I.* Greensboro, NC: Center for Creative Leadership.

Stagner, R. (1958). The gullibility of personnel managers. *Personnel Psychology, II,* 347–352.

Stahl, M. J. (1983). Achievement, power, and managerial motivation: Selecting managerial talent with the job choice exercise. *Personnel Psychology, 36,* 775–789.

Stein, A. H., and Bailey, M. M. (1973). The socialization of achievement orientation in females. *Psychological Bulletin, 80,* 345–366.

Stogdill, R. M. (1948). Personal factors associated with leadership: A survey of the literature. *Journal of Psychology, 25,* 35–71.

Taylor, M. S., Locke, E. A., Lee, C. and Gist, M. E. (1984). Type A behavior and faculty research productivity: What are the mechanisms? *Organizational Behavior and Human Performance, 34,* 402–418.

Thorndike, R. L., and Hagen, E. P. (1969). *Measurement and evaluation in psychology and education.* New York: Wiley.

Thornton, G. C. III (1980). Psychometric properties of self-appraisals of job performance. *Personnel Psychology, 33,* 263–272.

Ulrich, L., and Trumbo, D. (1965). The selection interview since 1949. *Psychological Bulletin, 63,* 100–116.

Vinitsky, M. (1973). A forty-year followup on the vocational interests of psychologists and their relationship to career development. *American Psychologist, 28,* 1000–1009.

Wagner, R. (1949). The employment interview: A critical summary. *Personnel Psychology, 2,* 17–46.

Wanous, J. P. (1980). *Organizational entry: Recruitment, selection, and socialization of newcomers.* Reading, MA: Addison-Wesley.

Waters, L. K., and Waters, C. S. (1970). Peer nominations as predictors of short-term sales performance. *Journal of Applied Psychology, 54,* 42–44.

Webster, E. C. (1964). *Decision making in the employment interview.* Montreal: Eagle.

Webster, E. C. (1982). *The employment interview: A social judgment approach.* Ontario, Canada: S.I.P. Publications.

Whyte, W. H. Jr. (1957). *The organization man.* New York: Doubleday.

Willingham, W. W. (1959). On deriving standard scores for peer nominations with subgroups of unequal size. *Psychological Reports, 5,* 397–403.

Wollack, L., and Guttman, F. (1960). Prediction of academic grades and post-OCS performance of junior officers with a battery of speeded tests. *U. S. Naval Personnel Research Field Activity.*

Wright, O. R., Jr. (1969). Summary of research on the selection interview since 1964. *Personnel Psychology, 22,* 391–413.

Yukl, G. A. (1981). *Leadership in organizations.* Englewood Cliffs, NJ: Prentice-Hall.

Zammuto, R. F., London, M., and Rowland, K. M. (1982). Organization and rater differences in performance appraisals. *Personnel Psychology, 35,* 643–658.

Zedeck, S., Tziner, A., and Middlestadt, S. E. (1983). Interviewer validity and reliability: An individual analysis approach. *Personnel Psychology, 36,* 355–370.

11

STAFFING ORGANIZATIONS
Review and Implications

AIMS OF THE CHAPTER

At this point we must face the problem of review and integration. In this chapter, then, we:

1. Summarize some of the major points made,
2. Note how some of the procedures and processes we have outlined can be applied in specific kinds of circumstances, and
3. Present ways by which job seekers can take advantage of the material to find a job in which they can be both satisfied and productive.

Prior to discussing each of these elements in Chapter 11, however, it is important to place the staffing of organizations in context, i.e., to repeat some of the material presented in Chapter 1. Specifically, it is important to remember that any staffing system cannot resolve all organizational problems. So, while we've noted throughout the book that people make the organization what it is, most situations do not permit starting from scratch. The reality is that organizations can be helped to be more effective through a variety of strategies including hiring new people and/or moving incumbents. Training, management development, and education, changes in organizational design and structure, adopting new accounting systems, creating innovations, and acquiring or merging with other companies are all ways by which organizations can be made more productive and more satisfying—and the selection and placement of new and current employees can also help.

How do we know which way to go? This is a key issue for organizations, especially when some unforeseen turbulence either within or outside the organization emerges. The turbulence might be conflict between the heads of Marketing and Personnel, or it could be the announcement of a major innovation by a competitor. When such turbulence exists, management obviously attempts to grapple with it and, if possible, to prevent recurrences. When fighting fires, for example, we put them out and try to prevent them in the future. In organizations this means the emergency is handled and attempts are made to insure that at least this particular form of emergency does not occur again.

Most frameworks for organizational effectiveness emphasize the necessity to focus on the many systems and subsystems of organizations as a remedy for preventing unexpected turbulence. For example, Katz and Kahn (1978) say that there are five major subsystems in all organizations, and for the total organization to be effective, all the subsystems must be functioning effectively. The five subsystems they specify are presented in Table 11–1.

What is important in Table 11–1 is the variety of issues that

Production Subsystems

The primary cycles of activity that yield the eventual output or organizations; the production process. Technology, division of labor, design of jobs.

Supportive Subsystems

Providing the materials to be produced and the delivery of products and services; supporting actual productivity; interacting with the larger environment for procurement of materials and disposition of goods produced.

Maintenance Subsystems

Maintaining both personnel and equipment; recruitment, socialization, training, compensation and reward (prestige, job satisfaction) systems; provisions for keeping equipment up and running.

Adaptive Subsystems

Monitoring of external changes and translating that information so the meaning for the organization is clear; product research, market research, long-range planning, research and development.

Managerial Subsystems

The activities for controlling, coordinating, and directing the other organizational subsystems; decision-making; conflict resolution; coordinating internal structures to meet external requirements; the authority subsystem.

Based on Katz and Kahn, (1978).

require attention for an organization to function effectively. Obviously, if the organization has the right people in place in the various subsystems, then the probabilities for success are improved; that is why good staffing is so important. Organizational diagnosis might reveal, however, that people who *could* do the job are in place but they have not been provided with the kinds of skills necessary to do so—a case for training. Or, suppose we confront a competitor's innovation; a solution might be to acquire or merge with the competitor. The point here is that there is a tendency in organizations to put all of the blame for ineffectiveness on the people in the organization and to fail to realize that those people may simply not have created the kinds of structures, processes, and procedures under which they could have been more successful. Just because our opening framework emphasizes the reciprocal nature of individuals and organizations does not mean that the most appropriate or best structures and processes will emerge in an organization!

The reason for this background to the review of staffing procedures is to caution against ever having a simplistic view of what is required to make an organization effective. As should be clear from Table 11-1, the number and variety of issues requiring attention in any organization is astounding—to have one be really effective is impossible to comprehend! We carry around an image of the managers in organizations as fantastic jugglers, keeping all of the organization's subsystems in the air at the same time, treating each as it comes up (or down) for attention, and trying to have the whole thing look like a polished act. It is an enormous task and a good staffing process can help, but it certainly is not the whole answer to organizational problems.

REVIEW OF STAFFING PROCEDURES

In this first section we review the major components of an optimal staffing system. In doing so, the major points made in earlier parts of the book will be reiterated.

Measurement of Job, Organization, and Context

We began in Chapter 2 by stating that a good staffing system must be based on an analysis of the (1) organization in which people are required to work; (2) the environment in which the organization must compete for resources (both physical and human) and market its products; and (3) the jobs which are performed in the organization.

The majority of the chapter was devoted to describing and comparing a variety of procedures designed to generate lists of the task activities that comprise jobs and the knowledge, skills, and abilities (KSAs) required to perform them. We showed that all good techniques of job analysis involve establishing the tasks to be performed in behavioral terms, some rating of the KSAs needed to perform the activities, some conclusions about the criticality of tasks and KSAs, and a judgment about the potential of staffing procedures (compared, say, to training) as a strategy for insuring the availability of competent staff.

Job and organization analysis information generated by these procedures is the foundation for all of the staffing procedures discussed in the rest of the book. Some examples are as follows:

1. Realistic job previews used in recruitment depend on adequate information about the job and organization.
2. Career ladders and promotions must be structured around information about jobs which indicates that lower level jobs provide experiences that are relevant for subsequent jobs.
3. The design and development of tests used in selection consist of signs and samples of job tasks as identified in a job analysis.
4. Tests of KSAs used in selection must be KSAs which the job analysis indicates are critically important to the adequate performance of significant tasks.

5. The standards (criteria) by which we judge people's performance must represent measures of their performance on important job tasks.
6. Organizational analysis can reveal other important criteria to be predicted. For example, an organizational goal may be lower turnover and higher quality of work life.
7. Judgments about which KSAs or tasks to include in selection procedures as opposed to training programs must be based on job analysis information.
8. Information about the reward attributes of jobs is useful in recruitment and in achieving desired levels of turnover.
9. The design of tests through content validity procedures will help insure criterion-related validity, that the test will "make sense" to test-takers, and will be acceptable to the courts. All of these possibilities depend on job analysis.
10. Not directly related to the topics discussed in this book, job analysis information is also centrally important in designing pay and compensation systems (e.g., Nash & Carroll, 1975) and training programs (e.g., Goldstein, 1986).

The ideal staffing process, then, must begin with measurement of the jobs and the organization in which the jobs occur.

Measuring Performance

Chapter 3 focused on the various ways we index whether individuals are meeting the standards of behavior identified in the job analysis—are they adequately performing the tasks which the job analysis indicated were part of their responsibility? These criteria of job performance must be collected if we are to make informed judgments both about incumbents and the degree to which selection procedures are providing the organization with a competent workforce.

In describing the various kinds of selection criteria (performance ratings, production, and personnel data), the importance of high quality data was continuously emphasized. Judgments of people's performance must be *relevant* to the tasks they are required to do, they must be *reliable, uncontaminated* and *practical.* Whereas in job analysis we attempt to document the task and KSA requirements of a job, in criterion measurement we attempt to document the degree to which a job incumbent has accomplished those tasks. In a sense, a good performance evaluation system establishes goals both for job incumbents and for an organization's recruitment, selection, and training programs. That is, the job of personnel is to be sure the people brought to the job can and will *do* the job.

The emphasis in Chapter 3 was clearly on job performance, but other kinds of important criteria were also mentioned in the chapter and later. For example, job satisfaction and commitment, absenteeism and turnover, as well as creativity, were all referred to. The issue to remember about criteria is that staffing programs should try to predict those kinds of criteria that are important for long-term organizational survival and organizational effectiveness. Precisely what these criteria are may vary from organization to organization —at Bell Labs it is creativity and innovation, at Frito-Lay it is high quality service—but in effective organizations, explicit choices are made about those goals. The goals, in turn, help focus the efforts, including the efforts of staffing, to goal accomplishment.

Recruitment: Retaining and Attracting Staff

Information about the kinds of jobs to be staffed, the kinds of people (KSAs) required to staff them and the kinds of people likely to stay with an organization and be effective should be used to determine recruitment activities. We strongly emphasized that recruitment from internal sources requires a carefully developed human resources management plan including, obviously, organizational attempts to retain the most qualified employees. Turnover, and its hypothesized antecedents job satisfaction and organizational commitment, became staffing issues not only because people had to be replaced but because good people would not be available for openings.

Chapter 4, then, stressed the idea that successful employee performance (as well as attendance and commitment) are most likely when the goal of recruitment is the attraction and retention of people who fit or match both the KSAs of available openings and the nature or kind of work situation in which the job exists. Finally, if the organization plans to keep its employees and profit from those employees' experiences, involvement, and commitment, attention must be directed to employees' career issues. Again, understanding what must be accomplished by the organization and the role of its human resources must be the basis not only of external recruitment but of career planning and promotional practices for internal employees as well.

Validation

It is one thing to do job analyses, criterion development, and recruitment and another to be able to demonstrate that assessment at selection yields superior employees. The techniques and procedures for establishing validity were presented in Chapters 5 and 6. Two major theses emerged from these chapters. First, evaluating the effectiveness of staffing procedures is a systematic, well developed technology dependent upon empirical verification, not armchair theorizing. Second, all predictor-criterion relationships are really tests of *constructs* or *hypotheses,* whether implicitly or explicitly stated.

The goal of validation efforts is the test of the construct—are we correct in the hypothesis that doing well on predictor X yields superior performance on criterion Y? It was shown that, in pursuit of validity, a content-oriented strategy made most sense. That is, we should focus on the content of the job in developing the predictor or the criterion in a criterion-related study. The criterion-related validation strategies—predictive validity and concurrent validity—were thoroughly presented, as were legal issues in the use of tests.

The bottom line in validation was shown to be the necessity for job relevance and empirical documentation.

Utility

In validation work, we ascertain the degree to which our selection procedures allow us to make accurate predictions about subsequent work performance of job applicants. In Chapter 7 we described a variety of situational variables which affect the practical utility of these procedures. The important considerations discussed were the influence of the selection ratio, the base rate, and the range of individual differences in performance. In short, a large applicant pool from whom only a few persons need to be selected with the current employee staff performing at varying levels of effectiveness constitutes the ideal situation for using valid staffing procedures. A strong case was made for the inclusion of assessments of the dollar contribution of staffing efforts because of the need to evaluate the relative worth of various personnel efforts and to make various organizational members aware of the value of its human resources.

Hiring Procedures

Chapters 8, 9, and 10 presented a very wide range of options useful in assessing candidates for jobs. In some sense, the very breadth of choices available may make it difficult to choose. However, our purpose in being relatively comprehensive was to show that the typical "application blank and interview" selection process

FIGURE 11-1. DIAGRAM OF THE SEQUENTIAL NATURE OF THE STAFFING PROCESS.

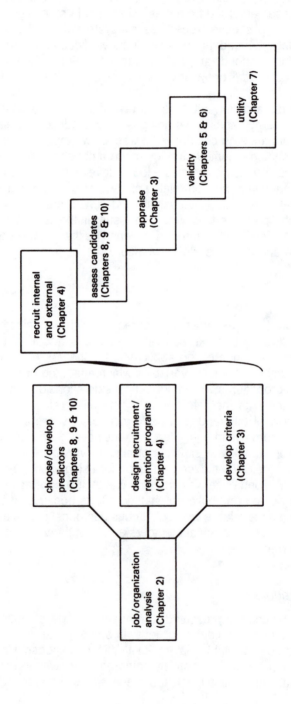

does not represent the state of the art. In other words, we wanted to reveal how many other good ideas there are that can be used to make hiring or promotion decisions in a wide range of circumstances. A second reason for discussing various alternatives is that these procedures each provide different information about job candidates. The greater the variety of valid information available, the more accurate predictions of job performance will be.

Summary

Figure 11–1 diagrams the stages of an ideal staffing program as briefly described above. Obviously every organization will not be able to carry out all of these steps for every job. Practical issues, then, can dictate the necessity to take shortcuts, to skip steps, to do less than an optimal job. It is important to keep Figure 11–1 in mind when *not* doing the optimal so that the tradeoffs in circumventing the ideal can be made explicit. In the next section of the chapter, these are the issues that are addressed.

PRACTICAL SOLUTIONS TO POSSIBLE PROBLEMS

Figure 11–1 can be erroneously interpreted as something that only the largest companies, with a lot of money to invest and large samples, can accomplish. This would be an erroneous interpretation for a number of reasons. First, we want to show in this section how easy it is to use the principles and procedures we have tried to teach you even when time is short, the company is small, and/or the job may not even exist yet but people have to be hired.

Our purpose in this section is to present some situations, then, that may not be the "classic" case and show how the problems were addressed. The important learning in this section is that when confronted by a staffing problem, it is possible to fall back on the framework in Figure 11–1 and the concepts presented earlier for clues about what can be done.

The examples to be presented all depend heavily on a job analysis as the first step, no matter how rudimentary the analysis is. The message here is that job analysis is the absolute first step no matter what the circumstances may be; if nothing else, we must be sure that the selection procedures used are as content valid as possible. The examples present a variety of techniques useful in generating information about candidates for jobs. One strategy emphasizes cognitive ability tests, another uses simulations and interviews, and a third requires the development of a method for forecasting the future so people can be hired for a job that does not yet exist. What we want to show here is how all of the strategies and procedures so far discussed can be brought together to actually produce a procedure for making informed decisions about applicants for jobs.

The "I Need to Hire Someone Now" Problem

No matter what the problem is, always start with at least a cursory job analysis. Pick the procedure from Chapter 2 with which you feel most comfortable and which best suits your purpose. Specify the variety of tasks to be done and the standards of performance to which you will hold the employee. Think of activities you could ask a person to do that correspond to the job activities required.

Make the content of your assessment like the job content. For example, say you need a short-order cook. Would you trust an interview to hire a cook? Before reading this book you may have, but now you would have applicants cook the kinds of things you want them to do on the job. The logic here is that you do not want to fly on an airplane on which the pilot was selected based only on an interview, so why should you serve food cooked by a person hired only by an interview?

The same principle applies to hiring salespersons, bricklayers, dishwashers, secretaries, office managers, foremen, or what have you. Let content validity be your guide in designing some exercise, simulation, or activity.

Another possibility is to call the local State Employment Service office after doing the job analysis. Describe the kind of person desired—remember to concentrate on *important* job *skills*. Because State Employment Services have General Aptitude Test Battery data on people, they may have applicants available who fit the descriptions you provide.

While waiting for an applicant, devise some weights for the importance of the different components of the job you have open. You will probably do some *implicit* weighting in the presence of an applicant, so why not be as explicit as possible? Such weighting will also serve as a guideline for the kinds of information you will want an interview to generate if you decide to do one (and *everyone* seems to).

After developing these weights, think carefully about the kinds of rewards the job offers. Chapters 3 and 4 again can be used here.

Providing applicants with such information may help make the decision more two-way and places some of the burden of responsibility for the decision on the applicant, too.

The clue to making such immediate kinds of decisions is to be systematic. While decisions made in this fashion may be of unknown validity, they are *more apt* to be valid because they are based on principles discussed throughout this book which have proven important in relatively rigorous research efforts.

The "We're Too Small for This Kind of Stuff" Problem

There are at least four ways of applying the materials in this book to the "we're too small problem: 1) through validity generalization 2) through synthetic validity 3) through content validity 4) through Management/Professional Recruitment.

Validity generalization. One way to circumvent the "too small" problem is to use the results of validity generalization analyses as a guide for development and/or selection of selection procedures. Recall from Chapter 8 that validity generalization analyses indicate that cognitive ability tests, at least, appear to have validity for particular job groups regardless of the organizational context. Other similar reviews (Hunter & Hunter, 1984; Schmitt, Gooding, Noe, & Kirsch, 1984) can be used as information regarding which types of tests are likely to measure the knowledge, skills, and abilities required in a particular job. For example, a small company should be able to use a clerical ability test for clerical jobs and expect it to be valid. Or, a firm interested in an auto mechanic should be able to use psychomotor and/or spatial perception measures. Companies interested in hiring professional technical people should be able to use a test of general cognitive aptitude with a degree of confidence. Again, it is necessary that a consideration of the job responsibilities and KSAs indicate that the jobs for which selection procedures are needed be similar to those jobs on which validity generalization data have been collected.

We also mentioned earlier (Chapter 8) that there are several consortia of companies in similar industries that have shared data in a way that allowed validation of selection procedures with very large sample sizes. Similar cooperative efforts among small companies could be used to develop relatively sophisticated selection procedures. Specific examples of solutions to the "small company" problem are described in the following sections.

Synthetic Validity. Guion (1965), for example, showed that even concurrent criterion related validation studies using cognitive ability tests can be carried out in small organizations. His approach to circumventing the small sample size problem was to use an approach called *synthetic validity*. In this procedure, a careful job analysis is used to identify the components of the job that are most crucial. For each such component, measures previously shown to be predictive of these components are then identified. With the meta-analysis of ability-performance relationships and the validity generalization work cited above, we have a much better base of information on which to identify these components. These predictors can then be weighted by their validity and used in a battery of procedures for gathering information on applicants and making a statement about their probability of success.

Guion used this synthetic validity idea in a small company employing only forty-eight people from stock boy to president. In no case were more than three people doing the same kind of work. He took the following steps:

1. *Job analysis.* Every position in the company was analyzed. Each was shown to consist of one or more of seven categories of job responsibility (job components): salesmanship, creative business judgment, customer relations, routine judgment, leadership, ability to handle detail work, and ability to organize work.

2. *Performance appraisal.* A relatively detailed appraisal system was designed based on the job analysis. Great care was taken to insure that halo, leniency errors, and so forth would not contaminate the reliability of the ratings. All employees were evaluated.

3. *Administration of tests.* A battery of tests was chosen and administered to all forty-eight employees. The battery included tests from the Employee Aptitude Survey (various abilities), the Guilford-Zimmerman Temperament Survey (G-ZTS; motivation), the Management Aptitude Inventory (management ability), and others, for a total of nineteen subtest scores.

4. *Test-Criteria intercorrelations.* The seven criteria were intercorrelated with the nineteen test scores. Through multiple correlation, the two test scores accounting for the largest proportion of each of the seven criteria were then selected as a "battery" for each criterion. Expectancy tables were prepared for each criterion, showing the probability of a person being rated superior given different scores on the battery for that criterion.

5. *Application.* During the year following the preliminary work, thirteen people were hired. Each was hired for a particular position by (a) identifying the job components (from the seven)

associated with the position under consideration, (b) administering those "batteries" that assessed the components, and (c) selecting people who were judged to have a good chance of success. 76 percent of those predicted to be "superior" were so rated.

Note that the development of the "battery" for each job component followed the concurrent validity model.

Today, it would be much better to use the accumulated evidence concerning the validity of procedures used in similar jobs. The important point is that there are a number of procedures which will yield positive results when their development follows the systematic job analysis, criterion development, validity-oriented model we have emphasized. These steps, however, can be adapted in many ways to accommodate practical constraints.

Content Validation. One of your authors (Schmitt and Ostroff, 1985) has participated in another example of the development of selection procedures for a relatively small group of people, the 39 emergency telephone operators in a medium sized urban area. These operators were required to answer phone calls from people in emergency situations requiring police, fire, or medical attention.

This project consisted of three major components:

- A job analysis to determine the tasks involved in performing the job of emergency telephone operator and the knowledge, skills, and abilities necessary to perform those tasks.
- The development of exercises which sample the KSAs needed for adequate job performance.
- The evaluation of the psychometric properties of the exercises and their content validity.

1. The **job analysis** procedure used was the one outlined in Chapter 2 called C-JAM (Levine, 1983). Task statements and KSAs were generated in group meetings. Both tasks and KSAs were then rated using the C-JAM scales described in Chapter 2 and the interjudge consistency of those ratings was assessed. Six major KSA dimensions were identified: communication skills, cooperativeness, emotional control, judgment, memory, and clerical/technical skills.

Both KSAs and task statements played a role in the construction of a variety of selection tests. Each test devised centered around two or more of the KSA dimensions. An attempt was made to devise a test of a given KSA dimension that resembled the actual telephone operator tasks for which that KSA was required. The tests constructed were based on tasks rated as most important and resembled components of the job as closely as possible. Expert

TABLE 11-2. *EXAMINATION BY SKILL DIMENSION MATRIX.*

DIMENSION	ORAL DIRECTIONS	INTERVIEW	SIMULATION
Communication Skills		X	X
Emotional Control		X	X
Judgment		X	X
Cooperativeness		X	X
Memory	X		
Clerical/Technical Skills	X		

job incumbents who helped in test administration were asked to review each test item and indicate whether or not it was essential to the performance of each major task dimension. These data generally confirmed the content validity of the various test components, though some minor additions and deletions were indicated by this review.

2. The **examination plan** consisted of three consecutive phases: a) an oral direction/typing test; b) a situational interview, and c) a phone call simulation test. The Examination Plan by Skills matrix is given in Table 11-2.

a. The *oral directions/typing test* was designed to measure the applicant's memory ability and technical/clerical skills. This test consisted of four components: spelling; telephone call recordings; monitoring; and typing. The first three components of the exam were administered via a tape recorder; applicants listened to the information and questions presented on tape and responded in writing on answer forms.

The spelling test required applicants to properly spell common street names and places presented on the tape, an obviously critical skill for an emergency operator. The telephone call portion of the test was actually a series of scripted conversations between complainants (callers) and operators. Here the candidate had to listen to the conversations and accurately record the pertinent information, as shown in Figure 11-2.

The third portion of the oral directions test was a monitoring exercise resembling tasks required for monitoring police units. Applicants listened to a series of statements which gave information about police units, their location, and activities. Following the presentation of these statements, questions were asked about the location of a unit, what type of call the officers were responding to, etc. Applicants recorded the information on their answer forms.

address of incident	city	location/building name
caller's name	phone #	caller's address
nature of incident		description of subjects/vehicles
complaint against		other information

Scores were based on the accuracy of the information recorded regarding the police units' locations and activities.

The final portion of the exam was a typing test. The typing test developed matched the kind of typing performed on the job. For this test, applicants type information printed on standardized forms into blank forms. The forms were exactly like the ones used in the phone call portion of the exam (See Figure 11–2). Scoring was based on speed (the number of blanks typed in each form) and accuracy (the number of errors made while typing).

b. *The situational interview,* first proposed by Latham, Saari, Purcell, and Campion (1980), is a structured interview in which applicants respond to a series of job-related incidents (See Chapter 10). In developing our modification of situation interview questions for the emergency operator's job, we began with the collection of critical incidents (Flanagan, 1954, see Chapter 2). Job incumbents were asked to identify incidents in which particularly good or poor job behavior had been exhibited by some operator. The list of critical incidents was analyzed and edited by the investigators and several subject matter experts (SME). Incidents were then translated into relevant interview questions in which job *applicants* were asked to indicate how they would behave in each of the presented situations. Since applicants were unlikely to have the job experience necessary to deal with the critical incidents, it was essential to translate these critical incidents into questions with which job candidates would have some knowledge and/or experience.

As an illustration of the transformation of critical incidents into interview questions, consider the following example of a question developed for the situational interview. To demonstrate communication skill, the following critical incident was suggested by experienced workers:

> A caller becomes abusive when talking to an operator. The operator gets mad and verbally abuses the caller using derogatory language.

This incident was transformed into the following interview question:

> How would you react if you were a sales clerk, waitress, or service station attendant and one of your customers talked back to you, indicated you should have known something you did not, or told you that you were not waiting on them fast enough?

Seventeen interview questions were developed in order to evaluate the applicants on KSA dimensions of communication skills, emotional control, judgment, and cooperativeness. Since the interview questions were based on incidents of critical job behavior, tasks important to the job were the items in the interview questions. All of these interview questions posed situations which were familiar to inexperienced job applicants.

A set of standardized BARS-type (Smith and Kendall, 1963) rating scales (see Chapter 3) was devised to aid the interviewer-raters in making more objective judgments of applicants' performance in the situational interview. The interview rating guide consisted of a set of twelve scales. On each scale, the dimension was listed along with a set of the interview questions which were likely to elicit candidate responses relevant to that particular dimension. Also listed were potential good and poor answers to each of the interview questions within each of the dimensions. Interview-raters were instructed to review the interview questions relevant for that particular scale, consider the examples of good and poor answers to those questions, then make a rating on a five-point scale ranging from excellent to poor based on the applicant's responses. A total interview score for the applicant was computed by adding together the scores received on each scale. One example of a rating scale is reproduced as Figure 11–3.

c. *The phone call simulation* placed job candidates in a role-playing exercise. The applicants played the role of an operator taking calls from complainants. An experienced operator played the role of a caller. This exercise assessed applicants' communication skills, emotional control, and judgment by focusing on the important tasks related to obtaining and recording critical information accurately.

Applicants talked with the caller and obtained the information necessary to send help. Some callers were hysterical or emotional. The candidates had a variety of questions they needed to ask each caller in order to elicit the appropriate information. The information

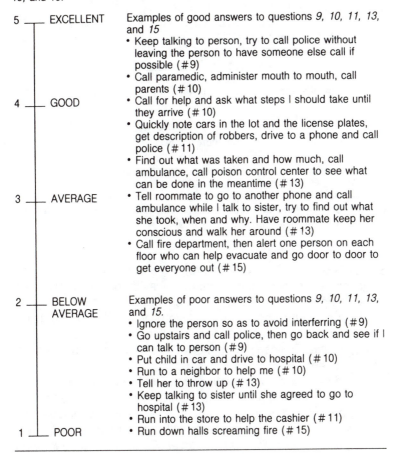

In making your rating on this scale, consider answers to questions *9, 10, 11, 13,* and *15.*

5 — EXCELLENT

Examples of good answers to questions *9, 10, 11, 13,* and *15*
- Keep talking to person, try to call police without leaving the person to have someone else call if possible (#9)
- Call paramedic, administer mouth to mouth, call parents (#10)

4 — GOOD
- Call for help and ask what steps I should take until they arrive (#10)
- Quickly note cars in the lot and the license plates, get description of robbers, drive to a phone and call police (#11)
- Find out what was taken and how much, call ambulance, call poison control center to see what can be done in the meantime (#13)

3 — AVERAGE
- Tell roommate to go to another phone and call ambulance while I talk to sister, try to find out what she took, when and why. Have roommate keep her conscious and walk her around (#13)
- Call fire department, then alert one person on each floor who can help evacuate and go door to door to get everyone out (#15)

2 — BELOW AVERAGE

Examples of poor answers to questions *9, 10, 11, 13,* and *15.*
- Ignore the person so as to avoid interferring (#9)
- Go upstairs and call police, then go back and see if I can talk to person (#9)
- Put child in car and drive to hospital (#10)
- Run to a neighbor to help me (#10)
- Tell her to throw up (#13)
- Keep talking to sister until she agreed to go to hospital (#13)
- Run into the store to help the cashier (#11)

1 — POOR
- Run down halls screaming fire (#15)

obtained was recorded on a standardized form, the same form used during the Oral Directions/Typing test, hence all candidates were familiar with this aspect of the simulation.

The technician, playing the caller, was in the next room using special phone equipment to speak with the applicant. A series of six phone call scripts (see Figure 11–4) were written to guide the technician in making calls. One practice call was given to allow applicants to acquaint themselves with the procedure. The phone call conversations were tape recorded so that raters could later listen to the tape and judge applicants' abilities. The role-playing operator was given extensive practice and instruction regarding the necessity to give the same information to all candidate callers.

FIGURE 11–4. *SAMPLE PHONE CALL SCRIPT.*

CALLER:	*(Angry)* I'm really mad and I've had enough of this. I have to work the morning shift and I get up really early. The morning shift starts at 6 o'clock. I work at Olds and I need my sleep. This is just ridiculous and it goes on every night. I can't believe it . . .
CBO:	Should interrupt at some point and ask what the problem is, get address, caller's name, etc.
CALLER:	(Gives this information to caller *when asked*
	• name: Henry Abbott (or Harriete Abbott)
	• incident: Neighbors dog barking furiously
	• caller's address: 2728 W. Landsdown
	• phone #: 378-5493
	• city: Okemos
	• neighbor's address: 2792 W. Landsdown
	(when caller asks for this address, also say:)
	I wish you'd hurry up and take care of this. I really need my sleep. You know, I have to work very early in the morning. This goes on every night and I'm tired of it . . .
CBO:	Should interrupt and continue getting information by asking questions -complaint against: don't know neighbor's name . . .

Since all conversations were recorded and evaluations were based on those recordings, non-standard behavior on the part of the role-playing technician could be taken into account.

Scoring for the phone call simulation consisted of two parts: (1) scoring of the standardized forms applicants completed; and (2) ratings of the applicants' communication skill, emotional control, and judgment.

3. **Psychometric evaluation** of the tests included a review of their content validity and reliability. The development of these exercises clearly relied on a content-oriented validation technique. The procedure used was in accordance with the standards established in the *Uniform Guidelines on Employee Selection Procedures.* As stated in the *Guidelines,* a selection procedure can be validated by a content-oriented strategy if it is representative of the important aspects of performance on the job. The tests developed matched the important tasks performed on the job based on information provided by SMEs in the job analysis. Further, the Guidelines specify that a job analysis which focuses on work behaviors and associated tasks is required. The job analysis procedure outlined above provided specific job behaviors as well as their importance and necessity to the job.

Content-oriented validity is usually not an appropriate strategy when the selection procedure involves knowledge, skills, or abilities which an employee will be expected to learn on the job. The initial C-JAM (job analysis; see Chapter 3) ratings of the KSA statements by job incumbents provided a basis for delineating KSAs necessary for newly hired workers and those KSAs learned on the job or learned through training; the tests devised concentrated only on those dimensions which were necessary for new workers to possess. Further, skills and abilities which were necessary, but required some training, were modified to accommodate inexperienced workers. For example, the standardized forms used to record information in the Oral Directions Test and the Phone Call Simulation were modified and were used in written form rather than on a computer system; the situational interview questions were translated from critical job incidents to experiences a person could encounter in everyday life.

The selection strategy involved multiple hurdles and both compensatory and noncompensatory scoring (see Chapters 5 and 6). Applicants who met or exceeded the specified cutoff scores in the Oral Directions/Typing Test phase of the examination process proceeded with the situational interview and phone call simulation in which a compensatory scoring scheme was employed. The use of minimum cutoff scores was justified by information gathered in job analysis interviews which indicated people needed minimal memory and technical/clerical skills (primarily assessed in the Oral Directions Test) and that other skills were more important in separating the marginal employee from the truly superior worker. Hence, the Interview and Phone Call Simulation were used to rank order candidates who had passed the earlier Oral Directions Test.

Another advantage of this type of selection procedure is that it provides a more realistic preview of the job (RSP; see discussion of RJPs in Chapter 4). Applicants gain a clearer understanding of the job in question as they perform behaviors that are required on the actual job.

A final attraction of this project was the extensive involvement of supervisory personnel and job incumbents in all phases of the effort. While this is a useful strategy in any project, this involvement insured that all proposed selection instruments were job-related. The involvement was also necessary to meet the administrative requirements of the emergency center in which the jobs existed. That is, police personnel had previously conducted the selection interview of candidates, and they wished to have continued input into the hiring decision. To accommodate these desires, Civil Service Personnel screened most of the low qualified applicants, making the interview procedure less burdensome. Of course, the usual affirmative action demands were also present and needed consideration.

Because of these requirements, applicants proceeded through two phases of testing. Civil Service personnel administered an Oral

Directions/Typing test designed for ease in administration to small groups of people. Police and supervisory personnel administered the situational interview and the phone call simulation.

In this example, then, we see a comprehensive staffing procedure being developed for a job employing relatively few people. Note the central role of the job analysis, the heavy use of simulations, the use of rating scales for judging candidate performance even in an interview, the involvement of supervisors and incumbents, and the care taken to adhere to legal issues in selection.

Robinson (1981) provides a similar example for a job in the private sector *where only one person was to be hired*. The small business was a general contracting firm which built about 60 single family homes and six multifamily projects in 1979. At that time, it had 10 employees and sales of about $10 million. They drew plans for buildings and made cost estimates and then invited subcontractor bids for various aspects of the work. Company personnel supervised construction and then sold the properties to others or kept them for investment purposes. Company personnel felt that business growth indicated the need for an additional construction superintendent.

A job analysis panel consisting of the company president, production and financial vice-presidents, and the construction superintendent identified 11 broad objectives and 71 tasks, of which 20 were deemed critical (see Figure 11–5). Job objectives were ranked independently from most to least important by the panel members, and a composite ranking was computed.

Based upon consideration of the critical tasks, an assessment battery was constructed, as in Schmitt and Ostroff (1986), using work sample procedures. The test battery consisted of the following elements:

1. *Blueprint Reading Test.* An architect was employed to help the panel identify common architectural errors and to incorporate them in drawings of buildings which the company had built. Applicants were asked to mark the location of the errors on the architectural drawings and the test was scored for the number of errors detected.

2. *Scrambled Subcontractor Test.* In this test, the applicants were provided a list of subcontractors (e.g., electrical, plumbing, roofing, etc.) and were asked to list them in their appropriate order of appearance on the site. The order of subcontractor appearance is critical in avoiding unnecessary delays and consequent large interest expenses from lengthy construction time. The most appropriate order for the subcontractors coming to the job was determined by the construction superintendent and the vice-president for production.

	BR	SS	CER	ST	SI
Insure prompt adherence to oral commitments	X			X	
Do a walk-through inspection with customer of production supervisor			X		
Complete superintendent's quality control checklist at specified intervals or phase of construction			X		
Differentiate between possible and impossible conditions on the various classifications of construction (Section 8, custom, commercial, etc.)	X		X		
Schedule work and materials in accordance with critical path set by company		X			
Inspect work progress daily and determine adherence to critical path		X	X		
Adjust schedule in accordance with work progress/delays			X		
Notify subcontractors and suppliers of accelerated or delayed progress to negotiate their time in			X		
Read and interpret plans and specifications	X				
Correct and document errors in plans	X				
Recognize when on-site changes create problems in other areas on the building	X				
Identify common errors made by lay-out person or architect	X				
Recognize deviations from the plants or code.	X		X		
Call for subcontractor when job is ready for that phase of operation		X		X	
Ask subcontractor about work methods, production, availability of workmen					X
Inspect a subcontractor's work			X		
Identify opportunities for theft and vandalism, and specify or take counter-measures, depending upon costs/benefits					X
Recognize violations of OSHA safety standards					
Keep an inventory of company equipment and tools					X

"X" indicates tests used to estimate task performance capability. BR = Blueprint Reading; SS = Scrambled Subcontractor; CER = Construction Error Recognition; ST = Scheduling Test; SI = Structured Interview.
From Robinson, (1981).

3. *Construction Error Recognition Test.* By interviewing the job analysis panel and a number of subcontractors, a list of 25 common and expensive construction errors was generated and an 8' by 12' shed was constructed incorporating the errors. Applicants were given unlimited time to inspect the shed and note the errors on a pad of paper; their score was the number of errors detected.

4. *Scheduling Test.* This test was an assessment center exercise in which applicants were required to change the job assignments of the people they supervised because of an unexpected development. Their performance in this exercise was rated by a team of company assessors. The objective of the exercise was to

assess candidates' ability to plan, organize, schedule, anticipate, and analyze problems, and to test their judgment.

5. *Structured Interview.* A structured interview conducted by the president and production vice-president covered various aspects of the relationship between the construction superintendent and building inspectors, safety procedures, company philosophy, and business ethics.

A newspaper ad generated 49 resumes which were screened down to 17 based on "goodness of fit" to the job objectives and tasks. The results of implementing this job-relevant selection procedure are described as follows by Robinson (1981, pp. 82–83):

> The 17 candidates were telephoned to establish provisional availability. The job objectives were read, and applicants were asked if they could achieve these objectives. The selection process was described, and applicants were invited to call the telephone receptionist at the company to make an appointment for testing. All 17 candidates telephoned, expressed their availability, and all 17 appeared for testing. Each was given a copy of the objectives and tasks and asked to review them at leisure. This would be the first time any of them had seen the tasks. Upon reading this information, one applicant disqualified himself.

"Blueprint Reading" test results assumed a neat bivariate distribution, with eight each in high- and low-performing groups. The "Scrambled Subcontractor" test disqualified one, leaving seven. The "Construction Error Recognition" test eliminated four and left three in the field. These three were given the "Scheduling Test" and the structured interview. One candidate stood out clearly as the best suited to the job. An offer was extended and accepted. More than a year later the fit was reported to be satisfactory.

Management recruitment. In Chapter 4 we mentioned the use of special management recruiting firms that charge a fee to find high level managerial/professional personnel. As we noted, those fees are substantial, typically one-third of the first year's salary of the person who is being recruited. Given the large amount of money expended, how does a firm use a "headhunter" most effectively? By this time, you can probably guess parts of the answer.

The firm should supply the recruiter with detailed information about what types of work the person would be expected to do, what kinds of knowledge, skills, and abilities might be required, what past work experiences might best prepare a candidate, what type of expectations the firm has for the recruit's development, promotion, and information on the organization's "climate." In short, the firm should perform the elements of a job/organization analysis as outlined in Chapter 2.

In evaluating the work of the recruiter, the firm should expect that information on potential candidates include a careful analysis of the candidate's KSAs and how they fit the "blueprint" provided. In other words, there should be evidence that the specifications provided regarding a capable candidate have been considered and "measured" in a thorough fashion.

In deciding whether or not to engage a particular executive/professional recruiter, we might ask how the recruiter will make her or his recommendation, what previous experience she or he has in recruiting similar personnel, and what type of background training qualifies the recruiter for their work. The investment a firm makes in the recruiter and the person recruited is substantial, and the best approach is to collect information about the position, recruiter, and the candidates in a systematic and job-related fashion.

Clearly, these examples represent procedures that could be carried out in small businesses. Equally obvious is the fact that these procedures take some time and effort to design and implement successfully. However, in most organizations, the human element is extremely critical and the time and effort expense in making appropriate selections may be the best resource investment the company makes (recall the discussion of utility in Chapter 7). While the procedures developed for emergency telephone operator and construction superintendent may be time-consuming and expensive, it is possible that they can be used repeatedly in the same organization given future need. Further, these procedures often have significant side benefits; they may result in clearer definition of company objectives, may suggest changes in company compensation plans, or may suggest that employee training be instituted or updated.

The "We Can't Make the Job Satisfying" Problem

In Chapter 2 we introduced the idea of worker reward attributes analyses as part of job and organization analyses. The idea was that as part of the selection procedure, we should analyze what the company offers its employees by way of reward for their effort and commitment. Very frequently, such analysis may lead to the conclusion that some significant rewards are lacking and company resources are simply not adequate to supply these rewards. And, as shown in Chapter 4, dissatisfaction and low commitment can yield turnover. While it is beyond the scope of this text to discuss in detail all potential solutions to this problem, we suggest exploring some of the alternatives which may be relatively low in cost.

1. Redesigning jobs or rotating jobs may be rewarding to some individuals, particularly if employees want to learn the business. A job in a small company, then, could clearly have some educational value to the employee.

2. Flexibility in working hours may be another significant low-cost reward to employees who have non-work obligations they must fulfill.

3. Decision-making regarding the work environment may help increase morale and a spirit of teamwork. In the emergency telephone operator example described previously, the supervisor frequently organized efforts to increase the "livability" of the work area. A break area with refrigerator and microwave was contributed by employees; the group organized itself to paint and redecorate their work space and to set up an aquarium. These must be activities the workers themselves want to do or they can be seen as manipulations by management to get them to contribute their time and money.

4. Of course, input to decisions about how work is done and organized may also be solicited from employees in firms of any size. Appropriately administered and followed up, such "participative systems" can be a powerful force in building a more productive company as well as a more satisfied and committed work force.

5. Use the realistic job preview to weed out job candidates who may not be able to "stand the heat." While the literature on the RJP suggests that the loss of candidates is not severe, some preliminary self-weeding could happen in a really onerous situation. Of course, when the situation is so bad that a company certainly does not want anyone to know about it, it may be time to take steps to *improve* the situation and stop looking for a person who can "take the heat."

In *Parkinson's Law*, Parkinson (1957) describes (with tongue in cheek) how a terrible job can be filled merely by proper recruiting. The kind of ad required is as follows:

Wanted—An archaeologist with high academic qualifications willing to spend 15 years in excavating the Inca tombs at Helsdump on the Alligator River. Knighthood or equivalent honor guaranteed. Pension payable but never yet claimed. Salary of £200 (or $6,000 U.S.) per year. Apply in triplicate to the Director of the Grubbenburow Institute, Sickdale, IL, USA.

Parkinson goes on to describe the benefits of such an ad:

Here the advantages and drawbacks are neatly balanced. There is no need to insist that candidates must be patient, tough, intrepid and single. The terms of the advertisement have eliminated all who are not. It is unnecessary to require that candidates must be mad on excavating tombs. Mad is just what they certainly will be. Having thus reduced the possible applicants to a maximum of 3, the terms of the advertisement place the salary just too low to attract 2 of them and the promised honor *just* high enough to interest the third. We may suppose that, in this case, the offer of a K.C.M.G. would have produced two applications, the offer of an O.B.E., none. The result is a single candidate. He is off his head but that does not matter. He is the man we want (Parkinson, 1957, pp. 54–55).

The "Job Doesn't Exist Yet" Problem

Occasionally, in both large and small organizations, we encounter the need to hire people for a job that is just being created because of technological change and/or company expansion. How do we analyze a job that doesn't exist and establish the requisite knowledge, skills, and abilities to do it?

One of your authors has been involved in an interesting project like this (Schneider and Schechter, 1986). What made the effort particularly interesting was that it concerned supervisors, rather than operative employees. The logic underlying the project was that the job of the operating employees (telephone salespersons) was changing in a number of significant ways so the question we asked was: if the job changes, and the kinds of people doing the new job are different from the people who did the old job, how does the supervisor's job change? To answer this question we went through the following steps:

1. A traditional job analysis was accomplished for the present supervisory job including specification of the tasks to be accomplished (including incumbent ratings of their importance and the amount of time spent doing them) and the KSAs necessary to perform the important tasks. For each KSA identified, SME judgments were, in turn, made about the importance of the KSA for doing the tasks (see Goldstein, 1986 for details about this form of job analysis).

2. A workshop of SMEs was planned to accomplish three goals:

    a. Define the nature of the job being supervised three to five years from the time of the workshop.

    b. Rate the importance of and time spent on the existing task statements for the supervisory job of the future.

  c. Rate the importance of the KSAs to accomplish the important tasks of the supervisory job of the future.

3. Attending the workshop was the team of job analysis consultants and five persons in the organization knowledgeable about the current supervisory job and the kinds of changes likely to occur in the job being supervised. These two groups of SMEs generated a list of the changes in the job and the organization that had to be considered in doing the job analysis of the future:

  a. Increased computerization of the job of the future permitting accurate monitoring of performance as well as improved efficiency.

  b. Increased complexity of the job of the future requiring more highly skilled people being hired and more intensive training of those hired.

  c. A change in the job from order-taking to active selling requiring more assertive people being hired.

  d. Increased competition on price in the marketplace making service a major goal of the salesperson.

Given these kinds of predictions about the nature of the technology of the job, the people who will be doing the job, and the market in which the organization functions, the chore of the workshop was to literally predict what the *supervisor* of this job would be doing and the KSAs he or she would need to do it.

4. As part of the job analysis of the job of the future, not only were the KSAs rated for their importance, but the SMEs made judgments about how the KSAs were to be acquired. That is, were supervisors to be selected already having the KSAs or were those selected going to be trained in the KSAs. If the latter case, then those selected would have to be competent enough to be trainable. In this particular project, the SMEs agreed that candidates should be hired who already possessed many of the skills and abilities of supervisors (define goals, plan, coordinate others, and so on) and that the task-specific knowledge required would be primarily provided in training.

Analyses of the data generated in the workshop against the data coming from the "job of the present" analysis revealed that those KSAs currently the most important were going to *increase* in importance for the job of the future. Whether this is a phenomenon that will characterize other studies of jobs of the future is not known yet.

This project suggests an important issue in job analysis: job analysis techniques uniformly address the status quo in that they focus on the world of today. In organizations that operate in an ever-changing world, jobs will also be ever-changing. It seems that any help we can get in defining what jobs will look like and, thus, what kinds of people they will require, could be of considerable strategic advantage.

Precisely how one validates selection procedures for jobs that are not quite yet in existence may seem a perplexing problem, but it is not intractable. For example, suppose a simulation of the job is created and used for selection. It (the simulation) could serve as a *criterion* for establishing the validity of a paper and pencil cognitive ability test that might be an inexpensive screening procedure. It (the simulation) could also serve as a *predictor* of training performance and, at a later point in time, the validity of the training program as a predictor of job performance could be accomplished.

The point here, as in our other examples, is that the foundation of such an effort rests on the application of comprehensive job analytic procedures.

IMPLICATIONS FOR THE JOB SEEKER

Throughout this book, we have discussed selection from the organization's viewpoint. That is, we have discussed how organizations organize and operate to try and insure the recruitment and selection of a competent work force. Those same procedures, however, also have implications for the way in which an individual chooses a job or organization. The stakes for the individual are just as significant, and in the last section of the book, we provide suggestions for selecting a job and organization.

Job and Organization Analysis

Before or during the application process, job seekers should do their homework regarding the job for which they apply. What are the job responsibilities? Whom would I report to? What are the possibilities for promotions? What are the pay rates and fringe benefits and of what value are they to me? What are expectations in the company regarding job performance, and how will I be evaluated? What are the organization's expectations regarding dress, community involvement, attendance at company functions? What is the status of the organization—financially and technologically, and what are its human resource policies? Certainly we should have answers to as many of these questions as possible before accepting a position, but research done early in the application process (before a job interview) can do much to direct our information search during the interview and other components of the job application process.

What kinds of sources of information exist? Perhaps the best source of information about a particular job and organization is incumbents. People who work at a job in a company not only have general opinions about them but they can be a source of very explicit, *critical*, information. Use of the word *critical* here should serve as a reminder—use Flanagan's (1954) critical incident methodology described so many times, especially in Chapters 2 and 3.

For example, ask people to describe actual examples that occur in the organization about issues that concern you. How do supervisors treat you? Is hard work rewarded? What are the attendance/punctuality rules and procedures? Is promotion from within? Remember, have them cite specific incidents: what were the circumstances; who was involved; what happened; and so on.

Information about specific jobs/organizations will also be available from one or more of the following sources:

1. Friends/family
2. Clergy
3. State employment services
4. Employment agencies
5. School counselors (both high school and college)
6. News articles in newspapers (e.g., *Wall Street Journal*) and magazines (e.g., *Fortune, Business Week*) for larger companies (and *Inc.* for smaller companies).

The message is that you should have knowledge when you apply for a job. Indeed, if the RJP literature is correct, the more realistic your information is for the job you take, the more satisfied you will be at it. Be prepared with knowledge!

Recruitment

In searching for a job it is sometimes a problem just finding appropriate job opportunities. This process of finding job opportunities is similar to an organization looking for job applicants. In recruitment of job opportunities, the best way to start is with a realistic assessment of one's interests and capabilities. In this regard, one should examine his or her educational and experience background; even standardized interest or aptitude batteries can be used to make these assessments. Most high schools and colleges have testing facilities and experienced test administrators and interpreters. As we showed, interest inventories, in particular, can be very useful data in making broad occupational choices; people, not only organizations, can use them. These standardized tests and an interview with a trained career counselor may suggest occupations that were not previously considered.

The next step in recruitment is to consider the jobs, organizations, and careers available that may fit your interests and capabilities. A standard source of information about various jobs that we discussed in Chapter 2 was the Dictionary of Occupational Titles (DOT). The DOT was constructed so that it could serve a career counseling function, and it has a wealth of information including job descriptions for more than 20,000 jobs. In addition to the narrative job descriptions, it also presents data on the abilities, interests, and temperaments of individuals who occupy those jobs. Most people looking for jobs are tied to a specific geographic area. The next step would be to locate companies that locally employ individuals in these jobs. In this context, local chambers of commerce, state employment agencies, or even the telephone book may be of help.

Once you have identified companies that may have jobs for which you believe you may qualify, then write and/or call the personnel officer in the company. Describe the job or jobs you are looking for and for which you feel you are qualified and why you are particularly interested in/qualified to work in their organization. The more information you have about the job or organization, the more likely it is that they will be impressed by and interested in you.

Remember, recruitment goes on internally as well as externally. This means that it is important for you to continually process information about opportunities inside your company. This is accomplished by making yourself known to people who (a) have information and (b) have access to jobs. This may sound very manipulative but, as the expression goes, whose career is this, anyhow. As noted in Chapter 4, London and Stumpf (1982) have done an excellent job of showing how individuals can take control of their own career and not wait for "the organization" to do it for them.

The Selection Process

Assuming one or more companies decide to pursue your application and request that you go through their formal selection process, there are a number of precautions suggested by the research on hiring procedures outlined in Chapters 8, 9, and 10. If asked to respond to biographical forms, be honest but also be sure to mention all possible job relevant experiences and why you perceive them to be relevant. If you are asked for names of individuals who can write a letter of reference, be sure to ask those individuals if they are willing to serve in that role. If standardized tests are required, find out, if possible, what those tests are and do some research regarding the test. If you are familiar with the test, its general content and format, you should be more relaxed when taking it.

An interview is part of the selection process in every company. If you have done your background research on the company, you will be able to ask informed questions if the opportunity arises and you may be able to anticipate and prepare for the kinds of questions that may be asked. Recall the similar-to-me effect on interviewer judgments; this effect suggests you be concerned about your dress and physical appearance. You should view the interview as an opportunity to find out about the company and whether or not you want to work in the organization. The degree to which the interviewer is informative, professional, and forthright in answering your questions can be an important source of information about how the organization views its human resources (Schmitt & Coyle, 1976).

Finally, and perhaps most importantly, most interviewers are untrained and most interviews are open-ended. Both facts allow you, as the interviewee, to almost guarantee that the interviewer will focus on what you say. What you say is a function of how well prepared you are regarding the points you want to get across. For example:

1. Your strengths, with examples of situations in which you have displayed them.
2. Your hopes, with examples of what you know you will have to do to make them reality.
3. How you work with others and the kinds of people you particularly enjoy working with.
4. Your short- and long-range plans.

The motto is: treat the interview as an opportunity to say the things you would have said if the interviewer had been a well-trained one who knew what she or he was looking for.

Systematic Evaluation and Decision-Making

Just as organizations should not be making decisions based on hunches, job applicants should not be haphazard or rely on their "gut" impressions of organizations in deciding where to work. As organizations are evaluated, you should keep notes on those things we suggested in the job/organization analysis. When job offers are made, you can then review each opportunity on the dimensions critical to you as a person and decide on the relative merits of each organization in an informed manner. If you have done a careful analysis of what is important to you (flexible hours, pay, promotion opportunities, coworkers, etc.) and if you have gathered information on these dimensions for each opportunity that presents itself, then organization and job choices can be optimal.

Utility

For an organization, consideration of utility most often involves an economic analysis of the contributions of employee skill levels relative to the costs incurred in making decisions. For an individual, utility considerations involve a consideration of the input (work, commitment, etc.) relative to the return (challenging and interesting work, pay, etc.). In choosing an organization wisely, it is important to consider what you value most and how employment in various organizations will have an impact on securing those things that are most valued. In this context, both work and non-work values will be considered. Certainly, issues relating to commuting time, quality of community life, possibility of spouse's employment, and other issues are of significant concern to individuals and by necessity to organizations as well.

SUMMARY

In this last chapter we summarized the major issues dealt with in previous chapters. We also outlined and provided examples of ways in which organizations with limited resources and numbers of people can apply the techniques discussed in this book. Finally, we discussed ways in which individuals can benefit from the same procedures and research when they pursue the selection of a job/organization/career.

By concluding with the role of individual responsibility in accomplishing a match of individual to organization, we come full circle to the idea that individual and organization effectiveness are inextricably intertwined. Both the individual and the organization have responsibilities to and for each other, and together they can pursue effectiveness through goal accomplishment. Just as organizations must carefully plan for the kinds of staff they need, so must individuals plan for the environment in which they can achieve. The list is long for both parties, but dedication to the specification of goals and objectives on both parts, followed by pursuit of likely avenues to achievement can surely yield both individual and organizational success.

REFERENCES

Flanagan, J. C. (1954). The critical incident technique. *Psychological Bulletin, 51,* 317–358.

Goldstein, I. L. (1968). *Training: Program development and evaluation,* Rev. Ed. Monterey, CA: Brooks-Cole.

Goldstein, I. L. (1986). *Training in organizations: Needs assessment, development and evaluation, 2nd ed.* Monterey, CA: Brooks-Cole.

Guion, R. M. (1965). *Personnel testing.* New York: McGraw-Hill.

Hunter, J. E., and Hunter, R. F. (1984). Validity and utility of alternative predictors of job performance. *Psychological Bulletin, 96,* 72–95.

Katz, D., and Kahn, R. L. (1978). *The social psychology of organizations,* 2nd ed. New York: Wiley.

Latham, G. P., Saari, L. M., Purcell, E. D., and Campion, M. A. (1980). The situational interview. *Journal of Applied Psychology, 65,* 422–427.

Levine, E. L. (1983). *Everything you always wanted to know about job analysis.* Tampa, FL: Mariner Publishing Company.

London, M., and Stumpf, S. A. (1982). *Managing careers.* Reading, MA: Addison-Wesley.

Nash, A. N., & Carroll, S. J., Jr. (1975). *The management of compensation.* Monterey, CA: Brooks-Cole.

Parkinson, C. N. (1957). *Parkinson's law and other studies in administration.* Boston: Houghton-Mifflin.

Robinson, D. D. (1981). Content-oriented personnel selection in a small business setting. *Personnel Psychology, 34,* 77–87.

Schmitt, N., and Coyle, B. W. (1976). Applicant decisions in the employment interview. *Journal of Applied Psychology, 61,* 184–192.

Schmitt, N., Gooding, R. Z., Noe, R. A., and Kirsch, M. (1984). Meta-analysis of validity studies published between 1964 and 1982 and the investigation of study characteristics. *Personnel Psychology, 37,* 407–422.

Schmitt, N., and Ostroff, C. (1986). Operationalizing the "behavioral consistency" approach: Selection test development based on a content-oriented strategy. *Personnel Psychology,* in press.

Schneider, B., and Schechter, D. (1985). *Strategic needs analysis.* Unpublished manuscript, Department of Psychology, University of Maryland, College Park.

Schneider, B., and Schechter, D. (1986). Job analysis of the future job: Procedure and implications. Working paper, Department of Psychology, University of Maryland, College Park, MD.

Smith, P. C., and Kendall, L. M. (1963). Retranslation of expectations: An approach to the construction of unambiguous anchors for rating scales. *Journal of Applied Psychology, 47,* 149–155.

APPENDIX

UNIFORM GUIDELINES ON EMPLOYEE SELECTION PROCEDURES

GENERAL PRINCIPLES

§ 1607.1 Statement of purpose.

A. *Need for uniformity—Issuing agencies.* The Federal government's need for a uniform set of principles on the question of the use of tests and other selection procedures has long been recognized. The Equal Employment Opportunity Commission, the Civil Service Commission, the Department of Labor, and the Department of Justice jointly have adopted these uniform guidelines to meet that need, and to apply the same principles to the Federal Government as are applied to other employers.

B. *Purpose of guidelines.* These guidelines incorporate a single set of principles which are designed to assist employers, labor organizations, employment agencies, and licensing and certification boards to comply with requirements of Federal law prohibiting employment practices which discriminate on grounds of race, color, religion, sex, and national origin. They are designed to provide a framework for determining the proper use of tests and other selection procedures. These guidelines do not require a user to conduct validity studies of selection procedures where no adverse impact results. However, all users are encouraged to use selection procedures which are valid, especially users operating under merit principles.

C. *Relation to prior guidelines.* These guidelines are based upon and supersede previously issued guidelines on employee selection procedures. These guidelines have been built upon court decisions, the previously issued guidelines of the agencies, and the practical experience of the agencies, as well as the standards of the psychological profession. These guidelines are intended to be consistent with existing law.

§ 1607.2 Scope.

A. *Application of guidelines.* These guidelines will be applied by the Equal Employment Opportunity Commission in the enforcement of title VII of the Civil Rights Act of 1964, as amended by the Equal Employment Opportunity Act of 1972 (hereinafter "Title VII"); by the Department of Labor, and the contract compliance agencies until the transfer of authority contemplated by the President's Reorganization Plan No. 1 of

1978, in the administration and enforcement of Executive Order 11246, as amended by Executive Order 11375 (hereinafter "Executive Order 11246"); by the Civil Service Commission and other Federal agencies subject to section 717 of Title VII; by the Civil Service Commission in exercising its responsibilities toward State and local governments under section 208(b)(1) of the Intergovernmental-Personnel Act; by the Department of Justice in exercising its responsibilities under Federal law; by the Office of Revenue Sharing of the Department of the Treasury under the State and Local Fiscal Assistance Act of 1972, as amended; and by any other Federal agency which adopts them.

B. *Employment decisions.* These guidelines apply to tests and other selection procedures which are used as a basis for any employment decision. Employment decisions include but are not limited to hiring, promotion, demotion, membership (for example, in a labor organization), referral, retention, and licensing and certification, to the extent that licensing and certification may be covered by Federal equal employment opportunity law. Other selection decisions, such as selection for training or transfer, may also be considered employment decisions if they lead to any of the decisions listed above.

C. *Selection procedures.* These guidelines apply only to selection procedures which are used as a basis for making employment decisions. For example, the use of recruiting procedures designed to attract members of a particular race, sex, or ethnic group, which were previously denied employment opportunities or which are currently underutilized, may be necessary to bring an employer into compliance with Federal law, and is frequently an essential element of any effective affirmative action program; but recruitment practices are not considered by these guidelines to be selection procedues. Similarly, these guidelines do not pertain to the question of the lawfulness of a seniority system within the meaning of section 703(h), Executive Order 11246 or other provisions of Federal law or regulation, except to the extent that such systems utilize selection procedures to determine qualifications or abilities to perform the job. Nothing in these guidelines is intended or should be interpreted as discouraging the use of a selection procedure for the purpose of determining qualifications or for the purpose of selection on the basis of relative qualifications, if the selection procedure had been validated in accord with these guidelines for each such purpose for which it is to be used.

D. *Limitations.* These guidelines apply only to persons subject to Title VII, Executive Order 11246, or other equal employment opportunity requirements of Federal law. These guidelines do not apply to responsibilities under the Age Discrimination in Employment Act of 1967, as amended, not to discriminate on the basis of age, or under sections 501, 503, and 504 of the Rehabilitation Act of 1973, not to discriminate on the basis of handicap.

E. *Indian preference not affected.* These guidelines do not restrict any obligation imposed or right granted by Federal law to users to extend a preference in employment to Indians living on or near an Indian reservation in connection with employment opportunities on or near an Indian reservation.

§ 1607.3 *Discrimination defined: Relationship between use of selection procedures and discrimination.*

A. *Procedure having adverse impact constitutes discrimination unless justified.* The use of any selection procedure which has an adverse impact on the hiring, promotion, or other employment or membership opportunities of members of any race, sex, or ethnic group will be considered to be discriminatory and inconsistent with these guidelines, unless the procedure has been validated in accordance with these guidelines, or the provisions of section 6 below are satisfied.

B. *Consideration of suitable alternative selection procedures.* Where two or more selection procedures are available which serve the user's legitimate interest in efficient and trustworthy workmanship, and which are substantially equally valid for a given purpose, the user should use the procedure which has been demonstrated to have the lesser adverse impact. Accordingly, whenever a validity study is called for by these guidelines, the user should include, as a part of the validity study, an investigation of suitable alternative selection procedures and suitable alternative methods of using the selection procedure which have as little adverse impact as possible, to determine the appropriateness of using or validating them in accord with these guidelines. If a user has made a reasonable effort to become aware of such alternative procedures and validity has been demonstrated in accord with these guidelines, the use of the test or other selection procedure may continue until such time as it should reasonably be reviewed for currency. Whenever the user is shown an alternative selection procedure with evidence of less adverse impact and substantial evidence of validity for the same job in similar circumstances, the user should investigate it to determine the appropriateness of using or validating it in accord with these guidelines. This subsection is not intended to preclude the combination of procedures into a significantly more valid procedure, if the use of such a combination has been shown to be in compliance with the guidelines.

§ 1607.4   Information on impact.

A. *Records concerning impact.* Each user should maintain and have available for inspection records or other information which will disclose the impact which its tests and other selection procedures have upon employment opportunities of persons by identifiable race, sex, or ethnic group as set forth in subparagraph B below in order to determine compliance with these guidelines. Where there are large numbers of applicants and procedures are administered frequently, such information may be retained on a sample basis, provided that the sample is appropriate in terms of the applicant population and adequate in size.

B. *Applicable race, sex, and ethnic groups for recordkeeping.* The records called for by this section are to be maintained by sex, and the following races and ethnic groups: Blacks (Negroes), American Indians (including Alaskan Natives), Asians (including Pacific Islanders), Hispanic (including persons of Mexican, Puerto Rican, Cuban, Central or South American, or other Spanish origin or culture regardless of race), whites (Caucasians) other than Hispanic, and totals. The race, sex, and ethnic classifications called for by this section are consistent with the Equal Employment Opportunity Standard Form 100, Employer Information Report EEO-1 series of reports. The user should adopt safeguards to insure that the records required by this paragraph are used for appropriate purposes such as determining adverse impact, or (where required) for developing and monitoring affirmative action programs, and that such records are not used improperly. See sections 4E and 17(4), below.

C. *Evaluation of selection rates. The "bottom line."* If the information called for by sections 4A and B above shows that the total selection process for a job has an adverse impact, the individual components of the selection process should be evaluated for adverse impact. If this information shows that the total selection process does not have an adverse impact, the Federal enforcement agencies, in the exercise of their administrative and prosecutorial discretion, in usual circumstances, will not expect a user to evaluate the individual components for adverse impact, or to validate such individual components, and will not take enforcement action based upon adverse impact of any component of that process, including the separate parts of a multipart selection procedure or any separate procedure that is used as an alternative method of selection. However, in the following circumstances the Federal enforcement agencies will expect a user to evaluate the individual components for adverse impact and may, where appropriate, take enforcement action with respect to the individual components: (1) Where the selection procedure is a significant factor in the continuation of patterns of assignments of incumbent employees caused by prior discriminatory employment practices, (2) where the weight of court decisions or administrative interpretations hold that a specific procedure (such as height or weight requirements or no-arrest records) is not job related in the same or similar circumstances. In unusual circumstances, other than those listed in (1) and (2) above, the Federal enforcement agencies may request a user to evaluate the individual components for adverse impact and may, where appropriate, take enforcement action with respect to the individual component.

D. *Adverse impact and the "four-fifths rule."* A selection rate for any race, sex, or ethnic group which is less than four-fifths (4/5) (or eighty percent) of the rate for the group with the highest rate will generally be regarded by the Federal enforcement agencies as evidence of adverse impact, while a greater than four-fifths rate will generally not be regarded by Federal enforcement agencies as evidence of adverse impact. Smaller differences in selection rate may nevertheless constitute adverse impact, where they are significant in both statistical and practical terms or where a user's actions have discouraged applicants disproportionately on grounds of race, sex, or ethnic group. Greater differences in selection rate may not constitute adverse impact where the differences are based on small numbers and are not statistically significant, or where special recruiting or other programs cause the pool of minority or female candidates to be atypical of the normal pool of applicants from that group. Where the user's evidence concerning the impact of a selection procedure indicates adverse impact but is based upon numbers which are too small to be reliable, evidence concerning the impact of the procedure over a longer period of time and/or evidence concerning the impact which the selection procedure had when used in the same manner in similar circumstances elsewhere may be considered in determining adverse impact. Where the user has not maintained data on adverse impact as required by the documentation section of applicable guidelines, the Federal enforcement agencies may draw an inference of adverse impact of the selection process from the failure of the user to maintain such data, if the user has an underutilization of a group in the job category, as compared to the group's representation in the relevant labor market or, in the case of jobs filled from within, the applicable work force.

E. *Consideration of user's equal employment opportunity posture.* In carrying out their obligations, the Federal enforcement agencies will consider the general posture of the user with respect to equal employment opportunity for the job or group of jobs in question. Where a user has adopted an affirmative action program, the Federal enforcement agencies will consider the provisions of that program, including the goals and timetables which the user has adopted and the progress which the user has made in carrying out that program and in meeting the goals and timetables. While such affirmative action programs may in design and execution be race, color, sex, or ethnic conscious, selection procedures under such programs should be based upon the ability or relative ability to do the work.

(Approved by the Office of Management and Budget under control number 3046–0017)
(Pub. L. No. 96–511, 94 Stat. 2812 (44 U.S.C. 3501 et seq.))
[43 FR 38295, 38312, Aug. 25, 1978, as amended at 46 FR 63268, Dec. 31, 1981]

§ 1607.5   *General standards for validity studies.*

A. *Acceptable types of validity studies.* For the purposes of satisfying these guidelines, users may rely upon criterion-related validity studies, content validity studies or construct validity studies, in accordance with the standards set forth in the technical standards of these guidelines, section 14 below. New strategies for showing the validity of selection procedures will be evaluated as they become accepted by the psychological profession.

B. *Criterion-related, content, and construct validity.* Evidence of the validity of a test or other selection procedure by a criterion-related validity study should consist of empirical data demonstrating that the selection procedure is predictive of or significantly correlated with important elements of job performance. See section 14B below. Evidence of the validity of a test or other selection procedure by a content validity study should consist of data showing that the content of the selection procedure is representative of important aspects of performance on the job for which the candidates are to be evaluated. See 14C below. Evidence of the validity of a test or other selection procedure through a construct validity study should consist of data showing that the procedure measures the degree to which candidates have identifiable characteristics which have been determined to be important in successful performance in the job for which the candidates are to be evaluated. See section 14D below.

C. *Guidelines are consistent with professional standards.* The provisions of these guidelines relating to validation of selection procedures are intended to be consistent with generally accepted professional standards for evaluating standardized tests and other selection procedures, such as those described in the Standards for Educational and Psychological Tests prepared by a joint committee of the American Psychological Association, the American Educational Research Association, and the National Council on Measurement in Education (American Psychological Association, Washington, D.C., 1974) (hereinafter "A.P.A. Standards") and standard textbooks and journals in the field of personnel selection.

D. *Need for documentation of validity.* For any selection procedure which is part of a selection process which has an adverse impact and which selection procedure has an adverse impact, each user should maintain and have available such documentation as is described in section 15 below.

E. *Accuracy and standardization.* Validity studies should be carried out under conditions which assure insofar as possible the adequacy and accuracy of the research and the report. Selection procedures should be administered and scored under standardized conditions.

F. *Caution against selection on basis of knowledges, skills, or ability learned in brief orientation period.* In general, users should avoid making employment decisions on the basis of measures of knowledges, skills, or abilities which are normally learned in a brief orientation period, and which have an adverse impact.

G. *Method of use of selection procedures.* The evidence of both the validity and utility of a selection procedure should support the method the user chooses for operational use of the procedure, if that method of use has a greater adverse impact than another method of use. Evidence which may be sufficient to support the use of a selection procedure on a pass/fail (screening) basis may be insufficient to support the use of the same procedure on a ranking basis under these guidelines. Thus, if a user decides to use a selection procedure on a ranking basis, and that method of use has a greater adverse impact than use on an appropriate pass/fail basis (see section 5H below), the user should have sufficient evidence of validity and utility to support the use on a ranking basis. See sections 3B, 14B (5) and (6), and 14C (8) and (9).

H. *Cutoff scores.* Where cutoff scores are used, they should normally be set so as to be reasonable and consistent with normal expectations of acceptable proficiency within the work force. Where applicants are ranked on the basis of properly validated selection procedures and those applicants scoring below a higher cutoff score than appropriate in light of such expectations have little or no chance of being selected for employment, the higher cutoff score may be appropriate, but the degree of adverse impact should be considered.

I. *Use of selection procedures for higher level jobs.* If job progression structures are so established that employees will probably, within a reasonable period of time and in a majority of cases, progress to a higher level, it may be considered that the applicants are being evaluated for a job or jobs at the higher level. However, where job progression is not so nearly automatic, or the time span is such that higher level jobs or employees' potential may be expected to change in significant ways, it should be considered that applicants are being evaluated for a job at or near the entry level. A "reasonable period of time" will vary for different jobs and employment situations but will seldom be more than 5 years. Use of selection procedures to evaluate applicants for a higher level job would not be appropriate:

(1) If the majority of those remaining employed do not progress to the higher level job;

(2) If there is a reason to doubt that the higher level job will continue to require essentially similar skills during the progression period; or

(3) If the selection procedures measure knowledges, skills, or abilities required for advancement which would be expected to develop principally from the training or experience on the job.

J. *Interim use of selection procedures.* Users may continue the use of a selection procedure which is not at the moment fully supported by the required evidence of validity, provided: (1) The user has available substantial evidence of validity, and (2) the user has in progress, when technically feasible, a study which is designed to produce the additional evidence required by these guidelines within a reasonable time. If such a study is not technically feasible, see section 6B. If the study does not demonstrate validity, this provision of these guidelines for interim use shall not constitute a defense in any action, nor shall it relieve the user of any obligations arising under Federal law.

K. *Review of validity studies for currency.* Whenever validity has been shown in accord with these guidelines for the use of a particular selection procedure for a job or group of jobs, additional studies need not be performed until such time as the validity study is subject to review as provided in section 3B above. There are no absolutes in the area of determining the currency of a validity study. All circumstances concerning the study, including the validation strategy used, and changes in the relevant labor market and the job should be considered in the determination of when a validity study is outdated.

§ 1607.6   Use of selection procedures which have not been validated.

A. *Use of alternate selection procedures to eliminate adverse impact.* A user may choose to utilize alternative selection procedures in order to eliminate adverse impact or as part of an affirmative action program. See section 13 below. Such alternative procedures should eliminate the adverse impact in the total selection process, should be lawful and should be as job related as possible.

B. *Where validity studies cannot or need not be performed.* There are circumstances in which a user cannot or need not utilize the validation techniques contemplated by these guidelines. In such circumstances, the user should utilize selection procedures which are as job related as possible and which will minimize or eliminate adverse impact, as set forth below.

(1) *Where informal or unscored procedures are used.* When an informal or unscored selection procedure which has an adverse impact is utilized, the user should eliminate the adverse impact, or modify the procedure to one which is a formal, scored or quantified measure or combination of measures and then validate the procedure in accord with these guidelines, or otherwise justify continued use of the procedure in accord with Federal law.

(2) *Where formal and scored procedures are used.* When a formal and scored selection procedure is used which has an adverse impact, the validation techniques contemplated by these guidelines usually should be followed if technically feasible. Where the user cannot or need not follow the validation techniques anticipated by these guidelines, the user should either modify the procedure to eliminate adverse impact or otherwise justify continued use of the procedure in accord with Federal law.

§ 1607.7   Use of other validity studies.

A. *Validity studies not conducted by the user.* Users may, under certain circumstances, support the use of selection procedures by validity studies conducted by other users or conducted by test publishers or distributors and described in test manuals. While publishers of selection procedures have a professional obligation to provide evidence of validity which meets generally accepted professional standards (see section 5C above), users are cautioned that they are responsible for compliance with these guidelines. Accordingly, users seeking to obtain selection procedures from publishers and distributors should be careful to determine that, in the event the user becomes subject to the validity requirements of these guidelines, the necessary information to support validity has been determined and will be made available to the user.

B. *Use of criterion-related validity evidence from other sources.* Criterion-related validity studies conducted by one test user, or described in test manuals and the professional literature, will be considered acceptable for use by another user when the following requirements are met:

(1) *Validity evidence.* Evidence from the available studies meeting the standards of section 14B below clearly demonstrates that the selection procedure is valid;

(2) *Job similarity.* The incumbents in the user's job and the incumbents in the job or group of jobs on which the validity study was conducted perform substantially the same major work behaviors, as shown by appropriate job analyses both on the job or group of jobs on which the validity study was performed and on the job for which the selection procedure is to be used; and

(3) *Fairness evidence.* The studies include a study of test fairness for each race, sex, and ethnic group which constitutes a significant factor in the borrowing user's relevant labor market for the job or jobs in question. If the studies under consideration satisfy (1) and (2) above but do not contain an investigation of test fairness, and it is not technically feasible for the borrowing user to conduct an internal study of test fairness, the borrowing user may utilize the study until studies conducted elsewhere meeting the requirements of these guidelines show test unfairness, or until such time as it becomes technically feasible to conduct an internal study of test fairness and the results of that study can be acted upon. Users obtaining selection procedures from publishers should consider, as one factor in the decision to purchase a particular selection procedure, the availability of evidence concerning test fairness.

C. *Validity evidence from multiunit study.* If validity evidence from a study covering more than one unit within an organization statisfies the requirements of section 14B below, evidence of validity specific to each unit will not be required unless there are variables which are likely to affect validity significantly.

D. *Other significant variables.* If there are variables in the other studies which are likely to affect validity significantly, the user may not rely upon such studies, but will be expected either to conduct an internal validity study or to comply with section 6 above.

§ 1607.8   Cooperative studies.

A. *Encouragement of cooperative studies.* The agencies issuing these guidelines encourage employers, labor organizations, and employment agencies to cooperate in research, development, search for lawful alternatives, and validity studies in order to achieve procedures which are consistent with these guidelines.

B. *Standards for use of cooperative studies.* If validity evidence from a cooperative study satisfies the requirements of section 14 below, evidence of validity specific to each user will not be required unless there are variables in the user's situation which are likely to affect validity significantly.

§ 1607.9   No assumption of validity.

A. *Unacceptable substitutes for evidence of validity.* Under no circumstances will the general reputation of a test or other selection procedures, its author or its publisher, or casual reports of it's validity be accepted in lieu of evidence of validity. Specifically ruled out are: assumptions of validity based on a procedure's name or descriptive labels; all forms of promotional literature; data bearing on the frequency of a procedure's usage; testimonial statements and credentials of sellers, users, or consultants; and other nonempirical or anecdotal accounts of selection practices or selection outcomes.

B. *Encouragement of professional supervision.* Professional supervision of selection activities is encouraged but is not a substitute for documented evidence of validity. The enforcement agencies will take into account the fact that a thorough job analysis was conducted and that careful development and use of a selection procedure in accordance with professional standards enhance the probability that the selection procedure is valid for the job.

§ 1607.10   Employment agencies and employment services.

A. *Where selection procedures are devised by agency.* An employment agency, including private employment agencies and State employment agencies, which agrees to a request by an employer or labor organization to device and utilize a selection procedure should follow the standards in these guidelines for determining adverse impact. If adverse impact exists the agency should comply with these guidelines. An employment agency is not relieved of its obligation herein because the user did not request such validation or has requested the use of some lesser standard of validation than is provided in these guidelines. The use of an employment agency does not relieve an employer or labor organization or other user of its responsibilities under Federal law to provide equal employment opportunity or its obligations as a user under these guidelines.

B. *Where selection procedures are devised elsewhere.* Where an employment agency or service is requested to administer a selection procedure which has been devised elsewhere and to make referrals pursuant to the results, the employment agency or service should maintain and have available evidence of the impact of the selection and referral procedures which it administers. If adverse impact results the agency or service should comply with these guidelines. If the agency or service seeks to comply with these guidelines by reliance upon validity studies or other data in the possession of the employer, it should obtain and have available such information.

§ 1607.11   Disparate treatment.

The principles of disparate or unequal treatment must be distinguished from the concepts of validation. A selection procedure—even though validated against job performance in accordance with these guidelines—cannot be imposed upon members of a race, sex, or ethnic group where other employees, applicants, or members have not been subjected to that standard. Disparate treatment occurs where members of a race, sex, or ethnic group have been denied the same employment, promotion, membership, or other employment opportunities as have been available to other employees or applicants. Those employees or applicants who have been denied equal treatment, because of prior discriminatory practices or policies, must at least be afforded the same opportunities as had existed for other employees or applicants during the period of discrimination. Thus, the persons who were in the class of persons discriminated against during the period the user followed the discriminatory practices should be allowed the opportunity to qualify under less stringent selection procedures previously followed, unless the user demonstrates that the increased standards are required by business necessity. This section does not prohibit a user who has not previously followed merit standards from adopting merit standards which are in compliance with these guidelines; nor does it preclude a user who has previously used invalid or unvalidated selection procedures from developing and using procedures which are in accord with these guidelines.

§ 1607.12   Retesting of applicants.

Users should provide a reasonable opportunity for retesting and reconsideration. Where examinations are administered periodically with public notice, such reasonable opportunity exists, unless persons who have previously been tested are precluded from retesting. The user may however take reasonable steps to preserve the security of its procedures.

§ 1607.13   Affirmative action.

A. Affirmative action obligations. The use of selection procedures which have been validated pursuant to these guidelines does not relieve users of any obligations they may have to undertake affirmative action to assure equal employment opportunity. Nothing in these guidelines is intended to preclude the use of lawful selection procedures which assist in remedying the effects of prior discriminatory practices, or the achievement of affirmative action objectives.

B. *Encouragement of voluntary affirmative action programs.* These guidelines are also intended to encourage the adoption and implementation of voluntary affirmative action programs by users who have no obligation under Federal law to adopt them; but are not intended to impose any new obligations in that regard. The agencies issuing and endorsing these guidelines endorse for all private employers and reaffirm for all governmental employers the Equal Employment Opportunity Coordinating Council's "Policy Statement on Affirmative Action Programs for State and Local Government Agencies" (41 FR 38814, September 13, 1976). That policy statement is attached hereto as appendix, section 17.

TECHNICAL STANDARDS

§ 1607.14   Technical standards for validity studies.

The following minimum standards, as applicable, should be met in conducting a validity study. Nothing in these guidelines is intended to preclude the development and use of other professionally acceptable techniques with respect to validation of selection procedures. Where it is not technically feasible for a user to conduct a validity study, the user has the obligation otherwise to comply with these guidelines. See sections 6 and 7 above.

A. *Validity studies should be based on review of information about the job.* Any validity study should be based upon a review of information about the job for which the selection procedure is to be used. The review should include a job analysis except as provided in section 14B(3) below with respect to criterion-related validity. Any method of job analysis may be used if it provides the information required for the specific validation strategy used.

B. *Technical standards for criterion-related validity studies.* (1) *Technical feasibility.* Users choosing to validate a selection procedure by a criterion-related validity strategy should determine whether it is technically feasible (as defined in section 16) to conduct such a study in the particular employment context. The determination of the number of persons necessary to permit the conduct of a meaningful criterion-related study should be made by the user on the basis of all relevant information concerning the selection procedure, the potential sample and the employment situation. Where appropriate, jobs with substantially the same major work behaviors may be grouped together for validity studies, in order to obtain an adequate sample. These guidelines do not require a user to hire or promote persons for the purpose of making it possible to conduct a criterion-related study.

(2) *Analysis of the job.* There should be a review of job information to determine measures of work behavior(s) or performance that are relevant to the job or group of jobs in question. These measures or criteria are relevant to the extent that they represent critical or important job duties, work behaviors or work outcomes as developed from the review of job information. The possibility of bias should be considered both in selection of the criterion measures and their application. In view of the possibility of bias in subjective evaluations, supervisory rating techniques and instructions to raters should be carefully developed. All criterion measures and the methods for gathering data need to be examined for freedom from factors which would unfairly alter scores of members of any group. The relevance of criteria and their freedom from bias are of particular concern when there are significant differences in measures of job performance for different groups.

(3) *Criterion measures.* Proper safeguards should be taken to insure that scores on selection procedures do not enter into any judgments of employee adequacy that are to be used as criterion measures. Whatever criteria are used should represent important or critical work behavior(s) or work outcomes. Certain criteria may be used without a full job analysis if the user can show the importance of the criteria to the particular employment context. These criteria include but are not limited to production rate, error rate, tardiness, absenteeism, and length of service. A standardized rating of overall work performance may be used where a study of the job shows that it is an appropriate criterion. Where performance in training is used as a criterion, success in training should be properly measured and the relevance of the training should be shown either through a comparison of the content of the training program with the critical or important work behavior(s) of the job(s), or through a demonstration of the relationship between measures of performance in training and measures of job performance. Measures of relative success in training include but are not limited to instructor evaluations, performance samples, or tests. Criterion measures consisting of paper and pencil tests will be closely reviewed for job relevance.

(4) *Representativeness of the sample.* Whether the study is predictive or concurrent, the sample subjects should insofar as feasible be representative of the candidates normally available in the relevant labor market for the job or group of jobs in question, and should insofar as feasible include the races, sexes, and ethnic groups normally available in the relevant job market. In determining the representativeness of the sample in a concurrent validity study, the user should take into account the extent to which the specific knowledges or skills which are the primary focus of the test are those which employees learn on the job.

Where samples are combined or compared, attention should be given to see that such samples are comparable in terms of the actual job they perform, the length of time on the job where time on the job is likely to affect performance, and other relevant factors likely to affect validity differences; or that these factors are included in the design of the study and their effects identified.

(5) *Statistical relationships.* The degree of relationship between selection procedure scores and criterion measures should be examined and computed, using professionally acceptable statistical procedures. Generally, a selection procedure is considered related to the criterion, for the purposes of these guidelines, when the

relationship between performance on the procedure and performance on the criterion measure is statistically significant at the 0.05 level of significance, which means that it is sufficiently high as to have a probability of no more than one (1) in twenty (20) to have occurred by chance. Absence of a statistically significant relationship between a selection procedure and job performance should not necessarily discourage other investigations of the validity of that selection procedure.

(6) *Operational use of selection procedures.* Users should evaluate each selection procedure to assure that it is appropriate for operational use, including establishment of cutoff scores or rank ordering. Generally, if other factors reman the same, the greater the magnitude of the relationship (e.g., correlation coefficent) between performance on a selection procedure and one or more criteria of performance on the job, and the greater the importance and number of aspects of job performance covered by the criteria, the more likely it is that the procedure will be appropriate for use. Reliance upon a selection procedure which is significantly related to a criterion measure, but which is based upon a study involving a large number of subjects and has a low correlation coefficient will be subject to close review if it has a large adverse impact. Sole reliance upon a single selection instrument which is related to only one of many job duties or aspects of job performance will also be subject to close review. The appropriateness of a selection procedure is best evaluated in each particular situation and there are no minimum correlation coefficients applicable to all employment situations. In determining whether a selection procedure is appropriate for operational use the following considerations should also be taken into account: The degree of adverse impact of the procedure, the availability of other selection procedures of greater or substantially equal validity.

(7) *Overstatement of validity findings.* Users should avoid reliance upon techniques which tend to overestimate validity findings as a result of capitalization on chance unless an appropriate safeguard is taken. Reliance upon a few selection procedures or criteria of successful job performance when many selection procedures or criteria of performance have been studied, or the use of optimal statistical weights for selection procedures computed in one sample, are techniques which tend to inflate validity estimates as a result of chance. Use of a large sample is one safeguard: cross-validation is another.

(8) *Fairness.* This section generally calls for studies of unfairness where technically feasible. The concept of fairness or unfairness of selection procedures is a developing concept. In addition, fairness studies generally require substantial numbers of employees in the job or group of jobs being studied. For these reasons, the Federal enforcement agencies recognize that the obligation to conduct studies of fairness imposed by the guidelines generally will be upon users or groups of users with a large number of persons in a job class, or test developers; and that small users utilizing their own selection procedures will generally not be obligated to conduct such studies because it will be technically infeasible for them to do so.

(a) *Unfairness defined.* When members of one race, sex, or ethnic group characteristically obtain lower scores on a selection procedure than members of another group, and the differences in scores are not reflected in differences in a measure of job performance, use of the selection procedure may unfairly deny opportunities to members of the group that obtains the lower scores.

(b) *Investigation of fairness.* Where a selection procedure results in an adverse impact on a race, sex, or ethnic group identified in accordance with the classifications set forth in section 4 above and that group is a significant factor in the relevant labor market, the user generally should investigate the possible existence of unfairness for that group if it is technically feasible to do so. The greater the severity of the adverse impact on a group, the greater the need to investigate the possible existence of unfairness. Where the weight of evidence from other studies shows that the selection procedure predicts fairly for the group in question and for the same or similar jobs, such evidence may be relied on in connection with the selection procedure at issue.

(c) *General considerations in fairness investigations.* Users conducting a study of fairness should review the A.P.A. Standards regarding investigation of possible bias in testing. An investigation of fairness of a selection procedure depends on both evidence of validity and the manner in which the selection procedure is to be used in a particular employment context. Fairness of a selection procedure cannot necessarily be specified in advance without investigating these factors. Investigation of fairness of a selection procedure in samples where the range of scores on selection procedures or criterion measures is severely restricted for any subgroup sample (as compared to other subgroup samples) may produce misleading evidence of unfairness. That factor should accordingly be taken into account in conducting such studies and before reliance is placed on the results.

(d) *When unfairness is shown.* If unfairness is demonstrated through a showing that members of a particular group perform better or poorer on the job than their scores on the selection procedure would indicate through comparison with how members of other groups perform, the user may either revise or replace the selection instrument in accordance with these guidelines, or may continue to use the selection instrument operationally with appropriate revisions in its use to assure compatibility between the probability of successful job performance and the probability of being selected.

(e) *Technical feasibility of fairness studies.* In addition to the general conditions needed for technical feasibility for the conduct of a criterion-related study (see section 16, below) an investigation of fairness requires the following:

(i) An adequate sample of persons in each group available for the study to achieve findings of statistical significance. Guidelines do not require a user to hire or promote persons on the basis of group classifications for the purpose of making it possible to conduct a study of fairness; but the user has the obligation otherwise to comply with these guidelines.

(ii) The samples for each group should be comparable in terms of the actual job they perform, length of time on the job where time on the job is likely to affect performance, and other relevant factors likely to affect validity differences; or such factors should be included in the design of the study and their effects identified.

(f) *Continued use of selection procedures when fairness studies not feasible.* If a study of fairness should otherwise be performed, but is not technically feasible, a selection procedure may be used which has otherwise met the validity standards of these guidelines, unless the technical infeasibility resulted from discriminatory employment practices which are demonstrated by facts other than past failure to conform with requirements for validation of selection procedures. However, when it becomes technically feasible for the user to perform a study of fairness and such a study is otherwise called for, the user should conduct the study of fairness.

C. *Technical standards for content validity studies*—(1) *Appropriateness of content validity studies.* Users choosing to validate a selection procedure by a content validity strategy should determine whether it is appropriate to conduct such a study in the particular employment context. A selection procedure can be supported by a content validity strategy to the extent that it is a representative sample of the content of the job. Selection procedures which purport to measure knowledges, skills, or abilities may in certain circumstances be justified by content validity, although they may not be representative samples, if the knowledge, skill, or ability measured by the selection procedure can be operationally defined as provided in section 14C(4) below, and if that knowledge, skill, or ability is a necessary prerequisite to successful job performance.

A selection procedure based upon inferences about mental processes cannot be supported solely or primarily on the basis of content validity. Thus, a content strategy is not appropriate for demonstrating the validity of selection procedures which purport to measure traits or constructs, such as intelligence, aptitude, personality, commonsense, judgment, leadership, and spatial ability. Content validity is also not an appropriate strategy when the selection procedure involves knowledges, skills, or abilities which an employee will be expected to learn on the job.

(2) *Job analysis for content validity.* There should be a job analysis which includes an analysis of the important work behavior(s) required for successful performance and their relative importance and, if the behavior results in work product(s), an analysis of the work product(s). Any job analysis should focus on the work behavior(s) and the tasks associated with them. If work behavior(s) are not observable, the job analysis should identify and analyze those aspects of the behavior(s) that can be observed and the observed work products. The work behavior(s) selected for measurement should be critical work behavior(s) and/or important work behavior(s) constituting most of the job.

(3) *Development of selection procedures.* A selection procedure designed to measure the work behavior may be developed specifically from the job and job analysis in question, or may have been previously developed by the user, or by other users or by a test publisher.

(4) *Standards for demonstrating content validity.* To demonstrate the content validity of a selection procedure, a user should show that the behavior(s) demonstrated in the selection procedure are a representative sample of the behavior(s) of the job in question or that the selection procedure provides a representative sample of the work product of the job. In the case of a selection procedure measuring a knowledge, skill, or ability, the knowledge, skill, or ability being measured should be operationally defined. In the case of a selection procedure measuring a knowledge, the knowledge being measured should be operationally defined as that body of learned information which is used in and is a necessary prerequisite for observable aspects of work behavior of the job. In the case of skills or abilities, the skill or ability being measured should be operationally defined in terms of observable aspects of work behavior of the job. For any selection procedure measuring a knowledge, skill, or ability the user should show that (a) the selection procedure measures and is a representative sample of that knowledge, skill, or ability; and (b) that knowledge, skill, or ability is used in and is a necessary prerequisite to performance of critical or important work behavior(s). In addition, to be content valid, a selection procedure measuring a skill or ability should either closely approximate an observable work behavior, or its product should closely approximate an observable work product. If a test purports to sample a work behavior or to provide a sample of a work product, the manner and setting of the selection procedure and its level and complexity should closely approximate the work situation. The closer the content and the context of the selection procedure are to work samples or work behaviors, the stronger is the basis for showing content validity. As the content of the selection procedure less resembles a work behavior, or the setting and manner

of the administration of the selection procedure less resemble the work situation, or the result less resembles a work product, the less likely the selection procedure is to be content valid, and the greater the need for other evidence of validity.

(5) *Reliability.* The reliability of selection procedures justified on the basis of content validity should be a matter of concern to the user. Whenever it is feasible, appropriate statistical estimates should be made of the reliability of the selection procedure.

(6) *Prior training or experience.* A requirement for or evaluation of specific prior training or experience based on content validity, including a specification of level or amount of training or experience, should be justified on the basis of the relationship between the content of the training or experience and the content of the job for which the training or experience is to be required or evaluated. The critical consideration is the resemblance between the specific behaviors, products, knowledges, skills, or abilities in the experience or training and the specific behaviors, products, knowledges, skills, or abilities required on the job, whether or not there is close resemblance between the experience or training as a whole and the job as a whole.

(7) *Content validity of training success.* Where a measure of success in a training program is used as a selection procedure and the content of a training program is justified on the basis of content validity, the use should be justified on the relationship between the content of the training program and the content of the job.

(8) *Operational use.* A selection procedure which is supported on the basis of content validity may be used for a job if it represents a critical work behavior (i.e., a behavior which is necessary for performance of the job) or work behaviors which constitute most of the important parts of the job.

(9) *Ranking based on content validity studies.* If a user can show, by a job analysis or otherwise, that a higher score on a content valid selection procedure is likely to result in better job performance, the results may be used to rank persons who score above minimum levels. Where a selection procedure supported solely or primarily by content validity is used to rank job candidates, the selection procedure should measure those aspects of performance which differentiate among levels of job performance.

D. *Technical standards for construct validity studies—* (1) *Appropriateness of construct validity studies.* Construct validity is a more complex strategy than either criterion-related or content validity. Construct validation is a relatively new and developing procedure in the employment field, and there is at present a lack of substantial literature extending the concept to employment practices. The user should be aware that the effort to obtain sufficient empirical support for construct validity is both an extensive and arduous effort involving a series of research studies, which include criterion related validity studies and which may include content validity studies. Users choosing to justify use of a selection procedure by this strategy should therefore take particular care to assure that the validity study meets the standards set forth below.

(2) *Job analysis for construct validity studies.* There should be a job analysis. This job analysis should show the work behavior(s) required for successful performance of the job, or the groups of jobs being studied, the critical or important work behavior(s) in the job or group of jobs being studied, and an identification of the construct(s) believed to underlie successful performance of these critical or important work behaviors in the job or jobs in question. Each construct should be named and defined, so as to distinguish it from other constructs. If a group of jobs is being studied the jobs should have in common one or more critical or important work behaviors at a comparable level of complexity.

(3) *Relationship to the job.* A selection procedure should then be identified or

developed which measures the construct identified in accord with subparagraph (2) above. The user should show by empirical evidence that the selection procedure is validly related to the construct and that the construct is validly related to the performance of critical or important work behavior(s). The relationship between the construct as measured by the selection procedure and the related work behavior(s) should be supported by empirical evidence from one or more criterion-related studies involving the job or jobs in question which satisfy the provisions of section 14B above.

(4) *Use of construct validity study without new criterion-related evidence*—(a) *Standards for use.* Until such time as professional literature provides more guidance on the use of construct validity in employment situations, the Federal agencies will accept a claim of construct validity without a criterion-related study which satisfies section 14B above only when the selection procedure has been used elsewhere in a situation in which a criterion-related study has been conducted and the use of a criterion-related validity study in this context meets the standards for transportability of criterion-related validity studies as set forth above in section 7. However, if a study pertains to a number of jobs having common critical or important work behaviors at a comparable level of complexity, and the evidence satisfies subparagraphs 14B (2) and (3) above for those jobs with criterion-related validity evidence for those jobs, the selection procedure may be used for all the jobs to which the study pertains. If construct validity is to be generalized to other jobs or groups of jobs not in the group studied, the Federal enforcement agencies will expect at a minimum additional empirical research evidence meeting the standards of subparagraphs section 14B (2) and (3) above for the additional jobs or groups of jobs.

(b) *Determination of common work behaviors.* In determining whether two or more jobs have one or more work behavior(s) in common, the user should compare the observed work behavior(s) in each of the jobs and should compare the observed work product(s) in each of the jobs. If neither the observed work behavior(s) in each of the jobs nor the observed work product(s) in each of the jobs are the same, the Federal enforcement agencies will presume that the work behavior(s) in each job are different. If the work behaviors are not observable, then evidence of similarity of work products and any other relevant research evidence will be considered in determining whether the work behavior(s) in the two jobs are the same.

DOCUMENTATION OF IMPACT AND VALIDITY EVIDENCE

§ 1607.15   Documentation of impact and validity evidence.

A. *Required information.* Users of selection procedures other than those users complying with section 15A(1) below should maintain and have available for each job information on adverse impact of the selection process for that job and, where it is determined a selection process has an adverse impact, evidence of validity as set forth below.

(1) *Simplified recordkeeping for users with less than 100 employees.* In order to minimize recordkeeping burdens on employers who employ one hundred (100) or fewer employees, and other users not required to file EEO–1, et seq., reports, such users may satisfy the requirements of this section 15 if they maintain and have available records showing, for each year:

(a) The number of persons hired, promoted, and terminated for each job, by sex, and where appropriate by race and national origin;

(b) The number of applicants for hire and promotion by sex and where appropriate by race and national origin; and

(c) The selection procedures utilized (either standardized or not standardized).

These records should be maintained for each race or national origin group (see section 4 above) constituting more than two percent (2%) of the labor force in the relevant labor area. However, it is not necessary to maintain records by race and/or national origin (see § 4 above) if one race or national origin group in the relevant labor area constitutes more than ninety-eight percent (98%) of the labor force in the area. If the user has reason to believe that a selection procedure has an adverse impact, the user should maintain any available evidence of validity for that procedure (see sections 7A and 8).

(2) *Information on impact*—(a) *Collection of information on impact.* Users of selection procedures other than those complying with section 15A(1) above should maintain and have available for each job records or other information showing whether the total selection process for that job has an adverse impact on any of the groups for which records are called for by sections 4B above. Adverse impact determinations should be made at least annually for each such group which constitutes at least 2 percent of the labor force in the relevant labor area or 2 percent of the applicable workforce. Where a total selection process for a job has an adverse impact, the user should maintain and have available records or other information showing which components have an adverse impact. Where the total selection process for a job does not have an adverse impact, information need not be maintained for individual components except in circumstances set forth in subsection 15A(2)(b) below. If the determination of adverse impact is made using a procedure other than the "four-fifths rule," as defined in the first sentence of section 4D above, a justification, consistent with section 4D above, for the procedure used to determine adverse impact should be available.

(b) *When adverse impact has been eliminated in the total selection process.* Whenever the total selection process for a particular job has had an adverse impact, as defined in section 4 above, in any year, but no longer has an adverse impact, the user should maintain and have available the information on individual components of the selection process required in the preceding paragraph for the period in which there was adverse impact. In addition, the user should continue to collect such information for at least two (2) years after the adverse impact has been eliminated.

(c) *When data insufficient to determine impact.* Where there has been an insufficient number of selections to determine whether there is an adverse impact of the total selection process for a particular job, the user should continue to collect, maintain and have available the information on individual components of the selection process required in section 15(A)(2)(a) above until the information is sufficient to determine that the overall selection process does not have an adverse impact as defined in section 4 above, or until the job has changed substantially.

(3) *Documentation of validity evidence.*—(a) *types of evidence.* Where a total selection process has an adverse impact (see section 4 above) the user should maintain and have available for each component of that process which has an adverse impact, one or more of the following types of documentation evidence:

(i) Documentation evidence showing criterion-related validity of the selection procedure (see section 15B, below).

(ii) Documentation evidence showing content validity of the selection procedure (see section 15C, below).

(iii) Documentation evidence showing construct validity of the selection procedure (see section 15D, below).

(iv) Documentation evidence from other studies showing validity of the selection procedure in the user's facility (see section 15E, below).

(v) Documentation evidence showing why a validity study cannot or need not be performed and why continued use of the procedure is consistent with Federal law.

(b) *Form of report.* This evidence should be compiled in a reasonably complete and organized manner to permit direct evaluation of the validity of the selection procedure. Previously written employer or consultant reports of validity, or reports describing validity studies completed before the issuance of these guidelines are acceptable if they are complete in regard to the documentation requirements contained in this section, or if they satisfied requirements of guidelines which were in effect when the validity study was completed. If they are not complete, the required additional documentation should be appended. If necessary information is not available the report of the validity study may still be used as documentation, but its adequacy will be evaluated in terms of compliance with the requirements of these guidelines.

(c) *Completeness.* In the event that evidence of validity is reviewed by an enforcement agency, the validation reports completed after the effective date of these guidelines are expected to contain the information set forth below. Evidence denoted by use of the word "(Essential)" is considered critical. If information denoted essential is not included, the report will be considered incomplete unless the user affirmatively demonstrates either its unavailability due to circumstances beyond the user's control or special circumstances of the user's study which make the information irrelevant. Evidence not so denoted is desirable but its absence will not be a basis for considering a report incomplete. The user should maintain and have available the information called for under the heading "Source Data" in sections 15B(11) and 15D(11). While it is a necessary part of the study, it need not be submitted with the report. All statistical results should be organized and presented in tabular or graphic form to the extent feasible.

B. *Criterion-related validity studies.* Reports of criterion-related validity for a selection procedure should include the following information:

(1) *User(s), location(s), and date(s) of study.* Dates and location(s) of the job analysis or review of job information, the date(s) and location(s) of the administration of the selection procedures and collection of criterion data, and the time between collection of data on selection procedures and criterion measures should be provided (Essential). If the study was conducted at several locations, the address of each location, including city and State, should be shown.

(2) *Problem and setting.* An explicit definition of the purpose(s) of the study and the circumstances in which the study was conducted should be provided. A description of existing selection procedures and cutoff scores, if any, should be provided.

(3) *Job analysis or review of job information.* A description of the procedure used to analyze the job or group of jobs, or to review the job information should be provided (Essential). Where a review of job information results in criteria which may be used without a full job analysis (see section 14B(3)), the basis for the selection of these criteria should be reported (Essential). Where a job analysis is required a complete

description of the work behavior(s) or work outcome(s), and measures of their criticality or importance should be provided (Essential). The report should describe the basis on which the behavior(s) or outcome(s) were determined to be critical or important, such as the proportion of time spent on the respective behaviors, their level of difficulty, their frequency of performance, the consequences of error, or other appropriate factors (Essential). Where two or more jobs are grouped for a validity study, the information called for in this subsection should be provided for each of the jobs, and the justification for the grouping (see section 14B(1)) should be provided (Essential).

(4) *Job titles and codes.* It is desirable to provide the user's job title(s) for the job(s) in question and the corresponding job title(s) and code(s) from U.S. Employment Service's Dictionary of Occupational Titles.

(5) *Criterion measures.* The bases for the selection of the criterion measures should be provided, together with references to the evidence considered in making the selection of criterion measures (essential). A full description of all criteria on which data were collected and means by which they were observed, recorded, evaluated, and quantified, should be provided (essential). If rating techniques are used as criterion measures, the appraisal form(s) and instructions to the rater(s) should be included as part of the validation evidence, or should be explicitly described and available (essential). All steps taken to insure that criterion measures are free from factors which would unfairly alter the scores of members of any group should be described (essential).

(6) *Sample description.* A description of how the research sample was identified and selected should be included (essential). The race, sex, and ethnic composition of the sample, including those groups set forth in section 4A above, should be described (essential). This description should include the size of each subgroup (essential). A description of how the research sample compares with the relevant labor market or work force, the method by which the relevant labor market or work force was defined, and a discussion of the likely effects on validity of differences between the sample and the relevant labor market or work force, are also desirable. Descriptions of educational levels, length of service, and age are also desirable.

(7) *Description of selection procedures.* Any measure, combination of measures, or procedure studied should be completely and explicitly described or attached (essential). If commercially available selection procedures are studied, they should be described by title, form, and publisher (essential). Reports of reliability estimates and how they were established are desirable.

(8) *Techniques and results.* Methods used in analyzing data should be described (essential). Measures of central tendency (e.g., means) and measures of dispersion (e.g., standard deviations and ranges) for all selection procedures and all criteria should be reported for each race, sex, and ethnic group which constitutes a significant factor in the relevant labor market (essential). The magnitude and direction of all relationships between selection procedures and criterion measures investigated should be reported for each relevant race, sex, and ethnic group and for the total group (essential). Where groups are too small to obtain reliable evidence of the magnitude of the relationship, need not be reported separately. Statements regarding the statistical significance of results should be made (essential). Any statistical adjustments, such as for less then perfect reliability or for restriction of score range in the selection procedure or criterion should be described and explained; and uncorrected correlation coefficients should also be shown (essential). Where the statistical technique catego-

rizes continuous data, such as biserial correlation and the phi coefficient, the categories and the bases on which they were determined should be described and explained (essential). Studies of test fairness should be included where called for by the requirements of section 14B(8) (essential). These studies should include the rationale by which a selection procedure was determined to be fair to the group(s) in question. Where test fairness or unfairness has been demonstrated on the basis of other studies, a bibliography of the relevant studies should be included (essential). If the bibliography includes unpublished studies, copies of these studies, or adequate abstracts or summaries, should be attached (essential). Where revisions have been made in a selection procedure to assure compatability between successful job performance and the probability of being selected, the studies underlying such revisions should be included (essential). All statistical results should be organized and presented by relevant race, sex, and ethnic group (essential).

(9) *Alternative procedures investigated.* The selection procedures investigated and available evidence of their impact should be identified (essential). The scope, method, and findings of the investigation, and the conclusions reached in light of the findings, should be fully described (essential).

(10) *Uses and applications.* The methods considered for use of the selection procedure (e.g., as a screening device with a cutoff score, for grouping or ranking, or combined with other procedures in a battery) and available evidence of their impact should be described (essential). This description should include the rationale for choosing the method for operational use, and the evidence of the validity and utility of the procedure as it is to be used (essential). The purpose for which the procedure is to be used (e.g., hiring, transfer, promotion) should be described (essential). If weights are assigned to different parts of the selection procedure, these weights and the validity of the weighted composite should be reported (essential). If the selection procedure is used with a cutoff score, the user should describe the way in which normal expectations of proficiency within the work force were determined and the way in which the cutoff score was determined (essential).

(11) *Source data.* Each user should maintain records showing all pertinent information about individual sample members and raters where they are used, in studies involving the validation of selection procedures. These records should be made available upon request of a compliance agency. In the case of individual sample members these data should include scores on the selection procedure(s), scores on criterion measures, age, sex, race, or ethnic group status, and experience on the specific job on which the validation study was conducted, and may also include such things as education, training, and prior job experience, but should not include names and social security numbers. Records should be maintained which show the ratings given to each sample member by each rater.

(12) *Contact person.* The name, mailing address, and telephone number of the person who may be contacted for further information about the validity study should be provided (essential).

(13) *Accuracy and completeness.* The report should describe the steps taken to assure the accuracy and completeness of the collection, analysis, and report of data and results.

C. *Content validity studies.* Reports of content validity for a selection procedure should include the following information:

(1) *User(s), location(s) and date(s) of study.* Dates and location(s) of the job analysis should be shown (essential).

(2) *Problem and setting.* An explicit definition of the purpose(s) of the study and the circumstances in which the study was conducted should be provided. A description of existing selection procedures and cutoff scores, if any, should be provided.

(3) *Job analysis—Content of the job.* A description of the method used to analyze the job should be provided (essential). The work behavior(s), the associated tasks, and, if the behavior results in a work product, the work products should be completely described (essential). Measures of criticality and/or importance of the work behavior(s) and the method of determining these measures should be provided (essential). Where the job analysis also identified the knowledges, skills, and abilities used in work behavior(s), an operational definition for each knowledge in terms of a body of learned information and for each skill and ability in terms of observable behaviors and outcomes, and the relationship between each knowledge, skill, or ability and each work behavior, as well as the method used to determine this relationship, should be provided (essential). The work situation should be described, including the setting in which work behavior(s) are performed, and where appropriate, the manner in which knowledges, skills, or abilities are used, and the complexity and difficulty of the knowledge, skill, or ability as used in the work behavior(s).

(4) *Selection procedure and its content.* Selection procedures, including those constructed by or for the user, specific training requirements, composites of selection procedures, and any other procedure supported by content validity, should be completely and explicitly described or attached (essential). If commercially available selection procedures are used, they should be described by title, form, and publisher (essential). The behaviors measured or sampled by the selection procedure should be explicitly described (essential). Where the selection procedure purports to measure a knowledge, skill, or ability, evidence that the selection procedure measures and is a representative sample of the knowledge, skill, or ability should be provided (essential).

(5) *Relationship between the selection procedure and the job.* The evidence demonstrating that the selection procedure is a representative work sample, a representative sample of the work behavior(s), or a representative sample of a knowledge, skill, or ability as used as a part of a work behavior and necessary for that behavior should be provided (essential). The user should identify the work behavior(s) which each item or part of the selection procedure is intended to sample or measure (essential). Where the selection procedure purports to sample a work behavior or to provide a sample of a work product, a comparison should be provided of the manner, setting, and the level of complexity of the selection procedure with those of the work situation (essential). If any steps were taken to reduce adverse impact on a race, sex, or ethnic group in the content of the procedure or in its administration, these steps should be described. Establishment of time limits, if any, and how these limits are related to the speed with which duties must be performed on the job, should be explained. Measures of central tend- ency (e.g., means) and measures of dispersion (e.g., standard deviations) and estimates of realibility should be reported for all selection procedures if available. Such reports should be made for relevant race, sex, and ethnic subgroups, at least on a statistically reliable sample basis.

(6) *Alternative procedures investigated.* The alternative selection procedures investigated and available evidence of their impact should be identified (essential). The

scope, method, and findings of the investigation, and the conclusions reached in light of the findings, should be fully described (essential).

(7) *Uses and applications.* The methods considered for use of the selection procedure (e.g., as a screening device with a cutoff score, for grouping or ranking, or combined with other procedures in a battery) and available evidence of their impact should be described (essential). This description should include the rationale for choosing the method for operational use, and the evidence of the validity and utility of the procedure as it is to be used (essential). The purpose for which the procedure is to be used (e.g., hiring, transfer, promotion) should be described (essential). If the selection procedure is used with a cutoff score, the user should describe the way in which normal expectations of proficiency within the work force were determined and the way in which the cutoff score was determined (essential). In addition, if the selection procedure is to be used for ranking, the user should specify the evidence showing that a higher score on the selection procedure is likely to result in better job performance.

(8) *Contact person.* The name, mailing address, and telephone number of the person who may be contacted for further information about the validity study should be provided (essential).

(9) *Accuracy and completeness.* The report should describe the steps taken to assure the accuracy and completeness of the collection, analysis, and report of data and results.

D. *Construct validity studies.* Reports of construct validity for a selection procedure should include the following information:

(1) *User(s), location(s), and date(s) of study.* Date(s) and location(s) of the job analysis and the gathering of other evidence called for by these guidelines should be provided (essential).

(2) *Problem and setting.* An explicit definition of the purpose(s) of the study and the circumstances in which the study was conducted should be provided. A description of existing selection procedures and cutoff scores, if any, should be provided.

(3) *Construct definition.* A clear definition of the construct(s) which are believed to underlie successful performance of the critical or important work behavior(s) should be provided (essential). This definition should include the levels of construct performance relevant to the job(s) for which the selection procedure is to be used (essential). There should be a summary of the position of the construction, the psychological literature, or in the absence of such a position, a description of the way in which the definition and measurement of the construct was developed and the psychological theory underlying it (essential). Any quantitative data which identify or define the job constructs, such as factor analyses, should be provided (essential).

(4) *Job analysis.* A description of the method used to analyze the job should be provided (essential). A complete description of the work behavior(s) and, to the extent appropriate, work outcomes and measures of their criticality and/or importance should be provided (essential). The report should also describe the basis on which the behavior(s) or outcomes were determined to be important, such as their level of difficulty, their frequency of performance, the consequences of error or other appropriate factors (essential). Where jobs are grouped or compared for the purposes of generalizing validity evidence, the work behavior(s) and work product(s) for each of the jobs should be described, and conclusions concerning the similarity of the jobs in terms of observable work behaviors or work products should be made (essential).

(5) *Job titles and codes.* It is desirable to provide the selection procedure user's job title(s) for the job(s) in question and the corresponding job title(s) and code(s) from the United States Employment Service's dictionary of occupational titles.

(6) *Selection procedure.* The selection procedure used as a measure of the construct should be completely and explicitly described or attached (essential). If commercially available selection procedures are used, they should be identified by title, form and publisher (essential). The research evidence of the relationship between the selection procedure and the construct, such as factor structure, should be included (essential). Measures of central tendency, variability and reliability of the selection procedure should be provided (essential). Whenever feasible, these measures should be provided separately for each relevant race, sex, and ethnic group.

(7) *Relationship to job performance.* The criterion related study(ies) and other empirical evidence of the relationship between the construct measured by the selection procedure and the related work behavior(s) for the job or jobs in question should be provided (essential). Documentation of the criterion-related study(ies) should satisfy the provisions of section 15B above or section 15E(1) below, except for studies conducted prior to the effective date of these guidelines (essential). Where a study pertains to a group of jobs, and, on the basis of the study, validity is asserted for a job in the group, the observed work behaviors and the observed work products for each of the jobs should be described (essential). Any other evidence used in determining whether the work behavior(s) in each of the jobs is the same should be fully described (essential).

(8) *Alternative procedures investigated.* The alternative selection procedures investigated and available evidence of their impact should be identified (essential). The scope, method, and findings of the investigation, and the conclusions reached in light of the findings should be fully described (essential).

(9) *Uses and applications.* The methods considered for use of the selection procedure (e.g., as a screening device with a cutoff score, for grouping or ranking, or combined with other procedures in a battery) and available evidence of their impact should be described (essential). This description should include the rationale for choosing the method for operational use, and the evidence of the validity and utility of the procedure as it is to be used (essential). The purpose for which the procedure is to be used (e.g., hiring, transfer, promotion) should be described (essential). If weights are assigned to different parts of the selection procedure, these weights and the validity of the weighted composite should be reported (essential). If the selection procedure is used with a cutoff score, the user should describe the way in which normal expectations of proficiency within the work force were determined and the way in which the cutoff score was determined (essential).

(10) *Accuracy and completeness.* The report should describe the steps taken to assure the accuracy and completeness of the collection, analysis, and report of data and results.

(11) *Source data.* Each user should maintain records showing all pertinent information relating to its study of construct validity.

(12) *Contact person.* The name, mailing address, and telephone number of the individual who may be contacted for further information about the validity study should be provided (essential).

E. *Evidence of validity from other studies.* When validity of a selection procedure is supported by studies not done by the user, the evidence from the original study or studies should be compiled in a manner similar to that required in the appropriate section of this section 15 above. In addition, the following evidence should be supplied:

(1) *Evidence from criterion-related validity studies.*—a. *Job information.* A description of the important job behavior(s) of the user's job and the basis on which the behaviors were determined to be important should be provided (essential). A full description of the basis for determining that these important work behaviors are the same as those of the job in the original study (or studies) should be provided (essential).

b. *Relevance of criteria.* A full description of the basis on which the criteria used in the original studies are determined to be relevant for the user should be provided (essential).

c. *Other variables.* The similarity of important applicant pool or sample characteristics reported in the original studies to those of the user should be described (essential). A description of the comparison between the race, sex and ethnic composition of the user's relevant labor market and the sample in the original validity studies should be provided (essential).

d. *Use of the selection procedure.* A full description should be provided showing that the use to be made of the selection procedure is consistent with the findings of the original validity studies (essential).

e. *Bibliography.* A bibliography of reports of validity of the selection procedure for the job or jobs in question should be provided (essential). Where any of the studies included an investigation of test fairness, the results of this investigation should be provided (essential). Copies of reports published in journals that are not commonly available should be described in detail or attached (essential). Where a user is relying upon unpublished studies, a reasonable effort should be made to obtain these studies. If these unpublished studies are the sole source of validity evidence they should be described in detail or attached (essential). If these studies are not available, the name and address of the source, an adequate abstract or summary of the validity study and data, and a contact person in the source organization should be provided (essential).

(2) *Evidence from content validity studies.* See section 14C(3) and section 15C above.

(3) *Evidence from construct validity studies.* See sections 14D(2) and 15D above.

F. *Evidence of validity from cooperative studies.* Where a selection procedure has been validated through a cooperative study, evidence that the study satisfies the requirements of sections 7, 8 and 15E should be provided (essential).

G. *Selection for higher level job.* If a selection procedure is used to evaluate candidates for jobs at a higher level than those for which they will initially be employed, the validity evidence should satisfy the documentation provisions of this section 15 for the higher level job or jobs, and in addition, the user should provide: (1) a description of the job progression structure, formal or informal; (2) the data showing how many employees progress to the higher level job and the length of time needed to make this progression; and (3) an identification of any anticipated changes in the higher level job. In addition, if the test measures a knowledge, skill or ability, the user should provide evidence that the knowledge, skill, or ability is required for the higher level job and the basis for the conclusion that the knowledge, skill, or ability is not expected to develop from the training or experience on the job.

H. *Interim use of selection procedures.* If a selection procedure is being used on an interim basis because the procedure is not fully supported by the required evidence of validity, the user should maintain and have available (1) substantial evidence of validity for the procedure, and (2) a report showing the date on which the study to gather the additional evidence commenced, the estimated completion date of the study, and a description of the data to be collected (essential).

(Approved by the Office of Management and Budget under control number 3046–0017)

(Pub. L. No. 96–511. 94 Stat. 2812 (44 U.S.C. 3501 et seq.))

[43 FR 38295, 38312, Aug. 25, 1978, as amended at 46 FR 63268, Dec. 31, 1981]

DEFINITIONS

§ 1607.16   Definitions.

The following definitions shall apply throughout these guidelines:

A. *Ability.* A present competence to perform an observable behavior or a behavior which results in an observable product.

B. *Adverse impact.* A substantially different rate of selection in hiring, promotion, or other employment decision which works to the disadvantage of members of a race, sex, or ethnic group. See section 4 of these guidelines.

C. *Compliance with these guidelines.* Use of a selection procedure is in compliance with these guidelines if such use has been validated in accord with these guidelines (as defined below), or if such use does not result in adverse impact on any race, sex, or ethnic group (see section 4, above), or, in unusual circumstances, if use of the procedure is otherwise justified in accord with Federal law. See section 6B, above.

D. *Content validity.* Demonstrated by data showing that the content of a selection procedure is representative of important aspects of performance on the job. See section 5B and section 14C.

E. *Construct validity.* Demonstrated by data showing that the selection procedure measures the degree to which candidates have identifiable characteristics which have been determined to be important for successful job performance. See section 5B and section 14D.

F. *Criterion-related validity.* Demonstrated by empirical data showing that the selection procedure is predictive of or significantly correlated with important elements of work behavior. See sections 5B and 14B.

G. *Employer.* Any employer subject to the provisions of the Civil Rights Act of 1964, as amended, including State or local governments and any Federal agency subject to the provisions of section 717 of the Civil Rights Act of 1964, as amended, and any Federal contractor or subcontractor or federally assisted construction contractor or subcontactor covered by Executive Order 11246, as amended.

H. *Employment agency.* Any employment agency subject to the provisions of the Civil Rights Act of 1964, as amended.

I. *Enforcement action.* For the purposes of section 4 a proceeding by a Federal enforcement agency such as a lawsuit or an administrative proceeding leading to debarment from or withholding, suspension, or termination of Federal Government contracts or the suspension or withholding of Federal Government funds; but not a finding of reasonable cause or a concilation process or the issuance of right to sue letters under title VII or under Executive Order 11246 where such finding, conciliation, or issuance of notice of right to sue is based upon an individual complaint.

J. *Enforcement agency.* Any agency of the executive branch of the Federal Government which adopts these guidelines for purposes of the enforcement of the equal employment opportunity laws or which has responsibility for securing compliance with them.

K. *Job analysis.* A detailed statement of work behaviors and other information relevant to the job.

L. *Job description.* A general statement of job duties and responsibilities.

M. *Knowledge.* A body of information applied directly to the performance of a function.

N. *Labor organization.* Any labor organization subject to the provisions of the Civil Rights Act of 1964, as amended, and any committee subject thereto controlling apprenticeship or other training.

O. *Observable.* Able to be seen, heard, or otherwise perceived by a person other than the person performing the action.

P. *Race, sex, or ethnic group.* Any group of persons identifiable on the grounds of race, color, religion, sex, or national origin.

Q. *Selection procedure.* Any measure, combination of measures, or procedure used as a basis for any employment decision. Selection procedures include the full range of assessment techniques from traditional paper and pencil tests, performance tests, training programs, or probationary periods and physical, educational, and work experience requirements through informal or casual interviews and unscored application forms.

R. *Selection rate.* The proportion of applicants or candidates who are hired, promoted, or otherwise selected.

S. *Should.* The term "should" as used in these guidelines is intended to connote action which is necessary to achieve compliance with the guidelines, while recognizing that there are circumstances where alternative courses of action are open to users.

T. *Skill.* A present, observable competence to perform a learned psychomoter act.

U. *Technical feasibility.* The existence of conditions permitting the conduct of meaningful criterion-related validity studies. These conditions include: (1) An adequate sample of persons available for the study to achieve findings of statistical significance; (2) having or being able to obtain a sufficient range of scores on the selection procedure and job performance measures to produce validity results which can be expected to be representative of the results if the ranges normally expected were utilized; and (3) having or being able to devise unbiased, reliable and relevant measures of job performance or other criteria of employee adequacy. See section 14B(2). With respect to investigation of possible unfairness, the same considerations are applicable to each group for which the study is made. See section 14B(8).

V. *Unfairness of selection procedure.* A condition in which members of one race, sex, or ethnic group characteristically obtain lower scores on a selection procedure than members of another group, and the differences are not reflected in differences in measures of job performance. See section 14B(7).

W. *User.* Any employer, labor organization, employment agency, or licensing or certification board, to the extent it may be covered by Federal equal employment opportunity law, which uses a selection procedure as a basis for any employment decision. Whenever an employer, labor organization, or employment agency is required by law to restrict recruitment for any occupation to those applicants who h e met licensing or certification requirements, the licensing or certifying authority to the extent it may be covered by Federal equal employment opportunity law will be considered the user with respect to those licensing or certification requirements. Whenever a State employment agency or service does no more than administer or monitor a procedure as permitted by Department of Labor regulations, and does so without making referrals or taking any other action on the basis of the results, the State employment agency will not be deemed to be a user.

X. *Validated in accord with these guidelines or properly validated.* A demonstration that one or more validity study or studies meeting the standards of these guidelines has been conducted, including investigation and, where appropriate, use of suitable alternative selection procedures as contemplated by section 3B, and has produced evidence of validity sufficient to warrant use of the procedure for the intended purpose under the standards of these guidelines.

Y. *Work behavior.* An activity performed to achieve the objectives of the job. Work behaviors involve observable (physical) components and unobservable (mental) components. A work behavior consists of the performance of one or more tasks. Knowledges, skills, and abilities are not behaviors, although they may be applied in work behaviors.

NAME INDEX

SUBJECT INDEX

ACKNOWLEDGMENTS

Figures 2–1, 2–2 Workshop Materials by Sidney A. Fine.

Table 2–1 Zaltman, G., Duncan, R. and Holbek, J. *Innovations and Organization*. p. 171. Copyright © 1973 by John Wiley & Sons, Inc. Reprinted by permission.

Figure 2–3 Summary Chart of Worker Functions adapted from Sidney A. Fine and Wretha W. Wiley (1974).

Figure 2–4 Ernest S. Primoff

Figure 2–5 *Position Analysis Questionnaire,* Copyright © 1969 by Purdue Research Foundation, West Lafayette, IN 47907. Reprinted with permission.

Tables 2–2, 2–3, 2–5 Levine, E. L. *Everything You Always Wanted to Know About Job Analysis*. Tampa: Workforce Dynamics. (P.O. Box 291335, Tampa, FL 33687) 1983.

Table 2–6 From Arthur N. Turner and Paul R. Lawrence, *Industrial Jobs and the Worker: An Investigation of Response to Task Attributes.* Boston: Division of Research, Harvard Business School, 1965, p. 33. Used with permission.

Table 2–7 Peters, L. H. and O'Connor, E. J. (1980). Situational constraints and work outcomes. *Academy of Management Review, 5,* 391–397. Reprinted by with permission.

Table 3–1 Seashore, S. E., Indik, B. P., and Georgeopoulos, B. S. Relationships among criteria of job performance. *Journal of Applied Psychology, 44,* 195–202. Copyright 1960 by the American Psychological Association. Reprinted by permission of the publisher and author.

Table 3–2 Lent, R. H., Aurbach, H. A., and Levin, L. S. Predictors, criteria, and significant results. *Personnel Psychology, 24,* 519–533, 1971.

Table 3–3 Wayne F. Cascio, *Applied Psychology in Personnel Management, 2nd. Ed.,* Copyright © 1982, p. 103 Reprinted by permission of Pentice-Hall, Inc., Englewood Cliffs, NJ.

Table 3–4 How do your performance appraisals perform? *Employment Relations Today.* Executive Enterprises Publication Co. 33 West 60th Street New York, NY. Reprinted with permission.

Table 3–5 Wexley, K.N. The performance appraisal interview. Paper presented at Johns Hopkins University, 1982. Reprinted with permission of the author.

Figure 3–2 Steers, R. M. and Rhodes, S. R. Major influences in employee attendance. *Journal of Applied Psychology, 63,* 391–407. Copyright 1978 by the American Psychological Association. Reprinted with permission of the publisher and author.

Figure 3–3 Mobley, W. H., Horner, S. O., and Hollingsworth, T. An evaluation of precursors of hospital employee turnover. *Journal of Applied Psychology, 63,* 408–414. Copyright 1978 by the American Psychological Association. Reprinted with permission of the publisher and author.

Figure 3–4 Adapted by permission from *Readings in Personnel and Human Resource Management* by R. S. Schuler and Youngblood (Eds.). Copyright by West Publishing Co.

Figure 3–6 Campbell, J. P., Dunnette, M. D., Arvey, R. D., and Hellernik, L. W. The development and evaluation of behaviorally based rating scales. *Journal of Applied Psychology, 57,* 15–22. Copyright 1973 by the American Psychological Association. Reprinted with permission of the publisher and author.

Figure 3–7 G. P. Latham and K. N. Wexely, *Increasing Productivity Through Performance,* © 1981, Addison-Wesley, Reading, MA. Pg. 237 (chart). Reprinted with permission.

Figure 3–10 Landy, F. J. and Farr, J. L. A process model of performance rating. *Psychological Bulletin, 87,* 72–107, 1980.

Figure 3–11 Blum, M. L. and Naylor, J. C. *Industrial Psychology: Its Theoretical and Social Foundations.* 1968. Harper & Row. Reprinted with permission of the author.

Figure 4–1 Survey Research Center, *Michigan Organizational Assessment Package, Progress Report II,* August, 1975. Ann Arbor, MI: Institute for Social Research, The University of Michigan.

Figure 4–3 Manuel London and Stephen A. Stumpf, *Managing Careers,* © 1982, Addison-Wesley, Reading, MA. Pg. 140, Figure 5.5. Reprinted with permission.

Figure 4–4 Reprinted with permission from Stumpf, S. A. and Hanrahan, N. M., Designing career management practices to fit strategic management objectives, in Schuler, R. and S. Youngblood (Eds.). *Readings in Personnel and Human Resource Managements, 2nd. Ed.,* St. Paul, MN: West, 1984, p. 331.

Tables 4–1 and 4–2 Reprinted by permission from Personnel Policies Forum, copyright 1979 by the Bureau of National Affairs, Inc., Washington, DC.

Table 4–3 From K. M. Rowland and G. R. Ferris, *Personnel Management.* Copyright © 1982 by Allyn and Bacon, Inc. Used with permission.

Figure 6–5 Richard D. Arvey, *Fairness in Selecting Employees,* © 1979, Addison-Wesley, Reading, MA. Pg. 49, Figure 3.1. Reprinted with permission.

Figure 6–7 Campbell, John P. *Comments on Content Validity: A Procedural Manual.* Published by the Minneapolis Civil Service, 1973. Used with permission.

Figure 7–3 Schmidt, F. L., Hunter, J. E., McKenzie, R., and Muldrow, T. Impact of valid selection procedures on workforce productivity. *Journal of Applied Psychology, 64,* 609–626. Copyright 1979 by the American Psychological Association. Reprinted with permission of the publisher and author.

Figures 7–5 and 10–4 Dreher, G. F. and Sackett, P. R. *Perspectives on Employee Staffing and Selection.* © 1983 by Richard D. Irwin, Inc., Homewood, IL. Used with permission.

Table 8–3 William W. Ruch. Copyright 1982, Psychological Services, Inc. Reproduced by permission.

Tables 8–4 and 10–1 Adapted from Edwin E. Ghiselli, *The Validity of Occupational Aptitude Tests,* pp. 34, 37, 41, 44, 46, 48, 50, 56. Copyright © 1966, John Wiley & Sons, New York. Reprinted by permission.

Tables 8–5 and 8–6 Hunter, J. E. and Hunter, R. Validity and utility of alternative predictors of job performance. *Psychological Bulletin, 96,* 72–95. Copyright 1984 by the American Psychological Association. Reprinted with permission of the publisher and author.

Table 9–1 and Figure 9–1 Adapted from Fleishman, E. A. 1977, The Physical Abilities Analysis Manual. Bethesda, MD.

Figure 9–2 Adapted from Cooper, M. A., Schemmer, F. M., Gebhardt, D. Marshall-Mies, J., and Fleishman, E. A. 1982. *Development and Validation of Physical Ability Tests for Jobs in the Electric Power Industry.* Bethesda, MD. Advanced Resources Research Organization.

Figure 9–4 Siegel, A. I. The miniature job training and evaluation approach: Additional findings. *Personnel Psychology, 36,* 41–56, 1983. Used with permission of the publisher.

Figure 9–5 Reprinted from Schmidt, F. L., Caplan, J. R., Bemis, S. E., Decuin, R., Dunn, L., and Antone, L. (1979). *The Behavioral Consistency Method of Unassembled Examining.* Washington DC: U.S. Office of Personnel Management. Used with permission of the author.

Chapter 10 "A manager must . . . " adapted from Miner, J. B. Twenty years of research on role motivation theory of managerial effectiveness. *Personnel Psychology, 31,* 739–760, 1978. Used with permission of the author.

Table 10–2 Mills, C. J. and Bohannon, W. E. Personality characteristics of effective state police officers. *Journal of Applied Psychology, 65,* 680–684. Copyright 1980 by the American Psychological Association. Reprinted by permission of the publisher and author.

Table 10–3 Borman, W. C., Rosse, R. L. and Abrahams, N. M. An empirical construct validity approach to studying predictor-job performance links. *Journal of Applied Psychology, 65,* 662–671. Copyright 1980 by the American Psychological Association. Reprinted by permission of the publisher and author.

Table 10–4 Dolliver, R. H., Irvin, J. A., and Bigley, S. E. Twelve-year follow-up of the strong vocational interest blank. *Journal of Counseling Psychology, 19,* 212–217. Copyright 1972 by the American Psychological Association. Reprinted with permission of the publisher and author.

Figure 10–1 Vinitsky, M. A forty-year follow-up on the vocational interests of psychologists and their relationship to career development. *American Psychologist, 28,* 1001. Copyright 1973 by the American Psychological Association. Reprinted with permission of the publisher and author.

Figure 10–2 Reproduced by permission of the Distributor, Consulting Psychologists Press, Inc., Palo Alto, CA 94306 for the publisher Stanford University Press. From the manual for the Strong-

Campbell Interest Inventory, Form 325 by David Campbell and Jo-Ida Hansen. Copyright 1974, 1977, 1981 by the Board of Trustees of Leland Stanford Junior University.

Figure 10–3   Holland, J. L. (1985). *Making Vocational Choices: A Theory of Vocational Personalities and Work Environment.* Englewood Cliffs, NJ: Prentice-Hall. Reprinted by permission of the publisher and author.

Table 10–7   England, G. W. 1971. *Development and Use of Weighted Application Blanks.* Used with permission of the author.

Table 10–11   Hakel, M. D. Employment interviewing. From K. M. Rowland and G. R. Ferris, *Personnel Management.* Copyright © 1982 by Allyn and Bacon, Inc. Reprinted with permission of the publisher and author.

Figure 10–5   Mabe, P. A. and West, S. G. Validity of self-evaluation of ability: A review and meta-analysis. *Journal of Applied Psychology, 67,* 280–296. Copyright 1982 by the American Psychological Association. Reprinted by permission of the publisher and author.

Table 11–1   Katz, D. and Kahn, R. L. *The Social Psychology of Organizations, 2nd ed.,* Copyright © 1978, John Wiley & Sons, New York. Reprinted with permission of the publisher and author.

Figure 11–5   Robinson, D. D. Content-oriented personnel selection in a small business setting. *Personnel Psychology, 34,* 77–87, 1981. Reprinted with permission of the publisher and author.